Course Success Guide

to accompany

Psychology

Fourth Edition

Lester M. Sdorow
Lafayette College

Prepared by
M. Lisa Valentino
Seminole Community College

McGraw Hill

Boston Burr Ridge, IL Dubuque, IA Madison, WI New York San Francisco St. Louis
Bangkok Bogotá Caracas Lisbon London Madrid
Mexico City Milan New Delhi Seoul Singapore Sydney Taipei Toronto

McGraw-Hill

A Division of The ***McGraw-Hill*** *Companies*

Course Success Guide to accompany
PSYCHOLOGY

3 4 5 6 7 8 9 0 CRS/CRS 6 5 4 3 2 1 0 9

ISBN 0-697-25289-2

www.mhhe.com

Contents

Preface

Dear Psychology Student:

Welcome to the study of psychology!

This Course Success Guide to accompany *Psychology*, fourth edition by Lester Sdorow has been developed to help you optimize your study strategy and time. The guide represents an integrated approach to learning psychology. The hope is that this study guide will allow you to gain deeper understanding of the basic ideas presented in the text by focusing attention on the link between concepts, hypotheses, real-world research results, and the principles of psychology described in each chapter.

The Course Success Guide will enable you to verify facts, principles, and methods discussed in the textbook. Its proper use as a supplement to the text, will reinforce your knowledge. Each chapter of the study guide is divided into the following sections:

LEARNING OBJECTIVES

The Learning Objectives can be used in two different ways. First, you can examine the objectives before you read the chapter in the text to get an overview of the major topics that will be covered. Pay attention to the terms, concepts, and names mentioned in the objectives. Second, after you have completed reading the chapter, return to the objectives; you should now be able to perform the activities described in the objectives. You may want to write your responses to the objectives so that you can review them again before an exam. If you find an objective that seems unclear to you, return to the textbook and reread that section. The page numbers following each objective refer to the location of the material in the textbook.

COMPREHENSIVE GUIDED REVIEW

Each chapter in the textbook is summarized in a Comprehensive Guided Review, structured as a fill-in-the-blanks exercise. This exercise will help point out the terms or sections of the textbook you need to review. When all of the blanks have been correctly filled in, you will have a thorough summary of the chapter for future reference and review.

MINI-REVIEWS

The most effective study strategies are those that rely on concentrated study sessions, interspersed with short breaks and lots of review. To encourage this type of study strategy, you will be advised to take a short study break at the end of each section of the Comprehensive Guided Review. Mini-reviews are provided after each break point to encourage you to review the material before moving on to study a new topic. Most of the Mini-reviews are matching exercises requiring you to match the key terms with their definitions or key people with their contributions to the field of psychology. Remember, if at any point you cannot complete a task, go back and reread the corresponding section of the textbook.

KEY RESEARCH FINDINGS

As you will learn in the first chapters of the textbook, scientific research is critical to psychology. The Key Research Finding Section is intended to reinforce the important research contributions presented in the text. The key research studies are page-referenced to the textbook. Be sure to familiarize yourself with these important contributions to psychology. Upon completion of this section of the Course Success Guide you should be able to describe the results and conclusions of each key research finding listed.

PRACTICE TESTS

At the end of each chapter you will find two Practice Tests consisting of multiple choice and essay questions. The sample questions are similar to those that you might see on an exam. Each question is referenced to the correct learning objective, and page number of textbook.

Practice Test A offers at least one question for each learning objective. The questions in this first practice test tend to be oriented to require a factual understanding of concepts. The number of questions in this practice test will vary depending on the number of learning objectives in the chapter. Practice Test B, a twenty question test, tends to be oriented toward conceptual understanding and application of concepts.

ANSWER RECORD

To allow you to check your answers to the practice tests, the answer record provides a brief explanation for each correct or incorrect answer for all of the multiple choice questions and several key points that should be included in a correct answer to the essay questions. Use this feedback to help you understand your mistakes in the Practice Tests. If you miss a question, you should review the corresponding learning objective and pages in the textbook as well.

I hope that you find this Course Success Guide useful and that it will bolster your understanding of the discipline of psychology.

M. Lisa Valentino
Psychology Professor
Seminole Community College

Acknowledgments

This Course Success Guide is dedicated to all the students with which I have had, and will have, the pleasure of teaching. You are the reason I teach; I hope that your study of psychology is full of joy, excitement and wonder.

Additionally, it is also dedicated to my family, my husband, Bill; daughter Erin; and sons, Justin and Brian. I thank them for their understanding and support as this edition took shape.

Finally, my heartfelt thanks go to Kristen Mellitt, editorial assistant, and Meera Dash, senior developmental editor for their confidence, patience, and trust. I could not find two more dedicated professionals. It has been a pleasure. Thank you.

1 The Nature of Psychology

LEARNING OBJECTIVES

After studying this chapter, you should be able to:

1. Define psychology and explain why psychology is a science. (p. 4)

2. List eight important historical figures who are associated with the philosophical roots of psychology and explain their positions relative to the traditions of rationalism versus empiricism. (p. 5-7)

3. List two important historical figures who are associated with the scientific (physiological) origins of psychology, mentioning the study of nerve conduction and brain functioning. (p. 7)

4. List the developers of psychophysics, evolution, and differential psychology and explain the significance of these theories in the development of psychology. (p.7-8)

5. Describe the contributions of Wilhelm Wundt to the growth of psychology. (p. 8-9)

6. Describe the leader, goals, methods, and weaknesses of the early school of psychology known as structuralism. (p. 9-10)

7. List four important figures in the development of functionalism and describe the goals and contributions of this early school of psychology. (p. 10-11)

8. List two important figures in the development of behaviorism, describe the "proper" object of study for behaviorists, and indicate the place of behaviorism in contemporary psychology. (p. 11-12)

9. Briefly describe the leaders and origins of Gestalt psychology and explain its important features and concepts, as well as the nature of its influence on contemporary psychology. (p. 12-13)

10. Briefly describe the origins of psychoanalysis, briefly explaining several important Freudian concepts, and then summarize the significant impact and weaknesses of this perspective. (p. 13-14)

11. List and contrast the important emphases of contemporary behavioral, psychoanalytic, and humanistic perspectives, mentioning the significant individuals, concepts, and concerns associated with each of these perspectives. (p. 15-17)

12. List and contrast the important emphases of contemporary cognitive, biopsychological, and social-cultural perspectives, mentioning the significant individuals, concepts, and concerns associated with each of these perspectives. (p. 17-19)

13. List and briefly describe six major academic fields of specialization within modern psychology, and then offer examples that explain the difference between basic research and applied research. (p. 19-21)

14. List and briefly describe seven major professional fields of specialization within modern psychology, and then distinguish among clinical psychology, counseling psychology, and psychiatry. Mention three emerging fields of professional psychology. (p. 21-22)

15. Describe the many obstacles that faced professional women during the early years of psychology, emphasizing the concept of separate spheres and the significance of the Experimentalists. (p. 23-24)

16. List and describe the major accomplishments of three important early psychologists who were women, emphasizing the contributions of Mary Whiton Calkins. (p. 24-26)

COMPREHENSIVE GUIDED REVIEW

The word__(1)___ was created from two Greek terms:_(2)__, meaning "soul," and logos, meaning "the study of." Thus, the initial definition of psychology was "the study of the __(3)_." However, this definition has evolved over the past hundred-plus years; in the late nineteenth century psychology was defined as the "science of__(4)__." In the 1920's the definition changed again to become the "__(5)__ study of__(6)__," and again in the 1960's to its present form as the "____(7)____ study of behavior and mental processes." Since the late nineteenth century psychology has been numbered among the scientific disciplines. Psychology is a science because it relies on the ___(8)___.

I. The History of Psychology: In discussing the history of psychology, it is important to maintain a delicate balance between the intellectual approach called__(9)___, which sees the past within the context of current knowledge, and __(10)___, the approach that considers and evaluates claims with an understanding of the knowledge, methods, and values of the era in which the claim was first proposed. Psychology is credited with having its foundations in two disciplines: __(11)____, which relies more on reasoning for its source of knowledge, and __(12)____, which relies more on objective, systematic observation.

Philosophical Roots of Psychology: The areas of interest within psychology date back to the philosophers of ancient Greece. Downplaying the idea of gaining knowledge through the senses, __(13)____ believed that people enter the world with inborn knowledge, a position called___(14)__. Plato also believed that we could access knowledge through reasoning. This philosophical approach was known as__(15)___. Plato's pupil ___(16)___was more willing to accept the notion of sensory experiences as a way to obtain knowledge. This philosophy was called__(17)__.

During the early Christian and medieval eras, the dominant Western authority on psychological questions was __(18)__, who wrote his views on memory, emotion, and motivation. His type of study was typical of the nonscientific approach to psychology at the time. ___(19)____ guided most of the beliefs during this time in the Christian West. As a result, empiricism and _(20)___ investigations became the domain of the Islamic intellectuals. It was___ _(21)__ ____, better known as Avicenna, who kept alive the teachings of Aristotle until the dawn of the Renaissance.

__(22)___ was the first modern rationalist. He insisted that we should doubt everything that is not obvious by reasoning. Francis Bacon joined him in his claims and inspired the modern scientific attitude of__(23)__and systematic observation. ___(24)____is considered the founder of applied science. On the other hand, __(25)__ disagreed with the rationalists and believed knowledgewas acquired primarily through the senses; he believed that each of us is born a blank slate, or _____(26)______. Furthermore, his concern with the relative importance of heredity and environment is known today as the issue of nature versus _(27)___. _____(28)___struck a compromise between ___(29)____'s strict rationalism and Locke's strict empiricism by arguing that knowledge is the product of inborn faculties that organize input from the environment.

Scientific Roots of Psychology: By the mid nineteenth century, the search to understand the psychological nature of humans began to shift away from ____(30)______toward the more empirically oriented physiologists. Hermann ___(31)_____conducted research that identified that nerve impulse conduction was not instantaneous and that the speed of the nerve impulse could be measured. Pierre ___(32)___, a contemporary of von Helmholtz's, is recognized as a leading brain researcher who studied the effects of damage to specific structures on the behavior of animals. Another nineteenth-century scientist, Gustav_(33)_, quantified the relationship between physical stimulation and mental experience using the technique of _(34)_. The German physicist Ernst _____(35)___influenced Fechner to use this technique.

The scientists of the nineteenth century were also strongly influenced by the theory of __(36)__ developed by Charles Darwin. This theory claims that physical characteristics that promote survival are more likely to pass to offspring, because individuals with such characteristics have a better chance of living long enough to reproduce. This concept is known as______(37)______. Darwin's cousin, Sir Francis __(38)________, used evolutionary theory and profoundly influenced psychology. He argued that natural selection could account for the development of human abilities, a belief that led him to found the field of______(39)_______. James McKeen_____(40)_______ brought Galton's influence to American psychology. Cattell coined the term_______(41)____to describe various tests of vision, hearing, and physical skills, and later established his own business, the______(42)__ Corporation, which is still active in the development of tests that assess abilities,___(43)_____, and personality.

The Growth of Psychology as a Scientific Discipline: Psychology did not become a separate discipline until the late ____(44)______ century. Most psychologists attribute the founding of psychology to_______(45)_________. He established the first formal psychological lab in the year ____(46)_____, at the University of___(47)_____, in Germany. Many of the most renowned psychologists in the world studied at Wundt's lab. The early growth of psychology was marked by competing approaches, known as__(48)______, which often reflected the efforts of pioneers who synthesized ___(49)_____ and science. These schools differed in three significant ways: their goal of study, their object of study, and their__(50)____of study.

The Early Schools of Psychology:

Structuralism aimed to analyze the mind according to its component elements and to discover how the elements interact. Edward ____(51)_____, one of Wundt's students, popularized this short-lived school. He used the method of having subjects report mental experiences evoked by specific stimuli; this method was called__(52)______. This method was aimed at analyzing complex mental experiences into what Titchener considered to be three basic elements: images, __(53)____, and sensations. One of his major contributions was the discovery that complex tastes were comprised of four basic tastes:____(54)____, sour,__(55)_____, and bitter.

Structuralism's demise was due more in part to its reliance on _____(56)_____. This method limited researchers to the study of___(57)_____ mental experience of relatively intelligent, verbally skillful adults. The reports were__(58)__within the same subject over repeated presentations of a particular stimulus and were____(59)_____ between different participants. Most important, the very act of_____(60)______ changed the conscious experience that was being reported.

Functionalism, an American school of thought, emerged in response to the limited focus on analyzing the contents of the mind. Instead, it sought to determine how the mind affects what people do. Functionalism's ideas were influenced by Charles ____(61)___'s theory of evolution, especially his concept of______(62)________. The functionalists reasoned that the____(63)_____ mind evolved because it promoted the___(64)_______ of individual human beings. Probably one of the most noted functionalists was ______(65)__________. He viewed the mind as a stream of____(66)_____, unsuited to analysis by the ___(67)____methods of the structuralists. He was not interested in laboratory research; James used his laboratory only for_____(68)____ and instead sought to study how people function in the real world. As a result of their convictions, the functionalists broadened their subject populations to include animals, ____(69)_____, and people with ___(70)_____. The functionalists expanded psychology's subject matter to include memory, ____(71)______, and personality. Although John Dewey extended functionalism and applied it to the improvement of____(72)______practices, the title "the founder of applied psychology" belongs to ____(73)_____. Although hired to run William James's lab at____(74)______, he conducted research and wrote books on the application of psychology to __(75)___, industry, ____(76)_____, psychotherapy, and film criticism.

The school of psychology that dominated the discipline for half a century beginning in 1913 was **behaviorism**. According to this school, psychology is a purely______(77)______ branch of natural science. Its theoretical goal is the ____(78)____and control of behavior. For the behaviorist, ______(79)______ is not the proper object of study; rather the proper subject matter for psychological research is __(80)____ behavior. John B. ___(81)______ is considered the founder of behaviorism. He denied that mental processes could cause behavior, but did not deny the existence of the__(82)_____. Hence we can have the _____(83)______ of hunger but it is the body or the environment, not the experience, that causes us to eat. As a result of this conviction, as well as other factors, the study of the _____(84)______ declined in psychology.

Max___(85)____countered the attempt to analyze the mind into its component parts and the_(86)__view that a human being is a passive responder to environmental stimuli. He founded a school of psychology known as **Gestalt psychology**, often best known by its chief tenet, "The whole is different from the sum of its _(87)_." The term *Gestalt* means "__(88)__" or organized whole and underscores the belief that we perceive wholes rather than individual parts. The founding of Gestalt psychology is credited with a vacation trip taken by Wertheimer in which he dreamt about the ____(89)_____, the appearance of apparent motion in the absence of actual motion. Wertheimer continued to study the phi phenomenon using a device called a ___(90)____and concluded that the mind does not respond ___(91)_____ to discrete stimuli, but instead __(92)__ stimuli into coherent wholes. This finding gave a new direction to psychology. Although Wertheimer is created with being the founder of Gestalt psychology, Wolfgang ____(93)_____ and Kurt ____(94)_____ promoted Gestalt psychology as a natural ___(95)_____ and applied it to the study of _______(96)_______. Finally, one cannot conclude this section without mentioning Kurt ____(97)____, a pioneer researcher who applied Gestalt principles to ___(98)______, small-group behavior, and leadership styles.

Psychoanalysis was founded by _______(99)_______ as the result of his attempts to treat patients suffering from physical symptoms with no apparent physical cause. Freud's treatment of this phenomenon, known as_(100)____, led him to conclude that the disorder resulted from unconscious psychological conflicts between sexual enjoyment and cultural prohibitions that were then "converted" into physical symptoms. Freud believed that_(101)____ motives influenced all behavior. This belief is known as _______(102)_________. Freud also claimed that: a) unconscious motives are usually related to __(103)____ or aggression; b) unconscious memories of __(104)____ years affect later development of the personality and c) unconscious influences explain ____(105)_____ behavior.

Psychoanalysis has not been without criticism. The major ones are: (a) The____(106)______ mind can be too easily used to explain any behavior for which there is no obvious cause. (b) There has been a failure to provide adequate evidence through ___(107)______ research.; and finally, (c) Results drawn from ________(108)______ alone cannot be generalized to all people.

Stop and take a break at this point.

Don't feel guilty about taking short rests during your study sessions. As you'll learn in the chapter on memory, your short-term memory is limited in the amount of information it can hold. Once it is full you need to give it time to transfer information into the more permanent warehouse, or long-term memory. So do it. A short break (fifteen minutes or so) can actually help your ability to remember and recall studied material.

Now that you've taken that short break, let's try brief review of the history of psychology section before moving on to the next section. Please turn the page to begin.

Mini-review of Key Figures in the History of Psychology: Before you go on, review your understanding of the historical schools by matching these famous people to their beliefs or significant achievement. (If you can't remember who someone is, remember to go back and review that section of the text.)

Historical Figure

_____ 1. Wilhelm Wundt
_____2. Plato
_____3. Gustav Fechner
_____4. Max Wertheimer
_____5. Francis Bacon
_____6. Kurt Lewin
_____7. Immanuel Kant
_____ 8. Hermann von Helmholtz
_____ 9. J. McKeen Cattell
_____10. Pierre Flourens
_____ 11. Ernst Weber
_____ 12. Aristotle
_____ 13. Sir Francis Galton
_____14. Edward Titchener
_____15. Saint Augustine
_____16. Abu Ibn Sina
_____17. René Descartes
_____18. William James
_____19. Wolfgang Kohler
_____20. John Dewey
_____21. Hugo Münsterberg
_____22. John Watson
_____23. John Locke
_____ 24. Charles Darwin
_____25. Kurt Koffka
_____26. Sigmund Freud

Contribution to Psychology

A. Believed that people enter the world with inborn knowledge
B. More willing than Plato to accept sensory experiences as a way to acquire knowledge
C. Dominant Western authority on psychological questions in the Christian and medieval eras
D. Kept alive the teachings of Aristotle during the Middle Ages; better known as Avicenna
E. The first modern rationalist; insisted we should doubt all that is not obvious by reasoning
F. Inspired the modern scientific attitude of skepticism
G. Believed we are all born *tabula rasa,* or blank slate
H. Claimed knowledge comes from inborn faculties that organize environmental input
I. Conducted research that identified the speed of nerve impulses
J. Studied the effects of brain damage on behavior of animals during the nineteenth century
K. Examined relationships between physical stimulation and mental experience; psychophysicist
L. Developed the technique of psychophysics
M. Developed the concept of natural selection
N. Founder of differential psychology
O. Coined the term mental test; founded the Psychological Corporation
P. Considered to be the founder of the discipline of psychology
Q. Used introspection to analyze elements of complex experiences; popularized Structuralism
R Most noted functionalist; viewed the mind as a stream of consciousness
S. Founder of behaviorism; studied overt actions
T. Founded Gestalt psychology; dreamed about the phi phenomenon
U. Applied Gestalt psychology to the study of problem solving
V. Promoted Gestalt Psychology as a natural science
W. Pioneer researcher into social conflict, leadership styles and small-group behavior
X. Believed that all behavior was the result of unconscious conflict related to sex and aggression
Y. Extended functionalism and applied it to improvement of education
Z. Founder of applied psychology; applied psychology to law and industry

Check your answers. If you missed any of these go back and review pages 4-16 in your text

Mini-review of Historical Schools of Psychology: Remember the five historical schools of psychology from the previous section of this chapter? These schools differed from one another in their object of study, their goal of study and their method of study. Before you go on to the Contemporary Psychological Perspectives , review your understanding of these historical schools by filling in this summary table. (The first line has been done for you.)

School	**Object of Study**	**Goal of Study**	**Method of Study**
Structuralism	Conscious experience	Analyze structure of the mind	Analytic introspection
Functionalism			
Behaviorism			
Gestalt Psychology			
Psychoanalysis			

II. Contemporary Psychological Perspectives: Today in psychology, instead of one predominant school of thought, rival perspectives have emerged. Thomas ___(109)____ attributes this to the absence of any unifying psychological model, or __________(110))__________, that determines what the appropriate goals, methods, and even subject matter should be. Today, there are_(111)_major perspectives. These include the **behavioral** perspective, the **psychoanalytic** perspective, the **humanistic** perspective the **cognitive** perspective, the **biopsychological** perspective, and the **Social-Cultural** perspective.

The behavioral perspective: _____(112)______, influenced by J. B. Watson, became the leading proponent of the behavioral perspective. He urged psychologists to ignore mental processes and limit psychology to the study of _____(113)____. Like Watson, he adopted the convictions of a utopian, publishing _____(114)______ in 1948. However he differed from Watson in that he stressed the role of the _(115)_____ of behavior in controlling behavior, rather than the role of environmental stimuli. In spite of Skinner's position against the study of mental processes, in recent years some behaviorists have begun to study the relationship between mental processes such as images and ____(116)___, which cannot be directly observed. These psychologists are called____(117)_ behaviorists. Their most influential leader has been Albert __(118)______.

The psychoanalytic perspective: This perspective is a descendant of the early school of psychology known as ___(119)_______. The psychoanalytic perspective emerged as Carl __(120)______ and Alfred __(121)_____ developed psychoanalytic theories that conflicted with Freud's emphasis on the biological drives of sex and aggression and placed more emphasis on ______(122)_______. They were later joined by other neo-Freudians such as Anna ___(123)____, Melanie __(124)______, Karen _(125)______, Erich_(126)__, Harry_____(127)____, and Erik ___(128)_____. Today, the perspective downplays the importance of biological drives and accepts the importance of early childhood experiences and the ______(129)______.

The humanistic perspective is called the ___(130)__ for its position as the first important alternative to the psychoanalytic and the behavioral perspectives. The humanistic perspective was founded by Abraham ___(131)___ on the premise that human beings have ______(132)_____ and are not merely pawns of unconscious motives or environmental stimuli. Maslow stressed the human being's natural tendency for _____(133)_____, or the realization of one's potential. The assumption that people have free will is key to ____(134)________ psychologists. Like Maslow, Carl __(135)___ held a positive view of human nature, emphasizing that the subject matter of psychology should be a person's unique, subjective _____(136)___ of the world, the main concern of ____(137)___ psychology. Rogers's _____(138)______ therapy is one of the major types of psychotherapy in use today. Although person-centered therapy has generated extensive scientific research, other aspects of humanistic psychology, such as techniques to encourage "_(139)__ experiences" and "___(140)___ raising," have received little scientific support. Nonetheless, although it has had little impact on _____(141)_______ psychology, humanistic psychology remains a most viable force in promoting the study of the positive aspects of the human experience, attending to a wide range of topics, such as love, _(142)______, and healthy personality development.

The cognitive perspective combines aspects of ___(143)_____ psychology with aspects of the behavioral perspective. Like Gestalt psychologists, cognitive psychologists emphasize the ____(144)____ role of the mind in organizing perceptions, in ____(145)_______ information, and in interpreting experiences. Like ____(146)_______ psychologists, cognitive psychologists emphasize the need for objective, well-controlled ___(147)_______ studies. Thus, cognitive psychologists infer___(148)_____ from observable responses, without relying on introspective reports alone; and, unlike ___(149)_____, they claim that mental processes do affect behavior. The cognitive perspective owes much to Jean __(150)______ and his theory of a child's cognitive development, and Herbert ____(151)____ for his research on the human brain and information processing using ___(152)____ models.

The biological perspective: The interests of biological psychologists focus primarily on the___(153)___, the hormonal system, and the effects of___(154)___ on psychological functions. This perspective has developed in recent decades due to an increase in the interest in ____(155)______ processes and biological bases of behavior, along with the development of more sophisticated _____(156)_____ equipment. Some psychologists suggest that as a result of the increasing influence of this perspective, psychology may be moving toward an even broader definition as "the science of behavior and mental processes, and the ____(157)______ processes underlying them." Two important contributors to this growing field include Wilder ____(158)____, who mapped the brain using weak electrical currents and Nobel Prize-winner Roger ____(159)____, who studied the differential functions of the left and right hemispheres of the brain.

Over the past three decades, the **social-cultural perspective** has developed in reaction against the tendency to assume that all psychological research is automatically generalizable to other____(160)____. It has been suggested that the development of virtually instantaneous communication, or the "______ (161) ______," has contributed to the growth of this perspective. Harry ____(162)____, one of the founders of this perspective argues that psychologists should avoid ____(163)____, or the tendency to view other cultures by using our own as the standard. He argues that we should instead examine each culture and ask what is ______(164)____ and desirable for each one. Disagreements exist among supporters of this perspective; some advocate the need to study the effects of culture on human behavior and mental processes, an approach known as ____(165)____ psychology; others advocate the need to study ________(166)________, in which the goal is to identify universal psychological truths.

Take time for another break!
After your break try to complete this review of the six contemporary perspectives before you move on.

Contemporary Perspective in Psychology Mini-review

Perspective	**Belief as to Areas of Study**	**Important Contributors**
Behavioral perspective	*Ignores mental processes* *Focuses on overt behavior*	*J. B. Watson* *B. F. Skinner*
Psychoanalytic perspective		
Humanistic perspective		
Cognitive perspective		
Biopsychological perspective		
Social-cultural perspective		

You are staying right on track! Now you are ready to move on to the last section of the chapter.

III. Psychology as a Profession:

Academic Fields of Specialization: The main employment settings for psychologists are____(167)____ and universities. Most academic psychologists are interested in some type of research. ____(168)______ research is research that attempts to answer questions for their own sake. ____(169)______research attempts to solve a practical problem. The largest academic specialization in psychology is ________(170)______ psychology. These psychologists generally limit themselves to laboratory research into basic psychological processes like perception, memory, ____(171)________, thinking, language, motivation, and ____(172)______. Other areas of specialization within academic psychology include: behavioral ____(173)________, comparative psychology, ______(174)__________psychology, personality psychology, and social psychology.

Review the Academic Areas of Specialization in Psychology: Before going on to study about the professional fields in psychology, stop and review the differences in the characteristics of each field of academic psychology by matching the specialization with its description.

Field	Characteristics
A. Experimental	_____1. Examines brain structures, drug effects, recovery from injury
B. Behavioral neuroscience	_____2. Examines the effects of people on one another
C. Comparative	_____3. Studies the physical, cognitive, and social change over the life span
D. Developmental	_____4. Interested in similarities and differences in behavior of humans and animals
E. Personality	_____5. Studies differences in behavior among individuals
F. Social	_____6. Studies basic processes such as perception, learning, and memory; lab oriented

---

Stay on track. You're almost to the end of the chapter!

Professional Fields of Specialization: Professional psychologists often work ___(175)___ college and university classrooms and labs. The two largest field of professional psychology include clinical and ___(176)___ psychology. Both deal with the causes, ___(177)___, diagnosis, and ___(178)___ of psychological disorders. ___(179)___ psychologists deal more with problems of everyday living, whereas ___(180)___ psychologists generally treat more severe disorders. A ___(181)___ is not a psychologist but a medical doctor trained in medical approaches to treating psychological disorders. Professional psychology has numerous other areas of specialization in addition to clinical and counseling fields. Quiz yourself on these now.

Match the area of concentration with its functions:

Specialization	Area of Concentration
______ Clinical	1. Jury selection, eyewitness accounts, disputes, negotiations
______ Counseling	2. Improving curriculum, teaching
______ School	3. Placement, performance, behavior, adjustment, and counseling
______ Educational	4. Human factors, aspects of human body structure that must be considered in equipment design and displays
______ Industrial/Organizational	5. Prevention, diagnosis, and treatment of disorders
______ Engineering	6. Helping amateur and professional athletes improve performance
______ Forensic	7. Prevention of physical illness by promoting adherence to healthy behaviors
______ Sport	8. Productivity; working conditions; methods for hiring; training; management in business, industry, or government
______ Health	9. Marriage, school, career
______ Environmental	10. Designing neighborhoods to reduce noise, crowding, and other sources of stress

---

IV. Thinking About Psychology: What Role Did Women Play in the Growth of Psychology?

The chief factor in limiting professional opportunities for women was the notion of "___(182)___": roles defined by the customs and policies of the times that saw women in the positions of good ___(183)___, wives, and mothers. Women who pursued careers as scientists often had to forgo or postpone marriage and ___(184)___. Additionally, the claim that women lacked the personal and ___(185)___ abilities needed to succeed in higher education presented a substantially powerful barrier to ___(186)___ to higher education. The final barrier to women was their exclusion from the professional ___(187)___ that would have offered opportunities for education and professional ___(188)___.

Christine Ladd- ____(189)______ studied with von Helmholtz and although she was denied membership in Titchener's research society, the _____(190)______, her stature as a psychologist and advocate for the acceptance of women in professional circles was a milestone. Eventually, Margaret Floy __(191)_______, a former president of the American Psychological Association, was the first female admitted to the all-male society.

Mary Whiton Calkins became ____(192)__'s first psychology professor. She continued her studies at __(193)______but bore the brunt of discrimination. Although her dissertation was brilliant and she had the support of prominent figures such as Hugo__(194)_______ and William James, she was denied a ___(195)______ at Harvard. Despite the odds, she became the__(196)___women president of the_____(197)______(APA). Calkins criticized Watson's __(198)____ approach and argued that, contrary to being a__(199)___ responder to environmental stimuli, the human being is active and __(200)_____.

Congratulations! You have finished your guided review of chapter 1. Take a short break and then come back to review the chapter Learning Objectives, the Key Research Findings, and the Key Concepts.

KEY RESEARCH FINDINGS

Provide the details of the following key research studies in psychology:

1. **von Helmholtz (1821-1894):** Speed of nerve impulses (Page 7)
2. **Flourens (1794-1867):** Cerebellum damage and motor in coordination (Page 7)
3. **Fechner (1801-1887):** Relationship between physical and mnetal experiences (Page 8)
4. **Darwin (1809-1882):** Theory of Natural Selection (Page 8)
5. **Wundt (1832-1920):** Use of lab to study conscious mind (Page 8-9)
6. **Wertheimer (1880-1943):** Phi phenomenon (Page 12)
7. **Penfield (1891-1976):** Map of the human brain via stimulation. (Page 18)
8. **Sperry (1913-1994):** Brain hemispheric specialization (Page 18)

Now it is time for you to really test your retention of the material in this chapter by taking the practice tests.

PRACTICE TEST A

1. According to the textbook, the current, broad definition of psychology is the science of
   a. behavior.
   b. mental processes.
   c. unconscious processes.
   d. behavior and mental processes.

Obj: 1 Page: 4

2. Biology and psychology are both sciences because they
   a. study the brain.
   b. rely on statistics.
   c. share a common method.
   d. require specialized education.

Obj: 1 Page: 4

3. If he were alive today, the philosopher who would be most likely to believe that Head Start programs would improve the intellectual development of children would be
   a. Plato.
   b. John Locke.
   c. Immanuel Kant.
   d. René Descartes.

Obj: 2 Page: 6-7

4. If you insisted that "seeing is believing," you would show your belief in
   a. nativism.
   b. empiricism.
   c. rationalism.
   d. psychic determinism.

Obj: 3 Page: 6

5. The nineteenth-century scientist who noted that damage to specific brain structures affected particular behaviors was
   a. Roger Sperry.
   b. Wilhelm Wundt.
   c. Pierre Flourens.
   d. Hermann von Helmholtz.

Obj: 3 Page: 7

6. Research in differential psychology, a field founded by Francis Galton, would be most likely to
   a. use placebo control groups.
   b. determine the effect of exercise on academic performance.
   c. study factors that make certain individuals more stress-resistant than others.
   d. assess changes in the personality of a single subject across various life stages.

Obj: 4 Page: 8

7. The early school of psychology that tried to understand the relationship between stimuli and conscious experience was
   a. humanism.
   b. behaviorism.
   c. structuralism.
   d. psychoanalysis.

Obj: 5 Page: 9

8. Structuralism died out in part because it
   a. relied on analytic introspection.
   b. was limited to the study of brain structures.
   c. emphasized the study of unconscious processes.
   d. favored applied research over sound laboratory research.

Obj: 6 Page: 10

9. If you developed an intelligence test that assessed how well one's mind enables one to adapt to different environmental situations, you would be in the tradition of
   a. structuralism.
   b. functionalism.
   c. psychoanalysis.
   d. gestalt psychology.

Obj: 7 Page: 11

10. Functionalism differed from structuralism in favoring
    a. the study of the conscious mind.
    b. the study of the unconscious mind.
    c. limiting psychology to laboratory research.
    d. the application of psychology to everyday life.

Obj: 6 & 7 Page: 9-11

11. According to John B. Watson,
    a. the mind does not exist.
    b. the mind does not cause behavior.
    c. all behavior has unconscious causes.
    d. a true psychology of the human being must rely on analytic introspection.

Obj: 8 Page: 11

12. The school of psychology that believed that the mind actively organizes sensations into meaningful perceptions is
    a. behaviorism.
    b. structuralism.
    c. psychoanalysis.
    d. gestalt psychology.

Obj: 9 Page: 12

13. If a psychologist insisted that a person's recent fall down a flight of stairs was more attributable to unconscious self-loathing than to clumsiness, she would be supporting the Freudian notion of
    a. stimulus control.
    b. psychic determinism.
    c. positive reinforcement.
    d. psychophysical parallelism.

Obj: 10 Page: 14

14. A major criticism of Freud's theory is that it
    a. assumes people have free will.
    b. overgeneralizes from case studies.
    c. places too much faith in human rationality.
    d. views childhood as relatively unimportant to personality development.

Obj: 10 Page: 14

15. Contemporary psychological perspectives include
    a. structuralism.
    b. functionalism.
    c. gestalt psychology.
    d. cognitive psychology.

Obj: 12 Page: 15

16. B. F. Skinner would be most likely to attribute your desire to pursue a college education to
   a. your drive for self-actualization.
   b. an unconscious need to prove yourself.
   c. your past success in academic courses.
   d. intellectual interests inherited from your parents.

Obj: 11 Page: 15-16

17. Neo-Freudians, such as Anna Freud, Erich Fromm, and Erik Erikson, differ from traditional Freudians in
   a. placing less emphasis on the sex drive.
   b. stressing the overriding importance of the unconscious.
   c. viewing heredity as more important than life experiences.
   d. assuming that childhood experiences are important determinants of adult personalities.

Obj: 11 Page: 16

18. The psychological perspective that is concerned with studying the brain, the hormone system, and the effects of heredity on behavior is the
   a. differential perspective.
   b. neurochemical perspective.
   c. cerebrocortical perspective.
   d. biopsychological perspective.

Obj: 12 Page: 18

19. The main difference between a psychiatrist and a clinical psychologist is that the psychiatrist
   a. is a physician.
   b. might analyze dreams.
   c. relies strictly on Freudian theory.
   d. deals with more serious kinds of disorders.

Obj: 14 Page: 22

20. Mary Whiton Calkins became a pioneer in psychology despite being burdened by
   a. a bias against psychoanalysts.
   b. the notion of "separate spheres."
   c. being a member of Titchener's "Experimentalists" society.
   d. having to fulfill her responsibilities as a wife and mother.

Obj: 15 Page: 24-26

Check your answers to Practice Test A before going on.

PRACTICE TEST B

1. Historically speaking, psychology developed from
   a. biology and sociology.
   b. philosophy and science.
   c. neurology and education.
   d. science and empiricism.

Obj. : 2 Page: 5

2. If your professor were to arrange a debate between Plato and Aristotle at your school, a likely title might be
   a. "Historicism or Presentism: Which Is More Useful?"
   b. "Reasoning or Sensory Experience: Which Is the Source of Knowledge?"
   c. "Empiricism or Sensory Experience: Which Is More Scientific?"
   d. "Nature or Nurture: Which Is More Powerful in Determining Behavior?"

Obj.: 2 Page: 5

3. While reasoning is certainly important in psychology, its methods depend more on sensory experiences (observation, for example) to develop knowledge. This approach is called
   a. psychic determinism.
   b. presentism.
   c. empiricism.
   d. rationalism.

Obj.: 3 Page: 6

4. The contributions of von Helmholtz, Flourens and Fechner were important in the history of psychology because they showed that
   a. philosophical speculation was unsuitable for the study of the brain and nervous system.
   b. the contents of the mind were changed by studying it.
   c. the structure of the mind could be determined by introspection.
   d. rationalism was superior to empiricism in studying the brain and behavior.

Obj.: 3 Page: 7

5. A psychophysicist would be interested in which of the following questions?
   a. What are the relative contributions of heredity versus experience to a person's behavior?
   b. Can we learn about the world through reasoning and philosophical speculation?
   c. Are living species related ?
   d. How little can a stimulus change before a person actually notices the change?

Obj.: 4 Page: 8

6. One reason why Wilhelm Wundt is important in the history of psychology is that he
   a. helped establish psychology as an independent discipline, separate from philosophy.
   b. applied the theory of evolution to human as well as animal behavior.
   c. trained a whole generation of important psychologists.
   d. developed mental tests to measure various physical abilities and skills.

Obj.: 5 Page: 9

7. An early psychologist presents a subject with a sphere and asks the subject to report on what images, feelings, and sensations the sphere evokes. This psychologist is using the method known as
   a. analytic introspection.
   b. psychophysical measurement.
   c. philosophical speculation.
   d. stream of consciousness.

Obj.: 6 Page: 9

8. In contrast to the structuralists, functionalists such as James, Dewey, and Münsterberg encouraged
   a. the study of unconscious as well as conscious determinants of behavior.
   b. limiting psychological studies to healthy, intelligent, male adults.
   c. applying psychology to solve practical everyday problems.
   d. restricting psychological study to overt, observable behavior.

Obj. : 7 Page: 10-11

9. With which of the following statements would John Watson strongly agree?
   a. Psychology should study the adult mind and its development through the life span.
   b. Psychology should concern itself with improving education, law, and industry.
   c. Psychology should be totally objective and aim to predict and control behavior.
   d. Psychology should emphasize the influence of unconscious motivations.

Obj.: 8 Page: 11

10. When a good chorus performs, you do not perceive the voices of the individual singers, that is, your mind forms a(n)
   a. introspection
   b. gestalt.
   c. phi.
   d. stream of consciousness

Obj.: 9 Page: 12-13

11. The core concept in the psychoanalytic approach is the importance of
   a. observable behavior.
   b. natural selection.
   c. perception as an active organizing process.
   d. unconscious motivations.

Obj: 10 Page: 13-14

12. Whenever Billy brings a storybook to his father, his father gives him attention and reads him a story. Whenever Bobby brings a storybook to his father, his father pushes it aside and criticizes Bobby for being demanding. As students, Billy loves to read and study, while Bobby dislikes anything that requires reading. This example demonstrates that
   a. a utopian society is an impossibility.
   b. psychic determinism is a key concept in contemporary psychology.
   c. nature is as important as nurture in determining what behaviors or characteristics develop in a person.
   d. what happens after we perform a behavior will influence whether that behavior occurs again.

Obj.: 11 Page: 15-16

13. What do behavioral psychologists and cognitive psychologists have in common?
 a. They both believe in the importance of objective, well-controlled laboratory research.
 b. They both emphasize the importance of unconscious motivations.
 c. They both deny the importance of mental processes and imagery.
 d. They both consider heredity an overriding factor in human development.

Obj.: 11& 12 Page: 17-18

14. A researcher finds that when he stimulates certain segments of a patient's brain, the person either has a vivid memory or involuntarily moves a body part. This research reflects which psychological perspective?
 a. Social-cultural.
 b. Biopsychological.
 c. Cognitive.
 d. Behavioral.

Obj.: 12 Page: 18

15. A researcher studies 3,000 North American men and finds they prefer competitive athletic activities over activities that involve artistic creativity. This researcher declares that such preferences apply to all men. This researcher may be ignoring the
 a. existential perspective.
 b. influences of society and culture.
 c. biological processes that underlie these preferences.
 d. importance of anxiety and the need for security.

Obj: 12 Page: 18

16. Dr. Ramos, a psychologist, uses behavioral principles to manage her classes. She believes that her forgetting an appointment with the dean was due to her unconscious conflicts about him. She feels best when she feels she is fulfilling her potential as a writer. When feeling low, she engages in vigorous exercise to increase her level of pleasure-creating brain chemicals. In other words, Dr. Ramos may be described as
 a. not ethnocentric.
 b. rational.
 c. eclectic.
 d. empirical.

Obj.: 12 Page: 19

17. Dr. Lee is studying color perception. Dr. Patel is studying children's memories for disturbing events, while Dr. Polk is studying how we recognize the emotional states of others. Most likely, these individuals are
 a. experimental psychologists.
 b. cognitive behaviorists.
 c. comparative psychologists.
 d. humanistic psychologists.

Obj.: 13 Page: 20

18. A new manufacturing process requires development of a piece of machinery with a very complex control panel made up of dials, levers, and meters. In order to design this new control panel to promote worker safety, errorless performance, and maximum comfort of use, the manufacturer would be wise to consult with a(n)
 a. forensic psychologist.
 b. comparative psychologist.
 c. engineering psychologist.
 d. environmental psychologist.

Obj.: 14 Page: 22

19. The year is 1920. Tom and Laura are both exceptional psychology students who have a special interest in children. Tom is encouraged by his professors to pursue doctoral studies and become a developmental psychologist. Laura is encouraged by her professors to become a child-care worker in an orphanage. Such differences in career guidance are in keeping with the notion of
 a. psychic determinism.
 b. eclecticism.
 c. ethnocentrism.
 d. separate spheres.

Obj.: 15 Page: 23

20. Considered the first great American women psychologist, she studied with William James, but was never allowed to register for courses at Harvard University. She developed the first psychology laboratory at a women's college and invented the paired-associates technique, which is still used today to study memory. Her name was
 a. Christine Ladd-Franklin
 b. Mary Whiton Calkins
 c. Karen Horney.
 d. Margaret Floy Washburn

Obj.: 16 Page: 24-26

ESSAY QUESTIONS

1. Explain what is meant by the social-cultural perspective in psychology. Why has this perspective gained importance in recent years?

Obj.: 12 Page: 19

2. A clinical psychologist and a developmental psychologist are asked to comment on the recent suicides of the members of the Heaven's Gate cult. What aspects of human behavior are each of these professionals likely to emphasize, given their specializations?

Obj.: 14 Page: 19-21

ANSWER RECORD FOR CHAPTER 1

Comprehensive Guided Review:

1. *psychology*
2. *psyche*
3. soul
4. mental life
5. scientific
6. behavior
7. scientific
8. scientific method
9. presentism
10. historicism
11. philosophy
12. science
13. Plato
14. nativism
15. rationalism
16. Aristotle
17. empiricism
18. Saint. Augustine
19. Religious dogma
20. scientific
21. Abu Ibn Sina
22. Descartes
23. skepticism
24. Descartes
25. John Locke
26. *tabula rasa*
27. nurture
28. Immanuel Kant
29. Descartes
30. philosophical reasoning
31. von Helmholtz
32. Flourens
33. Fechner
34. psychophysics
35. Weber
36. evolution
37. natural selection
38. Galton
39. differential psychology
40. Cattell
41. mental test
42. Psychological
43. intelligence
44. nineteenth
45. Wilhelm Wundt
46. 1879
47. Leipzig
48. schools
49. philosophy
50. method
51. Titchener
52. analytic introspection
53. feelings
54. sweet
55. salty
56. introspection
57. conscious
58. inconsistent
59. different
60. introspecting
61. Darwin
62. natural selection
63. conscious
64. survival
65. William James
66. consciousness
67. introspective
68. demonstrations
69. children
70. mental disorders
71. thinking
72. educational
73. Hugo Münsterberg
74. Harvard
75. law
76. education
77. objective experimental
78. prediction
79. introspection
80. overt
81. Watson
82. mind
83. mental experience
84. mind
85. Wertheimer
86. behavioral
87. parts
88. form
89. phi phenomenon
90. tachistoscope
91. passively
92. organizes
93. Kohler
94. Koffka
95. science
96. problem solving
97. Lewin
98. social conflict,
99. Sigmund Freud
100. conversion hysteria
101. unconscious
102. psychic determinism
103. sex
104. early
105. irrational
106. unconscious
107. empirical
108. case studies

Mini-review of Key Figures in the History of Psychology:

1. P; 2. A; 3. K; 4. T; 5. F; 6. W; 7. H; 8. I; 9. O; 10. J; 11. L; 12. B; 13. N; 14. Q; 15. C; 16. D; 17. E; 18. R; 19. V; 20. Y; 21. Z; 22. S; 23. G; 24. M; 25. U; 26. X

Mini-review of Historical Schools of Psychology:

School	Object of Study	Goal of Study	Method of Study
Structuralism	*Conscious experience*	*Analyze structure of the mind*	*Analytic introspection*
Functionalism	*Conscious experience*	*Study functions of the mind*	*Introspection and measures of performance*
Behaviorism	*Observable behavior*	*Controlling behavior*	*Observation and experiments*
Gestalt Psychology	*Conscious experience*	*Demonstration of holistic Nature of the mind*	*Introspection and demonstrations*
Psychoanalysis	*Unconscious motivation*	*Understanding personality*	*Clinical case studies*

109. Kuhn
110. scientific paradigm
111. six
112. B. F. Skinner
113. observable behavior
114. *Walden Two*
115. consequences
116. thoughts
117. cognitive behaviorists
118. Bandura
119. psychoanalysis
120. Jung
121. Adler
122. social relationships
123. Freud
124. Klein
125. Horney
126. Fromm
127. Stack Sullivan
128. Erikson
129. unconscious mind
130. third force
131. Maslow
132. free will
133. self-actualization
134. existential
135. Rogers
136. mental experiences
137. phenomenological
138. person-centered
139. growth
140. consciousness
141. academic
142. altruism
143. Gestalt
144. active
145. processing
146. behavioral
147. laboratory
148. mental processes
149. behaviorists
150. Piaget
151. Simon
152. computer
153. brain
154. heredity
155. mental
156. research
157. physiological
158. Penfield
159. Sperry
160. cultures
161. shrinking of our planet
162. Triandis
163. ethnocentrism
164. normal
165. cultural
166. cross-cultural psychology

Mini -review of Contemporary Perspectives in Psychology:

Perspective	**Belief as to Areas of Study**	**Important Contributors**
Behavioral perspective *Page 15-16*	*Ignores mental processes Focuses on overt behavior*	*J. B. Watson, B. F. Skinner*
Psychoanalytic perspective *Page 16-17*	*Stresses importance of childhood experiences and unconscious motivations*	*S. Freud, A. Freud, C. Jung, A. Adler, K. Horney, M. Klein, E. Fromm, E. Erikson, H. Stack Sullivan*
Humanistic perspective *Page 17*	*Stresses role of free will Studies the individual's subjective experience of the world*	*A. Maslow, C. Rogers*
Cognitive perspective *Page 17-18*	*Stresses the role of the active mind Infers mental processes from observable responses*	*J. Piaget, H. Simon*
Biopsychological perspective: *Page 18*	*Studies the brain, hormones, and genetic Influences on behavior and mental processes*	*W. Penfield, R. Sperry*
Social-cultural perspective *Page 18-19*	*Stresses the importance of viewing behavior and mental processes within their cultural context.*	*H. Triandis*

167. colleges
168. Basic
169. Applied
170. experimental
171. learning
172. emotion
173. neuroscience
174. developmental
175. outside
176. counseling
177. prevention
178. treatment
179. Counseling
180. clinical
181. psychiatrist
182. separate spheres
183. daughters
184. parenthood
185. intellectual
186. admission
187. networks
188. advancement
189. Franklin
190. Experimentalists
191. Washburn
192. Wellesley College
193. Harvard
194. Münsterberg
195. doctorate
196. first
197. American Psychological Association
198. behavioral
199. passive
200. purposive

Academic Specializations in Psychology Matching Quiz:

A. 6 Experimental
B. 1 Behavioral neuroscience
C. 4 Comparative
D. 3 Developmental
E. 5 Personality
F. 2 Social

Professional Specializations in Psychology Matching Quiz:

__5__Clinical
__9__Counseling
__3__School
__2__Educational
__8__Industrial/Organizational
__4__Engineering
__1__Forensic
__6__Sport
__7__Health
__10__Environmental

Practice Test A:

1. a. Incorrect: This is the behaviorist definition and is only a piece of today's definition.
   b. Incorrect: Mental processes are not the only thing that psychologists study.
   c. Incorrect: Unconscious processes are the concerns of psychoanalytic psychologists, but not all.
   d. Correct: Today's psychologists are concerned with both behavior and mental processes.

2. a. Incorrect: It is not what a scientist studies, but how.
   b. Incorrect: It is not what a scientist studies, but how.
   c. Correct: It is the common method used to study something that makes a scientist a scientist.
   d. Incorrect: It is not what a scientist studies, but how.

3. a. Incorrect: Plato believed that knowledge is inborn.
   b. Correct: John Locke believed that we are all born a blank slate and the environment makes us.
   c. Incorrect: Immanuel Kant thought knowledge was the product of mental faculties.
   d. Incorrect: René Descartes also believed that we are born with knowledge.

4. a. Incorrect: Nativism argues that we are born with inborn knowledge.
   b. Correct: Empiricism argues that knowledge is gained through sensory experience.
   c. Incorrect: Rationalism argues that reasoning gives us access to knowledge.
   d. Incorrect: Psychic determinism is Freud's term for the reason behind accidental behavior.

5 a. Incorrect: Roger Sperry did his brain research in the twentieth century.
   b. Incorrect: Wilhelm Wundt was interested in the conscious mind, not the brain.
   c. Correct: Pierre Flourens lived from 1794 to 1867 and studied the brains of animals.
   d. Incorrect: Hermann von Helmholtz studied nerve conduction, not the brain

6. a. Incorrect: Differential psychologists examine the effects of a variable on an individual, not variations among human beings.
   b. Incorrect: Differential psychologists examine the effects of a variable on an individual, not variations among human beings.
   c. Correct: Differential psychologists do examine stress response differences among individuals.
   d. Incorrect: Differential psychologists examine the effects of a variable on an individual, not variations among human beings.

7. a. Incorrect: Humanism was not an early school of psychology.
   b. Incorrect: Behaviorism was interested in overt behavior, not conscious experiences.
   c. Correct: Structuralists studied the relationship between stimuli and conscious experiences.
   d. Incorrect: Psychoanalysis was interested in studying the unconscious, not the conscious.

8. **a. Correct: Structuralism died out in part due to problems with its methodology, analytic introspection.**
   b. Incorrect: Structuralism did not study brain structure.
   c. Incorrect: Structuralism did not study the unconscious.
   d. Incorrect: Structuralism relied on laboratory research, not real-world study.

9. a. Incorrect: Structuralists were interested in structure, not function.
   b. Correct: Functionalists were interested in how the mind functioned to allow for adaptation.
   c. Incorrect: Psychoanalysts were interested in the unconscious mind, not intelligence.
   d. Incorrect: Gestalt psychologists were interested in wholes, not pieces of the individual.

10. a. Incorrect: Structuralists and functionalists were interested in the conscious mind.
    b. Incorrect: Neither view focused on the unconscious mind..
    c. Incorrect: Functionalists did not limit their study to the lab; structuralists did.
    d. **Correct: Functionalists were more concerned with application to everyday life.**

11. a. Incorrect: Watson did not deny the existence of the mind.
    b. **Correct: Watson felt that although the mind may exist, it did not cause behavior.**
    c. Incorrect: Watson did not feel that the unconscious was important.
    d. Incorrect: Watson relied on observation of overt actions, not introspection.

12. a. Incorrect: Behaviorism did not concern itself with the mind.
    b. Incorrect: Structuralism was more concerned with how the mind is structured than how it organizes information.
    c. Incorrect: Psychoanalysis was more concerned with unconscious conflicts than perceptions.
    d. **Correct: Gestalt psychologists were interested in studying how the mind organizes sensations.**

13. a. Incorrect: Freud did not discuss stimulus control.
    b. **Correct: Psychic determinism refers to an individual's action being the result of unconscious processes.**
    c. Incorrect: Positive reinforcement is a behavioral term, not a Freudian term.
    d. Incorrect: Psychophysical parallelism is a made-up term

14. a. Incorrect: Freud did not believe people had free will.
    b. **Correct: Freud relied heavily on case studies.**
    c. Incorrect: Freud was more concerned with the irrational side of humans.
    d. Incorrect: Freud's theory placed large emphasis on childhood conflicts.

15. a. Incorrect: Structuralism is no longer a viable school of psychology.
    b. Incorrect: Functionalism is no longer a viable school of psychology.
    c. Incorrect: Gestalt psychology is no longer a viable school of psychology.
    d. **Correct: Cognitive Psychology is currently an active perspective in psychology.**

16. a. Incorrect: Skinner never discussed self-actualization; it was not overtly measurable.
    b. Incorrect: Skinner was concerned with overt behavior, not the unconscious.
    c. **Correct: Skinner felt that our past experiences influence our later actions.**
    d. Incorrect: As a behaviorist Skinner did not agree that we were born with any inborn tendencies, rather that they developed as a result of our experiences in the world.

17. a. **Correct: The neo-Freudians placed less emphasis on the role of sex and aggression.**
    b. Incorrect: All Freudians agree that the unconscious is important.
    c. Incorrect: All Freudians agree that childhood experiences are more important then heredity.
    d. Incorrect: All Freudians agree that childhood experiences are more important then heredity.

18. a. Incorrect: Differential psychology studies the differences between individuals.
    b. Incorrect: Not a name of a perspective in psychology.
    c. Incorrect: Not a name of a perspective in psychology.
    d. **Correct: The biopsychological perspective is concerned with the study of the physical body and its relation to behavior.**

19. a. **Correct: A psychiatrist is a medical doctor, or physician; a clinical psychologist is not.**
    b. Incorrect: A psychoanalyst might analyze dreams.
    c. Incorrect: A psychiatrist would probably rely more on the biopsychological perspective than psychoanalytic.
    d. Incorrect: Both individuals would treat people with serious psychological disorders.

20. a. Incorrect: She was not a psychoanalyst.
    b. **Correct: She was a woman trying to work in psychology before the women's rights movement.**
    c. Incorrect: She was never allowed to join this male-only society.
    d. Incorrect: Like most female scientists of her time, she never married.

Practice Test B:

1. a. Incorrect: Biology is a branch of science and sociology is a new a discipline like psychology.
   b. Correct: Psychology has it's methodology roots in Science and philosophy for it questions.
   c. Incorrect: Neurology is the medical study of the nervous system.
   d. Incorrect: These choices are the same thing, both refer to a method of thought.

2. a. Incorrect: Neither Plato, nor Aristotle, were concerned with Historicism or Presentism.
   b. Correct: Plato argued for the use of reasoning, Aristotle for the use of sensory experience.
   c. Incorrect: Neither of these philosophers was an empiricist.
   d. Incorrect: Both of these Philosophers agreed in the inborn nature of knowledge.

3. a. Incorrect: Psychic determinism is a Freudian term referring to the influence of the unconscious on behavior.
   b. Incorrect: Presentism refers to an intellectual approach that see the past in the context of current knowledge.
   c. Correct: Empiricism is a philosophical school that accepts sensory experience as a source of knowledge.
   d. Incorrect: Rationalism refers to the philosophical school that argues the reasoning gives us knowledge.

4. **a. Correct: All three men used scientific study to demonstrate things that had not been shown using philosophical reasoning.**
   b. Incorrect: None of these men studied the contents of the mind.
   c. Incorrect: None of the three used introspection.
   d. Incorrect: Rationalism was not ascribed to by any of these men.

5. a. Incorrect: Psychophysicists are not interested in the nature-nurture debate.
   b. Incorrect: Psychophysicists do not use reasoning as a method of study.
   c. Incorrect: Psychophysicists are not interested in evolutionary things.
   d. Correct: Psychophysicists are interested in the relationship between stimuli and perceptions.

6 a. Incorrect: Wundt only established the first Lab in psychology, it was his students that helped establish the discipline.
   b. Incorrect: Wundt was not interested in evolution.
   c. Correct: Wundt trained numerous (more than thirty) famous psychologists that helped to spread the discipline.
   d. Incorrect: Wundt used introspection to examine the conscious mind.

7. **a. Correct: In introspection a subject describes their experience of a stimuli.**
   b. Incorrect: A psychophysical measurement is a made up word.
   c. Incorrect: The techniques describe in this question is one in which were are reporting sensory experiences, not reasoning.
   d. Incorrect: Stream of consciousness is William James's description of the mind.

8. a. Incorrect: Functionalists did not study the unconscious.
   b. Incorrect: Functionalists studied a broad range of subjects, including children and the mentally ill.
   c. Correct: Functionalists did want to see psychology solve problems of everyday life.
   d. Incorrect: It was the Behaviorists that restricted psychology to the study of overt behaviors.

9. a. Incorrect: To a behaviorist only overt observable behavior is OK to study
   b. Incorrect: To a behaviorist only overt observable behavior is OK to study.
   c. Correct: Watson was a behaviorist.
   d. Incorrect: To a behaviorist only overt observable behavior is OK to study

10. a. Incorrect: Introspection refers to breaking things down into parts, you don't do that at a choral presentation.
    b. Correct: The word Gestalt means organized whole.
    c. Incorrect: The phi phenomenon refers to the appearance of apparent motion.
    d. Incorrect: Stream of consciousness refers to William James's notion of the mind.

11. a. Incorrect: Psychoanalytic perspective is concerned with the unconscious
    b. Incorrect: Psychoanalytic perspective is concerned with the unconscious.
    c. Incorrect: Psychoanalytic perspective is concerned with the unconscious.
    d. Correct: Psychoanalytic perspective is concerned with the unconscious.

12. a. Incorrect: The question only gives information on a behavior, its consequence, and the outcome.
    b. Incorrect: The question does not give information on any unconscious motivations.
    c. Incorrect: No information is given on the genetics of Billy and Bobby.
    d. Correct: The question describes a behavior, its consequence, and the differential outcome.

13. **a. Correct: Both cognitive and behavioral psychologists use well-controlled laboratory research.**
    b. Incorrect: Neither believes in the influence of the unconscious.
    c. Incorrect: Cognitive psychologists study mental processes; behaviorists do not.
    d. Incorrect: Neither view addressed the role of heredity.

14. a. Incorrect: Social-cultural psychologists are interested in the role of society and culture, not the brain.
    b. Correct: Biopsychological psychologists do study the brain.
    c. Incorrect: Cognitive psychologists are interested in mental processes.
    d. Incorrect: Behavioral psychologists study overt actions.

15. a. Incorrect: Existential psychology is more concerned with individuals and how they respond to the reality, not making generalizations about all men.
    b. Correct: Social-cultural perspective points out that we need to take societal and cultural influences into account; examining only North American men does not allow for generalizations to all men.
    c. Incorrect: By limiting study to men we can rule out most biological differences.
    d. Incorrect: This is irrelevant in this study.

16. a. Incorrect: Ethnocentric refers to judging another culture by the standards of your own; Dr. Ramos is not doing this.
    b. Incorrect: Rational behavior is behavior that requires conscious thought and reasoning; again, she is not doing this.
    c. Correct: Eclectic refers to the adoption or appreciation of multiple theoretical views to explain behavior. Dr. Ramos is using psychoanalytic, humanistic and biopsychological perspectives.
    d. Incorrect: Empirical refers to a method of knowing about the world based on sensory experiences, not describing behavior from numerous perspectives.

17. **A. Correct: Experimental psychologists study perception, memory, and emotions.**
    B. Incorrect: Cognitive psychologists are interested in thinking and mental processes.
    C. Incorrect: Comparative psychologists study similarities and differences between psychological processes in humans and animals.
    D. Incorrect: Humanistic psychology is a perspective concerned with studying the individuals' attainment of their full potential.

18. a. Incorrect: Forensic psychologists work to improve the legal system, not industry.
    b. Incorrect: Comparative psychologists study similarities and differences between psychological processes in humans and animals.
    c. Correct: Engineering psychologists apply psychological principles to the design of equipment and instruments.
    d. Incorrect: Environmental psychologists use psychological principles to improve the physical environment, not machines.

19. a. Incorrect: Psychic determinism refers to the role of the unconscious in behavior not the differential treatment of men and women professionally.
    b. Incorrect: Eclecticism refers to the adoption or appreciation of multiple theoretical views to explain behavior not the differential treatment of men and women professionally.
    c. Incorrect: Ethnocentric refers to judging another culture by the standards of your own not the differential treatment of men and women professionally.
    d. Correct: The notion of separate spheres refers to the differential treatment of men and women professionally.

20. a. Incorrect: Christine Ladd-Franklin studied under Hermann von Helmholtz, not William James.
    b. Correct: Mary Whiton Calkins studied under William James and was denied formal admission and a doctorate from Harvard.
    c. Incorrect: Karen Horney was a neo-Freudian and did not study under James.
    d. Incorrect: Margaret Floy Washburn was Titchener's first female doctoral student.

Essay Questions:

1. The social-cultural perspective argues for an increase in the attention to the effects that social and cultural factors have on behavior, and an increase in the study of these as variables. One reason for the recent increase in interest in this perspective is the development of more rapid communication tools (phone, fax, telephone, radio, e-mail) and transportation (plane), making it easier to reach distance places, in effect "shrinking our planet" and making it more likely that people from different cultures will interact.

2. A clinical psychologist would be most concerned with any evidence of symptoms of depression, substance and/or alcohol abuse in the members of the cult during the time just before the suicides. The developmental psychologist, on the other hand, would be more focused on any significant life events or social changes that had occurred in the lives of the cult members during their development years, particularly childhood and adolescence.

2 Psychology as a Science

LEARNING OBJECTIVES

After studying this chapter, you should be able to:

1. Describe the strengths and weaknesses of common sense, appeals to authority, reasoning, and unsystematic observation as everyday sources of knowledge. (p. 32-34)
2. List and explain the two core assumptions on which the scientific method is based, mentioning the significance of critical thinking. (P. 35-36)
3. List and explain the five steps of the scientific method by referring to a classic study of interpersonal attraction. (p. 35-36)
4. Explain how a recent study on the ability to detect drunkenness seriously questions the validity of everyday wisdom. (p. 36-37)
5. List and offer illustrative examples of the goals of scientific research, emphasizing key concepts such as operational definition, theory, etc. (p. 37-39)
6. List and describe five research methods that describe behavior, emphasizing the strengths and weaknesses of each. (p. 40-46)
7. Explain the nature of correlational research in making predictions about behavior, distinguishing between positive and negative correlations. (p. 46-47)
8. Distinguish between correlational and experimental research, emphasizing the strengths and weaknesses of each of these research techniques and explaining why the experiment allows scientists to examine cause-and-effect relationships. (p. 47-48)
9. Define internal validity and explain the key elements of the experimental method, referring to key concepts such as confounding variables, random assignment, and the various types of bias. (p. 48-51)
10. Define external validity and explain the importance of this concept in understanding the results of psychological research. (p. 51-52)
11. Describe the function of descriptive statistics, then list and explain three measures of central tendency and three measures of variability. (p. 53-54)
12. Describe what information is summarized in a coefficient of correlation. (p. 54-56)
13. Describe the function of inferential statistics, emphasizing concepts such as statistical significance in explaining behavior. (p. 56)
14. Describe the core concept of meta-analysis. (p. 56)
15. List and explain six important principles relevant to the ethical treatment of human beings in research. (p. 57-59)
16. Summarize the important issues in the controversy regarding the use of animals in scientific research, distinguishing between advocates of animal rights versus animal welfare. (p. 59-61)

COMPREHENSIVE GUIDED REVIEW

I. Sources of Knowledge: Everyday sources of knowledge include **common sense, appeal to authority, reasoning,** and **unsystematic observation** . __(1)__ relies on the assumption that if people share a belief, then it must be true. This approach to psychology is often called__(2)__ psychology. This approach to knowledge is one that many introductory psychology students use when they begin the course. A problem with this approach is that scientific research studies often demonstrate the beliefs to be false.

In contrast to common sense, the **appeal to authority** path to knowledge relies on the use of__(3)__. A problem with this source of knowledge is that authorities can be__(4)__. The inadequacy of this source of knowledge is strongly shown when two authorities disagree. As with common sense, the best solution to a disagreement comes from__(5)__. As you remember from Chapter 1, the problems associated with relying on authorities led René__(6)__to argue that true knowledge comes through correct **reasoning.** This path to knowledge argues that the accuracy of your position depends on the correctness of the__(7)__ you offer in support of it.

The fourth common path used to obtain knowledge is **unsystematic observation.** This approach can be traced back to John__(8)__, who countered Descartes and insisted that true knowledge comes through the__(9)__. Remember that Locke felt that the only way to obtain knowledge was through__(10)__ or, as he called it, experience. This theoretical position was known as__(11)__. However, because this type of observation depends on selective reporting and anecdotal reports, it is often inaccurate. __(12)__observation is a more dependable source of knowledge. As scientists, psychologists rely on the more dependable method of systematic observation, or the **scientific method,** as their path to knowledge.

The Scientific Method: Because of the weaknesses in the popular approaches, scientists prefer the__(13)__ method. This method is based on certain__(14)__ and follows a formal series of steps. Scientists have three basic assumptions about the world. First, they believe that there is__(15)__ in the universe. In other words they believe that relationships among events are lawful and__(16)__. Second, scientists believe that every event has a natural, potentially__(17)__ cause. This belief is called__(18)__ and in its strictest form rules out the acceptance of free will and supernatural influences as causes of human behavior.

The third belief of scientists is that open-minded__(19)__ is the best attitude. **Skepticism** requires that a scientist receive solid__(20)__ before accepting any claims. This attitude requires the individual to maintain a delicate balance between__(21)__ and gullibility. This is particularly important in psychology since many "truths" are tentative, and research findings often depend on both the time and__(22)__ in which the research occurred.

Skepticism is the basis of__(23)__, a valuable method of thinking for nonscientists as well as scientists. **Critical thinking** involves the__(24)__ of claims and assumptions, and is characterized by three steps. A critical thinker must first__(25)__ what claim is being made. Then, a critical thinker will examine the __(26)__ in support of the claim. In examining the claim and evidence, the critical thinker asks if the claim is supported by __(27)__evidence or by personal opinions or beliefs. Finally, the critical thinker will consider any possible alternative__(28)__of the claim. If there is a better explanation, the critical thinker will reserve acceptance or rejection of the claim.

As skeptics, psychologists rely on the use of the__(29)__ method to gain knowledge about behavior and mental processes. This method is systematic and, although there is some variance, most scientists use a similar approach in conducting scientific research. The steps are: 1) Provide a__(30)__; 2) Conduct the study; 3) Analyze the__(31)__; 4)__(32)__the research findings and 5)__(33)__ the study

Scientists begin their research studies by providing a__(34)__. This step involves identifying the problem,__(35)__the literature, choosing a research__(36)__, and stating a research **hypothesis.** A __(37)__is a testable prediction about the relationship between two or more events or characteristics. Once the hypothesis is clear, the second step is to__(38)__ the study. In this step the scientist carries out the research procedure and__(39)__ data. After conducting the study, the researcher must then __(40)__ the data. This process is typically done using mathematical calculations called **statistics.** Additionally, during this step the researcher will discuss the__(41)__ of the findings. The fourth step in the research process is to__(42)__ the research findings. Research psychologists do this by presenting papers at professional meetings and publishing articles in professional__(43)__. This final step in the research method is to__(44)__ the study so as to strengthen confidence in the findings. **Replication** involves repeating a study a second or third time. Some replications are exact; others involve variations.

Take one of your study breaks right now.

Review the Scientific Method: Fill in the blanks below to describe the research process:

1. Provide a_____	2. ______ the study	3. _________ the data.	4. ________ the findings	5. ________the study
a. Identify the ___________	a. ________ the procedure	a. Apply________ to the data	a. Present a paper at ___________	a. ________ exact research study
b. Review relevant ___________	b. Collect the ________	b. Discuss________ of research findings	b. Publish an article in ___________	b. Replicate study with _________
c. Decide on the ___________				
d. State the ___________				

In a formal research report, the researcher__(45)__ the study. In the first section of a published report, the author presents the rationale for the study, the research question, or__(46)__. The second section of the report describes the __(47)__ used in conducting the study, including the subjects, apparatus, and procedures. The third section of the report presents the results and__(48)__ analysis. The final section of a report presents the researcher's discussion of the __(49)__ of the study.

On page 35 in the textbook, you find a detailed account of a study by Byrne, Ervin, and Lamberth (1970) in which they researched interpersonal attraction. Dr. Sdorow has provided a summary of the study's steps. First, the researcher conducted **archival research** of__(50)__studies on interpersonal attraction. The__(51)__that was decided on was a **field experiment** in which the researchers studied college students in a __(52)__ setting. The subjects were given a **questionnaire** or list of__(53)__ and then observed. The researchers used **statistics** to__(54)__and interpret the data. They found that the research supported the hypothesis that students would be attracted to those like themselves.

Quiz on Understanding Research Descriptions: On page 36 in the textbook, you will find the section entitled "Anatomy of a Contemporary Research Study." These sections appear throughout the textbook. They are designed to help you understand the scientific method as it is applied in all areas of psychology. On this particular page, you will find a summary of a study of drunken behavior conducted in 1983 by James Langenbucher and Peter Nathan. Use this account to quiz yourself on your ability to understand the scientific method. Identify the rationale, hypothesis, procedures, statistics, and conclusions of the Langenbucher and Nathan research study below.

What was the rationale for the study?

What procedures were used to test the hypothesis?

What were the conclusions of the authors?

II. Goals of Scientific Research: Psychologists do not just conduct research for research's sake: like other scientists they pursue common goals. The four goals of psychological research are the **description, prediction, explanation,** and **control** of behavior and mental processes.

_(55)__ involves citing the observable characteristics of an event, object, or individual. However, the descriptions are not arbitrary; scientific descriptions must be__(56)__. Scientists describe only those things that are__(57)_ to the research. Obtaining good scientific descriptions typically requires good__(58)_ skills. **Precision** is another important characteristic of good descriptions. To be considered__(59)_, the descriptions must be concrete, not abstract. This skill generally involves__(60)_, or the use of numbers to represent events or characteristics. In psychology, precision is achieved through the__(61)__, which define behaviors or qualities in terms of the procedures used to measure them.

Psychologists do not limit themselves to the descriptions of things; they are also interested in making__(62)_ about interrelationships among variables. **Predictions** are made in the form of__(63)_, which are usually derived from **theories.** A__(64)_ summarizes and explains research findings and often attempts to unite diverse research findings.

When psychologists go beyond the goals of description and prediction, they are often interested in__(65)_ variables and__(66)_ their effect on the behavior and mental processes. Thus, their research is directed at the goal of__(67)_. In psychology, the notion of control is used in two ways. First, it is critical in__(68)_. Second, psychologists try to __(69)_ their research findings to the control of behavior in everyday life, such as helping people alleviate maladaptive habits.

Psychologists are often able to predict and control behavior and mental processes. However, identifying the causes of behavior, mental and physiological processes, or__(70)_, is the ultimate goal of psychology. In other words, psychologists may be able to__(71)_ that students who study more often do better on exams, and may be able to (72)_ student's exam scores by controlling their study time, without knowing why studying more leads to higher exam scores. The goal of explanation is the answer to the question of "_(73)__" the students did better.

Remember the six perspectives presented in Chapter 1 of the text? (biopsychological, behavioral, cognitive, psychoanalytic, humanistic, and social-cultural) The__(74)_ that a psychologist favors will influence the explanation that is examined in that psychologist's research. Each of the particular perspectives might explain a student's Type A behavior differently. A cognitive psychologist might say that the behavior is linked to her _(75). A humanistic psychologist might say that the behavior was rooted in her__(76)_ of inadequacy. A __(77)__psychologist would most likely attribute her behavior to unconscious conflicts, while a_(78)__would say the behavior is the result of an imbalance of chemicals in her brain. The behavioral psychologist would most likely link the behavior to the person's __(79)_. Finally, the social-cultural psychologist would credit a person's actions to her __(80)__.

Quiz on Goals of Psychological Research: Match the goal with its question.

Goal	**Question**
______Description	1. Can I predict it?
______Prediction	2. What causes it?
______Control	3. What are its characteristics?
______Explanation	4. Can I make it happen?

III. Methods of Psychological Research: Psychologists rely on the scientific method to answer questions about the __(81)_, prediction, control, and__(82)_ of behavior and mental processes. The specific procedures used in each study vary according to the specific_(83)_being addressed. **Descriptive research** pursues the goal of__(84)_, **correlational research** the goal of__(85)__, and **experimental research** is directed at the goals of control and_(86)_

In **descriptive** research, the researcher simply records what is seen through __(87)__ observation. Variations of this type of research include **naturalistic observation, case studies, surveys, psychological testing,** and **archival research.** In ____(88)____, subjects are observed in their natural environment. To minimize the influence that the presence of the observer might have upon the behavior of the person being observed, the observer is as low-profile, or __(89)___, as possible.

Although the advantage of this approach is the potential discovery of something that could not be seen in the more artificial constraints of a__(90)__, this type of observation has its limitations. First, hasty__(91)__are often not applicable beyond the environment in which the observations were made; second, it does not allow the researcher to determine__(92)__ relationships. Examples of the use of naturalistic observation cited in the text include checking the wear rate of floor tiles in a museum, and the observation of__(93)__by Jane Goodall. The study of animal behavior in the natural environment is called__(94)__.

Case studies are in-depth studies of a__(95)__ designed to gain as much information as possible about a variety of phenomena. The__(96)__ researcher attempts to obtain information about the individual's thoughts, feelings, life experiences, and social relationships. This method is often used in ___(97)__studies of individuals with psychological disorders. A well-known case study is the published account of the therapy sessions that__(98)___ underwent to treat her multiple personality disorder. Like other types of___(99)__methods, the case study method has its shortcomings: case studies __(100)__ determine which particular variables caused the behavior; and the results of a single case study cannot be __(101)__ to all people.

Surveys are designed to gather large amounts of information about the__(102)__, behaviors, and __(103)__ of many people and are commonly presented in one of two forms, either a written__(104)__or a personal interview. Good __(105)__use clearly worded questions that do not introduce__(106)__, or the tendency to respond in a particular way. One problem most frequently encountered with surveys pertains to the__(107)__ of the response. Also related to this is the interactive effect of __(108)__differences between test takers and survey structure. An additional shortcoming in survey research, as with all descriptive studies, is the__(109)__ of the results.

Surveys do not include everyone of interest. Instead, the researchers often select a group of people to represent the __(110)__, or whole. This group is referred to as the__(111)__. Representativeness of the **sample** is important if the researchers want to generalize beyond it. Ideally, researchers should sample subjects who__(112)__ the **population** of interest. However, because researchers often know little information about the populations, in most cases researchers use ____(113)___sampling. By using random sampling, researchers can more__(114)__ state that what they find to be true for the sample is likely to be true for the population as a whole. The textbook discusses an example of a survey done without proper sampling procedures in the *Literary Digest* poll of 1936.

Take a minute to think about the generalizability of Gallup polls during presidential elections or the Nielsen ratings of TV shows. Many TV news programs now conduct surveys on various issues: sexual harassment, rape trials, the environment, the economy, and so on. How generalizable are the results of these surveys? What about the fact that to participate in some of these surveys you often have to dial a 900 number and pay anywhere from 50 cents to $4 to have your opinion recorded? Would that be an example of unbiased sampling?

The fourth type of descriptive research is__(115)__, which generates a formal sample of a person's behavior. Good **psychological tests** have the advantage of allowing researchers and others to make__(116)__ decisions about a subject's behavior. A good test demonstrates three important principles of test construction. These are **standardization, reliability,** and__(117)__.

The first characteristic of a good test is__(118)__. There are two kinds; one ensures that the test is scored in a __(119)__ manner and the other involves the establishment of__(120)__, which are standards with which those who take the tests are compared. The second characteristic of a good test is__(121)__. This is the degree to which a test gives__(122)__ results. Reliability is often determined by a __(123)__ method in which the subjects are given a test at two different times and then the scores are compared. The third characteristic of a good test is **validity.** ___(124)____refers to the extent to which a test measures what it is supposed to measure. There are four types of validity: ____(125)__validity, wherein a test appears to measure what it is supposed to measure; __(126)__ validity, wherein the items that are contained in the test are a representative sample of what is being tested; __(127)__ validity, which refers to the extent to which the test measures the supposed concept, or construct, it presumes to measure; and__(128)__validity, which indicates that the test accurately predicts behavior related to what the test is supposed to measure.

The final type of descriptive research discussed in the text is __(129)__. It is potentially the largest source of knowledge, wherein one examines collections of letters, __(130)__, tapes, videos, or other materials. Archives are especially valuable sources of__(131) material. The uses of archival research are virtually without limit, as are the questions that may be addressed.

Correlational research is directed at the goal of__(132)__. A correlation refers to the degree of__(133)_between two or more variables. Remember that a__(134)__ is an event, behavior, condition, or characteristic that has two or more values. Correlations are either positive or negative. When the correlation is__(135)__, the values of both variables go together in the same direction; both increase, or both decrease. When the correlation is__(136)__, the values of the variables go in opposite directions; as one increases, the other decreases. The value of a correlation can range from 0, meaning there is *no* relationship and 1.00, meaning the relationship is__(137)__. A limitation of correlational research is its inability to identify__(138)__. Thus, when two variables are__(139)__, psychologists must be careful not to conclude that one caused the other. Remember: correlation does not imply__(140)__.

__(141)____is used to determine whether there is a cause and effect relationship between variables. The simplest experiment uses two equivalent groups: the__(142)__ group, which is exposed to the condition you want to manipulate, and the__(143)__ group, which is not exposed to the condition. The__(144)__ variable is what the experimenter manipulates or changes. The__(145)__ variable is what the experimenter measures.

For example, pretend that you are an educational psychologist and you are interested in researching whether using a study guide improves students' performance on tests. To conduct this study, you would select two equivalent groups of students from the course. One group is assigned to study a chapter from the study guide and read the textbook. The second group reads only the textbook. An exam follows. In this case, the group that studies both the study guide and the textbook is the__(146)__ group and the group that studies only the textbook is the__(147)__ group. Reading a chapter from the study guide or not reading a chapter from the study guide is the__(148)__ variable in this study, and how each group performs on the test is the__(149)__ variable. Remember that the hypothesis in an experimental study questions whether the independent variable__(150)__the effect on the dependent variable.

In order to be able to reach good, generalizable conclusions, the experimenter must do more than just__(151)__ the **independent variable.** The experimenter must also control any extraneous factors whose effects would be __(152)__ with those of the independent variable. Such factors are known as__(153)____. **Confounding variables** may be associated with the experimental procedure, or something about the subjects or experimenter(s). (The "Pepsi Challenge" experiment discussed in your textbook provides an example of the importance of controlling potential confounding__(154)__ variables.) When experimenters control for confounding variables, they are said to promote the __(155)____ validity of the study.

Experimenters increase the chance that the **experimental** and **control** groups will be initially equivalent by relying on **random assignment.** In__(156)__ assignment, every subject has the same likelihood of being assigned to any of the groups. In addition to randomly assigning subjects to groups, experimenters still have other subject variables to control. One of the most important is **subject bias.** This is the tendency of people who know they are participants in a study to behave in a way__(157)__ than they normally do. If there is the possibility of__(158)__ occurring, the experimenter might have to become unobtrusive or__(159)__ the subjects about the true nature of the study. This, however, is considered __(160)__, and it is of great concern, so much so that the American Psychological Association, or APA, has developed guidelines for **informed consent.**

Another concern in experimental studies is that of **experimenter effects,** or the influence that the__(161)__ personal qualities, actions, and data treatment has on the outcome of the study. Additionally, the experimenter s __(162)__ about the outcome of the study is of special concern since it can lead to an experimenter__(163)__ effec in which the experimenter's unintentional actions contribute to or influence the outcome of the study. An example o this is the tendency of subjects to behave in accordance with the experimenter's expectancy. This is called the __(164)__. Smiling at subjects in one group and not at those in the other is just one example of actions that might promote an experimenter effect.

A classic example of an experimenter effect was demonstrated by Rosenthal and Jacobson in 1968. The researchers found that when teachers were led to believe that their students were fast learners, their students performed__(165)__. But when the teachers were told that their students were slow learners, their student's performance was__(166). This has come to be known as the__(167)__ effect. To control for possible experimenter effects, researchers often use a procedure in which neither the experimenter nor the subject knows what condition each is assigned to. This is known as a__(168)__.

Anatomy of a Classic Research Study: Can Experimenter Expectancies Affect the Behavior of Laboratory Rats?

In this classic study, "maze-bright" or "maze-dull" rats were used. Practice your skills at reading research studies by answering the questions below:

What was the rationale for the study?

What procedures were used to test the hypothesis?

What were the conclusions of the authors?

In addition to being concerned with **internal validity** issues, experimenters must also watch **external validity.** This concept relates to the extent to which experimenters can__(169)__ their research findings. This is an important issue in psychology because of the heavy reliance on white rats and college students as__(170)__. Another problem is the use of __(171)__. To what extent can findings using volunteers be generalized? The only way to determine whether the results of research studies have__(172)__ is to replicate them, repeatedly.

Congratulations. You have finished the section on methods of psychological research!
Stop and take a short break at this point and then do the mini-review when you come back.

Mini-review of Research Methods in Psychology: Match each research term with its correct description.

________1 descriptive	A. Research in which the researcher simply records what is seen through systematic observation
________2. correlational	B. Research in which subjects are observed in their natural environment
________3. naturalistic observation	C. An in-depth study of a single person; is often used in clinical studies
________4. survey	D. Method designed to gather large amounts of information about the attitudes, behaviors, opinions of many people
________5. psychological testing	E. A group of people selected to represent the whole
________6. archival research	F. All individuals of interest; the group that researchers wish to generalize about
________7. experimental	G. Generation of a formal sample of a person's behavior; has the advantage of allowing researchers and others to make unbiased decisions about a subject's behavior
________8. case study	H. The degree to which a test gives consistent results
________9. reliability	I. The assurance that the test is scored in a consistent manner and in accordance with norms
________10. validity	J. Refers to the extent to which a test measures what it is supposed to measure
________11. standardization	K. Method used to identify the degree of relationship between two or more variables; does not imply causation
________12. confounding variable	L. Used to determine whether there is a cause and effect relationship between variables
________13. independent variable	M. A type of descriptive research wherein one examines collections of letters, manuscripts, tapes, videos, or other materials
________14. dependent variable	N. In an experiment, the group exposed to the condition you want to manipulate
________15. experimenter effect	O. In an experiment, the group not exposed to the condition
________16. population	P. The variable that the experimenter manipulates or changes
________17. sample	Q. The variable that the experimenter measures
________18. subject bias	R. Any extraneous factors whose effects would be confused with those of the independent variable
________19. random sampling	S. Giving every subject the same likelihood of being assigned to any of the groups
________20. control group	T. The tendency of people who know they are participants in a study to behave in a way other than they normally do
________21. experimental group	U. The influence that the experimenter's personal qualities, actions and data treatment has on the results of the study
________22. double-blind	V. A procedure in which neither the experimenter nor the subject knows what condition the subjects are assigned to

IV. Statistical Analysis of Research Data: In order to make sense of data, psychologists use __(173)__. Psychologists use three different types: **descriptive statistics,** which__(174)__ data, **correlational statistics,** which determine__(175)__, and **inferential statistics,** which test research__(176)__.

__(177)__statistics are concerned with painting a picture about data or a set of scores. Descriptive statistics include **measures of central tendency** and **measures of variability**. Measures of__(178)__ use a single number to represent the group of scores. The three different measures of central tendency are the **mean,**__(179)__, and **mode.**

The__(180)__ is the most frequent score in a set of scores. To find the mode you simply look for the score or scores that occur most__(181)__. The **median** is the__(182)__ score. To calculate the median you must__(183)__ the scores from high to low and then find the middlemost score. The median is the__(184)__ point, or the 50-percent point. Hence, unlike the mode, which is determined by frequency, the median is determined by its__(185)__.

The _(186)_ is the measure of central tendency you use to compute your grades; it is the arithmetic average. To find the _(187)_, you add all of the scores and divide by the total number of scores. Since you add up each score, every score is represented in the final value. Thus, the mean is the most_(188)_ measure of central tendency. It is no determined solely by position or frequency. The_(189)_ is the measure of central tendency used most often by psychologists.

People use the term_(190)_ all the time. Advertisers use it to persuade you to buy their product. The problem is that the term *average* can refer to the_(191)_, median, or mean, and advertisers rarely tell you which of the three alternatives they are using, thus creating misleading impressions.

The **measures of variability** used in psychology include the **range, variance,** and_(192)_. The **range** simply refers to the difference between the highest and the lowest score in any set of scores. You may have five scores, but in calculating the range you use only_(193)_: the highest and the lowest. The range is easy to find, but it can be misleading since it uses only the most_(194)_ scores. A better **measure of variability** or_(195)_ should include the mean as one of its calculations, since it would account for the differences among all of the scores. That calculation is called the **standard deviation.** The_(196)_ deviation represents the degree of dispersion or variability of scores around their mean and is the square root of a measure of variability called the_(197)_.

Once you know a measure of central tendency, in most cases the mean, and a measure of variability, in most cases the standard deviation or variance, you have the essential information that you need to describe your data.

In **correlational statistics** we are interested in_(198)_ one set of scores from another. A_(199)_ is expressed as a correlation coefficient. A coefficient has two elements: the sign, which can be either plus or minus, which indicates the _(200)_ of the relationship between the two variables; and the number, which represents the_(201)_ of the relationship. Remember that a_(202)_ correlation indicates that high scores on one variable correlate with high scores on the other variable, and a_(203)_ correlation means that low scores on one variable relate to a high score on the other. The value of the correlation coefficient can range from minus 1.00 to 0.00 to plus 1.00. The _(204)_ the correlation value, the better your prediction will be. Finally, remember a correlation does not say anything about _(205)_.

_(206)_ statistics allows researchers to answer the question of whether the difference observed between the experimental and treatment groups is the result of chance, or the result of the actual independent variable manipulation. If there is a low probability that the difference is due to_(207)_, then the difference is said to be **statistically significant** and is attributable to the_(208)_variable. To determine the probability, researchers perform a statistical test for the significance of the difference between the groups. There are many types of inferential tests. One of the main tests is the_(209)_, which is used to compare two sets of scores (for example, the experimental versus the control group). Another type of inferential test is the_(210)_ (or ANOVA). This is an F test for _(211)_ in which there are more than two groups.

Statistical tests evaluate the differences between the _(212)_ and control groups on your descriptive measures and show you the degree to which these differences are_(213)_significant. Then you will know whether the difference(s) were _(214)_ or simply occurred by chance. However, statistical significance does not necessarily mean _(215)_ significance. For example, a drug may cause experimental subjects to lose significantly more weight than_(216)_ subjects, but if that difference was only one pound it may not be practical to take the drug.

Congratulations. You have finished the section on the use of statistics in psychology. You deserve a study break! Complete the mini-review when you return and then move on to the end of the chapter.

Mini-review of Statistics: Match the statistic with its application.

Statistic		**Application**
A. mode	______1.	Statistics that summarize data
B. standard deviation	______2.	Indicates there is a low probability that the difference between the experimental and control groups is due to chance
C. correlation coefficient	______3.	Measures that use a single number to represent the group of scores
D. mean	______4.	The most frequent score in a set of scores
E. t-test	______5.	The middle score
F. statistical significance	______6.	Includes the mean as one of its calculations; accounts for the differences between all of the scores
G. inferential statistic	______7.	The measure of central tendency you use to compute your grade average
H. median	______8.	The difference between the highest and the lowest score in any sct of scores
I. range	______9.	The standard deviation squared
J. variance	______10.	Statistics that test research hypotheses
K. descriptive statistics	______11.	A measurement that indicates the direction and strength of the relationship between the two variables
L. correlational statistics	______12.	One of the main inferential statistical tests used to compare two sets of scores
M. central tendency	______13.	The F-test; a type of inferential test for experiments in which we more than two groups are tested
N. analysis of variance	______14.	Statistics that determine relationships; or predict one score from another

V. Thinking About Psychology: What Are the Ethics of Psychological Research?

The American Psychological Association (APA) has a code for the ethical treatment of human and animal subjects. This code of ethics has certain requirements that researchers must meet when working with subjects. The code for the treatment of human subjects states:

1. Subjects must be__(217)__ of all aspects of the research procedure that might influence their decision to participate. This is known as **informed consent.**
2. No one can be__(218)__ to participate.
3. A subjects may__(219)__ at any time.
4. A subject must be protected from physical__(220)__ and mental distress
5. If the subject does experience harm or distress, the researcher must try to__(221)__ it.
6. Information gained from a subject must be held__(222)__.

Although this code of ethics specifically mentions the right of a subject to__(223)__ consent, the textbook cites a number of studies in which researchers used **deception** to reduce__(224)__. In such instances, the experimenter not only has to justify the use of deception but is also obligated to **debrief** the subjects.__(225)__ involves explaining the research and relieving any distress the subjects might have experienced.

In addition to a code of treatment for human subjects, the APA has guidelines for the treatment of animal subjects. Animal__(226)__ supporters oppose all laboratory research using animals, regardless of its scientific merit or practical benefits. Animal__(227)__ supporters would permit laboratory research on animals when its potential benefits outweigh any pain and distress caused to the animals. Currently the APA guidelines are closer to the views of the animal__(228)__ advocates. The standards require that animals be treated with__(229)__, housed in clean cages, and given adequate food and water. Additionally, researchers must__(230)__ the pain and suffering of the animal. All institutions that receive federal research grants that involve experiments using animals must have an animal subjects__(231)__ that reviews all research procedures to ensure that they meet ethical guidelines.

Why do psychologists study animals? First, to__(232)__ about animal behavior. Second, using animals makes it easier to __(233)__ extraneous factors. Third, __(234)__ changes across the life span can be more easily studied. Fourth, research on animals can generate__(235)__ that can then be tested on humans. Fifth, the research may benefit both humans and animals.

KEY RESEARCH FINDINGS

Provide the details of the following key research studies in psychology:

1. **Kozar et al. (1993):** Showed that free-throw percentage tended to increase after time-outs. (Page 32)
2. **Byrne, Ervin, & Lamberth (1970):** Showed that partners who had similar attitudes rated each other as more likeable, stood closer to each other, and were more likely to recall each others names than partners who had dissimilar attitudes. (Page 35-36)
3. **Langenbucher & Nathan (1983):** Showed that people with experience in observing drinkers may be unable to determine whether a person is drunk or sober. (Page 36-37)
4. **Webb et al. (1966):** Showed that the tiles at the most popular museum exhibit (hatching chicks) had to be replaced every six weeks. (Page 40)
5. **Goodall (1990):** Demonstrated that chimpanzee behavior in natural setting is different than in captivity. (Page 41)
6. **Chen, Lee & Stevenson (1995):** Demonstrated cultural differences in the use of extreme points on a questionnaire scale. (Page 43)
7. **Zweigenhaft (1977):** Showed that the size of an individual's signature was related to his or her self-esteem. (Page 45)
8. **Moore (1984):** Found that the number of acknowledgments given to women in journals increased from 1959 to 1979. (Page 46)
9. **Coke-Pepsi Slugfest (1976):** Demonstrated the effects of confounding variables. (Page 49)
10. **Harris & Rosenthal (1985):** Demonstrated that an experimenter's personal qualities can affect subjects behavior. (Page 49)
11. **Rosenthal & Jacobson (1968):** Demonstrated that teachers' expectancies for the performance of their students affect how well children perform. (Page 50)
12. **Rosenthal & Fode (1963):** Showed that the performance of rats could be attributed to experimenter bias. (Page 50)

Congratulations! You have finished your comprehensive review of Chapter 2. Now it is time for you to test what you have learned. Do the practice tests below.

PRACTICE TEST A

1. If you assume that a belief is true simply because you share it with many people, your belief would be based on
   a. common sense.
   b. deductive reasoning.
   c. an appeal to authority.
   d. unsystematic observation.

Obj.: 1 Page: 32

2. If you attribute your friend's depressed mood to an evil spirit, you would be violating the scientific assumption of
   a. free will.
   b. determinism.
   c. randomization.
   d. phenomenalism.

Obj.: 2 Page: 34

3 . In which step of the scientific method did Byrne have the subjects complete the survey in his research on the nature of the relationship between similarity and interpersonal attraction?
   a. Step 2: the analysis of data stage.
   b. Step 2. the communication stage.
   c. Step 2: the conducting of the study stage.
   d. Step 1: the rationale stage.

Obj.: 3 Page: 35-36

4. What was the rationale of the authors in the Langenbucher and Nathan study on drunkenness?
   a. The researchers took bartenders, social drinkers, and police officers and asked them to determine if an individual was drunk by observation of them.
   b. The researchers analyzed the data with statistics.
   c. The researchers wanted to test the commonly held belief that drunkness could be easily detected.
   d. The authors implied that without special training it is difficult to determine the sobriety of an individual.

Obj.: 4 Page: 36-37

5. If you define intelligence as a score on the Wechsler Intelligence Scale, you would be using a(n)
   a. lexical definition.
   b. unobtrusive measure.
   c. operational definition.
   d. commonsense explanation.

Obj.: 5 Page: 38

6. The prediction that "people high in psychological hardiness will be less likely to become ill than will people low in psychological hardiness" is an example of
   a. a fact
   b. a hypothesis.
   c. inductive reasoning.
   d. an operational definition.

Obj.: 5 Page: 38

7. A child psychologist spends three hours a week watching and recording the play patterns of 3-year-old children in a nursery school. This is an example of (a)
   a. case study.
   b. archival research.
   c. experimental research.
   d. naturalistic observation.

Obj.: 6 Page: 40

8. The largest of the following correlations is
   a. .37
   b. .00
   c. -.01
   d. -.93

Obj.: 7 Page: 46

9. There is a positive correlation between educational level and a deadly form of skin cancer called malignant melanoma. This means that
   a. attending college inhibits the growth of cancer cells.
   b. if you drop out of college today you will reduce your risk of skin cancer.
   c. the stress of college adversely affects the immune system's ability to destroy cancer cells.
   d. adults who have only a high school education will be less likely to develop malignant melanoma than will adults with a college education.

Obj.: 7 Page: 46

10. A researcher is interested in testing how cohabitation and marital stability are related. What type of research method should be used?
   a. an experimental study.
   b. a case study.
   c. a measure of central tendency.
   d. a correlational study.

Obj.: 8 Page: 47-48

11. A social psychologist compares the performance of runners who race against time to the performance of runners who race against other people. The dependent variable would be the
   a. running times.
   b. sex of the runners.
   c. nature of the running track.
   d. kind of opponent (time or other people).

Obj.: 9 Page: 47

12. If you can demonstrate that the results of your research study can be replicated, then you are providing evidence of
   a. content validity.
   b. external validity.
   c. reliability.
   d. construct validity.

Obj.: 10 Page: 51-52

13. Given the numbers 2, 3, 22, 10, 3, 7, 9, the median is
    a. 3
    b. 7
    c. 8
    d. 10

Obj.: 11 Page: 53

14. The strongest association between two variables is represented by which one of the following correlation coefficients?
    a. +.25
    b. -.44
    c. +.44
    d. -.53

Obj.: 12 Page: 54-56

15. The branch of statistics that uses data from samples to make predictions about populations is called
    a. deductive statistics.
    b. parametric statistics.
    c. descriptive statistics.
    d. inferential statistics.

Obj.: 13 Page: 56

16. If a group of researchers wants to examine the results of many related research studies to determine the average size of the effect of the independent variable, what type of statistical technique should they use?
    a. correlation
    b. meta-analysis
    c. t tests
    d. analysis of variance

Obj.: 14 Page: 56

17. Upon completion of a research study the highest priority should be that subjects are
    a. debriefed.
    b. given the results of the study.
    c. told that they were not deceived even if they were.
    d. told that their responses are not necessarily confidential.

Obj.: 15 Page: 57-59

18. Psychologists are interested in studying animals for a variety of reasons. Among them is
    a. research with animals can generate hypotheses that can then be tested using humans.
    b. that it is easier to control potential confounding variables.
    c. that research on animals may benefit animals themselves.
    d. all of the above.

Obj.: 16 Page: 59-61

PRACTICE TEST B

1. Dr. Green writes a book called *A Diet to Make Your Children Geniuses*. On the book cover and on numerous television interview shows, Dr. Green is described as a renowned authority on children and nutrition. What question should a wise reader ask?
    a. Is there any scientific research to support the claims made by this supposed expert?
    b. Is the book really a best-seller all over the country, or just in my community?
    c. Do television interviewers regard Dr. Green as an expert on this topic?
    d. Do any other experts contradict Dr. Green's ideas and recommendations?

Obj.: 1 Page: 33

2. A television "health editor" reports that eating lots of broccoli and cauliflower lowers the risk of certain cancers. As a critical thinker, your first question should be
    a. Does the health editor believe this claim?
    b. Is this claim based on scientifically evaluated empirical data?
    c. Have I read or heard similar claims from other sources?
    d. Does the editor refer to authorities who support this claim?

Obj.: 2 Page: 35

3. Why is replication important in the scientific method?
   a. Repetition permits greater confidence that the findings are accurate.
   b. Communication allows other researchers to evaluate the findings offered.
   c. Publishing or presenting the data establishes the rationale for the study.
   d. Variations in the study will determine if there is a better explanation for the findings.

Obj.: 3 Page: 35

4. You know that by offering a reward, your children will clean their rooms, so you offer some type of reward every time you want the rooms cleaned. This is an example of the psychological goal of
   a. control.
   b. prediction.
   c. understanding.
   d. description.

Obj: 5 Page: 37-39

5. You are interested in studying the environmental factors that influence college students to drop out of school. The goal of this research is best represented by the psychological goal of
   a. explanation.
   b. control.
   c. prediction.
   d. understanding.

Obj.: 5 Page: 37-39

6. A man is hospitalized after attempting to set himself on fire several times. Which research method would be most useful in trying to understand his behavior?
   a. an experiment.
   b. naturalistic observation.
   c. a case study.
   d. a survey.

Obj.: 6 Page: 41

7. A researcher studying college students finds that the more hours students devote to watching television the lower they score on a test of creativity. These variables are most accurately described as
   a. having little correlation.
   b. positively correlated.
   c negatively correlated.
   d. being related in terms of cause and effect.

Obj.: 7 Page: 46

8. A researcher asks two groups of students to fast after midnight. The next morning the researcher gives a caffeine pill to one group and a neutral pill to the other, and then gives both groups a problem-solving task. Here, the independent variable is
   a. whether or not the students fasted.
   b. the control group's behavior.
   c. the score on the problem-solving task.
   d. ingestion of caffeine or a neutral pill.

Obj.: 8 Page: 47

9. If every person in a given population has an equal and independent chance of being selected, the sample chosen is known as a
   a. nonrepresentative sample.
   b. random sample.
   c. biased sample.
   d. nongeneralizable sample.

Obj.: 9 Page: 48-51

10. The only way to determine whether the results of research studies do, in fact, have external validity is to
    a. replicate them.
    b. check the predictive validity.
    c. check the content validity.
    d. eliminate subject bias.

Obj.: 10 Page: 51-52

11. Psychologists use ______________ statistics to test their research hypotheses, ___________________ statistics to summarize data, and ________________statistics to determine relationships between variables.
    a. descriptive, correlational, inferential
    b. correlational, descriptive, inferential
    c. inferential, correlational, descriptive
    d. inferential, descriptive, correlational

Obj.: 11 Page: 52-54

12. Professor Patel records student scores on the first psychology examination of the semester. She calculates the mean and median scores for the class, as well as the standard deviation. Her calculations serve to
    a. summarize the performance of the class as a whole.
    b. infer whether the results occurred by chance or not.
    c. describe the performance of individual students.
    d. correlate test performance with other variables.

Obj.: 11 Page: 53

13. A researcher calculates a correlation coefficient of .21 between the number of software programs on students' home computers and college GPA. What does this communicate about the relationship between these two factors?
  a. A higher number of home computer programs strongly predicts higher college GPAs.
  b. Having a greater number of different software programs on the home computer causes students to do better in college.
  c. There is a relatively weak relationship between the number of programs on home computers and college GPAs.
  d. A greater number of software programs on college students' home computers predicts lower GPAs.

Obj.: 12 Page: 56

14. Researchers use inferential statistics in their studies to help determine
  a. the internal and external validity of the research method employed.
  b. whether the changes found occurred by chance or were due to the impact of the independent variable.
  c. if there is a positive or negative association between two variables.
  d. how close a set of scores are to the mean and also how dispersed they are around that mean.

Obj.: 13 Page: 56

15. Dr. Ames is conducting archival research into the study habits of students in different countries. She gathers research findings from hundreds of studies and wants to determine the average size of the effect of culture. What statistical techniques would be the best for her to use with her data?
  a. the calculation of a mean and standard deviation only.
  b. an analysis of variance.
  c. a t test.
  d. a meta-analysis.

Obj.: 14 Page: 56

16. A human factors psychologist is testing whether the noise of a particular machine causes irritability and decreases performance. Research participants sign a statement that explains the nature of the study and that there might be discomfort during the procedure. Their signature indicates they understand the nature of the study and agree to participate. Those who sign the statement
  a. cannot withdraw at a later time.
  b. have given informed consent.
  c. may not be deceived.
  d. have been debriefed.

Obj.: 15 Page: 58

17. Animal rights advocates
  a. would permit laboratory research on animals.
  b. have the complete and unqualified support of the APA.
  c. would argue that the 5 percent of APA members who conduct research using animals represents an acceptable figure.
  d. do not accept the argument that research with animals is justified by the fact that it can lead to findings that may benefit humankind.

Obj.: 16 Page: 59-61

18. If an experimenter varies the loudness of music in a factory to observe its effect upon the rate of productivity, the dependent variable is the
  a. rate of productivity.
  b. loudness of the music.
  c. factory setting.
  d. subjects involved in the experiment.

Obj.: 8 Page: 47-48

19. The famous cases of Sybil, Eve White and Jane-A case of multiple personality, all show the use of the ______________ method.
  a. experimental
  b. interview
  c. survey
  d. case study

Obj.: 6 Page: 41-42

20. A researcher conducted a correlational study examining the relationship between drug usage and attitudes toward premarital sex among teenagers. The results indicated that as drug usage increased, attitudes became more permissive. What is wrong with the researcher's concluding that an increase in drug usage causes attitudes to become more permissive?
   a. The subjects may have lied about their attitudes.
   b. The relationship is not a consistent one.
   c. The researchers did not take into account that as the teenagers became adults, their attitudes would become less permissive.
   d. The researchers are attempting to conclude cause from a correlational study.

Obj.: 8 Page: 47-48

ESSAY QUESTIONS

1. An instructor of introductory psychology wants to know if giving "more tests" (rather than "fewer tests") during the semester results in "more retention" of material "well after" the introductory course is over. Explain how the researcher might operationally define all of the terms in quotation marks.

Obj.: 5 Page: 37-39

2. Suppose you are having a discussion with your roommate about which science classes are good to take. You suggest psychology and your roommate argues that psychology is not a true science. He claims that psychology is all common sense. How would you counter your roommate's argument and defend the claim that psychology is a science?

Obj.: 2 Page: 34-35

ANSWER RECORD FOR CHAPTER 2

Comprehensive Guided Review:

1. Common sense	12. Systematic	23. critical thinking	34. rationale
2. lay	13. scientific	24. systematic evaluation	35. reviewing
3. experts	14. assumptions	25. identify	36. method
4. wrong	15. order	26. evidence	37 hypothesis
5. scientific research	16. predictable	27. empirical	38. conduct
6. Descartes	17. measurable	28. explanations	39. collects
7. reasons	18. determinism	29. scientific	40. analyze
8. Locke	19. skepticism	30. rationale	41. implications
9. senses	20. evidence	31. data	42. communicate
10. observation	21. cynicism	32. Communicate	43. journals
11. empiricism	22. place	33. Replicate	44. replicate

Review the scientific method:

1. Provide a *rationale*	2. *Conduct* the study	*3.* *Summarize* the data	4. *Communicate* the findings	5. *Replicate* the study
a Identify *problem of interest*	a. *Carry out* the procedure	a. Apply *statistics* to the data	a. Present a paper at *a professional meeting*	a. *Replicate* exact research study
b. Review the relevant *research literature*				
c. Decide on the *research procedures*	b. Collect the *data*	b. Discuss *implications* of research findings	b. Publish an article in a *research journal*	b. Replicate study with *variations*
d. State the *research hypothesis*				

45. describes	47. methods	49. implications	51. procedure	53. questions
46. Hypothesis	48 statistical	50. previous	52. real	54. summarize

Quiz on Understanding Research Descriptions:

What was the rationale for the study? *A legal court decision had stated that common sense could be used to determine drunkenness. The researchers wanted to know if this was true.*

What procedures were used to test the hypothesis? *Langenbucher and Nathan had bartenders, social drinkers, and police officers observe drinkers and provide a judgment as to whether they were drunk or not. The drinkers were then given a breathalyzer test to determine drunkenness.*

What were the conclusions of the authors? *The results indicated that none of the observers was very accurate in judging the drinkers' level of intoxication. They concluded that this meant that common sense could not be used as a method for determining whether someone is legally drunk or sober.*

---

55. Description
56. systematic
57. relevant
58. observation
59. precise
60. measurements
61. operational definitions
62. predictions
63. hypotheses
64. theory
65. manipulating
66. measuring
67. control
68. experiments
69. apply
70. explanation
71. predict
72. control
73. why
74. perspective
75. beliefs
76. feelings
77. psychoanalytic
78. biopsychologist
79. environment
80. culture

Quiz on Goals of Psychological Research:

__3__ Description __1__ Prediction __4__ Control __2__ Explanation

81. description
82. explanation
83. goal
84. description
85. prediction
86. explanation
87. systematic
88. naturalistic observation
89. unobtrusive
90. laboratory
91. generalizations
92. cause and effect
93. chimps
94. ethology
95. single person
96. case study
97. clinical
98. Sybil
99. descriptive
100. cannot
101. generalized
102. attitudes
103. opinions
104. questionnaire
105. surveys
106. bias
107. honesty
108. social-cultural
109. generalizability
110. population
111. sample
112. represent
113. random
114. accurately
115. psychological testing
116. unbiased
117. validity
118. standardization
119. consistent
120. norms
121. reliability
122. consistent
123. test-retest
124. Validity
125. face
126. content
127. construct
128. predictive
129. archival research
130. manuscripts
131. historical
132. prediction
133. relationship
134. variable
135. positive
136. negative
137. perfect
138. causes
139. correlated
140. causation
141. Experimental research
142. experimental
143. control
144. independent
145. dependent
146. experimental
147. control
148. independent
149. dependent
150. causes
151. manipulate
152. confused
153. confounding variables
154. procedural
155. internal
156. random
157. other
158. subject bias
159. misinform
160. deception
161. experimenter's
162. expectancy
163. bias
164. self-fulfilling prophecy
165. well
166. poor
167. Pygmalion
168. double-blind
169. generalize
170. subjects
171. volunteers
172. external validity

Anatomy of a Classic Research Study: Can Experimenter Expectancies Affect the Behavior of Laboratory Rats?

What was the rationale for the study? *The rationale was to demonstrate the potential influence of experimenter bias on the outcome of research studies.*

What procedures were used to test the hypothesis? *The methods used in this classic study were that students were told that their rats were either "maze-bright" or "maze-dull, ", although all rats were the same.*

What were the conclusions of the authors? *The results indicated that the supposed "maze-bright" rats learned the maze much faster than the "maze-dull" rats. The researchers concluded that experimenter expectation could influence the outcome of research.*

Mini-review of Research Methods in Psychology:

1.	A	4.	D	7.	L	10.	J	13.	P	16.	F	19.	S
2.	K	5.	G	8.	C	11.	I	14.	Q	17.	E	20.	O
3.	B	6.	M	9.	H	12.	R	15.	U	18.	T	21.	N
												22.	V

173. statistics
174. summarize
175. relationships
176. hypotheses
177. Descriptive
178. central tendency
179. median
180. mode
181. often
182. middle
183. arrange
184. halfway
185. position
186. mean
187. mean
188. representative
189. mean
190. *average*
191. mode
192. standard deviation
193. two
194. extreme
195. dispersion
196. standard
197. variance
198. predicting
199. correlation
200. direction
201. strength
202. positive
203. negative
204. higher
205. causation
206. Inferential
207. chance
208. independent
209. t test
210. analysis of variance
211. experiments
212. experimental
213. statistically
214. real
215. practical
216. control

Mini-review of Statistics:
1. K; 2. F; 3. M; 4. A; 5. H; 6. B; 7. D; 8. I; 9. J; 10. G; 11. C; 12. E; 13. N; 14. L

217. informed
218. forced
219. withdraw
220. harm
221. alleviate
222. confidential
223. informed
224. subject bias
225. Debriefing
226. rights
227. welfare
228. welfare
229. respect
230. limit
231. committee
232. learn
233. control
234. developmental
235. hypotheses

Practice Test A:

1. **a. Correct: Commonsense beliefs are beliefs that are held because they are common to others.**
   b. Incorrect: Deductive reasoning is a method of thinking that involves examining information presented.
   c. Incorrect: Appeal to authority is the acceptance of something because an authority states that it is so.
   d. Incorrect: Unsystematic observation involves beliefs based on causal observations of events.

2. a. Incorrect: Free will is a Humanistic concept representing the belief that humans are capable of choices.
   b. Correct: Determinism refers to the scientific assumption that every event has a physical, potentially measurable cause; demons are supernatural causes.
   c. Incorrect: Randomization refers to the assignment of subjects to treatment conditions, or the selection of subjects.
   d. Incorrect: This is not a concept discussed in the text.

3. a. Incorrect: Step 1 is not the analysis of data stage.
   b. Incorrect: Step 2 is not the communication stage.
   c. **Correct: Step 2 is the stage in which the study is conducted and measurements are made; this is what is being described.**
   d. Incorrect: Although step 1 is the rationale stage, the description is on the methods used, not the rationale.

4. a. Incorrect: This is a description of the methods used, not the rationale.
   b. Incorrect: This is a description of the data analysis.
   c. **Correct: This is a description of the reasons why the study was conducted, or the rationale.**
   d. Incorrect: This is a description of the conclusions of the study.

5. a. Incorrect: A lexical definition is a dictionary definition; this is not the dictionary definition of intelligence.
   b. Incorrect: In intelligence tests the tester is present, therefore obtrusive.
   c. **Correct: An operational definition defines the term in the way it will be measured; that is what is being done here.**
   d. Incorrect: The term *commonsense explanation* was not discussed in your text.

6. a. Incorrect: A fact is a known concept; this statement is a guess.
   b. **Correct: A hypothesis is a statement that makes an educated prediction about what might occur in a research study. That describes the statement presented.**
   c. Incorrect: Inductive reasoning involves the use of logical thinking to test problems.
   d. Incorrect: An operational definition defines the term in the way it will be measured; it does not make a prediction.

7. a. Incorrect: A case study would involve the measurement of only one 3-year-old child, not children.
   b. Incorrect: Archival research involves examining relevant research studies that have been previously published.
   c. Incorrect: In an experiment there would be manipulation of an independent variable.
   d. **Correct: In naturalistic observation the subjects are watched in their real-world setting.**

8. a. Incorrect: In determining largest value, only the numerical part of the correlation coefficient is examined;, the value closest to one is the largest;. .37 is not closest to 1.00.
   b. Incorrect: In determining largest value, only the numerical part of the correlation coefficient is examined;, the value closest to one is the largest;. 0.00 is not closest to 1.00.
   c. Incorrect: In determining largest value, only the numerical part of the correlation coefficient is examined;, the value closest to one is the largest;. .01 is not closest to 1.00.
   d. **Correct: In determining largest value, only the numerical part of the correlation coefficient is examined;, the value closest to one is the largest;. .93 is closest to 1.00.**

9. a. Incorrect: A positive correlation means the more education you have the more likely you are to have cancer; this would mean the cancer cells would be encouraged, not inhibited.
   b. Incorrect: A positive correlation means the more education you have the more likely you are to have cancer; it does not mean that college causes cancer.
   c. Incorrect: A positive correlation means the more education you have the more likely you are to have cancer; it does not indicate anything concerning causality.
   d. **Correct: A positive correlation means the more education you have the more likely you are to have cancer; thus someone with a high school education would be at lower risk than someone with a college education.**

10. a. Incorrect: An experiment is interested in causality, not predictive relationships.
    b. Incorrect: A case study only measures one individual, thus predictive relationships cannot be established.
    c. Incorrect: Measures of central tendency are descriptive statistics, not a research method.
    d. **Correct: Correlational studies examine predictive relationships.**

11. a. **Correct: The dependent variable is the variable that is measured, in this case the running times.**
    b. Incorrect: The dependent variable is the variable that is measured, in this case the running times.
    c. Incorrect: The dependent variable is the variable that is measured, in this case the running times.
    d. Incorrect: The dependent variable is the variable that is measured, in this case the running times.

12. a. Incorrect: Content validity is a form of internal validity of a test. It refers to whether the items in a test are a good representation of what is being tested.
    b. Correct: Replication establishes external validity.
    c. Incorrect: Reliability refers to the characteristic of consistency of psychological tests.
    d. Incorrect: Construct validity is a form of internal validity of a test. It refers to whether the test measures what is supposed to.

13. a. Incorrect: The median is the middle score in a data set, in this case, 7. (Remember, you must rank the scores from highest to lowest before finding the median.)
    b. Correct: The median is the middle score in a data set, in this case, 7.
    c. Incorrect: The median is the middle score in a data set, in this case, 7. (Remember, you must rank the scores from highest to lowest before finding the median.)
    d. Incorrect: The median is the middle score in a data set, in this case, 7. (Remember, you must rank the scores from highest to lowest before finding the median.)

14. a. Incorrect: The strongest association between variables is shown by a correlation closest to 1.0 or -1.0.; + .25 is not the closest of the choices given.
    b. Incorrect: The strongest association between variables is shown by a correlation.closest to 1.0 or -1.0.; -.44 is not the closest of the choices given.
    c. Incorrect: The strongest association between variables is shown by a correlation closest to 1.0 or -1.0.; + .44 is not the closest of the choices given.
    d. Correct: The strongest association between variables is shown by a correlation closest to 1.0 or -1.0.; -.53 is the closest of the choices given.

15. a. Incorrect: There is no branch of statistics called deductive statistics.
    b. Incorrect: Parametric statistics are a branch of inferential statistics but are not discussed in your text.
    c. Incorrect: Descriptive statisitcs paint a picture of the sample; they do not allow for inferences about a population.
    d. Correct: Inferential statistics are used to make inferences about a population from a sample.

16. a. Incorrect: Correlational studies are used to establish predictive relationships.
    b. Correct: Meta-analysis is a new form of statistical analysis that allows researchers to determine the average size of the effect of the independent variable.
    c. Incorrect: t tests are used to determine if there is a significant difference between two groups.
    d. Incorrect: An analysis of variance is used to compare two or more groups of data.

17. **a. Correct: Ethical guidelines state that human subjects should be informed; if deception is necessary then the subject should be told immediately at the end of the testing the reason for the deception.**
    b. Incorrect: The experimenter is not obligated to share the results.
    c. Incorrect: This, in itself, is deception.
    d. Incorrect: Their responses are confidential and should not be shared. The data may be published, but confidentiality must be preserved.

18. a. Incorrect: The item is correct, but is not the sole correct answer.
    b. Incorrect: The item is correct, but is not the sole correct answer.
    c. Incorrect: The item is correct, but is not the sole correct answer.
    d. Correct: This item was prepared purposely to remind you of a common variation of a multiple-choice item. It is important to determine the truth or falsity of each item as you read the question.

Practice Test B:

1. **a. Correct: Wise readers base decisions to accept claims on scientific evidence.**
    b. Incorrect: Wise readers base decisions to accept claims on scientific evidence, not on popularity.
    c. Incorrect: Wise readers base decisions to accept claims on scientific evidence, not on an expert's opinion.
    d. Incorrect: Wise readers base decisions to accept claims on scientific evidence, not on the expert's perceived popularity.

2. a. Incorrect: Critical thinkers base decisions to accept claims on scientific evidence, not on expert opinion.
    b. Correct: Critical thinkers base decisions to accept claims on scientific evidence.
    c. Incorrect: Critical thinkers base decisions to accept claims on scientific evidence.
    d. Incorrect: Critical thinkers base decisions to accept claims on scientific evidence, not on the opinions of authorities.

3. **a. Correct: The more often scientists can show an outcome, the more confident they are that the outcome did not occur by chance.**
   b. Incorrect: Replication refers to the repeating of the study, not communicating about it.
   c. Incorrect: Replication refers to the repeating of the study, not publication of it.
   d. Incorrect: Replications do not always have variations.

4. **a. Correct: When you try to manipulate something, you are working at the goal of control.**
   b. Incorrect: Prediction does not involve any manipulation.
   c. Incorrect: You can manipulate behavior with understanding it.
   d. Incorrect: You are manipulating behavior, not describing it.

5. a. Incorrect: In this case, you are describing relationships between factors, not explaining them.
   b. Incorrect: In this case, you are describing relationships between factors, not controlling them.
   c. Correct: In this case, you are describing relationships between factors to make predictions.
   d. Incorrect: In this case, you are describing relationships between factors, not trying to understand them.

6. a. Incorrect: Experiments generally involve manipulations of groups of subjects, not just one.
   b. Incorrect: You would not be able to observe him in his real setting while he was hospitalized.
   c. Correct: A case study would provide an in-depth look at the subject.
   d. Incorrect: A survey is used to gather descriptive information from a larger sample than one person.

7. a. Incorrect: You can predict one factor from the other; they are correlated.
   b. Incorrect: As TV watching increases, creativity scores go down. This is a negative correlation.
   c. Correct: As TV watching increases, creativity scores go down. This is a negative correlation.
   d. Incorrect: Correlation does not imply causation.

8. a. Incorrect: Whether or not the subjects fasted was not what was controlled.
   b. Incorrect: The independent variable is what the experimenter controls, not the behavior of the subject.
   c. Incorrect: The independent variable is what the experimenter controls, not the behavior of the subject.
   d. Correct: The independent variable, in this case the ingestion of caffeine pills, is what the experimenter controls.

9. a. Incorrect: Nonrepresentative samples are biased samples; if everyone has a chance of being chosen, then random sampling has been used.
   b. Correct: If everyone has a chance of being chosen, then random sampling has been used.
   c. Incorrect: In a biased sample not everyone has a chance of being chosen.
   d. Incorrect: A nongeneralizable sample is one that is biased.

10. **a. Correct: Replication leads to more confidence in your results, leading to external validity.**
    b. Incorrect: Predictive validity refers to whether the results predict behavior.
    c. Incorrect: Content validity refers to whether the test items are representative of the thing being tested.
    d. Incorrect: Eliminating subject bias does not influence external validity.

11. a. Incorrect: Inferential tests are used to test hypotheses, descriptive are used to summarize data, and correlational are used to determine relationships.
    b. Incorrect: Inferential tests are used to test hypotheses, descriptive are used to summarize data, and correlational are used to determine relationships.
    c. Incorrect: Inferential tests are used to test hypotheses, descriptive are used to summarize data, and correlational are used to determine relationships.
    d. Correct: Inferential tests are used to test hypotheses, descriptive are used to summarize data, and correlational are used to determine relationships.

12. **a. Correct: Mean, median, and mode are descriptive measures that describe the class.**
    b. Incorrect: Mean, median, and mode are descriptive measures that describe, not inferential measures.
    c. Incorrect: Mean, median, and mode are descriptive measures that describe the whole class, not individual students.
    d. Incorrect: Mean, median, and mode are descriptive measures that describe, not correlational measures that predict.

13. a. Incorrect: A correlation coefficient of .2 is not a very strong one.
    b. Incorrect: Correlation does not imply causation.
    c. Correct: A correlation coefficient of .21 is not a very strong one but it does indicate a relationship.
    d. Incorrect: A correlation of .21 is positive, indicating that as the number of computer programs goes up, so would GPA.

14. a. Incorrect: Inferential statistics are used to test hypotheses, or whether the difference is due to the independent variable.
    b. Correct: Inferential statistics are used to test hypotheses, or whether the difference is due to the independent variable.
    c. Incorrect: Inferential statistics do not identify correlations.
    d. Incorrect: Inferential statistic do not measure dispersion.

15. a. Incorrect: These are methods of description, not inferential measures.
    b. Incorrect: ANOVA is used in experimental studies with more then two groups.
    c. Incorrect: t tests are used in experimental studies involving two groups.
    d. Correct: A meta-analysis is used to determine the average size of the effect of a variable from any studies.

16. a. Incorrect: APA guidelines say subjects can withdraw at any time.
    b. Correct: Informed consent means that subjects have been told about the study and agree to participate.
    c. Incorrect: The investigator may have misinformed the subjects and would then debrief them at a later time.
    d. Incorrect: Debriefing occurs after the study is completed and the subjects are told of the true goals of the study.

17. a. Incorrect: Animal rights activists do not believe that any research on animals is justified.
    b. Incorrect: The APA supports animal research under ethical guidelines.
    c. Incorrect: Animal rights activists do not believe that any research on animals is justified.
    d. Correct: Animal rights activists do not believe that any research on animals is justified.

18. **a. Correct: The dependent variable is what the experimenter measures in an experiment, in this case the rate of productivity.**
    b. Incorrect: The dependent variable is what the experimenter measures in an experiment; in this case the loudness of music is what is manipulated.
    c. Incorrect: The dependent variable is what the experimenter measures in an experiment, in this case the rate of productivity.
    d. Incorrect: The dependent variable is what the experimenter measures in an experiment, in this case the rate of productivity.

19. a. Incorrect: An in-depth study of one person is a case study, not an expedient. These are all studies of one person.
    b. Incorrect: An in-depth study of one person is a case study, not an interview.
    c. Incorrect: An in-depth study of one person is a case study, not a survey.
    d. Correct: These are all in-depth studies of one person, or case studies.

20. a. Incorrect: Correlation does not imply causation.
    b. Incorrect: Correlation does not imply causation.
    c. Incorrect: Correlation does not imply causation.
    d. Correct: Correlation does not imply causation.

Essay Questions:

1. "More tests" might be operationally defined as " six tests per semester" as compared to fewer tests (defined as "two tests per semester"). "More retention" might be defined as a "higher score" on a comprehensive test of knowledge of introductory psychology. "Well after" might be defined as "three years" after completion of the course. Note that all definitions involve *measurable* factors.

2. You would need to explain to your roommate that a science is a science because it uses a particular method of knowing about the world. That way of knowing is the scientific method. You would then explain that psychology also uses the scientific method to answer questions about the behavior and mental processes of living organisms.

3 Behavioral Neuroscience

LEARNING OBJECTIVES

After studying this chapter, you should be able to:

1. Describe the domain of behavioral neuroscience, and explain how study of brain-behavior relationships dates back to the beginnings of functionalism. (p. 66-67)

2. Draw a diagram delineating the major divisions of the nervous system and their general functions. (p. 67-68)

3. Describe the functions of three types of neurons, describe their roles in reflexive behavior, and distinguish neurons from glial cells. (p. 68)

4. Draw a diagram of a neuron, labeling its parts and indicating the function of each part. (p. 68-69)

5. Describe the neuron at rest, mentioning the chemicals involved in resting potential, and then explain the changes involved in the action potential, mentioning the all-or-none law and the nodes of Ranvier. (p. 70-72)

6. Describe the process of synaptic transmission and explain the role of the neurotransmitters in that process, emphasizing the effects of acetylcholine and six other neurotransmitters. (p. 72-74)

7. Summarize the classic study that resulted in the discovery of endorphins, and offer an overview of subsequent research findings regarding endorphins. (p. 75)

8. Distinguish between neurotransmitters versus hormones and endocrine versus exocrine glands. (p. 76)

9. Explain why the pituitary gland is called the master gland, and then describe the effects of seven pituitary hormones. (p. 76-77)

10. List and describe two other sets of glands and explain how their secretions affect psychological functioning, mentioning the effects of anabolic steroid use. (p. 78)

11. List the four sources of knowledge regarding brain functioning, emphasizing the history and current use of the EEG and the distinct rhythms it records. (p. 78-80)

12. Draw a diagram of the hindbrain, delineating its four structures and their functions. (p. 80-81)

13. Draw a diagram of the midbrain, delineating two of its structures and their functions. (p. 81-82)

14. Draw a diagram of the forebrain, delineating its major structures, substructures, and their functions. (p. 82-84)

15. Describe in detail the structure and functioning of the lobes of the cerebral cortex, mentioning the primary and association areas and the concept of the homunculi. (p. 84-85)

16. Describe the contributions of Wilder Penfield to our understanding of the distribution of functions in the cerebral cortex. (p. 85-87)

17. Explain how positron-emission tomography allows scientists to observe ongoing brain function, and contrast this with the type of information garnered from computed tomography and magnetic resonance imaging. (p. 87-88)

18. Locate Broca's area and Wernicke's area on a diagram of the brain and explain how these two structures are involved in language production and comprehension. (p. 88-89)

19. Explain how the non-science-based practice of phrenology developed into a scientific interest in identifying the location of specific functions, and then describe the contemporary perspective on localization of function and explain how prosopagnosia supports this perspective. (p. 89-91)

20. Explain the concept of neural plasticity, describe the process by which lost functions are recovered after damage to the brain, and relate these to the controversial procedure called neural grafting. (p. 91-93)

21. Distinguish between dualism and monism, and explain how these perspectives are related to Roger Sperry's concept of emergent interactionism. (p. 93-94)

22. Critically evaluate popular notions of left-brained and right-brained people, and then summarize the findings regarding the relationship between handedness and longevity. (p. 94-96)

23. Describe three techniques used to study hemispheric specialization, and explain how studies of individuals with cerebral damage have also contributed to our understanding of brain functioning. (p. 97-99)

COMPREHENSIVE GUIDED REVIEW:

The field of **behavioral neuroscience** focuses on the study of the relationship between __(1)__ processes (such as brain activity) and __(2)__ processes (such as memory). In the clinical account on page 66 in your textbook, a case of neglect syndrome is discussed. This inability to attend to an entire side of one's body is generally the result of damage to the individual's __(3)__. A ____(4)_____would study the patient's brain to determine the cause of the syndrome. Although the__(5)__ have been declared by Congress to be "The Decade of the Brain," interest in behavioral neuroscience is not new. __(6)__predicted that researchers would discover the physiological processes underlying psychoanalysis. At about the same time, William __(7), strongly influenced by Darwin's theory of evolution, stressed the close association between psychology and biology.

I. The Nervous System: The brain is part of the nervous system, the chief means of communication within the body. The nervous system is organized into two major divisions: the ___(8)__nervous system, which contains the brain and the __(9)_ cord; and the __(10)__ nervous system, which contains the nerves allowing communication between the central nervous system and the glands, sensory organs, skeletal muscles, and internal body organs.

The **peripheral nervous system** is organized into two systems: the **somatic nervous system** and the **autonomic nervous system.** The __(11)__ nervous system includes afferent, or sensory, nerves which send messages from the sensory organs to the central system, and motor efferent nerves, which send messages from the central system to the skeletal muscles. The ___(12)__ nervous system controls automatic, involuntary responses through its two divisions: the ___(13)__ nervous system, which arouses the body to prepare it for action; and the ____(14)__ nervous system, which calms the body to conserve energy.

The Neuron: The nervous system is comprised of cells specialized for the transmission and reception of information. These cells are called __(15). ___(16)__neurons send messages along sensory nerves to the brain or spinal cord.__(17)__ neurons send messages along motor nerves to the glands, the cardiac muscle, and the skeletal muscles, as well as to the smooth muscles of the arteries, small intestine, and other internal organs. Though the focus is on neurons, the nervous system contains many more **glial** cells. These __(18)_ cells furnish physical support, supply nutritive elements, help in metabolic waste removal and message transmission facilitation, as well as aiding in regeneration of damaged neurons in the peripheral nervous system.

The Neural Impulse: To understand the function of the neuron and the role of neuronal communication, it will help first to study the structure and function of the spinal cord. The _____(19)___ is a long, tubelike structure enclosed in the protective spinal column. It extends from the __(20)__ to the tip of the spine. It contains __(21)__ that convey sensory messages from the body to the brain and motor messages from the brain to the body. In an important study, ____(22)____ demonstrated the limb-withdrawal reflex in the frog. He showed that the __(23)__ did not require input from the brain. We now know that reflexes involve sensory neurons making connections with **interneurons** located in the spinal cord, which in turn make connections with motor neurons. The job of these __(24)__ is to mediate the incoming sensory and outgoing motor messages.

In addition to knowing the structure and function of the spinal cord, knowing something about the structure of the neuron will further aid in understanding how neurons communicate information. The basic structure of the neuron is characterized by the __(25)__ (or cell body), which contains the **nucleus;** and __(26)__, which are short, branching fibers that receive messages. Dendrites are covered by dendritic __(27)__, which provide additional surface area for the reception of messages. The final basic feature is the __(28)__. It is a thin fiber that sends messages. Bundles of axons form the __(29)__ in the peripheral nervous system.

Today we know that the neuron conveys its message using a ____(30)____, although it took centuries of research for us to reach that conclusion. René __(31)__ first speculated that the body is controlled by vital spirits that he believed flowed through the nerves. Isaac __(32)__ put forth an alternative view, that information is conveyed throughout the body by the vibration of nerves. Luigi __(33)__ first demonstrated that the nerve impulse is electrical in nature. He took this conclusion to the extreme when he argued that __(34)__ was the basic life force, although he was never able to confirm his ideas. It took more than two centuries before researchers identified the nature of neural communication and its __(35)__-chemical process.

It was not until 1952 that Hodgkin & Huxley discovered the nature of transmission of the electrical impulse along the length of the axon, called ____(36)____. They found that in its inactive state, there is an electrical condition produced by the differences between the __(37)__ fluid (the fluid inside the neuron) and the extracelluar fluid (the fluid __(38)__ the neuron). These fluids contain electrically charged particles called __(39)__. The main positive ions are __(40)__ and potassium, and the main negative ions are proteins and __(41)__.

We now know that the electrical nature of neural conduction is due to changes in ion concentration across the axon __(42)__. In the inactive state of the resting cell, the __(43)__ fluid ends up with an excess of negative ions and the extracellular fluid ends up with an excess of __(44)__ ions. Hence, the inside of the resting neuron is __(45)__ relative to the outside, as in a battery. In this state, the neuron is said to be **polarized.** The inside has an electrical charge of -70 millivolts (mv) relative to the __(46)__.

When a neuron is stimulated by other neurons or by a sensory organ, the neuronal membrane becomes more __(47)__ to positively charged sodium ions, which, attracted by the negative ions inside, rush into the neuron. This very important process is called **depolarization.** As __(48)__ continues to rush in, the inside of the cell becomes less negative relative to the outside, and if the neuron reaches its firing __(49)__ (about -60 mv in a motor neuron), an **action potential** occurs at the site where the axon leaves the cell body. Hence, an ____(50)____ is a change in the electrical charge across the axonal membrane. The inside of the membrane becomes more electrically __(51)__ than the outside and reaches a threshold level. Once the potential has occurred, that point on the axonal membrane quickly restores its resting potential through a process called __(52)__. If the axon''s __(53)__ does not reach the cells **firing threshold**, a neural impulse, or action potential, will not occur. Thus, neural impulses, or ____(54)____, either exist at full strength or they do not. This is known as the __(55)__ law.

Once researchers had identified the mechanism by which the electrical change occurred, the next question became, How does the neural __(56)__ travel along the length of the neuron? Research into this question showed that the __(57)__ of neural conduction depends partly on whether the axon is surrounded by the fatty sheath of **myelin.** Additionally the French anatomist Louis Antoine __(58)__ showed that in myelinated axons there are small areas along the axon that are not covered by the sheath, exposing small __(59)__ he called the **nodes of Ranvier.** In __(60)__ axons, like most of the neurons in our nervous system, the action potential apparently jumps from one node to the next, resulting in very rapid conduction. Nonmyelinated fibers do not have such nodes, hence conduction in them is __(61)__.

If you were to examine a dissected brain, you would find that the inside matter of the brain is mostly __(62)__,while the outside matter is mostly __(63)__. Why? Because __(64)__ is a white substance and the inside of the brain contains many myelinated axons. Some neurological diseases result from problems with myelin. One example is the disease **multiple sclerosis (MS).** In MS, portions of the myelin sheaths in neurons in the brain and ____(65)____ are destroyed, disrupting axonal conduction. This leads individuals to experience ____(66)____, sensory disturbances, memory loss, and cognitive deterioration.

Synaptic Transmission: In the late nineteenth century, Camillo__(67)__ argued that neurons were physically connected to one another, while Santiago ____(68)____ argued that neurons were not physically connected. __(69)__ finally found evidence to show that neurons communicated across tiny gaps. Charles Sherrington coined the term __(70)__ to refer to these gaps. This led to another question: If neural impulses only function within a single neuron, and neurons are separated by__(71)__, how do neurons send information from one neuron to another? The answer to this question came to Otto__(72)__ in a dream. He then conducted an experiment to show that a stimulated nerve released a__(73)__, which he later identified as **acetylcholine.** The process Loewi described is known as____(74)____.

__(75)__ is now known to be one of a group of chemicals called as **neurotransmitters.** __(76)__ are stored in round packets, called **synaptic vesicles,** located in the intracellular fluid of small bumps that project from the end branches of axons. These protuberances are called **synaptic knobs.** Once researchers had identified the chemicals, a major question still remained: How is the information transmitted? Research indicates that four processes are involved in synaptic transmission:

1) Upon reaching the end of an __(77)__, the nerve impulse causes a chemical reaction that makes some__(78)__ vesicles release neurotransmitter molecules into the synapse.
2) The neurotransmitter molecules diffuse across the synaptic__(79)__ and reach the dendrites of another neuron.
3) The neurotransmitter molecules attach to__(80)__ receptor sites.
4) The excitatory__(81)__ molecules slightly____(82)____ the membrane of this next neuron and, with the combined action of other neurotransmitters, may raise it to its firing threshold. It is equally significant to note that some neurotransmitters are __(83)__, in that they inhibit the neuron from depolarizing. These inhibitory neurotransmitters then inhibit the neuron from firing an __(84)__. It is only when the combined effects of __(85)__ neurotransmitters exceed the combined effects of inhibitory transmitters that the neuron will fire.

After the neurotransmitters have done their job, they disengage from the receptor sites and are either broken down by enzymes or are taken back into their source neuron. This process is called ___(86)___.

Take a short break at this point.
When you come back, complete the mini-review of neurotransmission before going on.

Mini-review of Neural Transmission: Place the following actions in their correct sequence to describe the combined effects of the neural impulse and synaptic transmission in neuronal communication.

_______ A. The intracellular fluid has an excess of negative ions and the extracellular fluid has an excess of positive ions; the neuron is **polarized.**

_______ B. In cell 1 the nerve impulse reaches the end of the axon and makes some vesicles release neurotransmitter molecules into the **synapse.**

_______ C. The neurotransmitter molecules attach to dendritic receptor sites.

_______ D. The neurotransmitter molecules diffuse across the **synaptic gap** and reach the dendrites of neuron 2.

_______ E. The combined action of many neurotransmitters raise neuron 2 to its firing threshold.

_______ F. The excitatory neurotransmitter molecules slightly depolarize the membrane of neuron 2.

_______ G. The cell membrane becomes more permeable to positively charged sodium ions, which rush into the neuron.

_______ H. The inside of the axon becomes increasingly negative relative to the outside.

_______ I. **Reuptake** takes place. The neurotransmitters disengage from the receptor sites and are either broken down by enzymes or taken back into their source neuron.

_______ J. The neuron reaches its firing threshold and an action potential occurs at the site where the axon leaves the cell body.

_______ K. The axonal membrane quickly restores its resting potential through a process called **repolarization.**

II. Neurotransmitters: The nervous system uses many different _(87)____, each having its own characteristics and influences. Below is a summary of the different types of neurotransmitters and their known actions.

Acetylcholine is found at synapses between the neurons of the __(88)_ system and related organs, such as the heart, and in synapses between motor neurons and_(89)_ fibers. The drug _(90)_ prevents it from attaching to receptor sites on muscle fibers, causing muscle paralysis and eventual death. In the brain, it helps regulate_(91)_ processes, but its action can be impaired by drugs, for example, __(92)_, or by diseases such as Alzheimer's.

Dopamine is an _(93)_neurotransmitter implicated in the rewarding effects of pleasure-inducing activities and is directly involved in the ability to perform smooth muscle movements. Low levels of dopamine are found in people with __(94)__ disease due to a destruction of the dopamine neurons in the brain. In contrast, high levels are found in _(95)_, whose symptoms are alleviated by dopamine blockers.

Norepinephrine is believed to be involved in_(96)_ states and, in rats, it stimulates neurons that regulate_(97)_. Many antidepressant medications work by increasing the_(98)_ in the brain. Another neurotransmitter believed to be involved in depressive moods is **serotonin.** Too-low levels of_(99)_ have been linked to suicide attempts in depressed individuals.

GABA, or gamma aminobutyric acid, is an inhibitory___(100)____ neurotransmitter that helps promote muscle __(101)___ and inhibits anxiety. The drug Valium is believed to work by promoting the actions of_(102)_ **Glutamic acid** is the major_(103)_ amino acid neurotransmitter and is believed to be involved in_(104)_ formation.

Substance P is an excitatory protein in a class of neurotransmitters called _(105)_. It plays an apparent role in the transmission of_(106)_ impulses in the spinal cord. ______(107)_ Is gaining increased attention from researchers interested in its role in migraine headaches. Other neuropeptides that have received attention recently have been the **endorphins,** because of their role in relieving pain and inducing_(108)_.

Anatomy of a Classic Research Study: Does the Brain Contain Its Own Opiate Receptors?
In the study summarized on page 75 of the textbook, ______(109)______ (1973) discovered opiate receptors in the brains of animals. They discovered the receptors by injecting a_(110)_ drug and found that the drug attached itself to receptors in areas of the brain associated with pain perception and emotionality. They inferred that the brain had its own _(111)_ chemicals. A surge of research by others found that_(112)_ act at the synapses in the brain that inhibit pain impulses. This led to speculation that endorphins evolved partly because they provided_(113)_ relief. Additional supporting evidence came from heat-induced__(114)_ behavior of mice. A drug called__(115)_ blocked the pain-relieving effects of the endorphins, decreasing the tolerance the mice had for radiant heat. Endorphin secretion is stimulated by various forms of__(116)_, ranging from pain to vigorous exercise. Endorphins may also be responsible for feelings of euphoria.

Take one of your study breaks right now. When you come back, do the mini-review of neurotransmitters.

Mini-review of Neurotransmitters: Match the neurotransmitter with its action.

Neurotransmitter	**Actions**
1. Substance P	____ A. Too-low levels have been linked to suicide attempts in depressed individuals
2. Endorphins	_____B. Relieves pain and induces euphoria.
3. Norepinephrine	_____C. Neuropeptide that plays a role in the transmission of pain impulses in the spinal cord: implicated in migraine headaches
4. Acetylcholine	_____D. Inhibitory amino acid neurotransmitter; helps to promote muscle relaxation and inhibit anxiety
5. GABA	_____E. Excitatory amino acid neurotransmitter; involved in memory formation
6. Dopamine	____ F. Involved in mood states; antidepressant medications work by increasing its level in the brain
7. Serotonin	_____G. Found at synapses between the neurons of the parasympathetic system and related organs; curare prevents it from attaching to receptor sites
8. Glutamic acid	_____H. Inhibitory neurotransmitter implicated in the rewarding effects of pleasure-inducing activities; directly involved in the ability to perform smooth muscle movements. Low levels are found in Parkinson's patients

Congratulations! You are staying right on track. Let's go on!

III. The Endocrine System: The glands in the endocrine system secrete chemical messengers, or _(117)_, which are transported by the_(118)_ and capable of producing behavioral effects. These glands contrast with _(119)_ glands, such as the sweat glands, which secrete their chemicals onto the body surface.

(Figure 3.5 on page 76 in your textbook illustrates the locations of the major endocrine glands. It might help to refer to it as you review this section.)

The **pituitary gland**, known as the "____(120)____," secretes hormones that affect the activity of many other glands. It in turn is regulated by the__(121)_ structure known as the **hypothalamus.** Feedback from__(122)_ circulating in the blood stimulate the__(123)_ to signal the pituitary gland to increase or decrease its secretion of hormones. As the master gland, the_(124)_ gland releases an assortment of hormones that have a wide variety of direct effects. Pituitary hormones include __(125)_, which acts on kidney tissue to promote water retention and enhance memory processes by stimulating acetylcholine; and __(126)_, which stimulates labor contractions but may impair memory during pregnancy. Other pituitary hormones include___(127)___, which stimulates the physical development of bones and muscles; _(128)_, which facilitates milk production and may be implicated in stress-related infertility; and___(129)___ hormone, which promotes the secretion of hormones by the thyroid gland. The hormone__(130)_ is released by the thyroid gland and is needed for normal metabolism, physical growth, and brain development.

In addition to the (131) and **thyroid** glands, other endocrine glands release important hormones. These include the **adrenal gland** and the **gonads.** The (132) glands secrete hormones such as **aldosterone,** which helps regulate the excretion of (133) and potassium, and (134), a hormone that helps the body respond to stress. The adrenal (135) also secretes **epinephrine** and **norepinephrine.** (136) inhibits eating and enhances memory storage and retrieval, while (137) appears to arouse the body to take action. The (138), or the sex glands, secrete (139) in males, and (140) and progesterone in females. These hormones are involved in the development of secondary sex characteristics.

Wow! Time for another short study break and review!

Mini-review of the Endocrine System and Hormones: Match the hormone to its action:

Hormone:	**Action:**
____1. Growth hormone	A. Regulates arousal and biological rhythms
____2. Prolactin	B. Increases blood sugar
____3. Vasopressin	C. Regulates the uterus to maintain pregnancy
____4. Oxytocin	D. Inhibits eating; enhances memory storage and retrieval
____5. Aldosterone	E. Stimulates growth
____6. Cortisol	F. Regulates the excretion of sodium and potassium
____7. Testosterone	G. Regulates the development of male reproductive system
____8. Estrogen	H. Regulates metabolism and response to stress
____9. Progesterone	I. Stimulates uterine contractions during labor
____10. Thyroxin	J. Regulates metabolism and growth
____11. Glucagon	K. Promotes water retention by kidneys; involved in memory formation
____12. Melatonin	L. Stimulates milk production
____13. Epinephrine	M. Regulates the development of female sex characteristics
____14. Norepinephrine	N. Arouses the body to take action

IV. The Brain:

Functions: The brain is a 3-pound organ comprised of hundreds of billions of (141), each of which may communicate with thousands of others. Much of what we know comes from studies of brain (142); electrical (143) of the brain; recording of the electricity produced by brain activity, using the (144), or EEG; and computer scanning techniques.

Hans (145) first used the EEG to measure the electrical activity of the brain. Berger identified the (146) rhythm, a relatively slow brain-wave rhythm associated with relaxed, unfocused mental states. He also identified (147) rhythm, a relatively fast rhythm associated with active and alert mental states.

Before beginning the next sections, you may find it beneficial to open your textbook to page 80. As you review the next sections on the structures of the hindbrain, midbrain, and forebrain, refer to Figure 3.6, which shows the location of most of the major structures of these brain sections.

Functions of the Hindbrain: The (148) governs the ability to survive from moment to moment. Some of the more important structures located in the hindbrain include the **medulla,** the **pons,** the **cerebellum,** and the **reticular formation.** The (149), or medulla, is a most crucial part of the hindbrain. It is related to (150) and connects the brain and the spinal cord. It regulates your breathing, (151), and blood pressure and, when called upon, will induce coughing, vomiting, or swallowing. Lying above the medulla is the (152). It serves as a "bridge" connecting the (153) to the hindbrain and regulates the (154) cycle. The (155), or "little brain", controls the timing of well-learned sequences of movement that are too rapid to be controlled consciously. A little higher up in the hindbrain and passing from the hindbrain to the midbrain is the (156), a diffuse network of neurons that helps maintain vigilance and an optimal level of brain (157). It acts as a (158), allowing you to attend to important stimuli and ignoring unimportant ones. The role of the reticular formation in attention is demonstrated by the "____(159)____" in which you can be involved in a conversation with someone but can respond if you hear something of significance from across the room.

Functions of the Midbrain: The __(160)__ of mammals is relatively small and contains the **tectum** and the **substantia nigra.** At the roof of the midbrain is the __(161)__, which mediates certain reflexive responses to visual and auditory stimuli and helps to identify stimuli. Particularly graceful movements depend on the __(162)__. When the substantia nigra is affected by degenerative disease, __(163)__ disease results, producing its normally characteristic shuffling gait and hand tremors. These symptoms are caused by a __(164)__ deficit. Treatment involves intake of __(165)__, a precursor of dopamine in the brain.

Functions of the Forebrain: Above the hindbrain and midbrain is the __(166)__, which serves the "higher functions" of learning, __(167)__, thinking, emotion, and personality. The forebrain consists of the **thalamus,** the **limbic system,** and the **cerebral cortex.** A classic case of damage to the forebrain is that of Phineus __(168)__, whose forebrain was damaged by an exploding tamping rod. While there was little apparent change in his __(169)__ ability, the injury did lead to dramatic changes in emotion and __(170)__. In addition to the case study of Gage, there is additional supporting evidence that forebrain disorders are associated with __(171)__ behavior, including criminality.

Located in the center of the forebrain is the __(172)__, through which extends the brain stem. The thalamus serves as a sensory __(173)__ for taste, body, visual, and auditory sensations, but not for __(174)__. The __(175)__ surrounds the thalamus and lines the border between the two cerebral hemispheres. It serves to promote __(176)__ and, therefore, continuation of the species. There are four components of the limbic system: the **hypothalamus, septum,** the **amygdala,** and the **hippocampus.** The __(177)__ helps regulate sexual behavior, body temperature, eating, emotion, and drinking. The role of the hypothalamus in __(178)__ was accidentally discovered by Olds & Milner (1954). Their identification of a "__(179)__" in the hypothalamus has been subject to more recent research showing that although the __(180)__ plays a central role, it is but one of a group of structures that, when stimulated, induce feelings of __(181)__.

The __(182)__ continuously evaluates information from the environment, thereby inducing appropriate emotional responses. It helps you decide what to do if you opened your car door to find yourself eye to eye with a pit bull dog frothing at the mouth. Charles Whitman, the mass slayer in the 1966 Texas tower massacre, was found to have a tumor pressing on his amygdala. The __(183)__, on the other hand, is the limbic system structure that plays the greatest role in forming memories of your evaluation of information from the environment. Damage to this structure has been linked to __(184)__ associated with Alzheimer's disease.

The final structure of the forebrain is the __(185)__. This is the thin outer layer of the uppermost portion of the forebrain called the __(186)__. The most obvious and significant feature is the folds, or __(187)__. The cerebrum is divided into two halves; called the cerebral __(188)__. These in turn are divided into four __(189)__, each with two major areas. The lobes are known as the **frontal, parietal, occipital,** and **temporal.** The lobes each contain a __(190)__ area that serves either sensory or motor functions and __(191)__ areas that integrate information from the primary areas. Association areas are involved in behaviors such as speaking, __(192)__, and recognizing objects.

The __(193)__ lobes contain the primary motor cortex which controls __(194)__. Stimulation of the rear of the right or left frontal lobe induces limb movements on the __(195)__ side of the body. This phenomenon is known as __(196)__ control. The __(197)__ area is the primary cortical area of the frontal lobes. The primary cortical areas of the other lobes process __(198)__ information. Running parallel to the motor cortex of the frontal lobes are the primary cortical areas of the __(199)__ lobes. This cortical area is known as the __(200)__ cortex because it processes bodily senses such as pain, touch, and temperature. Both the somatosensory cortex and motor cortexes have particular areas that control __(201)__ portions of the body. The map of these representations is known as a __(202)__. We know of the existence of the homunculi due to the work of neurosurgeon Wilder __(203)__. Penfield used __(204)__ stimulation of the surface of the human brain and identified regions of the brain involved in specific body movement and sensations.

The primary cortical area for the temporal lobes is the __(205)__ cortex. It receives input from both ears but more so from the contralateral ear. The __(206)__ lobes contain the primary cortical area for vision. This area integrates the information from your __(207)__. The input from your right visual field is processed by your __(208)__ visual cortex and the information from the left visual field is processed by the right.

To help you stay on track, it's time to take a short study break. When you return, quickly review the structures of the brain and their functions before you move on.

Mini-review of Brain Structures and Their Functions:

Brain Structure:

______1. cortical association areas
______2. medulla
______3. pons
______4. cerebellum
______5. reticular formation
______6. tectum
______7. substantia nigra
______8. temporal lobe
______9. thalamus
______10. limbic system
______11. hypothalamus
______12. occipital lobe
______13. amygdala
______14. hippocampus
______15. cerebral cortex
______16. frontal lobe
______17. parietal lobe

Function:

A. Contains the primary cortical area for vision and integrates the information from your eye.
B. The "little brain"; controls the timing of well-learned sequences of movement that are too rapid to be controlled consciously
C. Contains the somatosensory cortex; it processes bodily senses such as pain, touch, and temperature
D. Is related to survival and connects the brain and the spinal cord, regulates your breathing, heart rate, and blood pressure and, when called upon, will induce coughing, vomiting, or swallowing
E. It serves as a "bridge" connecting the cerebellum to the hindbrain and regulates the sleep-wake cycle
F. Located in the center of the forebrain; serves as a sensory relay station for taste, body, visual, and auditory sensations, but not for smell
G. A diffuse network of neurons that helps maintain vigilance and an optimal level of brain arousal
H. Located at the roof of the midbrain; mediates certain reflexive responses to visual and auditory stimuli and helps to identify stimuli
I. Surrounds the thalamus and lines the border between the two cerebral hemispheres. It serves to promote survival and, therefore, continuation of the species
J. Involved in graceful movements; when its function degenerates, Parkinson's disease results
K. Helps regulate sexual behavior, body temperature, eating, emotion, and drinking
L. Contains the primary motor cortex; stimulation of the rear of this structure induces limb movements on the opposite side of the body
M. Integrates information from the primary cortical areas
N. Continuously evaluates information from the environment, thereby inducing appropriate emotional responses
O. Contains the auditory cortex
P. Is the limbic system structure that plays the greatest role in forming memories; damage to this structure has been implicated in the memory loss associated with Alzheimer's disease
Q. Is the thin outer layer of the uppermost portion of the forebrain called the cerebrum

---

In recent years, ____(209)____ have been added to the tools that are used to study the brain. These include __(210)__ **(PET),** which allows researchers to measure ongoing activity in particular regions of the brain and____(211)____ **(CT)** and _____(212)_____ **(MRI),** which are both used more for displaying brain structures. The CT takes many__(213)__ of the brain, while the MRI uses powerful__(214)__ to create detailed pictures of the brain. Both CT and MRI have been used to detect_(215)_ abnormalities in the brain. Very recently a new type of MRI called_(216)_ MRI has begun to be used. **Functional MRI** detects increases in__(217)__ to particular brain regions that are more active at particular times. This technique allows researchers to examine what brain structures may be working together.

It is important to note that areas of the brain do not work independently of one another. The (218) of different areas of the brain underlie many psychological functions. For example, the association areas of the (219) cortex integrate information involved in thinking, planning, and problem solving. Another example of the integration of different brain structures lies in the process of speech. Speech involves the interaction of the association cortex of the frontal and (220) lobes. In almost all right-handers and most left-handers speech appears to be controlled by the (221) hemisphere. In the left (222) lobe, **Broca's area** appears to control the (223) of speech while in the left (224) lobe, Wernicke's area appears to control (225), or the understanding of speech. Damage to either of these areas produces a disruption of language known as (226). Thus **Broca's aphasics** have trouble with (227) of language, while **Wernicke's aphasics** have a problem with (228) speech.

Localization of Brain Functions: A controversial issue in behavioral neuroscience has been the question about the extent to which psychological functions can be (229) within particular areas of the brain. The idea of **localization of function** originated with Franz Joseph (230). Gall devised a system for associating depressions and bumps in the skull with (231) abilities and personality. The practice of reading these bumps was known as (232). **Phrenology** had scientific shortcomings and its followers were never able to provide scientific support for it. In contrast to the views of phrenologists, Pierre Flourens and Karl Lashley proposed that psychological functions depended on the (233) of different areas of the brain. Currently, most behavioral neuroscientists favor a (234) between the views of Gall and Lashley. They view the brain as a collection of structures that interact flexibly. This interaction is not only shown in speech. Your ability to recognize faces depends on the interaction of (235) cortex in the (236) and temporal lobes. Individuals with damage to these areas exhibit **prosopagnosia,** or the inability to recognize (237).

Plasticity of the Brain: Although much of what is known about the functions of various brain structures comes from deficits demonstrated by individuals with brain (238), the human brain appears to be remarkable in its ability to (239) from experience and promote adaptive behavior. In doing so, the brain is said to show (240). Recovery from brain damage has been shown to occur through (241), in which nearby neurons grow new axon branches to replace those lost by damaged neurons. This growth is much more likely to occur in (242) organisms, and in humans only occurs in the (243) nervous system. Another mechanism of recovery from brain damage that has been suggested is that one area of the brain may substitute for a damaged area. This is know as the principle of (244). **Equipotentiality** has been demonstrated in children who have undergone a (245) for the treatment of epilepsy. In this case, the remaining (246) often takes over the function of the missing hemisphere. (247) is a controversial treatment in which healthy tissue is transplanted into the damaged brain or spinal cord to promote better recovery. Animal research with this technique has been promising, and researchers have tried, with some success, to apply the technique to the treatment of (248) disease patients. The technique remains controversial, because it involves the potential use of healthy (249) brain tissue.

The Mind-Brain Problem: An additional question that is raised by research into the brain is whether mental processes equate to the (250). Historically, (251) favored the concept of **dualism,** which views the mind as an immaterial substance (252) from the brain. The alternative view, called **monism,** proposes that the mind and brain are the same. Recently, a new position has been proposed by Nobel Prize-winner Roger (253). His view is known as **emergent interactionism,** in which he claims that the mind arises from the (254) of the brain. However, in spite of all of the advances in behavioral neuroscience, this question remains a (255) one.

V. Thinking About Psychology: Do the Cerebral Hemispheres Serve Different Functions?

We have discussed the fact that the (256) hemisphere appears to be involved in speech in most individuals and the popular press is full of references to "left brained" and "right brained" individuals. Is it true then that the cerebral hemispheres control different psychological functions? Researchers have finally reached some agreement on this topic. Although most researchers do not claim that (257) hemisphere has complete responsibility for any function, they do agree that, in general, the left hemisphere appears to be better at (258), sequential, analytical, rational, and mathematical functions, while the (259) hemisphere appears to be best at nonverbal, spatial, holistic, emotional, and creative functions. Evidence for this comes from three types of studies: intact brain studies, damaged brain studies, and split brain studies.

Intact brains studies using (260) recordings have produced evidence that people produce greater electrical activity in the left hemisphere while performing (261) tasks, and greater activity in the right hemisphere during (262) tasks. The evidence from a damaged brains comes mostly from (263) disorders; however, right hemispheric damage has been show to produce a (264) syndrome in which patients act as if the left side of their body does not exist.

Finally, the evidence from split brain studies involves the severing of the __(265)__, thus separating the cerebral hemispheres. Roger Sperry and his colleagues have demonstrated that when split brain patients were asked to complete __(266)__ tasks, the left hand (i.e. right hemisphere) was much better at the task then the right.

Anatomy of a Contemporary Research Study: Is Left-handedness a Pathological Condition?
Remember that in Chapter 1 we discussed how to read and understand psychological literature?
Take a moment to read the summary of the study provided on pages 95-96 in your textbook. Then answer the following questions. In this study what were the

a. rationale?

b. hypothesis?

c. method?

d. results?

e. Finally, what did the authors conclude their results meant?

KEY RESEARCH FINDINGS

Provide the details of the following key research studies in psychology:

1. **Tranel (1995):** Reports a case study of a patient with sensory neglect syndrome (Page 66)
2. **Hales (1730):** Demonstrated the role the spinal cord plays in limb reflexes in a frog (Page 68)
3. **Galvani (1786):** Demonstrated that the nerve impulse is electrical in nature (Page 69)
4. **Hodgkin & Huxley (1952):** Demonstrated the electrochemical process in neural transmission (Page 70)
5. **Nicoll & Madison (1982):** Showed that under general anesthesia you become unconscious because you were given a drug that prevented the axons of the brain responsible for consciousness from depolarizing. (Page 70)
6. **Ranvier (1871):** Identified the small gaps in the myelin sheath. (Page 71)
7. **Ramòn y Cajal (1937/1966):** Identified the synapse as a gap between neurons. (Page 72)
8. **Loewi (1921):** Demonstrated the chemical nature of synaptic transmission in the frog. (Page 72)
9. **Pert & Snyder (1973):** Demonstrated the existence of naturally occurring endorphins in the brain. (Page 75)
10. **Miczek, Thompson, & Shuster (1982):** Defeated mice were given naloxone and flicked their tails as quickly as they had before being defeated. (Page 75)
11. **Berger (1924):** Developed a procedure for recording the electrical activity in the brain; identified alpha and beta rhythms. (Page 79-80)
12. **Moruzzi & Magoun (1949):** Awakened sleeping cats by stimulating the reticular formation. (Page 81)
13. **Gage (1848):** Case study of an individual with forebrain damage. (Page 82)
14. **Fritsch & Hitzig (1870):** Demonstrated that electrical stimulation of the cerebral cortex in the frontal lobe produces limb movements on the opposite side of the body. (Page 84)
15. **Penfield (1891-1976):** Developed Montreal procedure for brain surgery; demonstrated that regions governing movement formed an upside-down map of the body in the primary cortical areas. (Page 86)
16. **Breathnach (1989):** Provided CT evidence linking Broca's aphasia to damage in Broca's area. (Page 88)
17. **Bach-y-Rita (1990) & Fox (1984):** Showed that intact brain areas take over functions of damaged areas. (Page 91)
18. **Fine, Meldrum & Patel (1990):** Performed transplantation of fetal GABA neurons that induced epileptic seizures in rats. (Page 92)
19. **Bernstein & Goldberg (1989)**: Performed grafts of fetal spinal cord cells reduced the seventy of rat hindlimb deficits. (Page 92)
20. **Loring & Sheer (1984):** Demonstrated differential EEG activity in the left and right hemispheres during verbal and spatial tasks. (Page 97)

21. **Moscovitch & Behrmann (1994):** Demonstrated that damage to right parietal cortex produces sensory neglect syndrome. (Page 98)
22. **Gazzaniga (1967):** Demonstrated that split-brain patients performed a block-design task better with the left hand. (Page 100)

Now that you have finished the comprehensive review, it is time to really test yourself. Take the two practice exams.

PRACTICE TEST A

1. A behavioral neuroscientist would not be interested in which of the following research questions?
   a. How does a specific drug affect an individual's ability to remember factual data?
   b. How does a change in an individual's hormone level affect the tendency for antisocial behavior?
   c. Does a change in exercise level affect the emotional state of an individual?
   d. Are female interviewers more effective in convincing males to disclose confidential information?

Obj.: 1 Page: 66-67

2. Imagine that you arrive at a class only to discover that there will be a surprise quiz. Immediately, your heart rate increases, your mouth goes dry, and you begin to sweat. This reflects activity in the
   a. endocrine system.
   b. somatic nervous system.
   c. sympathetic nervous system.
   d. parasympathetic nervous system.

Obj.: 2 Page: 68

3. A diving accident completely severes the spinal cord of a diver at mid-chest level. He would most likely experience
   a. initial leg paralysis, which would gradually disappear over time.
   b. permanent leg paralysis and permanent loss of feeling in the legs.
   c. almost immediate death due to destruction of control centers for breathing and heart rate.
   d. permanent loss of feeling in the body at the level of the injury, but retention of feeling above and below it.

Obj.: 3 Page: 68

4. The branchlike extension from a neuron with the specialized function of receiving messages from surrounding neurons is the
   a. axon.
   b. dendrite.
   c. synapse.
   d. terminal button.

Obj.: 3 Page: 68

5. When a neuron reaches its firing threshold, a surge of
   a. sodium ions rush into the axon.
   b. protein ions rush into the axon.
   c. chloride ions rush into the axon.
   d. protein ions rush out of the axon.

Obj.: 5 Page: 70

6. Your ability to perform the smooth movements required for writing, dancing, or playing basketball depends on neurons that secrete
   a. dopamine.
   b. serotonin.
   c. endorphins.
   d. norepinephrine.

Obj.: 6 Page: 74

7. Neurons communicate with one another through chemical substances called
   a. neurotransmitters.
   b. hormones.
   c. thyroxine.
   d. myelin.

Obj.: 6 Page: 72-74

8. If naloxone blocked the so-called runner's high in people who normally experience it, the runner's high would probably be caused by neurons associated with
   a. serotonin.
   b. endorphins.
   c. substance P.
   d. norepinephrine.

Obj.: 7 Page: 75

9. A woman who goes into premature labor may be secreting insufficient amounts of
   a. oxytocin.
   b. estrogen.
   c. progesterone.
   d. testosterone.

Obj.: 9 Page: 77

10. The gonads produce the sex hormones. Which of the groupings below indicates the correct relationship between gonad and hormone(s)
   a. ovaries--estrogen/testes--progesterone
   b. ovaries--estradiol and progesterone/testes--testosterone
   c. hypothalamus---estrogen and testosterone
   d. ovaries---testosterone and progesterone/testes--estradiol

Obj.: 10 Page: 78

11. Electroencephalography (EEG) is a technique used in studying the brain by
   a. implanting electrodes into the brain and thereby monitoring brain-wave activity.
   b. placing electrodes outside the brain and thereby monitoring brain-wave activity.
   c. taking X-ray images of the brain.
   d. producing lesions in specific structures in the brain.

Obj.: 11 Page: 78-80

12. A classical pianist suffers a stroke and can no longer play the piano with proper timing, though she can use all of her fingers to strike the correct keys. The stroke probably affected her
   a. cerebellum.
   b. motor cortex.
   c. corpus callosum.
   d. somatosensory cortex.

Obj.: 12 Page: 81

13. If a neural grafting technique is perfected for the treatment of Parkinson's disease, it would most likely involve the transplantation (from one person to another) of tissue from the
   a. cerebellum.
   b. hippocampus.
   c. motor cortex.
   d. substantia nigra.

Obj.: 13 Page: 81

14. An arrow from a careless archer pierces the brain of a bystander. The victim survives, recalls events from before the accident, but cannot form new memories. The arrow probably destroyed the
   a. pons.
   b. hippocampus.
   c. hypothalamus.
   d. parietal lobes.

Obj.: 14 Page: 83

15 The auditory cortex is the primary cortical area of the
   a. occipital lobe.
   b. temporal lobe.
   c. frontal lobe.
   d. parietal lobe.

Obj.: 15 Page: 84-85

16. Wilder Penfield is best known for his development of
   a. the EEG machine and PET scans.
   b. the Montreal procedure and mapping of the cortex.
   c. the Montreal procedure and PET scans of the brain.
   d. mapping the cerebral cortex with EEG recordings.

Obj.: 16 Page: 86

17. A PET scan measures the
   a. amount of glucose used in regions of the brain.
   b. electrical activity of the brain.
   c. magnetic fields of the brain.
   d. speed of polarization-depolarization in a neuron.

Obj. : 17 Page: 87-88

18. Damage to either Broca's or Wernicke's area of the cerebral cortex will, in most cases, cause
   a. aphasia.
   b. motor coordination.
   c. stuttering.
   d. prosopagnosia

Obj.:18 Page: 88-89

19. Phrenology was based on the erroneous assumption that
    a. brain structure could be determined by the bumps and depressions on the skull.
    b. psychological processes, especially memory, require the interaction of diverse areas of the brain.
    c. the effects of damage to the brain could be overcome by the process of regeneration.
    d. heredity affected the development of the brain.

Obj.: 19 Page: 89-91

20. Research on neural grafts in humans has primarily focused on which one of the following diseases or disorders?
    a. Parkinson's disease
    b. recovery of function due to severe head injury
    c. Alzheimer's disease
    d. the loss of function due to strokes

Obj.: 20 Page: 91-93

21. In reply to the question "What is the mind?" Descartes would favor which one of the following?
    a. a position known as monism
    b. a position known as dualism
    c. the belief that the mind is a material substance
    d. the belief that the corpus callosum was the site where the mind and brain interact

Obj.: 21 Page: 93-94

22. Evidence from split-brain research supporting the argument that the cerebral hemispheres serve different functions includes all but
    a. results gathered with the Wada test.
    b. the fact that anesthetization of the right hemisphere, but only rarely of the left hemisphere, induces temporary aphasia.
    c. the symptoms of the neglect syndrome.
    d. recent studies showing that the hemispheres can maintain separate streams of consciousness.

Obj.: 22 Page: 94-96

23. If a split-brain patient were to draw a map, he would probably perform
    a. better with his left hand.
    b. better with his right hand.
    c. equally well with both hands.
    d. better using a foot rather than a hand.

Obj.: 23 Page: 100

PRACTICE TEST B

1. A biological psychologist would not be interested in which of the following research questions?
    a. How does a specific drug affect an individual's ability to remember conceptual data?
    b. How does a change in an individual's hormone level affect the tendency for criminal behavior?
    c. Does a change in exercise level affect the emotional state of an individual?
    d. Are female interviewers more effective in convincing males to disclose confidential information?

Obj.: 1 Page: 66-67

2. In a large lecture hall, which of the following individuals is likely to be at the highest level of sympathetic arousal?
    a. Melissa Jones, who is daydreaming and staring out the window.
    b. Keith Smith, who is taking careful notes on the lecture.
    c. Professor Nguyen, who is lecturing on an unfamiliar topic.
    d. Bill Jones, who is thinking about a future term paper.

Obj.: 2 Page: 68

3. When Paula inhaled some pepper, she reflexively sneezed. Which statement most accurately describes what happened?
   a. Motor neurons carried a signal to the upper parts of the brain, which signaled the sensory neurons of the nose to carry out the sneeze.
   b. The glial cells transported nutrients to the sensory and motor nerves, which caused the facial muscles to flex.
   c. The pepper aroused the sympathetic system causing the body to prepare for action: namely a sneeze.
   d. Sensory neurons carried a signal to the interneuron of the spinal cord, which sent a message via the motor neurons to the muscles of the respiratory system.

Obj.: 3 Page: 68

4. Myelin sheaths serve the purpose of
   a. insulating the axon to speed neural transmission.
   b. providing oxygen to the soma.
   c. nourishing the neuron.
   d. retaining neurotransmitters.

Obj.: 4 Page: 68-69

5. The portion of the neuron that could be equated with the "highway of the nervous system" is the
   a. dendrite.
   b. cell body.
   c. axon.
   d. terminal button.

Obj.: 4 Page: 68-69

6. The firing of a neuron is most similar to :
   a. a bowl overflowing as more water slowly drips into it.
   b. the increase in daylight as the sun rises.
   c. a plane taking off and landing at its destination.
   d. a light coming on as one flips a light switch.

Obj.: 5 Page: 71

7. Which statement most accurately describes the process of synaptic transmission?
   a. Synaptic vesicles secrete neurotransmitters which diffuse over to the receptor sites on the dendrites of another neuron.
   b. As depolarization progresses, the firing threshold is reached and an action potential occurs.
   c. After firing, potassium ions rush out of the neuronal membrane in a process called repolarization.
   d. The action potential jumps from one node of Ranvier to the next, thus increasing the speed of transmission.

Obj.: 6 Page: 73

8. What "master" endocrine gland regulates many of the other endocrine glands by secreting hormones that affect those glands?
   a. adrenal gland
   b. thyroid gland
   c. pituitary gland
   d. thymus gland

Obj.: 9 Page: 76-77

9. You could be in deep conversation and yet recognize your name if someone in the room mentioned it. This vigilance is called the
   a. cocktail party phenomenon.
   b. reticular formation phenomenon.
   c. single focusing phenomenon.
   d. the blocking phenomenon.

Obj.: 12 Page: 80-81

10. Bonnie has a disease that disrupts the functioning of the hypothalamus. With which of the following areas of functioning is she likely to have serious difficulty?
   a. seeing, hearing, and tasting
   b. reading, writing, and fine movements
   c. thinking, problem solving, and visualizing
   d. eating, drinking, and body temperature control

Obj.: 14 Page: 83

11. A student visiting a behavioral neuroscience research center introduces herself to a patient who has had his hippocampus removed. A friendly and rather lengthy conversation follows. The next day, what is the patient likely to say when the student greets him in the hallway?
   a. "Why are you threatening to hurt me?"
   b. "Why do I keep eating even though I'm full?"
   c. "Do I know you?"
   d. "Why do I keep hearing strange sounds?"

Obj.: 14 Page: 83

12. Acetylcholine has been suggested to be involved in learning and memory and its degeneration related to Alzheimer's disease. Given what you know about the brain, in which structure would you expect to find a high percentage of acetylcholine receptors?
   a. pons
   b. reticular activating system
   c. hippocampus
   d. medulla

Obj.: 14 Page: 80

13. If you were to randomly select a portion of the cerebral cortex, it would most likely be a portion of the
   a. association cortex.
   b. cerebellum.
   c. sensory cortex.
   d. motor cortex.

Obj: 15 Page: 84-85

14. A gunshot wound to the right occipital lobe is likely to produce blindness in
   a. the right eye.
   b. the left eye.
   c. right visual fields of both eyes.
   d. left visual fields of both eyes.

Ob.j.: 16 Page: 86

15. If you want to measure ongoing brain activity in a certain region of the brain, you would most likely use a(n)
   a. MRI.
   b. CT scan.
   c. PET scan.
   d. surgical procedure similar to the one used by Penfield.

Obj.: 17 Page: 87-88

16. After a stroke, a patient is unable to speak. Later, his speech consists of short, telegraphic phrases. Most likely the stroke damaged neurons in
   a. the right occipital lobe.
   b. the cerebellum.
   c. Broca's area.
   d. the substantia nigra.

Obj.: 18 Page: 88

17. Which statement most accurately reflects current neuroscientific conclusions about whether psychological functions are spread out in different areas of the brain or localized in a specific area?
   a. Specialized brain structures interact flexibly with one another, but damage to any one of the structures disrupts the psychological functions
   b. Some psychological functions such as speech and fine motor movements are localized in only one area, but others are completely spread out.
   c. While cortical function are located in specific areas, the hindbrain and midbrain functions are quite spread out.
   d. Specific psychological functions are spread out over all the lobes of the cerebral cortex.

Obj.: 19 Page: 90-91

18. Roger Sperry differs from Wilder Penfield in that he
   a. is a monist while Penfield is more of a dualist.
   b. does not implicate the pineal gland while Penfield does.
   c. argues that the mind is not dependent on the brain while Penfield argues it is.
   d. does not support Fechner's position while Penfield does.

Obj.: 21 Page: 93-94

19. In most right-handed people, verbal abilities are governed
   a. primarily by the right hemisphere.
   b. primarily by the left hemisphere.
   c. equally by both hemispheres.
   d. by the occipital lobe.

Obj.: 22 Page: 94-96

20. A split-brain patient is blindfolded so that he cannot see his hands. A pen is placed in his left hand. He is asked to say out loud what is in his hand. What is likely to happen?
   a. He will correctly name it to be a pen.
   b. He will call it a "writing object" because his associations will be stimulated.
   c. He will not be able to hold the pen in his left hand because of damage to the corpus callosum.
   d. He will not be able to name it because his verbal left hemisphere will not know about the pen.

Obj.: 23 Page: 100

ESSAY QUESTIONS

1. From a behavioral science perspective, which of these items of folk wisdom is truer: "You can't teach an old dog new tricks" or "You're never too old to learn something new"?

Obj.: 20 Page: 91

2 Imagine meeting four different individuals who have sustained brain damage to different parts of their brains. Person A has a tumor in her thalamus. Person B has a tumor destroying her hypothalamus. Person C had a stroke that irreversibly damaged his temporal lobe, and Person D had a motorcycle accident that damaged his cerebellum. Describe the behavioral effects of each of these injuries.

Obj.: 12, 14, and 15 Page: 81-86

ANSWER RECORD FOR CHAPTER 3

Comprehensive Guided Review:

1. biological
2. psychological
3. brain
4. behavioral neuroscientist
5. 1990's
6. Freud
7. James
8. central
9. spinal
10. peripheral
11. somatic
12. autonomic
13. sympathetic
14. parasympathetic
15. neurons
16. Sensory
17. Motor
18. support
19. spinal cord
20. brain
21. neurons
22. Stephen Hales
23. reflex
24. interneurons
25. soma
26. dendrites
27. spines
28. axon
29. nerves
30. neural impulse
31. Descartes
32. Newton
33. Galvani
34. electricity
35. electro
36. axonal conduction
37. intracellular
38. outside
39. ions
40. sodium
41. chloride
42. membrane
43. intracellular
44. positive
45. negative
46. outside
47. permeable
48. sodium
49. threshold
50. action potential
51. positive
52. repolarization
53. depolarization
54. action potentials
55. all-or-none
56. impulse
57. speed
58. Ranvier
59. nodes
60. myelinated
61. slower
62. white
63. gray
64. myelin
65. spinal cord
66. muscle weakness
67. Golgi
68. Ramon y Cajal
69. Cajal
70. *synapses*
71. gaps
72. Loewi
73. chemical
74. synaptic transmission
75. Acetylcholine
76. Neurotransmitters
77. axon
78. synaptic
79. gap
80. dendritic
81. neurotransmitter
82. depolarize
83. inhibitory
84. action potential
85. excitatory
86. reuptake

Mini-review of Neural Transmission:

A. 1; B. 2; C. 4; D. 3; E. 8; F. 5; G. 6; H. 7; I. 11; J. 9; K. 10

87. neurotransmitters
88. parasympathetic
89. muscle
90. curare
91. memory
92. marijuana
93. inhibitory
94. Parkinson's
95. schizophrenia
96. mood
97. hunger
98. norepinephrine
99. serotonin
100. amino acid
101. relaxation
102. GABA
103. excitatory
104. memory
105. neuropeptides
106. pain
107. Substance P
108. euphoria
109. Pert & Snyder
110. morphinelike
111. opiate
112. endorphins
113. pain
114. tail-flicking
115. naloxone
116. stress

Mini-review of Neurotransmitters:
A. 7; B. 2; C. 1; D. 5; E. 8; F. 3; G. 4; H. 6

117. hormones
118. bloodstream
119. exocrine
120. master gland
121. brain
122. hormones
123. hypothalamus
124. pituitary
125. asopressin
126. oxytocin
127. growth hormone
128. prolactin
129. thyroid-stimulating
130. thyroxin
131. pituitary
132. adrenal
133. sodium
134. cortisol
135. medulla
136. Epinephrine
137. norepinephrine
138. gonads
139. testosterone
140. estrogen

Mini-review of Endocrine System:
1. E; 2. L; 3. K; 4. I; 5. F; 6. H; 7. G; 8. M; 9. C; 10. J; 11. B; 12. A; 13. D; 14. N

141. neurons
142. damage
143. stimulation
144. electro-encephalograph
145. Berger
146. alpha
147. beta
148. hindbrain
149. medulla oblongata
150. survival
151. heart rate
152. pons
153. cerebellum
154. sleep-wake
155. cerebellum
156. reticular formation
157. arousal
158. filter
159. cocktail party phenomenon
160. midbrain
161. tectum
162. substantia nigra
163. Parkinson's
164. dopamine
165. L-dopa
166. forebrain
167. memory
168. Gage
169. intellectual
170. personality
171. antisocial
172. thalamus
173. relay station
174. smell
175. limbic system
176. survival
177. hypothalamus
178. emotionality
179. pleasure center
180. hypothalamus
181. pleasure
182. amygdala
183. hippocampus
184. memory loss
185. cerebral cortex
186. cerebrum
187. convolutions
188. hemispheres
189. lobes
190. primary cortical
191. association
192. problem solving
193. frontal
194. movements
195. opposite
196. contralateral
197. motor
198. sensory
199. parietal
200. somatosensory
201. specific
202. homunculus
203. Penfield
204. electrical
205. auditory
206. occipital
207. eyes
208. left

Mini-review of Brain Structures and Functions:
1. M; 2. D; 3. E; 4. B; 5. G; 6. H; 7. J; 8. O; 9. F; 10. I; 11. K; 12. A; 13. N; 14. P; 15. Q; 16. L; 17. C

209. brain scans
210. positron-emission tomography
211. computed tomography
212. magnetic resonance imaging
213. X rays
214. magnetic fields
215. structural
216. functional
217. blood flow
218. integration
219. frontal
220. temporal
221. left
222. frontal
223. production
224. temporal
225. comprehension
226. aphasia
227. production
228. meaningful
229. localized
230. Gall
231. intellectual
232. phrenology
233. interaction
234. compromise
235. association
236. occipital
237. faces
238. damage
239. learn
240. neural plasticity
241. collateral sprouting
242. younger
243. peripheral
244. equipotentiality
245. hemispherectomy
246. hemisphere
247. Neural grafting
248. Parkinson's
249. fetal
250. mind
251. Descartes
252. separate
253. Sperry
254. activity
255. philosophical
256. left
257. either
258. verbal
259. right
260. EEG
261. verbal
262. spatial
263. language
264. sensory neglect
265. corpus callosum
266. spatial

Practice Test A:

1. a. Incorrect: Behavioral neuroscientists are interested in the relationship between the brain and behavior.
   b. Incorrect: Behavioral neuroscientists are interested in the relationship between the brain and behavior.
   c. Incorrect: Behavioral neuroscientists are interested in the relationship between the brain and behavior.
   d. Correct: Behavioral neuroscientists are interested in the relationship between the brain and behavior.

2. a. Incorrect: The endocrine system response is a much slower response.
   b. Incorrect: The somatic nervous system enervates the skeletal muscles and does not control fight or flight behavior.
   c. Correct: The sympathetic nervous system is responsible for the fight-or-flight behavior.
   d. Incorrect: The parasympathetic system is responsible for relaxing the body, not exciting it.

3. a. Incorrect: Severing the spinal cord would lead to permanent paralysis.
   b. Correct: Severing the spinal cord would lead to permanent paralysis.
   c. Incorrect: A mid-chest-level spinal cord cut would not cause death, only paralysis and sensory loss.
   d. Incorrect: A mid-chest-level spinal cord cut would not cause death, only paralysis and sensory loss.

4. a. Incorrect: The axon is the pathway that the action potential travels down.
   b. Correct: The dendrites are the long branchlike extensions that receive the message.
   c. Incorrect: The synapse is the connection between two neurons.
   d. Incorrect: Terminal buttom are the bulblike endings at the end of the axon that their neurotransmitters are released from.

5. **a. Correct: At threshold positive sodium ions rush *into* the axon.**
   b. Incorrect: At threshold positive sodium ions rush *into* the axon.
   c. Incorrect: At threshold positive sodium ions rush *into* the axon.
   d. Incorrect: At threshold positive sodium ions rush *into* the axon.

6. **a. Correct: Dopamine neurons are involved with smooth voluntary movements.**
   b. Incorrect: Serotonin neurons have been implicated in depression.
   c. Incorrect: Endorphins are neuropeptides chemicals involved in relieving pain.
   d. Incorrect: Norepinephrine is believed to be involved in moods.

7. **a. Correct: The chemicals released from the axon terminals are neurotransmitters.**
   b. Incorrect: Hormones are chemicals released into the blood by the endocrine system.
   c. Incorrect: Thyroxin is a hormone released by the thyroid gland.
   d. Incorrect: Myelin is the fatty substance that insulates the axon.

8. a. Incorrect: Naloxone has been shown to block endorphins.
   b. Correct: Naloxone has been shown to block endorphins.
   c. Incorrect: Naloxone has been shown to block endorphins.
   d. Incorrect: Naloxone has been shown to block endorphins.

9. a. Incorrect: Oxytocin is a hormone involved in inducing uterine contractions, thus would be elevated during labor.
   b. Incorrect: Estrogen regulates the development of female reproductive systems and secondary sex characteristics.
   c. Correct: Progesterone is responsible for regulating changes in the uterus to help maintain pregnancy.
   d. Incorrect: Testosterone regulates the development of the male reproductive system, all secondary sex characteristics, and sex drive.

10. a. Incorrect: The ovaries secrete progesterone, not the testes.
    b. Correct: Ovaries secrete estrogen and progesterone and the testes secrete testosterone.
    c. Incorrect: The hypothalamus is a brain structure that regulates the release of hormones.
    d. Incorrect: The ovaries do not secrete testosterone.

11. a. Incorrect: EEG recording does not require implantation of electrodes into the brain.
    b. Correct: EEG recordings are done by placing electrodes on the scalp outside the brain.
    c. Incorrect: EEG does not involve the use of x rays.
    d. Incorrect: EEG does not require lessening the brain.

12. **a. Correct: Cerebellum is involved in the control of timing of well-learned sequences of rapid movement.**
    b. Incorrect: Motor cortex controls the conscious movement of the fingers, not the automatic.
    c. Incorrect: Corpus callosum is the bridge of fibers that connect the left and right hemispheres.
    d. Incorrect: Somatosensory cortex controls the sensation of touch.

13. a. Incorrect: Cerebellum controls timing of well-learned sequences of movements.
    b. Incorrect: Hippocampal tissue is involved in memory formation.
    c. Incorrect: Motor cortex controls basic movement.
    d. Correct: Parkinson's disease has been shown to involve the substania nigra.

14. a. Incorrect: Pons has been shown to regulate the sleep-wake cycles.
    b. Correct: Hippocampal damage has been shown to disrupt the formation of new memories.
    c. Incorrect: Damage to the hypothalamus leads to disruption in behavior.
    d. Incorrect: Damage to the parietal lobes disrupts detection of sensory input.

15. a. Incorrect: Auditory cortex is located in the temporal lobe.
    b. Correct: Auditory cortex is located in the temporal lobe.
    c. Incorrect: Auditory cortex is located in the temporal lobe.
    d. Incorrect: Auditory cortex is located in the temporal lobe.

16. a. Incorrect: Wilder Penfield did not develop EEG or PET.
    b. Correct: Wilder Penfield is known for both of these.
    c. Incorrect: Wilder Penfield did not develop PET.
    d. Incorrect: Wilder Penfield did map the cortex, but not with EEG.

17. **a. Correct: PET scans use radioactive glucose to measure the amount of ongoing activity in specific regions of the brain.**
    b. Incorrect: PET scans do not measure the electrical activity; they use radioactive glucose to measure the amount of ongoing activity in specific regions of the brain.
    c. Incorrect: PET scans do not use magnetic fields; they use radioactive glucose to measure the amount of ongoing activity in specific regions of the brain.
    d. Incorrect: PET scans use radioactive glucose to measure the amount of ongoing activity in specific regions of the brain.

18. **a. Correct: Damage to Broca's or Wernicke's areas produces a language disturbance known as aphasia.**
    b. Incorrect: Damage to Broca's or Wernicke's areas produces a language disturbance known as aphasia.
    c. Incorrect: Damage to Broca's or Wernicke's areas produces a language disturbance known as aphasia.
    d. Incorrect: Damage to Broca's or Wernicke's areas produces a language disturbance known as aphasia.

19. **a. Correct: Phrenology was based on the incorrect assumption that the brain structure could be determined by the size and location of bumps on the skull.**
    b. Incorrect: Phrenology was based on the incorrect assumption that the brain structure could be determined by the size and location of bumps on the skull.
    c. Incorrect: Phrenology was based on the incorrect assumption that the brain structure could be determined by the size and location of bumps on the skull.
    d. Incorrect: Phrenology was based on the incorrect assumption that the brain structure could be determined by the size and location of bumps on the skull.

20. **a. Correct: The early research into neural transplantation centered around transplanting fetal substantia nigra neurons into patients with Parkinson's disease.**
    b. Incorrect: The early research into neural transplantation centered around transplanting fetal substantia nigra neurons into patients with Parkinson's disease.
    c. Incorrect: The early research into neural transplantation centered around transplanting fetal substantia nigra neurons into patients with Parkinson's disease.
    d. Incorrect: The early research into neural transplantation centered around transplanting fetal substantia nigra neurons into patients with Parkinson's disease.

21. a. Incorrect: Descartes believed that the mind and brain were two separate entities, a position known as dualism. Monism is the belief that the mind is a single material or immaterial substance.
    b. Correct. Descartes believed that the mind and brain were two separate entities, a position known as dualism.
    c. Incorrect: Descartes believed that the mind and brain were two separate entities, a position known as dualism. The dualists view the mind as an immaterial substance.
    d. Incorrect: Descartes believed it was the pineal gland.

22. a. Incorrect: Evidence from the Wada test supports the argument that the cerebral hemispheres serve different functions.
    b. Incorrect: This is a description of the Wada test and evidence from the Wada test supports the argument that the cerebral hemispheres serve different functions.
    c. Incorrect: Evidence from the studies of sensory neglect syndrome also supports the argument that the cerebral hemispheres serve different functions.
    d. Correct: There is no evidence that the two hemispheres can maintain separate streams of consciousness.

23. **a. Correct: The left hand is controlled by the right cerebral hemisphere, which is better at spatial location than the left.**
    b. Incorrect: The right hand is controlled by the left hemisphere, which is better at verbal skills.
    c. Incorrect: Due to the severing of the corpus callosum, the right hemisphere cannot communicate with the left hemisphere, thus only the left hand will be able to draw the accurate map.
    d. Incorrect: The foot will not draw any better than the hand.

Practice Test B:

1. a. Incorrect: A biological psychologist is interested in drug effects.
   b. Incorrect: A biological psychologist is interested in hormone changes.
   c. Incorrect: A biological psychologist is interested in changes in physiological states.
   d. Correct: A biological psychologist is not interested in changes in social effects.

2. a. Incorrect: Melissa is in a relaxed sate, not a fight-or-flight mode, which the sympathetic system governs.
   b. Incorrect: Keith is in a normal state of arousal, not a fight-or-flight mode, which the sympathetic system governs.
   c. Correct: The professor is in an anxious state and very aroused.
   d. Incorrect: Bill is in a state of non immediate threat, not a fight-or-flight mode, which the sympathetic system governs.

3. a. Incorrect: Motor neurons carry messages away from the CNS, not to it.
   b. Incorrect: Glial cells are support cells not transport cells
   c. Incorrect: Pepper cannot activate neurons.
   d. Correct: The Sensory neurons carry into the CNS, connect to interneurons, and then motor neurons carry the information back to the muscles.

4. **a. Correct: Myelin is a fatty substance that surrounds the axon, serving as an insulator.**
   b. Incorrect: Myelin is found around the axon, not the soma.
   c. Incorrect: Myelin does not nourish neurons; it protects the axon.
   d. Incorrect: Myelin does not have an effect on the neurotransmitter.

5. a. Incorrect: The dendrites are the branched ends where information is received.
   b. Incorrect: The cell body is the "powerhouse" unit of the cell; it houses the nucleus.
   c. Correct: The axon is the tubelike projection through which information flows.
   d. Incorrect: The terminal buttons are the bulblike endings at the end of the axon.

6. a. Incorrect: Neural impulses are sudden, not gradual.
   b. Incorrect: Neural impulses are sudden, not gradual.
   c. Incorrect: Neural impulses are sudden, not gradual.
   d. Correct: Neural impulses are sudden.

7. **a. Correct: Yes, in synaptic transmission the neurotransmitters diffuse across the synaptic gap.**
   b. Incorrect: Synaptic transmission refers to the release of the neurotransmitter, not the generation of the action potential.
   c. Incorrect: Synaptic transmission refers to the release of the neurotransmitter, not the exchange of ions in depolarization.
   d. Incorrect: Synaptic transmission refers to the release of the neurotransmitter, not the movement of action potential down the axon.

8. a. Incorrect: The adrenal gland is not the "master gland"; it does not regulate the actions of other glands.
   b. Incorrect: The thyroid gland is not the "master gland"; it does not regulate the actions of other glands.
   c. Correct: The pituitary gland is considered the "master gland" because it regulates the actions of all of the other glands.
   d. Incorrect: The thymus gland is not the "master gland"; it does not regulate the actions of other glands.

9. **a. Correct: This is known as the "cocktail party phenomenon".**
   b. Incorrect: Although the effect is attributed to the actions of the reticular formation, there is no such thing as the reticular formation phenomenon.
   c. Incorrect: There is no such thing as the single focusing phenomenon.
   d. Incorrect: The blocking phenomenon is a learning effect, not one of arousal or attention.

10. a. Incorrect: The hypothalamus is not involved in seeing, hearing, or tasting.
    b. Incorrect: The hypothalamus is not involved in reading, writing, or fine movements.
    c. Incorrect: The hypothalamus is not involved in thinking, problem solving or visualizing.
    d. Correct: The hypothalamus is suggested to be involved in eating, drinking, and temperature control.

11. a. Incorrect: The effects of hippocampal damage are seen in impaired memory formation.
    b. Incorrect: The effects of hippocampal damage are seen in impaired memory formation.
    c. Correct: The effects of hippocampal damage are seen in impaired memory formation.
    d. Incorrect: The effects of hippocampal damage are seen in impaired memory formation.

12. a. Incorrect: Pons does not appear to be directly involved in learning, memory, or Alzheimer's disease.
    b. Incorrect: Reticular formation does not appear to be directly involved in learning, memory, or Alzheimer's disease.
    c. Correct: The hippocampus does appear to be involved in learning, memory, and Alzheimer's disease.
    d. Incorrect: The medulla does not appear to be directly involved in learning, memory, or Alzheimer's disease.

13. **a. Correct: The majority of the cortex is made up of association cortex.**
    b. Incorrect: The cerebellum is not a cortical structure.
    c. Incorrect: Only a small part of the occipital, temporal, and parietal cortex is considered sensory cortex.
    d. Incorrect: The motor cortex is a very small strip in the frontal lobe.

14. a. Incorrect: Only a portion of the image from the right eye goes to the right occipital lobe.
    b. Incorrect: Only a portion of the image from the left eye goes to the right occipital lobe.
    c. Incorrect: The right visual field is processed by the left occipital lobe.
    d. Correct: Due to the partial contralateral control in the visual system, the right occipital lobe would process information from the left visual field of both eyes.

15. a. Incorrect: MRI measures structural abnormalities, not function.
    b. Incorrect: CT uses X rays to provide images of structures; it does not measure brain activity.
    c. Correct: PET measures activity levels in different structures.
    d. Incorrect: Penfield did not measure ongoing activity; he produced it with electrical stimulation to the brain.

16. a. Incorrect: The occipital lobe is involved in vision, not speech production.
    b. Incorrect: the cerebellum is involved in well-learned movements, not speech production.
    c. Correct: Damage to Broca's area is believed to impair speech production.
    d. Incorrect: The substantia nigra is involved in regulating sleep-wake cycles, not speech production.

17. **a. Correct: This is a compromise between localization and full interaction and is the current view.**
    b. Incorrect: Psychologists feel that more than just speech and motor movements are localized.
    c. Incorrect: Hindbrain and midbrain systems appear to have specific functions.
    d. Incorrect: Research suggests that some functions are localized in specific areas of the brain.

18. a. Incorrect: Sperry is not a monist.
    b. Incorrect: Penfield did not implicate the pineal gland, Descartes did.
    c. Incorrect: Penfield felt that the mind was not dependent on the brain.
    d. Correct: Sperry' views of emergent interactionism are different from Fechner and Penfield.

19. A. Incorrect: In almost all individuals verbal abilities appear to be a left hemispheric function.
    B. Correct: In almost all individuals verbal abilities appear to be a left hemispheric function.
    C. Incorrect: In almost all individuals verbal abilities appear to be a left hemispheric function.
    D. Incorrect: In almost all individuals verbal abilities appear to be a left hemispheric function.

20. a. Incorrect: The information from the left hand will go to the right hemisphere, which is the nonverbal hemisphere.
    b. Incorrect: The information from the left hand will go to the right hemisphere, which is the nonverbal hemisphere.
    c. Incorrect: The corpus callosum does not regulate motor functions.
    d. Correct: The information from the left hand will go to the right hemisphere, which is the nonverbal hemisphere.

Essay Questions:

1. Research suggests that the human brain is characterized by neural plasticity. That is, it can always learn from experience and promote adaptive behavior. The brain forms new synaptic connections throughout life, indicating that one can always learn and change.

2. Person A would mostly show impairments in her senses of sight, taste, hearing, and touch, but not in smell.
   Person B would show impairment in eating, drinking, and body temperature control.
   Person C would show impairments in hearing and possibly in speech comprehension.
   Person D would show impairments in the coordination of well-learned movements.

4 Human Development

LEARNING OBJECTIVES

After studying this chapter, you should be able to:

1. Describe the domain of developmental psychology and offer a brief overview of the history of this area of psychology. (p. 106)

2. Explain what is meant by the "nature versus nurture" controversy and how this is related to Darwin's concept of natural selection and contemporary research on behavioral genetics, mentioning a recent study on gender differences in jealousy. (p. 106-107)

3. Summarize the basic genetic principles presented and distinguish between phenotype and genotype, and the concept of polygenic characteristics and heritability. (p. 108-109)

4. Explain how family studies and twin studies offer insight into the relative contributions of heredity and environment to development, summarizing the important findings of representative studies. (p. 109-111)

5. List and describe the important features of three research techniques unique to developmental psychology, mentioning their strengths and weaknesses. (p. 111-112)

6. Describe the stages and processes of prenatal development, mentioning some of the problems that may arise from genetic defects and teratogens. (p. 112-114)

7. Describe the important events and features of infant and child physical and perceptual development, mentioning the results of the classic study of the development of depth perception in infants. (p. 115-118)

8. Describe and explain Piaget's stage theory of cognitive development, describing the changes in cognitive abilities at each stage, and making reference to the concept of schema and the processes of assimilation and accommodation. Briefly mention how culture may influence the timing of these cognitive changes. (p. 118-120)

9. Describe and explain Erikson's stage theory of psychosocial development, listing the important psychosocial crisis that characterizes each stage. (p. 120-121)

10. Define attachment, and explain the contributions of Bowlby, Harlow, and Ainsworth to our understanding of this aspect of emotional development, describing how the Strange Situation is used to evaluate the attachment style of children. (p. 121-122)

11. Describe three parenting styles and how they affect children's behavior and development. (p. 122-123)

12. Summarize what is presently known about the effects of day care, marital discord, and peer relationships on children's development. (p. 123-125)

13. Explain what is meant by gender-role development, emphasizing the perspectives of social-learning and gender-schema theory. (p. 125-126)

14. Present an overview of Kohlberg's stage theory of moral development, describing the characteristics of each level, and then summarize the criticisms surrounding this theory, emphasizing the work of Gilligan. (p. 126-129)

15. Explain the concepts of both the social clock and adolescence and describe how cultural and historical factors can influence various cohorts. (p. 129-130)

16. Summarize the physical, cognitive, psychosocial, and peer relationship changes that occur during adolescence in our culture. (p. 130-134)

17. Explain when adulthood begins in our culture and summarize the physical, cognitive, and psychosocial changes that are associated with adulthood in our culture, emphasizing the impact of marital status and single parenthood. (p. 134-138)

18. Describe the important developmental issues of middle adulthood, emphasizing the concept of generativity versus stagnation and evaluating the concept of the "empty nest syndrome." (p.138-139)

19. Describe the important developmental issues of late adulthood, emphasizing the issues of integrity versus despair, coping with the death of a spouse, and preparing for one's own death. (p. 140-141)

20. Summarize current findings regarding any sex differences in cognitive abilities, social behavior, personality, and aggression, noting the implications of the various explanations for those sex differences that have been identified. (p. 141-145)

COMPREHENSIVE GUIDED REVIEW

The scientific study of human development began in the 1870s, a decade that saw the appearance of the "baby biography." The __(1)__s saw the beginning of research on child development after infancy, most notably by G. Stanley __(2)__. Since then, and especially from the 1950s forward, psychology began to study human development across the entire ____(3)____. Through this research we know that infant development depends largely on learning, but that much also depends on____(4)____, or the sequential unfolding of inherited predispositions. Today, **developmental psychology** is a field that studies the physical,____(5)_____, cognitive, and psychosocial changes that take place across the life span.

I. The Nature of Developmental Psychology: From its very beginnings, one of the main concerns in the study of human development has been the issue of__(6)__ versus nurture. This controversy has continued since the era of ancient Greece. Aristotle's thesis was that we are born__(7)____ knowledge and that the experiences of life are etched on a blank slate, or *tabula rasa*. Plato, on the other hand, believed that we are born___(8)___ knowledge. Thus, Plato championed the position of___(9)____, and Aristotle championed the____(10)____ side of the debate. Centuries later the positions remained, though more intensely defended. In the mid nineteenth century it was Charles__(11)__who favored nature and John Locke who argued the__(12)__ side. Darwin's position was based on a process known as _____(13)_____. Darwin's cousin, Francis Galton, was the champion of___(14)___ over ___(15)___, and even coined the phrase. Physical traits, he reasoned, helped our ancestors survive. Thus, people who were superior on those traits were the fittest to reproduce. He traced the genealogy of geniuses and concluded that it runs in ____(16)____. Although aware of the role of the environment, he nonetheless concluded that __(17)__is produced by nature. Helmholtz, on the other hand, championed the ___(18)___ side of the controversy. Watson and Skinner also downplayed _____(19)_____, but with the waning of behaviorism in the 1960s, a new field, known as **behavioral genetics,** has emerged. This field studies how heredity and life experiences____(20)____ in affecting development. Over the past twenty to thirty years behavioral geneticists have found evidence for a ____(21)____ basis for characteristics of empathy, intelligence, and possibly even the tendency towards divorce. Recently, researchers have also been examining the role of heredity in social relationships.

Anatomy of a Contemporary Research Study: Are Social Relationships Governed by Predispositions Molded by Evolution? *As you have in past chapters, read the summary of the study by Buss and his colleagues presented on pages 107 and 108 in your textbook. Then answer the following questions:*

What was the rationale for the study?

What methods did the authors use to test their hypothesis?

What was the outcome of the study and what did the authors conclude the results meant?

In order to understand fully, and appreciate the nature of the research and findings in the field of behavioral genetics, a basic understanding of __(22)___ is needed. The founding of the science of **genetics** is attributed to Gregor____(23), an Austrian monk. Mendel studied the inheritance of physical traits in _____(24)_____. Current genetic science has come a long way since Mendel's time. We now know that genetic information is contained in all cells in our bodies on 23 **chromosomes.** ___(25)___ are long, thin strands made up of **deoxyribonucleic acid,** or ___(26)___ DNA molecules contain segments known as __(27)___, which direct the synthesis of **ribonucleic acid,** or **RNA.** __(28)___ then directs the formation or synthesis of proteins, which are responsible for the structure and function of our body. Thus, **genes** do not directly induce us to engage in particular behaviors; they do, however, influence the ___(29)___ factors within our body, for example our hormones, neurotransmitters, and brain structure. These factors then influence the ___(30)___ that we would engage in particular actions.

Genes occur in pairs. Each member of the pair may represent a different __(31)_. As a result, outward appearance may not indicate genetic structure. One member of the gene pair may be said to be **dominant** and the other said to be **recessive.** __(32)___genes take precedence over __(33)__ genes. As a result, genetic scientists distinguish between our__(34)__ and our **phenotype. Genotype** refers to our genetic inheritance and ____(35)___refers to the overall expression, or the outward appearance. Various genotypes include those with two dominant, two recessive, or a dominant and recessive gene. Adding to the complexity of understanding the genetic nature of behavioral characteristics and traits is their **polygenic** nature. Genetic scientists use the term ____(36)___ to refer to the fact that many characteristics are governed by more than one set of genes.

Heritability is another concept that is important in the research that attempts to identify the relative contributions of heredity and environment. _____(37)____ refers to the proportion of variability in a trait across a population. The variability in intelligence, for example, can be measured by a heritability ____(38)__. The values range from 0.0, where heritability accounts for ___(39)__of the variability in intelligence, to 1.0, where heritability accounts for __(40)__ of the variability.

There are four basic procedures, each concerned with the study of similarities between relatives, that are used to assess the __(41)__, or relative contribution of nature versus nurture. These include **family studies,** __(42)__ studies, and two different kind of **twin studies.** ___(43)__ studies examine the similarities between relatives with varying degrees of genetic similarity. **Adoption** studies measure the ___(44)__ in particular traits between adopted children and their biological parents and those same adopted children and their adoptive parents. The first type of twin studies compares ____(45)___ to fraternal twins. The last type compares identical twins reared ___(46)___.

All of the methods mentioned have limitations. Since members of the same family live and grow up together, __(47)__ studies cannot rule out that the correlation is not actually due to the similarity in the ___(48). In adoption studies, the environment has not been fully controlled for either. Although the postnatal environment is different, research indicates that the __(49)__ environment may also play an important role in development. In studies that compare identical twins to fraternal twins, the ___(50)___ degree of similarity of identical twins may be due to the fact that the similarity in their _____(51)__ traits leads the environment to have the same type of effect on them. Finally, in the comparisons of ____(52)____ twins reared apart, the similarity might be due to coincidence or the twins may have been reared in similar-enough environments. Thus it is important to note that no type of study provides undeniable proof that ___(53)__ plays a more important part than environment in human development. Current-day _____(54)_______ are careful to keep in mind that regardless of the influence of genetics on development, the importance of behavioral influences should not be ignored.

Research Methods in Developmental Psychology: Developmental psychologists use all of the research methods of psychology that were discussed in Chapter 2. However, in order to examine questions unique to development, specialized methodologies, unique to developmental psychology, have been developed. These include **longitudinal research, cross-sectional research,** and **cohort-sequential research.** A___(55)____ research design follows the same group of subjects over a period of time. It has the advantage of permitting psychologists to study the ___(56)__ group of individuals as they change over the course of their life spans. However, it has several weaknesses. These include the ___(57)__ of time the study takes and the extensive___(58)_ commitment required, as well as the attrition of subjects. The longer a study lasts, the more likely it is for subjects to move away, refuse to continue, or even to die. The ___(59)__ nature of the sample in longitudinal studies makes it unwise to ___(60)__ results from long term-longitudinal studies to other adults.

In____(61)___ research, psychologists consider groups of subjects of different ages at the same point in time. Each of the age groups is called a **cohort**. This design controls for the weaknesses of the ___(62)__ design, however it has its own problems. The most significant problem with this type of design is that differences between __(63)__ may be due to circumstances unique to a particular age cohort and not to true age-related changes. ____(64)____ research attempts to deal with the shortcomings of both the longitudinal and cross-sectional studies. Cohort-sequential research begins as a ____(65)___ study of different cohorts and then follows the cohorts ___(66)___.

Time for your first study break in this chapter. Remember, don't feel guilty about taking time out for a short break from studying. It's more beneficial than reading right through.

As always, to help you stay on track, do the mini-review before you continue.

Mini-review on the Nature of Development: Match each term with its correct description.

_____1. cohort-sequential research
_____2. genes
_____3. RNA
_____4. longitudinal research
_____5. genotype
_____6. phenotype
_____7. dominant
_____8. recessive
_____9. twin studies
____10. heritability
____11. chromosomes
____12. polygenic
____13. adoption studies
____14. cross-sectional research
____15. maturation
____16. family studies

A. Our overt expression of our inheritance as seen in our appearance or behavior
B. Segments that compose DNA molecules
C. Our genetic inheritance
D. Characteristics governed by more than one pair of genes
E. Sequential unfolding of inherited predispositions
F. Long, thin strands made up of DNA that contain the genes
G. Directs the formation or synthesis of proteins
H. Genes that take precedence over other genes
I. Proportion of variability in a trait across a population
J. Examines the similarities between relatives with varying degrees of genetic similarity
K. Genes that are expressed only when two identical genes are present
L. Measures the correlation in particular traits between adopted children and their biological parents and those same adopted children and their adoptive parents
M. Compares identical to fraternal twins, or identical twins reared apart
N. Has the advantage of permitting psychologists to study the same group of individuals as they change over the course of their life spans
O. Has the problem that differences observed between cohorts may be due to circumstances unique to a particular age cohort, not to true age-related changes
P. Research that begins as a study of different cohorts and then follows the cohorts throughout time

II. Prenatal Development: Every living organism begins as a single__(67)__. That cell evolves into a complex __(68)__ organism during the prenatal period of development. The ______(69)___period is divided into three stages: the **germinal, embryonic,** and **fetal**. The ______(70)___stage begins with conception, when a sperm unites with an egg (ovum) to form a one-celled **zygote.** This unification occurs in the __(71)__tubes of the woman. With its 23 pairs of chromosomes and the genes they contain, the __(72)__ becomes a multicelled ball that, by the end of the second week of conception, attaches to the wall of the uterus. The attachment to the uterine wall marks the beginning of the __(73)__ stage. This stage lasts for __(74)__ weeks. During this stage the__(75)__ is nourished through the placenta and begins to develop specialized organs. The growth of these specialized body organs appears to be regulated by genes and governed by cell-adhesion __(76)__. As the embryonic stage terminates, the __(77)__ is beating, and the 1-inch-long embryo has facial features, limbs, fingers, and toes. ____(78)___determines whether the embryo becomes a male or a female. Embryos that inherit a ___(79)__ chromosome are genetic males; those that inherit an __(80)__ chromosome are genetic females. At the termination of the embryonic period the primitive gonads of the male embryo secrete __(81)__. This in turn stimulates the development of__(82)__ sex organs.

The last stage of prenatal development is the __(83)__ stage. This stage lasts from the beginning of the third month until __(84)__. By the __(85)__ month movement is felt, and by the seventh month all of the major organs have become functional, and if born prematurely, the fetus would have a chance at survival. During the final three months of prenatal development the __(86)__ dramatically increases in size.

Most of the time prenatal development progresses and produces a normal infant, however in some cases __(87)__ defects produce physical and psychological syndromes. One such example is **Down syndrome**. Down syndrome is a associated with ____(88)___ and abnormal physical development. ____(89)____ are noxious substances such as drugs or viruses that can also can cause defects, as in the case of the rubella__(90)_. Another potential **teratogen** is the X ray. The use of __(91)__ such as cocaine, nicotine, or marijuana may also cause abnormal development. ____(92)__ may produce a syndrome that leads to facial deformities and mental retardation, called **fetal alcohol syndrome.** Some of the effects may not appear for a number of _____(93)_after birth.

III. Infant and Child Development: Childhood extends from birth until puberty and begins with ____(94)__, a period of rapid physical, cognitive, and psychosocial growth, extending from birth to age two. Developmental psychologists study changes in physical, perceptual, cognitive, and__(95)__ development.

Physical Development: Through __(96)__ and learning the infant quickly develops motor skills that go beyond reflexes. Although the sequence of development of motor skills is___(97)__, timing does___(98)__ among infants. In addition to rapid___(99)__ development, infancy is also a period of rapid brain development. Though these changes are governed by maturation, research has also indicated that they may be affected by___(100)_. Following infancy, growth rate slows and motor coordination improves.

Perceptual Development: Research has shown that newborn infants have more highly developed sensory, __(101)_, and cognitive abilities than William James, for example, believed. By recording changes in their eye movements, head movements, body movements, sucking behavior, or physiological responses, researchers have been able to determine that infants have well-developed ____(102)__abilities. Many creative studies have examined the__(103)___ abilities of newborns and found that these abilities are remarkably well developed at birth. The Anatomy of a Classic Research Study section on page 117 in your textbook discusses one such study, by _____(104)_____.

Anatomy of a Classic Research Study: When Do Infants Develop Depth Perception? *Use your understanding of how to read psychological research and summarize the findings of this study.*

What was the rationale for the study?

What methods did the authors use to test their hypothesis?

What was the outcome of the study and what did the authors conclude the results meant?

Other research has shown that infants have the ability to localize sounds, and can even match the emotional tone of sounds to the emotional tone of ____(105)____ expressions.

Cognitive Development: The rapid motor and perceptual development the infancy period is paralleled by rapid ____(106)____ development. Jean____(107)____ put forth the first formal theory of cognitive development. According to Piaget, beginning in infancy and ending in adolescence, children pass through____(108)____ distinct, increasingly sophisticated cognitive stages. These are: **sensorimotor, preoperational, concrete operational,** and **formal operational.** The first three stages will be discussed now and the last stage, ____(109)____, will be discussed later in the chapter.

The____(110)____ stage is the period during which the infant learns to coordinate sensory experiences and motor behavior. ____(111)____, or mental models that incorporate the characteristics of persons, objects, events, procedures, or situations, are formed during this stage. **Schemes** permit behavioral adaptation to environmental change. They also change as the result of **assimilation** and **accommodation.** By 8 months, infants normally demonstrate the____(112)____of **object permanence.** This not only shows that they have reached the point in their development when they can retain ____(113)____images of a physical object even after the object is no longer in sight, but it also signifies the beginning of____(114)____ thought, or the use of symbols to stand for physical objects.

The____(115)____ stage normally ranges from 2 to 7 years. A number of events occur. The stage is called preoperational because it is believed that the child cannot perform____(116)____ (i.e., mental manipulations of reality that are reversible). During this stage there is rapid improvement in the use of____(117)____. There is also development of the ability to____(118)____, as shown by the capacity for **transductive reasoning.** Finally, the child learns to overcome what Piaget calls____(119)____, which is the inability to perceive reality from the perspective of another person.

Piaget's third stage is the____(120)____ stage. It normally lasts from age 7 to age 12. During this stage the child learns to reason ____(121)____, but is limited to reasoning about objects that are ____(122)____ present. The ability to make transitive inferences develops and the child learns ____(123)____, or the realization that changing the form of something does not change the amount.

Cross-cultural studies of Piagetian stages of development have indicated that children throughout the world tend to pass through the stages in the____(124)____ order, although the____(125)____ may often vary. For example, the effect of____(126)____ experience was demonstrated in a study conducted in a Mexican village with children whose parents were pottery makers. The results indicated that the children who helped their parents in making pottery learned conservation skills much____(127)____ than other children.

Psychosocial Development: Erik____(128)____, one of the first researchers to consider cultural differences in psychosocial development, proposes another stage-oriented theory of development in which each stage of development involves a ____(129)____ to be overcome. The childhood conflicts include **trust versus mistrust** during the ____(130)____ year, **autonomy versus shame and doubt** during the second year, **initiative versus guilt** beginning at the age of 3, and **industry versus inferiority** from 6 to puberty.

Erikson argues that the first ____(131)____conflict occurs in the first year. It centers on the infant's development of____(132)____. Erikson contends that one of the most important factors in the development of trust is the development of a social ____(133)____, or a strong emotional bond between an infant and its caregiver. Three important researchers into the development of attachment are John Bowlby, Harry Harlow, and Mary Ainsworth. ____(134)____ became interested in the effects of maternal deprivation and studied orphans whose parents were killed in World War II. Bowlby favors an ____(135)____ viewpoint. He suggests that children need attachment because their____(136)____ depends on adult caregivers. This is similar to Sigmund ____(137)____'s view that a child attaches to the mother because she provides nourishment. Harry ____(138)____'s significant research with infant monkeys and "surrogate mothers" showed, however, that physical contact is ____(139)____ important than nourishment in promoting infant attachment to the mother. Harlow's research has sparked a lot of interest in the role of attachment in ____(140)____ psychosocial development. Mary ____(141)____ has conducted extensive research on the mother-infant relationship and distinguishes being a **securely attached** versus an

__(142)_ attached infant. Ainsworth suggests that an infant whose mother is sensitive, accepting, and affectionate will become __(143)__ attached and will, in strange situations, use the mother as a base from which to explore the world. Currently, research suggests that attachment patterns are __(144)_ of later behavior, even of romantic styles.

According to Erikson, the second psychosocial conflict that children face occurs during the_(145)__ year. Here the child explores the physical environment and learns __(146)__. This leads to the development of a greater sense of independence from the parents during the_(147)__ versus shame and doubt stage. The third of Erikson's stages is known as_(148)___versus guilt. Here, at about 3 years of age, a child deals with the development of a sense of right and wrong. The child begins to show __(149)__ in play and social relations. Additionally, the child develops the ability to control _(150)___. At age 6, Erikson claims, children enter the __(151)_ versus inferiority stage. The industrious child is one who achieves___(152)_ and as a result is likely to feel competent and happy.

Psychologists suggest that one of the most important factors in the psychosocial development of a child is the child-rearing practices of parents, particularly their approach to _(153)_. **Permissive parents** set few rules and rarely punish; but permissiveness is_(154)_. The children of _(155)_ parents are often less likely to adopt positive standards of behavior. **Authoritarian parents,** on the other hand, set strict rules and rely on __(156)_. Of concern is that physical discipline will lead to child _(157)_. A cycle may occur in which children who are abused may become abusive parents.

Diana _(158)__ has found that **authoritative parenting** appears to be the most effective approach to parenting. This approach involves being warm and loving while insisting on appropriate behavior. Within well-defined limits, _(159)__ is encouraged. __(160)__ parents explain the reasons for their rules and permit verbal disagreement. Their children then internalize standards of behavior and are socially competent,__(161)___, and socially responsible.

__(162)___is another controversial factor in child rearing. Studies have indicated that high-quality day care does ___(163)__ have adverse effects on preschoolers. Preschoolers are affected __(164)___ by the absence of their mothers during the day than by the overall amount of time their mothers spend with them when they are home. But concerns remain. Belsky (1988) reports that day care of more than __(165)__ hours a week in the first year of life is associated with_(166)_ attachment during infancy and greater noncompliance and aggressiveness in early childhood. The findings of this and other studies remain controversial. Many argue that the data are merely ___(167)_.

In addition to being influenced by _(168)____ style and day care, children are affected by the quality of their parents' marital relations. Recent research has shown that parental_(169)__ spills over to the parent-child relationship. Children exposed to marital discord suffer greater _(170)_ distress, and marital discord has been shown to undermine the child's feelings of emotional ___(171)__ and may lead to adjustment problems in childhood and adulthood. Research on the effects of _(172)_ on children has produced inconsistent findings. This is partly due to the fact that there are so many _(173)__in the divorce situation. Nonetheless, it does appear that children from divorced families have a greater sense of well-being than children from _(174)_ families with intense parental conflict.

Another important factor in the psychosocial development of children is their interaction with **peers.** _(175)___ provide the context for social and emotional growth of the child. Ninety-five percent of childhood friendships are between members of the_(176)_ sex. Girls tend to have fewer and more _(177)_ friendships among their peers than do boys. Additionally, _(178)_ are important peers and birth order has been shown to be a factor in social development. __(179)_ children are less socially popular than last-born children. Research shows that the only child does not suffer from the absence of siblings.

One of the most important aspects of psychosocial development is the development of **gender roles.** __(180)___ are behavior patterns considered to be appropriate for males or females in a given culture. __(181)_ offered the first formal theory of gender-role development and conceptualized the_(182)__ conflict, in which a child of 5 or 6 years of age adopts the gender role of the same-sex parent. There is little, if any, _(183)__ support for Freud's claims. **Social learning theory** emphasizes the importance of __(184)_learning and reinforcement. "Do as I do" may be more powerful than "Do as I say." Traditional gender roles may be perpetuated by the presence of men and women in positions in which they model__(185)__ gender roles. An alternative to the social learning theory has been proposed by Sandra __(186)_. Known as the **gender-schema theory,** this theory argues that __(187)__ leads the child to develop specific gender-related behaviors that in turn lead to the development of a gender __(188)__. As a result of the__(189)__ schemes the child engages in behavior that is consistent with that schema.

An often overlooked aspect of development is the development of **morality.** Freud felt that morality arose from the resolution of the__(190)__ conflict. Again, there is no research support for Freud's claims regarding the Oedipal conflict. Lawrence___(191)___,however, has formulated a **cognitive-developmental theory** of morality in which he argues that there are three levels of moral reasoning: **preconventional, conventional,** and **postconventional morality.** Each level contains two stages. Kohlberg agrees with Piaget in that as we progress to higher levels of moral reasoning we become more concerned with ___(192)__ than with the consequences of the action. According to Kohlberg, at the ___(193)___ level the individual is more concerned with the consequences of the actions. Stages at this level include the __(194)__ and obedience level and the instrumental-relativist orientation. This characterizes the reasoning of a child under 9 years of age. At the ____(195)__ level, usually reached by late childhood or early adulthood, the concern is the upholding of conventional laws and values. __(196)__ to parents and authority figures is favored. Stages at this level include the "good boy-nice girl" and "society-maintaining" orientations. The final level of reasoning is the ___(197)___ level. At this level the interest is on adherence to ___(198)__ principles. Stages at this level include social-contract orientation and the universal ethical principle orientation.

As with most theories in psychology, Kohlberg's theory has not gone without criticism. The first centers on the fact that Kohlberg is testing moral __(199)___, not moral action, and moral actions may not reflect moral reasoning. Second, is the argument that the theory does not take into account the influence of the___(200)__ in which the moral reasoning takes place. Additionally, the ____(201)____of the theory beyond Western culture has been questioned. Finally, Carol Gilligan has questioned the applicability of the theory to ____(202)_. She claims that Kohlberg's theory is based on a male view of morality.

To keep your attention focused, remember that it is important to take short breaks. Now is a good time to do that. Take a short study break. When you return, do the mini-review before moving on to the next section.

Mini-review of Prenatal, Infant and Childhood Development: Match each term with its correct description.

________A. germinal period
________B. Down syndrome
________C. embryonic period
________D. securely attached
________E. preconventional morality
________F. fetal period
________G. fetal alcohol syndrome
________H. zygote
________I. Authoritarian parents
________J. conservation
________K. initiative versus guilt
________L. cell-adhesion molecules
________M. XY
________N. attachment
________O. industry versus inferiority
________P. schemes
________Q. XX
________R. Mary Ainsworth
________S. teratogen
________T. object permanence
________U. infancy
________V. sensorimotor
________W. Harry Harlow
________X. preoperational
________Y. concrete operational
________Z. authoritative parenting
________Aa. conventional morality
________Bb. representational thought
________Cc. egocentrism
________Dd. trust versus mistrust
________Ee. John Bowlby
________Ff. postconventional morality
________Gg. autonomy versus shame and doubt
________Hh. Permissive parents
________Ii. gender-roles

1. The attachment to the uterine wall marks the beginning of this stage
2. Begins with conception, when a sperm unites with an egg (ovum)
3. A genetic male
4. Prenatal stage in which movement is felt; all of the major organs have become functional, and a premature birth has a chance at survival
5. Associated with mental retardation and abnormal physical development
6. Noxious substances such as drugs or viruses, which can also can cause birth defects
7. Syndrome that leads to facial deformities and mental retardation
8. A period of rapid physical, cognitive, and psychosocial growth, extending from birth to age 2
9. The stage during which the infant learns to coordinate sensory experiences and motor behavior
10. A genetic female
11. The use of symbols to stand for physical objects
12. Mental models that incorporate the characteristics of persons, objects, events, procedures, or situations
13. The ability to retain mental images of a physical object even after the object is no longer in sight
14. The Piagetian stage in which the child cannot perform conservation
15. The inability to perceive reality from the perspective of another person
16. The stage in which the child learns to reason logically, but is limited to reasoning about objects that are present
17. The knowledge that mental manipulations of reality are reversible
18. A strong emotional bond between an infant and its caregiver
19. The first of Erikson's psychosocial conflicts; occurs in the first year
20. Researcher who suggests that children need attachment because their survival depends on adult caregivers
21. Conducted research with infant monkeys and "surrogate mothers"
22. Conducted extensive research on the mother-infant relationship; developed the Strange Situation test
23. Parents who set strict rules and rely on punishment
24. An infant whose mother is more sensitive, accepting, and affectionate will be this
25. Erikson's stage in which the child explores the physical environment and learns independence
26. Erikson's stage in which the child deals with the development of a sense of right and wrong
27. Parents who set few rules and rarely punish
28. The most effective approach to parenting; involves being warm and loving while insisting on appropriate behavior
29. Erikson's stage in which successes are important to the development of the child
30. The cell that results from the unification of the sperm and egg
31. Governs the growth of specialized organs in the embryo
32. Behavior patterns considered to be appropriate for males or females in a given culture
33. Stage of morality in which the individual is more concerned with the consequences of the actions
34. Stage of morality in which the concern is the upholding of conventional laws and values
35. Stage of morality in which the individual is concerned with ethical principles

IV. Adolescent Development: Today, it is understood that there are physical, cognitive, and psychosocial developmental changes that occur across the__(203)__ life span. This is different from the assumption of earlier days, when it was thought that development was complete by the end of__(204)__. While __(205)__ factors and **social clocks** may make generations similar in their development, cultural and__(206)__ factors over the past four or more decades have produced profound differences between one generation and another. **Adolescence** is the transition period that occurs between childhood and (207). Formal study of this period began with the work of G. Stanley (208). (209) is unknown in nonindustrialized countries, instead adulthood begins with the onset of puberty and is celebrated with ceremonial rites of passages.

In the domain of **physical development** the most significant changes are the changes of (210). The physical changes in adolescence include not only rapid growth in (211) for girls (ages 10-12) and boys (ages 12-14) but also the (212) of primary sex characteristics and secondary sex characteristics. The (213) -induced physical changes that enable us to engage in sexual reproduction and the bodily changes stimulated by the sex hormones, but are unrelated to sexual reproduction, characterize this period of development. These physical changes are triggered by the increased secretion of the sex hormone (214) for boys, and the sex hormone (215) for girls. While boys typically have their first (216) between the ages of 13 and 15, girls exhibit earlier physical maturation and typically experience (217) between the ages of 11 and 13.

Not all changes in adolescence are the result of (218) fluctuations, and many are attributable to life events. However, the physical changes of puberty all combined can cause emotional distress. Research has shown that adolescents who know what to expect find puberty less distressing than those who are not informed, as in the case of girls knowledge of menarche.

Cognitive Development: According to Piaget, at age 12 many adolescents pass from the concrete operational stage to the (219) stage. The adolescent who reaches this stage engages in thinking that is (220). Formal operational thought has much in common with (221) thinking. In this form of thinking, a person solves problems by taking what is known, making (222) about what is not known, and then (223) testing the hypotheses. Research has shown that, although adolescents may solve more sophisticated abstract problems than children, formal operational thought may develop (224) than Piaget assumed. However , other research suggests that this stage may not be universal, as Piaget thinks but it may be related to the exposure to scientific thinking in (225) coursework.

Psychosocial Development: Erikson observes that psychosocial development continues through adolescence into adulthood and old age. He argues that the most important psychosocial tasks of adolescence are the formation of a personal (226) and the development of healthy relationships with peers and parents. Thus he entitles this period of development the period of identity versus (227). He feels that the adolescent grapples with the questions of "Who am I?", "What do I believe is important?" and "What are my (228) in life?" Characteristics of this crisis include: a) identifying one's (229) and goals; b) questioning the nature of (230); c) dealing with ethical, political, and religious beliefs; and d) experiencing (231) between parental and peer influences. Erikson's theory of adolescence has received support from (232) studies showing that adolescents typically move from a state of role confusion to a state of identity achievement. However, Carol Gilligan believes that Erikson's theory applies more to (233) than to females and should take into account cultural factors.

In the process of establishing their (234), another characteristic of this period of development is that adolescents experience conflict with their (235). Despite some normal conflicts, research has shown that most adolescents have (236) relations with their parents. Negative identities and relationships appear to be related to (237) management of the adolescent. Adolescents have more (238) friendships than younger children, with female relationships more intimate than those between males. This may be due to the increased (239) reasoning capabilities of the adolescent. The onset of (240) is associated with the conflict between the urge to engage in sexual relations and societal values against (241) sex. Unwanted teen pregnancies are much more common among (242) Than among Europeans. This fact is attributable to ignorance about (243) and the fact that many sexually active adolescents have not yet reached the formal operational stage of cognitive development. The use of psychoactive drugs, particularly (244), can be related to the behaviors of parents, peers, and the occurrence of negative life events.

V. Adult Development: There is no one single event that automatically signifies the onset of adulthood in all cultures. In Western cultures adulthood begins when adolescents become independent of their parents and assume responsibility for themselves.

Physical Development: The adult's physical peak is reached in the _(245)_; after this the basal metabolism rate decreases, necessitating increasing attention to diet and exercise. _(246)_changes also occur. As men age, they produce _(247)_ sperm and have more difficulty achieving penile erections. Between their forties and fifties, women experience _(248)_, which signals an end to child-bearing years, but does not mean an end to sexuality. Gradual physical changes begin to occur in middle age with changes in _(249)_, requiring some adults to wear glasses; however, marked changes in physical abilities usually do not occur until _(250)_ adulthood. Research has shown that people who maintain an active lifestyle exhibit a highly correlated _(251)_ rate of decline.

Cognitive Development: _(252)_ studies have shown that there is a decline in intelligence as we age, although, _(253)_ studies suggest that the decline does not begin until around age 60. Further research suggests that this decline holds for _(254)_ intelligence, the ability to reason and process information, not for _(255)_ intelligence, the ability to gain and retain knowledge. Psychologists have suggested that the decline in cognitive features may be accounted for by: a) a reduction in the _(256)_ of processing information; b) a decrease in the efficient use of _(257)_; and c) the fact that the elderly have not been in _(258)_ for a long time. It is clear that staying cognitively _(259)_ is associated with better physical, social, and emotional well-being. One factor that accounts for cognitive deterioration is the loss of brain cells.

Psychosocial Development: _(260)_ adulthood is from age 20 to age 40, middle adulthood from age 40 to age 65, and late adulthood from age 65 on. The similarities shown within these common age groups have been suggested to be the influence of the___(261)___. However, more recent research is suggesting that there is increased__(262)_ in age-appropriate behavior in adulthood.

Erikson claims that the first major task of adulthood is__(263)_ versus isolation. Intimate relationships involve strong emotional _(264)_ and personal commitment. Research has supported Erikson's belief that the development of the capacity for _(265)_ depends on the successful formation of a psychosocial _(266)_ in adolescence. Additional research has shown that

a) while _(267)__ are especially concerned with future career considerations, _(268)_ are equally concerned with career and family considerations;

b) men tend to be more concerned than women with the potential spouse's physical ___(269)__, while women tend to be more concerned with the spouse's potential earning capacity;

c) other important factors in whether a marriage will succeed are similarity, the willingness to discuss marital problems, and openness. One of the hallmarks of an unhappy marriage is the tendency of a spouse to offer negative explanations for the other spouse's behavior. Unhappy couples tend to be at higher risk for __(270)_; and d) though _(271)_ is a joyous part of marriage, it can also be one of life's greatest stresses.

_(272)_ notes that during the transition to middle adulthood, men commonly experience a midlife crisis, though research has shown it to be _(273)_ intense than he thought. Additionally there appears to be a difference in the life _(274)_ of men and women, with men typically focused on their careers and women more focused on marriage and children along with careers. According to Erikson, the main task of middle adulthood is the resolution of the conflict of generativity versus _(275)_. Those who achieve _(276)_ are less self-absorbed and more concerned with being a productive worker, spouse, and parent. One way of achieving this is to be a _(277)_for a younger person.

There is evidence that the "_(278)__" syndrome should he replaced by the notion of a "partly empty nest syndrome," since parents experience more distress after the _(279)_ child leaves home than after the last child leaves home. New trends in indicate that the "_(280)_nest syndrome" may be becoming more prevalent in Western cultures as young adults return home after finding it difficult to live independently.

Now that people are living for longer psychologists have begun to study development in _(281)_ adulthood. For Erikson, the main psychosocial task of this stage is to resolve the conflict of integrity versus _(282)_ Reminiscing and being active are positive factors in attaining and maintaining _(283)_. In attaining integrity Erikson argues that the individual has _(285)_ of a fear of death.

Death is inevitable. One of the greatest psychosocial challenges is the death of a spouse. Bereaved spouses are more prone to experience __(284)__, illnesses, or even death immediately after the death of their spouse. Our cultural acceptance of death has changed since the start of the __(286)__ century. Unlike in the past, many people today die alone in hospitals. The __(287)__ movement is a most promising development that attempts to counter this fact. Elisabeth __(288)__ has identified five stages experienced by terminally ill patients as they prepare for death. The stages are **denial, anger, bargaining, depression,** and **acceptance.** However, research has suggested that not all terminally patients go through all the stages in the same order.

Mini-review on Adolescent and Adult Development: Match each term with its correct description.

1. generativity versus stagnation
2. estrogen
3. identity versus role confusion
4. adolescence
5. testosterone
6. Carol Gilligan
7. "crowded nest syndrome"
8. crystallized intelligence
9. formal operational thought
10. menarche
11. Elisabeth Kübler-Ross
12. integrity versus despair
13. twenties
14. "empty nest" syndrome
15. adulthood
16. forties
17. fluid intelligence
18. intimacy versus isolation
19. hospice

______A. The transition period that occurs between childhood and adulthood
______B. The male sex hormone
______C. The ability to reason and process information
______D. The onset of the female menstruation cycle
______E. Cognitive stage in which thinking is abstract
______F. The developmental stage in which questions of "Who am I?" arise
______G. Believes that Erikson's theory applies more to males than to females
______H. Begins when adolescents become independent of their parents and assume responsibility for themselves
______I. The adult's physical peak is reached at this age
______J. The experience of distress by the parent after the last child leaves home
______K. Middle age begins at this age
______L. The ability to gain and retain knowledge
______M. The female sex hormone
______N. The first major task of adulthood according to Erikson
______O. In this stage reminiscing and being active are positive factors; the individual develops decreased fear of death
______P. The phenomenon of young adults returning home to live with parents after finding it difficult to live independently
______Q. Allows dying individuals to be cared for and die at home or in a homelike atmosphere
______R. Has identified five stages experienced by terminally ill patients as they prepare for death
______S. Stage in which the individual is most likely to become a mentor

VI. Thinking about Psychology: Are There Significant Sex Differences?

In the early nineteenth century __(289)__ stimulated an interest in the scientific study of sex differences. He assumed that females and males __(290)__ physical and psychological differences that helped them function in their specific roles. His ideas were countered by numerous early researchers who claimed that sex differences were the result of __(291)__ factors. Today, researchers are most concerned with sex differences in cognitive abilities, and psychosocial differences.

Early cognitive research seems to indicate that females tend to have better __(292)__ abilities, while males tend to have better __(293)__ abilities. However the adequacy of research on this latter finding has been questioned. Recent research has suggested that sex differences in verbal abilities have __(294)__ and currently are virtually non existent, and when a difference does exist it often disappears by __(295)__. Benbow and Stanley, on the other hand, present data to support the fact that, on average, males perform better than females in __(296)__. They attribute this difference to __(297)__, not environment. Their conclusion has provoked controversy. More recently, a __(298)__ was conducted and found, aside from males having higher scores on standardized tests, there were no overall gender differences in abilities such as calculating.

In examining differences in psychosocial development, researchers have focused on personality and __(299)__. Meta-analyses of research studies on personality differences indicate that males tend to be more assertive then females and generally have higher __(300)__. Females, on the other hand, tend to be slightly more extroverted, caring, and __(301)__. These differences appear to be stable throughout life. Additionally, females have a reputation for being more emotionally sensitive than men. This suggested difference depends on how __(302)__ is measured. In addition, males are reported to be more aggressive than females. Research has supported the latter finding by demonstrating that __(303)__ tend to be more physically aggressive. Recently however, the difference has been attributed more to gender __(304)__.

If sex factors do exist, what might they be? Two possible factors are __(305)__ differences and differences in physical structure. In the past there was some evidence to suggest that __(306)__ sex differences were due, at least in part, to hormonal differences and there was also strong evidence for a hormonal basis for sex differences in __(307)__ behavior. More recently however, studies have shown a __(308)__ of the sex differences between North American males and females over the past two decades. This evidence is interpreted to indicate that cognitive sex differences are possibly caused more by __(309)__ than biological factors. Unfortunately, after more than 20 years of research, no sex differences have emerged that are significant enough to predict how males and females will behave.

Congratulations! You have finished your guided review of Chapter 4. Review the following key research studies and then prepare yourself to take the practice tests.

KEY RESEARCH FINDINGS

1. **Galton (1869):** Research into hereditary nature of genius. (Page 107)
2. **Buss, Larsen, Westen & Semmelroth (1992) :** Examined heritability of social relationships. (Page 107)
3. **Price & Gottesman (1991) :** Researched heritability of body fat. (Page 110)
4. **Plomin, Loehlin, & Defries (1985) :** Conducted an adoption study on genetic nature of intelligence. (Page 110)
5. **Lykken et al. (1993):** Examined heritability of vocational interests. (Page 110)
6. **Waller et al. (1990):** Examined the heritability of religious values. (Page 110)
7. **Bouchard et al. (1990):** Examined twins reared apart. (Page 110)
8. **Mulligan & Moss (1991):** Examined sexuality across ages. (Page 112)
9. **Adams et al. (1990):** Studied alcohol use in old age. (Page 112)
10. **Pettersen, Yonas, & Fisch (1980):** Examined defensive eye blinking in newborns. (Page 114)
11. **Snodgrass (1994):** Studied cocaine influence on fetal development. (Page 114)
12. **Day & Richardson (1994):** Examined nicotine influence on fetal development. (Page 114)
13. **Fied & Watkinson (1990):** Studied marijuana influence on fetal development. (Page 114)
14. **Diamond (1988):** Examined effects of environment on brain development. (Page 115)
15. **Camel, Withers, & Greenough (1986):** Measured the effects of enriched environments on rat brains. (Page 115)
16. **Aslin & Smith (1988):** Examined focal ability in newborns. (Page 116)
17. **Field (1982):** Showed newborns' ability for emotional expression. (Page 116)
18. **Gibson & Walk (1960):** Used visual cliff to study depth perception. (Page 117)
19. **Morrongiello, Fenwick, & Chance (1990):** Examined infants' ability to localize sounds. (Page 118)
20. **Price-Williams, Gordon, & Ramirez (1969):** Examined cultural differences in acquisition of conservation. (Page 120)
21. **Hiatt, Campos, & Emde (1980):** Examined the ability of infants to express basic emotions. (Page 121)
22. **Harlow & Zimmerman (1959):** Examined the attachment behavior of infant monkeys. (Page 121)
23. **Ainsworth (1993):** Developed the Strange Situation test of attachment. (Page 122)
24. **Erel & Burman (1995)**: Conducted meta-analysis effects of parental discord on children. (Page 124)
25. **Kurtz (1995):** Examined differences between children of divorced parents and intact families. (Page 124)
26. **Newcomb, Bukowski, & Pattee (1993):** Conducted a meta-analysis of peer relationships and popularity. (Page 124)
27. **Parten (1932):** Examined changes in play behavior of children from 2 to 4 years of age. (Page 124)
28. **Domino (1992):** Conducted a cross-cultural study of competition in children. (Page 125)

29. **Rubin, Provenzano & Luria (1974):** Examined sex differences in descriptions of newborns. (Page 125)
30. **Lytton & Romney (1991):** Conducted meta-analysis of social influences on gender-role development. (Page 125)
31. **Snarey, Reimer & Kohlberg (1985):** Study of moral reasoning of Israeli adolescents. (Page 128)
32. **Lei (1994):** Examined the progression of moral reasoning in Taiwanese children and young adults. (Page 129)
33. **Barnett, Quackenbush & Sinisi (1995):** Tested claims of sex difference in notions of morality. (Page 129)
34. **Hendrixson (1989):** Examined moral reasoning differences in males and females. (Page 129)
35. **Rierdan & Koff (1990):** Examined girls' stress level concerning onset of menarche. (Page 131)
36. **Renner et al. (1990):** Examined understanding of abstract concepts in adolescents. (Page 132)
37. **Streitmatter (1993):** Conducted a longitudinal study of adolescent identity. (Page 133)
38. **Zhang & Thomas (1994):** Compared conformity behavior in adolescents cross-culturally. (Page 133)
39. **Gfellner & Hundleby (1994):** Surveyed Canadian students on drug usage. (Page 134)
40. **Dennerstein, Smith & Morse (1994):** Examined relationship between health, menopausal status, and happiness in women. (Page 135)
41. **Rogers, Meyer, & Mortel (1990):** Examined the benefits of activity on health in later life. (Page 136)
42. **Schaie (1989):** Examined speed of information processing in older adults. (Page 136)
43. **Ratner et al. (1987):** Examined the relation between cognitive activity and memory in old age. (Page 136)
44. **Levitz-Jones & Orlofsky (1985):** Examined adult women's intimacy and the relation with identity formation in adolescence. (Page 137)
45. **Inglis & Greenglass (1989):** Examined men and women's differences in desire to marry. (Page 137)
46. **Ben-Shlomo et al. (1993):** Examined mortality differences between married and single middle-aged men. (Page 137)
47. **O'Leary & Smith (1991):** Examined reasons for increase in divorce. (Page 138)
48. **Swann, Hixon & De La Ronde (1992):** Examined factors that keep spouses with abusive partners. (Page 138)
49. **Alvarado et al. (1995):** Examined relationship between belief in afterlife and death anxiety. (Page 140)

PRACTICE TEST A

1. Until the 1950s, developmental psychology was synonymous with
   a. gerontology.
   b. sociobiology.
   c. child psychology.
   d. behavioral genetics.

Obj.: 1 Page: 106

2. The study of the relationship between heredity and behavior is called
   a. eugenics.
   b. phylogeny.
   c. anthropometry.
   d. behavioral genetics.

Obj.: 2 Page: 107

3. Your genotype
   a. refers to your genetic inheritance.
   b. is always influenced by the environment as well as your inheritance.
   c. is the overt expression of your inheritance in your appearance or behavior.
   d. refers to the influence of chemical factors on your genes.

Obj.: 3 Page: 108-109

4. It appears that the best method for determining the relative influence of nurture and nature is to study the similarities between
   a. fraternal and identical twins reared in the same environment.
   b. identical twins reared in different families.
   c. family members who live together.
   d. adopted children and their biological parents.

Obj.: 4 Page: 109-111

5. A psychologist studies the gross motor ability of a group of adults at 50 years old, again at 60 years old, and finally at 70 years old. This is an example of
   a. longitudinal research.
   b. cross-sectional research.
   c. cohort-sequential research.
   d. quasi-experimental research.

Obj.: 5 Page: 111

6. Which list of stages is in developmental order?
   a. embryonic, germinal, fetal
   b. fetal, embryonic, germinal
   c. embryonic, fetal, germinal
   d. germinal, embryonic, fetal

Obj.: 6 Page: 112-114

7. Research on infant rats raised in enriched environments has found that they have an increase in the
   a. number of neurons in their brains.
   b. number of dendrites on their brain neurons.
   c. length of the axons on their brain neurons.
   d. diameter of the axons on their brain neurons.

Obj.: 7 Page: 115-116

8. A child who stands in front of the television without realizing that he or she is blocking other people's view of it is exhibiting
   a. egotism.
   b. egocentrism.
   c. ego-idealism.
   d. egocentration.

Obj.: 8 Page: 119

9. According to Erikson, a balance between spontaneity and restraint is reached when the individual successfully resolves the conflict of
   a. initiative versus guilt.
   b. trust versus mistrust.
   c. autonomy versus shame and doubt.
   d. industry versus inferiority.

Obj.: 9 Page: 120-121

10. The intense emotional tie that develops between a primary caregiver and an infant is called
    a. dependency.
    b. attachment.
    c. bonding.
    d. exclusiveness.

Obj.: 10 Page: 121-122

11. According to Diana Baumrind, what is the most effective approach to parenting?
    a. authoritative
    b. laissez-faire
    c. authoritarian
    d. permissive

Obj.: 11 Page: 122-123

12. Recent research on the effects of day care on children indicates that
    a. more then 20 hours of day care in the first year of life is associated with insecure attachment and greater aggressiveness in early childhood
    b. even high quality day care is detrimental to the child's development of attachments.
    c. infants in day care do not become insecurely attached and do well in school.
    d. both a and c

Obj.: 12 Page: 124

13. In regard to gender-role development, social-learning theory stresses
    a. observational learning and punishment.
    b. positive reinforcement.
    c. observational learning and positive reinforcement.
    d. the resolution of conflicts associated with infantile sexuality.

Obj.: 13 Page: 125-126

14. According to Kohlberg, students who do not cheat on exams because they fear the teacher will punish them are at the
    a. concrete level of moral development.
    b. conventional level of moral development.
    c. preconventional level of moral development.
    d. postconventional level of moral development.

Obj.: 14 Page: 128

15. In American culture, what marks the passage from adolescence to adulthood?
    a. High school graduation
    b. Moving away from home
    c. Securing a full-time job
    d. Any of the above could be a marker for this transition

Obj.: 15 Page: 129-130

16. A junior high school student shows excellent ability in designing and conducting experiments to test basic principles regarding the movement of objects. The student has probably reached what Piaget called the
    a. sensorimotor stage.
    b. preoperational stage.
    c. formal operational stage.
    d. concrete operational stage.

Obj.: 16 Page: 131

17. Elderly persons would be most likely to show a decline in fluid intelligence if, for example, they
    a. lost the ability to swim.
    b. forgot the names of old friends.
    c. could no longer solve algebra problems.
    d. could no longer form new memories of daily events.

Obj.: 17 Page: 136

18. According to Levinson, at midlife men must come to terms with their
    a. life's dream.
    b. approaching mortality.
    c. inability to have more children.
    d. loss of hair and gain in weight.

Obj.: 18 Page: 139

19. Erikson claims that successful aging in the late adulthood period is the result of
    a. achieving integrity.
    b. conducting a life review.
    c. being successful in your career.
    d. all of the above.

Obj.: 19 Page: 140-141

20. Though the reasons are not yet clear, on average, adolescent males are most clearly superior to females in scores on standardized tests of
    a. verbal ability.
    b. spatial ability.
    c. mathematical ability.
    d. social ability.

Obj.: 20 Page: 143

PRACTICE TEST B

1. Today, the central issue for psychologists studying human development is this question:
    a. How much do heredity and experience each influence development?
    b. What drives the physical changes of maturation?
    c. Does behavior change all through the life span?
    d. Can one use the scientific method to study change all through the life span?

Obj.: 2 Page: 106

2. Sue has just had a prenatal test examining her unborn baby's genetic make-up and the doctor has told her that her baby's genotype is XY. What sex is her baby?
    a. male
    b. female
    c. Sex is a trait that is determined by multifactorial inheritance, so you need more information.
    d. none of the above, this genotype is abnormal.

Obj.: 3 Page: 108-109

3. A researcher measures altruism (willingness to help others) in a group of 4-year-olds. He measures this trait again when that same group is age 14, then again at 24 and 50. This study is an example of
    a. longitudinal research.
    b. cross-sectional research.
    c. cohort-sequential research.
    d. observational research.

Obj.: 5 Page: 111

4. Robin reports that last night she felt her developing fetus move for the first time. Most likely, she has been pregnant for about
    a. 2 weeks.
    b. 8 weeks.
    c. 16 weeks.
    d. 24 weeks.

Obj.: 6 Page: 114

5. Cindy is in the final phase of her pregnancy. Developmental psychologists would say that she is in the________period.
    a. embryonic
    b. fetal
    c. germinal
    d. transition

Obj.: 6 Page: 114

6. Rina was born into a small, impoverished family living in relative isolation. She has no toys and she spends most of her time sitting or sleeping in a corner of a dark hut. Sula was born into a large family where all take turns caring for and interacting with her. She has many simple objects to handle and safe spaces to explore. If the findings of animal research can be generalized to human beings, what is likely to happen?
   a. Rina will develop some form of retardation, such as Down syndrome.
   b. Sula's brain will develop more dendrites and more synaptic connections.
   c. Rina will be more responsive to caretakers when they are actually present.
   d. Sula will be shy and quiet because of the high level of stimulation she experiences.

Obj.:7 Page: 116

7. Little Lisa has a schema that includes all creatures that fly through the air, that is, they are "birdies." Her father points to a colorful creature flying through the air and says, "That's a butterfly." In Piagetian terms, Lisa will now have to
   a. assimilate.
   b. accommodate.
   c. conserve.
   d. reason.

Obj.: 8 Page: 119

8. Four-year-old Amanda answers the telephone. The adult on the line asks Amanda if her mother is at home. Amanda keeps nodding her head, but the caller hears silence and keeps repeating the question. Finally the caller hangs up in frustration. Amanda's behavior is an example of
   a. assimilation.
   b. object permanence.
   c. egocentrism.
   d. conservation.

Obj.: 8 Page: 119

9. Ms. Lee assigns some household chores to her 8-year-old and praises him for doing them regularly and well. She also assists the child with schoolwork and encourages his participation in a singing group. According to Erik Erikson, this child is likely to
   a. enjoy his industriousness rather than experience inferiority.
   b. show great initiative rather than guilt.
   c. increase his feelings of trust in adults and teachers.
   d. become securely rather than insecurely attached.

Obj.: 9 Page: 122

10. Beth is 9 months old and cries inconsolably when an unfamiliar person offers to carry her and feed her. Beth is demonstrating
   a. object permanence.
   b. stranger anxiety.
   c. mistrust rather than trust.
   d. overdependence.

Obj.: 10 Page: 121

11. Little Billy is allowed almost total freedom, and his parents seldom punish inappropriate behavior in hopes of encouraging self-reliance and initiative. This parenting style is
   a. authoritarian.
   b. authoritative.
   c. permissive.
   d. democratic.

Obj.: 11 Page: 122

12. Your girlfriend Sasha has just given birth. She knows that you are taking a psychology class and asks you about what is known about the effects of day care on children. You tell her:
   a. Never put your child in day care. Children in day care usually are socially and cognitively delayed.
   b. It doesn't matter. Good-quality day care has no significant effects on children.
   c. She should put her child in day care right away. Children in day care usually score very high on intelligence tests.
   d. Good-quality day care for infants is fine, but it is best to limit it to no more than 20 hours until the child is 1 year old.

Obj.: 12 Page: 123-125

13. Carl and Carla are 4 years old and are both fascinated by the brightly colored beads on their mother's bureau and they wear them proudly. Their father rushes to buy Carla her own set of beads but criticizes Carl for wearing the beads. Carla comes to love wearing colorful jewelry, while Carl doesn't. Which theory insists that this is the way gender roles are acquired?
   a. Freudian theory
   b. Social learning theory
   c. Gender schema theory
   d. Evolutionary theory

Obj.:13 Page: 125

14. According to Kohlberg, a person who believes that Heinz should steal the drug so his wife can live to cook his supper is at which level of moral development?
   a. Punishment and obedience orientation.
   b. Instrumental relativist orientation.
   c. Society maintaining orientation.
   d. Goodby-nice girl orientation.

Obj.: 14 Page: 126-129

15. Fred and Sue are young adults whose family and friends expect them to marry soon. Psychologists call this expectation on the part of society
   a. a developmental task.
   b. matchmaking.
   c. the social clock.
   d. a rite of passage.

Obj.: 15 Page: 129-130

16. Jill has begun to think about difficult issues like homelessness and social injustice. She recently engaged you in a debate on the meaning of life. How old is Jill?
   a. 4 years old
   b. 8 years old
   c. 10 years old
   d. 15 years old

Obj.: 16 Page: 130-134

17. Recently, a former president of the United States parachuted out of an airplane and a 63-year-old woman gave birth to a baby. These events demonstrate that
   a. the "social clock" operating in our society has become more variable.
   b. there is strong social pressure in our society never to become "old."
   c. individuals can maintain their physical capacities into old age, but not their intellectual capacities.
   d. while crystallized intelligence declines with age, fluid intelligence does not.

Obj.: 17 Page: 136

18. Your older brother is 45 years old and has decided to serve as a mentor for an underprivileged child. Erik Erikson would say that your brother is working toward the development of
   a. intimacy.
   b. integrity.
   c. stagnation.
   d. generativity.

Obj.: 18 Page: 139

19. Your grandfather asks you to name what developmental psychologists consider to be the most important social task of late adulthood. You would most likely tell him that is was
   a. achieving integrity.
   b. conducting a life review.
   c. being successful in your career.
   d. all of the above.

Obj.: 19 Page: 140-141

20. Your mother argues that you should not encourage your daughter to take higher level math classes She claims that as a girl your daughter is genetically inferior to boys in math skills. Based on the information you have learned in this chapter, how would you respond to her?
   a. You would agree with her. Recent studies have shown that girls are genetically incapable of learning higher math skills.
   b. You would disagree. Recent studies have shown that although boys do better on standardized tests in math, there is no gender difference in math ability.
   c. You would disagree. Recent studies have shown that girls are better then boys in math abilities like calculating.
   d. You would partially agree and tell her that girls can do as well as boys in math until they are teenagers and then they lose their ability.

Ob.j: 20 Page: 143

ESSAY QUESTIONS

1. How do contemporary developmental psychologists study the relationship between nature and nurture? Which of these techniques is most useful in understanding the relative contributions of either genetics or environment to development?

Obj.: 4 Page: 109-111

2. Suppose that your grandmother had taken a developmental psychology course back in 1930. How would the topics covered in your grandmother's class differ from those covered in current developmental psychology courses?

Obj.: 1 Page: 106

ANSWER RECORD FOR CHAPTER 4

Comprehensive Guided Review:

1. 1890
2. Hall
3. life span
4. maturation
5. perceptual
6. nature
7. without
8. with
9. nature
10. nurture
11. Darwin
12. nurture
13. natural selection
14. nature
15. nurture
16. families
17. intelligence
18. nurture
19. heredity
20. interact
21. hereditary
22. genetics
23. Mendel
24. pea pods
25. Chromosomes
26. DNA
27. genes
28. RNA
29. physiological
30. likelihood
31. trait
32. Dominant
33. recessive
34. genotype
35. phenotype
36. polygenic
37. Heritability
38. score
39. none
40. all
41. heritability
42. adoption
43. Family
44. correlation
45. identical
46. apart
47. family
48. environment
49. prenatal
50. higher
51. physical
52. identical
53. heredity
54. behavioral geneticists
55. longitudinal
56. same
57. length
58. financial
59. selective
60. generalize
61. cross-sectional
62. longitudinal
63. cohorts
64. Cohort-sequential
65. cross-sectional
66. longitudinally

Antomy of a Contemporary Research Study: Are Social Relationships Governed by Predispositions Molded by Evolution?

What was the rationale for the study?

Buss believed that social relationships were governed by hereditary factors. He argued that as a result of natural selection men would demonstrate more sexual jealousy and that women would show more emotional jealousy.

What methods did the authors use to test their hypothesis?

Buss surveyed 202 undergraduate students as to what would stress them more in an intimate social relationship.

What was the outcome of the study and what did the authors conclude the results meant?

The results indicated that men showed more sexual jealousy and women showed more emotional jealousy. The author feels that this indicates a possible hereditary basis for social relationship formation.

Mini-review on the Nature of Development:
1. P; 2. B; 3. G; 4. N; 5. C; 6. A; 7. H; 8. K; 9. M; 10. I; 11. F; 12. D; 13. L; 14. O; 15. E; 16. J

67. cell
68. multi-celled
69. prenatal
70. germinal
71. fallopian
72 zygote
73. embryonic
74. six
75. embryo
76. molecules
77. heart
78. Heredity
79. Y
80. X
81. Testosterone
82. male
83. fetal
84. birth
85. fourth
86. fetus
87. genetic
88. mental retardation
89. Teratogens
90. virus
91. drugs
92. Alcohol
93. years
94. infancy
95. psychosocial
96. maturation
97. consistent
98. vary
99. motor
100. experience
101. perceptual
102. sensory
103. perceptual
104. Gibson & Walk

Anatomy of a Classic Research Study: When Do Infants Develop Depth Perception?

What was the rationale for the study?
Gibson & Walk were interested in how sophisticated infants' perceptual abilities were.

What methods did the authors use to test their hypothesis?
Gibson & Walk (1960) used a "visual cliff" to study depth perception in infants.

What was the outcome of the study and what did the authors conclude the results meant?
The results demonstrated that the infants would not cross from the "shallow" side to the "deep" side of the cliff. The researchers concluded that this meant infants as young as 6 months could perceive depth, and that depth perception is present by 6 months of age.

---

105. facial
106. cognitive
107. Piaget
108. four
109. formal operational
110. sensorimotor
111. Schemes
112. schema
113. mental
114. representational
115. preoperational
116. operations
117. language
118. reason
119. egocentrism
120. concrete operational
121. logically
122. physically
123. conservation
124. same
125. timing
126. cultural
127. earlier
128. Erikson
129. conflict
130. first
131. social
132. trust
133. attachment
134. Bowlby
135. evolutionary
136. survival
137. Freud
138. Harlow
139. more
140. human
141. Ainsworth
142. insecurely
143. securely
144. predictive
145. second
146. self-care
147. autonomy
148. initiative
149. initiative
150. impulses
151. industry
152. success
153. discipline
154. undesirable
155. permissive
156. punishment
157. abuse
158. Baumrind
159. independence
160. Authoritative
161. self-reliant
162. Day care
163. not
164. less
165. 20
166. insecure
167. correlational
168. parenting
169. discord
170. emotional
171. security
172. divorce
173. variables
174. intact
175. Friendships
176. same
177. intimate
178. siblings
179. Firstborn
180. Gender roles
181. Freud
182. Oedipus
183. research
184. observational
185. stereotypic
186. Bem
187. social learning
188. Gender schema
189. gender
190. Oedipus
191. Kohlberg
192. motives
193. preconventional
194. punishment
195. conventional
196. Obedience
197. postconventional
198. ethical
199. reasoning
200. situation
201. generalizability
202. Females

Mini-review of Prenatal, Infant and Child Development:
A. 2; B. 5; C. 1; D. 24; E. 33; F. 4; G. 7; H. 30; I. 23; J. 17; K. 26; L. 31; M. 3; N. 18; O. 29; P. 12; Q. 10; R. 22; S. 6; T. 13; U. 8; V. 9; W. 21; X. 14; Y. 16; Z. 28; Aa. 34; Bb. 11; Cc. 15; Dd. 19; Ee. 20; Ff. 35; Gg. 25; Hh. 27; Ii. 32

203. entire
204. childhood
205. biological
206. political
207. adulthood
208. Hall
209. Adolescence
210. puberty
211. height
212. maturation
213. hormone
214. testosterone
215. estrogen
216. ejaculation
217. menarche
218. hormonal
219. formal operational
220. abstract
221. scientific
222. hypotheses
223. systematically
224. earlier
225. academic
226. identity
227. role confusion
228. goals
229. values
230. reality.
231. conflict
232. longitudinal
233. males
234. identity
235. parents
236. positive
237. parental
238. intimate
239. cognitive
240. puberty
241. premarital
242. Americans
243. contraception
244. alcohol
245. twenties
246. Sexual
247. fewer
248. menopause
249. vision
250. late
251. slower
252. Cross-sectional
253. longitudinal
254. fluid
255. crystallized
256. speed
257. attention
258. school
259. active
260. Early
261. social clock
262. variability
263. intimacy
264. attachment
265. intimacy
266. identity
267. men
268. women
269. attractiveness
270. divorce
271. parenthood
272. Levinson
273. less
274. dreams
275. stagnation
276. generativity
277. mentor
278. empty nest
279. first
280. crowded
281. late
282. despair
283. integrity
284. depression
285. less
286. twentyth
287. hospice
288. Kübler-Ross

Mini-review on Adolescence and Adult Development:
A. 4; B. 5; C. 17; D. 10; E .9; F. 3; G. 6; H. 15; I. 13; J. 14; K. 16; L. 8; M. 2; N. 18; O. 12; P. 7; Q. 19: R. 11; S. 1

289. Galton
290. evolved
291. social
292. verbal
293. spatial
294. declined
295. adolescence
296. mathematics.
297. heredity
298. meta-analysis
299. aggression
300. self-esteem
301. nurturing
302. empathy
303. males
304. roles
305. hormonal
306. cognitive
307. play
308. narrowing
309. social

Practice Test A:

1. a. Incorrect: Gerontology is the study of aging, and developmental psychology was the study of children until the 1950s.
   b. Incorrect: Sociobiology is the study of the interaction of social behavior and biology.
   c. **Correct: Developmental psychology was the study of children until the 1950s.**
   d. Incorrect: Behavioral genetics is the field of study that examines how heredity and life experience interact in affecting development.

2. a. Incorrect: Eugenics is the movement that encourages only genetically superior people to have children.
   b. Incorrect: Phylogeny is not discussed in the chapter.
   c. Incorrect: Anthropometry is not discussed in this chapter
   d. **Correct: Behavioral genetics is the field of study that examines how heredity and life experience interact in affecting development.**

3. a. **Correct: Your genotype refers to your genetic inheritance.**
   b. Incorrect: This should read "often, but not always."
   c. Incorrect: The overt expression of your genetic makeup is your phenotype.
   d. Incorrect: No term is given for this.

4. a. Incorrect: This is not the best method.
   b. **Correct: Because identical twins share identical genetic makeups, and virtually identical prenatal environments, if there are differences in behaviors they can be attributed to environmental effects.**
   c. Incorrect: Results are difficult to explain because family members, although similar in genetic makeup, are genetically different.
   d. Incorrect: While this approach has been productive, it does not match the method of studying identical twins reared apart.

5 a. **Correct: Longitudinal methods follow the same group of subjects over time.**
b. Incorrect: Cross-sectional studies study different age groups of subjects at the same moment in time.
c. Incorrect: Cohort-sequential research is a combination of longitudinal and cross-sectional methods in which different age groups of subjects are followed over time.
d. Incorrect: Quasi-experimental methods are experiments in which the experimenter has not randomly assigned subjects to treatment conditions.

6. a. Incorrect: Germinal occurs first.
b. Incorrect: Fetal is the third stage.
c. Incorrect: Embryonic is the second stage.
d. **Correct: Germinal, embryonic, fetal is the correct sequence.**

7. a. Incorrect: The rats did not have more neurons, just more dendrites.
b. **Correct: The rats did not have more neurons, just more dendrites.**
c. Incorrect: The axon lengths had not changed.
d. Incorrect: The size of the axons had not changed.

8 a. Incorrect: The correct term for this is egocentrism.
b. **Correct: The correct term for this is egocentrism.**
c. Incorrect: The correct term for this is egocentrism.
d. Incorrect: The correct term for this is egocentrism.

9. a. **Correct: Erikson claims that the stage of initiative verus guilt is the stage in which the child develops a balance between spontaneity and restraint.**
b. Incorrect: In trust verus mistrust the child learns to develop a sense of security.
c. Incorrect: During the autonomy versus shame and doubt stage the child develops a sense of independence.
d. Incorrect: In the stage of industry versus inferiority, the child develops a sense of self-confidence.

10. a. Incorrect: The intense bond between a child and caregiver is called attachment.
b. **Correct: The intense bond between a child and caregiver is called attachment.**
c. Incorrect: The intense bond between a child and caregiver is called attachment.
d. Incorrect: The intense bond between a child and caregiver is called attachment.

11. a. **Correct: Baumrind argues that authoritative parenting is the most effective because it leads to children becoming socially competent, independent, and responsible.**
b. Incorrect: She does not categorize parenting this way.
c. Incorrect: Setting strict rules and relying on punishment is undesirable.
d. Incorrect: Setting few rules and rarely punishing misbehavior are also undesirable according to Baumrind.

12. a. Incorrect: Although this answer is correct, it is not the *best* answer provided.
b. Incorrect: High quality child care has not been shown to be detrimental to the development of attachments.
c. Incorrect: As with answer a, this choice is also correct, but not the *best* choice.
d. **Correct: This is the best choice since both a and c are correct.**

13. a. Incorrect: Social learning theory does not stress only punishment. This is but one of three major factors.
b. Incorrect: Social learning theory does not stress only reinforcement. This is but one of three major factors.
c. **Correct: This is the correct choice.**
d. Incorrect: This is Freudian theory, not social learning theory.

14. a. Incorrect: Kohlberg does not have a concrete level of moral reasoning.
b. Incorrect: Conventional level morality is concerned with following rules and laws.
c. **Correct: Preconventional level morality is concerned with avoidance of punishments or getting rewards.**
d. Incorrect: Postconventional morality is based on universal principles.

15. a. Incorrect: This is a correct answer but it is not the only correct choice, and not the best choice.
b. Incorrect: This is a correct answer but it is not the only correct choice, and not the best choice.
c. Incorrect: This is a correct answer, but it is not the only correct choice, and not the best choice.
d. **Correct: Since all three choices are correct, this is the best choice.**

16. a. Incorrect: Sensorimotor thought is not symbolic thought.
b. Incorrect: Preoperational thinking is symbolic thought but the child is not capable of manipulating the symbols.
c. **Correct: Formal operational thought is thought in which the child is able to test abstract ideas systematically.**
d. Incorrect: Concrete operational thinkers limit their thinking to the current, concrete world.

17. a. Incorrect: Remembering how to swim is considered procedural intelligence, not fluid.
b. Incorrect: Forgetting the names of friends would be a memory problem, not a decline in intelligence.
c. **Correct: Solving algebra problems would be considered an example of fluid intelligence.**
d. Incorrect: This is an example of a memory storage problem.

18. a. **Correct: Levinson claims that midlife men must come to terms with their life's dream, or resolve the contradiction between pursuit of the dream and realization of a sense of morality.**
b. Incorrect: Levinson claims that midlife men must come to terms with their life's dream, or resolve the contradiction between pursuit of the dream and realization of a sense of morality.
c. Incorrect: Levinson claims that midlife men must come to terms with their life's dream, or resolve the contradiction between pursuit of the dream and realization of a sense of morality.
d. Incorrect: Levinson claims that midlife men must come to terms with their life's dream, or resolve the contradiction between pursuit of the dream and realization of a sense of morality.

19. a. **Correct: Erikson claims that successful aging is the result of the achievement of integrity, or a sense of reflecting back on a meaningful life.**
b. Incorrect: Erikson claims that integrity is obtained via a life review, but it is not the review that leads to the successful aging, it is the outcome of the review.
c. Incorrect: Career success, according to Erikson, has little impact on success in aging.
d. Incorrect: Only choice a is correct.

20. a. Incorrect: Females tend to score higher in verbal tasks as children; in adolescence the differences are negligible.
b. Incorrect: There is no apparent sex difference in spatial abilities, and those that have been observed appear to have no practical impact.
c. **Correct: Males do have higher scores on standardized tests of mathematics.**
d. Incorrect: Although sex differences have been observed in personality and aggression, neither sex is considered superior in social ability.

Practice Test B:

1. a. **Correct: Developmental psychologists are still puzzled by the nature versus nurture controversy.**
b. Incorrect: Developmental psychologists are confident that maturation is a biological process.
c. Incorrect: Developmental psychologists know that there is developmental change throughout life.
d. Incorrect: Developmental psychologists do use the scientific method to study development.

2. a. **Correct: The genotype of a male is XY.**
b. Incorrect: The genotype of a female is XX.
c. Incorrect: Sex is determined by the type of chromosomes in the 23rd pair.
d. Incorrect: XY is a normal male.

3. a. **Correct: Longitudinal studies study the same subjects at different times.**
b. Incorrect: Cross-sectional studies study different age groups at the same time.
c. Incorrect: Cohort-sequential research follows different cohorts throughout time.
d. Incorrect: Observational research observes subjects.

4. a. Incorrect: No movement is felt in the germinal period. A zygote does not have arms and legs yet.
b. Incorrect: At 8 weeks, the embryonic period is ending; the child is not yet a fetus.
c. **Correct: Most pregnant women feel movement for the first time at 4 months.**
d. Incorrect: The fetus would be big enough prior to 7 months for the pregnant woman to feel it move.

5. a. Incorrect: The embryonic period is the second period of prenatal development.
b. **Correct: The fetal period is the prenatal period just prior to birth.**
c. Incorrect: The germinal period is the first period of prenatal development.
d. Incorrect: Transition is not a phase in prenatal development.

6. a. Incorrect: Down syndrome is a genetic disorder, not the result of environment.
b. **Correct: Research shows that enriched environment leads to enhanced brain development.**
c. Incorrect: Research shows that neglected children are not more responsive.
d. Incorrect: Research suggests that enriched environments lead to enhanced brain development; this has not been associated with interpersonal behavior

7. a. Incorrect: Assimilation is to add to existing schemes.
b. **Correct: Accommodation is to change an existing scheme to fit new information.**
c. Incorrect: Conservation refers to the ability of a child to know that amounts do not change when appearance does.
d. Incorrect: Reasoning refers to logical thinking; Lisa is not reasoning.

8. a. Incorrect: Assimilation refers to the adding of information to an existing scheme.
   b. Incorrect: Object permanence refers to a child's knowledge that an object exists without its being present.
   c. Correct: Egocentrism refers to children's lack of knowledge that others hold a viewpoint different from theirs. Amanda doesn't realize that the person on the phone cannot see her head.
   d. Incorrect: Conservation refers to the ability of a child to know that amounts don't change when appearance does.

9. **a. Correct: The successes that the child experiences will help lead to industriousness or competence.**
   b. Incorrect: In developing initiative, the child would develop independence, not competence.
   c. Incorrect: The 8-year-old child should have already developed trust.
   d. Incorrect: Children develop attachments during the first year, not at 8 years.

10. a. Incorrect: Object permanence refers to a child's knowledge that an object exists without its being present.
   b. Correct: Stranger anxiety refers to children's distress when approached by someone they do not know.
   c. Incorrect: Beth is nervous; however, she is not showing a lack of trust.
   d. Incorrect: It is normal for 9-month-olds to cry when their caregiver is gone. This is part of the development of attachment.

11. a. Incorrect: Authoritarian parents are very strict and use punishment.
   b. Incorrect: Authoritative parents set well-defined limits but explain them.
   c. Correct: Permissive parents do not set limits and allow kids full freedom.
   d. Incorrect: This is a fake term. Psychologists do not use the term *democratic parenting*.

12. a. Incorrect: Studies have shown that good-quality day care is not harmful for children.
   b. Incorrect: Studies have shown that poor-quality care can be harmful to children.
   c. Incorrect: Studies have shown that children who attended day care before age 2 do not do as well in high school.
   d. Correct: Studies have shown that infants in day care under 20 hours per week in the first year do develop secure attachments.

13. a. Incorrect: Freudian theory claims that gender identity is the result of identification with the same-sex parent.
   b. Correct: Social learning theory says that stereotypic gender roles are reinforced by the child's parent.
   c. Incorrect: Gender schema theory would go on to say that a child would develop stereotypic gender role schemas as a result of the father's action.
   d. Incorrect: Evolutionary theory claims that gender roles develop through natural selection, not the actions of parents.

14. a. Incorrect: Heinz is not avoiding punishment; he is looking for food rewards.
   b. Correct: In this reasoning, Heinz would be looking for food, or a reward.
   c. Incorrect: It is not a law that his wife cook for him; thus he is not trying to uphold any laws in this reasoning.
   d. Incorrect: In this reasoning, Heinz would be looking for food, or a reward, not a social convention.

15. a. Incorrect: Marriage is not a developmental task.
   b. Incorrect: Matchmaking is the act of getting them together.
   c. Correct: Social expectations to do something at a given time, like get married, are said to be governed by social clocks.
   d. Incorrect: The expectation of marriage is not a rite of passage; they do not need to marry to move on in development.

16. a. Incorrect: Jill is engaging in abstract thought; according to Piaget, 4-year-olds are preoperational thinkers and are not able to do this.
   b. Incorrect: Jill is engaging in abstract thought; according to Piaget, 8-year-olds are concrete operational thinkers and are not able to do this.
   c. Incorrect: Jill is engaging in abstract thought; according to Piaget, 10-year-olds are concrete operational thinkers and are not able to do this.
   d. Correct: At 15, Jill would be in formal operational thought and capable of abstract reasoning according to Piaget.

17. **a. Correct: The social clock refers to things that are appropriate for a given age; neither of these events is considered age-appropriate by a traditional social clock.**
   b. Incorrect: Both of these individuals are not doing typical behavior for their age; however, neither is denying his or her age.
   c. Incorrect: Neither of these examples refers to cognitive capabilities.
   d. Incorrect: Neither jumping from an airplane nor giving birth is a measure of intelligence.

18. a. Incorrect: To develop intimacy, he would need to develop a close personal relationship with a peer.
    b. Incorrect: In developing integrity, your brother would be retrospective about his life.
    c. Incorrect: Stagnation refers to someone who is socially withdrawn and self-centered; your brother is giving of himself.
    d. Correct: Erikson claims generativity is the giving of something to society; mentoring is one way to give to better society.

19. **a. Correct: Erikson felt that successful aging would lead to integrity and decreased fear of death.**
    b. Incorrect: An individual can conduct a life review and not be successful at acceptance of their life; this would not be aging.
    c. Incorrect: Career success is not enough. To be successful in old age, you also need social and personal success.
    d. Incorrect: Since B and C are incorrect, this is incorrect also.

20. a. Incorrect: Current studies are suggesting that there is not a biological sex difference in math ability.
    b. Correct: Current studies are suggesting that there is not a biological sex difference in math ability.
    c. Incorrect: Current studies are suggesting that there is not a biological difference in math ability.
    d. Incorrect: Current studies are suggesting that there is not a biological sex difference in math ability.

Essay Questions:

1. They study various pairs of relatives. Family studies involve similarities between relatives with varying degrees of genetic similarity. The general finding is that the closer a genetic relationship, the more alike they tend to be on a variety of traits. Twin studies are superior for this purpose. The similarities of identical versus fraternal twins can be compared.

   Better than family studies are adoption studies. The general finding is that adoptees are more similar to their biological parents than to their adoptive parents. Most useful of all are studies of identical twins reared apart. The general finding is for greater similarity between identical twins reared apart than between fraternal twins reared together.

2. Your grandmother's course would have concentrated on the infancy and childhood periods. The prenatal environment as well as the adulthood period would not be mentioned. The studies used would mostly consist of baby biographies. Freudian theory and behavioral theories would be the major theories presented.

5 Sensation and Perception

LEARNING OBJECTIVES

After studying this chapter, you should be able to:

1. Distinguish between sensation and perception, explaining how prosopagnosia offers insight into the distinction between these two processes. (p. 152)

2. Describe the general process by which sensation occurs in any sense modality. (p. 152)

3. Describe the domain of psychophysics, and then explain the concepts of absolute threshold and difference threshold (jnd), noting the elements of the modern approach of signal-detection theory. (p. 152-154)

4. Define and offer examples of sensory adaptation. (p. 154-155)

5. Explain the physical basis of our sense of vision, noting our sensitivity to only the visible spectrum, and the significance of the amplitude, brightness, and saturation of a light. (p. 155-156)

6. Draw a diagram of the eye, labeling its structures and delineating their functions regarding vision. Then trace the process by which vision occurs, from transduction in the retina to its final interpretation and organization in the visual cortex. (p. 156-160)

7. Describe the process of visual sensation, relating this to the processes of dark adaptation and color vision. (p. 160-162)

8. Compare and contrast the important features of the Young-Helmholtz theory of color vision with Hering's opponent-process theory, noting how the second theory explains the phenomenon of color blindness. (p. 162-164)

9. Compare the important features of Helmholtz's constructionist theory with Gibson's ecological theory. (p. 164)

10. List, describe, and offer examples of the Gestalt principles of perceptual organization, noting the disagreement among those who support the Gestalt position, feature-detector theory, and spatial frequency filter theory. (p. 164-166)

11. List and describe the binocular and monocular cues for depth perception, and then explain how three types of perceptual constancies allow us to maintain stability in our perceptions. (p. 167-170)

12. Describe the process by which illusions are created, and summarize the controversy that surrounds the nature of the moon illusion. (p. 170-171)

13. Summarize the findings of the classic study of the effects of early experience on the development of neural pathways, and relate this to current findings on this issue. (p. 171-174)

14. Label a diagram of the auditory system, designating the outer, middle, and inner ear, and delineating the functions of its various structures, and then trace the path of an auditory stimulus from the tympanic membrane to its final interpretation in the auditory cortex. (p. 174-175)

15. List and describe the four factors involved in auditory perception, mentioning the significance of place theory, frequency theory, and volley theory as well as the types of deafness. (p. 175-179)

16. Summarize what is known about the process of olfactory perception and how it differs from the other sensory processes, emphasizing the strong emotional impact of certain odors, and mentioning the significance of pheromones on the sexual behavior of animals. (p. 179-181)

17. Label a diagram of the tongue indicating the location of the taste buds and the location of papillae more sensitive to particular tastes, distinguishing between taste and flavor. (p. 181-182)

18. List the three skin senses and describe the processes of touch, temperature, and nociception, mentioning gate-control theory and how endorphin secretion affects our perception of pain. (p. 182-184)

19. List and describe five techniques for reducing pain and summarize the findings regarding how these techniques work. (p. 184-185)

20. List and describe the two body senses, mentioning where the relevant sensory receptors are located in the body, and how knowledge about the vestibular sense has been applied to reduce motion sickness. (p. 185-187)

21. Explain why psychologists remain skeptical regarding claims of ESP. (p. 187-190)

COMPREHENSIVE GUIDED REVIEW

I. Sensory processes are important to our everyday life. As you will remember from Chapter 1, the first psychological studies were concerned with understanding the connections between___(1)__ processes and the physical world. The study of the relationship between the physical characteristics of stimuli and the conscious experiences they produce is known as __(2)___. It was developed by Ernst Weber and Gustav Fechner in the nineteenth century. Currently, psychologists differentiate between the processes of **sensation** and **perception.** Both processes begin with a __(3)__, or a form of energy, that impacts a sensory organ. __(4)___ is the process that detects stimuli from the body or environment. ___(5)___ is the process that organizes sensations into meaningful patterns.

The disorder **prosopagnosia** clearly depicts the difference between sensation and perception. In___(6)___ an individual is able to see objects clearly; they are, however, unable to identify them by sight. The most famous example of this disorder is Dr. P., or "the man who mistook his wife for a hat." Dr. P. could recognize people by their__(7)__, but not by their faces. He had visual___(8)__; he could see peoples faces but could not perceive them; he could not___(9)__ the facial features into recognizable features.

Sensation depends on specialized___(10)__ called **sensory receptors.** These receptors detect stimuli and convert them into neural___(11)___. This process is known as **sensory transduction.** Sensory___(12)___ do not detect all environmental stimuli. The minimum level of stimulation that can be detected___(13)__ percent of the time is defined as the **absolute threshold** (or limen). An example of an___(14)___ would be the amount of salt needed on a French fry before you detect a "salty taste." The absolute threshold is affected by factors other than the___(15)__ of the stimulus. Because of this, researchers devised **signal detection theory,** which assumes that the detection of a stimulus depends on both the intensity of the stimulus and the physical and__(16)__ state of the individual. A major psychological characteristic of this theory is the concept of **response bias,** or how___(17)__ a person is to report the presence of a particular stimulus. ____(18)____ theory has application in numerous areas. Identifying bombs by using X-ray machines or understanding how different individuals respond differently to pain treatments are just two examples.

Signal-detection theorists identify four different types of reports. They are known as hits, misses, false alarms, and correct rejections. To illustrate the differences between each type of report, assume you are watching the street waiting for a particular "target" to occur, the appearance of a friend's car. There are four possible outcomes: a) You think you see the car, and it's really there; this would be considered a__(19)_; b) You think you see the car, but it's really not there. This would be considered a __(20)__; c) You don't see the car and it's really not there; this would be a ____(21)____; d) You don't see the car, but it's really there; this is called a__(22)__.

Signal detection involves more than just determining the presence or absence of a stimulus; we also must be able to detect a difference in stimulus ___(23)___. Therefore psychologists have identified the **difference threshold.** The ___(24)___ threshold is the minimum amount of change in stimulation an individual can detect. For example, if you turned the light-dimmer switch in your car, how much would the intensity of the light have to change before you could detect it? Weber and___(25)___ referred to the difference threshold as the "just noticeable difference," or ___(26)___. Their research showed that the amount of change in intensity needed to produce a **jnd** is a constant fraction of the___(27)___ stimulus. This is known as___(28)___ **law.**

Sensory adaptation is the tendency of sensory receptors to respond less and less to an___(29)___ stimulus. For example, when you first walk into a friend's apartment you notice the smell of the fish that had been cooked for dinner. But, you will not notice the scent for long. The longer you are in the apartment, the less you will notice the smell. Psychologists suggest that___(30)___ allows us to detect potentially important changes in our world while ignoring unchanging, or unimportant aspects. Research has shown that sensory adaption abilities may change as we age. Older individuals adapt ___(31)___ and return to normal sensitivity slower than younger people.

It's too early for a study break, but take time for a quick review to be sure that you understand and are remembering what you have studied.

Mini-review on Sensory Processes: Match each term with its correct definition.

________1. response bias
________2. difference threshold
________3. sensation
________4. prosopagnosia
________5. sensory transduction
________6. perception
________7. signal-detection theory
________8. sensory receptors
________9. absolute threshold
________10. Weber's law
________11. sensory adaptation
________12. psychophysics

A. The study of the relationship between the physical characteristics of stimuli and the conscious experiences they produce
B. The process that detects stimuli from the body or environment
C. The process that organizes sensations into meaningful patterns
D. The disorder in which an individual is able to see objects clearly but unable to identify them by sight
E. Cells that detect stimuli and convert them into neural impulses
F. The mechanism by which we detect environmental stimuli and convert them into neural impulses
G. The minimum level of stimulation that can be detected 50 percent of the time
H. Assumes that the detection of a stimulus depends on both the intensity of the stimulus, and the physical and psychological state of the individual
I. How prepared a person is to report the presence of a particular stimulus
J. The minimum amount of change in stimulation an individual can detect
K. States that the amount of change in intensity needed to produce a **jnd** is a constant fraction of the stimulus
L. The tendency of sensory receptors to respond less and less to an unchanging stimulus

---

II. Vision: The sensory system that received the most research attention is the ___(32)___ system. This is because it is the system that humans rely on the most. **Vision** relies on the use of our___(33)___ to sense light that is reflected by objects in the environment. The objects reflect the light of the **visible spectrum,** a narrow band of___(34)___ from a substantially broader **electromagnetic spectrum.**

Light has three___(35)___ properties: **wavelength, amplitude,** and **composition.** Each property leads to a perceptual, or psychological, property. The first physical property ,___(36)___, or the distance between two wave peaks measured in nanometers, determines the psychological quality of **hue,** or ___(37)___. The visible spectrum ranges from short wavelengths at the___(38)___ end of the spectrum (380 nanometers) to___(39)___ wavelengths at the red end (760 nanometers). Humans are unable to detect ultraviolet or infrared light because we lack the visual___(40)___ to detect these wavelengths.

The second physical property is __(41)_, or the height of the wavelength. This determines the psychological quality of **brightness,** or perceived__(42)__. The final physical property is composition and refers to the__(43)__ of a light's wavelength. Composition determines the psychological quality of **saturation.** A highly__(44)__ light will be seen as a truer color than a less saturated one. For example, a more saturated blue light would be seen as "bluer" than a less saturated one.

The Visual System: *(It may help to open your text to page 156 and look at Figure 5.3 as you study this section).* The__(45)__ is a fluid-filled sphere encased in a shape-maintaining tough white membrane called the **sclera.** At the front of the__(46)__ is the transparent **cornea.** The **iris** is a band of__(47)__ that lies behind the cornea, determines eye color, and regulates the amount of light that enters through the **pupil.** Research has shown that the size of the pupil is affected by a variety of psychological factors, including our level of__(48)__ or interest in a particular stimulus. In a psychologically aroused state the pupils__(49)__. This phenomenon has allowed psychologists to use the pupil to monitor the effectiveness of therapy for the treatment of__(50)_.

After passing through the pupil,__(51)__ is focused by the **lens** onto the **retina,** the light-sensitive carpet of **photoreceptors.** Ciliary muscles attached to the lens control **accommodation,** the process by which the lens changes __(52)__ to permit us to focus on objects at different distances. Research has shown that alcohol and ____(53)__ disrupt accommodation. The two most common conditions that affect one's ability to focus are **myopia** and **hyperopia.** When the eyeball becomes elongated,____(54)__, or near-sightedness, occurs. By contrast, when the eyeball is shortened, ____(55)_, or far-sightedness, occurs.

The image cast upon the retina is____(56)___, a phenomenon that taxed the genius of da Vinci and Descartes. We now know that we see the world right side up because of the way the visual system is wired. The__(57)__ pathways simply flip the image so that it appears right side up.

The retina contains specialized cells called **photoreceptors.** The__(58)__ were first identified by Heinrich Müller and respond when stimulated by light. There are two types of photoreceptors located in the retina of the human eye: **rods** and__(59)__. The rods and cones stimulate__(60)__ cells which in turn, stimulate ganglion cells, the axons of which form the optic nerves.

The__(61)_, which are sensitive to low illumination, are more densely packed in the periphery of the eye, and are important in night vision and peripheral vision. The **cones** are sensitive to__(62)__ illumination and provide color vision. It is the__(63)__ that provide our most acute vision. The cones__(64)__ in density as one approaches the center of the eye and, at the center, are the only photosensitive cells. This area of dense cones is known as the __(65)__. We use **smooth pursuit movements** and **saccadic movements** of the eye to keep objects __(66)__ on the **foveae.** The ____(67)___ movements help our eyes track moving objects. __(68)__ disrupts the action of the ocular muscles that control the smooth pursuit movements. The "Anatomy of a Contemporary Research Study" section of your text describes a study conducted by Bahill and LaRitz in which they studied the ability of subjects to use smooth pursuit movements to keep their eyes on the ball.

Anatomy of a Contemporary Research Study: Can Batters Really Keep Their Eye on the Ball?
Read the summary of the study on page 159 in your text and then answer the following questions:

What was the rationale for the study?

What methods did the authors use to test the hypothesis?

What was the outcome of the study and what did the authors conclude the results meant?

As you scan the environment, your smooth pursuit movements are complemented by ___(69)___ movements, or the continuous darting movements that bring new portions of scenes into focus on the fovea. After each saccadic movement the eye will then___(70)___ on a target for a quarter of a second. Visual information is picked up during these brief fixations.

The___(71)___ images are coded as neural impulses and are sent to the brain along the optic nerves. Of interest is the ___(72)___ spot, or the point on the retina at which the optic nerve leaves the back of the eye. This area was first identified by Edmé___(73)___. The spot is "blind" because there are___(74)___ rods or cones located at this spot.

The Brain: (*It may help to open your text to page 161 and look at Figure 5.7 as you study this section.)*
The optic nerves travel under the___(75)___ lobes and meet at the **optic chiasm**. Impulses from the eye divide at the optic ___(76)___; half remain to be conducted to the same side of the brain, while the other half cross over to the opposite side. The axons from the portion of the eye close to the___(77)___ cross to the opposite side of the brain. The axons from the side nearer the ear travel to the___(78)___ side of the brain. Some axons travel to the tectum in the___(79)___, which controls visual reflexes. Most of the axons go to the___(80)___, the sensory relay station of the brain. The thalamus transmits visual information to the **visual cortex** of the___(81)___ lobes. Damage to the visual cortex sometimes produces a___(82)___, or blind spot in the visual field. However, these are often not noticed since the brain fills in the missing details as it creates the overall visual___(83)___.

Retinal information about objects in the right visual field are processed in the___(84)___ occipital lobe, and retinal information in the left visual field is processed in the right visual field. (*Remember from Chapter 3 that all sensory information entering the body is processed by the opposite hemisphere of the brain.*) The visual cortex has been "mapped" and as a result, people who have gone blind may eventually benefit from a microprocessing system that permits stimulation of electrodes attached to the visual___(85)___. The electrodes are stimulated to produce patterns of spots of lights called___(86)___.

How is the neural impulse initiated by the photoreceptors? **Visual sensation** depends on___(87)___, which, when stimulated by light, break down and then resynthesize. The pigment for the ___(88)___ is rhodopsin, and for the cones it is___(89)___. The initial breakdown of the photopigment leads to the creation of the neural ___(90)___, which are sent along the optic nerves to the brain. The photoreceptors are also important in the processes of___(91)___and color vision.

Dark adaptation is the process by which your eyes become more___(92)___ to light. When you enter a dark room, often you have difficulty finding your way around. This is because your___(93)___ have had their photopigment "bleached" out. The photoreceptors need to increase their production of___(94)___ and iodopsin. The___(95)___ become less sensitive to light, while the rods become more sensitive. This process takes time. The cones will reach their maximum sensitivity at approximately ___(96)___ minutes, but the___(97)___ will take almost 30. So, since you owe your ability to see under___(98)___ illumination to your rods, you won't see very well in the dark for about a half hour. Impairment of this process is common in aging individuals and has been suggested to be related to the high proportion of nighttime automobile accidents that involve older drivers.

Because of the complexity of the visual system, several theories and a considerable amount of research have been generated as to try to explain **color vision**. The two major theories include the **Tri-chromatic** and the___(99)___ theories. The___(100)___, also known as the Young-Helmholtz theory, assumes that there are three types of cones, maximally sensitive to red, green, or blue light. George___(101)___ (1964) provided confirming evidence for the theory in research that earned him a Nobel Prize. Mixing colored lights is an___(102)___ process, whereas mixing ___(103)___is a subtractive process.

The **opponent-process theory** was proposed partly to explain the phenomenon of___(104)___, or the occurrence of images that persist after the removal of the visual stimulus. As the name of the theory implies, it assumes that there are ___(105)___, blue-yellow, and black-white opponent processes. The black-white process determines the ___(106)___of what we see. The theory argues that stimulation of one process___(107)___ the other. Confirming evidence for the theory was provided by ____(108)____ et al. in 1966. These researchers found cells in the__(109)__ that send impulses when their cones are stimulated by red and stop sending impulses when the cones are stimulated by green. They additionally found other cells that acted in the opposite fashion. (That is, the cells send messages when their cones are stimulated by green and stop sending impulses when their cones are stimulated by red.)

The trichromatic theory cannot, by itself, explain either **afterimages** or___(110)____. The___(111)__ theory, on the other hand, can. Research has identified three types of color vision: **trichromats, dichromats,** and **monochromats**. People with normal color vision are__(112)__, they have red, blue, and green photo pigments. People who are color blind are __(113)__; they lack one kind of iodopsin. Most commonly dichromats are__(114)__ color blind. Finally, people who are completely color blind are__(115)_. Color blindness is a genetic trait that appears to be carried on the __(116)__ chromosome. As a result males are more likely to demonstrate the trait than females. *(Remember, females have two X chromosomes and therefore must inherit a color blindness gene from both mother and father. A male has only one X chromosome, thus only has to inherit the gene from his mother.)*

Which theory is correct in explaining color vision? Today, the answer is___(117)_! The suggestion is that the trichromatic and opponent process theories combine to give us our visual__(118). Impulses from the red, green, or blue cones of the __(119)__ are sent to the opponent-processing cells in the ganglion cells and then sent farther up to the thalamus and visual cortex.

Visual__(120)__ provide the raw materials that are organized into meaningful patterns by **visual perception.** The basic assumption of___(121)__'s constructionist theory is that we learn through experience to convert sensations into accurate perceptions. The basic assumption of Gibson's__(122)__ theory is that visual perception depends mainly on inborn mechanisms that automatically convert sensations into perceptions of stimuli. While recent research *(one example is the visual cliff studies discussed in Chapter 4)* supports__(123)__'s theory, many perception researchers have traditionally believed that we "construct" our perceptions on what Helmholtz called unconscious inferences.

To perceive__(124)__, we distinguish meaningful shapes or patterns from environmental stimuli. To accomplish **form perception,** we must distinguish a shape, or figure, from a background, such as the black letters against this white page. This process is known as__(125)__ perception. The ____(126)__ psychologists feel that form perception is an active, not a passive, process. They suggest that our__(127)__ impose themselves on our sensations to form perceptions. This is called **top-down processing.** The Gestaltists have identified four principles that govern form perception. They are:

1)___(128)__: Stimuli that are close together will tend to be perceived as parts of the same form.
2)___(129)__: Stimuli that are similar to one another will tend to be perceived as parts of the same form.
3)___(130)__: We tend to fill in minor gaps in the forms we perceive.
4)___(131)__: We tend to group stimuli into forms that follow continuous lines or patterns.

Although there is some support for the Gestalt position that forms are perceived as__(132), rather than parts, there is also evidence for_(133)__ and Wiesel's (1979) **feature detector theory.** Gestalt psychologists would claim that we perceive the letter *A*__(134)_; feature-detector theorists, on the other hand, assume that we construct the *A* from its component lines and angles. Results from Hubel and Wiesel's research lead to the conclusion that we construct our visual perceptions from **feature-detector cells** in the visual __(135)_. This evidence provides an anatomical basis for **illusory contours.** An alternative theory, the **spatial frequency filter theory** holds that perception is based on the detection and analysis of__(136)__ in patterns of light and dark. These variations are called **spatial frequencies.**

If we lived in a two-dimensional world, ___(137)_ perception would be enough. However, we do not. Thus the visual system must have a mechanism for **depth perception.** Since the images on the retina are two-dimensional, we must perceive_(138)__, or the ability to judge the distance of objects, by using different types of cues. Constructionist theorists maintain that we perceive depth through the use of **binocular** and **monocular** cues. __(139)_ cues require the interaction of both eyes. One example of a binocular cue is____(140)___, the degree of difference between the images of an object that are focused on the two retinas. Another binocular cue is __(141)_, the degree to which the eyes turn inward to focus on an object. __(142)__ cues require only one eye. Examples of monocular cues are:

1) Accommodation: The perception of distance is a function of the change in__(143)__ of the retina
2) ____(144)____: The tendency to perceive objects that are closer to you as moving faster than more distant objects.
3) __(145)__: The tendency for objects that overlap to appear closer.
4) Relative size: The relative__(146)__ of objects is used. If two objects are at the same distance away, the smaller of two objects will appear farther away.
5) Linear perspective: Parallel objects seem to get__(147)__ together as they get farther away.
6) Elevation: Objects that appear__(148)__ in the visual field seem to be farther away.
7) __(149)__ patterns: Areas in a shadow tend to recede, while areas in the light tend to stand out.
8) ____(150)____: Depends on the clarity of objects; distant objects appear hazier.
9) Texture gradient: The texture of an object is__(151)__ when it is near and finer when it is far.

Additionally,___(152)___ allow us to continue to perceive an object as stable in size, shape, color, and brightness. Although the image focused on the retina may change, the features of an object will be perceived as___(153)__. We then interpret the change to mean something. For example:

a) ___(154)__ constancy: A change in retinal size is interpreted as a change in distance, not in the size of the actual object.
b) __(155)__ constancy: Objects of known shape will appear to maintain their normal shape regardless of the angle from which you view it.
c) ___(156)__ constancy: Perception of an object is related to the surroundings of the object. A white shirt is interpreted as equally bright in dim or bright light.

Visual illusions are the__(157)__ of a visual cue. Psychologists have used visual illusions to try to understand normal visual perception. The **moon illusion** is a classic example of a visual__(158)__. Objects, such as the moon, that are closer to the horizon appear many times larger than when high overhead. There are two explanations for this phenomenon: a) The apparent-distance hypothesis. This states that the brain assumes that the moon must be__(159)__ at the apparently more distant location—the horizon. To the contrary, however, research has shown that the sky looks farther away__(160)__ than it does at the horizon. If the apparent-distance hypothesis were correct, the moon should appear larger overhead; b) The__(161)__ hypothesis. This hypothesis suggests that the moon illusion is attributable to the different amounts of space, or its relative size as compared to its surroundings. The moon overhead is smaller due to all of the space around it.

Visual perception depends not only on the interaction of the eyes and the brain, but also on life__(162)__. The study featured in the "Anatomy of a Classic Research Study" section in your textbook examines the relationship between visual perception and life experiences.

Anatomy of a Classic Research Study: Can Early Experience Affect the Development of the Visua Pathways?
Read the summary on page 172 in your textbook. Then practice your critical reading skills by answering the following questions about the study:

What was the rationale for the study?

What methods did the authors use to test the hypothesis?

What was the outcome of the study and what did the authors conclude the results meant?

Additional evidence for the role of experience in visual perception comes from studies by Max von___(163)__, who studied subjects who had been blind from birth and later gained a sense of vision. Von Senden found that although these newly sighted individuals were able to distinguish___(164)__, and separate figure from ground, they had difficulty in__(165)__ objects they had learned to identify by touch. Additionally, __(166)__ factors have also been shown to play a role in visual perception. This is evidenced by the case of a __(167)__ who lived in a dense forest and had never seen an open plain. To him, buffalo at a distance were perceived as insects. The role of cultural experience is further supported by the classic Ponzo illusion.

Now that we have finished our discussion of the visual system, this is a good place to take a break.

Mini-review on Visual System: Complete the mini-review of the visual system before you go on to study the other sensory systems.

___________1. retinal disparity
___________2. cones
___________3. wavelength
___________4. lens
___________5. retina
___________6. saccadic movements
___________7. cornea
___________8. opponent-process theory
___________9. fovea
___________10. photopigment
___________11. accommodation
___________12. amplitude
___________13. sclera
___________14. hue
___________15. brightness
___________16. myopia
___________17. proximity
___________18. binocular cues
___________19. monocular cues
___________20. rods
___________21. pupil
___________22. saturation
___________23. smooth pursuit movements
___________24. iris
___________25. elevation
___________26. visual perception
___________27. aerial perspective
___________28. hyperopia
___________29. optic chiasm
___________30. tri-chromatic theory
___________31. relative size
___________32. similarity
___________33. trichromats
___________34. dichromats
___________35. dark adaptation
___________36. texture gradient
___________37. monochromats
___________38. closure
___________39. form perception
___________40. spatial frequency filter theory
___________41. continuity
___________42. motion parallax
___________43. depth perception
___________44. interposition

A. The distance between two wave peaks measured in nanometers
B. The height of the wavelength; determines the psychological quality of brightness
C. The purity of the light's wavelength; determines the psychological quality of vividness
D. The perceptual quality of color of light
E. The tough white membrane of the eye
F. The transparent outer layer of the eye
G. Lies behind the cornea and determines eye color; regulates the amount of light that enters
H. Psychologists have used this portion of the eye to monitor the effectiveness of therapy
I. The process by which the lens changes shape
J. The structure that focuses the light after it enters the eye
K. The light-sensitive carpet of photoreceptors
L. The eyeball becomes elongated; near-sightedness occurs
M. The eyeball is shortened; far sightedness occurs
N. Depends on the clarity of objects-distant objects appear hazier
O. Photoreceptors which are sensitive to low illumination: are important in night vision
P. The area of dense cones in the center of the retina
Q. Movements that help our eyes track moving objects
R. Photoreceptors sensitive to high illumination; provide color vision
S. The continuous darting movements that bring new portions of scenes into focus on the fovea
T. A chemical that, when stimulated by light, breaks down and then resynthesizes
U. The process by which your eyes become more sensitive to light
V. Also known as the Young-Helmholtz theory, assumes that there are three types of cones
W. Argues that stimulation of one process opposes the other
X. Term for normal color vision; these individuals have red, blue, and green photopigments
Y. The site at which the optic nerves from each eye meet and cross
Z. Term for people who are color blind but lack only one kind of iodopsin
Aa. Term for people who are completely color blind
Bb. The process by which visual sensations are organized into meaningful patterns
Cc. Objects of known shape will appear to maintain their normal shape regardless of the angle from which you view it
Dd. The perceptual quality that corresponds with the intensity of light
Ee. Process by which distinction is made between meaningful shapes or patterns
Ff. Stimuli that are close together will tend to be perceived as parts of the same form
Gg. Stimuli that are similar to one another will tend to be perceived as parts of the same form
Hh. Gestalt rule that states that we tend to fill in minor gaps in the forms we perceive
Ii. Theory holds that perception is based on the detection and analysis of variations in patterns of light and dark
Jj. Gestalt rule that states that we tend to group stimuli into forms that follow continuous lines or patterns
Kk. The ability to judge the distance of objects
Ll. Depth-perception cues that require the use of one eye
Mm. Depth-perception cues that require the interaction of both eyes
Nn. The degree of difference between the images of an object that are focused on the two retinas

____________45.	linear perspective	Oo.	The degree to which the eyes turn inward to focus on an object
____________46.	shape constancy	Pp.	The texture of an object is coarser when it is near and finer when it is far
____________47.	convergence	Qq.	The tendency to perceive objects that are closer to you as moving faster than more distant objects
____________48.	shading patterns	Rr.	The tendency for objects that overlap to appear closer
		Ss.	If two objects are at the same distance away, the smaller of two objects will appear farther away
		Tt.	Parallel objects seem to get closer together as they get farther away
		Uu.	Objects that appear higher in the visual field seem to be farther away
		Vv.	Areas in a shadow tend to recede, while areas in the light tend to stand out

III. Hearing (Audition): The auditory system is responsible for our ability to detect___(168)__. Sound is produced by ______(169)___ carried by air, water, or other mediums. Sound waves are comprised of a series of bunching-spreading ___(170)___ or cycles that are transmitted through a sound medium. Because sound waves require a___(171)__, sound does not exist in a vacuum. The height of the sound wave is called its___(172)___, and the number of cycles that pass through a point in a second is called the____(173)___. Frequency is measured in hertz (Hz).

The Auditory System: *(It may help you to refer to Figure 5.21 on page 175 in your textbook while reviewing the structure and function of the auditory system.)*

The auditory system involves the___(174)___ as the sense organ. The ear is divided into three parts the **outer,** the **middle,** and the **inner ear.** The ___(175)__ear includes the pinna, the auditory canal, and the tympanic membrane (eardrum). The____(176)___ ear includes the malleus (hammer), incus (anvil), and stapes (stirrup), and the____(177)___ ear includes the oval window and the cochlea.

Sound waves are gathered by the___(178)___ and pass through the external auditory canal to the eardrum, or tympanic membrane. The sound waves cause the___(179)___ to vibrate. These vibrations are transferred to the small bones, or ____(180)__, in the middle ear. First the malleus, or the hammer, vibrates; then the___(181)___, or the anvil, and finally the stapes, or stirrup, vibrate. Vibrations of the stapes are conveyed to the_____(182)_____, a membrane that is part of the cochlea. These vibrations continue as waves through the fluid-filled chamber that runs the length of the____(183)___ and set in motion the **basilar membrane.** Movement of this membrane causes bending of hair cells that trigger impulses that travel along the axons of the neurons and form the___(184)__ nerve. As in vision, impulses eventually reach the__(185)__. From there, the impulses are relayed to the auditory____(186)__ of the brain.

Auditory Perception: Your ability to perceive sounds of all kinds depends on **pitch perception, loudness perception, timbre perception,** and **sound localization.**

The frequency of a sound determines its___(187)__. There is no one theory that explains everything about pitch perception, but rather there are three overlapping theories that account for high-, low-, and medium-pitched sounds, respectively. The three major theories of pitch perception are:

1) The___(188)__ theory assumes that particular points on the basilar membrane vibrate maximally in response to sound waves of particular frequencies; the theory fails to explain pitch perception much below 1,000 Hz.
2) The___(189)__ theory assumes that the basilar membrane vibrates as a whole in direct proportion to the frequency of the sound waves striking the eardrum; explains the perception of pitch below 1,000 Hz.
3) The__(190)__ theory provides strong support for explaining pitch perception in the range of 1,000 Hz to 5,000 Hz.

Sounds also vary in intensity, or___(191)__, as well as pitch. Loudness Perception depends on both the number and the ___(192)___of hair cells that are stimulated on the basilar membrane. The unit of sound intensity is called the__(193)__. Over time, loud sounds, or high decibel sounds, can lead to hearing impairment for high-frequency sounds. In extreme cases an individual can end up with **conduction deafness,** in which there is a problem with the ____(194)____portions of the outer or middle ear. ____(195)__ deafness is most often treated with hearing aids; however, deafness that is the result of deterioration of the ossicles can be restored. Deteriorating ossicles are replaced with____(196)__ ones. Deafness that responds poorly to treatment is generally the result of problems with the__(197)_ ear, the basilar membrane, or the auditory nerve. This is known as___(198)_ **deafness.** In some cases of nerve deafness, __(199)__ implants have provided at least a restoration of rudimentary hearing.

Timbre is the___(200)_ of a sound, reflecting a unique mixture of sound waves. It is__(201)_ that lets us identify the source of a sound and distinguish, for example, a violin from a cello or a warbler from a crow. However, we are capable of determining the (202)_ of sounds because we have two ears. We can identify sounds that arrive at each of the ears with identical or different__(203)_ and at the same or different times. The auditory cortex has cells that respond to these two factors of intensity and__(204)_ time.

Stop here and review the auditory system before going on to study the remaining systems.

Mini-review of the Auditory System: Match each term with its correct definition.

_______1. hertz	A. The height of the sound wave
_______2. outer ear	B. The number of cycles that pass through a point in a second
_______3. frequency	C. Unit that frequency is measured in
_______4. place theory	D. Includes the pinna, the auditory canal, and the tympanic membrane (eardrum)
_______5. conduction deafness	E. Includes the malleus (hammer), incus (anvil), and stapes (stirrup)
	F. Includes the oval window and the cochlea
_______6. middle ear	G. Is determined by the frequency of a sound
_______7. volley theory	H. This theory assumes that particular points on the basilar membrane vibrate maximally in response to sound waves of particular frequencies
_______8. nerve deafness	
_______9. amplitude	I. The quality of a sound; lets us identify the source of a sound
_______10. inner ear.	J. This theory explains the perception of pitch below 1,000 Hz
_______11. timbre	K. This theory provides strong support for explaining pitch perception in the range of 1,000 Hz to 5,000 Hz
_______12. frequency theory	
_______13. decibel	L. The intensity of sound
_______14. pitch	M. The unit of sound intensity
_______15. loudness	N. Deafness that is most often treated with hearing aids
	O. Deafness that responds poorly to treatment; is generally the result of problems with the inner ear, the basilar membrane or the auditory nerve

IV. Chemical Senses: The chemical senses allow us to identify things based on their chemical content. The two chemical senses in the human include **smell** and **taste**.

Psychologists have relatively little knowledge of how the actions of the **olfactory system** lead to the sensation and perception of _(205)_. This is due to the complex nature of studying smells. The little research that has been conducted has indicated that molecules carried in inhaled__(206)_ stimulate smell receptor cells in the nasal passages. Distinctive firing __(207)_of receptor cells evoke different odors. It has been suggested that neural impulses from the receptor cells travel along the__(208)_ nerve directly to the frontal lobes of the brain. *(Remember from Chapter 3, smell is the only one of the external senses whose information does not get processed by the thalamus before reaching the cortex.)* Although the ___(209)__does not process the olfactory information before the cortex, the limbic system does receive extensive input from the olfactory system. This may account for the powerful___(210)_ effects of smells.

Researchers have not reached agreement on a set of basic odors; however,__(211)_ are commonly recognized. They are ethereal, camphoraceous, musky, floral, pepperminty, pungent and putrid. All other smells, it has been suggested, are (212)_of these. One theory of smell, the **stereochemical theory,** argues that smell receptors responsive to particular odors are sensitive to__(213)_ of a particular size or shape. This theory has failed to receive consistent research support.

The human sense of smell has a low___(214)___. Studies of college students have shown that they could identify their own odor, and women have been shown to recognize the smell of infants they had held briefly. As important as smell is for humans, smell may be even more important to other animals. For example, secretions such as aphrodisin (a vaginal **pheromone** released by female hamsters) has been shown to stimulate___(215)___ behavior. The addition of sex ___(216)___ to human fragrances, however, has produced inconsistent results.

The other chemical sense is___(217)___, or **gustation.** Taste depends on the use of taste buds, which line the grooves between the papillae of the___(218)___. The taste buds contain receptor cells that send neural impulses when stimulated by molecules dissolved in___(219)___. Research has shown that taste sensitivity varies with the number of taste___(220)___. Taste buds are replaced quite rapidly, although the rate declines with age. Avicenna proposed that there were four basic tastes: sweet, sour,___(221)___, and bitter, a description still accepted today. Flavor and taste are not one and the same. ___(222)___ is more complex than taste, and appears to involve both taste and smell.

V. Skin Senses: The **skin, or cutaneous,** senses include our senses of touch, ___(223)___and pain. These senses allow us to identify objects,___(224)___ feelings, and be protected from injury. There does not appear to be a simple one-to-one relationship between specific kinds of receptors and specific skin senses. Skin sensation appears to be determined by the___(225)___ of stimulation.

The sense of **Touch** is a system so precise that it can substitute for___(226)___. This is evidenced by the___(227)___ system or, more recently, the innovation of a camera worn on eyeglasses and a special electronic vest that transmits vibrations to the skin. Touch appears to be important in the development of our social___(228)___. Touch sensitivity depends on the ___(229)___ of the receptors.

The thermal sense of___(230)___ detection allows us to detect changes in external temperature. Research has shown that the skin contains receptors for warm and___(231)___. In the seventeenth century John Locke demonstrated how temperature sensations depended on detecting___(232)___ in skin temperature. More recent research has confirmed this fact.

The nociceptive sense of___(233)___ protects us from injury. The main pain receptors, or___(234)___, are free nerve endings in the skin. Two types of neurons transmit pain impulses. A-delta fibers carry sharp, or___(235)___, pain, and C fibers carry ___(236)___pain. One chemical substance implicated in pain is bradykinin, a substance that accumulates at the site of an ___(237)___. Research has shown that aspirin and___(238)___ may inhibit the release of *bradykinin.* An injury or intense stimulation causes many of the pain receptor neurons to transmit impulses by releasing **substance P** from their___(239)___.

The most influential theory of pain is the **gate-control theory.** It assumes that impulses pass through the substantia gelatinosa, which provides a "gate" for pain impulses. The gates can be closed by the body's natural opiates, the ___(240)___. This process is demonstrated by the ___(241)___ effect, wherein if soldiers interpreted their wounds as a ticket home, they needed less morphine than did civilians with similar wounds.

___(242)___work to reduce pain by stimulating the release of endorphins. The analgesic effects of___(243)___ are mediated by stimulating the release of endorphins through the insertion of fine needles into the body. Naloxone, a drug that blocks the effects of___(244)___, inhibits the analgesic effects of acupuncture. This offers evidence for the role of ___(245)___ in acupuncture. A more modern technique of___(246)___ relief involves the use of **transcutaneous electrical nerve stimulation (TENS).** Here,___(247)___ stimulation is applied to sites on the body. As with placebos and acupuncture, TENS may relieve pain by stimulating the release of___(248)___. Hypnosis also relieves pain, although apparently not by stimulating the release of endorphins. Finally, pain may be controlled by resorting to___(249)___ means, such as distracting thoughts or stimuli, as is the case in listening to music while seated in a dentist's chair.

VI. Body Senses: The **body senses** include the **kinesthetic sense** and the **vestibular sense.** The ___(250)___ sense informs you of the position of your joints, tension in your muscles, and movement in your extremities. This information is provided by special ___(251)___ in the joints, muscles, and tendons. Alcohol impairs kinesthetic feedback, thus impairing movements by disrupting our sense of limb___(252)__. The__(253)__ sense informs you of your position in space, assisting in balance and orientation. The chief organs are the **semicircular canals** and the **otolith organs.** The __(254)__ organs detect horizontal or vertical linear movement of the head, and the semicircular canals help us maintain ____(255)__ and keep the eyes fixed on a target. When the semicircular canals are affected by movement and consequent fluid-level changes, the __(256)__cells bend and trigger impulses to the cerebellum, helping to maintain balance. By permitting __(257)__movements of the head, the semicircular canals allow the eyes to remain fixed on a target. This is caused by the **vestibulo-ocular reflex.**

The vestibular sense may also induce___(258)___ sickness, although repeated stimulation may produce an increase in tolerance. One view holds that motion sickness is induced by conflict between vestibular and___(259)__ sensations. Drugs that inhibit neural activity in the____(260)____ may reduce motion sickness. Motion sickness can also be reduced by psychological means.

You are staying right on track. Keep up the good work! Take time for another short study break. Don't forget to complete the mini-review before you move on to study ESP.

Mini-review on Chemical, Skin and Body Senses: Match each term with its correct description.

_______1. C fibers
_______2. olfactory system
_______3. otolith organs
_______4. stereochemical theory
_______5. transcutaneous nerve stimulation (TENS)
_______6. A-delta fibers
_______7. pheromone
_______8. gate-control theory
_______9. touch
_______10. vestibular sense
_______11. endorphins
_______12. gustation
_______13. taste buds
_______14. bradykinin
_______15. temperature
_______16. cutaneous sense
_______17. nociceptors
_______18. substance P
_______19. semicircular canals
_______20. kinesthetic sense
_______21. naloxone
_______22. pain

A. The sense that appears to be important in the development of our social attachments
B. The sense that allows us to detect changes in external temperature
C. The sense that protects us from injury
D. The main pain receptors; free nerve endings in the skin
E. Fibers that carry sharp, or pricking, pain
F. Organs that help us maintain balance and keep the eyes fixed on a target
G. The body's natural opiates
H. Sensory receptors for sense of taste
I. Fibers that carry dull pain
J. The system responsible for sensation and perception of smell
K. Sense that allows us to identify objects, communicate feelings, and be protected us from injury
L. A chemical substance implicated in pain; accumulates at the inflammation site
M. A substance released from pain receptors at the time of injury or intense stimulation
N. Argues that smell receptors responsive to particular odors are sensitive to molecules of a particular size or shape
O. The most influential theory of pain; assumes that impulses pass through the substantia gelatinosa, which provides a "gate" for pain impulses
P. The sense of taste
Q. A drug that blocks the effects of opiates
R. A more modern technique of pain relief; involves the use of electrical stimulation that is applied to sites on the body
S. Sense that informs you of the position of your joints, tension in your muscles, and movement in your extremities
T. Sense that informs you of your position in space, assisting in balance and orientation
U. Organs that detect horizontal or vertical linear movement of the head
V. Chemicals released by animals that affect the behavior of other animals

VII. Thinking About Psychology: Why Do Psychologists Discount ESP?

ESP, or____(261)____, is defined as perception independent of sensory receptors. ESP and related phenomena are the topics of the field of___(262)__. These topics do not receive much widespread acceptance within mainstream psychology and most of the parapsychological activities are considered paranormal. Alleged paranormal abilities include **mental telepathy, clairvoyance, precognition, déja vu,** and **psychokinesis.**

__(263)__is the ability to perceive the thoughts of others without having any sensory contact with them. __(264)__ is the ability to perceive objects or events without having any sensory contact with them. __(265)__ is the ability to perceive events in the future; this is not to be confused with__(266)__, a feeling that one has experienced a present experience sometime in the past. Finally,__(267)__ (PK) is closely allied with ESP. PK is the ability to control objects with the mind alone.

Despite popular acceptance of **parapsychology,** most psychologists remain__(268)__ about alleged paranormal activities. Although some academic researchers have attempted to study paranormal activity using legitimate __(269)__ methods, problems remain with paranormal research. These include:

a) Demonstrations are, in general, poorly__(270)__.
b) __(271)__ events are too readily accepted as evidence of paranormal phenomena.
c) Instances of fraud occur all too often.
d) Magic tricks are used.
e) Researchers have difficulty__(272)__ paranormal events.
f) There is no satisfactory explanation for paranormal events.

Congratulations. You have completed the comprehensive guided review of Chapter 5. Review all of the key research presented in the chapter and then prepare yourself to take the practice tests.

KEY RESEARCH FINDINGS

Provide the details of the following key research studies in psychology:

1. **Sacks (1985):** Case study of man with prosopagnosia. (Page 152)
2. **Lloyd & Appel (1976):** Examined pain relief measures and response bias. (Page 154)
3. **Hollins, Delemos, & Goble (1991):** Examined sensory adaptation in skin receptors. (Page 155)
4. **Sturgen, Cooper, & Howell (1989):** Measured pupil response as related to anxiety. (Page 157)
5. **Fukuda, Kanada, & Saito (1990):** Examined the elasticity of the lens in aging subjects. (Page 157)
6. **Curcio et al. (1987):** Showed a relationship between acuity of vision and density of the cones in the fovea. (Page 158)
7. **Rayner (1993):** Examined saccadic movements and fixation length. (Page 159)
8. **Harbin, Durst, & Harbin (1989):** Examined the ability of athletes to maintain eye contact with a moving target. (Page 159))
9. **Vickers (1992):** Examined golfers' use of saccadic eye movements in relation to their putting ability. (Page 159)
10. **Homa (1983):** Showed that skimming increases the speed of page turning, but hurts reading comprehension. (Page 159)
11. **Livingstone & Hubel (1988):** Examined the integration of visual information by the visual cortex. (Page 160)
12. **Cha, Horch, & Normann (1992):** Examined ability to navigate a maze using phosphenes. (Page 160)
13. **Mortimer & Fell (1989):** Examined the relationship between dark adaptation, aging, and nighttime driving accidents. (Page 161)
14. **Adams, Courage, & Mercer (1994):** Showed poor color vision of newborn humans. (Page 162)
15. **Wald (1964):** Conducted a Nobel-prize winning study of color receptors in the eye. (Page 162)
16. **De Valois et al. (1966):** Provided evidence for the opponent-process theory of color vision. (Page 162)
17. **Cicerone & Nerger (1989):** Provided evidence for dichromatic type of color blindness. (Page 163)

18. **Rock, Gopnik, & Hall (1994):** Showed that subjects must have experience with reversible figures to reverse ambiguous figures. (Page 165)
19. **Kubovy & Wagemans (1995):** Provided evidence for role of proximity in grouping of stimuli. (Page 165)
20. **Hubel & Wiesel (1979):** Nobel Prize-winning study that led to the development of feature-detector theory of vision. (Page 166)
21. **Foley (1988):** Demonstrated that certain neurons respond to patterns with wide stripes, while others respond to patterns with narrow stripes. (Page 166)
22. **DeAngelis, Ohzawas & Freeman (1995):** Demonstrated cells in visual cortex that detect the degree of retinal disparity. (Page 167)
23. **Watten, Lie, & Birketvedt (1994):** Demonstrated that use of computer terminal leads to eye fatigue. (Page 167)
24. **Judge & Cumming (1986):** Examined response of neurons in tectum to accommodation of lens. (Page 168)
25. **Hofsten, Kellman, & Putaansuu (1992):** Demonstrated infants' use of motion parallax in depth perception. (Page 168)
26. **Higashiyama & Kitano (1991):** Demonstrated that relative size provides cue to distance perception. (Page 168)
27. **Arterberry, Yonas, & Benson (1989):** Demonstrated that 7-month old infants respond to texture-gradient cue. (Page 169)
28. **Slater (1992):** Presented evidence for size/shape constancies at birth. (Page 169)
29. **Farrimond (1990):** Demonstrated that alcohol disrupts perception of size constancy. (Page 170)
30. **Plug & Ross (1994):** Identified a variety of factors in the perception of the moon illusion. (Page 171)
31. **Blakemore & Cooper (1970):** Examined the influence of early experience on development of visual pathways. (Page 172)
32. **Turnbull (1961):** Studied the visual distance perception of the Bambuti Pygmies. (Page 173)
33. **Roberts & Schuele (1990):** Demonstrated that infection of middle ear in children is related to language and intellectual deficits. (Page 175)
34. **Takeuchi & Hulse (1993):** Demonstrated a possible critical period for the ability to detect specific pitch. (Page 176)
35. **Békésy (1957):** Researched the relationship between frequency and point at which maximal vibration occurred in the oval window. (Page 176).
36. **Danenberg, Loos-Cosgrove, & LoVerde (1987):** Examined hearing loss in an audience at a rock concert. (Page 177)
37. **Raloff (1982):** Examined the differences in hearing abilities cross-culturally. (Page 177)
38. **Tye-Murray, Spencer & Woodworth (1995):** Examined the hearing of cochlear implant recipients. (Page 177)
39. **Morrongiello et al. (1994):** Demonstrated that newborn human infants have the ability to localize sounds. (Page 178)
40. **Schaal (1988):** Examined infants ability to identify caregivers by odors. (Page 179)
41. **Lorig et al (1990):** Examined the influence of small concentrations of odors on mood. (Page 179)
42. **Schiffman, Suggs, & Sattely-Miller (1995):** Showed mood enhancements in subjects who wore cologne. (Page 180)
43. **Herz & Cupchik (1992):** Demonstrated the types of memories evoked by odors. (Page 180)
44. **Richardson & Zucco (1989):** Demonstrated no consistent relationship between chemical molecule shape and size to odor production. (Page 180)
45. **Bartoshuk & Beauchamp (1994):** Demonstrated that olfaction depends on stimulation of different receptors. (Page 180)
46. **Russell (1976):** Tested students in their ability to identify their own shirts by odor. (Page 180)
47. **Singer & Macrides (1990):** Studied the effects of aphrodisin, a vaginal pheromone, on copulatory behavior in hamsters. (Page 180)
48. **Maugh (1982); Filsinger et al (1984),** and **Weller & Weller (1995):** All three studies examined the role of pheromones in human sexual attraction. (Page 181)
49. **Bartoshuk (1991):** Demonstrated the relationship between flavor and smell. (Page 181)
50. **Catherwood (1993):** Examined infants reliance on the sense of touch at 8 months. (Page 182)
51. **Sumino & Dubner (1981):** Examined the types of thermal receptors in the human skin. (Page 183)

52. **Darian-Smith (1982):** Demonstrated that thermal receptors detect changes in skin temperature rather then actual temperatures. (Page 183)
53. **Dray & Perkins (1993):** Identified the collection of bradykinin at inflamation sites. (Page 183).
54. **Inoki et al. (1978):** Examined the effect of aspirin on bradykinin release and pain effects. (Page 183)
55. **Holland, Goldstein & Aronstam (1993):** Suggested a connection between gate-control theory of pain and substance P. (Page 184)
56. **Droste et al (1991):** Examined the correlation between pain and endorphin levels. (Page 184)
57. **Wang, Mao, & Han (1990):** Examined the role of endorphins in acupuncture pain relief. (Page 184)
58. **Marchaand et al (1993); Schwolow Wilckens & Roth (1988); Solomon & Guglielmo (1985),** and **Walsh et al (1995):** All studies examined the use of TENS for pain relief in various settings. (Page 184)
59. **Wang, Mao, & Han (1992):** Examined the effect of naloxone on pain relief using TENS. (Page 184)
60. **Chaves (1994):** Demonstrated the use of hypnosis as a pain-relief mechanism. (Page 184)
61. **Joubert & van Os (1989):** Examined naloxone effects on hypnotic pain relief. (Page 185)
62. **Vessey, Carlson & McGill (1994):** Demonstrated pain relief in children using distraction. (Page 185)
63. **Anderson, Baron, & Logan (1991):** Examined the use of music to diminish pain. (Page 185)
64. **Prud'homme, Cohen, & Kalaska (1994):** Demonstrated the activity in specific regions of somatosensory cortex with limb movements. (Page 185)
65. **Wang et al. (1993):** Demonstrated that alcohol intoxication impaired movement via disruptions of sense of limb position. (Page 185)
66. **Post et al. (1994):** Examined effects of alcohol intoxication on tracking of baseball. (Page 186)
67. **Antunano & Hernandez (1989):** Examined the incidence of motion sickness in paratroopers over numerous jumps. (Page 186)
68. **Messer & Griggs (1989)** and **Clarke (1991):** Examined the belief in the paranormal by college students. (Page 187).
69. **Ullman, Krippner, & Vaughan (1973):** Reported a successful demonstration of mental telepathy. (Page 187)
70. **Hearne (1989):** Reported an unsuccessful demonstration of mental telepathy. (Page 188)
71. **Sweat & Durm (1993):** Surveyed police departments on the success of clairvoyants and crime solutions. (Page 188)
72. **Palmer, Honorton, & Utts (1989):** Report by the National Academy of Science on the lack of evidence for paranormal activity. (Page 188)
73. **A Psychic Watergate (1981):** James Randi debunked the prediction of a woman with claims of precognition. (Page 189)

PRACTICE TEST A

1. The case of the man who mistook his wife's head for a hat illustrates the difference between
    a. sensation and cognition.
    b. perception and cognition.
    c. sensation and perception.
    d. psychophysics and signal detection.

Obj.: 1 Page: 152

2. Sensation involves
    a. organization and interpretation of a raw environmental input.
    b. stimulation of a receptor by a stimulus in the environment.
    c. detecting movement in our bodies
    d. psychological information about the environment.

Obj.:2 Page: 153

3. A psychologist presents you with a particular odor several times, each time varying its intensity, and asks you to report when you notice the odor. She would be testing your
    a. absolute threshold.
    b. relative threshold.
    c. subliminal threshold.
    d. differential threshold.

Obj.: 3 Page: 153

4. If you are presented with an unchanging stimulus, there will be a tendency for your sensory receptors to respond less and less to it. This is called
   a. sensory overload.
   b. sensory deprivation.
   c. sensory adaptation.
   d. sensory assimilation.

Obj.: 4 Page: 154-155

5. We are able to see objects because they
   a. reflect light.
   b. absorb light.
   c. refract light.
   d. are saturated with light.

Obj.: 5 Page: 155-156

6. If a person's left optic nerve is completely severed, he would be
   a. blind in his left eye.
   b. blind in his left visual field.
   c. blind in his right visual field.
   d. able to detect objects, but not identify them, with his left eye.

Obj.: 6 Page: 159-160

7. What occurs during dark adaptation?
   a. There is a shift from cone to rod vision.
   b. The cones inhibit the responsiveness of the rods.
   c. The rate of synthesizing iodopsin and rhodopsin decreases.
   d. The rods will reach their maximum sensitivity in about 10 minutes.

Obj.: 7 Page: 160-162

8. If you stare at a red surface and then at a white surface, you will see an afterimage that is
   a. red.
   b. blue.
   c. green.
   d. yellow.

Obj.: 8 Page: 163

9. Who would most likely support the ecological theory of visual perception?
   a. Hermann von Helmholtz
   b. James Gibson
   c. John Locke
   d. Thomas Young

Obj.: 9 Page: 164

10. What theory states that we construct our perception from the activity of certain brain cells that are sensitive to specific attributes of stimuli?
    a. spatial frequency filter theory
    b. figure-ground theory
    c. feature-detector theory
    d. constructionist theory

Obj.: 10 Page: 164-165

11. As you drive down a country road, you pass nearby cows faster than you pass distant mountains. This is an example of the depth perception cue known as
    a. convergence.
    b. accommodation.
    c. motion parallax.
    d. aerial perspective.

Obj.: 11 Page: 168

12. The best explanation of the moon illusion is suggested by
    a. the relative-size hypothesis.
    b. the apparent-distance hypothesis.
    c. the angle-of-view hypothesis.
    d. no one theory, though a modified version of the relative-size hypothesis may turn out to be the best candidate.

Obj.: 12 Page: 170-171

13. In Max von Senden's research on individuals who have been blind from birth and then gained their sense of vision as adults, what perceptual abilities appeared to be inborn and which appeared to require experience?
    a. Color vision and the ability to distinguish figure from ground appeared to be inborn; visual recognition appeared to require experience.
    b. Visual recognition appeared to be inborn; color vision and the ability to distinguish figure from ground appeared to require experience.
    c. Visual recognition and color vision appeared to be inborn, and the ability to distinguish figure from ground appeared to require experience.
    d. All visual perception appears to require previous experience during a critical period of development.

Obj.: 13 Page: 172

14. Chewing gum during an airplane descent aids the functioning of the
   a. pinna.
   b. cochlea.
   c. ossicles.
   d. eustachian tube.

Obj.: 14 Page: 175

15. If your friend were to argue that discrimination of different pitches occurs because sound waves of different frequency cause the cochlea's basilar membrane to vibrate in direct proportion to the frequency of the sound, which theory would your friend be proposing?
   a. Volley theory.
   b. Frequency theory.
   c. Place theory.
   d. Gate-control theory.

Obj.: 15 Page: 175-179

16. Pheromones are
   a. odors that attract sexual interest in animals.
   b. artificial chemicals produced for aphrodisiac purposes.
   c. perfume samples.
   d. the bond that connects sexual mates.

Obj.: 16 Page: 179-181

17. Where do you find the receptors for the detection of flavor?
   a. in the mouth.
   b. in the skin
   c. both a and d
   d. In the mucous membrane that lines the nasal cavity.

Obj.: 17 Page: 181

18. Touch sensations would be disrupted by damage to the
   a. frontal lobes.
   b. temporal lobes.
   c. parietal lobes.
   d. occipital lobes.

Obj.: 18 Page: 182

19. An effective pain reliever might inhibit the release of
   a. dopamine.
   b. endorphins.
   c. bradykinin.
   d. acetylcholine.

Obj.: 19 Page: 183

20. The kinesthetic sense enables one to
   a. perceive the movement of objects.
   b. detect the position of one's limbs.
   c. allegedly move objects with one's mind.
   d. sense changes in the temperature of objects.

Obj.: 20 Page: 185

21. If you could get the answers to this exam by reading your professor's mind, you would demonstrate
   a. precognition.
   b. clairvoyance.
   c. psychokinesis.
   d. mental telepathy.

Obj.: 21 Page: 187

PRACTICE TEST B

1. The muffled sounds you hear through your apartment's thin walls comprise ________. Your realization that those sounds are your neighbors arguing about money comprises ______________.
   a. sensation; perception
   b. perception; sensation
   c. sensation; transduction
   d. perception; the absolute threshold

Obj.: 1 Page: 152

2. Sensory ____________ detect stimuli and convert them into neural impulses through a process known as sensory ___________.
   a. receptors; processing
   b. unspecialized cells; transduction
   c. receptors; transduction
   d. transducers; receptors

Obj: 2 Page 152

3. On a hearing test, the technician needs to determine the smallest sound you can hear about half the time it occurs. This is a procedure involving
   a. the jnd.
   b. saccadic movements.
   c. absolute threshold.
   d. sensory adaptation.

Obj.: 3 Page: 153

4. Your friend lives in the flight path of a major airport. When you visit him, you are disturbed by the intense noise and vibration of passing planes. Your friend pays no attention to the noise and can sleep or talk right through it. Your friend's behavior is explained by the principle of
   a. response bias.
   b. the absolute threshold.
   c. sensory adaptation.
   d. sensory transduction.

Obj.: 4 Page: 154

5. You see your significant other across the room. Light from your significant other is focused by your __________ onto your ________.
   a. pupil; lens
   b. lens; retina
   c. retina; fovea
   d. fovea; pupil

Obj.: 5 Page: 156

6. Light entering the eye must first pass through a layer of
   a. rods.
   b. cones.
   c. ganglion cells.
   d. bipolar cells.

Obj.: 6 Page: 156-160

7. What sensory process explains the following phenomenon? It is the middle of the night, you get up to get a drink of water and turn on the light in your room. Upon returning to your room and turning off the lights, you are unable to see anything for a good 10 minutes and can't see well for 30.
   a. This example illustrates the principle of light adaptation. Your cones have been bleached and you need them to see in the dark.
   b. This example illustrates the principle of dark adaptation. Your cones have been bleached and you need them to see in the dark.
   c. This example illustrates the principle of light adaptation. Your rods have been bleached and you need them to see in the dark.
   d. This example illustrates the principle of dark adaptation. Your rod have been bleached and you need them to see in the dark.

Obj.: 7 Page: 161

8. In explaining color vision current day vision researchers claim that at the level of the cones color vision occurs via a(n) ________ process but along the neural path from cones to cortex the process is a(n) ____________ one.
   a. opponent ; trichromatic
   b. inhibitory; excitatory
   c. trichromatic; inhibitory
   d. trichromatic ; opponent

Obj: 8 Page: 162-164

9. You feel that perceptions are created by the brain through the use of inborn mechanisms that automatically convert sensations into perceptions. Which theory are you arguing?
   a. Helmholtz's ecological theory
   b. Gibson's constructionist theory
   c. Helmholtz's constructionist theory
   d. Gibson's ecological theory

Obj: 9 Page: 164

10.

```
* * * * * *
# # # # # #
* * * * * *
# # # # # #
```

In the above figure, the fact that we organize this image into rows of asterisks and pound signs illustrates the Gestalt principle of:
   a. proximity
   b. closure
   c. similarity
   d. figure-ground

Obj.: 10 Page: 165

11. Rodney lost sight in one eye after an accident. Yet he is able to drive his truck safely. To judge the distance of other vehicles, he makes use of
   a. monocular cues such as accommodation.
   b. retinal disparity and convergence.
   c. binocular cues such as interposition.
   d. size and shape constancies.

Obj.: 11 Page: 168

12. Which of the following best explains why we experience visual illusions?
   a. The visual image is processed right side up instead of upside down in the retina.
   b. The auditory system has misinterpreted the information it received.
   c. Image cues are misapplied.
   d. The individual is experiencing a psychotic episode.

Obj.: 12 Page: 171

13. The correct structure sequence that sound stimulates in the ear is
   a. eardrum, oval window, ossicles, and cochlea.
   b. oval window, ossicles, eardrum, and cochlea.
   c. cochlea, oval window, eardrum, and ossicles.
   d. eardrum, ossicles, oval window, and cochlea.

Obj.: 14 Page: 175

14. You get into a discussion with a classmate about how people are able to tell the difference between the pitch of sounds. If your friend were to argue that this occurs because sound waves of different frequency displace different regions on the cochlear basilar membrane, which theory would the friend be proposing?
   a. Volley theory.
   b. Frequency theory.
   c. Place theory.
   d. Gate-control theory

Obj.: 15 Page: 176

15. When Laura's date appears wearing a particular cologne, Laura is overcome with powerful memories of her first husband, who also wore that cologne. Most likely, this response occurs because
   a. the cologne releases one of the seven basic odors and the brain responds powerfully.
   b. there are many connections between the limbic system and the olfactory nerves.
   c. all olfactory stimuli are processed in the thalamus rather than the cortex.
   d. colognes containing pheromones are likely to release emotional and sexual memories.

Obj.: 16 Page: 180

16. Charlotte notices that whenever she has a head cold she tends to eat less. This is because
   a. stuffy noses decrease the experience of flavor in foods.
   b. mucus from a cold paralyzes the action of the taste buds on the tongue.
   c. the olfactory epithelium requires one of the seven basic smells to fire.
   d. the toxins produced by cold viruses damage the olfactory epithelium and papillae.

Obj.: 17 Page: 181

17. When Lucille first walks into the ocean, the water feels very cold. After a short time, it begins to feel very pleasant and comfortable. This change comes about because
   a. cold receptors are inhibited from firing and warm receptors transmit only warmth.
   b. temperature receptors in the skin adapt to the ongoing stimulation.
   c. nociceptive receptors continue to fire until some threshold is reached.
   d. warm and cold receptors fire simultaneously, thus producing the sensation of comfort.

Obj.: 18 Page: 183

18. After getting her finger caught in a drawer, Ruth holds her finger tightly, and this seems to reduce the pain somewhat. Most likely, this works because
   a. A-delta fibers cannot fire in response to the sharp pain caused by a closing drawer.
   b. touch sensations pass through a part of the spinal cord that closes the pain gate.
   c. pressure receptors fire and thus inhibit the firing of free nerve endings in the skin.
   d. touch releases substance P from the pain receptors and this reduces pain sensations.

Obj.: 19 Page: 184

19. What is the purpose of kinesthesis and the vestibular sense?
   a. They help us to interpret the auditory information the environment presents.
   b. They help us to interpret the sensory information the environment presents.
   c. They help us to integrate all the sensory input to the body.
   d. They help us to keep track of, orient, and regulate the position of our body and body parts in space.

Obj.: 20 Page: 186

20. The concept of ESP implies that
    a. when it comes to understanding how we know about the external environment, the scientific method is useless.
    b. the kinesthetic and vestibular senses respond to stimuli other than limb and head movements.
    c. it is possible to have knowledge of external stimuli without stimulation of the sensory receptors.
    d. there are several types of sensory receptors in the body that are still undiscovered.

Obj.: 21 Page: 187

ESSAY QUESTIONS

1. Your friend Sue has recently been having numerous "weird" things happen to her over the past few months. Her first symptom was that she lost her ability to see. Then a few week later, already blind, she lost her hearing and her sense of taste. The doctors have ruled out problems with her eyes, ears, and taste buds. They have hospitalized her and diagnosed a brain tumor. Based on your knowledge of how these sensory systems enter the brain, localize the tumor.

Obj.: 6, 15, 16 Page: 156-160; 175-179; 179-181

2. You told the server to "hold the anchovies" on your pizza. Describe how a bite or two of the pizza will lead you to determine whether or not anchovies are present.

Obj.: 17 Page: 179-181

ANSWER RECORD FOR CHAPTER 5

Comprehensive Guided Review:

1. sensory
2. psychophysics
3. stimulus
4. Sensation
5. Perception
6. prosopagnosia
7. voices
8. sensations
9. organize
10. cells
11. impulses
12. receptors
13. 50
14. absolute threshold
15. intensity
16. psychological
17. ready
18. Signal detection
19 hit
20. false alarm
21. correct rejection
22. miss
23. intensity
24. difference
25. Fechner
26. jnd
27. original
28. Weber's
29. unchanging
30. sensory adaptation
31. faster

Mini-review of Sensory Processes:
1. I; 2. J; 3. B; 4. D; 5. F; 6. C; 7. H; 8. E; 9. G; 10. K; 11. L; 12. A

32. visual
33. eyes
34. energy
35. physical
36. wavelength
37. color
38. violet
39. long
40. receptors
41. amplitude
42. intensity
43. purity
44. saturated
45. eye
46. sclera
47. muscles
48. arousal
49. dilate
50. phobias
51. light
52. shape
53. aging
54. myopia
55. hyperopia
56. upside down
57. neural
58. photoreceptors
59. cones
60. bipolar
61. rods
62. high
63. cones
64. increase
65. fovea
66. focused
67. smooth pursuit
68. Alcohol

Anatomy of a Contemporary Research Study: Can Batters Really Keep Their Eyes on the Ball?

What was the rationale for the study?
Studies had shown that professional athletes had faster smooth pursuit movements than amateurs. The authors wanted to know if the pros were truly keeping their eyes on the ball.

What methods did the authors use to test their hypothesis?
They had a device that pitched a ball over a plate at a consistent speed and path. They then recorded the eye movements of batters with a photoelectric device. Subjects were professional baseball players.

What was the outcome of the study and what did the authors conclude the results meant?
Results showed that the subjects tracked the ball to within 5 feet of the plate. Thus it was impossible to "keep your eye on the ball" any closer. They then suggest that good players calculate the speed and path, and their brain creates a perception of where they think the ball should be.

---

69. saccadic
70. fixate
71. retinal
72. blind
73. Mariotte
74. no
75. frontal
76. chiasm
77. nose
78. same
79. midbrain
80. thalamus
81. occipital
82. scotoma
83. perception
84. left
85. cortex
86. phosphenes
87. photopigments
88. rods
89. iodsopin
90. impulses
91. dark adaptation
92. sensitive
93. rods
94. rhodopsin
95. cones
96. 10
97. rods
98. low
99. opponent-process
100. trichromatic theory
101. Wald
102. additive
103. pigments
104. afterimages
105. red-green
106. brightness
107. inhibits
108. de Valois
109. thalamus
110. color blindness
111. opponent-process
112. trichromats
113. dichromats
114. red-green
115. monochromats
116. X
117. both
118. sensation
119. retina
120. sensations
121. Helmholtz
122. direct perception
123. Gibson
124. form
125. figure-ground
126. Gestalt
127. expectations
128. Proximity
129. Similarity
130. Closure
131. Continuity
132. wholes
133. Hubel
134. holistically
135. cortex
136. variations
137. form
138. depth
139. Binocular
140. retinal disparity
141. convergence
142. Monocular
143. shape
144. Motion parallax
145. Interposition
146. size
147. closer
148. higher
149. Shading
150. Aerial perspective
151. coarser
152. perceptual constancies
153. stable
154. Size
155. Shape
156. Brightness
157. misapplication
158. misperception
159. larger
160. overhead
161. relative-size
162. experiences

Anatomy of a Classic Research Study: Can Early Experience Affect the Development of the Visual Pathways?

What was the rationale for the study?
Blakemore and Cooper wanted to know if rearing kittens in limited visual environments would affect the development of visual feature detectors in the brain?

What methods did the authors use to test their hypothesis?
The authors raised kittens in darkness expect for a 5-hour period each day when they were placed in a large cylinder with either vertical or horizontal stripes. This was done from the age of 2 weeks until the kittens were 5 months old. The kittens' vision was tested after 5 months by waving a wand in front of them either horizontally or vertically.

What was the outcome of the study and what did the authors conclude the results meant?
Kittens raised with horizontal stripes only responded to the wand when it was waved horizontally, not vertically, and the opposite was true of the kittens reared with the vertical stripes. The authors concluded that the visual cortex has feature detectors for horizontal and vertical movements and that their development is dependent on experience.

---

163. Senden
164. colors
165. recognizing
166. cultural
167. Pygmy

Mini-review on Visual System:
1. Nn; 2. R; 3. A; 4. J; 5. K; 6. S; 7. F; 8. W; 9. P; 10. T; 11. I; 12. B; 13. E; 14. D; 15. Dd; 16. L; 17. Ff; 18. Mm; 19. Ll; 20. O; 21. H; 22. C; 23. Q; 24. G; 25. Uu; 26. Bb; 27. N; 28. M; 29. Y; 30. V; 31. Ss; 32. Gg; 33. X; 34. Z; 35. U; 36. Pp; 37. Aa; 38. Hh; 39. Ee; 40. Ii; 41. Jj; 42. Qq; 43. Kk; 44. Rr; 45. Tt; 46. Cc; 47. Oo; 48. Vv

168. sounds
169. vibrations
170. waves
171. medium
172. amplitude
173. frequency
174. ear
175. outer
176. middle
177. inner
178. pinna
179. eardrum
180. ossicles
181. incus
182. oval window
183. cochlea
184. auditory
185. thalamus
186. cortex
187. pitch
188. place
189. frequency
190. volley
191. loudness
192. firing thresholds
193. decibel
194. mechanical
195. Conduction
196. plastic
197. inner
198. nerve
199. cochlear
200. quality
201. timbre
202. source
203. intensities
204. arrival

Mini-review on Auditory System:
1. C; 2. D; 3. B; 4. H; 5. N; 6. F; 7. K; 8. O; 9. A; 10. F; 11. I; 12. J; 13. M; 14. G; 15. L

205. smell
206. air
207. patterns
208. olfactory
209. thalamus
210. emotional
211. seven
212. mixtures
213. molecules
214. threshold
215. copulatory
216. pheromones
217. taste
218. tongue
219. saliva
220. buds
221. salty
222. Flavor
223. temperature
224. communicate
225. pattern
226. sight
227. Braille
228. attachments
229. concentration
230. temperature
231. cold
232. changes
233. pain
234. nociceptors
235. pricking
236. dull
237. inflammation
238. morphine
239. axons
240. endorphins
241. Anzio
242. Placebos
243. acupuncture
244. opiates
245. opiates
246. pain
247. electrical
248. endorphins
249. outside
250. kinesthetic
251. receptors
252. position
253. vestibular
254. otolith
255. balance
256. hair
257. rotary
258. motion
259. visual
260. semicircular canals

Mini-review on Chemical, Skin and Body Senses:
1. I; 2. J; 3. U; 4. N; 5. R; 6. E; 7. V; 8. O; 9. A; 10. T; 11. G; 12. P; 13. H; 14. L; 15. B; 16. K; 17. D; 18. M; 19. F; 20. S; 21. Q; 22. C

261. extra sensory perception
262. parapsychology
263. Mental telepathy
264. Clairvoyance
265. Precognition
266. déjà vu
267. Psychokinesthesis
268. skeptical
269. scientific
270. controlled
271. Chance
272. replicating

Practice Test A:

1. a. Incorrect: Cognition is thinking; the man's problem was in recognition (perception) of what he saw (sensed).
   b. Incorrect: Cognition is thinking; the man's problem was in recognition (perception) of what he saw (sensed).
   c. **Correct: Cognition is thinking; the man's problem was in recognition (perception) of what he saw (sensed).**
   d. Incorrect: The man's problem was in recognition (perception) of what he saw (sensed).

2. a. Incorrect: The organization of raw environmental input is perception.
   b. **Correct: Sensation is the stimulation of a receptor by an environmental stimulus.**
   c. Incorrect: Detection of movement in our body involves sensation, but is not sensation alone.
   d. Incorrect: Sensation is the stimulation of a receptor by an environmental stimulus.

3. a. **Correct: This description is of a test of absolute threshold.**
   b. Incorrect: There is no such term mentioned in your text.
   c. Incorrect: The measurement is of the minimum amount of substance that your are able to detect; subliminal refers to information beneath awareness.
   d. Incorrect: There is a difference threshold mentioned in the text, but not a differential.

4. a. Incorrect: Sensory overload is not a term used in this chapter.
   b. Incorrect: Sensory deprivation refers to the absence of sensory input.
   c. **Correct: The description is the definition of sensory adaptation.**
   d. Incorrect: This term is also not discussed in the chapter.

5. a. **Correct: Light waves are refracted back into our eyes by the object that we are seeing.**
   b. Incorrect: If the object absorbed all the light, we would perceive it to be black due to the absence of any light reflected back to the eye.
   c. Incorrect: Prisms refract light by breaking it down into its different wavelengths or colors.
   d. Incorrect: The saturation of light is a characteristic that refers to the vividness of the light.

6. a. **Correct: The left optic nerve serves the left eye.**
   b. Incorrect: The left optic nerve carries all the information to the left eye.
   c. Incorrect: The left optic nerve serves the left eye.
   d. Incorrect: The left optic nerve carries all the sensory information to the left eye.

7. a. **Correct: Dark adaptation involves the transition from seeing in high light to seeing in the dark. This requires the shift from use of cones to use of rods.**
   b. Incorrect: The cones do not inhibit the rods.
   c. Incorrect: The rate of synthesizing rhodopsin would increase.
   d. Incorrect: The rods do not reach their maximum sensitivity for 20-30 minutes.

8. a. Incorrect: You will see the opponent color to red, which is green.
   b. Incorrect: You will see the opponent color to red, which is green.
   c. Correct: You will see the opponent color to red, which is green.
   d. Incorrect: You will see the opponent color to red, which is green.

9. a. Incorrect: von Helmholtz proposed the trichromatic theory of color vision.
   b. Correct: Gibson did propose the ecological theory of visual perception.
   c. Incorrect: John Locke did not propose a theory of vision.
   d. Incorrect: Thomas Young proposed the trichromatic theory of color vision.

10. a. Incorrect: Spatial frequency filter theory holds that perception depends on constructing figures based on detection of patterns of light and dark.
    b. Incorrect: Figure-ground theory does not exist; psychologists discuss figure-ground perception, which involves the distinction of an object from its surroundings.
    c. Correct: Feature-detector theory argues that our perception is constructed from the activity of certain brain cells sensitive to the attributes of the stimuli.
    d. Incorrect: Constructionist theory argues that we learn through experience to convert sensation into accurate perceptions.

11. a. Incorrect: Convergence is the degree to which eyes turn inward to focus on the object.
    b. Incorrect: Accommodation refers to a monocular cue to depth perception that involves the change of shape of the lens.
    c. Correct: Motion parallax is the tendency for objects closer to us to be perceived as being passed faster than those at a distance.
    d. Incorrect: aerial perspective is a depth-perception cue that objects closer to us appear clearer than those farther away.

12. a. Incorrect: The relative-size explanation does not fully explain this.
    b. Incorrect: The apparent-distance hypothesis claims that the horizon is perceived as farther away; however, evidence shows that this is not true.
    c. Incorrect: The angle-of-view hypothesis is not discussed in your text.
    d. Correct: Psychologists do not agree as to the explanation of the illusion; however they do feel that a modification of the relative-size hypothesis will turn out to be best.

13. **a. Correct: Color vision and figure-ground perception were present in the subjects immediately; however, visual recognition was not.**
    b. Incorrect: Color vision and figure-ground perception were present in the subjects immediately; however, visual recognition was not.
    c. Incorrect: Color vision and figure-ground perception were present in the subjects immediately; however, visual recognition was not.
    d. Incorrect: Color vision and figure-ground perception were present in the subjects immediately; however, visual recognition was not.

14. a. Incorrect: The pinna is the outer part of the ear; chewing gum relieves pressure in the eustachian tubes.
    b. Incorrect: The cochlea is a structure of the inner ear; chewing gum relieves pressure in the eustachian tubes.
    c. Incorrect: The ossicles are the small bones in the middle ear; chewing gum relieves pressure in the eustachian tubes.
    d. Correct: Chewing gum relieves pressure in the eustachian tubes.

15. a. Incorrect: Volley theory argues that sound waves of particular frequencies induce auditory neurons to fire in volleys.
    b. Correct: Frequency theory argues that the cochlear basilar membrane vibrates in direct proportion to the frequency of the sound.
    c. Incorrect: Place theory suggests that different places on the basilar membrane vibrate maximally in response to sound waves of specific frequencies.
    d. Incorrect: Gate-control theory is a theory of pain perception.

16. **a. Correct: Pheromones are odors that attract sexual interest in animals.**
    b. Incorrect: Pheromones have not been shown to be effective in humans.
    c. Incorrect: Although pheromones have been added to perfumes, they are not perfumes.
    d. Incorrect: Pheromones are odors that attract sexual interest in animals.

17. a. Incorrect: Flavor perception appears to involve both the senses of taste and smell, thus the receptors would be found in both the mouth and the nose.
    b. Incorrect: Flavor perception appears to involve both the senses of taste and smell, thus the receptors would be found in both the mouth and the nose.
    c. Correct: Flavor perception appears to involve both the senses of taste and smell, thus the receptors would be found in both the mouth and the nose.
    d. Incorrect: Flavor perception appears to involve both the senses of taste and smell, thus the receptors would be found in both the mount and the nose.

18. a. Incorrect: The somatosensory cortex is located in the parietal lobe.
    b. Incorrect: The somatosensory cortex is located in the parietal lobe.
    c. **Correct: The somatosensory cortex is located in the parietal lobe.**
    d. Incorrect: The somatosensory cortex is located in the parietal lobe.

19. a. Incorrect: Dopamine has not been shown to be involved in pain.
    b. Incorrect: Endorphins are believed to be involved in the closing of the pain gate, thus you would want to enhance their release.
    c. **Correct: Bradykinin accumulates at the site of the inflammation and thus is believed to be involved in pain.**
    d. Incorrect: Acetylcholine has not been implicated in pain.

20. a. Incorrect: The kinesthetic sense is the sense responsible for sensation of body, or limb movement.
    b. **Correct: The kinesthetic sense is the sense responsible for sensation of body or limb movement.**
    c. Incorrect: The kinesthetic sense is the sense responsible for sensation of body or limb movement. Mental telepathy is the alleged movement of objects using one's mind.
    d. Incorrect: The kinesthetic sense is the sense responsible for sensation of body, or limb movement.

21. a. Incorrect: Precognition is the alleged ability to perceive events in the future.
    b. Incorrect: Clairvoyance is the alleged ability to perceive objects or events without having sensory contact with them.
    c. Incorrect: Psychokinesis refers to the alleged ability to control objects with the mind alone.
    d. **Correct: Mental telepathy refers to the alleged ability to read someone's mind.**

Practice Test B

1. a. **Correct: Sensation is the hearing of sounds; perception is organizing them into meaningful units.**
   b. Incorrect: Sensation is the hearing of sounds; perception is organizing them into meaningful units.
   c. Incorrect: Sensation is the hearing of sounds; transduction is the mechanism by which sensation occurs.
   d. Incorrect: Perception is the process of organizing sensations into meaningful units; absolute threshold is the minimum amount of stimulation needed for a sensation.

2. a. Incorrect: Receptors do detect stimuli but the process is known as sensory transduction, not processing.
   b. Incorrect: Specialized cells do the processing, not unspecialized ones.
   c. **Correct: Receptors do detect stimuli and the process is known as sensory transduction.**
   d. Incorrect: The cells are not known as transducers.

3. a. Incorrect: The jnd refers to the difference between two stimuli.
   b. Incorrect: Saccadic movements bring new portions of the visual field into focus.
   c. **Correct: The absolute threshold is a measurement of the smallest amount of stimulation a system can detect.**
   d. Incorrect: Sensory adaptation is the tendency of receptors to respond only to changes in stimulation.

4. a. Incorrect: Response bias refers to the tendency to respond to those stimuli you expect.
   b. Incorrect: Absolute threshold refers to whether your friend senses the planes, not whether he responds to them.
   c. **Correct: Your friend always hears the planes, thus has adapted to the constant sounds; since they are new to you, you hear them.**
   d. Incorrect: Sensory transduction refers to the mechanism by which your ears process the sounds.

5. a. Incorrect: Light passes through the pupil, is focused by the lens onto the retina.
   b. **Correct: Light passes through the pupil, is focused by the lens onto the retina.**
   c. Incorrect; Light passes through the pupil, is focused by the lens onto the retina at the fovea.
   d. Incorrect: Light passes through the pupil, is focused by the lens onto the retina at the fovea.

6. a. Incorrect: The rods and cones are along the back wall of the eye.
   b. Incorrect: The rods and cones are lined along the back wall of the eye.
   c. **Correct: The ganglion cells are in front of the receptor cells in the retina of the eye.**
   d. Incorrect: There is no subcutaneous fat in the eye.

7. a. Incorrect: Light adaptation occurs when you go from dark to light.
   b. Incorrect: Dark adaptation involves shifting from using cones to using rods.
   c. Incorrect: Light adaptation occurs when you go from dark to light.
   d. Correct: Dark adaptation involves adjusting from being in light to seeing in the dark and involves shifting to the use of rods.

8. a. Incorrect: Opponent process has been shown to occur at the level of the brain.
   b. Incorrect: There are not any color vision theories that discuss inhibition in the cones.
   c. Incorrect: Trichromatic does occur in the cones, but there is no such thing as an inhibitory theory of color vision.
   d. Correct: Trichromatic theory explains color vision at the level of the cones; opponent process explains how the visual cortex works.

9. a. Incorrect: Helmholtz did not develop the ecological theory.
   b. Incorrect: Gibson did not develop the constructionist theory.
   c. Incorrect: Helmholtz's constructionist theory argues that we learn theory experience to create perceptions.
   d. Correct: Gibson's ecological theory argues that inborn mechanisms allow us to create perceptions from sensations.

10. a. Incorrect: The items are being grouped because they are alike, not because they are close to one another.
    b. Incorrect: The items are being grouped because they are alike, not because they made a pattern.
    c. Correct: The items are being grouped because they are alike.
    d. Incorrect: The items are all the figure.

11. **a. Correct: Depth perception using one eye uses monocular cues like accommodation.**
    b. Incorrect: Retinal disparity and convergence are binocular cues.
    c. Incorrect: Interposition is a monocular cue, not binocular.
    d. Incorrect: Size and shape constancies do not provide information on distance and depth.

12. a. Incorrect: Visual illusions are the result of misperception of sensory information.
    b. Incorrect: Visual illusions are the result of misperception of visual information.
    c. Correct: Visual illusions are the result of misperception of sensory information.
    d. Incorrect: Visual illusions are the result of misperception of sensory information.

13. a. Incorrect: The air stimulates the eardrum, which causes the ossicles (bones) in the middle ear to vibrate; the vibration is transferred to the oval window and the cochlea.
    b. Incorrect: The air stimulates the eardrum, which causes the ossicles (bones) in the middle ear to vibrate; the vibration is transferred to the oval window and the cochlea.
    c. Incorrect: The air stimulates the eardrum, which causes the ossicles (bones) in the middle ear to vibrate; the vibration is transferred to the oval window and the cochlea.
    d. Correct: The air stimulates the eardrum, which causes the ossicles (bones) in the middle ear to vibrate; the vibration is transferred to the oval window and the cochlea.

14. a. Incorrect: Volley theory argues that sound waves cause groups of auditory neurons to fire in volleys.
    b. Correct: Frequency theory argues that the basilar membrane vibrates as a whole in proportion to the frequency of the sound.
    c. Incorrect: Place theory states that hair cells at specific points on the membrane respond to different frequencies.
    d. Incorrect: Gate-control theory is a theory of pain, not sound.

15. a. Incorrect: The olfactory system has connections to the limbic system, which is involved in emotional responses.
    b. Correct: The olfactory system has connections to the limbic system, which is involved in emotional responses.
    c. Incorrect: Olfaction is the only one of the external senses whose input does not go to the thalamus before going to the cortex.
    d. Incorrect: Research into pheromones in humans has not indicated effects like those seen in animals.

16. **a. Correct: Flavors are related to both taste and smell.**
    b. Incorrect: The mucus of the cold blocks the olfactory receptors in the nose, not the taste buds.
    c. Incorrect: The type of smell does not matter.
    d. Incorrect: The mucus of the cold blocks, but does not damage the olfactory receptors.

17. a. Incorrect: Both the warm and cold receptors will adapt.
    b. Correct: The skin temperature receptors undergo sensory adaptation; they respond to changes in temperature.
    c. Incorrect: Nociceptive receptors do undergo sensory adaptation.
    d. Incorrect: Both the warm and cold receptors have undergone sensory adaptation.

18. a. Incorrect: The A-delta fibers do send the pain message, but it is blocked at the level of the spinal cord.
    b. Correct: Touch sensations do send a message that closes the pain gate at the level of the spinal cord.
    c. Incorrect: The blocking of the input occurs at the level of the spinal cord, not at the free nerve ending.
    d. Incorrect: It is the inhibition of substance P, not the release of substance P that reduces the pain.

19. a. Incorrect: These two senses allow for the ability to keep track of the heads position and maintain balance.
    b. Incorrect: These two senses allow for the ability to keep track of the heads position and maintain balance.
    c. Incorrect: These two senses allow for the ability to keep track of the heads position and maintain balance.
    d. Correct: These two senses allow for the ability to keep track of the heads position and maintain balance

20. a. Incorrect: Psychologists find the scientific method very useful; they claim that parapsychologists do not use it properly.
    b. Incorrect: These two senses allow for the ability to keep track of the heads position and maintain balance only.
    c. Correct: ESP suggests that it is possible to have knowledge of external sensory environments without sensory receptors.
    d. Incorrect: Parapsychologists do not feel that there are sensory receptors for ESP.

Essay Questions:

1. Since vision, audition, and taste are all affected by the tumor, the most logical place for the tumor to be is the thalamus. The initial inputs from all three sensory systems enter through the thalamus.

2. Chemical stimulation of the olfactory epithelium (smell) will be the first test of the anchovies' presence or absence; that is, we may smell them. If we are unsure, then we must taste the pizza. Chemical stimulation of the taste buds located on the papillae of the tongue will fire in response to the salty taste of the anchovies (especially on the sides of the tongue).

6 Consciousness

LEARNING OBJECTIVES

After studying this chapter, you should be able to:

1. Define consciousness and summarize the functionalist viewpoint regarding the qualities and purposes of consciousness. (p. 196-197)

2. Define daydreaming and describe its purposes. (p. 197)

3. Define attention and summarize the findings of research regarding the nature of attention, mentioning the "cocktail party phenomenon." (p. 197-198)

4. Summarize what is known about the circadian rhythm and how this is related to the experience of jet lag and issues of rotating shifts in the workplace. (p. 198-200)

5. Describe the sleep cycle, emphasizing the nature of REM sleep, and what is known about the duration of sleep. (p. 200-204)

6. Describe the important features of two theories that attempt to explain why we sleep. (p. 204-205)

7. List and describe three sleep disorders and how they are treated. (p. 205-207)

8. Beginning with the classic study by Calkins, summarize what is known about the content of dreams, mentioning the phenomenon of lucid dreams. (p. 207- 209)

9. List and describe four theories about why we dream, mentioning supportive evidence for each theory. (p.209-211)

10. Define hypnosis and briefly summarize the history of this phenomenon. (p. 212-213)

11. Explain the relationship between hypnotic induction and hypnotic susceptibility, and then summarize what is known about how hypnosis affects perception, cognition, and behavior. (p. 213-215)

12. List and explain two theories about the nature of hypnosis, citing supportive evidence for each theory. (p. 215-217)

13. Define meditation, and summarize what is known about its physiological and psychological effects. (p. 217-218)

14. Explain what psychoactive drugs are, and how they generally work, mentioning issues such as dependence and tolerance. (p. 219)

15. Describe and offer examples of the three general categories of psychoactive drugs, emphasizing their effects on psychological functioning. (p. 219-224)

16. Distinguish among three concepts of the unconscious, citing relevant research findings in support of each concept. (p. 225-230)

COMPREHENSIVE GUIDED REVIEW

I. The Nature of Consciousness: Questions as to the nature of__(1)__ have interested mankind since 1690, when John Locke wrote that "consciousness is the perception of what passes in a man's own mind." Two centuries after Locke, William James claimed that consciousness exhibits four features. First, because you feel it belongs to you, consciousness is__(2)_. Second, because you can attend to certain things while ignoring others, consciousness is __(3)__. Third, because its contents blend into one another, consciousness is__(4)__; and fourth, because its contents are in a constant state of flux, consciousness is __(5)__. William James likened consciousness to a__(6)_. The metaphor of "stream of consciousness" came to weave its way through the writings of James Joyce, among others. William James believed that consciousness was an__(7)__ development, enhancing our ability to adapt. Today, psychologists share a view similar to John Locke's concept of consciousness defining consciousness as the __(8)__of one's own mental activity, including thoughts, feelings, and sensations.

Daydreaming is a state of consciousness in which we voluntarily shift our attention from mental experiences stimulated by__(9)_ stimuli to mental experiences generated by the brain. Eric Klinger demonstrated that we may spend a large portion of our waking activity___(10)_. Psychologists have suggested four reasons why we daydream:

1) Daydreaming lets us mentally__(11)_ alternative courses of action;
2) Daydreaming keeps us mentally aroused in situations that provide __(12)__ external stimulation;
3) Daydreaming solves___(13)_; and
4) Daydreaming brings us pleasure.

Today's researchers are more interested in the__(14)__ of consciousness than any of the other features. Psychologists refer to the selectivity aspect of consciousness as__(15)__. The suggestion has been made that **attention** is adaptive because it keeps the consciousness from becoming chaotic; in other words, it gives__(16)_ and meaning. Research studies have been done examining the several factors that determine whether we will attend to a particular stimulus. Among them are the personal__(17)_ of the stimulus and a change in stimulation.

During the early part of the twentieth century, differing approaches eventually led to the claim by John__(18) that consciousness, being unobservable, was not a legitimate entity for scientific study. This__(19)_ position dominated and consequently subdued research on consciousness for more than five decades. However, Eastern influences, drugs, and the__(20)__ of the 1960s rekindled an interest in further research into the nature of consciousness and its altered states.

II. Sleep: The most obvious alternative to consciousness is ___(21)__. However, **sleep** is but one cyclical change in our physiological processes, or **biological rhythms.** There is still controversy surrounding the question of whether specific____(22)____ are inborn and therefore unchangeable.

Circadian rhythms are our__(23)_-hour sleep-wake cycles of psychological and physiological changes. Circadian rhythms are governed by the hormone__(24)_. (*Remember, it was discussed in Chapter 2 that increases in melatonin are correlated with sleepiness.*) Melatonin is secreted by the__(25)__ gland. This secretion is regulated by a region of the__(26)__ called the suprachiasmatic nucleus. Recent research has examined, with some success, the use of melatonin as a treatment for__(27)__.

Changes in the circadian rhythm are possible. Shortening your sleep cycle, or experiencing a ___(28)__, as you do when you fly from west to east, is a harder adjustment than a **phase delay.** Psychologists suggest that this is because you are countering the normal tendency for longer cycles. Research has shown that if subjects are allowed to adjust their cycle, without respect to any external cues, they normally adapt to a__(29)__-hour cycle, not 24. Thus, researchers suggest that, it is natural to lengthen the circadian cycle and this is why you are not as likely to experience symptoms of jet lag when flying from_____ _(30)_ _____.

Since shifts in__(31) cycles are a necessary part of life for approximately 25 percent of the American population, psychologists have researched ways to prevent the "jet lag" symptoms of these changes. Understanding the natural tendency for a longer circadian cycle led researchers to test the use of rotating shifts in which workers shift gradually. A

__(32)__ schedule, which uses the natural tendency to lengthen the circadian cycle by having workers rotate from night, to day, to evening, and back to night, provides better employee health, satisfaction, and higher productivity than a phase-advance schedule.

Patterns of Sleep: Although the__(33)__ (EEG) was developed in the 1930s, formal study of sleep and sleep cycles did not begin in earnest until the late 1960s. The EEG measures__(34)__-wave patterns. Since the 1960s research has indicated that each different point in the sleep cycle displays characteristic electroencephalograph (EEG) recording and physiologic changes.

As you move from a__(35)__ state through the various stages of sleep, there are characteristic changes in the EEG and physiologic arousal. First, as__(36)__ begins there is a shift from beta, to alpha, to theta waves on the EEG recording. Associated with this are__(37)__ in breathing rate, heart rate, muscle tension, rate of respiration, and body temperature and a slow, rolling eye movements. You are said to have entered__(38)__ sleep when the slow, rolling eye movements stop. Stage 1 is considered an initial__(39)__ stage of sleep. You move from stage 1 to stage 2, a deeper sleep characterized by periodic bursts of higher-frequency sleep__(40)__. From stage 2 you enter stage 3, marked by the appearance of extremely__(41)__-frequency delta waves. When at least 50 percent of the waves observed on the EEG are__(42)__ waves, you have entered stage 4 sleep, the deepest sleep. Approximately 20 to 40__(43)__ are spent in stage 4 sleep and then there is a reversal in the stages. You would than reach the **rapid eye movement** stage of sleep, or __(44)__. After a short period of **REM** sleep, approximately 10 minutes, you would return to stage 2 and begin the cycle over. Each complete cycle of sleep takes an average of__(45)__minutes to complete.

REM sleep, also known as__(46)__ sleep, earned its name because of the darting eye movements that characterize it. Stages 1 through 4 are not characterized by darting eye movements and are collectively called non-REM, or __(47)__ sleep. While in REM we are physiologically__(48)__, yet immobile and difficult to awaken. For this reason, REM sleep is also called __(49)__ sleep. And because we are paralyzed during REM sleep,__(50)__ (somnambulism) cannot occur. Thus, sleepwalking occurs only during__(51)__ sleep. REM sleep is also characterized by the spontaneous arousal of the__(52)__ organs. REM sleep is also associated with__(53)__.

Duration of Sleep: The need for sleep varies across the life span, with__(54)__ sleeping the most and elderly people the least. Studies examining the minimum amount of sleep needed have shown that any thing below__(55)__hours induces extreme drowsiness and mood disruptions. Additionally, further research suggests that most North Americans are chronically sleep__(56)__. Many people overcome the effects of inadequate nighttime sleep with daytime "__(57)__." Many cultures incorporate naps into their everyday lives. Research indicates that this is not a bad thing; in fact naps have been shown to__(58)__ alertness and improve performance.

Functions of Sleep: Considering the amount of time we spend sleeping, why do we sleep? Researchers have conducted countless studies examining this very question. Your text mentions two prominent theories: sleep as a restorative function and sleep as adaptive inactivity.

Sleep as Restorative: This most common sense view holds that sleep__(59)__ the body and mind. This idea is tested by observing the effects of sleep deprivation. In the case of Peter Tripp, sleep deprivation caused __(60)__and delusional thinking, which disappeared after a single night's sleep. More formal research offers evidence of the negative effects of sleep loss and the restorative effects of sleep. For example, studies have shown that sleep deprivation has been associated with a decline in the performance of__(61)__ and physical tasks, as well as an impairment in the function of the__(62)__ system. *(This is suggested as a possible explanation for why students often get sick immediately after finals week!)* Additional evidence for the __(63)__function of sleep comes from research showing that sleep, especially deep sleep, increases in duration on nights following vigorous exercise. However, despite the evidence of the restorative function of sleep, we do not know what it is that sleep restores.

Sleep as Adaptive Inactivity: There are two reasons to believe that sleep may be a period of adaptive inactivity. First, Webb (1992) argues that sleep evolved because it__(64)__ the sleeper from harm. Support for this view comes from __(65)__ studies of animal sleeping habits and durations. Data have shown that animals that have little to fear while they sleep, sleep____(66)__ than those that do. Second, evidence shows that sleep conserves____(67)___. Evidence for this view again comes from comparative studies of the sleep and food-finding behaviors of different animal species. These comparisons show a__(68)__ correlation between the length of sleep and the amount of time it takes to find food.

So why do we sleep? Recently, Wilse___(69)__ suggests that both of these theories of sleep are partly correct. Webb argues that the___(70)__ theory explains why sleepiness increases as sleep loss increases and the____(71)__ theory explains why sleep follows a circadian cycle.

Sleep Disorders: Although most individuals have no problems with sleep, some people have difficulties. The textbook discusses three common sleep disorders: insomnia, sleep apnea, and narcolepsy.

____(72)__is chronic difficulty in either falling asleep (sleep-onset insomnia) or staying asleep (sleep-maintenance insomnia). A third type of insomnia is early-morning awakening, where individuals sleep soundly through the night but consistently wake up__(73)__ than they want to. Treatment of insomnia often includes using sleeping___(74)__ to assist in falling asleep, but sleeping pills interfere with the sleep cycle, lose their effectiveness over time, and cause harmful side effects. For these reasons, alternative ways of treating insomnia are preferable. They include the following:

1) Using the sleep-related chemical, ___(75)__ (a precursor to the neurotransmitter serotonin, which is known to promote the onset of sleep)
2) Reducing presleep__(76)__ by avoiding exercise and caffeine products
3) Avoiding daytime____(77)__
4) Using___(78)__ intervention (trying to stay awake while lying in bed)
5) Using stimulus____(79)__ (arranging the bedtime situation to promote sleep)

___(80)___is a form of sleep-maintenance insomnia. It is a sleep-stop breathing-wake-breathe cycle. Victims of sleep apnea repeatedly are awakened during their sleep because they stop___(81)__. Often these individuals do not remember waking in the night and are often chronically sleepy during the day. Sleep apnea is caused either by the failure of the ___(82)__ centers of the brain to maintain normal breathing or by a collapse of the_(83)___, which is common in obese people.

___(84)__is the experience of repeated, sudden, irresistible daytime sleep attacks in which one immediately falls into REM sleep. Since narcolepsy is associated with the onset of___(85)___ sleep, it is often accompanied by, a loss of __(86)__ tension as well. Though the cause of narcolepsy is unclear, there seems to be a hereditary predisposition. Victims may benefit from naps or from___(87)___ drugs.

III. Dreams: Dreams are a storylike sequence of visual images commonly evoking strong emotions. The anatomy of a classic research study looks at the 1893 study done by Mary Whiton Calkins in which she attempted to answer the question, What are the characteristics of dreams?

Anatomy of a Classic Research Study: What Are the Characteristics of Dreams?
Read the summary of the research study on pages 207 and 208 in your textbook and answer the following questions:

What was the rationale for the study?

What methods did the authors use to test the hypothesis?

What was the outcome of the study and what did the authors conclude the results meant?

In addition to curiosity about the characteristics of dreams, humans have long been interested in the___(88)__ of dreams. Calvin Hall (1966) analyzed the content of thousands of dreams, and more recent research has confirmed his findings that most of our dreams pertain to the___(89)__ day. Some dreams are frightening; these are called _____(90)___.

Nightmares occur during____(91)____ sleep. By contrast, **night terrors** occur during____(92)____ sleep, stages 3 and 4. They are common in____(93)____ and may reflect a genetic predisposition.

The____(94)____ of dreams may be affected by immediate environmental stimuli, as indicated by Calkins. This has been shown in numerous research studies. In one study, researchers presented subjects with an____(95)____ after they entered REM sleep. About 20 percent of the dreams incorporated the odor. In another study, sleepers were sprayed with a water mist when they were in REM sleep. The subjects reported being in the rain, or similar ____(96)____ themes.

Lucid dreaming is an approach developed by Stephen LaBerge in which the dreamer is____(97)____ of dreaming and learns to direct their dreams.

The Purpose of Dreaming: Dream sleep (REM) is important. If deprived of it, and then allowed to sleep as long as they like, subjects show an____(98)____ in REM sleep. This is the REM____(99)____ effect and it suggests that dream sleep serves certain functions.

Perhaps the most common view of the function of dreaming is that dreams serve as wish____(100)____. Freud claimed that dreams serve as safe outlets for unconscious____(101)____ or aggressive impulses. He distinguished between a dream's ____(102)____ **content** (what can be verbally reported), and its **latent content** (which is the dream's____(103)____ meaning). Psychoanalysts have failed, however, to provide research support for dreaming as a form of wish fulfillment. This has led to the search for other functions of dreams.

A more recently researched topic has been the____(104)____ function of dreams. Anecdotal reports, the analysis of dreams occurring during REM sleep, and controlled experiments have shown that dreams help us to deal with emotional as well as practical problems. However, no studies have shown that dreams____(105)____ better emotional adjustment.

Another suggestion as to the purpose of dreams is that they are important to ____(106)____. Research studies over decades have indicated that____(107)____ memories are formed better after a good night's sleep. Also, other research has shown that the more____(108)____ sleep we have during the night, the better our memory will be for material learned the day before. (*Keep this in mind as you study for your next test! No more all-nighters. Get that good night's sleep so your memory will be at its best!*)

Most dream theorists argue that dreaming serves psychological functions. However, Hobson & McCarley (1977) argue that dreams are the by-products of the____(109)____'s attempt to make sense of spontaneous changes generated by the pons during REM sleep. This interpretation is known as the **activation-synthesis theory.** The theory argues that the forebrain detects brain activation and____(110)____ it into a dream.

To date, despite almost a century of research on dreams, there is no one best explanation of what functions are served by dreams.

Time for a well-earned study break. Remember, space out your study sessions and be sure to include time for sleep! Before moving on to study other altered states of consciousness, take time to complete the mini-review on sleep and dreams.

Mini-review on Sleep and Dreams: Match each term with its correct definition.

_______1. nightmares
_______2. stage 2
_______3. melatonin
_______4. daydreaming
_______5. early-morning awakening
_______6. phase-advance
_______7. NREM sleep
_______8. biological rhythms
_______9. stage 1
_______10. latent content
_______11. circadian rhythms
_______12. sleep-maintenance insomnia
_______13. sleep as a restorative function
_______14. sleepwalking
_______15. stage 4
_______16. narcolepsy
_______17. phase delay
_______18. dreams
_______19. EEG
_______20. stage 3
_______21. REM; rapid eye movement
_______22. somnambulism
_______23. lucid dreaming
_______24. sleep apnea
_______25. sleep as adaptive inactivity
_______26. sleep-onset insomnia
_______27. REM rebound effect
_______28. night terrors
_______29. manifest content

A. Frightening experiences that occur during NREM sleep
B. Dreaming in which the dreamer is conscious of dreaming
C. Chronic difficulty in falling asleep
D. A state of consciousness in which we voluntarily shift our attention from mental experiences stimulated by external stimuli to mental experiences generated by the brain
E. The cyclical change in physiological processes
F. Our 24-hour sleep-wake cycles of psychological and physiological changes
G. Circadian rhythms are governed by this hormone
H. A deeper sleep characterized by periodic bursts of higher-frequency sleep spindles
I. The shortening of your sleep cycle, the shift you experience when you fly west to east
J. What can be verbally reported from a dream
K. The lengthening of the circadian cycle, as when you fly from east to west
L. A technique that measures brain-wave activity
M. Initial stage of sleep when the slow, rolling eye movements stop
N. Stage of sleep characterized by darting eye movements
O. Term used to describe stages 1 through 4 of sleep
P. Term for the sleepwalking
Q. This phenomenon occurs only during NREM sleep; specifically during stages 3 and 4
R. Phase of sleep marked by the appearance of extremely low-frequency delta waves
S. Theory that holds that sleep restores the body and mind; explains why sleepiness increases as sleep loss increases
T. Stage of sleep that is the deepest sleep; at least 50 percent of the waves observed on the EEG are delta waves
U. Theory of sleep that argues that sleep may be a period of adaptive inactivity because it protects the sleeper from harm or conserves energy; explains why sleep follows a circadian cycle
V. A form of sleep-maintenance insomnia; it is a sleep-stop breathing-wake-breathe cycle
W. Portion of the dream that, according to Freud is the dream's hidden, or true, meaning
X. Experience of repeated, sudden, irresistible daytime sleep attacks followed immediately by falling into REM sleep
Y. Sleep disorder in which the individual has difficulty staying asleep
Z. Frightening experiences that occur during REM sleep
Aa. An increase in REM sleep seen if one is deprived of REM and then allowed to sleep an unlimited period of time
Bb. Sleep disorder where individuals sleep soundly through the night but consistently wake up earlier than they want to
Cc. A storylike sequence of visual images commonly evoking strong emotions

IV. Hypnosis: Hypnosis is an altered state of consciousness. It originated in the work of Anton__(111)__, who claimed he could cure illnesses by transmitting animal magnetism to his patients through a process known as mesmerism. In 1842, James Braid renamed mesmerism__(112)__.

The process of inducing a hypnotic state depends more on the__(113)__ of the subject than on the skills of the hypnotist. The aim of hypnosis is to create a relaxed, passive, and highly focused state of__(114)__. The subject gradually relinquishes more and more control of his or her thoughts,__(115)_, and behaviors to the hypnotist. People cannot be hypnotized against their will. Those individuals more susceptible to hypnosis have more active __(1 6) lives and have a high capacity for absorption in whatever they are doing. Hypnotizability can be__(117)_ by one of two tests: the Stanford Hypnotic Susceptibility Scale and the Harvard Group Scale of Hypnotic Susceptibility.

Most extreme claims as to the effects of hypnosis have been discredited. However, psychologists have identified a variety of effects. These include:

Perceptual Effects: A main effect is__(118)__. Hypnosis appears to work by distracting people from their pain.

Cognitive Effects: One of the chief effects of hypnosis is **hypermnesia,** or the enhancement of____(119)_. However, research has shown that some of the memories may be__(120)_, or inaccurate memories. In addition to the possibility of pseudomemories, another problem with hypnotically induced memories is the increased _(121)_ that the individual may experience, regardless of accuracy.

Behavioral Effects: Hypnosis has been shown to be effective in treating psychological and physical events such as headaches, surgical recuperation,__(122)_, and performance anxiety. Additionally, **posthypnotic suggestions** are often used and have been found to be ___(123)__. One concern is that hypnotized subjects might be induced to commit __(124)__ acts . Generally, there is no evidence that hypnotized subjects become mindless zombies; it is thought that hypnosis poses no risks.

In the late 1800s there was disagreement about whether hypnosis induced an__(125)_, or trance, state of consciousness. Today, the main theory of hypnosis as an altered state is the **neodissociation theory.** This theory originated from __(126)_'s (1978) classroom demonstration of what he called the **hidden observer.** He has used this concept to explain hypnotically induced___(127)__, using the cold pressor test. Additional evidence for the idea that hypnosis is a true altered state of awareness comes from EEG studies that show a different pattern of __(128)__ activity in the occipital lobe in hypnotized subjects told that the image they were seeing was blocked. Other research studies have shown differences in overall brain-wave patterns.

There are, however, those who insist that hypnotically induced effects are merely responses to personal and__(129)_ factors. Research done at Carleton University in Canada is used to support this. This research demonstrated that subjects acted under hypnosis as they had been__(130)_ they would. Also, evidence from age-__(131)__ studies has shown that people behave as an adult thinks a child would act, not in a true childlike manner. Neither side of this debate has provided clear evidence to discount the alternative position.

V. Meditation: Meditation is a procedure that uses mental exercises to achieve a__(132)_, highly focused state of consciousness. A westernized form of meditation is called____(133)____ (TM). The subjects concentrate on repeating a sound, or __(134)_. The early 1970s saw the introduction of the___(135)__, espoused by Herbert Benson. As in TM, the subject repeats a sound (other than a mantra).

Research has generated contradictory findings as to the effects of the use of__(136)_. Benson claims that meditation promotes a unique state of physical and mental ___(137)__. Some studies demonstrate that heart rate, oxygen consumption, and carbon dioxide expiration are__(138) in mediating subjects. Benson claims these results are due to the use of his technique. The claim, however, has been challenged by Holmes, who reviewed the literature and found no difference in__(139)__ arousal as the result of mediation. Whatever the outcome of this debate, meditation is as effective as other self-regulation techniques (such as stress management) and has been shown to be useful in preparing patients for surgery.

VI. Psychoactive Drugs: Psychoactive Drugs are chemicals that induce changes in moods,__(140)__, and behavior by affecting neural activity. ___(141)_ drugs exert their effects by altering synaptic activity, either by promoting or inhibiting it. Overall effects of these drugs depend on a number of factors including dosage, the user's __(142)__with the drug, the user's expectations, and the setting in which the drug is used.

All psychoactive drugs can cause psychological__(143)__, an intense desire to reach a drug-induced state of intoxication. Additionally, most psychoactive drugs may also lead to a physical dependence, or__(144)__ to the drug. Users of psychoactive drugs also often develop a__(145)__, or a decrease in the physiological responsiveness to the drug. As a result they require more of the drug to achieve the same effects. Finally, when users of psychoactive drugs stop taking the drug, they might experience__(146)__ symptoms.

Psychoactive drugs are divided into three general classifications: **depressants, stimulants,** and **hallucinogens.**

__(147)__include **alcohol, barbiturates, inhalants,** and **opiates.**
Alcohol promotes the effectiveness of__(148)__ by decreasing activity in brain centers that normally inhibit social behaviors such as sex and aggression or even helpfulness.
Barbiturates also facilitate the actions of GABA and include Seconal, which is used as a sleeping pill, and Pentothal, known as "__(149)__."
Inhalants include ether, chloroform, and__(150)__, also known as "laughing gas."
Opiates include opium, morphine, heroin, and codeine. The euphoric and pain-relieving effects of the opiates are caused by their binding to__(151) receptors, which act to block pain impulses and stimulate the brain's pleasure centers.

Stimulant drugs increase__(152)__. They include caffeine, nicotine,__(153)__, and cocaine.
Caffeine: Although it is a popular means of maintaining mental alertness, it may produce different effects. It does not help a drunken person sober up. At low doses it may improve attention and concentration, but at high doses it may impair sleep. Chronic use of caffeine may lead to__(154)__**,** marked by agitation, insomnia, and intense anxiety.
Nicotine works by stimulating certain__(155)__ receptors**.** This effect may increase the efficiency of information processing in the brain.
Amphetamines are synthetic stimulant drugs commonly known as "__(156)__." The amphetamines include Benzedrine, Dexedrine, and Methedrine. Amphetamines are commonly used as__(157)__ pills because they also suppress appetite and decrease basal metabolic rate. Chronic users may experience **amphetamine psychosis**.
Cocaine is an extract from the__(158)__ leaf and provides a brief, but intense, feeling of self-confidence and euphoria. It acts by preventing the__(159)__ of norepinephrine by neurons that secrete it. __(160)__ originally contained both caffeine and cocaine. Cocaine does have serious side effects as it causes__(161)__ and hallucinations, as Freud found out!

__(162)__ induce extreme alterations in consciousness. They produce experiences of visual hallucinations, a sense of timelessness, and feelings of__(163)__. The hallucinogens include psilocybin, mescaline, and phencyclidine. The most common hallucinogens are LSD and marijuana.
Psilocybin is present in__(164)__ and has been used in some cultures to induce mystical states of consciousness. The Mayans used a "magic mushroom" containing the drug in their religious rituals. The drug is widely used among those college students who use hallucinogens.
Mescaline, a chemical present in the__(165)__, acts by blocking serotonin receptors.
LSD's effects are powerful; it exerts its effects by influencing the__(166)__ brain receptors. A dose may induce a "trip" that involves hallucinations and even synesthesia. Indeed, "bad trips" can occur in which the alteration is so disturbing that it causes feelings of panic. The likelihood of a bad trip appears to vary as a function of the__(167)__ of the user, the user's expectations, and the setting in which the drug is used.
Cannabis sativa, or THC, is a constituent of the__(168)__ plant, cannabis sativa. Hemp has been popular for two of its other products,__(169)__ and hashish. Marijuana, when used__(170)__, makes time seem to pass more slowly and induces rich sensory experiences. Highly potent marijuana induces visual__(171)__. Marijuana was banned in the United States in 1937 because of claims that it led to wild sexual and __(172)__behavior. Research has shown that the drug does not promote aggression, but it clearly impairs coordination and vigilance while__(173)__. Marijuana has also been shown to impair__(174)__ formation.

Stop here and take another short break. When you return, complete the mini-review on hypnosis, meditation and psychoactive drugs before tackling the Thinking About Psychology section of the chapter.

Mini-review of hypnosis, meditation, and psychoactive drugs: Match each term with its correct definition.

_______1. psychoactive drugs
_______2. hypnosis
_______3. relaxation response
_______4. neodissociation theory
_______5. hypermnesia
_______6. meditation
_______7. stimulants
_______8. hallucinogens
_______9. caffeine
_______10. nicotine
_______11. amphetamines
_______12. cocaine
_______13. psilocybin
_______14. mescaline
_______15. LSD
_______16. cannabis sativa
_______17. marijuana
_______18. opiates
_______19. pseudomemories
_______20. posthypnotic suggestions
_______21. alcohol
_______22. barbiturates
_______23. hidden observer
_______24. transcendental mediation (TM)
_______25. depressants

A. Class of psychoactive drugs that includes alcohol, barbiturates, inhalants, and opiates
B. A dose may induce a "trip" that involves hallucinations and even synesthesia
C. Technique that that has been found to be effective in the treatment of obesity
D. Term for inaccurate memories
E. Class of psychoactive drugs that induce extreme alterations in consciousness; most common are LSD and marijuana
F. Chemicals that induce changes in moods and behavior by affecting neural activity
G. The theory of hypnosis as an altered state of consciousness
H. An altered state of consciousness; originated in the work of Anton Mesmer, who claimed he could cure illnesses by transmitting animal magnetism to his patients
I. The enhancement of memory
J. In moderate amounts, makes time seem to pass more slowly and induces rich sensory experiences; has also been shown to impair memory formation
K. A procedure that uses mental exercises to achieve a relaxed, highly focused state of consciousness
L. A westernized form of meditation; the subjects concentrate on repeating a sound, or mantra
M. Psychoactive drug that does not help a drunken person sober up. A stimulant, at low doses it may improve attention and concentration, but at high doses it may impair sleep
N. Psychoactive drug that promotes the effectiveness of GABA by decreasing activity in brain centers that normally inhibit social behaviors such as sex and aggression or even helpfulness
O. A form of relaxation espoused by Herbert Benson. The subject repeats a sound other than a mantra which leads to a relaxed state
P. A chemical present in the peyote cactus; acts by blocking serotonin receptors
Q. Class of psychoactive drugs that include caffeine, nicotine, and cocaine
R. Psychoactive drugs that facilitate the action of GABA, and include Seconal and Pentothal
S. Psychoactive drugs that include opium, morphine, heroin, and codeine; euphoric and pain-relieving effects are caused by their binding to endorphin receptors
T. Psychoactive drug that may increase the efficiency of information processing in the brain
U. Psychoactive drug that is an extract from the coca leaf and provides a brief, but intense, feeling of self-confidence and euphoria
V. Psychoactive drug that is present in mushrooms and has been used in some cultures to induce mystical states of consciousness
W. Synthetic stimulant drugs commonly known as speed; often used as diet pills
X. A constituent of the hemp plant; popular for two products, marijuana and hashish
Y. Hilgard's term for portion of consciousness not under hypnotic control

VI. Thinking About Psychology: Are We Affected by Unconscious Influences?

This question always provokes vigorous debate among psychologists. However, before the question can be answered, it is necessary to clarify what __(175)__ of unconscious process is being debated. Psychologists differentiate between, **perception__(176)__ awareness,** or the unconscious perception of stimuli that exceed our normal absolute threshold but fall outside our attention; __(177)__, or the unconscious perception of stimuli that are too weak to exceed the absolute threshold for detection; and the__(178)__ **unconscious,** the region of the mind containing thoughts and feelings that motivate without awareness.

Perception Without Awareness: There is substantial evidence that we can be influenced by stimuli that are above the __(179)__ but to which we are not attending. Research on attention has demonstrated the existence of perception without awareness, as in the case of__(180)__ listening. However, research has failed to provide any support for __(181)__. Perception without awareness has also been shown in studies of people with __(182)__, including prosopagnosia.

Awareness is not an all-or-none phenomenon; it is a__(183)__. When we focus our attention on one target we use __(184)__processing. When, on the other hand, we do one thing while focusing our attention on another, we are using __(185)__ processing.

Subliminal Perception: The main question here is, "Can subjects perceive stimuli that do__(186)__ exceed the absolute threshold?" The results are__(187)__; evidence from studies using words of varying emotional charge and cartoon faces showing varying emotional expressions indicate that visual stimulation can affect brain pathways. We can __(188)__ objects without having information reach consciousness. However, there is__(189)__ evidence that recordings played backward contain subliminal messages; even if they did, there is no evidence that people will obey them. There *is* evidence that popular__(190)__ subliminal tapes do not affect behavior.

Anatomy of a Contemporary Research Study: Are Subliminal Self-Help Audiotapes Effective?
Read and review the summary of this study on pages 227-228 in your textbook and then answer the following questions to test your understanding.

What was the rationale for the study?

What methods did the author use to test the hypothesis?

What was the outcome of the study and what did the authors conclude the results meant?

The Freudian Unconscious: Freud subscribed to the notion of __(191)__, or the belief that unconscious factors affect our behavior. He divided consciousness into three levels: **conscious**, or the aspect of the mind that has __(192)__ of fleeting images, feelings, and sensations; **preconscious,** or the aspect of the mind that houses memories of which we are __(193)__ at the moment, but can become aware of at will; and the **unconscious**, or the storehouse of__(194)__ feelings and memories of which we are unaware.

Recently, a new technique has been employed to study the unconscious. **Subliminal psychodynamic activation** is based on the assumption that __(195)__charged subliminal messages will alter the recipient's moods and behaviors. Overall, the results indicate that__(196)__ produces small, though statistically significant effects on moods and behaviors (Hardaway, 1990).

Congratulations! You have finished your guided review of the consciousness chapter. This chapter contains a great deal of information that can be applied in everyday life. Use this information wisely and in a manner that can enhance your ability to perform effectively.

KEY RESEARCH FINDINGS

The chapter contains numerous research citations; the key ones are listed below. Review these studies to be sure you understand their significance to the field.

1. **Segal & Luce (1966):** Case study of radio DJ who stayed awake for 200 hours. (Page 196)
2. **Bartusiak (1980):** Examined students' daydreaming behavior. (Page 197)
3. **Neisser & Becklen (1975):** Examined the selectivity of attention in students. (Page 198)
4. **Watts (1982):** Examined the relationship between circadian rhythm fit and roommate satisfaction. (Page 199)
5. **Haimon & Lavie (1996):** Studied the relationship between daylight levels and melatonin levels. (Page 199)
6. **MacFarlane et al. (1991):** Tested the effects of melatonin on sleep quality. (Page 199)
7. **Webb & Agnew (1974):** Demonstrated the lengthening of the circadian cycle in the absence of external cues. (Page 199)
8. **Czeisler, Moore-Ede, & Coleman (1982):** Examined the effects of different types of rotating shifts on health, life satisfaction, and productivity. (Page 200)
9. **Loomis, Harvey, & Hobart (1937):** First identified the use of EEG to measure brain-wave activity during sleep. (Page 201)
10. **Aserinsky & Kleitman (1953):** Associated REM sleep with dreaming. (Page 202)
11. **Webb (1985):** Examined the minimum amount of sleep possible without induction of drowsiness and mood alterations. (Page 203)
12. **Hicks, Johnson, & Pellegrini (1992):** Compared college students' satisfaction with their sleep with reports from 1978. (Page 204)
13. **Rodgers et al. (1995); Blagrove, Alexander, & Horne (1995);** and **Irwin et al. (1994):** Examined the effects of sleep deprivation on performance in physical and mental tasks and immune system response. (Page 205)
14. **Spring, Chiodo, & Bowen (1987):** Examined the effects of tryptophan on sleep. (Page 206)
15. **Mendelson, Maczaj, & Holt (1991):** Demonstrated the effectiveness of drug treatment on sleep apnea. (Page 206)
16. **Calkins (1893):** Examined the characteristic features of dreams. (Page 207)
17. **Hall (1966):** Conducted an analysis of the content of dreams. (Page 208)
18. **Wood, Bootzin, & Rosenhahn (1992):** Examined the presence of nightmares in college students after the San Francisco earthquake. (Page 208)
19. **Dement & Wolpert (1958):** Examined the relationship between environmental events and dream content. (Page 209)
20. **Gross & Lavie (1994):** Examined occurrence of dreams in sleep apnea patients. (Page 209)
21. **Dement (1960) :** Demonstrated the REM rebound effect. (Page 209)
22. **Cartwright (1978):** Conducted research into role of dreaming in problem solving. (Page 210)
23. **Cartwright (1991):** Examined the relationship between dreaming and depression in patients going through a divorce. (Page 210)
24. **Tilley & Empson (1978):** Examined the effects of REM deprivation on memory recall. (Page 210)
25. **Wallace & Kokoszka (1995):** Studied the relationship between people's fantasy lives and their ability to imagine some thing suggested to them. (Page 212)
26. **Lynn, Rhue, & Weekes (1990):** Demonstrated that people cannot be hypnotized against their will. (Page 213)
27. **Spanos, McNeil, & Stam (1982):** Examined the physical effects of hypnotic suggestions. (Page 213)
28. **Laurence & Perry (1983):** Examined the effects of hypnotic suggestion. (Page 214)
29. **Wojcikiewicz & Orlick (1987):** Examined the influence of posthypnotic suggestion on performance anxiety in college fencers. (Page 214)
30. **Orne & Evans (1965):** Examined whether hypnotized individuals would commit dangerous acts. (Page 214)
31. **Gibson (1991):** Provided counterevidence as to whether hypnotized individuals would commit harmful acts. (Page 214)
32. **Hilgard (1978):** Demonstrated the notion of the hidden observer in hypnotized individuals. (Page 215)
33. **Spiegel et al. (1985):** Examined EEG activity in the visual cortex during a hypnotic suggestion. (Page 216)

34. **Spanos & Hewitt (1980):** Using the cold pressor test, examined the intensity of pain the hidden observer reported compared to what the subjects had been led to expect. (Page 216)
35. **Orne (1951):** Examined behavior of hypnotized college students and age regression behavior.(Page 216)
36. **Wallace & Benson (1972):** Showed the physiological effects of the use of meditation. (Page 218)
37. **Benson et al (1994) :** Compared the self-esteem of high schoolers who used relaxation with those who did not. (Page 218)
38. **Muehlbach & Walsh (1995):** Examined the effects of caffeine usage in productivity in night-shift workers. (Page 222)
39. **Tranel & Damasio (1985):** Studied women suffering from prosopagnosia and their ability to distinguish between faces without being consciously aware. (Page 225)
40. **Underwood (1994):** Examined subliminal perception on TV in England. (Page 227)
41. **McConnell, Cutter, & McNeil (1958):** Examined the effects of subliminal advertising in a movie theater. (Page 227)
42. **Greenwald, Spangenberg, Pratkanis, & Eskenazi (1991):** Examined the effectiveness of subliminal self-help audiotapes. (Page 227)
43. **Hudesman, Page, & Rautiainen (1992):** Examined the effects subliminal psychodynamic activation on success of college students in a remedial math course. (Page 230)

Great job! You have finished your study of Chapter 6. Prepare yourself for your exam by taking the practice tests.

PRACTICE TEST A

1. "Consciousness is the perception of what passes in a man's own mind." This definition was put forth by which theorist?
   a. Peter Tripp
   b. William James
   c. John Locke
   d. James Joyce

Obj.: 1 Page: 196-197

2. The daydreaming is the
   a. drunken state caused by depressant drugs.
   b. mental state induced by posthypnotic suggestions.
   c. State we are in when we voluntarily shift our attention form external stimuli to mental fantasies..
   d. state of reverie associated with transcendental meditation.

Obj.: 2 Page: 197

3. We will attend to a given stimulus if it is
   a. personally important and stationary.
   b. expected or unusual.
   c. usual and personally important.
   d. important, moving, changing, or novel.

Obj.: 3 Page: 197-198

4. Research has found that shift workers perform best when they move from the night shift to the day shift to the swing shift. In regard to biological rhythms, this is an example of phase
   a. delay.
   b. advance.
   c. inversion.
   d. acceleration.

Obj.: 4 Page: 200

5. While lying on the beach in a relaxed state of mind, your mental state would be characterized by a higher proportion of
   a. beta waves.
   b. alpha waves.
   c. delta waves.
   d. theta waves.

Obj.: 5 Page: 201

6. After running a 57-mile race, individuals did not sleep longer than normal, but they did have more stage 4 sleep than usual. This supports which theory of why we need to sleep?
   a. To conserve energy, or adaptive inactivity
   b. To repair wear and tear on the body
   c. To dream
   d. To explain stimuli, or problem solving

Obj.: 6 Page: 204-205

7. Sleep apnea is the
   a. inability to dream while asleep.
   b. tendency to suffer from daytime sleep attacks.
   c. tendency to experience early-morning awakening.
   d. inability to sleep and breathe at the same time.

Obj.: 7 Page: 206

8. If you are experiencing a night terror, you are most likely to be in
   a. REM sleep.
   b. stage 1 sleep.
   c. stage 2 sleep.
   d. stage 4 sleep.

Obj.: 8 Page: 208

9. If you dreamed of flying like a bird, a psychoanalyst might interpret it to mean that you would like to be less socially inhibited. According to Sigmund Freud, the dream of your flying like a bird, itself, would be the
   a. latent content.
   b. abstract content.
   c. concrete content.
   d. manifest content.

Obj.: 9 Page: 209

10. Since the 1800s, scientists have debated whether hypnosis is an altered state of consciousness or a
   a. dissociated state.
   b. disordered but temporary state of heightened suggestibility.
   c. normal state of waking consciousness.
   d. placebo effect.

Obj.: 10 Page: 212-213

11. Suggesting to a hypnotized smoker that she will feel nauseous whenever she puts a cigarette to her lips is an example of
   a. mesmerism.
   b. hypermnesia.
   c. subliminal suggestion.
   d. posthypnotic suggestion.

Obj.: 11 Page: 214

12. Research evidence suggests that hypnotically, age-regressed subjects behave in a manner
   a. consistent with their present beliefs about past behavior.
   b. inconsistent with their present beliefs about past behavior.
   c. consistent with their childhood beliefs about past behavior.
   d. inconsistent with their childhood beliefs about past behavior.

Obj.: 12 Page: 215-217

13. The popular forms of meditation share techniques such as
   a. focusing on a sound, image, or object.
   b. lying down in a dark, soundless room.
   c. withdrawal of attention away from intruding images, feelings, and sensations.
   d. not b.

Obj.: 13 Page: 217

14. Psychoactive drugs are chemicals that induce changes in perception, mood, thinking, and behavior. They can cause addiction or ____________ and a decreased responsiveness to the drug, or ____________.
   a. tolerance, dependence
   b. withdrawal, tolerance
   c. dependence, withdrawal
   d. dependence, tolerance

Obj.: 14 Page: 219

15. Experimental research indicates promise in treating alcoholism by using drugs that block alcohol from stimulating receptors that rely on the neurotransmitter
   a. GABA.
   b. dopamine.
   c. acetylcholine.
   d. norepinephrine.

Obj.: 15 Page: 219

16. A person is rushed to an emergency room with symptoms of paranoid schizophrenia. Given that she is not schizophrenic, she probably is a heavy user of
   a. opiates.
   b. amphetamines.
   c. barbiturates.
   d. cannabis sativa.

Obj.: 15 Page: 222

17. The ability to perceive stimuli that do not exceed the absolute threshold is called
    a. hypermnesia.
    b. dissociation.
    c. subliminal perception.
    d. perception without awareness.

Obj.: 16 Page: 226

PRACTICE TEST B

1. Why is Peter Tripp's sleep-deprivation experience of limited scientific value?
    a. He was a disc jockey.
    b. The experiment was conducted in 1959.
    c. He began to hallucinate during the experiment and it had to be discontinued.
    d. The experiment was held in an uncontrolled environment.

Obj.: 1 Page: 196

2. What is the purpose or function of consciousness?
    a. To permit an internal dialogue with the self and imaginary others
    b. To make us more reflective, flexible, adaptive, and less reckless
    c. To escape from the immediate environment and to create other environments
    d. To experience the world in discrete pieces, one at a time

Obj.: 1 Page: 197

3. Research on daydreaming has shown that
    a. males are more likely to use daydreams to solve problems.
    b. older adults daydream more about current concerns than do younger adults.
    c. females are more likely than males to daydream while performing tasks.
    d. daydreams by females include more self-revelations.

Obj.: 2 Page: 197

4. One of your classmates is reading the text and you ask him a question. You get no response. What does your classmate's experience illustrate?
    a. automatic processing
    b. selective attention
    c. daydreaming
    d. meditation

Obj.: 3 Page: 197-198

5. To promote maximum safety and productivity in a manufacturing plant that operates 24 hours a day, how should the rotation of workers' shifts be carried out?
    a. Always move workers ahead to the next 8-hour shift
    b. Always move workers back to the previous 8-hour shift
    c. Always randomly vary the shift to which workers are rotated
    d. Always rotate shifts as often as possible to promote alertness

Obj.: 4 Page: 198-200

6. Which item most accurately describes the sequence of stages that characterizes the first sleep cycle?
    a. Stages 1, 2, 3, 4, REM
    b. Stages 1, 2, 3, 4, 3, 2, 1, REM
    c. REM, stages 1, 2, 3, 4
    d. Stages 1, 2, 3, 4, REM, 4, 3, 2, 1

Obj.: 5 Page: 201

7. Researchers have found that those deprived of sleep cannot perform physical and mental tasks efficiently. Their immune system also becomes impaired. These findings support the idea that sleep
    a. is restorative of bodily systems.
    b. is a social and cultural invention.
    c. has an adaptive and protective function.
    d. restores the body, but not the mind.

Obj.: 5 Page: 204

8. Kevin is asleep, his brain waves indicate high activity, and his blood pressure and heart rate are evaluated. Which of the following is not an additional characteristic of this type of sleep?
    a. A penile erection
    b. Rapid shifts of the eyes under closed lids
    c. Reports of vivid dreams upon being awakened
    d. Sleepwalking

Obj.: 5 Page: 200-204

9. The observation that bats and other animals with highly sensitive visual systems sleep during daylight and humans sleep during darkness when they are most vulnerable supports which theory of sleep function?
   a. Sleeping to promote self-preservation
   b. Sleeping as mental reprogramming
   c. Sleeping to overcome wear and tear
   d. Sleeping to conserve energy

Obj.: 6 Page: 204-205

10. As final exams approach, Rick develops sleep problems. He falls asleep quickly but keeps waking up several times during the night. He appears to be suffering from
   a. sleep-onset insomnia.
   b. sleep-maintenance insomnia.
   c. early-morning awakening.
   d. apneic insomnia.

Obj.: 7 Page: 206

11. Paul recounts his dream in which he flew a motor boat through the skies over Vienna. According to Freud, what aspect of the dream is now known?
   a. The manifest content
   b. The latent content
   c. The lucid content
   d. The symbolic content

Obj.: 9 Page: 209

12. You have a big botany exam today and spent last night cramming your head with all the details of the photosynthesis cycle. This morning you feel that you spent most of last night, after finally getting to sleep, dreaming of killer plants overtaking your room. Which theory of dreaming would explain why you had this increase in dreaming?
   a. You didn't increase your amount of dreaming; you just remember more of the dreams
   b. Dreaming as the brain's explanation for stimuli
   c. Activation-synthesis hypothesis
   d. Dreaming is an aid to memory formation

Obj.: 9 Page: 209-211

13. Eric is extremely overweight, and he has been advised to lose weight for health reasons. He has asked your opinion as to whether he should try a hypnotist to help him lose the weight. Which of the following is closest to the best advice you could give him?
   a. If his eating is stress related then he should try it because hypnosis has been shown to be effective with other stress-related illnesses
   b. Don't waste your money; hypnosis is not effective in relieving physical ailments
   c. Don't waste your money; hypnosis has been shown to help some physical ailments but not self initiated addictive ones
   d. Go for it; hypnosis has been shown to be effective in helping individuals overcome obesity and postsurgical pain

Obj.: 10 Page: 212-213

14. One of the problems associated with the use of hypnotically enhanced eyewitness testimony is that individuals hypnotized for this purpose
   a. tend to be overly confident of these memories, whether they reflect real events or not.
   b. begin to experience hypermnesia for many personal events.
   c. actively create additional and unrelated pseudomemories.
   d. often insist on adding details to their refreshed memories.

Obj.: 11 Page: 214

15. What type of effect of hypnosis is seen in hypermnesia?
   a. perceptual
   b. behavioral
   c. cognitive
   d. side

Obj.: 12 Page: 215-217

16. Your coworker Trudy tells you that she has just discovered a method that allows her to achieve a tranquil, highly focused state of consciousness. She tells you that it is very easy to do; all you have to do is seek out a peaceful place, maintain a comfortable seated position, focus on a sound or image, and withdraw your attention from external sensations. What altered state of consciousness is she describing?
   a. Hypnosis
   b. Sleep
   c. Meditation
   d. Delta sleep

Obj.: 13 Page: 218

17. After several weeks of occasional heroin use, Michael experiences an intense craving for the drug and feels chilled, nauseated, and irritable. In other words, Michael is
   a. addicted and experiencing withdrawal symptoms.
   b. developing a tolerance for the narcotic drug.
   c. psychologically dependent on the narcotic for pleasure.
   d. going to have hallucinations and other disturbed cognitions.

Obj.: 14 Page: 219

18. After her second cup of coffee, Lisa is ready to tackle that difficult computer programming problem. In other words,
   a. GABA is having a strong effect on her central nervous system.
   b. her nervous system is flooded with glutamate.
   c. caffeine has become bound to her endorphin receptors.
   d. her acetylcholine receptors have been stimulated.

Obj.: 15 Page: 222

19. An ad reads, "Work on your medical degree while at home... and asleep!" For $599 one will receive five audiotapes covering five basic medical school topics. These are to be played while the person is asleep. Based on your present level of knowledge, should one invest in these tapes?
   a. No. While such techniques may work for less complex knowledge, such as reading works of fiction, they do not work for factual material.
   b. No. Such tapes are known to work for behavioral changes such as smoking cessation or relaxation, but they do not work for mastering information.
   c. No. Memories cannot be formed during sleep, so the content of the tapes is lost.
   d. No. The content of the tapes will merely be incorporated into dreams.

Obj.: 16 Page: 225

20. Perception without awareness
   a. is usually an all-or-none phenomenon.
   b. involves both controlled and automatic processing.
   c. has been demonstrated only in cases of prosopagnosia.
   d. is impossible to demonstrate.

Obj.: 16 Page: 225-230

ESSAY QUESTIONS

1. If you always experience an extremely high level of test anxiety, are there any techniques or approaches available that may help you control your anxiety? Name them, and describe how they might be applied to control your anxiety.

Obj.: 10, 11, 13 Page: 212-218

2. If alcohol is a depressant, why are intoxicated individuals more willing to engage in arousing activities such as driving fast, aggression, or casual sex?

Obj.: 15 Page: 219

ANSWER RECORD FOR CHAPTER 6

Comprehensive Guided Review:

1. consciousness
2. personal
3. selective
4. continuous
5. changing
6. stream
7. evolutionary
8. awareness
9. external
10. daydreaming
11. rehearse
12. unstimulating
13. problems.
14. selectivity
15. attention
16. structure
17. importance
18. Watson
19. behavioristic
20. technology
21. Sleep
22. biological rhythms
23. 24
24. melatonin
25. pineal
26. hypothalamus
27. insomnia
28. phase advance
29. 25
30. east to west
31. circadian
32. phase-delay
33. electroencephalograph
34. brain
35. waking
36. relaxation
37. decreases
38. stage 1
39. light
40. spindles
41. low
42. delta
43. minutes
44. REM
45. 90
46. active
47. NREM
48. aroused
49. paradoxical
50. sleepwalking
51. NREM
52. sexual
53. dreaming
54. infants
55. four
56. deprived
57. naps
58. increase
59. restores
60. hallucinations
61. mental
62. immune
63. restorative
64. protects
65. comparative
66. longer
67. energy
68. negative
69. Webb
70. restorative
71. activation-inactivity
72. Insomnia
73. earlier
74. pills
75. tryptophan
76. arousal
77. napping
78. paradoxical
79. control
80. Sleep apnea
81. breathing
82. respiratory
83. windpipe
84. Narcolepsy
85. REM
86. muscle
87. stimulant

Anatomy of a Classic Research Study: What Are the Characteristics of Dreams?

What was the rationale for the study?

Mary Whiton Calkins was interested in the characteristics of dreams. She wanted to know if there were any common features of dreams.

What methods did the authors use to test their hypothesis?

She recorded her dreams and a colleague, Edmund Sanford, recorded his over an extended period of time.

What was the outcome of the study and what did the authors conclude the results meant?

She reported:

a) We dream every night.
b) We have about four dreams a night.
c) As the night progresses, we are more likely to be dreaming.
d) Most dreams are mundane and refer to recent life events.
e) Dreams may incorporate external stimuli.
f) What Calkins called "real thinking" occurs during sleep.
g) We can reason while dreaming and even, to an extent, control our dreams.
h) Dreams may disguise their true meaning.

---

88. meaning
89. preceding
90. nightmares
91. REM
92. NREM
93. childhood
94. content
95. odor
96. watery
97. conscious
98. increase
99. rebound
100. fulfillments
101. sexual
102. manifest
103. true
104. problem-solving
105. cause
106. memory
107. long-term
108. REM
109. forebrain
110. synthesizes

Mini-review of Sleep and Dreams:

1. Z; 2. H; 3. G; 4. D; 5. Bb; 6. I; 7. O; 8. E; 9. M; 10. W; 11. F; 12. Y; 13. S; 14. Q; 15. T; 16. X; 17 K; 18. Cc; 19. L; 20. R; 21. N; 22. P; 23. B; 24. V; 25. U; 26. C; 27. Aa; 28. A; 29. J

111. Mesmer
112. hypnosis
113. susceptibility
114. mind
115. perceptions
116. fantasy
117. measured
118. pain relief
119. recall
120. pseudomemories
121. confidence
122. obesity
123. effective
124. dangerous
125. altered
126. Hilgard
127. pain relief
128. electrical
129. situational
130. suggested
131. regression
132. tranquil
133. transcendental mediation
134. mantra
135. relaxation response
136. meditation
137. arousal
138. decreased
139. physiological
140. perception
141. Psychoactive
142. experience
143. dependence
144. addiction
145. tolerance
146. withdrawal
147. Depressants
148. GABA
149. truth serum
150. nitrous oxide
151. endorphin
152. arousal
153. amphetamines
154. caffeinism
155. acetylcholine
156. speed
157. diet
158. coca
159. reuptake
160. Coca-Cola
161. paranoia
162. Hallucinogens
163. depersonalization
164. mushrooms
165. peyote cactus
166. serotonin
167. state
168. hemp
169. marijuana
170. moderately
171. hallucinations
172. aggressive
173. driving
174. memory

Mini-review of Hypnosis, Meditation, and Psychoactive Drugs:
1. F; 2. H; 3. O; 4. G; 5. I; 6. K; 7. Q; 8. E; 9. M; 10. T; 11. W; 12. U; 13. V; 14. P; 15. B; 16. X; 17. J; 18. S; 19. D; 20. C; 21. N; 22. R; 23. Y; 24. L; 25. A

175. type
176. without
177. subliminal perception
178. Freudian
179. absolute threshold
180. dichotic
181. sleep learning
182. brain damage
183. continuum
184. controlled
185. automatic
186. not
187. mixed
188. recognize
189. no
190. self-help

Anatomy of a Contemporary Research Study: Are Subliminal Self-Help Audiotapes Effective?

What was the rationale for the study?
Greenwald, Spangenberg, Pratkanis, and Eskenazi were interested in whether the claims of self-help tape advertisers were valid.

What methods did the authors use to test the hypothesis?
The subjects were adults who listened to audiotapes that advertisers claimed would improve memory or self-esteem. The subjects were given pre- and post-tests.

What was the outcome of the study and what did the authors conclude the results meant?
The results indicated that there was a tendency for subjects to improve in memory or self-esteem, but the improvements were not related to the subliminal messages on the tape.

---

191. psychic determinism
192. awareness
193. unaware
194. repressed
195. emotionally
196. subliminal psychodynamic activation

Practice Test A:

1. a. Incorrect: Peter Trip was the radio DJ who went 200 hours without sleep.
   b. Incorrect: James saw consciousness as a stream.
   c. **Correct: This is a quote from John Locke.**
   d. Incorrect: James Joyce is a writer who was influenced by William James's view of consciousness.
2. a. Incorrect: Daydreaming is the term for the state in which we voluntarily shift our attention from external stimuli to mental fantasies.
   b. Incorrect: Daydreaming is the term for the state in which we voluntarily shift our attention from external stimuli to mental fantasies.
   c. **Correct: Daydreaming is the term for the state in which we voluntarily shift our attention from external stimuli to mental fantasies.**
   d. Incorrect: Daydreaming is the term for the state in which we voluntarily shift our attention from external stimuli to mental fantasies.

3. a. Incorrect: We do attend to a given stimulus if it is personally important, but not because it is stationary.
   b. Incorrect: We attend to stimuli that are important, moving, changing or novel.
   c. Incorrect: We attend to stimuli that are important, moving, changing or novel.
   d. Correct: We attend to stimuli that are, important, moving, changing, or novel.

4. **a. Correct: Research has shown that delaying the sleep cycle is best.**
   b. Incorrect: Research has shown that delaying the sleep cycle is best.
   c. Incorrect: Research has shown that delaying the sleep cycle is best.
   d. Incorrect: Research has shown that delaying the sleep cycle is best.

5. a. Incorrect: Beta waves are high-frequency waves indicative of an alert mental state.
   b. Correct: Alpha waves are low-frequency waves indicative of a relaxed, introspective state.
   c. Incorrect: Delta waves are extremely low-frequency waves indicative of a deep sleep state.
   d. Incorrect: Theta waves are characteristic of the middle sleep states.

6. a. Incorrect: This theory would have us sleep so we didn't do the run in the first place.
   b. Correct: This theory claims that we sleep to repair damages to the body tissues caused by the stress and wear and tear.
   c. Incorrect: This theory explains why we would go into REM sleep; however, after a lot of physical activity we spend more time in NREM than in REM.
   d. Incorrect: This theory is a about why we do REM sleep.

7. a. Incorrect: Sleep apnea is the inability to sleep and breathe at the same time.
   b. Incorrect: The tendency to suffer daytime sleep attacks is narcolepsy.
   c. Incorrect: The tendency to experience early-morning awakenings is a form of insomnia.
   d. Correct: Sleep apnea is the inability to sleep and breathe at the same time.

8. a. Incorrect: Night terrors are episodes in which people sit up suddenly and feel an intense fear They may speak incoherently and scream, but most likely will not remember the experience in the morning. Nightmares occur in stage 4 sleep.
   b. Incorrect: Night terrors are episodes in which people sit up suddenly and feel an intense fear. They may speak incoherently and scream, but most likely will not remember the experience in the morning. Nightmares occur in stage 4 sleep.
   c. Incorrect: Night terrors are episodes in which people sit up suddenly and feel an intense fear. They may speak incoherently and scream, but most likely will not remember the experience in the morning. Nightmares occur in stage 4 sleep.
   d. Correct: Night terrors are episodes in which people sit up suddenly and feel an intense fear. They may speak incoherently and scream, but most likely will not remember the experience in the morning. Nightmares occur in stage 4 sleep.

9. a. Incorrect: Latent content refers to the hidden meaning of the dream, or the underlying meaning.
   b. Incorrect: Freud did not coin a term called abstract content.
   c. Incorrect: Freud did not coin a term called concrete content.
   d. Correct: Manifest content of a dream refers to the actual storyline of the dream, or what is reported to have been dreamt.

10. a. Incorrect: Psychologists have not discussed hypnosis as a dissociated state.
    b. Correct: Some psychologists consider hypnosis as a temporary state of heightened suggestibility.
    c. Incorrect: Hypnosis is an induced state in which a person responds to suggestions; it is not a "normal" state of consciousness.
    d. Incorrect: A placebo effect is one in which subjects are not given anything but act as if they had been given a substance.

11. a. Incorrect: Mesmerism is the term that was applied to Mesmer's demonstrations of hypnosis.
    b. Incorrect: The term for suggestions such as this one, which are directed at having effects after the hypnosis, is posthypnotic suggestion.
    c. Incorrect: The term for suggestions such as this one, which are directed at having effects after the hypnosis, is posthypnotic suggestion.
    d. Correct: The term for suggestions such as this one, which are directed at having effects after the hypnosis, is a posthypnotic suggestion.

12. a. **Correct: Orne's 1951 study of college students showed that subjects acted according to their current beliefs about past behaviors.**
    b. Incorrect: Orne's 1951 study of college students showed that subjects acted according to their current beliefs about past behaviors.
    c. Incorrect: Orne's 1951 study of college students showed that subjects acted according to their current beliefs about past behaviors.
    d. Incorrect: Orne's 1951 study of college students showed that subjects acted according to their current beliefs about past behaviors.

13. a. Incorrect: While this is a correct answer it is not a complete one, thus not the best choice.
    b. Incorrect: Relaxation techniques do not require lying down or a dark room.
    c. Incorrect: While this is a correct answer it, like answer a, is not a complete one, thus not the best choice.
    d. **Correct: Since b is the only incorrect answer, this is the best choice.**

14. a. Incorrect: Dependence is another term for addiction and tolerance is the term for a decreased responsiveness to a drug.
    b. Incorrect: Dependence is another term for addiction and tolerance is the term for a decreased responsiveness to a drug.
    c. Incorrect: Dependence is another term for addiction and tolerance is the term for a decreased responsiveness to a drug.
    d. **Correct: Dependence is another term for addiction and tolerance is the term for a decreased responsiveness to a drug.**

15. a. **Correct: Research has shown that alcohol facilitates the action of GABA.**
    b. Incorrect: Research has shown that alcohol facilitates the action of GABA.
    c. Incorrect: Research has shown that alcohol facilitates the action of GABA.
    d. Incorrect: Research has shown that alcohol facilitates the action of GABA.

16. a. Incorrect: Opiates have been implicated in pain, not schizophrenic behaviors.
    b. **Correct: Chronic use of amphetamines has been shown to induce amphetamine psychosis which is similar to schizophrenic like behavior.**
    c. Incorrect: Barbiturates act to induce sleepiness.
    d. Incorrect: Cannabis sativa makes time pass slowly and induces rich, sensory experiences.

17. a. Incorrect: Perception of stimuli beneath absolute thresholds is called subliminal perception.
    b. Incorrect: Perception of stimuli beneath absolute thresholds is called subliminal perception.
    c. **Correct: Perception of stimuli beneath absolute thresholds is called subliminal perception.**
    d. Incorrect: Perception of stimuli beneath absolute thresholds is called subliminal perception.

Practice Test B:

1. a. Incorrect: Scientific value of is not determined by the subject's occupation.
   b. Incorrect: Scientific value is not determined by when the study was conducted.
   c. Incorrect: Scientific value is not determined by whether or not the results turn out as expected.
   d. **Correct: Good scientific data are obtained using a controlled, systematic method.**

2 a. Incorrect: Consciousness allows us to adapt to our environment and be reflexive and more flexible.
   b. **Correct: Consciousness allows us to adapt to our environment and be reflexive and more flexible.**
   c. Incorrect: Consciousness allows us to adapt to our environment and be reflexive and more flexible.
   d. Incorrect: Consciousness allows us to adapt to our environment and be reflexive and more flexible.

3. a. Incorrect: This is true for females, not males.
   b. Incorrect: The opposite is true.
   c. Incorrect: This is true for males, not females.
   d. **Correct: Females do more self-revealing in their daydreams**

4. a. Incorrect: Automatic processing refers to tasks done with out attention.
   b. **Correct: Your class mate is selectively attending to their textbook.**
   c. Incorrect: If your friend were daydreaming they would not be focused on an external stimuli like the textbook.
   d. Incorrect: If your friend were meditating they would be relaxed and not focused on the textbook.

5. **a. Correct: Using a phase-delay schedule shift allows the workers to take advantage of the natural tendency to lengthen the sleep cycle.**
b. Incorrect: This would require the workers to do a phase advance in their circadian rhythms.
c. Incorrect: Scheduled, predictable changes are more beneficial then random changes.
d. Incorrect: Too many changes in circadian cycles is too hard to adapt to.

6. a. Incorrect: You do not go directly into REM from stage 4.
b. Correct: You begin at stage 1, go down to 4, back up to 1 and then to REM.
c. Incorrect: You do not go directly into REM from waking.
d. Incorrect: You do not go directly into REM from stage 4.

7. **a. Correct: The fact that sleep allows the immune system to work at it optimal level, supports the restorative position.**
b. Incorrect: These events are not social and cultural inventions.
c. Incorrect: These functions are not protective functions.
d. Incorrect: Mental tasks involve functions of both the body and the mind.

8. a. Incorrect: Kevin is in REM sleep; penile erections are characteristic of REM
b. Incorrect: Kevin is in REM sleep; rapid eye movements are characteristic of REM
c. Incorrect: Kevin is in REM sleep; vivid dreams upon waking are characteristic of REM
d. Correct: Kevin is in REM sleep; limb paralysis is characteristic of REM, thus sleepwalking is not possible.

9. **a. Correct: The behaviors described are all directed at helping the species to survive.**
b. Incorrect: The fact that the bats sleep at night is not indicative of the need for mental reprogramming.
c. Incorrect: Sleeping at the same time every night and only when you are vulnerable does not support the idea of wear and tear.
d. Incorrect: The fact that they sleep at the same time every day does not support the theory of energy conservation.

10. a. Incorrect: Rick is not having problems going to sleep; he is having problems staying asleep.
b. Correct: Sleep-maintenance insomnia is having difficulty staying asleep; Rick is not having problems going to sleep; he is having problems staying asleep.
c. Incorrect: Rick is waking in the middle of the night, not only in the morning.
d. Incorrect: Rick is not havingany sleep apnea.

11. **a. Correct: The manifest content is what Paul remembers.**
b. Incorrect: The latent content would be the hidden, underlying meaning of Paul's dream.
c. Incorrect: Paul was asleep when he dreamt, therefore it was not a lucid dream.
d. Incorrect: The symbolic content is a made-up term.

12. a. Incorrect: This is not a theory of dreaming
b. Incorrect: The content of the dream is not related to the brain's explanation for stimuli.
c. Incorrect: the activation synthesis theory does not concern itself with the content of dreams.
d. Correct: The fact that you dreamt of plants represents your formation of the memories that you are forming.

13. a. Incorrect: Hypnosis has been shown to be effective for obesity regardless of its cause.
b. Incorrect: There is evidence that shows that hypnosis is effective in relieving physical postsurgical pain.
c. Incorrect: Hypnosis has been shown to be effective for obesity regardless of its cause
d. Correct: There is evidence that shows that hypnosis is effective in relieving obesity and physical postsurgical pain.

14. **a. Correct: Individuals who recall memories obtained via hypnosis tend to be more confident of the memories, regardless of their accuracy.**
b. Incorrect: Undergoing hypnosis does not always lead to hypermnesia.
c. Incorrect: Hypnotized individuals do not actively produce pseudomemories.
d. Incorrect: Hypnotized individuals do not add information to their memories.

15. a. Incorrect: Hypermnesia is not perceptual.
b. Incorrect: Hypermnesia is not behavioral.
c. Correct: Hypermnesia is cognitive.
d. Incorrect: This is an irrelevant answer.

16. a. Incorrect: Hypnosis is not a tranquil and highly focused state of consciousness.
b. Incorrect: Sleep is not a tranquil and highly focused state of consciousness.
c. Correct: Meditation is defined as a tranquil and highly focused state of consciousness.
d. Incorrect: Delta sleep is not a tranquil and highly focused state of consciousness.

17. **a. Correct: The symptoms listed are symptoms of withdrawal.**
    b. Incorrect: If he had developed a tolerance he would require more of the drug to experience the same effects.
    c. Incorrect: He is experiencing physical symptoms; psychological dependence does not lead to physical symptoms.
    d. Incorrect: Not all drugs produce hallucinations as a result of withdrawal.

18. a. Incorrect: Caffeine does not influence GABA.
    b. Correct: Caffeine leads to a release of glutamate into the nervous system.
    c. Incorrect: Caffeine does not bind to endorphin receptors.
    d. Incorrect: Caffeine does not stimulate acetylcholine receptors.

19. a. Incorrect: You do not attend to any information during your sleep.
    b. Incorrect: You do not attend to any information during your sleep.
    c. Correct: You do not attend to any information during your sleep.
    d. Incorrect: You do not attend to any information during your sleep.

20. a. Incorrect: Perception without awareness is often a partial phenomenon.
    b. Correct: Perception without awareness can be either automatic or controlled.
    c. Incorrect: It has also been demonstrated in dichotic listening and the neglect syndrome.
    d. Incorrect: It is not impossible to demonstrate, but controversy remains.

Essay Questions:

1. Techniques or approaches include hypnosis, posthypnotic suggestion, meditation, TM, the relaxation response, and stress management.

2. Alcohol intoxication seems to reduce one's inhibitions about risky behavior. In addition, intoxicated individuals appear unable to foresee the negative consequences of their behavior; that is, they exhibit "alcohol myopia." This leads to more extreme behaviors.

7 Learning

LEARNING OBJECTIVES

After studying this chapter, you should be able to:

1. Define learning and distinguish learning from reflexes, instincts and the behavioral changes resulting from maturation. (p. 236)

2. Summarize the history of interest in classical conditioning, emphasizing the core concept of learning by association. (p. 236-237)

3. List and explain the major concepts of classical conditioning by referring to Pavlov's classic experiment of the conditioning of the salivary response in a dog. (p. 237-238)

4. List and explain six important factors in classical conditioning, offering examples of each. (p. 237-240)

5. Summarize the classic "Little Albert" study, and then describe how classical conditioning may be applied in understanding the features of drug dependence and taste aversions. (p. 240-243)

6. Summarize what is known about the biological constraints on classical conditioning. (p. 244)

7. Explain the core concept of operant conditioning and summarize the history of interest in this type of learning. (p. 245-246)

8. Define behavioral contingency and then list and offer examples of six concepts related to positive reinforcement. (p. 246-249)

9. Distinguish among six schedules of reinforcement and explain how they influence the performance of a behavior. (p. 249-251)

10. Define negative reinforcement and describe two forms of negative reinforcement. (p. 251-252)

11. Distinguish between extinction and punishment as techniques that decrease the probability of a behavior, emphasizing the special issues that surround the use of punishment to change behavior. (p. 252-253)

12. Describe four areas where operant conditioning principles have been applied to change behavior (p. 254- 258)

13. Summarize what is known about the biological constraints on operant learning, mentioning instinctive drift and biological preparedness. (p. 258-259)

14. Explain the significance of prediction, expectancy, and blocking in the cognitive perspective on learning. (p. 259-260)

15. Explain the significance of the classic Tolman study of latent learning and Bandura's work on observational learning and social learning theory in supporting the cognitive view of learning. (p. 260-263)

16. Define biofeedback, summarize the history of research in this area, and then describe where biofeedback has been applied, offering a critical review of biofeedback research. (p. 264-267)

COMPREHENSIVE GUIDED REVIEW

Learning is a relatively permanent change in knowledge or behavior achieved as the result of___(1)___. It should not be confused with **reflexes, instincts,** or **maturation**. A__(2)__ is an inborn response to a specific stimulus, such as when a physician taps your knee with a small mallet and your knee jerks. An __(3)__ is an inborn complex behavior found in members of a species, such as grooming by cats. __(4)__ is a process by which a behavior appears in the natural course of individual development, such as crawling in human infants. Learning is more ___(5)__ and adaptive than any of these processes.

The scientific study of learning, which began in the late 1800s, was essentially dominated by___(6)__'s theory of evolution. For this reason, psychologists viewed learning as an adaptive process and used___(7)__ as subjects. Throughout research into learning, psychologists have identified three different types of learning: **classical conditioning, operant conditioning,** and **cognitive learning.** __(8)__conditioning is the association of a stimulus with a response. ___(9) conditioning is the association of behaviors with their consequences, and ___(10)___ deals with learning as the acquisition of information

I. Classical Conditioning: Classical conditioning grew from a tradition dating back to Aristotle. Aristotle believed that learning depended on___(11)___, or the occurrence of events in time (temporal contiguity), and space, (___(12)_ contiguity). Locke and Hume became known as__(13)__ because they agreed with Aristotle that learning depends on associating contiguous events. In the early part of the twentieth century, Pavlov demonstrated what he called the "_____(14)______," or the process by which a neutral stimulus acquired the characteristic of eliciting the salivary response in dogs. At first___(15)__ was disturbed by what he called "psychic reflexes" in the dog, but he eventually became so interested in the conditioned response that he spent the rest of his career studying them. ___(16)__, an American graduate student, presented a research paper on the knee jerk conditioned reflex the same year that Pavlov won the Nobel Prize for his research on digestion in the dog, but Twitmeyer was generally ignored. J. B. ___(17)__, a behaviorist, endorsed Pavlov's research in his APA presidential address in 1914. This was the impetus for a surge of interest in classical conditioning.

Acquisition of the Classically Conditioned Response: Given a stimulus that___(18)__ elicits a response, such as meat powder on the tongue of a dog, a blow to the knee, or a puff of air on the exposed eyeball, you have the foundation for conditioning. Because the initial stimulus-response relationship is unlearned, the stimulus is called the _____(19)_____**(UCS)** and the response is called the **unconditioned response (UCR).** A key concept to remember is that the UCS elicits the UCR. A ____(20)___ stimulus, or one that does not normally elicit the response, is chosen and paired trial by trial, with the UCS. By the end of training (___(21)__), the neutral stimulus will have acquired the properties of the UCS. If, when presented by itself, the neutral stimulus elicits the response, it comes to be known as the **conditioned stimulus (CS)** and the response comes to be known as the ____(22)______ **(CR).**

If, later, a newly conditioned CS (____(23)_____) is later paired with another neutral stimulus and that stimulus then elicits a new conditioned response,____(24)___ conditioning is said to occur. It has been suggested that this may be why music used in advertising makes you think of the product. Other applications of the classical conditioning model have taken many forms. Among those mentioned in your textbook are the word "__(25)___" which came to elicit salivation among college students; or research into controlling nocturnal enuresis, or bed wetting.

What factors influence classical conditioning? Generally, psychologists consider two main factors. First, is the issue of stimulus intensity and number of pairings in the initial acquisition. The____(26)__ the intensity of the UCS and the greater the number of pairings of the CS and the UCS, the greater the strength of conditioning. Second is the issue of the time interval between the CS and the___(27)__. The possibilities are:

1) ___(28)__ conditioning—the CS is presented and remains until at least the onset of the US.
2) ___(29)__ conditioning—the CS is presented first and ends before the onset of the US.
3) ___(30)__ conditioning—the CS and US begin and end together.
4) ___(31)__ conditioning—the onset of the UCS precedes the onset of the CS.

In general, the___(32)__ conditioning occurs with delayed conditioning, followed by trace and simultaneous. Backward conditioning is less effective.

Stimulus generalization is the process wherein the CR may occur in response to stimuli that are___(33)__ to the CS. _____(34)____ is the process wherein the organism responds to the CS but not to stimuli that are similar to it. **Extinction** is the process wherein there is a___(35)__ in the strength of the CS to elicit a CR. In contrast to acquisition, where the CS and UCS are paired, in___(36)__ the CS is presented alone. Extinction___(37)__ the CR; it does not eliminate it. This is confirmed by the occurrence of___(38)___. **Spontaneous recovery** is the event wherein, following extinction and a___(39)__ period, a CS will again elicit the CR. The CR, however, is___(40)__ and subject to faster (re-) extinction.

Although not as diabolical as___(41)__ predicted in his 1932 novel, *Brave New World*, there are general applications of classical conditioning in use today. These fall into three categories: the explanation of phobias, the explanation of drug ___(42)__, and the explanation of taste aversions.

Explaining Phobias: In a now classic study, John Watson & Rosalie Rayner demonstrated the ability to classically condition a__(43)__, or unrealistic or exaggerated fear.

Anatomy of a Classic Research Study: Can Classical Conditioning Explain Phobias? *Read all about the classic study on page 241 in your textbook and then answer the following questions.*

What was the rationale for the study?

What methods did the authors use to test their hypothesis?

What was the outcome of the study and what did the authors conclude the results meant?

Explaining Drug Dependence: Classical conditioning may even explain why, with continued use, people experience drug___(44)__. **Tolerance** occurs when higher and higher doses of a psychoactive drug are required to produce the same ___(45)__ effects. The suggestion is that physiological responses may be conditioned that are ___(46)___to what the drug would produce. For example, though heroin induces respiratory depression, stimuli associated with its administration induce respiratory___(47)__. The setting in which the drug is normally administered may account for a reduction in tolerance, and opposite effects may be stronger than usual.

Explaining Taste Aversions:_____(48)_____ involves the classical conditioning of an aversion to a taste that has been associated with a noxious stimulus. John___(49)____'s research on conditioned taste aversion in rats and his clever applications (injecting lithium chloride into the carcasses of sheep to discourage preying coyotes from eating sheep) have helped to provide an understanding of this phenomenon. Another application of____(50)_____ in taste aversion has been shown by Ilene Bernstein. Bernstein showed that a novel taste could be classically conditioned to be associated with nausea induced by___(51)___.

Anatomy of a Contemporary Research Study: Can Classical Conditioning Help Maintain the Appetites of Children Receiving Chemotherapy? *Read about the study on page 243 in your textbook and answer the following questions.*

What was the rationale for the study?

What methods did thre authors use to test their hypothesis?

What was the outcome of the study and what did the authors conclude the results meant?

____

Biological Constraints on Classical Conditioning: We now know that not every stimulus paired with a UCS can become a CS, contrary to what Pavlov stated. There are inherited___(52)___ constraints on the ease with which certain stimuli can be associated with certain responses. The first demonstration of the___(53)___ on the CS-UCS pairing was done in a study that attempted to replicate Watson & Rayner's "Little Albert" study using a watch glass as the CS. The limitations were again documented in a study by Garcia & Koelling (1966), which showed that rats have an inborn tendency to associate nausea and dizziness with___(54)___, but not with sights and sounds.

Stop here and take a short break. When you return complete the mini-review on classical conditioning before moving on to study about operant conditioning.

Mini-review of Classical Conditioning: Match the term with its correct description.

____1. backward conditioning
____2. conditioned stimulus (CS)
____3. reflex
____4. Ivan Pavlov
____5. operant conditioning
____6. simultaneous conditioning
____7. maturation
____8. spontaneous recovery
____9. unconditioned response (UCR)
____10. learning
____11. extinction
____12. stimulus discrimination
____13. Twitmeyer
____14. instinct
____15. trace conditioning
____16. cognitive learning
____17. classical conditioning
____18. J. B. Watson
____19. conditioned response (CR)
____20. conditioned taste aversion
____21. unconditioned stimulus (UCS)
____22. stimulus generalization
____23. higher-order conditioning
____24. delayed conditioning
____25. neutral stimulus

A. The process wherein the CR may occur in response to stimuli that are similar to the CS
B. A relatively permanent change in knowledge or behavior achieved as the result of experience
C. An inborn response to a specific stimulus, such as when a physician taps your knee with a small mallet and your knee jerks
D. An inborn complex behavior found in members of a species, such as grooming by cats
E. Considers learning as the acquisition of information
F. An American graduate student, who presented a research paper on the knee jerk reflex the same year that Pavlov won the Nobel Prize, but was generally ignored
G. A process by which a behavior appears in the natural course of individual development, such as crawling in human infants
H. The procedure in which the CS is presented first and ends before the onset of the US
I. The initial unlearned stimulus that elicits a response in classical conditioning
J. Classical conditioning of an aversion to a taste that has been associated with a noxious stimulus
K. A form of learning in which a neutral stimulus comes to elicit a response after being associated with a stimulus that already elicits that response
L. A behaviorist, he endorsed Pavlov's research in his APA presidential address in 1914 and was the impetus for the surge of interest in classical conditioning
M. In classical conditioning an unlearned, automatic response to a particular unconditioned stimulus
N. The stimulus that does not normally elicit the response.
O. A neutral stimulus that comes to elicit a particular conditioned response after being paired with an unconditioned stimulus that already elicits that response
P. Procedure in which the CS is presented and remains until at least the onset of the US
Q. The reappearance after a period of time of a conditioned response that has be subjected to extinction
R. In classical conditioning, the response to the CS
S. Demonstrated what he called the "conditional response," the

process by which a neutral stimulus acquired the characteristic of eliciting the salivary response in dogs

T. The classical conditioning procedure in which the CS and UCS begin and end together

U. The process wherein the organism responds to the CS but not to stimuli that are similar to it

V. The gradual disappearance of the conditioned response when the conditioned stimulus is repeatedly presented without being paired with the unconditioned stimulus

W. The procedure in which the onset of the UCS precedes the onset of the CS

X. B.F. Skinner's term for instrumental conditioning in which a behavior becomes more or less probable depending on its consequences

Y. The establishment of a CR to a neutral stimulus that has been paired with an existing CS

II. Operant Conditioning: While Russian physiologists were studying the relationship between stimuli and___(55)__, Thorndike was studying the relationship between actions and their consequences. ___(56)__'s puzzle box studies led him to develop the **law of effect,** which states that a behavior followed by a "__(57)_" state of affairs is strengthened and a behavior followed by an "annoying" state of affairs is___(58)_. This type of learning became known as___(59)_ conditioning. Thorndike's work inspired B. F. Skinner to research this phenomenon, which he called___(60)___ conditioning. ___(61)__ devoted his career to the study of the relationships between behaviors and their consequences, which he called **behavioral contingencies.** There are four: **positive reinforcement, negative reinforcement, extinction,** and **punishment.**

Positive Reinforcement: A__(62)__ is a consequence of a behavior that increases the likelihood that the behavior will occur again. In positive reinforcement, a behavior that is followed by the presentation of a desirable stimulus is__(63)__ to occur in the future. The desirable stimulus is the__(64)__ reinforcer. Deciding what will be a positive reinforcer is provided by the **Premack principle:** that a behavior that has an __(65)__ probability of occurring can be used as a positive reinforcer for a behavior that has a lower probability. Positive reinforcement is strengthened by three factors: increasing the__(66)__ (size) of the reinforcer, decreasing the interval between the behavior and the reinforcer, and increasing the number of__(67)__ of the behavior and the reinforcer.

There are two classes of positive reinforcers: primary **reinforcers,** which are biological and__(68)_, and **secondary** reinforcers, which become reinforcing by being__(69)__ with a primary reinforcer. Behaviors that have been positively reinforced do not occur continually for two reasons: a) behavior is controlled by discriminative stimuli (a process known as___(70)___), which inform the individual when a behavior will likely be reinforced, and b) the individual becomes increasingly__(71)__.

Positive reinforcement can be used to increase both behaviors already in a behavioral repertoire, as well as those that are new. In **shaping,** the individual is reinforced for successive___(72)__ of a new "target" behavior. Applications of __(73)__ have included various types of animal training, teaching Down syndrome children to jump a hurdle in preparation for the Special Olympics, and encouraging a professor to use more personal examples in class. **Chaining,** on the other hand, involves the reinforcement of already existing behaviors into a__(74)__ of behaviors. In backward __(75)__, a sequence of actions is taught by first reinforcing the final action in the chain and then working backward, until the subject performs all of the behavioral segments in sequence. In__(76)_ chaining, the first action of the chain is reinforced. Behavioral segments are added to the chain until the individual performs all of the segments in sequence. Applications of__(77)__ include flight training, teaching the use of a musical keyboard, and training mentally retarded people to make their beds.

Once an individual has been trained to perform a specific behavioral response their behavior is influenced by the __(78)__ **of reinforcement** that they are under. In a____(79)__ **schedule of reinforcement,** every instance of the desired behavior is reinforced. Under this schedule there is___(80)___ extinction when reinforcement stops. In some cases reinforcement is given only for some instances of a desired behavior; these are known as partial schedules of reinforcement, or____(81)____, and are more resistant to____(82)__. There are two kinds of partial schedules: ratio and ____(83)__; and, in turn, two kinds of ratio and interval schedules: fixed and___(84)___.

A___(85)__ schedule provides reinforcement after a specific number of responses. It produces high, steady response rates.

A variable___(86)__ schedule provides reinforcement after an unpredictable number of desired responses. It produces high, steady response rates which are more resistant to extinction than any other schedule.

A __(87)__-interval schedule provides reinforcement after a set period of time. It produces a drop in responding immediately after a reinforcement and an increase as the end of the interval approaches.

A variable-interval schedule provides reinforcement for the first desired response made after unpredictable periods of time, which vary around an average. It produces slow, steady rates of responding and is highly__(88)__ to extinction.

Overall,___(89)__ schedules produce faster responses than do interval schedules while variable schedules produce ____(90)___rates of responses than do fixed schedules.

Negative Reinforcement: In____(91)____, a behavior that brings about the removal of an aversive stimulus becomes more likely to occur. (*This is often confusing to students. Remember, negative reinforcement "satisfies" by taking something unwanted away, therefore the response likelihood goes up!*) There are two forms of negative reinforcement: learning to *end* something aversive, or___(92)__ learning, and learning to *prevent* something aversive, or___(93)__ learning. Overall, in **escape learning** the aversive stimulus itself is__(94)_, while in **avoidance learning** the_____(95)___ caused by anticipation of that stimulus is removed.

Extinction: As in classical conditioning, behaviors learned through operant conditioning are subject to___(96)__ and **spontaneous recovery**. An individual will stop responding if the reinforcement is taken away. In____(97)___ following extinction and a rest period, the organism will again engage in the response. The response is weaker however, and subject to___(98)__ extinction.

Punishment: Punishment___(99)__ the probability of a response by presenting something undesirable as a consequence of that response. As with reinforcement, there are two types of punishment:___(100)__ punishment, or punishment by application of an unwanted stimulus, and negative punishment, or punishment through the ___(101)__of a wanted stimulus. (*Be careful, do* not *confuse punishment with negative reinforcement. Negative reinforcement* increases *the probability of a response by* removing *something undesirable as a consequence of that response. Punishment* decreases *the likelihood of a behavior through either the application or removal of a stimulus.)* As a technique for ___(102)__ children, punishment for misbehavior can be effective in reducing the undesirable behavior; however, it is often used ineffectively. Effective punishment should be immediate, strong enough only to stop the undesirable behavior, and used__(103)__.

Applications of Operant Conditioning: B. F Skinner claimed that many of society's everyday problems could be eliminated through the use of___(104)__ conditioning. Today there are four general categories of application of operant conditioning. These include: **animal training, child rearing, educational improvements,** and the **understanding and treatment of psychological disorders.**

Animal Training: Skinner trained____(105)__ to guide missiles toward enemy ships by having them peck at an image of the target ship to obtain food pellets. More recently, pigeons have been trained to serve as air-sea rescue spotters. ____(106)__ have been trained to serve as aides to physically handicapped people.

Child Rearing: Skinner reared his daughter in an enclosure called the_____(107)____. Parents have effectively used ____(108)__ to eliminate their child's temper tantrums. Teachers promoted toothbrushing by positively reinforcing children for having clean teeth by posting their name on the classroom wall.

Educational Improvement: One application is the **token economy,** where teachers have used tokens to ____(109)____ students for appropriate conduct and academic behaviors.____(110)____ have been used to decrease TV watching, increase reading and improve social skills in mentally retarded adults. Pressey invented the teaching machine as an instrument for____(111)____ **instruction.** Today's use of **computer-assisted instruction** is a descendant of this approach.

Understanding and Treatment of Psychological Disorders: Operant conditioning has enhanced our understanding of disorders, particularly____(112)____. Seligman's research has been particularly influential in validating the concept of **learned**____(113)____ as an explanation for depression. Operant conditioning has also been used to change abnormal behaviors using a process known as____(114)____.

Biological Constraints on Operant Conditioning: Thorndike put forth the concept of____(115)____ to explain why it was easier to train cats to escape from puzzle boxes by stepping on a pedal than by scratching themselves. The animals appeared to____(116)____ tendencies to associate the performance of certain behaviors with certain consequences. Thorndike's observations and claims were not given any attention by his contemporaries and it was not until the ____(117)____s rediscovered the concept and applied it to account for the misbehavior of some animals that the idea of biological constraints on operant learning was accepted. The Brelands considered the failure of animals to learn some behaviors and the misbehavior of others as a reversion to____(118)____ behaviors, which they called **instinctive drift.** Seligman concluded that there is a continuum of____(119)____ for certain behaviors. The continuum moves from prepared to unprepared to contraprepared, as illustrated by this example: Humans are *prepared,* chimps are____(120)____, and dogs are *contraprepared* to use language.

This is a good point to take another of your short study breaks. To stay on track be sure to complete the mini-review of operant conditioning before moving on to the section on cognitive learning.

Mini-review on Operant Conditioning: Match each term with its correct description.

________1. positive punishment
________2. escape learning
________3. positive reinforcement
________4. secondary reinforcers
________5. belongingness
________6. behavioral contingencies
________7. variable-interval schedule
________8. the Premack principle
________9. law of effect
________10. fixed-ratio schedule
________11. negative punishment
________12. primary reinforcers
________13. behavior modification
________14. shaping
________15. negative reinforcement
________16. instinctive drift
________17. instrumental conditioning
________18. fixed-interval schedule
________19. operant conditioning
________20. extinction
________21. reinforcer

A. States that behaviors followed by satisfaction are strengthened and behaviors followed by annoyance are weakened
B. Thorndike's term for learning involving associations between behaviors and consequences
C. A behavior that when followed by a desirable stimulus that is given becomes more likely to occur in the future
D. Biological and unlearned reinforcers
E. Procedure in which the individualis reinforced for successive approximations of a new "target" behavior
F. B. F. Skinner's term for learning involving associations between behaviors and consequences
G. The relationships between behaviors and their consequences
H. A consequence that increases the likelihood that the behavior will occur again
I. States that a behavior that has a increased probability of occurring can be used as a positive reinforcer for a behavior that has a lower probability
J. Initially unlearned; become reinforcing by being associated with a biological phenomenon
K. Involves the reinforcement of already existing behaviors into a series of behaviors
L. Procedure in which every instance of the desired behavior is reinforced
M. Procedure in which reinforcement is given only for some instances of a desired behavior
N. Procedure that provides reinforcement after a specific number of responses; it produces high, steady response rates

________22. chaining	O. Term for learning that brings about the removal of an aversive stimulus
________23. continuous reinforcement	P. Term for satisfaction by taking something unwanted away; leads to an increase in the response
________24. variable-ratio schedule	Q. Provides reinforcement after an unpredictable number of desired responses
________25. partial reinforcement	R. Term for learning to prevent something aversive
________26. avoidance learning	S. Provides reinforcement after a set period of time
________27. punishment	T. The stopping of responding when reinforcement is taken away
________28. token economy	U. Provides reinforcement for the first desired response made after unpredictable periods of time, which vary around an average
	V. Decreases the probability of a response by presenting something undesirable as a consequence of that response
	W. Punishment by application of an unwanted stimulus
	X. Tokens are used to reward appropriate conduct
	Y. Punishment through the removal of a wanted stimulus
	Z. Term for the use of operant conditioning to change abnormal behaviors
	Aa. Thorndike's concept to explain why it was easier to train cats to escape from puzzle boxes by stepping on a pedal than by scratching themselves
	Bb. The Brelands term for the reversion of animals to species-specific behaviors.

III. Cognitive Learning: The traditional view of classical and operant conditioning is that they are explained by __(121)__ alone. But evidence has accumulated to show that mere contiguity of a neutral and an unconditioned stimulus is insufficient to produce__(122)__ conditioning, and mere contiguity of a behavior and a consequence is insufficient to produce ____(123)____. In contrast to the contiguity view, cognitive theorists believe that secondary reinforcers gain their ability to reinforce behaviors because they have reliably__(124)__ the occurrence of primary reinforcers.

A__(125)__ explanation of classical conditioning that rules out mere contiguity is offered by Rescorla (1988). Classical conditioning will occur only when the CS permits the individual to__(126)__ predict the occurrence of the UCS. This means that the individual is learning__(127)__ among events in the environment. Another source of evidence that supports a cognitive interpretation of classical conditioning is the phenomenon of__(128)__, in which a neutral stimulus paired with a CS, which already elicits a CR, will be less likely to become a CS itself. **Blocking** occurs because the neutral stimulus adds nothing to the occurrence of the__(129)__. The CS already __(130)__the UCS's occurrence. An additional source of evidence against a strictly contiguity-based view comes from research on conditioned____(131)____.

A trend of the cognitive revolution is to examine learning more in terms of the acquisition of__(132)__ than conditioning. This means that learning can occur without revealing itself in __(133)__ behavior, or performance. Tolman called learning in the absence of overt actions__(134)__ learning. Latent learning stimulated interest in __(135)__learning, in which an individual learns a behavior by watching others perform it. **Observational learning** is central to Bandura's____(136)____ **theory** which assumes that social behavior is learned through observation and mental processing of information.__(137)__ has identified four factors that account for observational learning: You must first __(138)__to the actions of the model, then you must__(139)__ the actions, next you must have the__(140)__ to perform the actions; and finally you must be__(141)__ to perform the actions.

Bandura first demonstrated the power of__(142)____ in his 1965 research on aggressiveness in children as a function of observing the filmed behavior of models. Recent research has extended this finding by comparing the behavior of children who watch violent television and those who watch "Mister Rogers' Neighborhood." Results indicated that those children who watch Mr. Rogers engaged in more positive__(143)__ behaviors.

IV. Thinking About Psychology: Is Biofeedback an Effective Means for Learning Self-Regulation of Physiological Processes?

Biofeedback is a form of __(144)__ conditioning that enables an individual to gain control over a normally involuntary physiological process (or better control of a voluntary process) when provided with auditory or visual feedback of about the state of that process. The feedback serves as a__(145)__ reinforcer for changes in the desired direction. It is much like watching where the arrow goes when you shoot at a target. How is this accomplished? There are three steps:

1) __(146)__changes in electrical activity of some portion of the body (muscles of the forehead, jaw, neck, head, etc.) This is done with sensors, usually electrodes, attached to the body.
2) __(147)__the changes in electrical activity so that they can be recorded and used to generate a feedback signal.
3) Present__(148)__ to the subject to indicate the state of the physiological process. The feedback might be in the form of light that gets brighter as heart rate increases or a tone that changes in pitch as muscle tension decreases.

Although the term__(149)__ was not coined until 1969, the ability to gain control over one's own physiological processes has been demonstrated by Indian yogis for centuries. There were few studies until the 1960s, partly because influential psychologists such as__(150)__ considered such control impossible. Biofeedback was popularized in the 1960s by reports of subjects who had learned to control their__(151)__ brain-wave patterns. But scientific credibility came with Neal __(152)__'s research with rats showing that they could be trained to gain voluntary control over physiological responses controlled solely by the autonomic nervous system. For unknown reasons, attempts to replicate Miller's findings__(153)__.

Though biofeedback has not proven to be an unqualified__(154)__, it has not proven to be a failure. A multitude of studies demonstrate its effectiveness. Some examples of physiological processes people have learned to control are: 1) Heart rate; 2) Brain waves; 3) gastrointestinal activity; 4) skeletal muscles; 5) muscle tension reduction during childbirth, gymnastics, sustained playing of musical instruments, tension headaches; 6) muscle tension increase in physical rehabilitation, foot movements in stroke victims, use of facial muscles after surgery; and 7) muscle strength.

Though widely used, there is still controversy concerning its effectiveness and practicality. To demonstrate its effectiveness, one must show that changes are caused by the__(155)__ and not other factors. In addition, instrumentation is costly, what may be statistically significant may not be__(156)__, what may work in the lab may not work in the clinic, and the effects may not last beyond the training sessions.

Congratulations! You have completed your comprehensive guided review of Chapter 7. Below you will find a list of the key research studies presented in the chapter. Be sure to review your understanding of their results.

KEY RESEARCH FINDINGS

Provide the details of the following key research studies in psychology:

1. **Cogan & Cogan (1984):** Paired the name *Pavlov* with lemonade over a series of trials to demonstrate classical conditioning. (Page 238)
2. **Mowrer & Mowrer (1938):** Used an electrified mattress pad to treat enuresis. (Page 238-239)
3. **Watson & Rayner (1920):** Demonstrated classical conditioning of a phobia. (Page 241)
4. **Garcia et al. (1956)**: Exposed rats to radiation and then presented them with a novel drink in a novel cage. (Page 242)
5. **Gustavson et al. (1974):** Discouraged coyotes from eating sheep by injecting lithium chloride into sheep carcasses. (Page 242)
6. **Schafe, Sollars, & Bernstein (1995):** Demonstration that a 30-minute interval is superior to a 10-second interval in the development of taste aversions. (Page 243)
7. **Bernstein (1978):** Based on the "Mapletoff" study; study suggested that cancer patients be given a novel-tasting food before receiving chemotherapy. (Page 243)

8. **Valentine (1930):** Attempted to replicate Watson and Rayner's study with "Little Albert" using an opera glass as the CS. (Page 244)
9. **Garcia & Koelling (1966):** Provided further support for biological constraints on conditioning when they found that rats have an inborn tendency to associate nausea and dizziness with tastes, but not with sights and sounds. (Page 244)
10. **Thorndike (1898):** Studied the behavior of cats in a puzzle box. (Page 245)
11. **Premack (1965):** Proposed the Premack principle. (Page 246)
12. **Wolfe (1936):** Demonstrated that chimps could obtain grapes by setting tokens into vending machines. (Page 246)
13. **Cameron & Cappello (1993):** Used shaping to train a child with Down syndrome to jump over a hurdle. (Page 248)
14. **Hur & Osborne (1993):** Used chaining to successfully train mentally retarded adults to perform steps in making a corsage. (Page 248)
15. **Ash & Holding (1990):** Used forward chaining to use the musical keyboard. (Page 248)
16. **McWilliams, Nietupski, & Hamre-Nietupski (1990):** Trained people with mental retardation to make their beds. (Page 248)
17. **Skinner (1956):** Discovered partial reinforcement schedules by accident when he ran short of food pellets. (Page 249)
18. **Roberts & Fanurik (1986):** Examined the effectiveness of operant conditioning in using seat belts. (Page 254)
19. **Skinner (1960):** Trained pigeons to guide missiles toward enemy ships. (Page 254)
20. **Stark (1981):** Trained pigeons to act as air-sea rescue spotters for the Coast Guard. (Page 254)
21. **Swain, Allard, & Holborn (1982):** Showed that teachers promoted toothbrushing by writing names on the board. (Page 256)
22. **Williams (1959):** Parents have used extinction to eliminate their children's temper tantrums. (Page 256)
23. **Smith et al. (1982):** Used verbal praise to increase participation in classroom discussions. (Page 256)
24. **Swiezy, Matson, & Box (1992):** Used token economies in classroom discussions. (Page 256)
25. **Wolfe, Mendes, & Factor (1984):** Used token economies to reduce television watching in children. (Page 256)
26. **Brown, Fuqua, & Otts (1986):** Used token economies to increase reading in students. (Page 256)
27. **Sandford, Elzinga, & Greainger (1987):** Used token economies to improve social skills in adults with mental retardation. (Page 256)
28. **Benjamin (1988):** Identified Sidney Pressey as the discoverer of programmed instruction. (Page 256)
29. **Seligman & Maier (1967):** Demonstrated learned helplessness in dogs. (Page 257)
30. **Woods, Higson & Tannahill (1984):** Showed successful use of token economies in training mental hospital patients to care for themselves. (Page 258)
31. **Breland & Breland (1961):** Suggested that the "misbehavior" of animals may be the result of instinctive drift. (Page 258-259)
32. **Seligman (1970):** Proposed the concept of a continuum of preparedness for association of behaviors. (Page 259)
33. **Shettleworth & Julergensen (1980):** Demonstrated that it is easier for a hamster to learn to dig than to wash its face to obtain positive reinforcement. (Page 259)
34. **Rescorla (1968):** Proposed a cognitive explanation for classical conditioning of rats. (Page 260)
35. **Kamin (1969):** Demonstrated the phenomenon of blocking in classical conditioning. (Page 260)
36. **Tolman (1932):** Proposed the concept of latent learning. (Page 261)
37. **Tolman & Hozik (1930):** Demonstrated that rats did not perform in a maze until rewarded for their performance. (Page 261)
38. **Keith & McVety (1988):** Showed that rats given an opportunity to observe a water maze before swimming through it for a food reward performed better than rats not given such an opportunity. (Page 261)
39. **Bandura (1986):** Identified factors associated with observational learning. (Page 262)
40. **Merckelbach, Arntz, & de Jong (1991):** Examined percentage of individuals with spider phobia that was the result of observational learning. (Page 262)
41. **Bandura (1965):** Demonstrated that children who had seen a model rewarded for being aggressive were more aggressive in their play. (Page 263)
42. **Huston, Watkins, & Kunkel (1989):** Demonstrated that children who watched altruistic television engaged in more positive social behaviors and children who watched violent television were more aggressive. (Page 263)

43. **Croce (1986):** Showed that at the end of training, the legs of bodybuilders who received biofeedback were stronger than those of bodybuilders who exercised without biofeedback. (Page 266).
44. **Gauthier, Cote, & French (1994):** Studied the use of biofeedback with women migraine headache sufferers. (Page 267)

PRACTICE TEST A

1. A relatively permanent change in knowledge or behavior resulting from experience is called
   a. instinct.
   b. learning.
   c. maturation.
   d. habituation.

Obj.: 1 Page: 236

2. The tradition from which classical conditioning emerged can be traced back to
   a. John Locke.
   b. David Hume.
   c. Ivan Pavlov.
   d. Aristotle.

Obj.: 2 Page: 236-237

3. In Pavlov's basic study, a dog salivates in response to meat powder placed on its tongue. A tone is then presented on several trials just before the meat powder. The dog eventually salivates in response to the tone. The tone is the
   a. conditioned response.
   b. conditioned stimulus.
   c. unconditioned response.
   d. unconditioned stimulus.

Obj.: 3 Page: 237

4. A biopsychologist tries to condition constriction of the blood vessels of the skin in response to a tone. She sounds a tone, which is turned off before she directs a blast of cold air at the subject's right hand (which makes its peripheral vessels constrict). This would be an example of
   a. trace conditioning.
   b. delayed conditioning.
   c. backward conditioning.
   d. simultaneous conditioning.

Obj.: 4 Page: 239

5. When one attempts to explain the role of classical conditioning in drug dependence,
   a. the drug is the CS and the physiological response is the UCR.
   b. stimuli may elicit effects opposite to those of the drug itself.
   c. one may notice tolerance, wherein no changes in the doses of the drug are necessary to produce the same response.
   d. one finds that the classical conditioning model does not apply.

Obj.: 5 Page: 240-243

6. Bernstein (1991) conducted a study on children receiving chemotherapy. Her findings showed that
   a. taste aversion is stronger to familiar foods than to novel-tasting foods.
   b. the majority of children who ate Mapletoff on the days they received chemotherapy chose Mapletoff.
   c. cancer patients should be given novel-tasting foods before receiving chemotherapy.
   d. Mapletoff did not affect the nausea-induced loss of appetite experienced by people undergoing cancer chemotherapy.

Obj.: 6 Page: 244

7. The statement "behavior that is followed by a satisfying state of affairs is strengthened" is related to the
   a. Garcia effect.
   b. law of effect.
   c. blocking effect.
   d. Premack principle.

Obj.: 7 Page: 245

8. You wear a new jacket and receive many compliments, which makes you more likely to wear the jacket. This is an example of
   a. extinction.
   b. spontaneous recovery.
   c. positive reinforcement.
   d. negative reinforcement.

Obj.: 8 Page: 246

9. A child is reinforced with praise by his parents on some occasions that he brings home an "A" on a spelling test. Sometimes they praise the child, sometimes they do not--in a completely unpredictable manner. The child is on a
   a. fixed-ratio schedule.
   b. fixed-interval schedule.
   c. variable-ratio schedule.
   d. variable-interval schedule.

Obj.: 9 Page: 250

10. You have a toothache, which motivates you to go to the dentist. The dentist fills a cavity, eliminating your pain. When you have a toothache in the future, you will be more likely to go to the dentist. This is an example of
   a. extinction.
   b. punishment.
   c. positive reinforcement.
   d. negative reinforcement.

Obj.: 10 Page: 251

11. You discover that a phone that has always worked no longer does. You immediately stop using it. In operant conditioning, this would be an example of
   a. extinction.
   b. punishment.
   c. negative reinforcement.
   d. intermittent reinforcement.

Obj.: 11 Page: 252

12. Computer-assisted instruction (CAI) is based on
   a. classical conditioning.
   b. operant conditioning.
   c. latent learning.
   d. the Premack principle.

Obj.: 12 Page: 254-258

13. You train a raccoon to take a tiny basketball and "dunk" it into a hoop. But at times the raccoon stops to wash the ball in a nearby puddle, much as it would wash food in the wild. This would be an example of
   a. extinction.
   b. latent learning.
   c. instinctive drift.
   d. spontaneous recovery.

Obj.: 13 Page: 259

14. Cognitive learning theorists believe that the ____ of a relationship between the CS and UCS is probably more important than timing or frequency.
   a. predictability
   b. strength
   c. quality
   d. severity

Obj.:14 Page: 259-260

15. Your friend, who drives a standard-shift car, suffers a leg injury and cannot drive home. Though you have only driven automatic-shift cars, you have observed other people drive cars with standard shifts. As a result, you succeed, despite shifting roughly, in driving your friend to the emergency room. This would be an example of
   a. blocking.
   b. latent learning.
   c. instinctive drift.
   d. learning without awareness.

Obj.: 15 Page: 261

16. Biofeedback became scientifically credible to many psychologists when
   a. B. F. Skinner endorsed it as a viable treatment for many conditions.
   b. they became aware that a Russian researcher demonstrated as early as 1885 that a patient could control his heart rate.
   c. Neal Miller reported success in training rats to gain voluntary control over physiological responses controlled solely by the autonomic nervous system.
   d. in the late 1960s many subjects reported they could control their alpha brain-wave patterns.

Obj.: 16 Page: 264-267

PRACTICE TEST B

1. After receiving a poor score on your English test for not reading your textbook, you now are very diligent about reading the text prior to each test. According to learning theorists, you have experienced
   a. maturation.
   b. associative learning.
   c. reflexive behavior.
   d. instinctual behavior.

Obj.: 1 Page: 236

2. Whenever it rains, Susie's mother becomes very anxious, especially when driving. She consistently tells the child that it's dangerous to drive in rain. At 18 months of age Susie has begun to demonstrate an anxiety response whenever it begins to rain. Susie's anxiety response is a result of
   a. an inborn fear of rain.
   b. an unresolved unconscious conflict.
   c. classical conditioning.
   d. instrumental conditioning.

Obj.: 2 Page: 236-237

3. As a child, Richard had to have many throat examinations. Every time the doctor would examine his throat, Richard would gag reflexively. Now, whenever the physician asks him to open his mouth, he gags. Which principle explains Richard's response?
   a. classical conditioning
   b. operant conditioning
   c. cognitive learning
   d. instinctual behavior

Obj.: 3 Page: 237

4. Assuming you have eaten sour lemons before, imagine eating a large, juicy, sour lemon. If your thinking about it causes your mouth to water, then your salivation would be referred to as a(n)
   a. conditioned stimulus.
   b. conditioned response.
   c. unconditioned stimulus.
   d. unconditioned response.

Obj.: 3 Page: 237-238

5. Warren's cat has learned to purr and rub against him whenever the cat hears the sound of the can opener. Lately, Warren has noticed that his cat behaves the same way if Warren uses his blender or his electric drill. Warren's cat is demonstrating
   a. extinction.
   b. stimulus generalization.
   c. trace conditioning.
   d. stimulus discrimination.

Obj.: 4 Page: 239

6. You have been previously conditioned to associate your dad with safety; your dad always wears a new aftershave and every time you are around your dad he smells like that aftershave. After a while you realize that whenever you smell that brand, you feel "safe". By what process did the aftershave become predictive of safety?
   a. operant conditioning
   b. instrumental conditioning
   c. shaping
   d. higher-order conditioning

Obj.: 4 Page: 239-240

7. While little Rosa is having her first experience with ice cream, several loud thunderclaps occur. These frighten Rosa. For years afterward she becomes fearful when offered ice cream. In this situation, Rosa
   a. has developed a phobia about ice cream.
   b. is demonstrating spontaneous recovery of a learned response.
   c. can extinguish her fear by avoiding all ice cream.
   d. will generalize her fear to both hot and cold foods.

Obj.: 5 Page: 241

8. An elementary school teacher states that students who complete their classroom assignment satisfactorily have extra time at recess. This results in more students completing their classroom assignment satisfactorily. This teacher is using
   a. primary reinforcers.
   b. positive reinforcement.
   c. shaping and chaining.
   d. negative reinforcement.

Obj.: 8 Page: 246

9. Little Ronnie loves candy. He has learned that having temper tantrums around his parents gets no extra candy, but tantruming when he is with the babysitter always results in extra candy. In other words, the babysitter is serving as a
   a. primary reinforcer.
   b. discriminative stimulus.
   c. negative reinforcer.
   d. punisher.

Obj.: 8 Page: 246

10. Laura commands her new puppy to "Shake!" lifts his paw, and then reinforces him. After several repetitions, she merely touches the dog's paw, says, "Shake!" and reinforces the dog. Later on, she merely extends her hand near the dog's paw and says "Shake!" The dog now raises his paw to "shake." In training her dog, Laura has used the technique called
   a. chaining.
   b. stimulus control.
   c. negative reinforcement.
   d. shaping.

Obj.: 8 Page: 247

11. Many people persist at fishing. Central to this form of behavior is the schedule of reinforcement known as a
   a. variable-interval schedule.
   b. fixed-interval schedule.
   c. continuous schedule.
   d. variable-ratio schedule.

Obj.: 9 Page: 249-251

12. When asked why you attend your psychology class you say, "So that I don't fail the course!" What type of conditioning is this an example of ?
   a. Escape conditioning
   b. extinction
   c. Avoidance conditioning
   d. Positive reinforcement

Obj: 10 Page: 251-252

13. Tammy finds writing papers to be a very aversive experience. Therefore, she never takes any classes that require term papers. Tammy's behavior is an example of
   a. escape learning.
   b. avoidance learning.
   c. cognitive learning.
   d. observational learning.

Obj.: 10 Page: 252

14. How are punishment and negative reinforcement different?
   a. Punishment involves aversive stimulation, while negative reinforcement involves pleasant or satisfying stimulation.
   b. Punishment feels satisfying to the person administering the punishment, while negative reinforcement does not.
   c. Punishment always involves pain or discomfort, while negative reinforcement involves removal of primary reinforcers.
   d. Punishment decreases the likelihood of a behavior occurring, while negative reinforcement increases that likelihood.

Obj.: 11 Page: 252

15. As a child, there was no way for Betty to avoid her parents' physical and psychological abuse. As an adult, she is very depressed and believes there is nothing she can do to escape her husband's physical abuse, nor does she believe she can change other negative factors in her life. Her situation may be described as one of
   a. continuous negative reinforcement.
   b. intermittent punishment.
   c. learned helplessness.
   d. behavior modification.

Obj.:12 Page: 257

16. The Brelands attributed the "misbehavior" of some animals to
   a. spontaneous recovery.
   b. chaining.
   c. instinctive drift.
   d. behavioral preparedness.

Obj.: 13 Page: 258-259

17. You observe an animal show in which a raccoon is trained that when it is given a coin it puts it into a slot that causes a sign to pop up. You notice that before the raccoon puts the coin into the slot he rubs it between his paws. What would psychologists atribute the paw-rubbing behavior to?
   a. classical conditioning
   b. observational learning
   c. instinctive drift
   d. maturation

Obj.: 13 Page: 258-259

18. When dolphins are undergoing operant learning, their trainers use fish as reinforcers, and each fish is accompanied by clicking a hand-held device. Later the clicks themselves serve as secondary reinforcers, and dolphins will work for the clicks alone. Cognitive researchers hold that dolphins will do this because
    a. the clicks have been associated with the primary reinforcers in time.
    b. the dolphins are too well fed to be willing to work for fish.
    c. the clicks reliably predict the presence of fish reinforcers.
    d. the dolphins are biologically unprepared to respond to clicks alone.

Obj.: 14 Page: 260

19. Rats given an opportunity to observe a water maze before swimming through it for a food reward performed better than rats not given such an opportunity. This provided evidence of what Tolman called
    a. observational learning.
    b. operant conditioning.
    c. "cognitive maps".
    d. reinforcement.

Obj.: 15 Page: 260-263

20. One problem with biofeedback is that you should be aware of its problems. One of them is that biofeedback
    a. provides noncontingent feedback.
    b. can create powerful placebo effects.
    c. does not work with children.
    d. has failed to demonstrate that alpha waves can be conditioned.

Obj.: 16 Page: 264-267

ESSAY QUESTIONS

1. Kelly's parents always leave her with the same babysitter when they go out. Within minutes of the sitter's arrival her parents are gone. Kelly's babysitter arrives at her birthday party; as soon as Kelly see her she begins to cry. Using Rescorla's cognitive model for explaining classical conditioning, explain why Kelly cried when she saw the babysitter.

Obj.: 14 Page: 259

2. How would you use shaping and positive reinforcement to train your new puppy to bring you her leash when you give the command, "Walk!" ?

Obj.: 8 Page: 247- 248

ANSWER RECORD FOR CHAPTER 7

Comprehensive Guided Review:

1. experience
2. reflex
3. instinct
4. Maturation
5. flexible
6. Darwin
7. animals
8. Classical
9. Operant
10. cognitive learning
11. contiguity
12. spatial
13. associationists
14. conditional response
15. Pavlov
16. Twitmeyer
17. Watson
18. automatically
19. unconditioned stimulus
20. neutral
21. acquisition
22. conditioned response
23. conditioned stimulus
24. higher-order
25. Pavlov
26. greater
27. UCS
28. delayed
29. trace
30. Simultaneous
31. backward
32. strongest
33. similar
34. Stimulus discrimination
35. reduction
36. extinction
37. inhibits
38. spontaneous recovery
39. rest
40. weaker
41. Huxley
42. dependence
43. phobia

Anatomy of a Classic Research Study: Can Classical Conditioning Explain Phobias?

What was the rationale for the study?
Watson and Rayner wanted to demonstrate that phobic behaviors could be classically conditioned.

What methods did the authors use to test their hypothesis?
Little Albert sat on a mattress and was presented with a white rat. Every time Albert reached out to touch the rat a loud noise was made from behind him.

What was the outcome of the study and what did the authors conclude the results meant?
Watson and Rayner (1920), successfully conditioned "Little Albert" to respond fearfully to furlike objects. Albert also demonstrated stimulus generalization. Watson and Rayner concluded that phobias could be learned and were not manifestations of the unconscious. Current ethical standards of psychological research would prevent the experimental induction of phobias in children. One question remains—whatever happened to "Little Albert"?

44. tolerance
45. physiological
46. opposite
47. excitation
48. Taste aversion
49. Garcia
50. classical condition
51. chemotherapy

Anatomy of a Contemporary Research Study: Can Classical Conditioning Help Maintain the Appetites of Children Receiving Chemotherapy?

What was the rationale for the study?
Bernstein felt that it was possible that loss of appetite in patients undergoing chemotherapy might be due to a conditioned taste aversion.
What methods did the authors use to test their hypothesis?
Bernstein assigned children receiving chemotherapy to one of three groups. One received a novel flavor of ice cream before their chemotherapy, the second received the novel ice cream on their days off from chemotherapy and the third group did not get the novel ice cream.

What was the outcome of the study and what did the authors conclude the results meant?
The results indicate that the group of children that received the ice cream just before their chemotherapy avoided eating the ice cream when given the choice. The other groups did not. This led to the suggestion that chemotherapy patients should be given a novel-tasting substance just prior to chemotherapy so that they develop an aversion to only that food and not all food.

52. biological
53. constraints
54. tastes

Mini-review of Classical Conditioning:
1. W; 2. O; 3. C; 4. S; 5. X; 6. T; 7. G; 8. Q; 9. M; 10.B; 11. V; 12. U; 13. F; 14. D; 15. H; 16. E; 17. K; 18. L; 19. R; 20. J; 21. I; 22. A; 23. Y; 24. P; 25. N

55. responses
56. Thorndike
57. satisfying
58. weakened
59. instrumental
60. operant
61. Skinner
62. reinforcer
63. more likely
64. positive
65. increased
66. magnitude
67. pairings
68. unlearned
69. associated
70. stimulus control
71. satiated
72. approximations
73. shaping
74. series
75. chaining
76. forward
77. chaining
78. schedule
79. continuous
80. rapid
81. partial reinforcement
82. extinction
83. interval
84. variable
85. fixed-ratio
86. ratio
87. Fixed
88. resistant
89. ratio
90. steadier
91. negative reinforcement
92. escape
93. avoidance
94. removed
95. emotional distress
96. extinction
97. spontaneous recovery
98. faster
99. decreases
100. positive
101. removal
102. disciplining
103. consistently
104. operant
105. pigeons
106. Monkeys
107. air crib
108. extinction
109. reward
110. Token economies
111. programmed
112. depression
113. helplessness
114. behavior modification
115. belongingness
116. inherit
117. Breland
118. species-specific
119. preparedness
120. unprepared

Mini-review of Operant Conditioning:
1. W; 2. O; 3. C; 4. J; 5. Aa; 6. G; 7. Q; 8. I; 9. A; 10. N; 11. Y; 12. D; 13. Z; 14. E; 15. P; 16. Bb; 17. B; 18. S; 19. F; 20. T; 21. H; 22. K; 23. L; 24. U; 25. M; 26. R; 27. V; 28. X

121. contiguity
122. classical
123. operant conditioning
124. predicted
125. cognitive
126. reliably
127. relations
128. blocking
129. UCS
130. predicts
131. taste aversion
132. knowledge
133. overt
134. latent
135. observational
136. social learning
137. Bandura
138. attend
139. remember
140. ability
141. motivated
142. observational learning
143. social
144. operant
145. positive
146. Detect
147. Amplify
148. feedback
149. biofeedback
150. Skinner
151. alpha
152. Miller
153. failed
154. success
155. feedback
156. clinically significant

Practice Test A:

1. a. Incorrect: An instinct is an inborn complex behavior.
   b. **Correct: This is the definition of learning.**
   c. Incorrect: Maturation is the sequential unfolding of inherited predispositions.
   d. Incorrect: Habituation is the decrease in response to a stimulus as a result of experience.

2. a. Incorrect: Locke agreed with Aristotle's view that learning depended on contiguity.
   b. Incorrect: Hume agreed with Aristotle's view that learning depended on contiguity.
   c. Incorrect: Pavlov focused his research on associative learning.
   d. **Correct: Aristotle was the first to suggest that learning depended on contiguity.**

3. a. Incorrect: The conditioned response is the salivation to the tone alone.
   b. **Correct: The tone is the conditioned stimulus.**
   c. Incorrect: The unconditioned response is the salivation to the meat powder.
   d. Incorrect: The unconditioned stimulus is the meat powder.

4. a. **Correct: In trace conditioning the CS is turned off before the UCS is presented; that is there is a trace of time between them.**
   b. Incorrect: In delayed conditioning the CS remains on until the UCS is present; that is, there is no delay.
   c. Incorrect: In backward conditioning the UCS is presented first.
   d. Incorrect: In simultaneous conditioning the UCS and CS are presented together, simultaneously.

5. a. Incorrect: The drug is the UCS and the response is the UCR.
   b. **Correct: Although heroin induces respiratory depression, the stimuli associated with its administration produce respiratory excitation.**
   c. Incorrect: The tolerance occurs to increasing doses of the drug needed to produce the same effects.
   d. Incorrect: It certainly appears to provide one explanation. Knowing how the model can explain something provides insight into how the model can be used to cure something.

6. a. Incorrect: This is opposite.
   b. Incorrect: They were the fewest who chose it.
   c. **Correct: The suggestion is that they would then develop a taste aversion to the novel food and not all food.**
   d. Incorrect: Because it's novel.

7. a. Incorrect: Garcia effect refers to biological preparedness and taste aversions.
   b. **Correct: This statement is a part of Thorndike's law of effect.**
   c. Incorrect: This statement is a part of Thorndike's law of effect.
   d. Incorrect: The Premack principle states that a more probable behavior can be used as a reinforcer for a less probable one.

8. a. Incorrect: Extinction is the cessation of behavior as a result of the disappearance of the reinforcement.
   b. Incorrect: Spontaneous recovery refers to the reemergence of extinguished behavior after a rest period.
   c. **Correct: Positive reinforcement is the application of a wanted stimulus (compliment) after a response (wearing the jacket).**
   d. Incorrect: Negative reinforcement is the removal of an unwanted stimulus after a response.

9. a. Incorrect: A fixed-ratio schedule would predictably reward the child after every x number of responses.
   b. Incorrect: A fixed-interval schedule would predictably reinforce the child for every response after every x amount of time
   c. Correct: In a variable-ratio schedule the reinforcement is unpredictable but is based on number of responses.
   d. Incorrect: In a variable-interval schedule the reinforcement is unpredictable and is based on the interval of time.

10. a. Incorrect: Extinction is the cessation of behavior as a result of the disappearance of the reinforcement.
    b. Incorrect: Punishment results from a response being followed by nonsatisfaction.
    c. Incorrect: Positive reinforcement is the application of a wanted stimulus after a response.
    d. Correct: Negative reinforcement is the removal of an unwanted stimulus (toothache) after a response (going to the dentist).

11. **a. Correct: Extinction is the cessation of behavior (using the phone) as a result of the disappearance of the reinforcement (working phone).**
    b. Incorrect: Punishment results from a response being followed repeatedly by nonsatisfaction.
    c. Incorrect: Negative reinforcement is the removal of an unwanted stimulus after a response.
    d. Incorrect: There is no such term as intermittent reinforcement.

12. a. Incorrect: CAI is based on shaping, or operant conditioning.
    b. Correct: CAI is based on shaping, or operant conditioning.
    c. Incorrect: Latent learning is learning in the absence of performance.
    d. Incorrect: The Premack principle states that a more probable behavior can be used as a reinforcer for a less probable one.

13. a. Incorrect: Extinction is the cessation of behavior (using the phone) as a result of the disappearance of the reinforcement (working phone).
    b. Incorrect: Latent learning is learning in the absence of performance.
    c. Correct: Instinctive drift is the appearance of species-specific behaviors that have not been reinforced in animal behavior.
    d. Incorrect: Spontaneous recovery refers to the reemergence of extinguished behavior after a rest period.

14. **a. Correct: Cognitive theorists emphasize whether there is predictability between the CS and UCS as most important.**
    b. Incorrect: Cognitive theorists emphasize whether there is predictability between the CS and UCS as most important.
    c. Incorrect: Cognitive theorists emphasize whether there is predictability between the CS and UCS as most important.
    d. Incorrect: Cognitive theorists emphasize whether there is predictability between the CS and UCS as most important.

15. a. Incorrect: Blocking refers to the process by which a neutral stimulus is paired with a conditioned stimulus that already elicits a CR, such that the new stimulus does not become a CS.
    b. Correct: Latent learning is learning in the absence of performance. You had learned to drive a stick shift but had not performed the response until now.
    c. Incorrect: Instinctive drift is the appearance of species specific n=behaviors that have not been reinforced in animal behavior.
    d. Incorrect: This is an example of latent learning, not learning without awareness.

16. a. Incorrect: Skinner considered it impossible to voluntarily control involuntary processes.
    b. Incorrect: Perhaps this was the first study of what we know as biofeedback but it certainly had a postponed, if any, effect.
    c. Correct: Neal Miller did report success with rats.
    d. Incorrect: Many of these reports were questioned.

Practice Test B:

1. a. Incorrect: Maturation is an unfolding of a inherited predispositions, it is not the result of experience.
   b. Correct: Associative learning is the modification of behavior as the result of experience with the environment.
   c. Incorrect: Reflexive behaviors are involuntary, automatic responses; reading your textbook is not automatic or involuntary.
   d. Incorrect: Instinctive behaviors are inborn complex behavior; reading your text is not an inborn behavior.

2. a. Incorrect: Susie's behavior is the result of an association between a conditioned stimulus (rain), an unconditioned stimulus (her mother's behavior), and a response (her fear). This is classical conditioning.
   b. Incorrect: Susie's behavior is the result of an association between a conditioned stimulus (rain), an unconditioned stimulus (her mother's behavior), and a response (her fear). This is classical conditioning.
   c. **Correct: Susie's behavior is the result of an association between a conditioned stimulus (rain), an unconditioned stimulus (her mother's behavior), and a response (her fear). This is classical conditioning.**
   d. Incorrect: Susie's behavior is the result of an association between a conditioned stimulus (rain), an unconditioned stimulus (her mother's behavior), and a response (her fear). This is classical conditioning.

3. **a. Correct: Richard has associated opening his mouth (CS) with throat exams (UCS). His gagging is a conditioned response.**
   b. Incorrect: Richard has associated opening his mouth (CS) with throat exams (UCS). His gagging is a conditioned response.
   c. Incorrect: Richard has associated opening his mouth (CS) with throat exams (UCS). His gagging is a conditioned response.
   d. Incorrect: Richard has associated opening his mouth (CS) with throat exams (UCS). His gagging is a conditioned response.

4. a. Incorrect: The salivation to the thought of the lemon is a response, not a stimulus.
   b. Correct: The salivation to the thought of the lemon is a conditioned response.
   c. Incorrect: The salivation to the thought of the lemon is a response, not a stimulus, and it is learned, not reflexive.
   d. Incorrect: The salivation to the thought of the lemon is a response, but it is not reflexive; it resulted from the previous association of lemons with the sour taste.

5. a. Incorrect: Extinction refers to the cessation of behavior after the CS is no longer paired with the UCS-UCR.
   b. Correct: The cat is responding to a stimulus similar to the original CS; this is stimulus generalization.
   c. Incorrect: Trace conditioning refers to the method of conditioning in which the CS is presented just prior to the UCS, and then turned off. In this example the original CS is not presented.
   d. Incorrect: In stimulus discrimination the cat would not respond to the blender or drill and only respond to the can opener.

6. a. Incorrect: You are associating a stimulus and response, not a response and a consequence.
   b. Incorrect: Operant and instrumental conditioning are the same thing; since a is incorrect, so is b.
   c. Incorrect: Your association has not been successively approximated, thus it has not been shaped.
   d. Correct: The aftershave smell is now a new CS associated with the old CS (your dad).

7. **a. Correct: Rosa has associated the thunderstorm with the novel taste of ice cream.**
   b. Incorrect: Rosa has associated the thunderstorm with the novel taste of ice cream.
   c. Incorrect: Rosa has associated the thunderstorm with the novel taste of ice cream.
   d. Incorrect: Rosa has associated the thunderstorm with the novel taste of ice cream.

8. a. Incorrect: Primary reinforcers are biologically based; recess time is not biological.
   b. Correct: The teacher gave the children something they wanted; they were "satisfied" and their assignment completing behavior increased.
   c. Incorrect: The teacher is not reinforcing successive approximation of assignment completion or trying to chain together a sequence of behaviors.
   d. Incorrect: Negative reinforcement is the removal of an unwanted stimulus to increase behavior.

9. a. Incorrect: The candy is the primary reinforcement, not the babysitter.
   b. Correct: The baby has discriminated between the parents and the babysitter and responds differently to each.
   c. Incorrect: Negative reinforcement is the removal of an unwanted stimulus to increase behavior.
   d. Incorrect: A punisher is a stimulus that decreases the likelihood of a behavior; the babysitter is increasing the occurrence of temper tantrums.

10. a. Incorrect: In chaining, multiple behaviors are put together into a sequence; Laura is training only one behavior.
    b. Incorrect: Stimulus control refers to the control of behavior by a discriminative stimulus. Laura is not a discriminative stimulus.
    c. Incorrect: Negative reinforcement is the removal of an unwanted stimulus to increase behavior; Laura is giving the puppy a wanted stimuli.
    d. Correct: Laura is reinforcing successive approximations of the paw-shaking behavior. This is shaping.

11. **a. Correct: You generally fish for varied intervals before catching anything.**
    b. Incorrect: Fish are not normally caught at set periods of time.
    c. Incorrect: You don't catch a fish every time you try!
    d. Incorrect: The variable portion is correct; the term "*ratio*" means number of responses.

12. a. Incorrect: In escape conditioning the response leads to end something aversive.
b. Incorrect: The behavior is not decreasing.
c. **Correct: You are going to class to avoid, or prevent, an aversive event.**
d. Incorrect: In this case the consequence of the response is the avoidance of an unwanted stimulus, not the giving of something wanted.

13. a. Incorrect: In escape conditioning the response leads to end something aversive, she is not ending the consequence, she is avoiding it.
b. **Correct: Tammy avoids any class that requires papers; the behavior leads to the prevention of something aversive.**
c. Incorrect: Cognitive learning refers to the acquisition of knowledge.
d. Incorrect: Tammy is not observing anyone else avoid the classes, thus this is not observational learning.

14. a. Incorrect: Punishment involves non-satisfying consequences and decreases behavior; reinforcement involves satisfying consequences and increases behavior.
b. Incorrect: Punishment involves non-satisfying consequences and decreases behavior; reinforcement involves satisfying consequences and increases behavior.
c. Incorrect: Punishment involves non-satisfying consequences and decreases behavior; reinforcement involves satisfying consequences and increases behavior.
d. **Correct: Punishment involves non-satisfying consequences and decreases behavior; reinforcement involves satisfying consequences and increases behavior.**

15. a. Incorrect: Negative reinforcement is satisfying and leads to an increase in behavior.
b. Incorrect: The punishment that she is experiencing is not intermittent; it is continuous.
c. **Correct: Learned helplessness is, as a result of previous experiences, when people believe that there is nothing they can do to change things.**
d. Incorrect: Betty's behavior is not being modified using operant conditioning.

16. a. Incorrect: Spontaneous recovery refers to the reemergence of the response after extinction.
b. Incorrect: Chaining refers to the process by which existing behaviors are trained to occur in a sequence.
c. **Correct: Instinctive drift is the term that the Brelands used to refer to the shift to more species-specific behavior, or the "misbehavior" of their animals.**
d. Incorrect: Behavioral preparedness is the degree to which members of a species are innately prepared to learn particular behaviors.

17. a. Incorrect: You have been associating a response with a consequence, this isn't classical conditioning.
b. Incorrect: The paw-rubbing behavior is not the operant response you wanted; it interferes with the desired response of just putting the coin in the slot.
c. **Correct: The paw-rubbing behavior is a species-specific behavior that the raccoon engages in; this is the result of what the Brelands called instinctive drift.**
d. Incorrect: The paw-rubbing behavior is present at birth; it does not emerge in a preprogrammed sequence, thus it is not maturation.

18. a. Incorrect: Cognitive theorists claim that more than contiguity is involved in associative learning.
b. Incorrect: Cognitive theorists have controlled for the satiation level of the animals.
c. **Correct: Cognitive theorists claim that secondary reinforcers become reinforcers because they have reliably predicted the occurrence of primary reinforcement in the past.**
d. Incorrect: If the dolphins were biologically unprepared to respond to the clicks they would not make the association between the clicks and food.

19. a. Incorrect: Observational learning refers to learning a behavior by observing the consequences that others receive for performing it, in this case another rat is not swimming in the maze
b. Incorrect: Although swimming to obtain a food reward is operant behavior, this is not how Tolman explained his results.
c. **Correct: The rats who observed the maze had the opportunity to develop mental representations, or "cognitive maps" of it.**
d. Incorrect: The rats were not being reinforced for observation of the maze.

20. a. Incorrect: Noncontigent feedback is used as a control for determining if biofeedback is effective.
b. **Correct: A potential possible with biofeedback is the potential of placebo effects due to the use of sophisticated equipment.**
c. Incorrect: Biofeedback has been used effectively to control hyperactivity in children.
d. Incorrect: Biofeedback control of alpha waves was reported in the 1960s, however, it has been hard to replicate.

Essay Questions:

1. The babysitter is the neutral stimulus in this conditioning and Kelly's parents leaving is the UCS. Kelly's crying to seeing the babysitter is the conditioned response. Rescorla would explain Kelly's behavior by saying that the babysitter (CS) predicts the occurrence of the parents leaving (UCS). Thus, Kelly cries because she expects her parents to leave.

2. First, remember to deliver the discriminative stimulus (command) "Walk!" at each repeated trial in the training. Then, first reinforce her for walking toward the easily seen and reached leash. Second, reinforce her only for walking toward and then mouthing the leash. After this is mastered, reinforce her for performing all these previous behaviors in addition to removing the leash from its usual place. Ultimately, reinforce her for walking to, picking up, and carrying the leash to you but only after you say, "Walk!"

8 Memory

LEARNING OBJECTIVES

After studying this chapter, you should be able to:

1. Define flashbulb memory and summarize what is known about this phenomenon of memory. (p. 272)

2. Define memory and summarize the Jamesian view of the functions of memory. (p. 272)

3. Summarize the important features of the Shiffrin & Atkinson information-processing model of memory, emphasizing the concepts of encoding, storage, and retrieval. (p. 273-274)

4. Describe the important features of sensory memory, emphasizing the results of Sperling's partial report study. (p. 274-276)

5. Describe the important features of short-term memory, mentioning the duration and capacity of working memory, and explaining how these can increase by maintenance rehearsal and chunking, and decrease by decay and displacement. (p. 276-277)

6. Explain the relationship between elaborative rehearsal and encoding in long-term memory. (p. 278)

7. Summarize the important features of Craik & Lockhart's levels of processing theory and explain how the findings regarding elaborative rehearsal support this theory. (p. 279)

8. Draw a diagram that describes and illustrates the relationships among the various kinds of memory that comprise long-term memory. (p. 279-281)

9. List and describe the important features of two theories that attempt to explain how semantic and episodic memories are organized in long-term memory. (p. 281-283)

10. Explain how two theories attempt to account for retrieval from long-term memory, mentioning the concept of constructive recall. (p. 283-284)

11. Summarize the methods and findings of Ebbinghaus's classic memory research, mentioning the serial-position effect, the methods of savings, and the forgetting curve. (p. 284-286)

12. List and explain four other approaches to explaining why we forget, distinguishing between retroactive and proactive interference, repression, the tip-of-the-tongue phenomenon and context- and state-dependent memory. (p. 286-292)

13. Summarize the important features of the SQ3R method of study, and explain how techniques such as overlearning, distributed practice, and use of the various mnemonic devices can improve one's memory. (p. 292-295)

14. Explain the significance of Lashley's early studies of animal memory and current research with aplysia in the understanding of where memories are stored in the brain, mentioning long-term potentiation, the role of the hippocampus, and "H. M." (p. 296-299)

15. Explain the roles of the neurotransmitter acetylcholine, the amino acid NMDA, the hormone epinephrine, and glucose in memory consolidation. (p. 299-301)

16. Summarize the important findings of studies on eyewitness identification, the accuracy of children's testimony, and the effect of biasing, or leading questions, on memory. (p. 301-305)

COMPREHENSIVE REVIEW

Memory is the process by which information is acquired,__(1)__ in the brain, later retrieved, and possibly forgotten. Do you recall where you were when the *Challenger* disaster occurred? If so, you are experiencing a ___(2)__ memory—a long-lasting memory of a surprising, important, emotionally arousing event. Recent research supports the idea that the formation of a **flashbulb memory** requires that the event be perceived as important and___(3)__, but exactly what accounts for flashbulb memories is still unclear. Some psychologists feel that flashbulb memories involve a special__(4)__ mechanism; others feel that memory relies more on experiences. They believe that we think more __(5)__ about more significant events, and this explains why flashbulb memories are so detailed. Support for this claim comes from a study done in 1993 with college students and their memories of the U.S. attack on Baghdad in the Persian Gulf War. Results indicated that although their memories of__(6)__ events were no less accurate than those of the attack on Baghdad, the students had more __(7)__in their memories of the Persian Gulf War. Thus, Weaver concludes that__(8)__ memories seem special because of the confidence we place in them.

I. Information Processing and Memory: During the past few decades research in to memory has been driven by the __(9)__ revolution in psychology. This perspective views the mind as an__(10)__ processor. The most influential model of memory is the Shiffrin & Atkinson (1969) **information-processing model.** This model assumes that memory involves three successive stages: **sensory memory,**__(11)__ **memory,** and **long-term memory.** (*It may help to refer to Figure 8.1 on page 274 in your textbook as you study the sections on information processing.)*

__(12)__memory stores exact replicas of stimuli impinging on each of the senses from less than 1 second (visual sensory memory) to 4 seconds (auditory sensory memory). The information is then transferred to short-term memory, which stores information for about__(13)__ seconds, unless you maintain it through a mental rehearsal. Information is then transferred to__(14)__ **memory,** where it is stored for a lifetime. The model compares processing at each stage to information processing by a__(15)__. It involves __(16)__, or converting information into a form that can be stored in memory; __(17)__, or the retention of information in memory; and__(18)__, the recovery of information from memory. The model notes that we are also subject to__(19)__, which is the failure to retrieve information from memory.

II. Sensory Memory:__(20)__ sensory memory is known as **iconic memory,** and auditory sensory memory is known as__(21)__ **memory.**

Visual Sensory Memory: Psychologists had determined that the reason we see smooth motion, as opposed to a series of picture frames is because of the actions of our__(22)__ sensory memory. It was known that visual sensory memory stored information for up to a__(23)__; however, psychologists wanted to know how much of the information that our visual receptors detect was actually transferred to sensory memory. That led to the classic research study by Sperling summarized on page 274 of your textbook.

Read the summary of George Sperling's classic study and then answer the questions below to test your understanding of the research.

Anatomy of a Classic Research Study: Do We Form Sensory Memories of All the Information That Stimulates Our Sensory Receptors?

What was the rationale for the study?

What methods did the authors use to test the hypothesis?

What was the outcome of the study and what did the authors conclude the results meant?

Auditory Sensory Memory:___(24)___ sensory memory blends together successive pieces of auditory information. It stores information___(25)___ than iconic memory, holding information for approximately 4 seconds. An area in the___(26)___ auditory cortex has been identified that processes echoic sensory memory.

III. Short-Term Memory: Short-term memory is known as the___(27)___ memory. Why? Because we work with it; we use it to manipulate information provided by either sensory memory or___(28)___ memory. Information that is transferred into short-term memory is represented by one of three codes: a visual code (___(29)___), an acoustic code (sounds), or a___(30)___ code (meanings).

Capacity: Short term memory has a___(31)___ capacity. Information is stored in___(32)___ (units of meaningful information), such as a number, a letter, or a word. The limit appears to be between 5 and___(33)___ chunks. George Miller called this the "magic___(34)___, plus or minus two." Miller also noted that the ability to chunk individual items can increase the amount of information stored in___(35)___ memory.

Duration: In addition to having limits on the amount of information that short-term memory can hold, the brain also has a limit to how___(36)___ the information can be held. Peterson & Peterson demonstrated that without ___(37)___, information is stored for no more than 20 seconds. But, if we use___(38)___ rehearsal by repeating the information to ourselves, we can store it in short-term memory for as long as we want. Research has suggested that the loss of information from short-term memory occurs primarily through a___(39)___ process in which the information fades over time. However, it has also been shown that short-term memories can be lost through ___(40)___ by new information.

Time for a short study break to allow for your short-term memory to process the information presented so far. Be sure to review before moving on to the next section of the text.

Mini-review of Sensory and Short-term Memory: Match each term with its correct description.

________1. memory	A. Capacity of short-term memory
________2. retrieval	B. Long-lasting memory of a surprising, important, emotionally arousing event
________3. long term memory	C. The most influential model of memory, assumes that memory involves processing in three successive stages
________4. iconic memory	D. Stores exact replicas of stimuli impinging on each of the senses from less than 1 second to 4 seconds
________5. storage	E. The process by which information is acquired, stored in the brain, later retrieved, and possibly forgotten
________6. seven, plus or minus two	F. Place where information is stored for a lifetime
________7. flashbulb memory	G. Auditory sensory memory
________8. echoic memory	H. Conversion of information into a form that can be stored in memory
________9. short term memory	I. The recovery of information from memory
________10. information-processing model	J. The failure to retrieve information from memory
________11. sensory memory	K. Visual sensory memory
________12. encoding	L. The retention of information in memory
________13. forgetting	M. Stores information for about 20 seconds, unless you maintain it through a mental rehearsal

IV. Long-Term Memory: ___(41)___ memory is the relatively permanent storage component. At best long-term memory can store a___(42)___ amount of information with great accuracy, while, at worst, it may fail to store at all. Long-term memory is encoded in various forms, stored in an___(43)___ manner, retrieved using cues, and forgotten through improper___(44)___ or insufficient cues.

Encoding: How is information encoded, or___(45)___, in long-term memory? It is encoded through a process that ___(46)___ organizes and integrates it with information already stored in long-term memory. This is known as **elaborative rehearsal,** as opposed to ___(47)___ rehearsal, where we simply hold information in short-term memory without trying to transfer it into long-term memory. ____(48)____ rehearsal is a superior method of encoding more detailed information. The increased____(49)__ of information using elaborative rehearsal supports Craik & Lockhart's **levels of processing theory.** Craik & Lockhart believe that it is the "__(50)__" at which we encode information that determines how well that information is stored. Listening only to a melody, without ever attending to the lyrics, is an example of a__(51)__ level of processing. Listening to the lyrics and thinking about their____(52)__ requires a much deeper level of processing, but will lead to better retention of the information, according to the theory.

Storage: Information is stored primarily as___(53)__ (where our memory is better) or as words. According to Endel Tulving, information is stored in two kinds of long-term memory: **procedural memory** (also known as___(54)__ memory), which includes memories of how to perform behaviors, and___(55)__ memory **(explicit memory)**, or memories of facts. Tulving further divides declarative memory into___(56)__ memory, which includes memories of general knowledge; and___(57)__ memory, which includes memories of personal experiences tied to particular times and places. There is evidence from electrical activity and ___(58)__ studies to support the idea that the brain evolved two different memory systems, one for___(59)__ memory and one for **declarative memory.** However, there are those who question the idea of multiple memory systems.

Whether or not you agree that long-term memory is organized into separate memory systems, one thing that everyone agrees on is that long-term memory has an___(60)__ structure. There are two theories that explain how information in these systems is organized. They are the **semantic network theory** and the **schema theory.**

Semantic Network Theory: This theory explains how___(61)__ information is meaningfully organized in long-term memory. The theory assumes that memories are stored as___(62)__ (concepts) connected by **links** (___(63)__ between two concepts). The retrieval of a node from memory stimulates activation of related nodes, so-called spreading___(64)__.

Schema Theory: An alternative to the network theory of memory organization, ___(65)__ theory is used to explain both ___(66)__ and semantic memory. This theory was first proposed by Frederick Bartlett, who argued that long-term memories were organized a parts of a schema, or___(67)__ structure that organizes knowledge and affects the encoding, storage, and retrieval of the knowledge.

Retrieval: According to the____(68)____ theory, the retrieval of information from long-term memory begins with searching a particular region of memory and then tracing the associations among memories (nodes) in that region. This process is analogous to looking for a book in the___(69)__. By contrast,____(70)_____ assumes that as we retrieve memories, we may alter them to make them consistent with our schemas. Ulric Neisser (1981) used John Dean's testimony at the Watergate hearings to provide support for the schema theory of memory___(71)__. He concluded that Dean used____(72)____, which is the distortion of memories by adding or changing details to fit the schema, in recalling his long-term memories of the events. Thus, there is support for the idea that___(73)__ do influence our recall of information. However, both theories argue that retrieval is clearly___(74)__, not haphazard, and at this time, neither has offered the best explanation of the storage and retrieval of long-term memories.

Forgetting: William James believed that___(75)__ was adaptive because it rids us of useless information that might impair the ability to remember useful information. However, sometimes, we even forget___(76)__ information as well. ____(77)____ was the first researcher to formally study **forgetting,** or the inability to remember previously stored information. He found that recall is worse for items in the___(78)__ of a list than at the beginning and the end of the list. This is known as the____(79)____. The better memory for items at the___(80)__ of the list is called the **primacy effect**, whereas the better memory for items at the end of the list is called the ___(81)__ effect.

What accounts for the **serial-position effect?** The fact that items at the beginning are subject to more rehearsal and hence are more readily placed into long-term memory is suggested to account for the___(82)__ effect. The **recency effect** appears to occur because the items at the end of the list remain readily accessible in___(83)__ memory. The items in the ____(84)____ of the list are neither placed firmly into long-term memory nor readily accessible in short-term memory.

Prior to Ebbinghaus, memory research had been unsystematic and__(85)__. Ebbinghaus introduced a new way to access memory. This is the **method of savings,** now called__(86)__. He showed that it takes__(87)__ trials to relearn a list than it does to learn it originally. ___(88)__ occurs because **relearning** improves the ___(89)__of information stored in memory. ___(90)__ has been used as a method of testing **implicit** memory. ___(91)__ memory is tested using other methods, such as a recognition test, that test your ability to recognize information that you have been exposed to previously; and___(92)__ tests, in which you are asked to remember all the information you can about the topic being presented.

Ebbinghaus also studied the__(93)__ at which we forget. Ebbinghaus's classic **forgetting curve** shows that most forgetting occurs in the first few__(94)__ and then slows. However, meaningless nonsense syllables show more__(95)__ initial forgetting than meaningful material. Various theories have been proposed to explain why forgetting occurs. These include **decay theory, interference theory, motivation theory** and **cue dependence theory.**

___(96)___**theory** argues that memories make an imprint in the memory system; over time that imprint weakens and disappears. Decay theory has received__(97)__ research support, as evidenced by the Jenkins & Dallenbach (1924) study in which subjects experienced better retention over time if they slept than if they were awake.

___(98)__**theory** appears to be a better explanation of forgetting than decay theory. It assumes that forgetting results from particular memories interfering with the retrieval of other memories. There are two types of interference: **proactive interference,** wherein___(99)__ memories interfere with new memories; and___(100)__ **interference,** wherein new memories interfere with old ones.

___(101)__**theory:** Freud argued that people forget through the process of__(102)__, in which emotionally threatening experiences are banished to the unconscious mind. Although research has not shown this to be a tenable position, some evidence suggests that we are more motivated to forget ___(103)__upsetting experiences. Beyond this there has been a considerable amount of research on the__(104)__ between motivation and forgetting that suggests we may be motivated to distort our recall of the past in ways that make it more consistent with present perceptions.

Cue-dependence Theory: Forgetting can sometimes be explained by the failure to have adequate ___(105)___. A good example is the **tip-of-the-**___(106)__ **phenomenon,** in which you cannot quite recall a familiar word but can recall parts of the word. Studies of this phenomenon support the concept of____(107)____, which states that recall will be best when cues present during encoding are also available during retrieval. These cues may be related to:

1) ___(108)___**-dependent memory.** In this instance you perform best where you learn. Controversy exists about whether the environment context is important when recall is required, but not when recognition is required.
2) ___(109)__**-dependent memory.** Internal states also affect our recall of information. If your internal state during encoding is similar to your internal state during retrieval you will recall more. People who learn in a drug-induced state recall better in that same state, depending, of course, on the nature of the drug.
3) ___(110)___**-dependent memory.** This is a form of state-dependent memory in which our recall of information that has been encoded in a particular mood will be best when we are in that mood again. Related to this is the phenomenon of__(111)__ memory which argues that there is a better tendency to recall mood consistent with ones' current mood.

Mini-review of Long-term Memory: Match each term with its correct description.

_______1. semantic network theory
_______2. semantic memory
_______3. elaborative rehearsal
_______4. serial-position effect
_______5. proactive interference
_______6. long-term memory
_______7. declarative memory
_______8. cue-dependence theory
_______9. maintenance rehearsal
_______10. procedural memory
_______11. repression
_______12. primacy effect
_______13. episodic memory
_______14. levels of processing theory
_______15. forgetting
_______16. decay theory
_______17. schema theory
_______18. mood-dependent memory
_______19. retroactive interference
_______20. constructive recall
_______21. recency effect
_______22. context-dependent memory
_______23. method of savings
_______24. tip-of-the-tongue phenomenon
_______25. relearning
_______26. interference theory
_______27. state-dependent memory
_______28. motivation theory

A. The relatively permanent storage component
B. Argues that internal states also affect our recall of information
C. Process that actively organizes and integrates it with information already stored in long-term memory
D. Process by which we simply hold information in short-term memory without trying to transfer it into long-term memory
E. Argues that it is the "depth" at which we encode information that determines how well that information is stored
F. Also known as implicit memory; includes memories of how to perform behaviors
G. Assumes that memories are stored as concepts connected by links
H. Inference wherein old memories interfere with new memories
I. Also known as explicit memory; memories of facts
J. Better memory for items at the end of the list
K. Memories of general knowledge
L. Term for when you cannot quite recall a familiar word but can recall parts of the word
M. Argues that long-term memories were organized as parts of a concept structure that affects the encoding, storage and retrieval of the knowledge
N. Current term for the fact that it takes fewer trials to relearn a list than it does to learn it originally
O. Memories of personal experiences tied to particular times and places
P. Assumes that forgetting results from particular memories interfering with the retrieval of other memories
Q. Effect that argues that recall is worse for items in the middle of a list than at the beginning and the end of the list
R. Ebbinghaus's method to access memory
S. States that recall will be best when cues present during encoding are also available during retrieval
T. The distortion of memories by adding or changing details to fit the schema
U. Process where new memories interfere with old ones
V. Better memory for items at the beginning of the list
W. The inability to remember previously stored information
X. Argues that memories make an imprint in the memory system; over time that imprint weakens and disappears
Y. Argues that forgetting occurs through the process of repression
Z. Process by which emotionally threatening experiences are banished to the unconscious mind
Aa. Argues that you perform best in the place where you learn
Bb. Is a form of state-dependent memory in which our recall of information that has been encoded in a particular mood will be best when we are in that mood again

V. Improving Your Memory: Memory can be improved by the use of effective ____(112)____ and by using mnemonic devices.

Effective Study Habits: Good study habits are the key to success in___(113)__. The first step to good study habits is establishing a__(114)__ of study times. Be sure to plan study sessions when you are most awake, alert, and __(115)__. The second step is to locate a good__(116)__ for effective studying. The best location for studying has good light, is quiet, comfortable, and free of__(117)__. Last, you should establish an effective study__(118)__.

The **SQ3R method** is a study technique that has proved helpful to many college students. The elements of this technique are: **Survey, Question, Read, Recite, Review.** This technique is different from rote memorization since it requires ___(119)___ of material and, when used properly, leads to a deeper level of processing.

1. **Survey** the main headings and subheadings to create a ___(120)___ for the information you are studying.
2. Ask yourself ___(121)___ about the topic to be answered as you read.
3. **Read** the material ___(122)___ to find the answers to the questions. The answers will be found not only in the paragraphs but in the tables, figures, illustrations, and definitions of terms in the margins.
4. ___(123)___**:** Say the information to yourself to see if you understand it. Do not leave a section until you are sure that you understand the answers to your questions.
5. **Review:** Every few days you should look again at the material and ___(124)___ yourself on the information. Continue to review the material to the point of ___(125)___ it. In other words, study the material until you feel you know all of it—and then go over it several more times.

In addition to the use of the SQ3R study technique, use the ___(126)___ practice schedule that we have encouraged in this study guide. In **distributed practice** you study in small increments and take short breaks, rather than massing your practice time together. Spacing study time is much more pleasant than cramming, and it makes more efficient use of your memory!

Using Mnemonic Devices: A ___(127)___ is a technique for organizing information to be memorized to make it easier to remember. Your textbook discusses four types: **method of loci, acronyms, pegword method,** and **link method.**
___(128)___ is useful for memorizing sets of items. To use a method of loci method for the material in this chapter you would memorize the concrete terms from this chapter and associate them with places and landmarks.
___(129)___ is obtained by taking a mental walk and visualizing all of the locations.
___(130)___ are terms formed with the first letters of a series of words.
___(131)___: This mnemonic device relies on both imagery and rhyming. For the method to work well, the image of the pegword object and the image of the object to be recalled should interact.
___(132)___: This method involves taking images of the items to be memorized and connecting them in sequence. One form is the narrative method, in which unrelated items are connected to one another in a story.

Time to practice what we preach; take a short study break. When you return, remember to review the previous section of the chapter using the mini-review on improving memory before you move on.

Mini-review of Memory Improvement Techniques: Fill in the correct words to describe the steps of the SQ3R technique and write yourself brief notes as to what to do at each step.

S________**:**
Q________**:**
R________**:**
R________**:**
R________**:**

VI. The Biopsychology of Memory: Many psychobiological researchers have conducted research into the neuroanatomy and ___(133)___ of memory, and today the research is revealing plenty. Karl ___(134)___ was one of the first researchers to show an interest in the biological basis of memory. Lashley's search for the ___(135)___, or memory trace, led to frustration. Undaunted, many researchers have continued to search for the **engram.** Among the studies are those conducted by Krupa, Thompson, & Thompson (1984), in which they identified an engram in the ___(136)___ of rabbits, and Kandel & Schwartz (1992) who identified a neural engram in a ___(137)___.

In ___(138)___ memory, the engram is suggested to be involved in the facilitation of the transmission of neural impulses at specific synapses. This is called **long-term potentiation,** which appears to depend on the release of a ___(139)___ that crosses synapses and stimulates other neurons in the relevant pathway. Researchers who study ___(140)___ are particularly interested in the hippocampus. Evidence pointing to the role of the ___(141)___ comes both from animal and human brain damage studies. Human evidence comes from___(142)__ patients and a case study of H. M. , whose temporal lobes, including most of his hippocampus, were removed. As a result of the surgery, H.M. developed **anterograde amnesia** and was no longer able to form new long-term___(143)__ memories. He could, however, form new procedural memories.

In addition to looking at a___(144)__ basis for memory, biopsychological researchers have studied the neurochemistry of memory as well. James McConnell's (1959) classic flatworm study appeared to indicate that the memory of the classically conditioned response had been encoded___(145)__ and distributed throughout the flatworm's body. Another study demonstrated the apparent chemical___(146)__ of memory, and in 1972 , a study by Unger, Desiderio & Parr claimed to isolate the protein-like substance *scotophobin*. However even more recently numerous scientists have failed to replicate memory transfers.

While___(147)__ studies continue to provoke controversy, such is not the case regarding the role of_____(148)__ in memory. Most strongly implicated is___(149)_, with its role in Alzheimer's disease. Autopsies of victims of Alzheimer's disease shows degeneration of the acetylcholine neurons that connect the___(150)__to other areas of the brain; drugs that___(151)__ acetylcholine receptors, when given to normal patients, induce Alzheimer's-like memory losses. However, this research is also not without difficulties. It would seem logical that if not enough acetylcholine were the problem, then___(152)__ brain levels of it would correct the problem. Unfortunately this has had limited success.

The most successful and exciting area of interest in the neurochemistry of memory surrounds the___(153)__ receptors. NMDA, an amino acid, binds to specific receptors in the hippocampus and enhances the___(154)__ of the synaptic transmission.

Additionally,__(155)__ appear to be involved in memory. Memory storage is promoted by administering the stimulant ___(156)__, which increases the release of epinephrine. Additionally, the release of___(157)__ has been implicated in memory formation. There is a positive___(158)__ between blood glucose levels and memory performance, and glucose tablets have been shown to improve memory temporarily in Alzheimer's patients. However, before you go out and ingest large amounts of sugar, realize that the greatest enhancement of memory is seen with___(159)__ amounts of glucose.

Take a moment to review this material before continuing on to the "Thinking about Psychology" section.

Mini-review of Biopsychology of Memory: Match each term with its correct description.

____1. Karl Lashley
____2. engram
____3. long-term potentiation
____4. H. M.
____5. anterograde amnesia
____6. scotophobin
____7. acetylcholine
____8. NMDA
____9. epinephrine

A. The physiological memory trace
B. An amino acid that binds to specific receptor in the hippocampus and enhances the efficiency of the synaptic transmission
C. Hormone believed to be involved in memory storage
D. Neurotransmitter believed to be involved in memory formation
E. First researcher to show an interest in the biological basis of memory
F. The inability to form new long-term memories
G. Proteinlike substance believed to be involved in memory transfer
H. Patient whose temporal lobes, including most of his hippocampus, were removed
I. The facilitation of the transmission of neural impulses at specific synapses

VII. Thinking About Psychology: Should We Trust Eyewitness Testimony?

In a famous case, Father Pagano was falsely identified by seven eyewitnesses as the gentleman bandit, Ronald Clouser. The possibility of convicting innocent people has led psychologists to study the factors that affect___(160)__. The main concern of this line of research has focused on the__(161)__ of children's testimony and the effects of leading questioning.

The research demonstrates that children are___(162)___ accurate than adults in their eyewitness accounts, in general because they are more subject to suggestion. Further research has shown that younger children are less accurate than older children and that children, overall, are more prone to___(163)___.

Although adults may be more accurate than children, a main factor in accuracy of testimony with adults is the ___(164)___ of questions. Elizabeth___(165)___ has demonstrated the influence of questioning on eyewitness testimony in many studies. A study by Loftus & Palmer is the focus of the Anatomy of a Contemporary Research Study.

Read the summary of this study on page 304 in your textbook and answer the following questions.

Anatomy of a Contemporary Research Study: Can Leading Questions Influence Eyewitness Testimony?

What was the rationale for this study?

What methods did the authors use to test their hypothesis?

What was the outcome of the study and what did the authors conclude the results meant?

Although leading questions have been shown to affect the___(166)___ of eyewitness testimony, further research has indicated that this may not be as powerful as expected. Eyewitness memory may be___(167)___ by mentally reinstating the physical setting of the event and___(168)___ eyewitnesses that some information will be false.

KEY RESEARCH FINDINGS

Provide the details of the following key research studies in psychology:

1. **Colegrove (1899):** Surveyed middle-aged adults on memories of what they were doing at the time Lincoln was shot. (Page 272)
2. **Conway et al. (1994):** Surveyed U.S. and British citizens on memories surrounding Margaret Thatcher's resignation. (Page 272)
3. **Weaver (1993):** Compared students' memories of attack on Baghdad with constructed vivid memories of an everyday event 6 and 12 months after the event. (Page 272)
4. **Sperling (1960):** Using a partial report procedure, measured amount of information stored in iconic memory. (Page 274)
5. **Conrad (1962):** Compared recall from short term memory of letters that were similar in sound and shape. (Page 276)
6. **Miller (1956):** Noted that short-term memory was limited to the "magic number seven." (Page 276)
7. **Chase & Simon (1973):** Compared chess experts to nonexperts in the ability to store memory of chess positions. (Page 277)
8. **Peterson & Peterson (1959):** Measured amount of time that information normally remains in short-term memory. (Page 277)
9. **Schilling & Weaver (1983):** Demonstrated the effects of distractors on retention of information in short-term memory. (Page 277)
10. **Nickerson & Adams (1979):** Examined the percent of Americans that could recognize the correct image on a penny. (Page 278)
11. **Rivera-Tovar & Jones (1990):** Examined that use of elaborative rehearsal in teaching children CPR. (Page 278)
12. **Lockhart & Craik (1990):** Tested memory differences based on level at which information was processed. (Page 279)
13. **Craik & Tulving (1975):** Provided support for the levels of precessing theory of memory. (Page 279)

14. **Klimesch, Schimke, & Schwaiger (1994):** Associated different memory types with different brain-wave activity. (Page 280)
15. **Schacter (1983):** Demonstrated that an Alzheimer's patient had differential deficits in procedural, episodic, and semantic memories. (Page 280)
16. **Ericsson & Polson (1988):** Demonstrated the ability of increasing memory through the use of categorizing. (Page 281)
17. **Bartlett (1932):** Found that British college students found the theme of a story but added, eliminated, or changed details to fit their own story schemas. (Page 283)
18. **Harris, Schoen, & Hensley (1992):** Found that American and Mexican students remembered stories that fit with their cultural expectations. (Page 283)
19. **Macklin (1994):** Demonstrated that a visual cue enabled children to remember a cereal better. (Page 283)
20. **Neisser (1981):** Examined John Dean's testimony and concluded that it fit with the use of schemas in construction of memories. (page 284)
21. **Ebbinghaus (1885/1913):** Demonstrated the forgetting curve and serial-position effect. (Page 284-285)
22. **Bahrick (1984):** Demonstrated the permanent nature of long-term memory. (Page 286)
23. **Jenkins & Dallenbach (1924):** Showed that subjects had better recall if they slept rather than if they remained awake. (Page 286)
24. **Hoemann & Keske (1995):** Suggested that sign language and verbal language may use different memory systems. (Page 287)
25. **Loftus & Burns (1982):** Demonstrated that subjects who had seen the violent version of a robbery had poorer recall of the details of the crime than did subjects who had seen the nonviolent version. (Page 288)
26. **Conway & Ross (1984):** Suggested that distorted memories of a study skills group may have reflected members' desire to have their participation pay off. (Page 288)
27. **Yarmey (1973):** Examined the use of cues in improving retrieval abilities and supported the concept of encoding specificity. (Page 289)
28. **Godden & Baddeley (1975):** Indicated that scuba divers who memorized and recalled lists of words in different locations recalled fewer words than when they memorized and recalled the words in the same location. (Page 290)
29. **Smith & Vela (1992):** Demonstrated that recognition was better in the same context as information was memorized. (Page 290)
30. **Eich et al. (1975):** Examined the influence of marijuana on memory formation and recall. (Page 291)
31. **Ehrlichman & Halpern (1988):** Investigated the influence of odors on recall of emotional memories. (Page 292)
32. **Flannagan & Blick (1989):** Indicated that students who used elaborative rehearsal recalled more information. (Page 293)
33. **Gathercole & Conway (1988):** Found that subjects who read terms out loud later remembered more of them than did subjects who read them silently, wrote them down, or heard them spoken by someone else. (Page 293)
34. **Driskell, Willis, & Cooper (1992):** Performed meta-analysis of the benefits of overlearning. (Page 293)
35. **Bouzid & Crawshaw (1987):** Demonstrated that distributed training in a word-processing seminar led to significantly faster and more accurate performance. (Page 293)
36. **Bower & Clark (1969):** Demonstrated that a group that used a narrative mnemonic device recalled more words than those that used mental rehearsal. (Page 295)
37. **Lashley (1950):** Unsuccessfully searched for the "engram," the physiological substrate for memory. (Page 297)
38. **Kandel & Schwartz (1982):** Successfully demonstrated the existence of an engram for a classically conditioned response in the snail. (Page 297)
39. **Krupa, Thompson & Thompson (1993):** Successfully demonstrated the existence of an engram for a classically conditioned response in the rabbit. (Page 297)
40. **Scoville & Milner (1957):** Case study of H. M. (Page 298)
41. **Cohen & Squire (1980):** Demonstrated that subjects with anterograde amnesia had the ability to form new procedural memories, but not declarative ones. (Page 299)
42. **McConnell, Jacobson, & Kimble (1959):** Demonstrated that both regenerated halves of flatworms learned to respond to the light at the same rate. (Page 299)
43. **Unger, Desiderio, & Parr (1972):** Demonstrated chemical transfer of memories in rats. (Page 299)
44. **Nissen, Knopman, & Schacter (1987):** Examined the role of acetylcholine in memory recall. (Page 300)

45. **Kim et al. (1991):** Showed that a drug that blocked NMDA receptors prevented the formation of a conditioned response. (Page 300)
46. **Cahill et al. (1994):** Demonstrated that an epinephrine blocker interfered with memory of an emotional story. (Page 300)
47. **Manning, Parsons, & Gold (1992):** Showed the effects of increased blood glucose levels on memory. (Page 301)
48. **Ceci, Ross, & Toglia (1987):** Demonstrated the effects of misleading questions on children's testimony. (Page 302)
49. **Gordon & Follmer (1994):** Examined the accuracy of testimony in 3- to 7-year-old children. (Page 303)
50. **Beal, Schmitt, & Dekle (1995):** Demonstrated the tendency for children to guess or make up answers when their memory is unclear. (Page 303)
51. **Loftus& Palmer (1974):** Examined the influence of leading questions on eyewitness testimony. (Page 304)
52. **Greene, Flynn, & Loftus (1982):** Examined the influence of a warning as to possible misleading information on eyewitness testimony. (Page 305)

Time to quiz yourself to be sure that your studying is leading to overlearning! Take the practice tests below and evaluate the areas that you need to go back and review.

PRACTICE TEST A

1. Many older Americans have unusually vivid memories of the circumstances in which they heard that the Japanese had attacked Pearl Harbor on December 7, 1941. These memories are called
   a. engrams.
   b. mnemonics.
   c. echoic memories.
   d. flashbulb memories.

Obj.: 1 Page: 272

2. The process by which we store information in the brain, later retrieved and eventually forgotten is called
   a. learning.
   b. memory.
   c. cognition.
   d. intelligence.

Obj.: 2 Page: 272

3. The stage of memory that can store a few items of unrehearsed information for up to about 20 seconds is called
   a. sensory memory.
   b. episodic memory.
   c. long-term memory.
   d. short-term memory.

Obj.: 3 Page: 273

4. To test the claims of his subjects Sperling (1960) initially used a
   a. partial-report procedure.
   b. whole-report procedure.
   c. questionnaire.
   d. random-report procedure.

Obj.: 4 Page: 274-276

5. When you attend to information in your sensory memory, it enters your
   a. engram.
   b. long-term memory.
   c. preconscious mind.
   d. short-term memory.

Obj.: 5 Page: 276

6. Repeating information to oneself to keep it in short-term memory is called
   a. maintenance rehearsal.
   b. elaborative rehearsal.
   c. cognitive rehearsal.
   d. processing rehearsal.

Obj.: 6 Page: 278

7. According to the levels of processing theory, your memories for material in this chapter will be strongest if they have been processed at the
   a. visual level.
   b. auditory level.
   c. semantic level.
   d. olfactory level.

Obj.: 7 Page: 279

8. Tulving argues that we have two kinds of long-term memory. What are they?
   a. procedural and episodic memory
   b. semantic and procedural memory
   c. declarative and semantic memory
   d. procedural and declarative memory

Obj.: 8 Page: 279-281

9. After suffering a stroke, a person recovers and learns how to cook gourmet meals, but forgets ever having learned how to cook them. This shows the difference between
   a. semantic memory and procedural memory.
   b. procedural memory and episodic memory.
   c. semantic memory and declarative memory.
   d. episodic memory and declarative memory.

Obj.: 9 Page: 281

10. The distortion of memories by adding or changing details to fit a schema is known as
   a. cognition.
   b. relearning.
   c. semantic networks.
   d. constructive recall.

Obj.: 10 Page: 283-284

11. The serial-position effect supports the distinction between
   a. short-term and long-term memory.
   b. procedural and declarative memory.
   c. maintenance and elaborative rehearsal.
   d. the method of savings and relearning.

Obj.: 11 Page: 284-286

12. On Monday you study for a biology test. On Tuesday you study for a psychology test. On Wednesday you take a psychology test. If material you studied on Monday interferes with your ability to recall information you studied on Tuesday, you would experience
   a. retrograde amnesia.
   b. anterograde amensia.
   c. proactive interference.
   d. retroactive interference.

Obj.: 12 Page: 287

13. A football quarterback memorizes his team's playbook by studying 2 hours a day for 10 days, rather than trying to master it in one 20-hour session. He would be making use of
   a. overlearning.
   b. massed practice.
   c. distributed practice.
   d. maintenance rehearsal.

Obj.: 13 Page: 293

14. A person suffers damage to the hippocampus. She would be *least* likely to have difficulty
   a. recalling where she had breakfast earlier today.
   b. remembering the names of people she met yesterday.
   c. studying this textbook chapter and taking an exam on it.
   d. learning how to use a CD player and retaining that ability later.

Obj.: 14 Page: 298-299

15. A freshman in the twenty-first century ingests a food supplement that enhances her ability to retain information she studies. The supplement probably increased her brain's level of
   a. GABA.
   b. dopamine.
   c. acetylcholine.
   d. glutamic acid.

Obj.: 15 Page: 300

16. Research by Elizabeth Loftus indicates that the accuracy of eyewitness recall may be affected by
   a. hypnosis.
   b. repression.
   c. leading questions.
   d. alcohol intoxication.

Obj.: 16 Page: 304-305

PRACTICE TEST B

1. You can remember with great detail where you were and what you were doing on the day of the Oklahoma City bombing. This is an example of
   a. a short-term memory.
   b. a flashblub memory.
   c. an engram.
   d. semantic memory.

Obj.: 1 Page: 272

2. At a shopping mall, your ability to find your way to your parked car easily demonstrates that you
   a. have a memory of the layout of the mall.
   b. are psychic.
   c. have learned by classical conditioning.
   d. have high intelligence.

Obj.: 2 Page: 273

3. On her personal computer, Celia blocks out a paragraph and then presses the "delete" key. This action is comparable to which memory-related process?
   a. encoding
   b. storage
   c. retrieval
   d. forgetting

Obj.: 3 Page: 273

4. The classic research study involving "partial reports" by George Sperling demonstrated that
   a. the sensory registers for all of the senses hold information for the same amount of time.
   b. iconic memory holds all the information that stimulates our visual receptors for less than a second.
   c. short-term memory holds all the information received by the sensory register.
   d. chunking can increase the amount of information held by short-term memory.

Obj.: 4 Page: 274-275

5. Why is short-term memory called "working memory"?
   a. It can attend to many streams of sensory data at the same time and has both long capacity and duration.
   b. It works hard to automatically extend its storage capacity.
   c. It functions to average out the length of time that sensory data remain in each sensory register.
   d. It continually processes selected sensory data and retrieves information from long-term memory.

Obj.: 5 Page: 276

6. If you had to learn a list of twenty items, you would be better off to break the list into two units of ten items each. This would permit you to take advantage of the
   a. primacy effect.
   b. recency effect.
   c. sequential-position effect.
   d. primacy and recency effects.

Obj.: 5 Page: 279

7. On an exam, in order to accurately remember the information contained in a chapter of your textbook, you must engage in
   a. echoic rehearsal.
   b. maintenance rehearsal.
   c. elaborative rehearsal.
   d. cue-dependent rehearsal.

Obj.: 6 Page: 278

8. Cathi decides to study for her psychology exam. According to Craik and Lockhart, which level of processing should she use to maximize her performance on the test?
   a. a visual level
   b. an echoic level
   c. semantic level
   d. an acoustic level

Obj.: 7 Page: 279

9. Remembering the exact date when Madame Curie discovered radium is an example of what type of memory?
   a. semantic memory
   b. declarative memory
   c. episodic memory
   d. procedural memory

Obj.: 8 Page: 280

10. A student attempts to remember all of the information required for a comprehensive examination at the end of a college course. The key factor that will determine his success in encoding such a vast amount of information is
    a. lots of time to study.
    b. careful organization of the material.
    c. use of cortical stimulants such as caffeine.
    d. intermittent naps.

Obj.: 9 Page: 281

11. John tells you that long term-memory is organized along concept maps. He claims that a specific cognitive structure organizes information and then affects how it is comes into the memory system, where it is placed and how it comes out. What theory of long-term memory organization is he arguing?
  a. semantic network theory
  b. explicit memory organization theory
  c. information processing theory
  d. schema theory

Obj.: 9 Page: 281

12. A class is asked to read and recall a short poem from memory. They begin well, falter in the middle, and do well again on the last line of the poem. Their increased accuracy for the line at the end of the poem is an example of the
  a. primacy effect.
  b. terminal effect.
  c. recency effect.
  d. Premack effect.

Obj.: 11 Page: 284

13. When Ramon's family moved, Ramon went to a new high school and had to learn the names of dozens of new teachers. Now he has great trouble remembering the names of his teachers from his first high school. This problem is an example of
  a. trace decay.
  b. motivated forgetting.
  c. retroactive interference.
  d. state-dependent forgetting.

Obj.: 12 Page: 287

14. There is a good chance that your grade on an essay exam will be higher if you study in the room where you will take the examination. This is an example of ____________dependent memory.
  a. state-
  b. context-
  c. mood-
  d. episodic-

Obj.: 12 Page: 290

15. A young second lieutenant witnessed the death of seventeen of his men when the truck that was following his overturned on a gravel road. He finds himself reliving that trauma. According to Freud, he forgot the accident because of
  a. proactive interference.
  b. decay.
  c. repression.
  d. unmotivated forgetting.

Obj.: 12 Page: 289

16. To improve one's study skills, a student should find a quiet, comfortable place to study because
  a. that will allow the student to take short naps and then resume studying quickly.
  b. everyone else will hear the sounds of the radio playing and the dog barking during the study session.
  c. most other stimuli are more interesting and absorbing than academic information.
  d. complete attention to the information to be remembered is the first step in short-term memory processing.

Obj.: 13 Page: 292

17. To recall if May has 30 or 31 days, Rodney recites the rhyme, "Thirty days has September, April, June and November, ...etc." This rhyme is a(n)
  a. mnemonic device.
  b. pegword method.
  c. acronym.
  d. narrative.

Obj.: 13 Page: 295

18. Lisa meets and has an extended conversation with H. M. this afternoon. The next morning, Lisa returns and greets H. M. in the hallway of the Montreal Neurological Institute. Most likely, H. M. would respond by asking,
  a. "Who are you?"
  b. "What is my name?"
  c. "Would you help me tie my shoe?"
  d. "How do you play tennis?"

Obj.: 14 Page: 298

19. Kim tells you that she heard that high glucose levels cause better memory so she has stocked up on high glucose foods and plans to eat them right before each of her exams. Based on your knowledge of the research on the effects of blood sugar on memory performance what should you tell Kim?
    a. "That's smart, I'm going to do it too."
    b. "Actually, she has it backward; low blood sugar causes better memory performance and the sugar that works best is sucrose, not glucose."
    c. "Be careful. Too much sugar can cause her to develop diabetes, and besides the effect only works for old people."
    d. "The data are only correlational, not causal; and the greatest improvement of memory comes from moderate amounts of glucose."

Obj.: 15 Page: 300

20. Arlene is investigating a bank robbery. She wants to make sure that her questioning does not alter the memory of her eyewitnesses. What can she do to lessen the likelihood that her questioning will influence her witnesses?
    a. Physically reenact what she thinks happened with her witnesses
    b. Hypnotize her witnesses and then question them
    c. She can't; leading questions have been shown to influence memories and nothing prevents this
    d. Have the witnesses mentally recreate the context of what happened just prior to the robbery and then instruct them to walk through the events

Obj.: 16 Page: 304

ESSAY QUESTIONS

1. John is a police officer investigating a robbery that occurred at a day-care center. He has asked your advice as to whether he should trust the testimony of the children. Summarize what John should keep in mind concerning the use of children as eyewitnesses?

Obj.: 16 Page: 302

2. List and give examples of five/six ways you can apply knowledge about memory to improve your study skills and, therefore, your performance on your next psychology examination.

Obj.: 13 Page: 292-295

ANSWER RECORD FOR CHAPTER 8

Comprehensive Guided Review:

1. stored
2. flashbulb
3. surprising
4. brain
5. deliberately
6. everyday
7. confidence
8. flashbulb
9. cognitive
10. information
11. short-term
12. Sensory
13. 20
14. long-term
15. computer
16. encoding
17. storage
18. retrieval
19. forgetting
20. Visual
21. echoic
22. iconic
23. second

Anatomy of a Classic Research Study: Do We Form Sensory Memories of All the Information That Stimulates Our Sensory Receptors?

What was the rationale for the study?
Sperling's (1960) goal was to test the traditional wisdom that sensory memory stores a relatively small amount of information that stimulates the sensory registers.

What methods did the authors use to test their hypothesis?
Subjects stared at a screen in which sets of 12 letters, arranged into three rows of 4, were projected. Presentations were very short (a half a second) in duration. The subjects were asked to report as many of the letters as possible (whole report) and as many letters as possible within a specific row (partial report).

What was the outcome of the study and what did the authors cpnclude the results meant?
Based on data obtained from a partial report, as opposed to a whole report, Sperling concluded that almost all of the information from visual receptors is stored as an image in iconic memory, but, as his subjects had claimed, the image fades rapidly. In a

sequential study, he found that when the delay period reached 1 second, almost all of the information in iconic memory had faded. In spite of this short duration, we can retain information in sensory memory by attending to it and transferring it into short-term memory.

---

24. Echoic
25. longer
26. primary
27. working
28. long term
29. images
30. semantic
31. limited
32. chunks
33. 9
34. seven
35. short-term
36. long
37. rehearsal
38. maintenance
39. decay
40. displacement

Mini-review of Sensory and Short-term Memory:
1. E; 2. I; 3. F; 4. K; 5. L; 6. A; 7. B; 8. G; 9. M; 10. C; 11. D; 12. H; 13. J

41. Long-term
42. massive
43. organized
44. storage
45. stored
46. actively
47. maintenance
48. Elaborative
49. encoding
50. depth
51. shallow
52. meaning
53. images
54. implicit
55. declarative
56. semantic
57. episodic
58. case
59. procedural
60. organized
61. semantic
62. nodes
63. connections
64. activation
65. schema
66. episodic
67. cognitive
68. semantic network
69. library
70. schema theory
71. organization
72. constructive recall
73. schemas
74. systematic
75. forgetting
76. useful
77. Ebbinghaus
78. middle
79. serial-position effect
80. beginning
81. recency
82. primacy
83. short-term
84. middle
85. anecdotal
86. relearning
87. fewer
88. Savings
89. retrieval
90. Relearning
91. Explicit
92. recall
93. rate
94. days
95. rapid
96. Decay
97. little
98. Interference
99. old
100. retroactive
101. Motivation
102. repression
103. emotionally
104. relationship
105. retrieval cues
106. tongue
107. encoding specificity
108. Context
109. State
110. Mood
111. mood-congruent

Mini-review of Long-term Memory:
1. G; 2. K; 3. C; 4. Q; 5. H; 6. A; 7. I; 8. S; 9. D; 10. F; 11. Z; 12. V; 13. O; 14. E; 15. W; 16. X; 17. M; 18. Bb; 19. U; 20. T; 21. J; 22. Aa; 23. R; 24. L; 25. N; 26. P; 27. B; 28. Y

112. study habits
113. school
114. schedule
115. motivated
116. place
117. distractions
118. technique
119. elaborative rehearsal
120. framework
121. Questions
122. carefully
123. Recite
124. quiz
125. overlearning
126. distributed
127. mnemonic device
128. Method of loci
129. Retrieval
130. Acronyms
131. Pegword method
132. Link method

Mini-review of Memory Improvement Techniques:
Survey: **Headings and subheadings; create framework**
Question: **Pose questions in head**
Read**: Everything! Paragraphs, captions; glossary**
Recite**: Say the information out loud!**
Review**: Go over the material over and over and over!**

133. neurochemistry
134. Lashley
135. engram
136. cerebellum
137. sea snail
138. human
139. molecule
140. long-term potentiation
141. hippocampus
142. Alzheimer's
143. declarative
144. structural
145. chemically
146. transfer
147. transfer
148. neurotransmitters
149. acetylcholine
150. hippocampus
151. blocks
152. elevating
153. NMDA
154. efficiency
155. hormones
156. amphetamine
157. glucose
158. correlation
159. moderate

Mini-review of Biopsychology of Memory:
1. E; 2. A; 3. I; 4. H; 5. F; 6. G; 7. D; 8. B; 9. C

160. eyewitness testimony
161. accuracy
162. less
163. guessing
164. wording
165. Loftus
166. recall
167. improved
168. warning

Anatomy of a Contemporary Research Study: Can Leading Questions Influence Eyewitness Testimony?

What was the rationale for this study?
Loftus and Palmer were interested in the effects of leading questions on the testimony of eyewitnesses.

What methods did the author use to test the hypothesis?
Subjects viewed one of seven films of two car accidents. Each film lasted between 5 to 30 seconds in length. The subjects were then asked different questions about the accidents. One group was asked if the cars "smashed" into each other. In each of the other groups the word smashed was replaced with another word ("contacted," "hit," "bumped" or "collided"). A week later the subjects were asked about the film.

What was the outcome of the study and what did the authors conclude the results meant?
The results indicated that the subjects' estimates of the speed of the cars was influenced by the word used in the question. "The subjects who were asked if the cars smashed into each other estimated the speed higher than the others. The authors conclude that the results indicate that memories of eyewitnesses are reconstructions, not exact replications, and can be influenced by subsequent questioning.

Practice Test A:

1. a. Incorrect: Engrams are physiological memory traces.
   b. Incorrect: Mnemonics are devices that facilitate memory.
   c. Incorrect: Echoic memories are auditory sensory memories.
   d. Correct: Flashbulb memories are vivid memories of emotional episodes.

2. a. Incorrect: Learning is an inferred change in potential behavior that results from experience.
   b. Correct: This is the definition of memory.
   c. Incorrect: Cognition refers to thinking processes.
   d. Incorrect: intelligence is the global capacity to act purposfully, think rationally, and deal effectively with the environment.

3. a. Incorrect: Sensory memory holds information for only fractions of a second, not 20 seconds.
   b. Incorrect: Episodic memory is a type of long term memory for time periods.
   c. Incorrect: Long-term memory is held permanently.
   d. Correct: Short-term memory can store small amounts of information for about 20 seconds without rehearsal.

4. a. Incorrect: Sperling used the partial-report method in which he asked his subjects to report a portion of the stimulus after beginning with the whole-report method.
   b. Correct: Sperling used the partial-report method in which he asked his subjects to report a portion of the stimulus after beginning with the whole-report method.
   c. Incorrect: Sperling used the partial-report method in which he asked his subjects to report a portion of the stimulus after beginning with the whole-report method.
   d. Incorrect: Sperling used the partial-report method in which he asked his subjects to report a portion of the stimulus after beginning with the whole-report method.

5. a. Incorrect: Engrams are physiological memory traces.
   b. Incorrect: Information that is attended to enters the short-term memory.
   c. Incorrect: Information that is attended to enters the short-term memory.
   d. Correct: Information that is attended to enters the short-term memory.

6. **a. Correct: Maintenance rehearsal keeps information in short-term memory.**
   b. Incorrect: This involves actively organizing new information to make it more meaningful and integrating it with material already in long-term memory.
   c. Incorrect: This would be a choice if it were not for the fact that maintenance rehearsal is precisely defined.
   d. Incorrect: Such a phrase is not used.

7. a. Incorrect: This is too shallow a level of processing; deeper levels lead to better retention of information, according to the theory.
   b. Incorrect: This is too shallow a level of processing; deeper levels lead to better retention of information, according to the theory
   c. Correct: This is the deeper level of processing needed to retain the information.
   d. Incorrect: This is not a level of processing presented in the theory.

8. a. Incorrect: Episodic is but one of two types of declarative memory.
   b. Incorrect: Semantic is but one of two types of declarative memory.
   c. Incorrect: Same as b, above.
   d. Correct: Note that declarative memory, however, is subdivided into semantic and episodic memory.

9. a. Incorrect: Semantic memory is not described here.
   b. Correct: Knowing how to cook is procedural memory; remembering that you have done them is episodic memory.
   c. Incorrect: Semantic is a type of declarative memory.
   d. Incorrect: Episodic is a type of declarative memory.

10. a. Incorrect: This is a definition of constructive recall, not cognition.
    b. Incorrect: This is a definition of constructive recall, not relearning.
    c. Incorrect: This is a definition of constructive recall, not semantic networks.
    d. Correct: This is a definition of constructive recall.

11. **a. Correct: Two types of serial-position effects are observed primacy effects (the information already transferred to LTM) and recency effects (the information still in STM)**
    b. Incorrect: According to Tulving, this is where we store long-term memory.
    c. Incorrect: These are encoding processes for long-term memory.
    d. Incorrect: Same concept, different terms.

12. a. Incorrect: Retrograde amnesia is the inability to remember long-term memories.
    b. Incorrect: Anterograde memories is the inability to store new long-term memories.
    c. Correct: Proactive interference occurs when old memories interfere with the ability to remember new memories.
    d. Incorrect: Retroactive interference occurs when new memories interfere with the ability to remember old information.

13. a. Incorrect: Overlearning refers to the practice of reviewing material even after you have fully learned it.
    b. Incorrect: The football payer is not cramming all his study into a small amount of time.
    c. Correct: The football player has spread his study out, or used distributed practice.
    d. Incorrect: maintenance rehearsal refers to repeating the information over and over; it keeps info in STM.

14. a. Incorrect: Persons with hippocampal damage have difficulty remembering new long-term memories.
    b. Incorrect: Persons with hippocampal damage have difficulty remembering new long-term memories.
    c. Incorrect: Persons with hippocampal damage have difficulty remembering new long-term memories.
    d. Correct: Hippocampal damage does not affect procedural memories, only declarative ones.

15. a. Incorrect: Acetylcholine is the neurotransmitter that has been implicated in enhancing memory.
    b. Incorrect: Acetylcholine is the neurotransmitter that has been implicated in enhancing memory.
    c. Correct: Acetylcholine is the neurotransmitter that has been implicated in enhancing memory.
    d. Incorrect: Acetylcholine is the neurotransmitter that has been implicated in enhancing memory.

16. a. Incorrect: Loftus does not research hypnosis.
    b. Incorrect: Loftus does not research the unconscious, or repression.
    c. Correct: Loftus has repeatedly shown the effects of leading questions on eyewitness testimony.
    d. Incorrect: Loftus does not research the effects of alcohol intoxication on memory.

Practice Test B:

1. a. Incorrect: Short-term memory is held for only 20 seconds without continuous rehearsal.
   b. Correct: A flashbulb memory is an intense, detailed memory of an event.
   c. Incorrect: An engram is a physiological memory trace.
   d. Incorrect: Semantic memory is a type of declarative memory of facts.

2. **a. Correct: The ability to travel around the mall is indicative of a memory of a previous experience at the mall.**
   b. Incorrect: Psychic powers have nothing to do with sensory experiences.
   c. Incorrect: Unless you park in the same locations, no associative learning has taken place.
   d. Incorrect: High intelligence is measured by an intelligence test, not whether you can find a parked car.

3. a. Incorrect: Encoding equates to putting information into the computer.
   b. Incorrect: Storage equates to putting the information on a disk or hard drive.
   c. Incorrect: Retrieval equates to calling a file up that has already been saved.
   d. **Correct: Forgetting equates to erasing a memory, or deleting a file.**

4. a. Incorrect: Sperling was not interested in the amount of time that information was held for.
   b. **Correct: Sperling's partial reports determined how much visual information could be held in sensory memory.**
   c. Incorrect: Sperling was not measuring short-term memory.
   d. Incorrect: Sperling was not measuring short-term memory.

5. a. Incorrect: Short-term memory does not hold information for a long duration nor does it hold a lot.
   b. Incorrect: To extend the capacity of short-term memory you must actively chunk information.
   c. Incorrect: Short-term memory does not affect the amount of information in sensory memory.
   d. **Correct: Short-term memory is continually working to process information.**

6. a. Incorrect: Primacy effect alone would only allow you to recall about the first 7 items.
   b. Incorrect: Recency effect alone would only allow you to recall the last 7 items.
   c. Incorrect: There is no such thing as a sequential-position effect.
   d. **Correct: Between the combination of the primacy and recency effects you should remember the 10 items on each list.**

7. a. Incorrect: There is no such thing as echoic rehearsal.
   b. Incorrect: Maintenance rehearsal allows information to stay in short-term memory due to its limited capacity, not a place you want the have to rely on for a test.
   c. **Correct: Elaborative rehearsal allows information to be placed into the unlimited long-term memory.**
   d. Incorrect: Cue-dependent rehearsal does not exist.

8. a. Incorrect: Visual level is a shallow level and will not allow for good performance on tests.
   b. Incorrect: Echoic level is a shallow level of processing and does not allow for good test performance.
   c. **Correct: Semantic level of processing is a deep level and does lead to better test performance.**
   d. Incorrect: An acoustic level is an auditory level of processing, that is a shallow level of processing and does not allow for good test performance.

9. a. Incorrect: This is not general knowledge.
   b. **Correct: This is factual information, or declarative memory.**
   c. Incorrect: This is not a memory of something that happened to you.
   d. Incorrect: This is not a memory of how to do something.

10. a. Incorrect: It is not necessarily how much you study but how well you study that leads to good performance.
    b. **Correct: The most important thing for success in school is careful organization of study material.**
    c. Incorrect: Caffeine will not allow you to process information any better.
    d. Incorrect: Naps without effective study techniques will not help performance.

11. a. Incorrect: Semantic network theory argues that information is placed at nodes, not organized by concepts.
    b. Incorrect: There is no such theory as explicit memory organization theory.
    c. Incorrect: Information-processing theory is a broad theory that argues that the brain works as an information processor, but does not specifically state how that processing is done.
    d. **Correct: Schema theory argues that memories are organized by cognitive structures called schemas.**

12. a. Incorrect: Primacy is related to their ability to recite the first lines well.
    b. Incorrect: There is no terminal effect.
    c. **Correct: Recency effect relates to the ability to remember the last, or most recent thing that comes in.**
    d. Incorrect: Premack effect does not refer to a memory phenomenon.

13. a. Incorrect: Trace decay refers to the decay of short-term memory; the names he is trying to remember are from long-term memory.
    b. Incorrect: Motivated forgetting refers to repression of information, not the interference of information.
    c. **Correct: Retroactive interference occurs when new information interferes with the memory of old information.**
    d. Incorrect: The failure to remember the names has nothing to do with Ramon's state.

14. a. Incorrect: The place where you study is the context, not the state.
    b. **Correct: Remembering better in the place you studied is called context-dependent memory.**
    c. Incorrect: The place where you study is the context, not your mood.
    d. Incorrect: There is no such thing as episodic-dependent memory.

15. a. Incorrect: Freud did not talk about proactive interference.
b. Incorrect: Freud did not talk about decay of memories.
c. Correct: Freud felt that memory failures took place via repression, a motivated form of forgetting.
d. Incorrect: Freud felt that memory failures took place via repression, a motivated form of forgetting.

16. a. Incorrect: A quiet study place helps to improve concentration and attention on the information to be studied.
b. Incorrect: A quiet study place helps to improve concentration and attention on the information to be studied.
c. Incorrect: A quiet study place helps to improve concentration and attention on the information to be studied.
d. Correct: A quiet study place helps to improve concentration and attention on the information to be studied.

17. **a. Correct: This is a device that allows you to remember something, thus it is a mnemonic device.**
b. Incorrect: This does not require associating items to objects that rhyme with the number 1, 2.
c. Incorrect: This does not rely on creating a word or term from the letters of the words to be remembered.
d. Incorrect: This does not rely on the technique of creating a story of the information used to remember it.

18. **a. Correct: H. M. cannot form any new long-term memories, therefore he will not remember having met Lisa.**
b. Incorrect: H. M. can remember things from before his surgery; therefore he remembers his own name.
c. Incorrect: H. M. has good procedural memory; he remembers how to do things.
d. Incorrect: H. M. has good procedural memory; he remembers how to do things.

19. a. Incorrect: Research has shown that only moderate amounts of blood glucose are related to better memory.
b. Incorrect: Research has shown that only moderate amounts of blood glucose are related to better memory.
c. Incorrect: Diabetes is not caused by eating too much sugar.
d. Correct: Although research has shown that there is a relationship, it is for blood glucose levels, and is only correlational data.

20. a. Incorrect: Physical reenactments may lead to misinformation.
b. Incorrect: As you learned in Chapter 6, hypnosis has not been shown to produce more accurate memories.
c. Incorrect: You can lessen the likelihood that questioning will influence the memory by warning them and having the person walk mentally through the event.
d. Correct: You can lessen the likelihood that questioning will influence the memory by warning them and having the person walk mentally through the event.

Essay Questions:

1. John should be aware that:
Children's testimony is not as reliable as adults' testimony.
Younger children are less accurate than older children.
Children are more easily influenced by leading questions.
Younger children are more likely to say they experienced something that they have only thought about, remember less information spontaneously, and provide fewer details then older children.
Children are more likely to guess when testifying repeatedly about the same event.

2. a) Schedule regular study sessions at a time of day (or night) when you know you are alert and motivated. This will help ensure more efficient attention to, and therefore encoding of information.
b) Studying should occur in a quiet, comfortable place also to facilitate greater attention and, therefore, better encoding of information.
c) Use the SQ3R method as an actual study technique. This stands for Survey, Question, and then Read, Recite, and Review. These techniques facilitate elaborative rehearsal of the material.
d) Consider overlearning the material because this reduces anxiety and increases confidence.
e) Make use of distributed rather than massed practice. That is, study for a few hours each day, rather than many hours just before the exam.
f) Make use of mnemonic devices.

9 Thinking and Language

LEARNING OBJECTIVES

After studying this chapter, you should be able to:

1. Describe the domain of cognitive psychology and the reasons for the "cognitive revolution." (p. 310)

2. Define thinking and summarize the historical controversy surrounding this psychological function. (p. 310-311)

3. Define concept, and distinguish between logical and natural concepts, emphasizing prototypes. (p. 311-313)

4. Define problem solving, describe four problem-solving strategies, and explain how mental sets and functional fixedness can interfere with effective problem solving. (p. 313-318)

5. Define creativity, and describe the characteristics of creative individuals, mentioning the results of a recent study about the inhibition of creativity. (p. 319-320)

6. Distinguish between divergent and convergent thinking, describe the strengths and weaknesses of the Remote Associates Test in evaluating creative behavior, and summarize what is known about ways to increase creativity. (p. 321-322)

7. Define decision making, and explain how the representativeness heuristic, the availability heuristic, and framing effects can all bias our decision making. (p. 323-325)

8. Summarize the important developments and issues in the area of artificial intelligence. (p. 325-326)

9. Define language, list and offer examples of the three characteristics of language that distinguish it from other types of communication. (p. 326-328)

10. Define grammar and then distinguish among phonemes and morphemes, syntax and semantics, offering examples of each. (p. 328-329)

11. Explain Chomsky's concept of transformational grammar, distinguishing between surface structure and deep structure, and explaining the concept of pragmatics. (p. 329)

12. Describe the stages of language acquisition, and then summarize the evidence regarding whether there is a critical period for language acquisition. (p. 330-333)

13. Compare and contrast the language acquisition theories of B. F. Skinner, Albert Bandura, and Noam Chomsky. (p. 333-334)

14. Explain the linguistic-relativity hypothesis, and summarize the important findings of the classic study evaluating this concept. (p. 334-335)

15. Summarize the findings regarding the impact of sexist language. (p. 336-337)

16. Summarize the results of the attempts to teach apes language and describe the nature of the controversy that surrounds recent attempts to do so. (p. 337-341)

COMPREHENSIVE GUIDED REVIEW

Creativity, artificial intelligence, and sign language are topics that fall within the domain of___(1)__ psychology, a field of psychology that combines William James's concern with mental processes and John Watson's concern with observable behavior. Thinking and language are two different yet interrelated cognitive activities. They enable you to __(2)__ ideas and communicate information and they too are areas of concern for cognitive psychologists.

I. Thinking: ____(3)__ is the purposeful manipulation of words, symbols, and images. Although we know now that forming concepts, solving___(4)__, being creative, and making decisions are processes that depend on thinking, as recently as 1925, J. B. Watson claimed that thinking was not a mental activity. In fact, he insisted that it was no more than__(5)__ speech. Margaret Floy Washburn agreed with Watson, and proposed the ___(6)_**theory of thinking.** However, a study by Smith et al. in 1947 provided convincing evidence___(7)__ Watson's claim. Smith paralyzed himself with___(8)__ and was put on a respirator. After the drug wore off, his report of the experience showed that he was able to think. The authors concluded that this indicated that____(9)__ was not dependent on **subvocal speech.** However, it was not until the "cognitive revolution" of the 1960s that the study of mental processes, or "___(10)__," was reintroduced to psychology. Today, cognitive psychologists study concept formation, problem solving, creativity, _____(11)___, and artificial intelligence under the domain of **cognition.**

Concept Formation: Concept formation is one of the basic cognitive processes. A **concept** represents a __(12)_of objects, events, qualities, or relations whose members share certain characteristics. There are two different kinds of concepts: **logical concepts** and **natural concepts.** A___(13)_concept is formed by identifying the specific features possessed by all members of the concept. Real-life logical concepts are not generally studied in the ___(14)__. Typically researchers create a new concept so that they can have more precise control over the__(15)__ of the concept. Features of a logical concept are usually identified through the use of___(16)__ testing.

__(17)__concepts, such as "love," are formed through everyday experience and tend to have "fuzzy boundaries." The difficulty in defining natural concepts prompted Rosch (1975) to propose that natural concepts are based on ___(18)__, the best representatives of a concept. More recently, researchers have become interested in studying natural concept __(19)_. In a study on artistic styles, Hartley & Homan (1981) showed that subjects were___(20)__ to identify a set of features that distinguished one artist from another, yet they could accurately__(21)__ a second set of paintings to the correct artist.

Problem Solving: ____(22)__ is the thought process that enables us to overcome obstacles in order to reach goals. Generally, a common series of steps are used to solve the problem. First, the problem is___(23)_; second, ___(24)_ is gathered; third, ___(25)__ are tried; and fourth, the results are___(26)__. There are four common problem-solving strategies: **trial and error, insight, algorithms,** and **heuristics**.

Trial and error is the__(27)__ problem-solving strategy. It involves trying one possible___(28)__ after another until you find one that works. While effective, trial and error is not always__(29)_.

Insight is an approach that depends on mental____(30)__ of information rather than on overt trial and error. It is often characterized by the "Aha!" experience—the__(31)__ realization of the solution to a problem. One of the most significant studies on insight was conducted by Kohler (1925) with the chimp ___(32)__, who piled boxes, by size, to get to the treat, a banana. The argument that Sultan displayed__(33)__ was challenged by several behaviorists who trained pigeons to emit, much to their surprise, similar insightful behavior. The behaviorists argued that Sultan's "insightful" behavior was nothing more than a series of__(34)__ behaviors.

An **algorithm** is a__(35)__ that, when followed step by step, ensures that the solution to a problem will be found. Physicians use__(36)__ to diagnose disorders by noting specific combinations of symptoms and characteristics of the patient. __(37)__ programs also rely on algorithms.

Heuristics are general principles, or "____ (38) ____," that guide problem solving. Unlike an algorithm, a__(39)__ does not guarantee the discovery of a solution, but it may be more__(40)__.

Impediments to Problem Solving: Past__(41)__ may sometimes hinder the ability to solve problems. Two different examples are **mental sets** and **functional fixedness**

Problem solving may be hindered by a____(42)____. This is a particular problem-solving strategy that has worked in the past, but that interferes with solving a problem that requires a new____(43)__. A classic example is found in the Luchins (1946)__(44)__ problem. Mental sets can be overcome by thinking visually instead of verbally, placing the problems in a different__(45)__, and by making assumptions__(46)__ to those that we normally make.

Functional fixedness is the second way in which past experience can impede our ability to solve problems. It is the inability to realize that a problem can be solved by using a____(47)__ object in an unusual way. The classic two-string problem is an example of____(48)____. As with mental sets, functional fixedness can be__(49)__. One of the best ways is to change, or ignore, the__(50)__ of familiar objects.

Creativity: Like other__(51)__ concepts, creativity cannot be defined by a specific set of features. Often we are able to ___(52)__ between creative and non creative solutions to problems but cannot identify what makes them__(53)__. Psychologists have attempted to define this "__(54)__" concept as a form of problem solving that is characterized by finding solutions that are unique as well as socially__(55)__. Creative people tend to

1) be more motivated by their__(56)__ interest in creative tasks than in extrinsic factors;
2) be above-average__(57)__;
3) prefer novelty;
4) favor__(58)__;
5) make__(59)__ judgments; and
6) be superior at__(60)__ verbal and visual thinking, and rational, reality-oriented thinking with irrational, imaginative thinking.

Anatomy of a Contemporary Research Study: Does Rewarding Creative Behavior Inhibit Creativity?
Read the summary of the study by Amabile on page 320-321 in your textbook and review your understanding by answering the following questions.

What was the rationale for the study?

What methods did the author use to test the hypothesis?

What was the outcome of the study and what did the author conclude the results meant?

Creativity and Divergent Thinking: Convergent thinking focuses on finding correct__(61)__ solutions to problems. __(62)__ **thinking** is the cognitive process by which a person considers a variety of potential solutions to artistic, literary, scientific, or practical problems. While an overemphasis on__(63)__ thinking may impair **divergent thinking** and, as a result, impair__(64)__, divergent thinking can be induced by **brainstorming.** In__(65)__, the thinkers are prompted to think up as many solutions as possible to the problem. The Remote Associates Test was developed to access divergent thinking and has been found to have a__(66)__ correlation with creativity. Research has also shown that divergent thinking can be cultivated and can be promoted by__(67)__ emotional states.

Decision Making: Decision making is a form of___(68)___ in which we try to make the best choice from among alternative judgments or courses of action. In making decisions, we weigh two factors. __(69)__ is the value we assign to a given alternative. A decision to play the lottery has__(70)__ utility due to the potential of winning but it also has a low___(71)__. Probability is our estimate of the___(72)__ that a given alternative will lead to a valued consequence. Decision making is subject, however, to certain___(73)__, such as a reliance on **heuristics.**

Heuristics and Decision Making: Two types of heuristics are involved: the **representativness heuristic** and the **availability heuristic**. In using the___(74)__ **heuristic**, we assume that the characteristics of a small sample are representative of its population, but, indeed, this may not be the case. On the other hand, the___(75)__ **heuristic** is the tendency to estimate the probability of an event by how easily relevant instances of the event come to mind. However, again, these instances may not reflect their actual probability.

The way in which questions are___(76)__ also influences decisions. This is known as the **framing effect.** For example, note the different effects of these comments: "I failed two quizzes this term" and "I earned an A on fourteen quizzes this term." Though both statements report the___(77), how would those respond who are interested in how well you did? It is the way that questions are framed that influences___(78)__, not the objective content.

Artificial Intelligence: AI is a field of study that integrates____(79)____ and cognitive psychology. This field was founder by Nobel prize winner Herbert___(80)__. Those who study AI try to simulate or improve on human___(81)__ by using computer programs. As an example, many AI researchers attempt to develop computer programs, so-called ___(82)__**systems,** that display expertise in specific domains of knowledge. Among the many expert programs available today are computer___(83)__ programs; Mycin (a program to help physicians diagnose___(84)__ diseases); Prospector (a program designed to help___(85)__ companies decide where to dig for minerals); and Dipmeter, which has helped analyze___(86)__ data from oil-well drillings. Most computer programs perform decision-making processes in **serial,** meaning they perform ___(87)__ step at a time. In contrast, the human brain performs decision making both in **serial** and **parallel.** When information is processed in___(88)__, several steps occur simultaneously and are then integrated.

Time for one of your study breaks. Take a brief breather from studying and when refreshed, review your comprehension of the previous material by completing the mini-review. Remember, if you are unsure of any of the answers while completing the mini-review, go back and reread that section of the chapter.

Mini-review of Cognition: Match each term with its correct description.

_______1. expert systems
_______2. divergent thinking
_______3. concept
_______4. framing effect
_______5. creativity
_______6. cognitive psychology
_______7. prototypes
_______8. thinking
_______9. Remote Associates Test
_______10. problem solving
_______11. availability heuristic
_______12. subvocal speech
_______13. insight
_______14. heuristics
_______15. logical concepts
_______16. representativeness heuristic
_______17. algorithm
_______18. utility
_______19. mental sets
_______20. artificial intelligence
_______21. decision making
_______22. convergent thinking
_______23. natural concepts
_______24. trial and error
_______25. functional fixedness
_______26. brainstorming
_______27. probability

A. Assumption that the characteristics of a small sample are representative of its population
B. A field of psychology that combines William James's concern with mental processes and John Watson's concern with observable behavior
C. The purposeful manipulation of words, symbols, and images
D. J. B. Watson's claim of what thinking was
E. A category of objects, events, qualities, or relations whose members share certain characteristics
F. Concept formed by identifying the specific features possessed by all members of the concept
G. When followed step by step, ensures that the solution to a problem will be found; physicians use these to diagnose disorders
H. Test developed to assess divergent thinking
I. Concepts formed through everyday experience; tend to have "fuzzy boundaries"
J. The best representatives of a concept
K. The thought process that enables us to overcome obstacles in order to reach goals
L. The value that we assign to a given alternative in decision making
M. The simplest problem-solving strategy; involves trying one possible solution after another
N. Approach that depends on mental manipulation of information; it is often characterized by the "Aha!" experience
O. General principles, or "rules of thumb," that guide problem solving
P. A particular problem-solving strategy that has worked in the past but interferes with solving a current problem
Q. Focuses on finding correct conventional solutions to problems
R. The inability to realize that a problem can be solved by using a familiar object in an unusual way
S. A "fuzzy" concept; a form of problem solving that is characterized by finding solutions that are unique as well as socially valued
T. The cognitive process by which a person considers a variety of potential solutions to artistic, literary, scientific, or practical problems
U. Type of thinking in which the individuals are prompted to think up as many solutions as possible to the problem
V. A form of problem solving in which we try to make the best choice from among alternative judgments or courses of action
W. Estimate of the likelihood that a given alternative will lead to a valued consequence
X. The tendency to estimate the probability of an event by how easily relevant instances of the event come to mind
Y. The way in which questions are posed; also influences decisions
Z. A field of study that integrates computer science and cognitive psychology
Aa. Computer programs that display expertise in specific domains of knowledge

II. Language: Language is a formal system of communication involving ___(89)___, whether spoken, written, or gestured, and rules for combining them. The languages of the world share three characteristics: **semanticity,** which indicates that true language conveys the thoughts of the communicator in a ___(90)___ way; **generativity,** which indicates that those who use the language can ___(91)___ its symbols in novel ways; and **displacement,** which indicates that language permits us to refer to objects and events that are not ___(92)___. Spoken ___(93)___ is only one form of communication. ___(94)___ can also occur without the use of language, as in the case of animals. ___(95)___ language in humans, for example, conveys meaning without words. Additionally, other animals communicate without true language; e.g., the ___(96)___ of the honeybee.

All true languages have__(97)___ that are governed by rules. ___(98)__ comprises the rules that govern the structure of all languages. The components of grammar include **phonology, syntax,** and **semantics.**

Phonology: All spoken languages are comprised of___(99)__, the basic sounds of a language. English contains about forty phonemes but the number varies based on__(100)_. Each phoneme is represented by a___(101)__ or combination of letters. Children have__(102)__ difficulty in pronouncing phonemes not found in their native language; thus psychologists have suggested that there may be a ___(103)__ period for language development. Individual phonemes and combinations of phonemes form____(104)_, the smallest meaningful units of language. _____(105)__are comprised of one or more **morphemes.**

Syntax is a system of rules that governs the acceptable__(106)__ of words in phrases and sentences.__(107)__ varies within different languages. For example, the normal order of verb and object are__(108)__ in Japanese and English. **Semantics** is the study of how language conveys___(109)__. Chomsky explains this ability to express the same meaning using different phrases by distinguishing between a language's **deep structure** and its___(110)__ **structure.** The _(111)_ **structure** is the underlying meaning of a statement, while the surface structure is the word ____(112)__that express the meaning. Chomsky calls the rules by which we generate surface to deep structures and deep to surface structures ____(113)___. However, the meaning of a statement also depends on the social___(114)__ in which the statement is made. **Pragmatics** is a branch of semantics that deals with the___(115)__ between language and its social context. As an example, you might say, "I can't wait for the next exam." You can say this in an___(116)__ way, indicating that you are prepared and confident, or in a sarcastic way, suggesting that the exam is a real burden and that possibly you are ill prepared and stressed.

The Acquisition of Language: The process of language acquisition appears to be___(117)_, with infants passing through distinct stages. Though the___(118)__ of the stages may vary, the order does not.

Stages in Language Acquisition: Briefly, the universal sequence is as follows:

1) First months—communication through__(119)__.
2) 4 to 6 months—____(120).
3) 9 months—babbling comes to be limited to the___(121)__ of the family's language.
4) 1 year— first words or___(122)__ **speech,** using single words to express whole sentences. Characterized by ___(123)__, such as saying "kitty" and meaning other four-legged animals, or___(124)_, such as saying "kitty" and only meaning the child's one cat.
5) 18 to 24 months—the use of two-word phrases. This type of speech is called___(125) **speech.**
6) __(126)___ years—children begin to go beyond referring to objects that are located in their immediate environments and also include parts of speech in addition to nouns and verbs.
7) 2 years and beyond—language develops rapidly. It is measured by a unit called the **mean length of utterance** (MLU), an index that assesses the child's level of language____(127)__.

Children are influenced by their mothers' speech, but often are confused by exceptions to grammatical rules, and thus, ___(128)__ occurs. This phenomenon is the application of grammatical rules without making necessary exceptions. For example, children will often___(129)__ "ed" to the end of all words, even when inappropriate. They soon come to learn the rules, rather than a specific instance of correct grammar, as shown in the classic study by___(130), with the "wug test."

Is There a Critical Period for Language Acquisition? Research has suggested that there may be a critical period for the___(131)__ of language. The case studies of Victor and Genie suggest that there is a **critical period** between childhood and adolescence in which language acquisition is___(132)__. However, remember that these two examples are of___(133)___ research and it is not wise to generalize from case studies. A stronger line of research on critical periods comes from that of adults who learn___(134)__ languages. This research shows that is clearly becomes progressively more___(135)__ as we get older.

Theories of Language Acquisition: The question of whether language is acquired solely through___(136)__ or acquired by___(137)__ of an inherited predisposition remains unresolved. Skinner (1957) claimed that language is acquired through learning, primarily through the positive___(138)__ of appropriate speech. Support for this position has come from studies showing that positive reinforcement may influence language___(139)___. Bandura (1977), however, supports the role of ___(140)__ learning in language acquisition, wherein children develop language primarily through imitating the vocabulary and grammatical constructions used by their parents and others. This latter assumption has been challenged by Noam___(141)_. He argues that children___(142)__ a **language acquisition device** a___(143)__ mechanism that makes them sensitive to phonemes, syntax, and semantics. Support for Chomsky's position comes from studies of___(144)__ children who were neither rewarded for using sign language nor able to learn it from a model. Nonetheless, these children developed their own___(145)__ system and communicated by using signs characteristic of sign language. More recent research has provided some support for the___(146)__ position, although, it seems that the positions of Chomsky, Skinner, and Bandura must be___(147)__ in order to explain how language is acquired.

The Relationship Between Language and Thinking: ___(148)__, expressed in his belief as to the relationship between language and thinking with his **linguistic relativity hypothesis.** This hypothesis assumes that our view of the world is___(149)__ by the particular language we speak. Critics, however, argue that on the contrary, thinking determines language. What does research have to say about the hypothesis? A study by Carmichael, Hogan, & Walter (1932)___(150)_ Whorf's hypothesis. In this study subjects were presented___(151)__ drawings of objects that were given one of two labels. When asked to draw the objects the subjects drew the objects so that they resembled the ___(152)__ they had been given. Another study that tested Whorf's hypothesis is featured in the "Anatomy of a Classic Research Study."

Anatomy of a Classic Research Study: Does Language Influence Our Perception of Colors?
Read the summary of Rosch study on page 335 in your textbook and answer the following questions to check your understanding of the information.

What was the rationale for the study ?

What methods did the author use to test the hypothesis?

What was the outcome of the study and what did the author conclude the results meant?

Linguistic Relativity and Sexist Language: Although the more recent research indicates that language does not determine how we___(153)___ about the world, it does suggest that language may certainly___(154)__ it. For example, the use of a masculine pronoun, albeit intended to refer to both men and women, nonetheless conveys___(155)__. Are you the female chairman of a committee? Indeed, because our use of language can affect the way we think about sex (___(156)__) roles, Whorf's hypothesis is suggested to have some merit, as long as it is used, to recognize that language influences thinking, though it does not___(157)__ it.

Take a short study break and then review the previous section in the mini-review before finishing the chapter.

Mini-review of Language: Match each term with its correct definition.

________1. semanticity	A. A formal system of communication involving symbols, whether spoken, written, or gestured, and rules for combining them
________2. linguistic relativity hypothesis	B. Indicates that true language conveys the thoughts of the communicator in a meaningful way
________3. telegraphic speech	C. Indicates that those who use the language can use its symbols in novel ways
________4. grammar	D. Indicates that language permits us to refer to objects and events that are not present
________5. semantics	E. Comprises the rules that govern the structure of all languages
________6. overextension	F. The basic sounds of a language
________7. phonemes	G. The smallest meaningful units of language
________8. generativity	H. A system of rules that governs the acceptable sequences of words in phrases and sentences
________9. deep structure	I. The study of how language conveys meaning
________10. morphemes	J. The underlying meaning of a statement
________11. mean length of utterance (MLU)	K. The word organization structure that expresses the meaning
________12. pragmatics	L. The rules by which we generate surface to deep structures and deep to surface structures
________13. language	M. A branch of semantics that deals with the relationship between language and its social context
________14. critical period	N. Use of single word to express whole sentences
________15. transformational grammar	O. Application of a word to more objects than it actually represents
________16. displacement	P. A measurement that assesses the child's level of language maturation
________17. holophrastic speech	Q. The use of two-word phrases
________18. underextension	R. The application of grammatical rules without making necessary exceptions; for example, adding "ed" to the end of all words, even when inappropriate
________19. surface structure	S. Application of a word to less than it actually represents
________20. syntax	T. A time between childhood and adolescence in which language acquisition is optimal
________21. language acquisition device	U. A brain mechanism that makes children sensitive to phonemes, syntax, and semantics
________22. overregularization	V. This hypothesis assumes that our view of the world is determined by the particular language we speak

III. Thinking About Psychology: Can Apes Use Language?

Teaching Chimpanzees to Use Language: The cases of the chimpanzees Gua and Viki both led to the conclusion that the vocal anatomy of apes is not designed for___(158)___ speech. The case of Washoe is a different story. The Gardners' chimp developed a repertoire of 132 signs, which she used to name ___(159)___and to describe the qualities of objects. They eventually taught four other chimps to use____(160)____ and Washoe eventually taught ASL to a young chimp that she adopted. Additional evidence came when the Premacks taught Sarah to use plastic chips as___(161)__. Duane Rumbaugh & Sue Savage-Rumbaugh taught Lana to use a____(162)___ to form sentences.

Controversy About Ape-language Research: Terrace, based on his analysis of tapes of conversations with ____(163)____ (a chimp he trained to use sign language), claims that apes do not learn true language. He argues that what they learned was merely to make signs, arrange forms, or press computer keys in a certain order to obtain __(164)__. Their use of language,____(165)___ claims, was no different from a pigeon who learns to peck a sequence of keys to get a food reward. Terrace's attack has not gone unchallenged, however. Francine Patterson taught___(166)___ to use more than three hundred signs and claims that Koko's speech has also displayed____(167)___. Patterson claims that Terrace uses isolated frames on which to base his conclusions. Recently, the strongest evidence supporting ape language comes from studies by Duane___(168)___ and Sue Savage-Rumbaugh. Their research with two chimpanzees, Austin and Sherman, as well as further research with Kanzi and Mulika, has shown that apes may use___(169)___ language.

KEY RESEARCH FINDINGS

Provide the details of the following key research studies in psychology:

1. **Smith et al. (1947):** Researched the argument that thinking equated to subvocal speech. (Page 310)
2. **Hartley & Homa (1981):** Studies of artistic styles showed that subjects could form a natural concept without identifying a set of defining features. (Page 313)
3. **Green & Gilhooly (1990):** Compared novice computer programmers on their use of problem-solving strategies. (Page 314)
4. **Metcalf & Wiebe (1987):** Examined whether insight was a gradual or predictable process or sudden and unpredictable. (Page 315)
5. **Kohler (1925):** Observed insightful behavior in a chimp named Sultan. (Page 315)
6. **Epstein et al. (1984):** Demonstrated apparent insight behavior in pigeons using chaining. (Page 315)
7. **Luchins (1946):** Examined problem solving using the water-jar problem (Page 317)
8. **Adelson (1984):** Demonstrated mental set in computer programers. (Page 317)
9. **Maier (1931):** Demonstrated the phenomenon of functional fixedness in the two-strings problem. (Page 318)
10. **Glucksberg & Danks (1968):** Showed that by using nonsense words to refer to familiar objects subjects were more likely to overcome functional fixedness. (Page 318)
11. **Rushton (1990):** Found that tests of creativity and tests of intelligence were correlated in undergraduate subjects. (Page 319)
12. **Fuchs-Beauchamp, Karnes, & Johnson (1993):** Found a correlation between children's intelligence scores and creativity. (Page 320)
13. **Amabile (1985):** Examined the influence of rewarding intrinsic behavior and effects on creativity (Page 320)
14. **Gilovich, Vallone, & Tversky (1985):** Examined the truth of a representativeness heuristic by testing the idea of having a "hot hand" in basketball. (Page 323)
15. **Tversky & Kahneman (1973):** Examined the availability heuristic and its effect on thinking. (Page 324)
16. **Levin, Schnittjer, & Thee (1988):** Demonstrated the influence of framing effects on decision making in college students. (Page 324)
17. **Kahneman & Tversky (1982):** Demonstrated the influence of framing effects on decision making. (Page 324)
18. **Brown (1973):** Developed the mean length of utterance as a measure to assess children's level of language maturation. (Page 331)
19. **Berko (1958):** Found that children would indeed apply grammatical rules to novel words like "wug." (Page 332)
20. **Johnson & Newport (1989):** Found that adult Korean and Chinese immigrants had a more difficult time learning a second language. (Page 333)
21. **Routh (1969):** Demonstrated the role of learning in infants' language development. The infants responded by increasing their production of the phonemes for which they were reinforced. (Page 333).
22. **Nelson (1977):** Demonstrated that 2-year-old's improved the complexity of their sentence structure when adults replied to them in more complex forms. (Page 333)
23. **Goldin-Meadow & Mylander (1983):** Demonstrated that deaf children spontaneously develop their own gestural system that has characteristics of true language. (Page 334)
24. **Bohannon & Stanowicz (1988):** Found that language development does depend on feedback from adults. (Page 334)
25. **Carmichael, Hogan, & Walter (1932):** Suggested that when subjects who were presented with ambiguous drawings of objects that were given either of two labels, subjects later drew pictures that looked more like the object that had been named than like the object they had seen. (Page 335)
26. **Rosch (1975):** Compared English-speaking college students to the Dani people on a color recall ability task. (Page 335)
27. **Hamilton (1988):** Examined the influence of sexist pronouns on thinking. (Page 337)
28. **Kellog (1933)** and **Hayes (1951):** Found that a chimp raised as a child would not develop verbal language. (Page 338)

29. **Gardner & Gardner (1969):** Taught Washoe ASL. (Page 338)
30. **Rumbaugh, Gill, & von Glasersfeld (1973):** Taught a chimp, Lana, to use a computer to communicate. (Page 339)
31. **Terrace et al. (1979):** Taught Nim Chimpsky to use sign language, but claimed that it was not true language. (Page 339)
32. **Savage-Rumbaugh et al. (1980):** Demonstrated that chimps Austin and Sherman, but not Lana, were able to categorize objects as edible or nonedible. (Page 340)
33. **Savage-Rumbaugh (1990):** Trained Pygmy chimps in Yerkish to a level superior to other apes. Also found that apes can respond to symbols referred to in human speech. (Page 340).

PRACTICE TEST A

1. The 1950s and 1960s saw a revolution in which strict behaviorism was replaced by a concern with studying both the mind and behavior. This revolution is known as the
   a. post behavioristic revolution.
   b. psychoanalytic revolution.
   c. cognitive revolution.
   d. Gestalt revolution.

Obj.: 1 Page: 310

2. The purposeful manipulation of words and images is
   a. thinking.
   b. language.
   c. the cognitive revolution.
   d. memory.

Obj.: 2 Page: 310-311

3. A prime number can be evenly divided only by itself or one. "Prime number" is an example of a(n)
   a. algorithm.
   b. heuristic.
   c. natural concept.
   d. logical concept.

Obj.: 3 Page: 311

4. An experienced chess player who could checkmate her opponent in two moves fails to notice that opportunity, and, instead, continues to follow a less effective approach that has worked in similar situations in the past. This failure to show flexibility in problem solving is an example of the influence of a
   a. prototype.
   b. mental set.
   c. expert system.
   d. framing effect.

Obj.: 4 Page: 317

5. A child who enjoys playing the piano begins to play often after his parents begin giving him five dollars every time that he practices. His loss of interest was most likely the product of
   a. pragmatics.
   b. overextension.
   c. overregularization.
   d. extrinsic motivation.

Obj.: 5 Page: 320-321

6. What cognitive process focuses on finding conventional "correct" solutions to problems?
   a. decision making
   b. divergent thinking
   c. convergent thinking
   d. creativity

Obj.: 6 Page: 321-322

7. If you meet three members of an ethnic group who act shy and unemotional and you decide that all members of that group share those traits, you would be exhibiting the
   a. availability heuristic.
   b. error of overextension.
   c. representativeness heuristic.
   d. fundamental attribution error.

Obj.: 7 Page: 323

8. The field that integrates computer science and cognitive psychology in studying information processing through the design of computer programs that appear to think like human beings is called
   a. pragmatics.
   b. heuristics.
   c. functionalism.
   d. artificial intelligence.

Obj.: 8 Page: 325

9. The sentence, "Yesterday, he zorked the brem in Antarctica," is most lacking in
   a. syntax.
   b. morphemes.
   c. semanticity.
   d. displacement.

Obj.: 9 Page: 326-327

10. The sentence, "John the book gave to Jane" violates proper English
   a. syntax.
   b. semantics.
   c. pragmatics.
   d. displacement.

Obj.: 10 Page: 328-329

11. The statement "She looks great for her age" would be interpreted as either sarcasm or flattery, depending on its social context and the speaker's tone of voice. This is an example of
   a. syntax.
   b. pragmatics.
   c. surface structure.
   d. linguistic relativity.

Obj.: 11 Page: 329

12. An infant's father has a beard. Because of this, she calls all men with beards "daddy." This is an example of
   a. generativity.
   b. overextension.
   c. overregularization.
   d. holophrastic speech.

Obj.: 12 Page: 330

13. A major difference among Skinner's, Bandura's, and Chomsky's accounts of language acquisition is that
   a. Bandura argues that language is acquired through learning, mainly through positive reinforcement.
   b. Chomsky insists that infants are born with the predisposition to develop language.
   c. Skinner assumes the existence of a language acquisition device.
   d. research on language acquisition using deaf children provides clear support for Bandura's position.

Obj.: 13 Page: 333-334

14. The assumption that one's perception of the world is molded by one's language is called the
   a. framing effect.
   b. holophrastic effect.
   c. representativeness heuristic.
   d. linguistic relativity hypothesis.

Obj.: 14 Page: 334-335

15. The research as to the impact of sexist language shows that
   a. language has no effect on the way we think.
   b. repeated exposure to male pronouns promotes the belief that an activity is more suitable for males.
   c. undergraduate students were not more likely to think that an individual referred to as "he" was male.
   d. subjects reported that language did not affect their thoughts as to gender roles.

Obj.: 15 Page: 336-337

16. Herbert Terrace takes the position that
   a. apes have learned true language.
   b. apes have not learned true language.
   c. the verbal behavior of apes provides support for the linguistic relativity hypothesis.
   d. continuing research in this area is fruitless.

Obj.: 16 Page: 337-341

PRACTICE TEST B

1. Language, memory, and thinking are all examples of
   a. observable behaviors.
   b. unconscious processes.
   c. human instincts.
   d. cognitive functions.

Obj.: 1 Page: 310

2. Which of the following theorists agreed with J. B. Watson that thinking was nothing more than subvocal speech?
   a. Nim Chimpsky
   b. Sigmund Freud
   c. Margaret Floy Washburn
   d. Scott Smith

Obj.: 2 Page: 310

3. In one culture "animals that may be eaten" include only cows, horses, and sheep, because they eat grass. In another culture, only dogs and cats may be eaten, because they eat meat. In each of these cultures, "animals that may be eaten" comprise a(n)
   a. natural concept.
   b. prototypical concept.
   c. logical concept.
   d. artificial concept.

Obj.: 3 Page: 311

4. When Letitia turns on her computer, she can hear it whirring, but nothing appears on her monitor. She asks herself, "Is it plugged into a power source?" "Is it connected to the computer?" In other words, she is
   a. identifying the problem.
   b. gathering information.
   c. trying a solution.
   d. evaluating the result.

Obj.: 4 Page: 313-314

5. Howard is a supervisor who has always used competition and individual rewards to promote productivity among his workers. However, now his workers come from an ethnic group where competitiveness is considered rude and individual rewards cause shame, so the workers productivity has decreased dramatically. Howard is completely lost as to what to do. Howard may be hindered by his
   a. divergent thinking.
   b. mental set.
   c. algorithms.
   d. framing effects.

Obj.: 4 Page: 317

6. Some research-oriented psychology students ask a professor to guide their research club. Based on previous research findings, more creative ideas are likely to come out of the club if
   a. their efforts are not evaluated or extrinsically rewarded.
   b. a cash prize is offered for the best and most creative research proposal.
   c. the most productive members of the club have their pictures published in the campus newspaper.
   d. the professor encourages competition among the club members.

Obj.: 5 Page: 320

7. If you attended a seminar on creative thinking, you would most likely be given exercises in
   a. convergent thinking.
   b. divergent thinking.
   c. brainstorming.
   d. positive emotions.

Obj.: 6 Page: 321-322

8. When you assume that the characteristics of a small sample are representative of its population, you are using the
   a. availability heuristic.
   b. representativeness heuristic.
   c. probability heuristic.
   d. utility heuristic.

Obj.: 7 Page: 323-325

9. Undergraduates rated the incidence of cheating at their school higher when told that "65 percent of students had cheated at some time in their college career" than when told that "35 percent of the students never had cheated." This is an example of
   a. a representativeness heuristic.
   b. a framing effect.
   c. stimulus generalization.
   d. an availability heuristic.

Obj.: 7 Page: 323-325

10. Recently a computer won a match against a world-renowned chess-player. Another computer surpassed a group of medical specialists in making correct diagnoses in difficult cases. A group of computer and cognitive scientists are developing a program that allows the computer to interact as a "therapist" might. These events involve
   a. representativeness heuristics.
   b. pragmatics.
   c. expert systems.
   d. convergent thinking.

Obj.: 8 Page: 325-326

11. A very disturbed schizophrenic patient talks a lot, but no one can understand what he is saying. In other words, this patient's speech lacks
   a. pragmatics.
   b. displacement.
   c. semanticity.
   d. generativity.

Obj.: 9 Page: 326

12. Which item represents the way human language is constructed?
   a. Phonemes form morphemes, which form words, which form sentences.
   b. Morphemes form phonemes, which form words, which form sentences.
   c. Syntax forms morphemes, which form words, which form sentences.
   d. Semantics form phonemes, which form morphemes, which form sentences.

Obj.: 10 Page: 328

13. The sentences "Jill ate the ice cream cone" and "The ice cream cone was eaten by Jill" both share the same
   a. syntax.
   b. surface structure.
   c. transformational grammar.
   d. deep structure.

Obj.: 11 Page: 329

14. Which of the following correctly presents the universal sequence of language development?
   a. crying, holophrases, telegraphic speech, babbling, cooing
   b. crying, cooing, holophrases, babbling, condensed speech
   c. crying, telegraphic speech, cooing, babbling, holophrases
   d. crying, cooing, babbling, holophrases, telegraphic speech

Obj.: 12 Page: 330-333

15. A 14-month old says "ba-tee." This may mean "Where is my bottle?" or "I want a bottle," or "That's a bottle." This baby is engaging in
   a. babbling.
   b. overextension.
   c. telegraphic speech.
   d. holophrastic speech.

Obj.: 12 Page: 330

16. Which statement most accurately reflects current thinking regarding how human beings acquire language?
   a. Human beings acquire language through both classical and operant conditioning processes.
   b. Human beings appear innately prepared for language, but acquire a specific language through learning processes.
   c. Human beings are naturally imitative, and, if reinforced for imitation, they will demonstrate overregularization.
   d. Human beings acquire language because there is a critical period for observation and imitation.

Obj.: 13 Page: 334

17. Some studies have investigated whether people whose languages contain fewer color names distinguish fewer colors. They have been the most influential studies of the linguistic relativity hypothesis. Their results
   a. contradict Whorf's hypothesis.
   b. support Whorf's hypothesis.
   c. provide definitive support for a learning theory approach to the relationship between language and thinking.
   d. are inconclusive.

Obj.: 14 Page: 334-335

18. The research on the use of sexist language indicated that:
   a. language does not influence the way in which we think about the world.
   b. language determines how we think about the world.
   c. language determines the way we think about the world.
   d. nothing so far; the research in inconclusive at this time.

Obj.: 15 Page: 336-337

19. The Gardners' claim that the fact that Washoe signed the term "water bird" supports the argument that Washoe is demonstrating which characteristic of language?
   a. semantics
   b. generativity
   c. displacement
   d. fluency

Obj.: 16 Page: 339

20. What conclusion did your textbook author conclude is the current state of research into ape language?
    a. Clearly apes are not capable of spoken language, but when taught ASL there are no apparent limits.
    b. Clearly apes are not capable of true language of any kind.
    c. Using ASL, a chimp can attain the level of approximately a 3-year-old human; it is unclear if this is an upper limit or a limit of training techniques.
    d. Chimps are capable of a highly complex communication system using grunts and facial expressions.

Obj.: 16 Page: 341

ESSAY QUESTIONS

1. You have a psychology exam tomorrow morning and have left your textbook and notes at a friend's house. You need these to study. Your car is out of gas. You have a problem. Identify the steps that you would undertake to solve this problem and describe one type of obstacle that might keep you from solving the problem.

Obj.: 4 Page: 314-318

2. What are the unique features that make human communication different from what occurs between a person and a dog or between dogs?

Obj.: 9 Page: 326-327

ANSWER RECORD FOR CHAPTER 9

Comprehensive Guided Review:

1. cognitive	13. logical	25. solutions	37. Computer	49. overcome
2. comprehend	14. laboratory	26. evaluated	38. rules of thumb	50. name
3. Thinking	15. definition	27. simplest	39. heuristic	51. natural
4. problems	16. hypothesis	28. solution	40. efficient	52. differentiate
5. subvocal	17. Natural	29. efficient	41. experiences	53. creative
6. motor	18. prototypes	30. manipulation	42. mental set	54. fuzzy
7. against	19. formation	31. sudden	43. strategy	55. valued
8. curare	20. unable	32. Sultan	44. water-jar	56. intrinsic
9. thinking	21. match	33. insight	45. context	57. intelligence
10. cognition	22. Problem solving	34. chained	46. opposite	58. complexity
11. decision making	23. identified	35. rule	47. familiar	59. independent
12. category	24. information	36. algorithms	48. functional fixedness	60. integrating

---

Anatomy of a Contemporary Research Study: Does Rewarding Creative Behavior Increase Creativity?

Read the summary of the study by Amabile on page 320-321 in your textbook and review your understanding by answering the following questions.

What was the rationale for the study?

Amabile (1989) claims that creative people are more motivated by intrinsic interest in creative tasks than by extrinsic factors. She felt that, in fact, creative people, rewarded with extrinsic reasons may lose interest.

What methods did the authors use to test their hypothesis?

Subjects were recruited through advertisements and asked to write two brief poems. After they wrote the first poem the subjects were divided into three groups. One group was given a questionnaire pertaining to intrinsic motivation, and a second group received a questionnaire dealing with extrinsic motivation, the final group did not get a questionnaire. The subjects then wrote the second poem, and the creativity of the poem was measured.

What was the outcome of the study and what did the author conclude the results meant?

The results supported the assumption. The group asked to think about extrinsic rewards showed a significant decrease in the creativity in their poems. Amabile felt that this supports her hypothesis.

---

61. conventional
62. Divergent
63. convergent
64. creativity
65. brainstorming
66. moderate
67. positive
68. problem solving
69. Utility
70. high
71. probability
72. likelihood
73. biases
74. representative
75. availability
76. framed
77. truth
78. Decisions
79. computer science
80. Simon
81. thinking
82. expert
83. chess
84. infectious
85. mining
86. geological
87. one
88. parallel

Mini-review of Cognition:
1. Aa; 2. T; 3. E; 4. Y; 5. S; 6. B; 7. J; 8. C; 9. H; 10. K; 11. X; 12. D; 13. N; 14. O; 15. F; 16. A; 17. C; 18. L; 19. P; 20. Z; 21. V; 22. Q; 23. I; 24. M; 25. R; 26. U; 27. W

89. symbols
90. meaningful
91. combine
92. present
93. language
94. Communication
95. Body
96. dance
97. structures
98. grammar
99. phonemes
100. dialect
101. letter
102. less
103. critical
104. morphemes
105. Words
106. arrangement
107. Syntax
108. reversed
109. meaning
110. surface
111. deep
112. arrangements
113. transformational grammar
114. context
115. relationship
116. enthusiastic
117. universal
118. timing
119. crying
120. babbling
121. phonemes
122. holophrastic
123. overextension
124. underextension
125. telegraphic
126. 2
127. maturation
128. overregularization
129. add
130. Berko
131. development
132. optimal
133. case study
134. second
135. difficult
136. learning
137. maturation
138. reinforcement
139. acquisition
140. observational
141. Chomsky
142. inherit
143. brain
144. deaf
145. gestural
146. learning
147. integrated
148. Whorf
149. determined
150. supports
151. ambiguous
152. label

Anatomy of a Classic Research Study: Does Language Influence Our Perception of Colors?
Read the summary of the Rosch study on page 335 in your textbook and answer the following questions to check your understanding of the information.

What was the rationale for the study?
Rosch was interested in whether language influences the perception of colors. Her hypothesis was that people from cultures with fewer color names can distinguish fewer colors.

What methods did the author use to test the hypothesis?
Rosch visited the Dani people of New Guinea, who have only two words for color. Dani and American subjects were asked to select a specific colored chip from among 160 colored chips.

What was the outcome of the study and what did the author conclude the results meant?
The results of her research showed that English-speaking college students and those from the Dani culture were both superior at recognizing nonfocal colors. This finding contradicted Whorf's hypothesis.

---

153. think
154. influence
155. sexism
156. gender
157. determine

Mini-review of Language:
1. B; 2. V; 3. Q; 4. E; 5. I; 6. O; 7. F; 8. C; 9. J; 10. G; 11. P; 12. M; 13. A; 14. T; 15. L; 16. D; 17. N; 18. S; 19. K; 20. H; 21. U; 22. R

158. producing
159. objects
160. sign language
161. words
162. computer
163. Nim Chimpsky
164. rewards
165. Terrace
166. Koko
167. generativity
168. Rumbaugh
169. true

Practice Test A:

1. a. Incorrect: Post-behavioristic revolution is not a term that psychologists used.
   b. Incorrect: Psychoanalysis did not emerge in the 1950s and 1960s. It has been around since the 1800s.
   c. Correct: The revolution was known as the cognitive revolution due to the increase in interest in studying the processes of the mind.
   d. Incorrect: Gestalt psychology influenced psychology before the 1950s.

2. **a. Correct: The purposeful manipulation of words and images is the definition of thinking.**
   b. Incorrect: The purposeful manipulation of words and images is the definition of thinking.
   c. Incorrect: The purposeful manipulation of words and images is the definition of thinking.
   d. Incorrect: The purposeful manipulation of words and images is the definition of thinking.

3. a. Incorrect: An algorithm is a problem-solving strategy that when followed ensures a correct solution.
   b. Incorrect: A heuristic is a problem-solving principle of rule of thumb.
   c. Incorrect: A natural concept cannot be logically defined; "prime number" is logically defined.
   d. Correct: A logical concept is defined by identifying the features of it, for example defining a "prime number" as one that is divisible only by itself.

4. a. Incorrect: In the situation described in the question the player is using a mental set, or a less effective approach that has worked in the past.
   b. Correct: In the situation described in the question the player is using a mental set, or a less effective approach that has worked in the past.
   c. Incorrect: In the situation described in the question the player is using a mental set, or a less effective approach that has worked in the past.
   d. Incorrect: In the situation described in the question the player is using a mental set, or a less effective approach that has worked in the past.

5. a. Incorrect: Pragmatics is the study of the relationship between language and social context and has nothing to do with how often the child practices.
   b. Incorrect: Overextension is a language error that children make when learning a language.
   c. Incorrect: Overregularization is a language error that children make when learning a language.
   d. Correct: Extrinsic motivation is providing a reward for performing a behavior.

6. a. Incorrect: Decision making is a form of problem solving in which one tries to make the best choice from among alternative judgments or courses of action.
   b. Incorrect: In divergent thinking an individual freely considers a variety of potential solutions to artistic, literary, scientific, or practical problems.
   c. Correct: In convergent thinking the person focuses on finding conventional correct solutions.
   d. Incorrect: Creativity generates novel, socially valued solutions to problems.

7. a. Incorrect: The availability heuristic is the tendency to estimate the probability of an event by how easily instances come to mind.
   b. Incorrect: Psychologists do not use the term "error of overextension."
   c. Correct: A representative heuristic is used when we assume that the characteristics of a small sample is representative of a larger population.
   d. Incorrect: A fundamental attribution error is a term not discussed in this chapter.

8. a. Incorrect: Pragmatics is the study of the relationship between language and social context and has nothing to do with how often the child practices.
   b. Incorrect: A heuristic is a problem-solving principle of rule of thumb.
   c. Incorrect: Functionalism is a school of psychology popular in the early 1900s.
   d. Correct: Artificial intelligence is the field of study that integrates computer science and cognitive psychology.

9. a. Incorrect: This sentence uses correct syntax.
   b. Incorrect: Morphemes are the smallest unit of a language and they are not violated in this example.
   c. Correct: This example lacks semanticity, or meaningfulness.
   d. Incorrect: The example does not lack displacement as it refers to objects that are not present.

10. **a. Correct: This example does not follow the proper rules of arrangement of words and phrases in sentences, or syntax.**
    b. Incorrect: This example does not follow the proper rules of arrangement of words and phrases in sentences, or syntax.
    c. Incorrect: This example does not follow the proper rules of arrangement of words and phrases in sentences, or syntax.
    d. Incorrect: This example does not follow the proper rules of arrangement of words and phrases in sentences, or syntax.

11. a. Incorrect: Syntax is the rules governing the arrangement of words in the sentence. This is not changing in the example.
b. **Correct: Pragmatics is the study of the relationship between the language and social context; this is changing with the tone in which the sentence is stated.**
c. Incorrect: Surface structure is the word arrangements, which aare not changing in this example.
d. Incorrect: Linguistic relativity refers to the theory that the world is molded by language.

12. a. Incorrect: Generativity refers to the ability to combine words in novel ways.
b. **Correct: Overextension refers to the tendency for children to apply a word to more objects than it actually represents; this is what is happening in this example.**
c. Incorrect: Overregularization is the application of a grammatical rule without making the necessary exceptions to it.
d. Incorrect: Holophrastic speech is speech characterized by single-word sentences.

13. a. Incorrect: This is Skinner's position.
b. **Correct: Chomsky does insist that infants are born with the predisposition to develop language.**
c. Incorrect: This is Chomsky's belief.
d. Incorrect: This research has provided support for Chomsky's position.

14. a. Incorrect: The assumption that one's perception of the world is molded by language is called the linguistic relativity hypothesis.
b. Incorrect: The assumption that one's perception of the world is molded by language is called the linguistic relativity hypothesis.
c. Incorrect: The assumption that one's perception of the world is molded by language is called the linguistic relativity hypothesis.
d. **Correct: The assumption that one's perception of the world is molded by language is called the linguistic relativity hypothesis.**

15. a. Incorrect: Hamilton showed in 1988 that sexist language (the use of "he") did have an effect on the perception of the reader.
b. **Correct: Hamilton showed in 1988 that sexist language (the use of "he") did have an effect on the perception of the reader.**
c. Incorrect: Hamilton showed in 1988 that sexist language (the use of "he") did have an effect on the perception of the reader.
d. Incorrect: Hamilton showed in 1988 that sexist language (the use of "he") did have an effect on the perception of the reader.

16. a. Incorrect: Terrace does not believe that apes have developed true language; he feels that they lack generativity.
b. **Correct: Terrace does not believe that apes have developed true language; he feels that they lack generativity.**
c. Incorrect: Terrace does not believe that apes have developed true language; he feels that they lack generativity.
d. Incorrect: Terrace does not believe that apes have developed true language; he feels that they lack generativity.

Practice Test B:

1. a. Incorrect: None of these phenomena is observable.
b. Incorrect: Language is not an unconscious phenomenon.
c. Incorrect: Instincts are biologically preprogrammed sequences of behaviors; none of these is a preprogrammed sequence.
d. **Correct: All three of these are cognitive functions.**

2. a. Incorrect: Nim Chimpsky is a chimp, not a psychological theorist.
b. Incorrect: Sigmund Freud was a psychoanalyst, not a behaviorist; he proposed that thought was an unconscious process.
c. **Correct: Margaret Floy Washburn agreed with Watson and developed the motor theory of thinking.**
d. Incorrect: Scott Smith is not a psychological theorist.

3. a. Incorrect: Natural concepts do not have clear definitions, as is illustrated in the example.
b. Incorrect: Prototypical concepts is not a correct term used by psychologists.
c. **Correct: Logical concepts have clear definitions that can be arrived at by hypothesis testing.**
d. Incorrect: Artificial concept is not a term used by psychologists.

4. a. Incorrect: In this example she has already identified the problem.
b. **Correct: She has identified the problem and now is gathering information about the problem.**
c. Incorrect: Solution testing involves trying an action; she is only questioning.
d. Incorrect: She could not evaluate a result until she has tried a solution.

5. a. Incorrect: Divergent thinking involves looking for a variety of possible solutions, not just conventional ones.
   b. Correct: Mental sets involve the use of strategies that have worked before but are not appropriate in the new situation. This is what Howard is doing.
   c. Incorrect: Algorithms are rules that if followed ensure a solution to the problem.
   d. Incorrect: Framing effects occur when the way a question is posed influences the interpretation of the problem.

6. **a. Correct: Amabile's research showed that when creative people are made to think about extrinsic rewards, their creativity decreases.**
   b. Incorrect: Amabile's research showed that when creative people are made to think about extrinsic rewards, their creativity decreases.
   c. Incorrect: Amabile's research showed that when creative people are made to think about extrinsic rewards, their creativity decreases.
   d. Incorrect: Amabile's research showed that when creative people are made to think about extrinsic rewards, their creativity decreases.

7. a. Incorrect: Convergent thinking involves the use of conventional means to solve problems, not creativity.
   b. Correct: Measures of divergent thinking are correlated with creativity.
   c. Incorrect: Brainstorming is a technique that encourages divergent thinking but is done in a group.
   d. Incorrect: Divergent thinking has been shown to be increased by positive emotional states, not creativity.

8. a. Incorrect: When using an availability heuristic you are basing your decisions on the tendency of that event to come to mind, not how representative it is.
   b. Correct: A representativeness heuristic bases decisions on generalization from the characteristics of a small sample.
   c. Incorrect: Psychologists do not use the term "probability heuristic."
   d. Incorrect: Utility refers to the value of a given alternative in a decision; there is not a utility heuristic.

9. a. Incorrect: A representativeness heuristic bases decisions on generalization from the characteristics of a small sample.
   b. Correct: Framing effects refer to the influence on decisions of the way a question is posed.
   c. Incorrect: Stimulus generalization is a concept from the learning chapter that refers to the tendency to give a learned response to similar stimuli.
   d. Incorrect: When using an availability heuristic you are basing your decisions on the tendency of that event to come to mind.

10. a. Incorrect: A representativeness heuristic bases decisions on generalization from the characteristics of a small sample; this would not allow the system to win.
    b. Incorrect: Pragmatics examines the relationship between language and its social context.
    c. Correct: An expert system is a computer system highly knowledgeable in a specific area, like chess.
    d. Incorrect: Convergent thinking involves problem solving using conventional methods; again, this would not allow the system to win a chess match.

11. a. Incorrect: Pragmatics involves the study of the relationship between language and its social context.
    b. Incorrect: Displacement is the characteristic of language that refers to the ability to refer to things not present.
    c. Correct: Semanticity refers to the meaningfulness of language.
    d. Incorrect: Generativity refers to the ability to combine words in novel and meaningful ways.

12. **a. Correct: Phonemes are the smallest unit of sound; morphemes are the smallest meaningful unit and form words, which form sentences.**
    b. Incorrect: Phonemes are the smallest unit of sound; morphemes are the smallest meaningful unit and form words, which form sentences.
    c. Incorrect: Phonemes are the smallest unit of sound; morphemes are the smallest meaningful unit and form words, which form sentences.
    d. Incorrect: Phonemes are the smallest unit of sound; morphemes are the smallest meaningful unit and form words, which form sentences.

13. a. Incorrect: Syntax refers to the rules that govern the acceptable arrangement of words and these sentences have different syntax.
    b. Incorrect: Surface structure refers to the arrangements of words in the sentences, which are different in these sentences.
    c. Incorrect: Transformational grammar refers to the conversion of surface structure to deep structures and vice versa.
    d. Correct: These sentences share the same deep structures, or underlying meaning.

14. a. Incorrect: Babies are born crying, they progress to cooing, then babbling, followed by holophrases and then telegraphic speech.
    b. Incorrect: Babies are born crying, they progress to cooing, then babbling, followed by holophrases and then telegraphic speech.
    c. Incorrect: Babies are born crying, they progress to cooing, then babbling, followed by holophrases and then telegraphic speech.
    d. Correct: Babies are born crying, they progress to cooing, then babbling, followed by holophrases and then telegraphic speech.

15. a. Incorrect: Babbling involves the repetition of phonemes; they are not representational.
b. Incorrect: Overextension refers to the use of words too broadly, just one concept.
c. Incorrect: Telegraphic speech is made-up of two-word sentences, "ba-tee" is a single "word."
d. Correct: Holophrastic speech refers to the use of one-word sentences to represent something; "ba-tee" is an example.

16. a. Incorrect: The research has suggested that a combination of Chomsky's, Skinner's, and Bandura's theories are needed to explain language.
b. Correct: The research has suggested that a combination of Chomsky's, Skinner's, and Bandura's theories are needed to explain language. This statement does that.
c. Incorrect: The research has suggested that a combination of Chomsky's, Skinner's, and Bandura's theories are needed to explain language.
d. Incorrect: The research has suggested that a combination of Chomsky's, Skinner's, and Bandura's theories are needed to explain language.

17. **a. Correct: Rosch's study with the Dani indicated that both Americans and Dani were equally effective in identifying colors, the opposite of what Whorf predicted.**
b. Incorrect: Rosch's study with the Dani indicated that both Americans and Dani were equally effective in identifying colors, the opposite of what Whorf predicted.
c. Incorrect: Rosch's study with the Dani indicated that both Americans and Dani were equally effective in identifying colors, the opposite of what a learning theory would predict.
d. Incorrect: Rosch's study with the Dani indicated that both Americans and Dani were equally effective in identifying colors, the opposite of what Whorf predicted.

18. a. Incorrect: The research has indicated that language does influence thinking but does not determine thought.
b. Incorrect: The research has indicated that language does influence thinking but does not determine thought.
c. Correct: The research has indicated that language does influence thinking but does not determine thought.
d. Incorrect: The research has indicated that language does influence thinking but does not determine thought.

19. a. Incorrect: Semantics is the study of the meanings of words.
b. Correct: Generativity refers to the characteristic of language referring to the ability to combine words in novel and meaningful ways.
c. Incorrect: Displacement refers to the ability to refer to objects that are not present; in the example, the object Washoe was referring to was present.
d. Incorrect: Fluency refers to the ability to understand the meaning of the symbol.

20. a. Incorrect: The recent research suggests that the level of ability the apes can attain may be limited.
b. Incorrect: The recent research does suggest that apes are capable of learning sign language.
c. Correct: The recent research does suggest that apes are capable of learning sign language, however, the level of ability the apes can attain may be limited.
d. Incorrect: The grunts and facial expressions of chimps are not complex.

Essay Questions:

1. The first step would be to identify the problem. Second, you would gather information about the problem. Third, you would try a solution, and fourth, you would evaluate the solution tried. If the solution failed you would try another. Two obstacles that might hinder your ability to solve the problem would be a mental set and functional fixedness.

2. Human language uses an agreed-upon series of symbols and an agreed-upon system of rules for combining those symbols. All human languages are characterized by:
1) semanticity or meaningfulness;
2) generativity or an infinite potential for novelty of expression; and
3) displacement or the ability to communicate about objects or events that are not immediately present.

While animal communication has semanticity and the communication of a few species has displacement, no animal communication has generativity.

10 Intelligence

LEARNING OBJECTIVES

After studying this chapter, you should be able to:

1. Define intelligence and summarize some of the difficulties in arriving at a satisfactory delineation of this concept. (p. 346)

2. Distinguish between and offer examples of achievement tests versus aptitude tests. (p. 346-347)

3. Describe the significant events and individuals in the history of intelligence testing. (p. 347-348)

4. Describe the origins of and principles underlying the Binet-Simon/Stanford-Binet intelligence tests and then summarize the strengths and weaknesses of this approach to intelligence testing. (p. 348-349)

5. List and describe the important features of three intelligence scales developed by David Wechsler (p. 349-350)

6. List and describe four important and often controversial issues surrounding the nature and use of intelligence scales, mentioning how researchers have attempted to respond to question of cultural bias. (p. 350-352)

7. Define mental retardation; describe the four levels of retardation and summarize what is presently known about the causes of mental retardation. (p. 353-355)

8. Describe historical and contemporary approaches to educating persons with mental retardation. (p. 355-356)

9. Define mental giftedness and summarize the findings of several important studies of the mentally gifted. (p. 356-358)

10. Summarize the contributions of Charles Spearman, Louis Thurstone, J. P. Guilford, as well as those of John Horn & Raymond Cattell regarding the nature of intelligence. (p. 359-361)

11. Summarize the important features of Robert Sternberg's triarchic theory of intelligence, offering examples of each type of intelligence delineated in the theory. (p. 361-362)

12. Describe and offer examples of the various types of intelligence delineated in Howard Gardner's theory of multiple intelligences. (p. 362-363)

13. Summarize the findings of historical and contemporary research regarding the relative contributions of heredity versus environment to intellectual capacity, emphasizing both family studies and adoption studies. (p. 363-368)

14. Summarize the research findings regarding the impact of intellectual enrichment programs such as Head Start. (p. 369-371)

COMPREHENSIVE GUIDED REVIEW

___(1)___ intelligent behavior is easier than defining it. As a ___(2)___ concept, it is not easily defined by a distinct set of features. The difficulty may be seen in the individual with below average intelligence who exhibits the ___(3)___savant syndrome. In this syndrome individuals' ability to ___(4)___ and relate to others socially is impaired, but they are capable of memorizing enormous amounts of material, thus displaying ___(5)___ behavior. Although it has been difficult to find a ___(6)___ acceptable definition, Wechsler, influenced by functionalism, proposed a definition of intelligence that has come to be the most widely accepted. He defined **intelligence** as the global capacity to act__(7)__, to think rationally, and to deal effectively with the environment.

I. Intelligence Testing: Modern interest in intelligence began with the development of tests of__(8)__ ability, which fell into one of three categories: **achievement tests, aptitude tests,** and **intelligence tests.** __(9)__ tests are used to assess knowledge of a particular subject. __(10)__ **tests** are used to predict the potential to perform well in a particular academic or vocational situation, and__(11)__ **tests** are a kind of aptitude test that assesses overall mental ability.

The history of intelligence testing has been traced back to the__(12)__. It suggests that they used intelligence tests beginning around 2200 B.C. to identify talented people to serve as__(13)__. However, ability testing did not become the subject of__(14)__ study until Francis Galton set up his anthropometric lab approximately 100 years ago.

Galton, influenced by__(15)__, devised a test to identify people with superior physical abilities and who would therefore be better adapted for survival. His interest in individual differences led to the development of__(16)__ **psychology,** a field concerned with both the cognitive and __(17)__ differences among people. It was James McKeen Cattell who introduced Galton's__(18)__ method in the United States. He administered Galton's tests, which he called__(19)__ *tests.*

The first formal test of general__(20)__ was the Binet-Simon scale and was published in 1905. As the result of an 1881 French educational reform law,__(21)__ was commissioned to develop a test to identify slow learners. Binet and Simon administered questions related to language,__(22)__, and arithmetic to children of all ages, and developed a test they called the *Binet-*__(23)__ *scale.* It employed the concept of__(24)__, defined as the number of items children at different age levels could pass. But since the concept of **mental age** often proved misleading, William Stern proposed the use of a__(25)__ of mental age to chronological age as a more appropriate determination of intelligence. This became known as the **intelligence quotient,** or__(26)__, and took the form mental age (MA)/chronological age (CA) × 100.

Henry__(27)__ translated the Binet-Simon scale into English and brought it to the United States. With additional changes to better suit children reared in America, a 1916 version, still in use today, was published as the __(28)__ *Intelligence Scale* (the test was revised in 1937, 1960, 1972, and 1986). During World War I, group tests were developed as an alternative to the__(29)__ individualized administration of the **Stanford-Binet;** among them, the *Army Alpha Test,* the *Army Beta Test,* and the still-used *Otis-Lennon Mental Abilities Tests* and *Armed Forces Qualification Test.*

Because of the marked__(30)__ of the growth of mental age after childhood, Stern's formulation was inadequate for adults. Wechsler replaced Stern's ratio IQ with a__(31)__ IQ, such that those who perform at the same level as their age peers receive an IQ of 100. Placing less emphasis on__(32)__ ability, Wechsler published the *Wechsler-Bellevue Intelligence Scale* in 1939. Later versions included the *Wechsler Intelligence Scale for*__(33)__ *(WISC)* in 1949, for ages 6 to 16; the *Wechsler* __(34)__ *Intelligence Scale (WAIS)* in 1955, for ages from late adolescence through adulthood; and the *Wechsler Preschool and Primary Scale of Intelligence* (__(35)__), for ages 4 to 6 ½. Three IQ scores are given: a verbal IQ, a__(36)__ IQ, and an overall IQ.

Issues in Intelligence Testing: As you recall from Chapter 1, a test must be **standardized, reliable,** and **valid.** __(37)__refers to both the establishment of performance norms on a test and uniformity in how the test is administered and scored. When an intelligence test is standardized, the average (__(38)__) score is set at 100, with a standard deviation of 15. When these data are applied to the__(39)__ *curve,* approximately 68 percent of the population will earn scores ranging from 85 to 115. __(40)__ is the degree to which a test gives consistent results. An individual's IQ score may change over the years.__(41)__ reliability measures are at least .9, thus intelligence tests are considered to be__(42)__ over the short run. However, there was a question as to the__(43)__ reliability of the tests. The Berkeley Growth Study found that mental ability__(44)__ steadily until adolescence, slows down, and then levels off at about the age of 20. __(45)__ is the extent to which a test measures what it is supposed to measure, as a thermometer should measure temperature. __(46)__ validity, the extent to which the test accurately predicts the behavior it is supposed to measure, is especially important. The intelligence tests have been shown to correlate __(47)__ with school performance, indicating that the tests are good, but not perfect__(48)_ of school performance.

Related to the validity issue is the question of whether intelligence tests are fair to__(49)__ groups, especially African Americans. This has made testing both a scientific and a__(50)__ issue. Judge Peckham's 1979 ruling that IQ tests violated the civil rights of African Americans was__(51)__ by the subsequent judgment of the National Academy of Science. Those opposed to Peckman's decision argued that the test was not__(52)__ against African American students because of its good predictive validity. In other words, the test did accurately__(53)__ the performance of both African American and white children. Critics of Peckman further suggested that the differences in the scores might be the result of differences in__(54)__ environments. One solution would be to compromise and use tests that are not affected by the test taker's__(55)__ background. Unfortunately, even the so-called __(56)__ tests have been, to date, biased against some minorities from our own or other cultures. This controversy remains an__(57)__ issue in psychology.

Time to take a study break. Remember, these breaks are important to allow you to time to organize the information mentally and keep your attention at peak levels.

Complete the mini-review before you proceed to the next section.

Mini-review of Intelligence Testing: Match each term with its correct description.

_______1. intelligence quotient
_______2. validity
_______3. culture free
_______4. intelligence tests
_______5. Army Alpha, Army Beta, and Otis-Lennon Tests
_______6. autistic savant syndrome
_______7. standardization
_______8. intelligence
_______9. WPPSI
_______10. differential psychology
_______11. Binet-Simon scale
_______12. deviation IQ
_______13. WISC
_______14. achievement tests
_______15. reliability
_______16. mental age
_______17. Stanford-Binet Intelligence Scale
_______18. aptitude tests
_______19. predictive validity
_______20. WAIS

A. In this syndrome, individuals' ability to communicate and relate to others socially is impaired, but they are capable of memorizing enormous amounts of material
B. The global capacity to act purposefully, to think rationally, and to deal effectively with the environment
C. Intelligence test for ages 4 to 6 ½
D. The degree to which a test gives consistent results
E. Tests used to assess knowledge of a particular subject
F. Field concerned with both the cognitive and behavioral differences among people
G. The first formal test of general intelligence
H. Based on the number of items children at different ages could pass
I. Ratio of mental age to chronological age: (MA)/(CA) × 100
J. Intelligence test for ages from late adolescence through adulthood
K. The extent to which a test measures what it is supposed to measure
L. Tests used to predict the potential to perform well in a particular academic or vocational situation
M. A 1916 version of the Binet-Simon scale, translated into English, with changes to better suit children reared in America; still in use today
N. World War I group tests developed as an alternative to the Stanford-Binet
O. Calculated such that those who perform at the same level as their age peers receive an IQ of 100
P. Intelligence test for ages 6 to 16
Q. Refers to both the establishment of performance norms on a test and uniformity in how the test is administered and scored
R. Tests that are not affected by the test taker's cultural background
S. The extent to which a test accurately predicts the behavior it is supposed to measure
T. A type of aptitude test that assesses overall mental ability

II. Extremes of Intelligence: Another controversial issue in psychology is the__(58)__ and education of people who fall at either extreme of the range of intelligence. Those who score below__(59)__ are usually considered mentally retarded and those who fall above 130 are usually considered__(60)__. However, these classifications are not based__(61)__ on IQ scores.

Classification of Mental Retardation: To be classified as____(62)____, a person must have an IQ below 70 and have difficulty performing in everyday life. There are four categories of retardation, including: **mild, moderate, severe,** and **profound retardation.**

1) __(63)__*retardation*—IQs between 50 and 70, able to care for themselves, work, be adequate parents;
2) *moderate retardation*—IQs between 35 and 49; may be__(64)__; may hold menial jobs, often in sheltered workshops; have difficulty with social relationships; and rarely marry;
3) __(65)__ *retardation*—IQs between 20 and 34; at most capable of learning rudimentary skills, but__(66)__ to care for themselves, to benefit from schooling, to hold jobs, or to maintain normal social relationships;
4) __(67)__ *retardation*—generally institutionalized, receiving no more than__(68)__ care

Causes of Mental Retardation: We now know that about 75 percent of the cases of mental retardation are caused, not by__(69)__, but by socio-cultural deprivation, so-called __(70)__ **retardation.** The remaining 25 percent are caused by forms of brain damage. Among them:

Ingestion effects during pregnancy—drugs, **fetal alcohol syndrome.**
Disease effects—rubella (__(71)__ measles).
Infection effects—herpes.
Malnutrition effects—a reduction in brain__(72)__ due to the severe malnutrition of mothers during pregnancy.
Exposure effects—prenatal exposure to____(73)____ may impair the normal migration of brain cells.
Oxygen deficits at birth—may lead to__(74)__, a most common cause of perinatal brain damage.
Genetic effects—as in the case of **PKU,** which leads to mental retardation by the age of 3. Some cases of mental retardation are caused by genetic defects that occur during gestation, as in the case of__(75)__ syndrome.

Education of Persons with Mental Retardation: Today the mildly retarded are called "__(76)__," and the__(77)__ retarded are called "trainable." Dissatisfaction with the approach of placing the educable mentally retarded in special classes led to __(78)__. In this approach, mandated by the Education for All Handicapped Children Act of 1975, mentally retarded children are placed is as many __(79)__classes as possible. However, the educational needs of the mentally retarded are not limited to__(80)__ training. They may also need training in self-care, home management, __(81)__ skills, and community mobility skills. The movement that has paralleled mainstreaming is__(82)__, the transfer from large institutional settings into community settings.

Mental Giftedness: At the other extreme from mental retardation are those individuals who are considered mentally __(83)__. Sir Francis__(84)__ began the study of the gifted in the late nineteenth century. Mentally gifted individuals are considered to be those who score above __(85)__on the IQ test along with exceptionally high scores on achievement tests in specific subjects, for example, mathematics.

The needs of the mentally gifted have traditionally received less attention than those of the mentally retarded, mostly due to the belief that gifted individuals peaked early, only to become academic, social, and vocational__(86)__ later in like. This view has changed. The most well-known organization for the gifted is __(87)__. The classic study in support of the viewpoint that the gifted are doomed to become academic, vocational, and social failures was that of William James __(88)__. He enrolled at__(89)__ at the age of 11, served on the faculty at Rice Institute, but ended up spending the rest of his life working at menial jobs. Lewis __(90)__'s Genetic Studies of Genius has countered the belief that mentally gifted individuals are doomed to become academic, vocational, and social failures; it is the focus of the "Anatomy of a Classic Research Study."

Anatomy of a Classic Research Study: What Is the Fate of Childhood Geniuses? *Read the summary of Terman's study on page 357 in you textbook and answer the following questions.*

What was the rationale for the study?

What methods did the author use to test the hypothesis?

What was the outcome of the study and what did the authors conclude the results meant?

More recently the results of the *Study of Mathematically Precocious Youth* by Benbow and Stanley emphasizes the need for intensive___(91)_, accelerated courses, and counseling for parents of gifted students. Their findings continue to support ___(92)__'s view.

To stay on track, stop here and take a short break.
Review the extremes of intelligence in the mini-review before continuing.

Mini-review of the Extremes of Intelligence: Match each term with its correct description.

________1. severe retardation
________2. Mensa
________3. mentally retarded
________4. Lewis Terman
________5. mild retardation
________6. mainstreaming
________7. moderate retardation
________8. William James Sidis
________9. cultural-familial retardation
________10. mentally gifted
________11. profound retardation
________12. *Education for All Handicapped Children Act of 1975*
________13. normalization

A. Have an IQ below 70 and have difficulty performing in everyday life
B. Enrolled at Harvard at the age of 11, served on the faculty at Rice Institute, but ended up spending the rest of his life working at menial jobs
C. Mandated that mentally retarded children are placed is as many normal classes as possible
D. IQ between 50 and 70; able to care for themselves, work, be adequate parents
E. Score above 130 on the intelligence test along with exceptionally high scores on achievement tests in specific subjects
F. Results from socio-cultural deprivation
G. IQ between 20 and 34; at most capable of learning rudimentary skills; unable to care for themselves; cannot maintain normal social relationships
H. Movement that argues that mentally retarded people need training in self-care, home management, consumer skills, and community mobility skills in community settings
I. Category of mentally retardation generally are institutionalized, receiving no more than custodial care
J. IQs between 35 and 49; may be trained; may hold menial jobs, often in sheltered workshops; have difficulty with social relationships; and rarely marry
K. The most well-known organization for the gifted
L. He conducted the Genetic Studies of Genius
M. Movement that argues that mentally retarded people should be placed into as many normal classes as possible

III. Theories of Intelligence: Is intelligence a general characteristic that affects all aspects of behavior, or are there different kinds of intelligence, with each affecting specific facets? This has been a question that psychologists interested in intelligence have grappled with. The most recent trend has been to assume that there are various __(93)__ of intelligence.

Factor-Analytic Theories of Intelligence:
Spearman's Theory of General Intelligence: ___(94)___'s view on intelligence was that it was the general ability to reason and solve problems in a variety of situations. About the same time that Binet was developing his intelligence test, ___(95)___was developing a theory that considered intelligence a general characteristic underlying a variety of behaviors. Spearman developed his theory of___(96)___ intelligence. Spearman used a___(97)___ technique called **factor analysis** to determine the degree of___(98)___ between performance on different tasks. When several tasks showed high intercorrelations, he presumed that there was a___(99)___ underlying factor. Initially he noted that performance on a wide variety of cognitive tasks tended to show high___(100)___ correlations with one another. This led him to conclude that performance on all of the tasks depended on the operation of a single underlying general intelligence factor, which he called "___(101)___"—a general intelligence factor. Since the correlations were always less than a perfect 1.00, he concluded that each behavior also depended on its own___(102)___ factor, which he called "s." Research has provided some support for the "g."

Thurstone's Theory of Primary Mental Abilities: Thurstone also used the___(103)___ approach but, unlike Spearman, concluded that there was___(104)___ general intelligence factor. He identified___(105)___ factors, which he called *primary mental abilities:* reasoning, word fluency,___(106)___ speed, verbal comprehension, spatial visualization, numerical calculation, and associative___(107)___.

Guilford's Theory of the Structure of the Intellect: Guilford used___(108)___ to identify 120 factors and, recently, increased it to 150. Each of the factors interacts along three dimensions of intelligence. The dimensions are: a) *Operations*—___(109)___ processes; b)___(110)___—information that a person is thinking about; and c) *Products*—___(111)___ of thinking about the information.

Horn and Cattell's Two-Factor Theory of Intelligence: This is the most recent___(112)___ theory. Two intelligence factors were identified: ___(113)___**intelligence**—reflecting thinking ability, memory capacity, and speed of information processing. Horn and Cattell believe that fluid intelligence is largely___(114)___, affected little by training, and declines in late adulthood; and ___(115)___**intelligence**—reflecting the acquisition of knowledge through education and experience. They believe that crystallized intelligence___(116)___ or remains the same in late adulthood.

At present, the question of which of the factor-analytic theories is best remains___(117)___. Certainly one criticism of these theories is that they assume that intelligence reflects only those cognitive abilities needed to perform in___(118)___. A theory that would consider a___(119)___ range of abilities would be more acceptable. Sternberg & Gardner have provided us with such a theory.

The Triarchic Theory of Intelligence: ___(120)___ and his colleagues surveyed people in a variety of settings and asked them to list what they believed were the main characteristics of intelligent people. The results showed that intelligent people were assumed to have good___(121)___ skills, good problem-solving abilities, and good social judgment. Sternberg's theory is based on his observations of how people process___(122)___. The theory claims that intelligence is comprised of___(123)___ kinds of abilities:

1) ___(124)___ *intelligence.* It is similar to the kind of intelligence considered by traditional theories and primarily reflects our verbal reasoning ability;
2) ___*(125)*___ *intelligence.* It is the ability to combine different experiences in insightful ways to solve novel problems. It reflects creativity; and
3) ___*(126)*___ *intelligence.* It is the ability to function in practical, everyday social situations, such as in the case of being *street smart.*

The theory recognizes that we must be able to function in settings other than___(127)___. Furthermore, the theory recognizes that we may excel in one kind of intelligence and not necessarily in the other two.

The Theory of Multiple Intelligences: Gardner's (1983) theory is based on the assumption that the brain has ___(128)___ separate systems for different adaptive abilities that he calls "intelligence." There are___(129)___ types: **linguistic, logical-mathematical, spatial, musical, bodily-kinesthetic, intrapersonal,** and **interpersonal.** Several of Gardner's kinds of intelligence are assessed by traditional intelligence tests. These include: *Linguistic intelligence:* the ability to__(130)__ through language; *Logical-mathematical intelligence:* the ability to analyze____(131)__ and solve mathematical problems; and ____(132)_*intelligence,* or the ability to perceive and arrange objects in the environment. The remaining kinds of intelligence are not assessed by traditional tests: *Musical intelligence* is the ability to analyze, __(133)__, or to play music; *Bodily-kinesthetic intelligence* is the ability to__(134)__ or manipulate objects effectively; *Intrapersonal intelligence* is the ability to know___(135)__ and understand what motivates your behavior; and *Interpersonal intelligence* is the ability to function in__(136)__ situations because you are able to understand the needs of other people and predict their behavior.

Stop and take another short study break. The previous section mentions a lot of names and theories, so be sure that you know who proposed what. To check your comprehension take the mini-review before moving on to the "Thinking about Psychology" section of the chapter.

Mini-review of Theories of Intelligence:

Part I: Match the psychologist with the theory of intelligence:

_______1. Gardner	A. The triarchic theory of intelligence
_______2. Spearman	B. The theory of multiple intelligences
_______3. Thurstone	C. Two-factor theory of intelligence
_______4. factor analysis	D. Theory of general intelligence
_______5. Sternberg	E. Theory of the structure of the intellect
_______6. Guilford	F. The statistical technique to determine the degree of correlation between performances on different tasks
_______7. Horn & Cattell	G. Theory of primary mental abilities

Part II: Briefly describe the tenets of each theory of intelligence:

Factor-analytic Theories of Intelligence:

Theory of General Intelligence

Theory of Primary Mental Abilities

Theory of the Structure of the Intellect

Two-Factor Theory of Intelligence

Non-factor Analysis Theories:

The Triarchic Theory of Intelligence

The Theory of Multiple Intelligences

IV. Thinking About Psychology: Does Intelligence Depend More on Nature or on Nurture?

Early Studies of Immigrants: In 1912, Goddard concluded that a very large proportion of Italians, Hungarians, Jews, and Russians were "___(137)__," which today we would call mildly retarded. Even after reevaluating his research, he concluded that these ethnic groups were__(138)_ inferior Goddard's claim was later reinforced by the work of Brigham, who found that __(139)_scored lower on IQ tests than did American-born whites. He attributed these differences in IQ scores to differences in___(140)__. What both Goddard and Brigham failed to realize was that there were a host of __(141)__ and environmental factors that could have accounted for their findings. In 1930, Brigham admitted that he had been wrong in assuming that the poorer performance of immigrants was attributable to heredity. Items on the Army Alpha Test illustrate the problem.

Research on the Influence of Heredity and Environment: Project Head Start was stimulated, in part, by the finding that blacks scored an average of__(142)_ points lower than whites on IQ tests. Those who supported Head Start attributed this difference to the poor_(143)_ conditions in which black children were more likely to be reared. In 1969,_(144)_ questioned whether programs such as Head Start could boost the intellectual level of deprived children. He based his doubts on the notion of_(145)_. He claimed that__(146)_ percent of the variability in intelligence can be explained by heredity and that this accounts for the difference in the IQ gap between white and black children. In the tradition of_(147)_, one of Jensen's chief supporters, Shockley (1972), proposed paying people with low IQs to undergo sterilization. Burt reported similar pro-heredity findings, but it was Kamin (1974) who discovered that data supporting the hereditary basis of intelligence had been__(148)_.

Family Studies of Intelligence: Studies of relatives and__(149)_ led to the conclusion that the size of the correlation in intelligence between relatives of varying degrees of genetic similarity is, by itself,__(150)_ for determining whether similarity is caused primarily by hereditary factors or by environmental factors.

__(151)_studies provide evidence for the genetic basis of intelligence. The genes inherited from the__(152)_ parents appear to exert a stronger influence on adoptees than does the environment provided by their adoptive parents (Bouchard & McGue, 1981). Overall, however, the conclusion that emerges from adoption study research is that intelligence is influenced both by heredity and environment, with neither_(153)_ the other.

Anatomy of a Contemporary Research Study: What is the Effect of Adoption on the Intellectual Development of Adopted Children? *Read the summary of the Scarr and Weinberg study on page 367 in your textbook and answer the following questions.*

What was the rationale for the study?

What methods did the author use to test their hypothesis?

What was the outcome of the study and what did the authors conclude the results meant?

Additional support for the influence of_(154)_ comes from family configuration studies. A survey of men in the Netherlands found that the larger their families and the later their birth orders, the _(155)_intelligent they tended to be. This finding has been explained by Zajonc's (1986)__(156)_ **model,** which assumes that each child is born into an intellectual environment that is dependent on the intelligence levels of his or her parents and siblings. The___(157)_ the number of children and the smaller the average interval between births, the lower will be what Zajonc calls the **average intellectual environment.** Zajonc continues to present evidence to support his **confluence model;** however, a recent National Institutes of Health study failed to show a__(158)_ between intelligence and the average interval between birth in a family. Moreover, it has been pointed out that the supporting research has shown only a correlational relationship, not a ___(159)_one.

Enhancing Intelligence: Intellectual Enrichment Programs: Additional support for the influence of the environment comes from the finding that the difference between the performance of whites and blacks on the SAT has __(160)_, as has the difference in intelligence between black and white children. The Venezuelan enrichment program illustrates how__(161)__ such programs can be. Even more evidence comes from__(162)__ in IQ scores in fourteen nations. Japanese children scored 11 points higher than American children, in keeping with their culture's emphasis on education. Indeed, it may not be in our best interest to study the relative importance of heredity and environment, as data could be used as support for__(163)__.

Congratulations! You have finished your review of Chapter 10. As always, it is now time to review the key research studies mentioned in the chapter and complete the test-readiness items. Continue to stay on track!

KEY RESEARCH FINDINGS

1. **Lynn & Wilson (1990):** Found that higher intelligence test scores in elementary school children were related to faster reaction times. (Page 348)
2. **Bayley (1955):** Found that mental ability increases through adolescence and levels off about at age 20. (Page 351)
3. **Linn (1982):** Found that first-year college grade-point averages could be more accurately predicted by using both SAT scores and high school GPA. (Page 351)
4. **Messick & Jungeblut (1981):** Found that SAT preparation courses had only a modest positive effect on SAT scores. (Page 351)
5. **Taylor (1990):** Claimed that standardized IQ tests were biased against African Americans. (Page 351)
6. **Lambert (1981):** Suggested that differences in IQ test scores between African Americans and white children might be more likely the result of social differences and experiences. (Page 352)
7. **Goddard (1912):** Asserted that the tendency for mental retardation or intelligence was inherited (Page 354)
8. **Griffiths, Paterson, & Harvie (1995):** Described the effect of diet in combatting phenylketonuria (PKU). (Page 355)
9. **Matson, DiLorenzo, & Esveldt-Dawson (1981):** Showed the usefulness of behavior modification in training patients with mental retardation to care for themselves. (Page 355)
10. **Wallace (1986):** Studied the effects of childhood genius in later years. (Page 357)
11. **Terman (1921-):** Continuing longitudinal study that has shown that gifted children tend to become socially, academically, physically, and vocationally superior adults. (Page 357)
12. **Cravens (1992):** Supported Terman's findings. (Page 357)
13. **Benbow & Stanley (1983):** Provided programs in science and math for youths who scored above 700 on SATs. (Page 358)
14. **Benbow, Arjmand & Walberg (1991):** Follow-up study to Benbow & Stanley that demonstrated the subjects had many outstanding educational achievements. (Page 358)
15. **Ceci & Liker (1986):** Found that the ability to handicap horse races was unrelated to general intelligence test scores. (Page 359)
16. **Guilford (1959):** Identified 120 factors that represented interactions among mental operations, contents, and products. (Page 360)
17. **Horn & Cattell (1966):** Applied factor analysis to develop a two-factor theory of intelligence. (Page 360)
18. **Sternberg et al. (1981):** Surveyed people who responded that intelligence was demonstrated by good verbal skills, social judgment, and problem-solving abilities. (Page 361)
19. **Sternberg (1994):** Developed a triarchic theory of intelligence based on his earlier survey. (Page 361)
20. **Ball, Mann, & Stamm (1994):** Supported the triarchic theory with a study of gifted students. (Page 362)
21. **Gardner (1983):** Developed a theory of multiple intelligences based on the brain's evolution of separate systems for different adaptive abilities. (Page 362)
22. **Brigham (1923):** Found that immigrants scored lower on army IQ tests than American-born whites and attributed this to heredity. (Page 365)
23. **Shockley (1972):** Suggested that Americans with lower-than-average IQ scores be paid by the government to undergo sterilization. (Page 365)
24. **Kamin (1974):** Discovered that data in support of a genetic study of IQ scores in twins had been falsified. (Page 365)
25. **Scarr & Carter-Saltzman (1979):** Found that the similarity in intelligence between twins is more likely genetic than environmental. (Page 366)

26. **Burt (1943, 1955, 1966):** Reported that the correlation in intelligence between identical twins reared apart was .771 in each of the studies. (Page 366)
27. **Loehlin, Horn, & Willerman (1994):** Found that the correlation in intelligence between adoptive parents and children is less than that between the children and their biological parents. (Page 367)
28. **Coon et al. (1990):** Found that the influence of the environment on adoptive children decreases with age. (Page 367)
29. **Scarr & Weinberg (1976):** Found that children raised by parents in a higher socioeconomic class scored about 20 points higher than other children of their group. (Page 367)
30. **Belmont & Marolla (1973):** Their survey showed that the later men were born in the birth order, the less intelligent they were. (Page 368)
31. **Zajonc (1976):** Developed a confluence model, which described an average intellectual environment as the key in predicting intelligence. (Page 368)
32. **Brackbill & Nichols (1982):** Did an NIH study that failed to find support for the confluence model. (Page 368)
33. **Sue & Okazaki (1990):** Hypothesized that differences between Asian Americans and others is due to simple adaptive behavior. (Page 370)

PRACTICE TEST A

1. "The global capacity to act purposefully, to think rationally, and to deal effectively with the environment" defines
   a. insight.
   b. creativity.
   c. intelligence.
   d. mental giftedness.

Obj.: 1 Page: 346

2. A test designed to predict your ability to benefit from training as a chef would be an
   a. aptitude test.
   b. expertise test.
   c. achievement test.
   d. intelligence test.

Obj.: 2 Page: 347

3. What was the first formal test of intelligence?
   a. Wechsler Adult Intelligence Scale
   b. Wechsler Intelligence Scale for Children
   c. Binet-Simon Scale
   d. Stanford-Binet Scale

Obj.: 3 Page: 347-348

4. Given a mental age of 8 and a chronological age of 16, a child would have an IQ of
   a. 2
   b. 8
   c. 50
   d. 128

Obj.: 4 Page: 348-349

5. The inadequacy of the ratio IQ was overcome by Wechsler when he replaced Stern's ratio IQ with
   a. deviation IQ.
   b. standardized IQ.
   c. normative IQ.
   d. verbal IQ.

Obj.: 5 Page: 349-350

6. You develop a new test of social intelligence and establish norms by administering it to groups varying in their sex, age, income, educational level, and geographic location. This procedure is an aspect of
   a. normalization.
   b. homogenization.
   c. standardization.
   d. factor analysis.

Obj.: 6 Page: 350

7. To be classified as mentally retarded, a person must have a low IQ and
   a. be completely dependent on others.
   b. have difficulty performing in everyday life.
   c. show evidence of brain damage.
   d. be completely untrainable.

Obj.: 7 Page: 353-355

8. The placement of mentally retarded students in as many normal classes as possible is called
   a. tracking.
   b. mainstreaming.
   c. normalization.
   d. deinstitutionalization.

Obj.: 8 Page: 355

9. A child is given numerous achievement tests and scores exceptionally well on them. The child also is given an IQ test, and scores 132. What term would psychologists use to categorize this child?
   a. mentally retarded
   b. profound intellect
   c. mentally gifted
   d. academically gifted

Obj.: 9 Page: 356

10. The statistical technique that determines the degree of correlation between performances on various tasks to determine the extent to which they reflect particular underlying characteristics is called
   a. confluence.
   b. psychometrics.
   c. synchronicity.
   d. factor analysis.

Obj.: 10 Page: 359

11. If you were an excellent problem solver, could recall virtually all the course material you study for exams, and rapidly perform mental arithmetic calculations, you would demonstrate excellent
   a. fluid intelligence.
   b. structural intelligence.
   c. experiential intelligence.
   d. crystallized intelligence.

Obj.: 10 Page: 360

12. According to the triarchic theory of intelligence, if you could change a flat tire, felt at ease when meeting new people, and performed well when interviewing for a job, you would be high in
   a. innate intelligence.
   b. contextual intelligence.
   c. componential intelligence.
   d. experiential intelligence.

Obj.: 11 Page: 361

13. According to the theory of multiple intelligences, if you realized why you had a short temper when confronted with minor frustrations, you would exhibit
   a. experiential intelligence.
   b. componential intelligence.
   c. interpersonal intelligence.
   d. intrapersonal intelligence.

Obj.: 12 Page: 362

14. The motivating assumption of Project Head Start was that the difference in the average IQ between blacks and whites was mainly attributable to differences in
   a. heredity.
   b. maturational rates.
   c. individual motivation.
   d. socioeconomic conditions.

Obj.: 13 Page: 365

15. Socioeconomically deprived children who attend Project Head Start show an average gain in IQ of about
   a. 5 points.
   b. 10 points.
   c. 14 points.
   d. 15 points.

Obj.: 14 Page: 369-371

PRACTICE TEST B

1. Finding a universally acceptable definition of intelligence is difficult because
   a. it is a concept formed by testing hypotheses about particular features that are common to all members of the concept.
   b. it is a natural concept, formed through everyday experience.
   c. intelligent behavior can be easily recognized and a description of that behavior is sufficient.
   d. it cannot be measured.

Obj.: 1 Page: 346

2 Your syllabus indicates that you will be taking a comprehensive examination at the end of this course. This examination is an example of a(n)
   a. achievement test.
   b. aptitude test.
   c. intelligence test.
   d. differential test.
Obj.: 2 Page: 346-347

3. A test designed to predict your ability to seek training as a computer specialist would be a(n)
   a. achievement test.
   b. intelligence test.
   c. aptitude test.
   d. computer knowledge test.
Obj.: 2 Page : 346-347

4. Galton was most inspired by
   a. Binet's definition of intelligence.
   b. Spearman's theory of general intelligence.
   c. Darwin's theory of evolution.
   d. Cattell's use of his anthropometric method.
Obj.: 3 Page: 347-348

5. Ultimate fairness of a test is related to its
   a. reliability.
   b. validity.
   c. ability to accommodate cross-cultural differences.
   d. ability to accommodate racial, gender, and religious differences.
Obj.: 3 Page: 347-348

6. According to the Binet-Simon scale, a child with a mental age of 5 and a chronological age of 10, would have an IQ of
   a. 50.
   b. 10.
   c. 5.
   d. 15.
Obj.: 4 Page: 348-349

7. On the original Binet-Simon test, 8-year-old Nicole can answer all the questions up to those designed for 10-year-olds. Nicole has a(n) __________ of 10.
   a. chronological age
   b. intellectual age
   c. intelligence quotient
   d. mental age
Obj.: 4 Page: 348

8. Luis completes a Wechsler scale and his overall score is 90. What may we conclude about Luis?
   a. He is mentally retarded.
   b. His IQ is barely within the normal range.
   c. His IQ is in the normal range.
   d. His IQ is in the gifted range.
Obj.: 5 Page: 350

9. Compared to the Stanford-Binet, the Wecshler-Bellevue Intelligence Scale
   a. stressed verbal ability.
   b. was developed to assess psychiatric patients with high verbal ability.
   c. provided separate scores for verbal and performance IQ.
   d. provided a total IQ score.
Obj.: 5 Page: 350

10. According to those who are critical of IQ tests, African American children tend to score somewhat lower on IQ tests because
   a. all African American children are deprived of optimal educational and cultural experiences.
   b. many African American children are not exposed to certain learning experiences common to whites.
   c. African American culture values accomplishments in areas other than academics.
   d. the prevalence of one-parent homes among African Americans hinders intellectual development.
Obj.: 6 Page: 351

11. You have been asked to give an individually administered intelligence test to your students. Your choices are
   a. the Army Beta and the Otis-Lennon Mental Abilities Test.
   b. the Otis-Lennon and the Stanford-Binet.
   c. the WAIS and the Stanford-Binet.
   d. the Army Alpha and the WAIS.
Obj.: 6 Page: 350-352

12. Dina scores about 65 on standard IQ tests. She is trained as a cashier, is married, and has a child. What may we conclude about Dina?
   a. Most likely her low IQ score is due to emotional difficulties.
   b. She may be classified as moderately retarded.
   c. Most likely she will need to reside in an institution.
   d. She is similar to about 85 percent of all retarded individuals.

Obj.: 7 Page: 353

13. After years of living in a large institution, Ed is moving to a large house in the same town where he was born. In his new home, Ed will live with other teenagers with mental retardation and will learn a curriculum designed to help him eventually live on his own and hold a job. Ed is undergoing
   a. mainstreaming.
   b. cultural-familial retardation.
   c. behavior modification.
   d. normalization.

Obj.: 8 Page: 355

14. Which item is out of place here?
   a. fluid intelligence
   b. Charles Spearman
   c. factor analysis
   d. "g" factor

Obj.: 10 Page: 359

15. A weakness of all the factor-analytic theories of intelligence is that they are all based on the assumption that
   a. intelligence is a very stable, lifelong characteristic, unaffected by environment.
   b. certain social groups are innately endowed with superior intellectual capacity.
   c. IQ tests really do evaluate potential rather than amount of knowledge acquired.
   d. intelligence is somehow related to school performance and achievement.

Obj.: 10 Page: 361

16. A strength of Sternberg's triarchic theory of intelligence is that it
   a. recognizes the existence of seven primary mental abilities.
   b. recognizes that intelligence implies superior functioning beyond academic performance.
   c. is based on several factors that can be easily measured by traditional IQ tests.
   d. can be applied across all ages, social classes, and ethnic groups.

Obj.: 11 Page: 361

17. What theorist(s) recognize that we must be able to function in settings outside of school, believe that intelligence can be improved by special training, and consider creative and practical intelligence?
   a. Gardner
   b. Sternberg
   c. Horn & Cattell
   d. Thurstone

Obj.: 11 Page: 361

18. According to Gardner, if you are good at presenting oral reports, you are exhibiting
   a. interpersonal intelligence.
   b. linguistic intelligence.
   c. experiential intelligence.
   d. spatial intelligence.

Obj.: 12 Page: 362-363

19. Dr. Lee replicates a large-scale study that compares the IQ scores of adopted children with those of their biological parents and their adoptive parents. Based on previous research, you would predict that which of these pairings would show the greatest positive correlation in IQ scores?
   a. adopted children and their biological parents
   b. adopted children and their adoptive parents
   c. adopted children and their adoptive siblings
   d. adopted children and their unrelated friends

Obj.: 13 Page: 367

20. According to the confluence model, the "average intellectual environment" will be lower
   a. the fewer the number of children in the family.
   b. the longer the average interval between births.
   c. the fewer the number of children and the longer the average interval between births.
   d. the greater the number of children and the smaller the average interval between births.

Obj.: 13 Page: 363-368

ESSAY QUESTIONS

1. Your friend Henry argues that intelligence tests are biased against minorities, particularly African Americans and should be outlawed. Based on the evidence presented in your textbook, briefly describe what you would tell Henry to counter his argument.

Obj.: 13 Page: 367

2. Below is a list of well-known individuals who have excelled in one or more areas of life. Apply Gardner's theory of multiple intelligences in describing what kind of intelligence(s) each possesses to a very high degree. Support your response by pointing to specific talents or skills these individuals need in their work.
   a) Nelson Mandela, President of South Africa
   b) Madeleine Albright, Secretary of State
   c) Tiger Woods, Golf Champion
   d) Tina Turner, Singer, Composer, Entertainer
   e) Maya Lin, Sculptress, Creator of the Vietnam Memorial

Obj.: 12 Page: 362-363

ANSWER RECORD FOR CHAPTER 10

Comprehensive Guided Review:

1. Recognizing	12. Chinese	23. Simon	34. Adult	46. Predictive
2. natural	13. civil servants	24. mental age	35. WPPSI	47. moderately
3. autistic	14. scientific	25. ratio	36. performance	48. predictors
4. communicate	15. Darwin	26. IQ	37. Standardization	49. minority
5. intelligent	16. differential	27. Goddard	38. mean	50. political
6. universally	17. behavioral	28. Stanford-Binet	39. normal	51. contradicted
7. purposefully	18. anthropometric	29. time-consuming	40. Reliability	52. biased
8. mental	19. mental	30. slowing	41. Test-retest	53. predict
9. Achievement	20. intelligence	31. deviation	42. reliable	54. rearing
10. Aptitude	21. Binet	32. verbal	43. long-term	55. cultural
11. intelligence	22. reasoning	33. Children	44. increases	56. culture-free
			45. Validity	57. unresolved

Mini-review on Intelligence Testing:

1. G; 2. K; 3. R; 4. T; 5. N; 6. A; 7. Q; 8. B; 9. C; 10. F; 11. I; 12. O; 13. P; 14. E; 15. D; 16. H; 17. M; 18. L; 19. S; 20. J

58. classification	64. trained	70. cultural-familial	77. moderately	84. Galton
59. 70	65. Severe	71. German	78. mainstreaming	85. 130
60. gifted	66. unable	72. cells	79. normal	86. failures
61. solely	67. Profound	73. X rays	80. academic	87. Mensa
62. mentally retarded	68. custodial	74. anoxia	81. consumer	88. Sidis
63. Mild	69. heredity	75. Down	82. normalization	89. Harvard
		76. educable	83. gifted	90. Terman

Anatomy of a Classic Research Study: What Is the Fate of Childhood Geniuses?

What was the rationale of the study?

Terman wanted to show that mentally gifted individuals were not doomed to later failure.

What methods did the author use to test the hypothesis?

The Stanford-Binet Intelligence Scale was administered to California children, and those scoring above 135 were identified. A longitudinal descriptive study has been completed on these children, measuring them every decade.

What was the outcome of the study and what did the authors conclude their results meant?
Terman's significant longitudinal research of the mentally gifted showed that, among other characteristics, they tend to become socially, physically, vocationally, and academically superior adults. Terman's study was not without weaknesses; among the factors were the subjects awarness that they were being studied, socioeconomic status, and better health.

---

91. training
92. Terman

Mini-review on the Extremes of Intelligence:
1. I; 2. K; 3. A; 4. L; 5. D; 6. M; 7. J; 8. B; 9. F; 10. E; 11. G; 12. C; 13. H

93. kinds
94. Binet
95. Spearman
96. general
97. statistical
98. correlation
99. single
100. positive
101. g
102. specific
103. factor-analytic
104. no
105. seven
106. perceptual
107. memory
108. factor analysis
109. thought
110. Contents
111. results
112. factor-analytic
113. Fluid
114. inherited
115. Crystallized
116. increases
117. unanswered
118. school
119. broader
120. Sternberg
121. verbal
122. information
123. three
124. Componential
125. Experiential
126. Contextual
127. school
128. evolved
129. seven
130. communicate
131. arguments
132. Spatial
133. compose
134. move
135. yourself
136. social

Mini-review on Theories of Intelligence:
Part I:
1. B; 2. D; 3. G; 4. F; 5. A; 6. E; 7. C

Part II:
Factor-Analytic Theories of Intelligence
Theory of General Intelligence: *Considered intelligence a general characteristic underlying a variety of behaviors, which he called "g"—a general intelligence factor, with special talents or "s" factors.*

Theory of Primary Mental Abilities: *Concluded that there was no general intelligence factor. He identified seven factors, which he called primary mental abilities: reasoning, word fluency, perceptual speed, verbal comprehension, spatial visualization, numerical calculation, and associative memory.*

Theory of the Structure of the Intellect: *Identified 120 factors and has recently increased it to 150. Each of the factors interacts along three dimensions of intelligence. The dimensions are:*
- *a) Operations—thought processes*
- *b) Contents—information that a person is thinking about*
- *c) Products—results of thinking about the information*

Two-Factor Theory of Intelligence: *Identifies two intelligence factors:*
Fluid intelligence—reflecting thinking ability, memory capacity, and speed of information processing; is largely inherited, affected little by training, and declines in late adulthood; crystalized intelligence—reflecting the acquisition of knowledge through education and experience; increases or remains the same in late adulthood.

Non-Factor Analysis Theories:
Triarchic Theory of Intelligence: *Argues that intelligent people have good verbal skills, good problem-solving abilities, and good social judgment.*
- *a) Componential intelligence-It is similar to the kind of intelligence considered by traditional theories and primarily reflects our verbal reasoning ability.*
- *b) Experiential intelligence-It is the ability to combine different experiences in insightful ways to solve novel problems. It reflects creativity.*
- *c) Contextual intelligence- It is the ability to function in practical, everyday social situations, such as in the case of being street smart.*

The Theory of Multiple Intelligences: *Based on the assumption that the brain has evolved separate systems for different adaptive abilities that he calls "intelligence." There are seven types:*

Linguistic intelligence is the ability to communicate through language.
Logical-mathematical intelligence is the ability to analyze arguments and solve mathematical problems.
Spatial intelligence is the ability to perceive and arrange objects in the environment.
Musical intelligence is the ability to analyze, compose, or play music.
Bodily-kinesthetic intelligence is the ability to move or manipulate objects effectively.
Intrapersonal intelligence is the ability to know yourself and understand what motivates your behavior.
Interpersonal intelligence is the ability to function in social situations because you are able to understand the needs of other people and predict their behavior.

137. feebleminded
138. intellectually
139. immigrants
140. heredity
141. cultural
142. 15
143. socioeconomic
144. Jensen
145. heritability
146. 80
147. eugenics
148. falsified
149. twins
150. inadequate
151. Adoption
152. biological
153. dominating

Anatomy of a Contemporary Research Study: What is the Effect of Adoption on the Intellectual Development of Adopted Children?

What was the rationale for the study?
They focused on the question of whether children from lower socioeconomic classes who are adopted by parents from higher socioeconomic classes should show little or no gain in IQ.

What methods did the author use to test the hypothesis?
Scarr & Weinberg (1976) conducted the Minnesota Adoption Study in which they measured the intelligence scores of African American children who had been adopted by white couples of higher socioeconomic status and compared them with the average intelligence score for African American children.

What was the outcome of the study and what did the authors conclude the results meant?
The results showed that the adopted children had a higher average IQ score than other African American students of same socioeconomic status reared by their biological parents. The results and a follow-up supported the authors' findings that nurture, as well as nature, is important in intellectual development.

---

154. environment
155. less
156. confluence
157. greater
158. relationship
159. causal
160. narrowed
161. effective
162. increases
163. discrimination

Practice Test A:

1. a. Incorrect: The global capacity to act purposefully, think rationally, and deal effectively with the environment is the definition of intelligence, not insight.
   b. Incorrect: The global capacity to act purposefully, think rationally, and deal effectively with the environment is the definition of intelligence, not creativity.
   c. **Correct: The global capacity to act purposefully, think rationally, and deal effectively with the environment is the definition of intelligence.**
   d. Incorrect: The global capacity to act purposefully, think rationally, and deal effectively with the environment is the definition of intelligence, not mental giftedness.

2. a. **Correct: Aptitude tests test your ability to benefit from instruction in a particular area.**
   b. Incorrect: There is no such thing as an expertise test.
   c. Incorrect: Achievement tests measure what you know or have learned about a specific topic.
   d. Incorrect: Intelligence tests assess overall mental ability.

3. a. Incorrect: Wechsler's tests were developed after the Binet-Simon scale.
   b. Incorrect: Wechsler's tests were developed after the Binet-Simon scale.
   c. **Correct: The Binet-Simon scale was the first test.**
   d. Incorrect: The Stanford -Binet test was a modification of the Binet-Simon scale for American children.

4. a. Incorrect: IQ = Mental age/Chronological age x 100, in this case 8/16 x 100= 50.
   b. Incorrect: IQ = Mental age/Chronological age x 100, in this case 8/16 x 100= 50.
   c. **Correct: IQ = Mental age/Chronological age x 100, in this case 8/16 x 100= 50.**
   d. Incorrect: IQ = Mental age/Chronological age x 100, in this case 8/16 x 100= 50.

5. a. **Correct: Wechsler calculated a deviation IQ in which the subject's performance is compared to others'.**
   b. Incorrect: One could argue that this alternative plays a role in defining IQ, but it is not known as a form of IQ.
   c. Incorrect: One could argue that this alternative plays a role in defining IQ, but it is not known as a form of IQ.
   d. Incorrect: Verbal IQ is but one aspect of a total IQ.

6. a. Incorrect: The process described is the process of standardizing a test.
   b. Incorrect: The process described is the process of standardizing a test.
   c. **Correct: The process described is the process of standardizing a test.**
   d. Incorrect: The process described is the process of standardizing a test.

7. a. Incorrect: Mildly mental retarded individuals can care for themselves and hold responsible jobs.
   b. **Correct: The definition of mental retardation states only that the individual has a low IQ score and has difficulty performing in everyday life.**
   c. Incorrect: Not all forms of retardation result from brain damage.
   d. Incorrect: The definition of mental retardation states only that the individual has a low IQ score and has difficulty performing in everyday life.

8. a. Incorrect: There is no such term as tracking.
   b. **Correct: Mainstreaming involve placing mentally retarded individuals in as many normal classes as possible.**
   c. Incorrect: Normalization refers to the movement that argues that mentally retarded individuals should be trained in life skills in specialized classes.
   d. Incorrect: Deinstitutionalization refer to the movement to keep mentally retarded individuals out of institutions.

9. a. Incorrect: Mental retardation IQ scores are below 70.
   b. Incorrect: This term is not used by psychologists.
   c. **Correct: This description meets the characteristics of giftedness.**
   d. Incorrect: This term is not used by psychologists.

10. a. Incorrect: Confluence is not a statistical method; it refers to a model that argues that an individual's intelligence depends on the level of intelligence of parents interacting with the number of children in the family and the interval between them.
   b. Incorrect: Psychometrics is not discussed in the chapter.
   c. Incorrect: Synchronicity is not discussed in the chapter.
   d. **Correct: Factor analysis is the statistical technique used to identify factors.**

11. a. **Correct: The recall of course material and ability to calculate math problems rapidly is an example of Fluid intelligence.**
   b. Incorrect: Structural intelligence is not a term used by psychologists.
   c. Incorrect: Experiential intelligence is Sternberg's term for the ability to use experiences in new, creative ways.
   d. Incorrect: Crystallized intelligence reflects knowledge gained through direct instruction.

12. a. Incorrect: Innate intelligence is not a term that Sternberg uses.
   b. **Correct: Contextual intelligence is street smarts, knowledge of the type described in this question.**
   c. Incorrect: Componential intelligence refers to the ability to be analytical and examine parts.
   d. Incorrect: Experiential intelligence is Sternberg's term for the ability to use experiences in new, creative ways.

13. a. Incorrect: Experiential intelligence is Sternberg's term for the ability to use experiences in new, creative ways; Gardner proposed the MI theory of intelligence.
   b. Incorrect: Componential intelligence is Sternberg's term for the ability to be analytical.
   c. Incorrect: Interpersonal intelligence is the ability to understand other people.
   d. **Correct: Intrapersonal intelligence is the understanding and knowledge of self.**

14. a. Incorrect: Head Start assumes that the differences in IQ scores is due to environmental, or socioeconomic, conditions.
   b. Incorrect: Head Start assumes that the differences in IQ scores is due to environmental, or socioeconomic, conditions.
   c. Incorrect: Head Start assumes that the differences in IQ scores is due to environmental, or socioeconomic, conditions.
   d. **Correct: Head Start assumes that the differences in IQ scores is due to environmental, or socioeconomic, conditions.**

15. a. Incorrect: The increase in IQ scores of children who attended Head Start was an average of about 10 points.
   b. **Correct: The increase in IQ scores of children who attended Head Start was an average of about 10 points.**
   c. Incorrect: The increase in IQ scores of children who attended Head Start was an average of about 10 points.
   d. Incorrect: The increase in IQ scores of children who attended Head Start was an average of about 10 points.

Practice Test B:

1. a. Incorrect: Intelligence is a natural concept, not a logical one; it cannot be defined using logical means.
   b. Correct: Intelligence is a natural concept, not a logical one; it cannot be defined.
   c. Incorrect: While intelligent behavior can be recognized, a description of it does not suffice as a definition of it.
   d. Incorrect: Indeed it can, otherwise there would be little or no use for intelligence tests.

2. **a. Correct: Achievement tests are tests that measure your knowledge of information learned.**
   b. Incorrect: Aptitude tests measure your potential to benefit from instruction.
   c. Incorrect: Intelligence tests are a type of aptitude test that measures mental ability.
   d. Incorrect: Differential tests do not exist.

3. a. Incorrect: This is a test that measures knowledge of a specific subject.
   b. Incorrect: This is a kind of aptitude test that assesses overall mental ability.
   c. Correct: Aptitude tests measure your potential to benefit from instruction.
   d. Incorrect: This is a test that measures knowledge of a specific subject.

4. a. Incorrect: Galton was inspired by his cousin, Charles Darwin, not Binet.
   b. Incorrect: Galton was inspired by his cousin, Charles Darwin; Spearman's work was not published until 1927.
   c. Correct: Galton was inspired by his cousin, Charles Darwin.
   d. Incorrect: Cattell introduced the anthropometric method in the United States.

5. a. Incorrect: This is the degree to which a test gives consistent results.
   b. Correct: Validity refers to whether a test tests what it proposes to test.
   c. Incorrect: These are culture-free tests, and there is a continuing surge of interest in developing them.
   d. Incorrect: Tests must be designed to measure what they are supposed to measure and either not be affected by such factors or take such factors into account when the norms are established.

6. **a. Correct: IQ is defined as MA/CA x 100, thus, 5/10 x 100= 50.**
   b. Incorrect: IQ is defined as MA/CA x 100, thus, 5/10 x 100= 50.
   c. Incorrect: IQ is defined as MA/CA x 100, thus, 5/10 x 100= 50.
   d. Incorrect: IQ is defined as MA/CA x 100, thus, 5/10 x 100= 50.

7. a. Incorrect. Chronological age is the amount of time since your birth; thus Nicole is 8.
   b. Incorrect: There is no such thing as intellectual age.
   c. Incorrect: Intelligence quotient is defined as MA/CA x 100, in this case 10/8 x 100= 150.
   d. Correct: Mental age is defined as the number of items passed in the Stanford-Binet intelligence test.

8. a. Incorrect: Normal intelligence scores fall between 70 and 129; thus Luis is normal.
   b. Incorrect: Normal intelligence scores fall between 70 and 129; thus Luis is normal.
   c. Correct: Normal intelligence scores fall between 70 and 129; thus Luis is normal.
   d. Incorrect: Normal intelligence scores fall between 70 and 129; thus Luis is normal.

9. a. Incorrect: The Stanford-Binet stressed verbal ability.
   b. Incorrect: This should read ". . . patients with low verbal ability."
   c. Correct: The Wechsler-Bellevue test provided two scores-a verbal, and a performance. The Binet test only provided an overall score.
   d. Incorrect: This was provided in later versions of the Wechsler test.

10. a. Incorrect: Those critical of the tests claim that the test is culturally biased. The problem for many African American children is that they are not provided with educational experiences similar to those of white children.
    b. Correct: Those critical of the tests claim that the test is culturally biased. The problem for many African American children is that they are not provided with educational experiences similar to those of white children.
    c. Incorrect: Those critical of the tests claim that the test is culturally biased. The problem for many African American children is that they are not provided with educational experiences similar to those of white children.
    d. Incorrect: Those critical of the tests claim that the test is culturally biased. The problem for many African American children is that they are not provided with educational experiences similar to those of white children.

11. a. Incorrect: The Army Alpha, Army Beta, and Otis-Lennon are group-administered tests.
    b. Incorrect: The Army Alpha, Army Beta, and Otis-Lennon are group-administered tests.
    c. Correct: The WAIS and the Stanford-Binet tests are individually administered tests of intelligence.
    d. Incorrect: The Army Alpha, Army Beta, and Otis-Lennon are group-administered tests.

12. a. Incorrect: IQ differences are not the result of emotional states.
b. Incorrect: The moderately retarded classification is between 35 and 49.
c. Incorrect: With an IQ score of 65 she would fall into the mild retardation category; most mildly retarded individuals are able to care for themselves, work, and be adequate parents.
d. Correct: With an IQ score of 65 she would fall into the mild retardation category; most mildly retarded individuals are able to care for themselves, work, and be adequate parents. About 85 percent of retarded individuals fall in this category.

13. a. Incorrect: Mainstreaming means that Ed would be placed in as many normal classes and environments as possible.
b. Incorrect: Cultural-familial retardation is a type of retardation, not an educational movement.
c. Incorrect: Behavior modification is a specific technique used to train trainable individuals, not an overall movement.
d. Correct: Normalization is the countermovement to mainstreaming in which it is argued that mentally retarded individuals need more specific training in life and job skills along with academics.

14. **a. Correct: Fluid intelligence was proposed by Horn & Cattell. The remaining items are parts of Spearman's theory of general intelligence.**
b. Incorrect: Fluid intelligence was proposed by Horn & Cattell. The remaining items are parts of Spearman's theory of general intelligence.
c. Incorrect: Fluid intelligence was proposed by Horn & Cattell. The remaining items are parts of Spearman's theory of general intelligence.
d. Incorrect: Fluid intelligence was proposed by Horn & Cattell. The remaining items are parts of Spearman's theory of general intelligence.

15. a. Incorrect: All theories of intelligence assume that it is a stable, lifelong characteristic.
b. Incorrect: Factor-analytic theories do not assume any hereditary nature to intelligence.
c. Incorrect: Factor-analytic theories place too much emphasis on school-related achievement.
d. Correct: Gardner & Sternberg, the major critics of factor-analytic theories, claim that Factor-analytic theories place too much emphasis on school-related achievement.

16. a. Incorrect: Sternberg's theory argues the existence of componential, experiential, and contextual intelligence, not seven primary abilities.
b. Correct: Sternberg's theory argues the existence of componential, experiential, and contextual intelligence, thus taking into account a broader concept of intelligence beyond academic performance.
c. Incorrect: Sternberg's theory argues the existence of componential, experiential, and contextual intelligence, thus making it more difficult to measure.
d. Incorrect: All theories of intelligence can be applied across age and social classes.

17. a. Incorrect: Gardner's position on these issues is not discussed in the text.
b. Correct: Sternberg believes that traditional models of intelligence place too much emphasis on academics and not enough on the other areas.
c. Incorrect: They would agree that special programs may increase both fluid and crystallized intelligence, but they do not address creative and practical intelligence.
d. Incorrect: Thurstone's position is not discussed in the text.

18. a. Incorrect: Interpersonal intelligence deals with one's ability to function well in social situations.
b. Correct: Linguistic intelligence emphasizes the ability to present oneself orally.
c. Incorrect: Experiential intelligence is Sternberg's form of creative intelligence.
d. Incorrect: Spatial intelligence deals with the ability to perceive and arrange objects in the environment.

19. **a. Correct: Previous research has shown that the IQ scores of adopted children correlate higher with their biological parents', providing evidence for a genetic basis for intelligence.**
b. Incorrect: Previous research has shown that the IQ scores of adopted children correlate higher with their biological parents', providing evidence for a genetic basis for intelligence.
c. Incorrect: Previous research has shown that the IQ scores of adopted children correlate higher with their biological parents', providing evidence for a genetic basis for intelligence.
d. Incorrect: Previous research has shown that the IQ scores of adopted children correlate higher with their biological parents', providing evidence for a genetic basis for intelligence.

20. a. Incorrect: Confluence model argues that the greater the number of children *and* the shorter the time between them the lower the IQ score due to the limited ability of the parents to spend time with the child.
    b. Incorrect: Confluence model argues that the greater the number of children *and* the shorter the time between them the lower the IQ score due to the limited ability of the parents to spend time with the child.
    c. Incorrect: Confluence model argues that the fewer the children and the longer the time between them the ***higher*** the IQ score due to the ability of the parents to spend time with the child.
    d. **Correct: Confluence model argues that the greater the number of children and the shorter the time between them the lower the IQ score due to the limited ability of the parents to spend time with the child.**

Essay Questions:

1. First, point out that the intelligence test has been shown to be a reliable and valid predictor of school performance. Second, point out that the fact that African Americans score lower on the test does not mean that the test is biased against them. The correlation between IQ and school performance is not perfect, indicating that other factors are also involved; one of these may be environmental. This is supported by the data that show that IQ tests do have good predictive validity for all ethnic groups. Further support for this finding comes from enrichment studies showing that participants in programs like Head Start demonstrate improvement in intellectual abilities.

2. a) Mandela: linguistic, intrapersonal, and interpersonal
   b) Albright: linguistic, intrapersonal, and interpersonal
   c) Woods: spatial, bodily-kinesthetic, intrapersonal, and interpersonal
   d) Turner: musical, bodily-kinesthetic, interpersonal
   e) Lin: spatial, intrapersonal

11 Motivation

LEARNING OBJECTIVES

After studying this chapter, you should be able to:

1. Define motivation and briefly mention the issues surrounding the use of this concept. (p. 376)

2. List and describe three identified sources of motivation, emphasizing the various theories associated with each of these sources. (p. 376-378)

3. Summarize what is known about the bodily, brain, and environmental factors involved in the regulation of the hunger motive and relate these to the issue of obesity. (p. 378-383)

4. Describe two eating disorders and summarize what is known about the biological and sociocultural causes of these disorders. (p. 383-386)

5. Describe the physiological, psychological, and historical factors that influence human sexual behavior. (p. 386-387)

6. Describe Alfred Kinsey's contributions to the understanding of American sexual behavior and explain the nature of the controversy that surrounded his work. (p. 388)

7. Describe the contributions of William Masters and Virginia Johnson to the understanding of sexual functioning, emphasizing the characteristics of the sexual response cycle. (p. 388-389)

8. Define sexual dysfunction and then describe several common male and female dysfunctions as well as how sex therapists attempt to treat them. (p. 390-391)

9. Define gender identity, and distinguish between gender identity disorder and sexual orientation, emphasizing recent findings regarding the origins of sexual orientation. (p. 391-394)

10. Describe the arousal motive and summarize the findings regarding the effects of optimal arousal, sensory deprivation, and sensation seeking on psychological functioning. (p. 394-397)

11. Describe achievement motivation and explain how it is related to the pursuit of success and goal setting. (p. 397-400)

12. Distinguish between intrinsic and extrinsic motivation and offer a brief overview of the various theories that seek to explain the findings in this area of motivation research. (p. 400-401)

13. Summarize how scientific knowledge about motivation has been applied to sports. (p. 401-405)

COMPREHENSIVE GUIDED REVIEW

Motivation refers to the psychological processes that arouse,___(1)___, and maintain behavior toward a goal. As it is not directly___(2)___, we must infer it from the behaviors that we observe. The concept of motivation is useful in explaining ___(3)___ in behavior over time.

I. Sources of Motivation include genes, drives, and__(4)__.

Genes: Early-twentieth-century psychologists, influenced by__(5)__ and led by William McDougall, attributed motivation to__(6)__, which are complex, inherited (that is, unlearned) behavior patterns characteristic of a species. In the 1920s, psychologists, influenced by John B.__(7)__, rejected **instincts** as factors in human motivation. Watson believed that human behavior was__(8)__, not instinctual. The__(9)__ credibility of instinct theorists declined for two reasons. First, the theorists attempted to__(10)__ almost all behavior as instinctive (you play sports, for example, because of a "competitive__(11)__") and second, because they failed to explain the behaviors they labeled as instinctive.

Though instinct theory, as applied to human behavior, is no longer favored by most, some scientists (sociobiologists) believe that human social behavior has a __(12)__ basis. **Sociobiology** is a field founded by Edward__(13)__ that examines the hereditary basis of human and animal behavior. Critics of__(14)__ argue that it places too much emphasis on the role of hereditary influences on behavior.

Drives: Clark__(15)__'s **drive-reduction theory** emerged to dominate psychology from the 1930s to the 1950s. According to Hull, a **need** caused by physiological__(16)__, such as a lack of food, water, or sex, induces a state of __(17)__called a **drive,** which motivates the individual to reduce it. Drive reduction aims at restoring__(18)__, a steady state of physiological equilibrium. In many cases, the process is mediated by the hypothalamus.

Drive-reduction theory can be used to__(19)__ behaviors such as eating or drinking; that is, we eat (drink) to reduce the __(20)__ of hunger (thirst). However, the theory cannot explain all human motivation; for example, why are people motivated to skydive?

Incentives: In contrast to an internal state of tension that "__(21)__" you toward a goal, an **incentive** is an __(22)__ stimulus that "pulls" you toward a goal. Stimuli that we perceive as__(23)__ are known as *positive* incentives, whereas stimuli we perceive as undesirable are known as__*(24)*__ incentives. Incentives are frequently associated with drives. Your hunger would "__(25)__" you to eat, but your favorite flavor would "pull" you toward a particular brand of pizza.

Maslow's Hierarchy of Needs: Abraham Maslow suggested that some needs have__(26)__ over others. Figure 11.1 on page 379 in your textbook shows Maslow's **hierarchy of needs.** For Maslow, the term__*(27)*__ refers to both physiological and psychological motives. He claims that you must first satisfy your basic__*(28)*__ needs before becoming motivated to satisfy your higher needs. According to Maslow the needs from highest to lowest are transcendence, self-actualization, __(29)__, belongingness and love, safety and security, and physiological. Few people satisfy all their lower needs; thus, fewer reach the top two levels. Research on conscientious objectors __(30)__ Maslow's position.

This is a good point to take one of your brief study breaks. Remember to review this section using the mini-review before going on.

Mini-review on Sources of Motivation: Match each term with its correct description.

________1. motivation	A. He suggested that some needs have priority over others
________2. instincts	B. An internal state of tension that "pushes" you toward a goal
________3. A drive	C. The psychological processes that arouse, direct, and maintain behavior toward a goal
________4. sociobiologists	D. An external stimulus that "pulls" you toward a goal
________5. Clark Hull	E. Complex, inherited (unlearned) behavior patterns characteristic of a species
________6. negative incentives	F. According to this theory, a need caused by physiological deprivation, such as a lack of food, water, or sex, induces a state of tension that we are motivated to reduce
________7. sociobiology	G. Motivating stimuli that we perceive as desirable
________8. drive-reduction theory	H. Scientists who believe that human social behavior has a genetic basis
________9. Abraham Maslow	I. Founder of drive-reduction theory
________10. incentive	J. Field founded by Edward Wilson that examines the hereditary basis of human and animal behavior
________11. positive incentives	K. Theory that claims you must first satisfy your basic physiological needs before becoming motivated to satisfy your higher needs
________12. hierarchy of needs theory	L. Motivating stimuli we perceive as undesirable

II. The Hunger Motive:

Factors That Regulate Hunger: Hunger and eating behaviors are complex. Psychologists have identified internal bodily factors, brain factors, as well as external__(31)__ factors, in the regulation of eating behavior.

Bodily Factors: The main body mechanisms involved in the regulation of hunger are in the mouth, the stomach, the __(32)__ intestine, the liver, and the pancreas. In the mouth,__(33)__ receptors play an important role by sending taste sensations to the brain, which favors the tastes of foods that contain nutrients you may lack. However, the mouth is not the sole regulator of food intake. Figure 11.2 on page 380 in your textbook illustrates the 1912 Cannon and Washburn study in which the researchers were concerned with the question, "How does the__(34)__ affect hunger?" Although they concluded that stomach contractions__(35)__ hunger, it was unclear whether the opposite was true and hunger might have caused the stomach contractions.

Later research has shown that the stomach, like the mouth, is not the sole means of regulating hunger but does play an important role. In addition to the contractions of the stomach, research has identified special ____(36)__cells in the stomach that detect the amount of food it contains. These receptors inform the__(37)__ of the amount of food by sending impulses along the **vagus nerve** to the brain,__(38)__ the level of hunger.

In the presence of food, the small intestine, the main site of digestion, secretes the__(39)__ *cholecystokinin,* which, in turn, signals the brain via the__(40)__ nerve, reducing the level of hunger. Of special importance is the hormone __(41)__, which is secreted by the pancreas. Insulin helps the blood__(42)__ enter the body cells for use in metabolism, promotes the__(43)__ of fat, and induces feelings of hunger. In fact, it is believed that insulin plays an even more important role than blood sugar, since hunger depends more on__(44)__ levels of insulin than on decreased levels of blood sugar.

Brain Factors: Although signals from the body regulate hunger, they do so through their effects on the brain, especially the__(45)__. The neurotransmitter__(46)__ promotes eating by stimulating receptors in the hypothalamus. Two areas of the hypothalamus are particularly significant in the regulation of hunger. Electrical stimulation of the____(47)____ *(VMH)* inhibits eating, while its destruction induces eating. Electrical stimulation of the *lateral hypothalamus (LH),* by contrast,__(48)__ eating, while its destruction inhibits eating. Recent research has suggested that **cholecystokinin**

inhibits eating by enhancing the neuronal activity in the___(49)__ and suppressing it in the VMH. How does damage to the hypothalamus affect hunger? It does so, in part, by altering the body's____(50)____, that is, its normal weight. Damage to the LH__(51)__ the set point and the organism eats less. Damage to the VHM__(52)__ the set point and the organism eats more to maintain its body weight.

Environmental Factors: All of the factors mentioned thus far are__(53)__ factors, but hunger in humans is regulated by external as well as internal factors. The mere sight of food, or even daydreaming about it, can induce feelings of hunger by ___(54)__ the level of insulin in the blood.

Obesity is a body weight more than__(55)__ percent above normal for one's height and build. An important factor in obesity is the body's **set point**, which reflects the amount of stored__(56)__ cells, which, once gained, are never lost. All you can do is shrink the__(57)__ of the cells.

Another important factor in __(58)__is the **basal metabolic rate.** This is the rate at which the body burns__(59)__. The _____(60)____ rate typically accounts for 65-75 percent of the calories that your body takes in. Some of us with __(61)__ metabolic rates can wolf down those milkshakes and cheeseburgers and gain nothing, while others, with low rates, must eat much less to keep the same waistlines. One way to boost basal metabolic rate is with__(62)__ exercise.

Your body alters its metabolic rate to defend its____(63)___, but what determines the set point? There is a strong __(64)__relationship between the weight of adoptees and their___(65)__ parents, but little relationship between the weight of adoptees and their adoptive parents. However, the set point __(66)__appear to be affected by early diet. Males whose mothers experienced famine during a__(67)__ period, including the third trimester of gestation and the first month after birth, were shown to be less likely to become__(68)__ than males who had been exposed to famine at other times during their development. Thus, even the__(69)__ between adoptees and their biological parents could be due to prenatal influences on the development of set points.

Obesity has also been linked to differences in__(70)__ to external food cues. Research conducted in the 1960s indicated that people feel ___(71)__in the presence of food and that obese people may be more responsive to those cues. Why? Maybe it is because food continues to taste good to obese people even after they are full. But the "__(72)__" of obese people does not seem to cause their obesity. Instead, their obesity may cause their externality. Current theory suggests that since many obese individuals are always__(73)__, they may be in a chronic state of hunger. Judith__(74)__ has shown that obese people have chronically high levels of insulin, which would make them hungrier, and thus more responsive to food cures.

Reactions to__(75)__ situations may also increase hunger and even cause overeating. Depression, loneliness, and similar negative emotions may spur an__(76)__ in eating, especially among the obese. Remember the__(77)__, the neurotransmitters that relieve pain and increase under stress? Well, endorphins stimulate____(78)__. In pigs, the drug __(79)__, an endorphin blocker, decreases eating behavior.

Eating Disorders: The idea that "thin is in" is prevalent in our society, more so for females than for males. What do you think of your body?

Anatomy of a Contemporary Research Study: How Satisfied Are Males and Females with Their Bodies?
Read the summary of the Fallon and Rozin (1985) study on page 383 and 384 in your textbook and answer the questions below.

What was the rationale for the study?

What methods did the authors use to test their hypothesis?

What was the outcome of the study and what did the authors conclude the results meant?

Anorexia nervosa is a sometimes fatal disorder in which the person becomes emaciated after going on a__(80)__ diet. People with anorexia nervosa view themselves as__(81)__, when in reality they are thin, and exhibit a preoccupation with food. __(82)__ is more common in females than in males. The causes of anorexia are unclear, though possible causes range from a malfunctioning__(83)__ to excessive secretion of cholecystokinin, to a conflict concerning social maturation, or a reaction to the accumulation of unwanted body fat during puberty. Physical treatment may require __(84)__ feeding. __(85)__ treatment may require therapy aimed at promoting more adaptive ways of thinking about food.

Bulimia nervosa is characterized by eating__(86)__. People with bulimia nervosa maintain their normal weight by self-induced__(87)__ or by enemas and laxatives. Bulimics also think excessively about food and fear becoming__(88)__. The causes of the disorder are unclear. There is some evidence to suggest a genetic__(89)__. Other possible causes include a low level of serotonin, abnormal secretion of__(90)__, or shifts in endorphin levels. Factors other than those associated with brain chemistry include engaging in activities that emphasize weight__(91)__, a situational emphasis on weight control, and families that fail to support social independence and emotional expression. Bulimics may become __(92)__ eaters, or people continually concerned about food. These individuals rationalize their eating behavior and are__(93)__ attuned to their internal hunger cues. __(94)__ and individual psychotherapy are equally effective in treating bulimia, with abstinence from bingeing and purging achieved in about 40 percent of the cases.

Time for another short break and review.

Mini-review of Hunger Motivation: Match each term with its correct description.

________1. ventromedial hypothalamus (VMH)	A. Its electrical stimulation promotes eating, while its destruction inhibits eating
________2. endorphins	B. Hormone secreted by the small intestine, which, in turn, signals the brain via the vagus nerve, reducing the level of hunger
________3. cholecystokinin	C. Secreted by the pancreas; helps blood sugar enter the body cells for use in metabolism, promotes the storage of fat, and induces feelings of hunger
________4. bulimia nervosa	D. Neurotransmitter that promotes eating by stimulating receptors in the hypothalamus
________5. basal metabolic rate	E. An endorphin blocker; decreases eating behavior
________6. norepinephrine	F. A body weight more than 20 percent above normal for one's height and build
________7. obesity	G. Its electrical stimulation inhibits eating, while its destruction induces eating
________8. naloxone	H. The rate at which the body burns calories; typically accounts for 65-75 percent of the calories that your body takes in
________9. lateral hypothalamus (LH)	I. Neurotransmitters that increase under stress; they relieve pain and stimulate hunger
________10. insulin	J. A sometimes fatal disorder in which the person becomes emaciated after going on a starvation diet
________11. anorexia nervosa	K. Eating disorder characterized by eating binges; people with the disorder maintain their normal weight by self-induced vomiting or by enemas and laxatives.

III. The Sex Motive: Examples of the power of the__(95)__ drive and the incentive value of sexual stimuli abound in our contemporary society. You may already be thinking of the myriad examples you have encountered in films, magazines, ads, talk shows, and on the "soaps." What accounts for the __(96)__of the sex drive?

Physiological Factors: The sex hormones secreted by the__(97)__ are the most important factors in sexual motivation. Their secretion is controlled by hormones released by the__(98)__ gland, which in turn is controlled by the hypothalamus. However, while__(99)__ have a direct effect on sexual development, their influence in motivating human sexual behavior is less clear. Research has indicated that__(100)__, in both males and females, motivates sexual behavior. Estrogen, on the other hand, has little impact on sexual__(101)__.

Psychological Factors:

Social-cultural Factors: By contrast to animals, whose sexual behavior is rigidly controlled by__(102)__, sociocultural factors are the main motivators for__(103)__. Consequently, humans vary markedly in their sexual behavior. The acceptance of pre-intercourse behaviors and masturbation varies considerably from one__(104)__ to another. In extreme cases, human beings may engage in **paraphilias,** which are ways of gaining sexual gratification that__(105)__ cultural norms.

In Western cultures, acceptable sexual behavior has__(106)__ over time. For the Greeks, bisexuality and masturbation were__(107)__. By contrast, during the __(108)__era it was believed that sexual activity should be aimed at procreation. A particularly unique example is that the Victorian emphasis on sexual__(109)__ led John Harvey Kellogg to invent what he claimed to be a nutritional "cure" for masturbation--cornflakes!

Kinsey's Surveys of Human Sexual Behavior: Reports of the nature of the human sexual response have historically stirred the emotions of readers, and criticism has gone to the extremes of__(110)__. The Lewis paper, the__(111)__report, and the research of Masters and Johnson produced everything from outrage to acceptance. More importantly, each in its own right produced knowledge.

Kinsey's findings__(112)__ the public. He reported that masturbation,__(113)__, premarital sex, extramarital sex, and other sexual behaviors were more common than people thought. One finding showed that most men, and almost half of all women, engaged in__(114)__ sexual intercourse; and most women, and almost all men engaged in masturbation. Scientists warned that care should be taken in__(115)__ Kinsey's findings to the general public since it included a mostly white, well-educated sample willing to talk about their sexual behaviors.

Since Kinsey's report, premarital sex in the United States has__(116)__. There appear to be four reasons for the increase. Casual sex has been portrayed in a__(117)__ light in the media; there are more effective and easily obtainable forms of__(118)__; modern medicine has reduced the fear of common venereal diseases; and the "double standard" has weakened. In the 1980s, however, increased fears about incurable diseases such as genital herpes and__(119)__ have reduced the incidence of premarital sexual activity. There is no question that the__(120)__of sexual conduct are dependent on the time period when they are studied. The literature is replete with examples of changes in sexual behavior.

Masters and Johnson's Research on the Human Sexual Response Cycle: The shocked response to Kinsey's survey was mild compared to thereaction to the research of Masters and__(121)__, who were not content with asking just about sexual behavior but instead__(122)__ and measured it. They identified four phases of the______(123)______ in men and women. The first two phases comprise the period of **foreplay**. Women chose__(124)__ as more important than either intercourse or afterplay, while men chose__(125)__as most important. __(126)__ also preferred to spend more time on foreplay and afterplay, appearing to enjoy the verbal and physical affection of sexual behavior. The phases of the sexual response cycle are:

1) The *excitement phase.* In this phase, mental or physical stimulation causes__(127)__.
2) The__(128)__ *phase.* In this phase, heart rate, blood pressure, muscle tension, and the rate of respiration increase.
3) The *orgasm phase.* In this phase, heart and breathing rates reach their peak, males __(129)__ *semen,* and both sexes experience intensely pleasurable sensations induced by rhythmic __(130)__contractions. Women find that stimulation of the clitoris is the most efficient way to achieve an__(131)__, although stimulation of the front wall of the vagina may also lead to orgasm. Although the__(132)__ of the orgasm is important, the finding that women who experienced orgasm after their partners felt less satisfied is problematic.
4) The__(133)__ *phase.* In this phase, blood leaves the genitals and sexual arousal lessens, especially for males, who now enter a__(134)__ period, during which they cannot achieve an orgasm. Females, however, are capable of multiple orgasms.

Sexual Dysfunctions, or chronic__(135)__ at different phases of the sexual response cycle, were also addressed by Masters and Johnson.

Male Sexual Dysfunctions: Among the most common male sexual dysfunctions are *erectile dysfunction, premature* __(136)__, and *retarded ejaculation.* __(137)__ dysfunctions occur when the male has an inability to attain or maintain an erection during the arousal phase of the sexual response cycle. Premature ejaculation, in which the male reaches the __(138)__ phase too rapidly for his female partner to be sexually satisfied, is reported to occur in one third of men.

Female Sexual Dysfunctions: Among women, the most common sexual dysfunctions include *orgasmic dysfunction* (the inability to reach the__(139)__ phase),__(140)__ (the experience of pain during or after intercourse), and *vaginismus* (the occurrence of__(141)__ in the muscle ring around the opening of the vagina). Women who experience orgasmic dysfunction tend to have greater sexual__(142)__, difficulty discussing sexual activities, and more negative attitudes toward__(143)__.

Sex Therapy: Masters and Johnson concluded that the__(144)__ causes of sexual dysfunction are usually sexual guilt, sexual ignorance, or anxiety about sexual performance. In treating sexual dysfunction, they begin by having the clients undergo a complete physical exam, followed by counseling to overcome guilt, and__(145)__ about sexual anatomy, motivation, and behavior. Their main technique in sex therapy is______(146)______, a process and procedure where, under guidance and instruction, partners participate in nongenital caressing, then genital caressing, and finally, intercourse. Although Masters and Johnson reported that more than two thirds of their clients showed (147), their failure to (148) define their terms, such as *improvement*, or to conduct follow-up research, led to continuing criticism. Nonetheless, studies of sex therapy by others have provided convincing evidence of its (149).

Gender identity refers to a person's (150) sense of sex. **Transsexualism** is a disorder of *gender* (151) in which a person who is physically a male or female feels like a member of the opposite sex. The extent to which heredity, hormonal imbalances, or childhood experiences contribute to (152) is unknown. Transsexuals may choose to undergo (153) to change the appearance of their sex organs, as well as hormone therapy to eliminate the physical characteristics of their original sex. Most transsexuals who undergo surgery report (154) with the results of the sex-change operation. Transsexualism should not be confused with **homosexuality**, a sexual (155).

Sexual orientation refers to one's sexual (156) toward persons of one's own sex or the opposite sex. (157) is a sexual orientation marked by a preference for sexual relations with members of one's own sex. Unlike the transsexual, the homosexual does not feel trapped in the body of the (158) sex. Female homosexuals are called (159), and male homosexuals are called "*gays*."

Theories of homosexuality abound, with none gaining widespread acceptance. (160) theories implicate herediarty and hormonal factors. Homosexuality runs in families, and identical twins are (161) likely to be homosexual than fraternal twins. Support for a hormonal basis comes from research showing that the administration of (162) produces a physiological response in males that is (163) between them and that produced by females.

Traditional views have favored a (164) interpretation, but there is no evidence that particular childhood experiences cause homosexuality. A more recent and controversial (165) theory of homosexuality holds that sexual orientation depends on the sex of the children with whom we are socializing when our sex drive first emerges. To date, no study on the origins of sexual orientation has identified any physiological or social factor that, by itself, can explain sexual orientation preferences.

Congratulations! You have finished another section. Time for another study break and review.

Mini-review of Sexual Motivation: Match each term with its correct description.

_______1. Masters and Johnson	A. Hormone that in both males and females motivates sexual behavior
_______2. testosterone	B. Phase of the sexual response cycle in which heart rate, blood pressure, muscle tension, and the rate of respiration increase
_______3. dyspareunia	C. Hormone that has little impact on sexual motivation
_______4. transsexualism	D. Phase of the sexual response cycle in which heart and breathing rates reach their peak, males ejaculate semen, and both sexes experience intensely pleasurable sensations induced by rhythmic muscle contractions
_______5. excitement phase	E. A female sexual dysfunction in which she is unable to reach the orgasm phase
_______6. erectile dysfunctions	F. Ways of gaining sexual gratification that violate cultural norms.
_______7. gays	G. He reported that masturbation, homosexuality, premarital sex, extramarital sex, and other sexual behaviors were more common than people thought
_______8. paraphilias	H. Conducted research on the human sexual response cycle by observing and measuring it
_______9. kinsey	I. Phase of the sexual response cycle in which mental or physical stimulation causes arousal
_______10. vaginismus	J. A female sexual dysfunction in which the woman has spasms in the muscle ring around the opening of the vagina
_______11. estrogen	K. Chronic problems at different phases of the sexual response cycle
_______12. sex therapy	L. Phase of the sexual response cycle in which blood leaves the genitals and sexual arousal lessens
_______13. homosexuality	M. Occurs when the male has an inability to attain or maintain an erection during the arousal phase of the sexual response cycle
_______14. premature ejaculation	N. Sexual dysfunction in which the male reaches the orgasm phase too rapidly for his female partner to be sexually satisfied; is reported to occur in one third of men
_______15. plateau phase	O. A female sexual dysfunction in which she experiences pain during or after intercourse
_______16. sexual orientation	P. Begins by having the clients undergo a complete physical exam, followed by counseling to overcome guilt, and education about sexual anatomy, motivation, and behavior
_______17. sensate focusing	Q. Main technique in sex therapy, a process and procedure where, under guidance and instruction, partners participate in nongenital caressing, then genital caressing, and finally, intercourse
_______18. lesbians	R. The person's perceived sense of sex
_______19. orgasmic dysfunction	S. A disorder of gender identity in which a person who is physically a male or female feels like a member of the opposite sex
_______20. gender identity	T. Refers to sexual attraction toward persons of one's own sex or the opposite sex
_______21. resolution phase	U. A sexual orientation marked by a preference for sexual relations with members of one's own sex
_______22. sexual dysfunctions	V. Term for male homosexuals
_______23. orgasm phase	W. Term for female homosexuals

IV. The Arousal Motive: __(166)__ is the general level of physiological activation of the brain and body. Brain arousal is believed to regulated by the____(167)___ and the endocrine and autonomic nervous system regulate body arousal.

In 1908, Yerkes & Dodson reported that animals performed tasks best at a__(168)__ level of stimulation, and that the more complex the task, the lower the level of optimal stimulation. Hebb later showed that humans perform best at a moderate level of arousal, with__(169)__ deteriorating under excessively high or low arousal levels. This relationship between arousal and performance became known as the__(170)__ law. Hebb also found that optimal arousal is higher for__(171)__ tasks than for complex tasks and for well-learned tasks than for novel tasks.

Optimal levels of arousal permit us to__(172)__ and attend to tasks, such as exams.__(173)__ promotes a lowering of the level of concentration, and overarousal impairs performance, interfering particularly with the retrieval of information from short-term memory. Research concerning the predictions made by the Yerkes-Dodson law have historically been inconsistent and flawed__(174)__, but many support the notion of optimal level of arousal for task performance.

Sensory Deprivation: We require__(175)__ stimulation for proper perceptual, cognitive, and emotional functioning. What happens to those who are denied such stimulation? ____(176)____ is the prolonged withdrawal of normal levels of external stimulation. When subject to deprivation, people may experience delusions,__(177)__, and emotional arousal caused by the brain's attempt to restore its optimal level of arousal. The anatomy of a classic research study examines the effects of sensory deprivation.

Anatomy of a Classic Research Study: What Are the Effects of Prolonged Sensory Deprivation? *Read the summary of the 1958 Hebb study on page 396 of your textbook and answer the following questions.*

What was the rationale for the study?

What methods did the authors use to test the hypothesis?

What was the outcome of the study and what did the authors conclude the results meant?

Inadequate external stimulation might__(178)__ us to seek external stimulation or to generate our own stimulation through alterations in brain activity. Flotation *restricted environment stimulation (REST)*, in which subjects float in a dark,__(179)__ tank filled with warm salt water, has been shown to be effective in reducing arousal __(180)__causing hallucinations, distress, or cognitive impairment and has been used to eliminate drug usage, treat_____(181)_____, and reduce blood pressure.

Sensation seeking is one's motivation to seek high or low levels of sensory__(182)__. People high in sensation seeking prefer activities that__(183)__ arousal levels, whereas__(184)__ sensation seekers prefer activities that decrease their arousal. Differences in sensation seeking are apparent in everyday life and have a strong__(185)__ component. Sensation seeking has been shown to be related to__(186)__ behavior, preferences in artistic style, and the tendency to engage in more dangerous activities.

V. The Achievement Motive: The__(187)__ motive is the desire for mastery, excellence, and accomplishment. Interest in studying social motivation was stimulated by Henry __(188)__'s (1938) research and more recently by McClelland and Atkinson. In the context of Maslow's needs hierarchy, the need for achievement would be associated with one of the higher levels, the need for__(189)__. Thus, it is suggested, the need for achievement would be __(190)__ in cultures, such as that of the United States, where people have satisfied their lower needs. Since 1950, there has been a change in this country. As themes of achievement have declined, so have the number of__(191)__ issued. Of course, since these data are__(192)__, it is not certain that changes in achievement motivation caused changes in practical achievements. In addition to the overall change in achievement motivation, there has been a change in the achievement motive over time for males and females, with__(193) showing a marked increase, possibly as a result of the women's movement's influences.

Need for Achievement: Murray referred to the achievement motive as the__(194)__*for achievement,* which reveals itself in efforts to meet high standards of performance or to compete successfully. It is measured by the ____(195)____

Test (TAT). The TAT is based on the assumption that our fantasies reveal our motives. The test consists of a series of drawings of people and the subject is asked to tell__(196)__ is happening, what led up to the picture, and what will happen later. People who score high in the need for achievement tend to__(197)__ at tasks in the face of difficulty, delay gratification in the pursuit of long-range goals, achieve greater success, and select moderately difficult challenges.

The need for achievement__(198)__ with the achievement situation. Your achievement behavior depends on ____(199)____ (the perceived rewards that accompany success in a particular area), __(200)__ (the perceived probability of success in a particular area), and_____ __(201)__ ____ (the motivation to avoid situations that might bring failure).

Research has also shown that the need for achievement may interact with__(202)__ to determine a person's performance. It also appears that early upbringing is an important factor, as parents who encourage__(202)__ and reward good performance foster a strong need. Finally, adults raised in a culture that does not foster achievement motivation can __(203)__ to develop it.

Goal Setting: Goals increase motivation and improve performance by providing__(204)__. They focus your attention, increase your effort, maintain your__(205)__, and encourage you to develop strategies for reaching them. ____(206)____ has been especially important in business and industry in stimulating productivity, using *management by objectives.* Recent research suggests that goals should be specific, challenging, __(207)__ rather than imposed, provide for feedback on the extent of progress, be short term, and be in a sequence that leads to a long-term goal.

Intrinsic Motivation: __(208)__ motivation is the desire to perform a task for its own sake. In contrast, **extrinsic motivation** is the desire to perform a task to gain__(209)__ rewards. Two theories provide possible answers to the observation that while extrinsic rewards may increase achievement motivation, they sometimes__(210)__ achievement motivation. __(211)__ **theory** assumes that extrinsic rewards decrease intrinsic motivation when a person attributes his or her performance to the extrinsic reward. **Cognitive-evaluation theory** holds that a reward perceived as providing information about a person's__(212)__ in an activity will increase his or her intrinsic motivation to perform that activity. But a reward perceived as an attempt to__*(213)*__ a person's behavior will decrease intrinsic motivation to perform that activity.

Stop here and review the sections on arousal and achievement motivation.

Mini-review of Arousal and Achievement Motivation: Match the term with its correct description.

________1. achievement motive	A. The perceived probability of success in a particular area
________2. cognitive-evaluative theory	B. The general level of physiological activation of the brain and body
________3. sensory deprivation	C. The statement of the relationship between arousal and performance; argues that performance is best at a moderate level of stimulation
________4. intrinsic motivation	D. The prolonged withdrawal of normal levels of external stimulation
________5. arousal	E. Subjects float in a dark, soundproof tank filled with warm salt water
________6. Yerkes-Dodson law	F. One's motivation to seek high or low levels of sensory stimulation
________7. Thematic Apperception Test	G. The desire for mastery, excellence, and accomplishment
________8. incentive value	H. He stimulated interest in studying social motivation
________9. Henry Murray	I. Theory holds that a reward perceived as providing information about a person's competence in an activity will increase intrinsic motivation, but will decrease if the reward is perceived as an attempt to control a person's behavior
________10. extrinsic motivation	J. A test that consists of a series of drawings of people; the subject is asked to tell what is happening
________11. sensation seeking	K. The perceived rewards that accompany success in a particular area.
________12. fear of failure	L. The motivation to avoid situations that might bring failure
________13. Flotation restricted environment stimulation (REST)	M. Serves to increase motivation and improve performance by providing incentives
________14. goals	N. The desire to perform a task for its own sake
________15. overjustification theory	O. The desire to perform a task to gain external rewards
________16. expectancy	P. Assumes that extrinsic rewards decrease intrinsic motivation when a person attributes his or her performance to the extrinsic reward

VI. Thinking About Psychology: What Is the Relationship Between Motivation and Sport?

__(214)__ psychology is the field of study that studies the relationship between psychological factors and sport performance. Researchers in **sport psychology** focus on two major areas of interest: the influence of the arousal motive and the achievement motive.

The Arousal Motive and Sport: Your degree of____(215)___ will influence your choice of sports, such as hang gliding versus bowling. People who play competitive sports are aware of "choking," a behavior that occurs when your anxiety makes you attend to normally ___(216)__ movements, such as foul shooting in basketball.
The__(217)__ law may explain why some athletes perform better during practice than during competition. During practice you may be at your__(218)__ level of arousal, a relatively nonstressful situation. There is no single optimal level of arousal during competition, but the optimal level of arousal will be lower for__(219)__ tasks and higher for the more skillful athlete. A good___(220)__ should be able to realize which players must be psyched up and which should be calmed down to achieve optimal levels of arousal during competition. Flotation___(221)__ has been useful in reducing overarousal.

The Achievement Motive and Sport: Research has shown that athletes with a high need for__(222)__ are motivated to seek competition that provides a fair test of their abilities. One way in which superior athletes make competition against lesser athletes more motivating is by giving themselves__(223)__. Goal setting is important in sport motivation. In general:

Athletes are more motivated by__(224)__ rewards than by extrinsic rewards.
Athletes perform best at an optimal level of__(225)__, which varies with the individual, the sport, and the position they play.
Athletes are influenced by their achievement motive, with their level enhanced by their need for achievement, proper use of____(226)___, and reliance on intrinsic rewards.

KEY RESEARCH FINDINGS

Provide the details of the following research studies in psychology:

1. **Maslow (1970):** Developed a theory of motivation based on a hierarchy of needs. (Page 378)
2. **Cannon & Washburn (1912):** Concluded that stomach contractions caused hunger. (Page 379)
3. **Wolkowitz et al. (1990):** Studied the relation of cholecystokinin to hunger. (Page 380)
4. **Hetherington & Ranson (1942):** Demonstrated that the ventromedial hypothalamus (VMH) is a key brain structure related to hunger. (Page 380)
5. **Stunkard, Stinnett, & Smoller (1986):** Indicated that heredity plays a larger role in obesity than habits learned from an adoptive family. (Page 382)
6. **Ravelli, Stein, & Susser (1976):** Showed that men exposed to famine during the third trimester of prenatal development through the first month after birth were less likely to become obese than men exposed to famine at other times during their development. (Page 382)
7. **Schachter (1971):** Concluded that obese people are more likely to feel hunger in the presence of external food cues. (Page 383)
8. **Rodin (1981):** Hypothesized that obese people have higher levels of insulin than others, which makes them more susceptible to external food cues. (Page 383)
9. **Baldwin, de la Riva, & Ebenezer (1990):** Demonstrated the effects of endorphins on hunger. (Page 383)
10. **Fallon & Rozin (1985):** Studied the perception of body images among men and women. (Page 384)
11. **Carlat & Camargo (1991):** Found that 85 percent of people with bulimia nervosa are female. (Page 385)
12. **Wilcox (1990):** Studied the effects of antidepressants on bulimia nervosa. (Page 385)
13. **Weber, Klesges, & Klesges (1988):** Suggested a link between restrained eating and binge eating. (Page 386)
14. **Heatherton, Polivy, & Herman (1989):** Suggested that restrained eaters are underresponsive to internal hunger cues and overresponsive to external hunger cues. (Page 386)
15. **Kinsey, Pomeroy, & Martin (1948):** Studied sexual behavior of men. (Page 388)
16. **Kinsey et al. (1953):** Examined sexual behavior of women. (Page 388)
17. **Lottes (1993):** Surveyed college students about sexual behavior. (Page 388)
18. **Masters & Johnson (1966):** Described the sexual response cycle of men and women. (Page 388)
19. **Denny, Field, & Quadagno (1984):** Reported differing sexual preferences between men and women. (Page 389)
20. **Darling, Davidson, & Cox (1991):** Reported that women whose partners had an orgasm before them felt less satisfied sexually. (Page 389)
21. **Masters & Johnson (1970):** Reported improvement of two-thirds of their sex-therapy clients. (Page 391)
22. **Kilmann et al. (1986):** Reported results of sex therapy by the American Association of Sex Educators, Counselors, and Therapists. (Page 391)
23. **Hamer et al. (1993):** Found a genetic marker on the X chromosome that they related to homosexuality. (Page 393)
24. **LeVay (1991):** Found differences in the structure of the hypothalamus between the brains of homosexuals and heterosexuals. (Page 393)
25. **Gallagher, McFalls, & Vreeland (1993):** Revealed that the most popular theory of homosexuality was the Freudian idea of a cold father and overly affectionate mother. (Page 393)
26. **McConaghy & Blaszcynski (1991):** Studied self-rating of sexuality and penile erection. (Page 394)
27. **Yerkes & Dodson (1908):** Demonstrated that animals performed tasks best at a moderate or optimal level of arousal. The more complex the task, the lower the level of optimal arousal. (Page 394).
28. **Hebb (1955):** Showed that the relationship between arousal and task performance in humans followed a U-shaped curve. (Page 394)
29. **Plass & Hill (1986):** Tested arithmetic performance of low-, moderate- and high-anxious children and determined that the anxiety level induced by the test affected performance. (Page 395)
30. **Hebb (1958):** Studied the effects of prolonged sensory deprivation. (Page 396)
31. **Humphreys & Revelle (1984):** Related the need for achievement with arousal level on given tasks. (Page 399)
32. **Rodgers & Hunter (1991):** Showed that management by objectives increased productivity in 68 of 70 studies. (Page 399)
33. **Locke & Latham (1985):** Suggested that setting specific goals is more effective than having no or vague goals. (Page 399)

34. **Lepper, Greene, & Nisbett (1973):** Showed that a reward for performance did not always increase subsequent performance. (Page 400)
35. **Triplett (1898):** Demonstrated that bicyclists rode faster when competing against others than when competing against a time. (Page 401)
36. **Weinberg et al. (1993):** Found that goal setting was an effective way to enhance performance. (Page 404)
37. **Lerner & Locke (1995):** Found that specific goal setting helped improve athletic performance better than "doing your best." (Page 404)
38. **Boyce (1992):** Studied the effect of specific goal setting on a college rifle-shooting team. (Page 404)

PRACTICE TEST A

1. The psychological process that arouses, directs, and maintains behavior toward a goal is called
   a. regression.
   b. motivation.
   c. aggregation.
   d. extroversion.

Obj.: 1 Page: 376

2. After playing a set of tennis, you feel thirsty. Your thirst would be an example of a(n)
   a. need.
   b. drive.
   c. reflex.
   d. instinct.

Obj.: 2 Page: 377

3. A researcher inserted an electrode into the brain of a rat. When he sent an electric current through the electrode, the rat began to eat. The site of the electrode was most likely the
   a. lateral hypothalamus.
   b. medial geniculate body.
   c. lateral geniculate body.
   d. ventromedial hypothalamus.

Obj.: 3 Page: 380

4. In 1983, Karen Carpenter died of heart failure caused by
   a. obesity.
   b. bulimia nervosa.
   c. extreme stress.
   d. anorexia nervosa.

Obj.: 4 Page: 383-386

5. The obtaining of sexual pleasure from dressing in clothing of the opposite sex is called
   a. bisexuality.
   b. homosexuality.
   c. transvestitism.
   d. transsexualism.

Obj.: 5 Page: 387

6. The first major formal survey of male and female sexual behavior was conducted by
   a. Freud.
   b. Kinsey.
   c. Masters and Johnson.
   d. Money.

Obj.: 6 Page: 388

7. The sex therapy in which partners first participate in nongenital caressing, then proceed to genital stimulation, and finally engage in sexual intercourse was prescribed by
   a. Kinsey.
   b. Dr. Ruth.
   c. Masters and Johnson.
   d. the American Association of Sex Educators, Counselors, and Therapists.

Obj.: 7 Page: 388-389

8. Dyspareunia is a condition in which
   a. males experience retarded ejaculation.
   b. females experience painful sexual intercourse.
   c. males can only maintain intermittent erections.
   d. females can achieve orgasm only through means other than sexual intercourse.

Obj. : 8 Page: 390

9. A person who is physically a member of one sex but feels psychologically like the opposite sex exhibits
   a. bisexuality.
   b. homosexuality.
   c. transvestitism.
   d. transsexualism

Obj.: 9 Page 391

10. The tendencies for police to engage in high-speed chases and for students to engage in unprotected sex are related to
    a. paraphilias.
    b. sensation seeking.
    c. sensory deprivation.
    d. need for achievement.

Obj.: 10 Page: 397

11. If you have a need for achievement, in testing your basketball shooting ability you would most likely choose to shoot
    a. lay-ups.
    b. from half court.
    c. from the foul line.
    d. at a 5-foot-tall basket.

Obj.: 11 Page: 398

12. The notion that an extrinsic reward will decrease intrinsic motivation when a person attributes his or her performance to that reward is called
    a. overextension theory.
    b. overjustification theory.
    c. overregularization theory.
    d. cognitive-evaluation theory.

Obj.: 12 Page: 401

13. The optimal level of arousal would probably be lowest for
    a. lifting weights.
    b. throwing a football.
    c. serving a tennis ball.
    d. making a shot on a pool table.

Obj.: 13 Page: 402

PRACTICE TEST B

1. In addition to explaining the reason for an observed behavior, the concept of motivation can also help us to understand
   a. fluctuations in behavior over time.
   b. outbursts of emotional behavior.
   c. how we solve complex problems.
   d. our attraction to others.

Obj.: 1 Page: 376

2. An instructor offers "extra credit" toward a test grade to those students willing to do some additional library research on a particular topic. This opportunity may be viewed as a
   a. positive incentive.
   b. negative incentive.
   c. drive-reduction incentive.
   d. homoeostatic incentive.

Obj.: 2 Page: 378

3. One reason that instinct theorists fell out of favor was that they
   a. could identify only a few behaviors that were instinctive.
   b. used circular reasoning.
   c. generalized their beliefs to humans by observing organisms lower on the phylogenic scale.
   d. favored nurture over nature.

Obj.: 2 Page: 376-378

4. College students who are motivated to do just well enough in their classes to make to a published Dean's list would be classified as operating at Maslow's ________ level of needs.
   a. self-actualization
   b. safety
   c. belongingness
   d. esteem

Obj.: 2 Page: 376-378

5. One Dutch study found that those who had been exposed to famine conditions immediately before and immediately after birth were less likely to be obese as adults, compared to others who had been exposed to famine at other times. This finding suggests that
   a. food deprivation leads to psychological maladjustment.
   b. obesity is less common among certain ethnic groups.
   c. the prenatal period may be critical in establishing set point and basal metabolic rate.
   d. food habits acquired during childhood affect adult weight levels.

Obj.: 3 Page: 382

6. It has been suggested that stress, an external factor, might
   a. usually result in overeating.
   b. cause nonobese people to overeat more than obese people do.
   c. induce overeating by stimulating the brain to secrete endorphins.
   d. normally have no effect on eating behavior.

Obj.: 3 Page: 382

7. Martha is constantly monitoring and controlling her food desires. On a hot summer day, she "gives in" and consumes ice cream. Later that evening, she engages in an immense eating binge followed by self-induced vomiting. Martha may be described as
   a. a bulimic who is a restrained eater.
   b. an anorexic who is overly responsive to internal cues.
   c. a person who is attempting to overcome her hereditary trend toward obesity.
   d. a person with an overabundance of cholecystokinin.

Obj.: 4 Page: 385-386

8. The Lesslykus tribe encourages masturbation and simulated intercourse among their prepubescent children. The Morelykus tribe discourages any sexual play among its prepubescent children. This example demonstrates that human sexual behavior
   a. tends to be freer and unrestricted among smaller tribal groups.
   b. varies greatly because of social and cultural norms.
   c. can range from normal to abnormal.
   d. is heavily influenced by hormonal factors.

Obj.: 5 Page: 387

9. Patricia is especially friendly to the men in her college classes. She should be aware that men may perceive her behavior as
   a. manipulative.
   b. flirtatious.
   c. domineering.
   d. controlling.

Obj.: 6 Page: 388

10. Melinda is experiencing an orgasm. The intense pleasure that she feels is caused by
   a. a peak level of lubrication.
   b. her memory of the affection expressed during the excitement phase.
   c. rhythmic muscle contractions and the release of endorphins.
   d. a sudden reversal of blood flow to the genitals.

Obj.: 7 Page: 389

11. How effective has sex therapy been found to be in treating sexual dysfunctions?
   a. not at all effective unless combined with drug therapy
   b. effective only for couples who really loved each other
   c. generally effective, with the best success rates in treating premature ejaculation and orgasmic dysfunction
   d. almost 100 percent effective with all the dysfunctions except for retarded ejaculation and dyspareunia

Obj.: 8 Page: 391

12. A person's self-perceived sex is her or his
   a. gender identity.
   b. unconscious sexuality.
   c. sexual orientation.
   d. autoeroticism.

Obj.: 9 Page: 391

13. Freud claimed that homosexuality is caused by
   a. hormonal factors.
   b. heredity and hormonal factors.
   c. repressed sexual aggression.
   d. a dominant, overly affectionate mother and an aloof, unemotional father.

Obj.: 9 Page: 391

14. For Jermaine, a perfect day consists of sleeping late, going for a slow walk in the woods, lunch with an old friend, reading for a few hours, and then a date that involves going to chamber music concert. For Kathleen, a perfect day consists of rising early, jogging for an hour or so on an urban street, a fast-food lunch at the mall, coaching a team of 7-year-olds in volleyball, and then leaving with a date for a weekend of white-water kayaking. These two individuals differ in their
    a. sensory deprivation levels.
    b. sensation-seeking level.
    c. achievement motivation.
    d. expectancy levels.

Obj.: 10 Page: 397

15. Your achievement behavior depends on
    a. the strength of your general need for achievement.
    b. the value of the incentive.
    c. your level of expectancy.
    d. all of the above.

Obj.: 11 Page: 397-400

16. A characteristic of people with a high need for achievement is that they
    a. have difficulty delaying gratification in the pursuit of long-term goals.
    b. prefer extremely difficult challenges.
    c. are motivated to seek competition that provides a fair test of their abilities.
    d. will perform best with a low level of arousal.

Obj.: 11 Page: 397-400

17. The intrinsic joy of being a poet is achieved by
    a. the enjoyment of your poetry by others.
    b. selling your poetry.
    c. the writing of the poetry itself.
    d. attending poetry seminars.

Obj. 12 Page: 400-401

18. An alternative to the theory that an extrinsic reward will decrease intrinsic motivation when a person attributes his or her performance to that reward is known as
    a. cognitive-evaluation theory.
    b. overregularization theory.
    c. overextension theory.
    d. overjustification theory.

Obj.: 12 Page: 400-401

19. Ben is a moderately-good tennis player. He usually chooses to play with opponents who are generally just a little better than he is. Most likely, Ben
    a. has a high need for sensation seeking.
    b. is motivated by extrinsic rewards.
    c. has low expectancies for success.
    d. has a high need for achievement.

Obj.: 13 Page: 403

20. When you "choke" during a sporting event, what happened?
    a. Your anxiety made you unaware of the normally automatic movements involved in playing
    b. You were more likely to have been at an optimal level of arousal
    c. You were so anxious that you performed below your normal level of activity
    d. You need to engage in additional training

Obj.: 13 Page: 401-405

ESSAY QUESTIONS

1. Assume your ultimate goal is to "get an A" in this course. How can you apply the principles of goal setting to reach that goal?

Obj.: 11 Page: 397-400

2. You are a sports psychologist. You have been asked to offer some pointers to your institution's basketball team members to help them achieve and sustain a high level of performance. You decide to apply your knowledge of the need for achievement. What would you tell them?

Obj.: 13 Page: 401-405

ANSWER RECORD FOR CHAPTER 11

Comprehensive Guided Review:

1. direct
2. observable
3. variations
4. incentives
5. Darwin
6. instincts
7. Watson
8. learned
9. scientific
10. explain
11. instinct
12. genetic
13. Wilson
14. sociobiology
15. Hull
16. deprivation
17. tension
18. homeostasis
19. explain
20. drive
21. pushes
22. external
23. desirable
24. negative
25. push
26. priority
27. need
28. physiological
29. esteem
30. supported

Mini-review of Sources of Motivation:
1. C; 2. E; 3. B; 4. H; 5. I; 6. L; 7. J; 8. F; 9. A; 10. D; 11. G; 12. K

31. environmental
32. small
33. taste
34. stomach
35. cause
36. receptor
37. brain
38. reducing
39. hormone
40. vagus
41. insulin
42. sugar
43. storage
44. increased
45. hypothalamus
46. norepinephrine
47. ventromedial hypothalamus
48. promotes
49. LH
50. set point
51. lowers
52. raises
53. internal
54. increasing
55. 20
56. fat
57. size
58. obesity
59. calories
60. basal metabolic
61. high
62. aerobic
63. set point
64. positive
65. biological
66. does
67. critical
68. obese
69. correlation
70. responsiveness
71. hungrier
72. externality
73. dieting
74. Rodin
75. stressful
76. increase
77. endorphins
78. hunger
79. naloxone

Anatomy of a Contemporary Research Study: How Satisfied Are Males and Females with Their Bodies?

What was the rationale for the study?
Fallon and Rozin (1985) studied the relationship between the body images that males and females have of themselves and eating disorders.

What methods did the authors use to test the hypothesis?
College students were asked to rate themselves on a continuum from very thin to very obese. Comparisons were made between males and females.

What was the outcome of the study and what did the authors conclude the results meant?
The results suggested that the tendency of women to have a negative body image may put more pressure on them to lose weight. Perhaps this contributes to the greater tendency of women to develop eating disorders.

---

80. starvation
81. fat
82. Anorexia
83. hypothalamus
84. intravenous
85. Psychological
86. binges
87. vomiting
88. obese
89. predisposition.
90. cholecystokinin
91. control
92. restrained
93. less
94. Group

Mini-review of Hunger Motivation:
1. G; 2. I; 3. B; 4. K; 5. H; 6. D; 7. F; 8. E; 9. A; 10. C; 11. J

95. sex
96. power
97. gonads
98. pituitary
99. hormones
100. testosterone
101. motivation
102. hormones
103. humans
104. culture
105. violate
106. varied
107. normal
108. Victorian
109. denial
110. censorship
111. Kinsey
112. shocked
113. homosexuality
114. premarital
115. generalizing
116. increased
117. positive
118. contraception
119. AIDS
120. norms
121. Johnson
122. observed
123. sexual response cycle
124. foreplay
125. intercourse
126. Women
127. arousal
128. plateau

129. ejaculate
130. muscle
131. orgasm
132. timing
133. resolution
134. refractory
135. problems
136. ejaculation
137. Erectile
138. orgasm
139. orgasm
140. dyspareunia
141. spasms
142. guilt
143. masturbation
144. psychological
145. education
146. sensate focusing
147. improvement
148. operationally
149. effectiveness
150. perceived
151. identity
152. transsexualism
153. surgery
154. satisfaction
155. orientation
156. attraction
157. Homosexuality
158. opposite
159. lesbians
160. Physiological
161. more
162. estrogen
163. intermediate
164. Freudian
165. learning

Mini-review of Sexual Motivation:
1. H; 2. A; 3. O; 4. S; 5. I; 6. M; 7. V; 8. F; 9. G; 10. J; 11. C; 12. P; 13. U; 14. N; 15. B; 16. T; 17. Q; 18. W; 19. E; 20. R; 21. L; 22. K; 23. D

166. Arousal
167. reticular formation
168. moderate
169. performance
170. Yerkes-Dodson
171. simple
172. concentrate
173. Underarousal
174. methodologically
175. sensory
176. Sensory deprivation
177. hallucinations

Anatomy of a Classic Research Study: What are the Effects of Prolonged Sensory Deprivation?

What was the rationale for the study?
Hebb and his colleagues examined the phenomenon of "brainwashing," using sensory deprivation.

What methods did the author use to test the hypothesis?
They conducted studies of sensory deprivation in which subjects were confined in soundproof rooms with restricted opportunity to experience visual and tactile sensations.

What was the outcome of the study and what did the authors conclude the results meant?
The results showed that the subjects found the lack of sensory stimulation so aversive they preferred to forgo a monetary incentive in favor of sensory stimulation.

---

178. motivate
179. soundproof
180. without
181. tension headaches
182. stimulation
183. increase
184. low
185. hereditary
186. sexual
187. achievement
188. Murray
189. esteem
190. stronger
191. patents
192. correlational
193. females
194. need
195. Thematic Apperception
196. what
197. persist
198. varies
199. incentive value
200. expectancy
201. fear of failure
202. independence
203. learn
204. incentives
205. persistence
206. Goal setting
207. self-defined
208. Intrinsic
209. external
210. decrease
211. Overjustification
212. competence
213. control

Mini-review of Arousal and Achievement Motivation:
1. G; 2. I; 3. D; 4. N; 5. B; 6. C; 7. J; 8. K; 9. H; 10. O; 11. F; 12. L; 13. E; 14. M; 15. P; 16. A

214. Sport
215. sensation seeking
216. automatic
217. Yerkes-Dodson
218. optimal
219. complex
220. coach
221. REST
222. achievement
223. handicaps
224. intrinsic
225. arousal
226. goal setting

Practice Test A:

1. a. Incorrect: The process that arouses, directs, and maintains behavior toward a goal is called motivation.
   b. Correct: The process that arouses, directs, and maintains behavior toward a goal is called motivation.
   c. Incorrect: The process that arouses, directs, and maintains behavior toward a goal is called motivation.
   d. Incorrect: The process that arouses, directs, and maintains behavior toward a goal is called motivation.

2. a. Incorrect: The need is defined as the motivated state, or the lack of water.
   b. Correct: The thirst is the drive or state of tension that results from the need.
   c. Incorrect: A reflex is an automatic response to external stimulation.
   d. Incorrect: An instinct is a complex, inherited behavior pattern that is present at birth.

3. **a. Correct: Electrical stimulation of the LH induces eating behavior.**
   b. Incorrect: Stimulation of the medial geniculate does not affect eating.
   c. Incorrect: Stimulation of the lateral geniculate does not affect eating.
   d. Incorrect: Stimulation of the VMH decreases eating behavior.

4. a. Incorrect: Karen Carpenter died as a result of heart failure brought on by anorexia.
   b. Incorrect: Karen Carpenter died as a result of heart failure brought on by anorexia.
   c. Incorrect: Karen Carpenter died as a result of heart failure brought on by anorexia.
   d. Correct: Karen Carpenter died as a result of heart failure brought on by anorexia.

5. a. Incorrect: Bisexuality is a sexual orientation.
   b. Incorrect: Homosexuality is a sexual orientation in which individuals are attracted to members of their own sex.
   c. Correct: Transvestitism is a paraphilia that involves obtaining sexual enjoyment from dressing in opposite-sex clothing.
   d. Incorrect: Transsexualism occurs when individuals feel that they are the opposite from their genetic sex.

6. a. Incorrect: Freud did not conduct surveys. He relied on case studies to make generalizations.
   b. Correct: Kinsey conducted the first survey of sexual behavior in 1953.
   c. Incorrect: This was the most recent major undertaking, conducted by Masters and Johnson.
   d. Incorrect: Money did not conduct such surveys.

7. a. Incorrect: Kinsey did not recommend any sex therapy; he conducted a survey.
   b. Incorrect: Dr. Ruth was not the originator of sex therapy.
   c. Correct: Masters and Johnson created the therapy method. It is called sensate focusing.
   d. Incorrect: The members of this organization were surveyed in the 1980s as to the effectiveness of therapy.

8. a. Incorrect: Dyspareunia is defined as a female sexual dysfunction in which the woman experiences pain during and/or after sexual intercourse.
   b. Correct: Dyspareunia is defined as a female sexual dysfunction in which the woman experiences pain during and/or after sexual intercourse.
   c. Incorrect: Dyspareunia is defined as a female sexual dysfunction in which the woman experiences pain during and/or after sexual intercourse.
   d. Incorrect: Dyspareunia is defined as a female sexual dysfunction in which the woman experiences pain during and/or after sexual intercourse.

9. a. Incorrect: Transsexuals are individuals who believe that they are the opposite sex from their genetic makeup; bisexuality is a sexual orientation.
   b. Incorrect: Transsexuals are individuals who believe that they are the opposite sex from their genetic makeup; homosexuality is a sexual orientation.
   c. Incorrect: Transsexuals are individuals who believe that they are the opposite sex from their genetic makeup. Transvestitism is a paraphilia in which the individual finds sexual pleasure in dressing in opposite-sex clothing.
   d. Correct: Transsexuals are individuals who believe that they are the opposite sex from their genetic makeup.

10. a. Incorrect: Paraphilias are a way of obtaining sexual gratification in ways that violate legal or cultural norms.
    b. Correct: High sensation-seeking need levels have been linked to these behaviors.
    c. Incorrect: Sensory deprivation is the prolonged withdrawal of normal levels of stimulation.
    d. Incorrect: The need for achievement has not been linked to any of these behaviors.

11. a. Incorrect: Individuals with a high need for achievement choose moderately difficult challenges, thus would not take the easy lay-up shot.
    b. Incorrect: Individuals with a high need for achievement choose moderately difficult challenges, thus would not take the extremely difficult shot from midcourt.
    c. **Correct: Individuals with a high need for achievement choose moderately difficult challenges, thus would take the mid-distance shot.**
    d. Incorrect: Individuals with a high need for achievement choose moderately difficult challenges, thus would not take the easy shot.

12. a. Incorrect: The notion that extrinsic reward decreases intrinsic motivation because people attribute their performance to the reward is called overjustification theory.
    b. **Correct: The notion that extrinsic reward decreases intrinsic motivation because people attribute their performance to the reward is called overjustification theory.**
    c. Incorrect: The notion that extrinsic reward decreases intrinsic motivation because people attribute their performance to the reward is called overjustification theory.
    d. Incorrect: The notion that extrinsic reward decreases intrinsic motivation because people attribute their performance to the reward is called overjustification theory.

13. a. Incorrect: This is a fairly easy task, thus would require higher levels of arousal.
    b. Incorrect: This a is fairly easy task, thus would require higher levels of arousal.
    c. Incorrect: This a is fairly easy task, thus would require higher levels of arousal.
    d. **Correct: This is the most complex task of the list, thus would require a lower level of arousal.**

Practice Test B:

1. **a. Correct: Motivation helps to explain both the why and the when of behaviors.**
    b. Incorrect: Motivation helps to explain both the why and the when of behaviors.
    c. Incorrect: Motivation helps to explain both the why and the when of behaviors.
    d. Incorrect: Motivation helps to explain both the why and the when of behaviors.

2. **a. Correct: This is an example of a positive incentive, or a desirable stimuli that pulls you toward the goal.**
    b. Incorrect: A negative incentive is a stimulus that is undesirable and leads us to steer away from it.
    c. Incorrect: There is no such thing as a drive-reduction incentive.
    d. Incorrect: There is no such thing as a homoeostatic incentive.

3. a. Incorrect: They attempted to explain almost all behavior as instinctive.
    b. Correct: Instinct theory lost favor because it was not able to explain behavior; the reasoning was circular, e.g., we play music because of a "music instinct."
    c. Incorrect: This is not cited as a reason for the disfavor they encountered.
    d. Incorrect: They favored nature over nurture.

4. a. Incorrect: The key words here are "*just well enough* to make the *published list,*" to be motivated for self-actualization individuals do something because they want it, not for how it looks to others.
    b. Incorrect: Getting on the Dean's list does not keep you safe.
    c. Incorrect: Being put on a published Dean's list does not allow you to be part of a group, thus it does not meet the belongingness need.
    d. Correct: The key words here are "*just well enough* to make the *published list*", the student wants the recognition, or esteem associated with the action.

5. a. Incorrect: The critical period in this study was during the prenatal and early infant years, thus suggesting a critical period in the development of body weight set point.
   b. Incorrect: The critical period in this study was during the prenatal and early infant years, thus suggesting a critical period in the development of body weight set point.
   c. **Correct: The critical period in this study was during the prenatal and early infant years, thus suggesting a critical period in the development of body weight set point.**
   d. Incorrect: The critical period in this study was during the prenatal and early infant years, thus suggesting a critical period in the development of body weight set point.

6. a. Incorrect: "Usually" should be replaced by "may" for this choice to be correct.
   b. Incorrect: The opposite is true.
   c. **Correct: Endorphins are increased during times of high stress and have been shown to increase eating behavior.**
   d. Incorrect: Stress normally does have an effect on eating.

7. **a. Correct: Martha's behavior is a classic description of a bulimic who shows signs of restrained eating.**
   b. Incorrect: Martha's behavior is a classic description of a bulimic who shows signs of restrained eating.
   c. Incorrect: Martha's behavior is a classic description of a bulimic who shows signs of restrained eating.
   d. Incorrect: Martha's behavior is a classic description of a bulimic who shows signs of restrained eating.

8. a. Incorrect: We have not been told of the size of the tribal groups, thus cannot conclude that tribal size is a factor.
   b. Correct: This result does demonstrate that sexual behavior varies among different cultures.
   c. Incorrect: The behaviors described are both considered normal and abnormal, depending on the viewpoint one takes.
   d. Incorrect: Hormonal factors do not differ in different cultures.

9. a. Incorrect: The behavior described is often perceived by males as flirtatious.
   b. Correct: The behavior described is often perceived by males as flirtatious.
   c. Incorrect: The behavior described is often perceived by males as flirtatious.
   d. Incorrect: The behavior described is often perceived by males as flirtatious.

10. a. Incorrect: Female and male orgasms are induced by rhythmic contractions of muscles and the release of endorphins.
    b. Incorrect: Female and male orgasms are induced by rhythmic contractions of muscles and the release of endorphins.
    c. **Correct: Female and male orgasms are induced by rhythmic contractions of muscles and the release of endorphins.**
    d. Incorrect: Female and male orgasms are induced by rhythmic contractions of muscles and the release of endorphins.

11. a. Incorrect: Surveys found that therapy was generally effective, with best rates in treatment of premature ejaculation and orgasmic dysfunction.
    b. Incorrect: Surveys found that therapy was generally effective, with best rates in treatment of premature ejaculation and orgasmic dysfunction.
    c. **Correct: Surveys found that therapy was generally effective, with best rates in treatment of premature ejaculation and orgasmic dysfunction.**
    d. Incorrect: Surveys found that therapy was generally effective, with best rates in treatment of premature ejaculation and orgasmic dysfunction.

12. **a. Correct: A person's self-perceived sex is called gender identity.**
    b. Incorrect: Unconscious sexuality is not a psychological term.
    c. Incorrect: Sexual orientation refers to the sexual attraction toward persons' of one's sex or opposite sex.
    d. Incorrect: A person's self-perceived sex is called gender identity.

13. a. Incorrect: Freud did not take hormonal factors into account.
    b. Incorrect: Freud emphasized the role of the unconscious, not hormones and heredity.
    c. Incorrect: According to Freud, this was not the root cause.
    d. Correct: Freud felt that male homosexuality resulted from an overly affectionate mother and an aloof unemotional father.

14. a. Incorrect: Neither individual is undergoing sensory deprivation.
    b. Correct: These two individuals differ in their sensation-seeking needs; Jermaine has low needs, Kathleen has high needs.
    c. Incorrect: There is not enough information about the achievement motivation of either individual.
    d. Incorrect: Expectancy level refers to the perceived probability of success in a particular area; again, we do not have enough information to determine this.

15. a. Incorrect: Achievement behavior depends on this, but not only this factor; it also depends on b and c.
 b. Incorrect: Achievement behavior depends on this, but not only this factor; it also depends on a and c.
 c. Incorrect: Achievement behavior depends on this, but not only this factor; it also depends on a and b.
 d. Correct: Since all three answers are correct, this is the best choice.

16. a. Incorrect: They do not have much difficulty in delaying gratification.
 b. Incorrect: They prefer moderately difficult challenges.
 c. Correct: People with high need for achievement are motivated to seek out fair tests of their abilities.
 d. Incorrect: They will perform best at an optimal level of arousal.

17. a. Incorrect: This is an extrinsic, or external, motivator.
 b. Incorrect: This is an extrinsic, or external, motivator.
 c. Correct: This is an internal motivator.
 d. Incorrect: This is an extrinsic, or external, motivator.

18. **a. Correct: This theory suggests that intrinsic motivation is increased if the reward is perceived as providing information about the person's competence, thus is an alternative.**
 b. Incorrect: Overregularization theory is not a theory of motivation.
 c. Incorrect: Overextension theory does not pertain to motivation.
 d. Incorrect: Overjustification theory is the theory being presented in the statement.

19. a. Incorrect: Ben probably has a high need for achievement since he chooses to seek out competition that provides a fair test of his abilities.
 b. Incorrect: Ben probably has a high need for achievement since he chooses to seek out competition that provides a fair test of his abilities.
 c. Incorrect: Ben probably has a high need for achievement since he chooses to seek out competition that provides a fair test of his abilities.
 d. Correct: Ben probably has a high need for achievement since he chooses to seek out competition that provides a fair test of his abilities.

20. **a. Correct: Athletes who "choke" experience increased awareness of typically automatic responses as a result of their anxiety.**
 b. Incorrect: Athletes who "choke" experience increased awareness of typically automatic responses as a result of their anxiety.
 c. Incorrect: Athletes who "choke" experience increased awareness of typically automatic responses as a result of their anxiety.
 d. Incorrect: Athletes who "choke" experience increased awareness of typically automatic responses as a result of their anxiety.

Essay Questions:

1. a) Set very specific, challenging subgoals rather than vague subgoals. Thus, "I will study one hour per day" is better than "I will increase my study time."
 b) Keep a record of my progress toward reaching that goal. Keep a daily chart on which I plot actual hours studied, pages read, etc.
 c) Set short-term goals to help me reach my ultimate goal. These may include things such as creating a summary table to show the relationship among concepts or dividing a chapter into thirds and writing a summary for each third.

2. Among the elements you would include: the case of Kathy Ormsby, the use of a handicap, the role of goal setting, the desire to seek competition that provides a fair test of one's ability, and the role of intrinsic reward.

12 Emotion

LEARNING OBJECTIVES

After studying this chapter, you should be able to:

1. Define emotion and list the three aspects of emotion that have been studied by psychologists. (p. 410)
2. Describe the functioning of the autonomic nervous system, the various brain structures, and the neurochemical system in the physiological basis of emotional experience. (p. 410-414)
3. Describe the role of the voice, facial expression, and body movements in the expression and communication of emotion. (p. 415-418)
4. Summarize the contributions of Robert Plutchik and Charles Darwin to our understanding of the experience of emotion. (p. 418-419)
5. Describe the two dimensions along which emotions are subjectively experienced. (p. 419)
6. List and describe two theories regarding our subjective experience of happiness. (p. 420-421)
7. List and describe three theories regarding our subjective experience of humor. (p. 421-422)
8. Describe the important characteristics of three biopsychological theories of emotion and summarize their respective strengths and weaknesses. (p. 423-427)
9. Describe the important characteristics of the facial-feedback theory of emotion. (p. 428-429)
10. List and describe the important features of two cognitive theories of emotion and briefly describe the supportive research for each of them. (p. 429-433)
11. Explain the underlying principle of the polygraph test, summarize the issues that surround its use, then explain the strengths and weaknesses of the Guilty Knowledge Test as an alternative to the polygraph. (p. 433-437)

COMPREHENSIVE GUIDED REVIEW

Although the concept is difficult to define, most psychologists agree that **emotion** is a motivated state marked by ___(1)___ arousal, expressive behavior, and mental experience, which varies in its ___(2)___ and pleasantness-unpleasantness. There are a variety of approaches one might take in the study of emotion. Some psychologists prefer to study the biological level (the ___(3)___ of emotion), others the ___(4)___ level (the expression of emotion), and still others the ___(5)___ level (the experience of emotion).

I. The Biopsychology of Emotion:

The Autonomic Nervous System and Emotion: Both the ___(6)___ and experience of emotion depend on the level of activity in the **autonomic nervous system.** Figure 12.1 on page 411 in your textbook illustrates the functions of the two branches of the autonomic system: the ___(7)___ **nervous system** and the **parasympathetic nervous system.** The interaction between the two systems contributes to changes in emotions. While the sympathetic nervous system relies on the neurotransmitter ___(8)___ to regulate its target organs, the parasympathetic system relies on ___(9)___ to regulate its target organs.

Activation of the sympathetic system may stimulate the___(10)__ response. Once a threat has been met or avoided, the sympathetic system becomes__(11)__ active and the parasympathetic system becomes__(12)__ active, calming the body. However, arousal is not a simple on-off phenomenon. Since the sympathetic nervous system stimulates the release of epinephrine and norepinephrine from the___(13)__ glands into the blood, the physiological arousal may persist for a while, even after the threat has disappeared.

What are some of the characteristics of sympathetic arousal? Among them are the experience of___(14)__, an increase in alertness, increased heart rate and breathing, dilation of the pupils, dryness of the mouth, goose bumps, and perspiration. Given that the real or perceived threat disappears, these__(15)__ changes will diminish in intensity, returning to a state of normalcy.

The Brain and Emotion: Autonomic system arousal is regulated by the **hypothalamus,** a component of the ______(16)_____. The___(17)__ helps control changes in breathing and heart output and also adds a positive or negative emotional component to memories. Other structures of the **limbic system** play a role in the experience of emotion. The __(18)__ also attaches labels to experiences, especially in dangerous, fear-evoking situations. The septum___(19)__ aversive emotional states, especially fear.

The______(20)____, which comprises the cerebral hemispheres, is also important in our processing of emotions. The cortex is believed to be involved in our__(21)__ experience of emotions. It appears that the__(22)__ hemisphere is more involved in positive emotions and the__(23)__ more involved in negative emotions. There is considerable evidence to support this conclusion. The first of type of evidence comes from studies by Richard Davidson, in which he measured the __(24)__activity of each hemisphere during different states of emotional arousal. In addition, the Wada test, which involves the selective__(25) of one cerebral hemisphere, has also provided evidence of the__(26)__ of emotionality. Finally, support for lateralization comes from studies of brain damage.

The Chemistry of Emotion: Research has shown that emotions depend on chemistry, relying on both hormones and __(27)__. Stressful situations cause the secretion of the hormones__(28)__ and norepinephrine, and levels of the neurotransmitters norepinephrine and serotonin have been implicated in __(29)__. In one study, levels of hormones were measured on the day subjects gave a public speech and on a day when they did not give a speech. The levels of epinephrine and__(30)__ (which also serve as neurotransmitters) increased on days when the subjects gave speeches. An increase was also noted in__(31)__ levels on days when the subjects gave speeches relative to days when they did not. The **endorphins** are another class of __(32)__that contribute to emotional experience. They provide relief from pain and evoke feelings of___(33)__.

II. The Expression of Emotion: Emotions cannot be directly observed by others; they are inferred from __(34)__of them, or from expressive behaviors. Behaviors that express emotions include vocal qualities, body movements, and __(35)__ expressions. There is a__(36)__ variety of emotional expression across cultures.

Vocal Qualities: We communicate our emotional state through changes in the rate, pitch, and loudness of our __(37)__. These__(38)__ features of speech are called **prosody.** Changes in vocal qualities tend to be__(39)__ from one person to another and from one culture to another. __(40)__ quality also affects social relations. Subjects who exhibit depression are more likely to be__(41)__. However, understanding __(42)__ may also have positive effects. Helping depressed individuals change their prosodic features can lead to more positive__(43)__ interactions, in turn improving mood state. The prosodic features of speech are regulated primarily by the__(44)__ cerebral hemisphere.

Body Movements: To study the extent to which we respond to the body movements of others, we must control for the influence of__(45)__ expressions or physical appearance. Walk & Homan (1984) did exactly this by having dancers wear small lights on their joints and perform in the__(46)_. The subjects__(47)__ identified the emotions represented by body movements only. This serves as evidence that emotional cues provided by_____(48)_____ are distinct from those provided by facial expressions or physical appearance. This ability to decode nonverbal behavior is__(49)__ in social interaction. Finally, we seem to prefer an __(50)__ level of nonverbal interaction in everyday social relations. We prefer people who are neither too nonverbally aloof nor too nonverbally intrusive.

Facial Expressions: Though we may believe that we are unbiased in our presentation, __(51)__ expressions have been shown to communicate true feelings. Research has shown that facial expressions convey both the intensity and the __(52)__ of our emotional states, as many card players would recognize. However, our recognition of facial expression might also depend on the __(53)__ context. As in the recognition of emotions from body movements, __(54)__ are superior to __(55)__ in recognizing emotions from facial expressions. Researchers have been able to distinguish __(56)__ emotional expressions from false ones. The face, for example, reveals when smiles are sincere or false. A __(57)__ smile is called the **Duchenne smile.**

Charles __(58)__ believed that facial expressions evolved because they promoted survival by communicating emotions, thus helping to distinguish friend from foe. Three lines of research support Darwin's view that facial expressions for basic emotions are __(59)__ and universal: 1) People who are blind from birth exhibit facial expressions representing the __(60)__ emotions, including joy, fear, anger, disgust, sadness, and surprise; 2) young infants produce facial expressions for the basic emotions; and 3) facial expressions for the basic emotions are __(61)__ across cultures.

Mini-review of the Biopsychology and the Expression of Emotion: Match each term with its correct description.

_______1. emotion
_______2. septum
_______3. norepinephrine
_______4. sympathetic nervous system
_______5. Wada test
_______6. Charles Darwin
_______7. hypothalamus
_______8. epinephrine and norepinephrine
_______9. prosody
_______10. parasympathetic nervous system
_______11. Duchenne smile
_______12. cerebral cortex
_______13. facial expressions
_______14. norepinephrine and serotonin
_______15. amygdala
_______16. acetylcholine
_______17. endorphins

A. Component of the limbic system that suppresses aversive emotional states, especially fear
B. The sympathetic nervous system relies on this neurotransmitter to regulate its target organs
C. The parasympathetic system relies on this neurotransmitter to regulate its target organs
D. Brain area believed to be involved in our subjective experience of emotions
E. Activation of this branch of the autonomic nervous system may stimulate the fight-or-flight response
F. Stressful situations cause the secretion of these hormones
G. Chemicals that provide relief from pain and evoke feelings of euphoria
H. Component of the limbic system that regulates autonomic system arousal; helps control changes in breathing and heart output and also adds a positive or negative emotional component to memories
I. Nonverbal features of speech that include changes in the rate, pitch, and loudness
J. Involves the selective anesthesia of one cerebral hemisphere; has provided evidence of the lateralization of emotionality
K. Neurotransmitters that have been implicated in depression
L. Once a threat has been met or avoided, this branch of the autonomic nervous system becomes more active, calming the body.
M. Component of the limbic system that attaches labels to experiences, especially in dangerous, fear-evoking situations
N. Body changes that convey both the intensity and the pleasantness of our emotional states
O. A natural smile
P. He believed that facial expressions evolved because they promoted survival by communicating emotions, thus helping to distinguish friend from foe
Q. A motivated state marked by physiological arousal, expressive behavior, and mental experience, which varies in its intensity and pleasantness-unpleasantness

III. The Experience of Emotion: There seem to be only a few basic emotions, from which all others are derived. Robert__(62)__(1980) considers joy, fear, anger, disgust, sadness, surprise, acceptance, and anticipation to be the basic emotions. These primary emotions are comprised of four pairs of__(63)__. There is evidence that the experience of emotion varies both in its__(64)__ and its pleasantness. Individuals who tend to experience intensely pleasant emotions are likely to experience intensely unpleasant ones, as in__(65)__ versus despair. People who tend to experience mildly pleasant emotions tend to experience mildly unpleasant emotions, as in gladness versus __(66)__. Emotions may impair the __(67)__ system and, as a result, make us more prone to illness. Depression has an adverse effect on the immune system, perhaps even__(68)__ the immune system in its attempt to retard the progression of cancer.

Happiness is __(69)__ correlated with intelligence, social skills, and family support. __(70)__ **theory** considers happiness to be the result of estimating that your life circumstances are more favorable than those of other people. ____(71)____**theory,** on the other hand, proposes that your experience of happiness depends not only on comparing yourself with others, but also on comparing yourself with yourself. The theory claims that your current state of happiness depends, in part, on the__(72)__ of your present circumstances with your past circumstances. As your circumstances improve, your level of happiness becomes__(73)__. There is a limit, however, as lottery winners have testified. These winners were no__(74)__ than they were in the past and actually found less pleasure in formerly enjoyable everyday experiences.

Humor: Happiness is enhanced by__(75)__, an emotional experience that plays a positive and productive role in everyday life. One surprising finding has been that humorous people may not feel as__(76)__ as they act. For example, some people use humor to maintain social distance and minimize __(77)__. Given that humorous people may not be as gregarious as they seem, what makes their humor amusing? One factor is the__(78)__ context in which the humor is expressed. While the use of__(79)__ tends to make one's experience of simple humor funnier, subtle, complex humor will seem less funny.

But what accounts for our response to humor when sober? The most popular theories include **disparagement theory, incongruity theory,** and **release theory.** Hobbes's__(80)__ **theory** claimed that we feel amused when humor makes us feel superior to other people. Research supporting this position found that we are especially amused when we dislike those to whom we are made to feel superior. Kant's __**(81)**__ **theory**, on the other hand, states that incongruous humor brings together incompatible ideas in a surprising outcome that violates our expectations. This theory explains why many jokes require__(82)__ and lose their humorous effect on the second telling. Finally, __(83)__ **theory** is based on Freud's claim that humor is an outlet for anxiety caused by repressed sexual or aggressive energy. Humor may raise your level of anxiety and then suddenly lower it, providing you with such relief that you laugh. Release theory explains the popularity of humor that plays on our sexual anxieties. In regard to aggression, one study showed that the subjects' laughter provided a cathartic experience, which released energy that would have provoked later aggression.

IV. Theories of Emotion: There are three general categories of theories of emotion: biopsychological theories, behavioral theories, and cognitive theories. The theories vary in the emphasis they place on__(84)__, behavior, and cognition.

Biopsychological Theories of Emotion:

The James-Lange Theory: William James claimed that physiological changes __(85)__ emotional experiences. Because Carl Lange made the same claim, the theory became known as the__(86)__ theory. The main premise of the theory is that specific patterns of__(87)__ changes are produced by emotional events. This is illustrated on page 424 in your textbook (Figure 12.5). By example, instead of the commonsense belief that "we see a snake, are frightened, and run," the theory claims, "we meet a snake, run, and are frightened."

The theory provoked criticism by Walter Cannon, who argued:

1) People are__(88)__ at perceiving the subtle physiological changes induced by the sympathetic nervous system.
2) Different emotions can be evoked by the__(89)__ patterns of physiological arousal.
3) Physiological changes that are dependent on adrenal hormone secretions are simply too__(90)__ to account for an instantaneous emotional experience.

Recent research has come to provide some credence for the temporarily disfavored James-Lange theory.

The Cannon-Bard Theory: After rejecting the James-Lange theory, Cannon and Bard put forth the theory that an emotion is produced when an event or object is perceived by the__(91)_, which conveys this information simultaneously to the cerebral cortex and to the skeletal and autonomic nervous system. (See Figure 12.7, textbook page 426.) The cortex uses__(92)__ to determine the nature of the perceived object or event, while the muscles and sympathetic system provide the physiological arousal that prepares the individual to take action. Unlike the James-Lange theory, this theory assumes that different emotions are associated with the__(93)__ state of physiological arousal.

The___(94)__ theory has failed to gain research support because the thalamus does not play the role it assumed. However, replacing the reference to the thalamus with a reference to the____(95)____, and the theory is supported by research. For example, research on victims of spinal cord damage has provided support for the Cannon-Bard theory, while contradicting the__(96)__ theory. This research shows that damage that prevents people from perceiving their bodily__(97)__ still allows them to experience distinct emotions. This supports Cannon-Bard's claim that emotional experience depends mainly on the__(98)__ perception of ongoing events, and violates the James-Lange assumption that emotional experience depends on the perception of bodily arousal.

The Opponent-process Theory: This theory holds that the mammalian brain has___(99)__ mechanisms that counteract strong positive or negative emotions by evoking an opposite emotional response to maintain **homeostasis.** Solomon (1980) argues that the__(100)__ emotion begins sometime after the onset of the first emotion and lasts longer than the first emotion. Additionally, if we experience the first emotion on repeated occasions, the opposing emotion grows __(101)__ and the emotion that is experienced becomes a compromise between the two emotional states. This theory provides support for a "happy medium" approach with__(102)__ in everything, including emotional experience.

Behavioral Theories of Emotion: The__(103)___ **theory** holds that our facial expressions affect our emotional experiences. Unlike the James-Lange theory, which is primarily concerned with the effect of __(104)__nervous system activity on emotion, facial-feedback theory is limited to the effect of facial expressions; this theory was put forth by Waynbaum in 1907. Contemporary facial-feedback theorists, led by Ekman, assume that__(105)__ has endowed us with facial expressions that provide different patterns of sensory feedback of muscle tension levels to the brain, thereby evoking different emotions. Despite receiving support from research, the theory has not received unqualified support. The best conclusion is that feedback from facial expressions is but one of__(106)__ factors defining our emotional experiences.

Cognitive Theories of Emotion: Cognitive theories are the most recent theories of emotion and stress the importance of thinking.

The Two-Factor Theory: Stanley Schachter's **two-factor theory** argues that physiological arousal and the ___(107)_ of a cause for that arousal produce the emotional experience. Schachter claims that when you experience __(108)_ arousal, you search for its source. Your attribution of a cause for your arousal__(109)__ the emotion that you experience. The major and original supportive research for two-factor theory of emotion was conducted in the 1960s. Since then, research has produced inconsistent findings. The "Anatomy of a Classic Research Study" describes Schachter and Singer's classic study of the role of attribution in the perception of emotion.

Anatomy of a Classic Research Study: Do Emotions Depend on the Attribution of a Cause for Our Physiological Arousal? *Read the summary of the study on page 429-430 in the textbook and answer the questions below.*

What was the rationale for the study?

What methodology did the authors use to test the hypothesis?

What was the outcome of the study and what did the authors conclude the results meant?

Richard Lazarus's____(110)__ **theory**, on the other hand, downplays the role of physiological arousal and assumes that our emotion at a given time depends on our interpretation of the situation we are in at that time. Unlike the two-factor theory, the cognitive-appraisal theory__(111)__ the role of physiological arousal. The research findings are mixed. An early study by Lazarus and colleagues found support for the theory; however, Robert Zajonc and others question whether the cognitive-appraisal is really essential to the__(112)__ of emotion.

In the face of these competing theories of emotion, the best a psychologist can conclude is that none of them is sufficient to explain emotion fully, though each may describe a process that contributes to it.

Mini-review of the Experience and Theories of Emotion: Match each term with its correct description.

______1. adaptation-level theory
______2. disparagement theory of humor
______3. two-factor theory
______4. Cannon-Bard Theory
______5. Robert Plutchik
______6. cognitive-appraisal theory
______7. incongruity theory of humor
______8. happiness
______9. facial-feedback theory
______10. James-Lange Theory
______11. opponent-process theory
______12. release theory of humor
______13. humor
______14. social-comparison theory

A. He considers joy, fear, anger, disgust, sadness, surprise, acceptance, and anticipation to be the basic emotions
B. This is positively correlated with intelligence, social skills, and family support
C. Theory that considers happiness to be the result of estimating that one's life circumstances are more favorable than those of other people
D. Theory that proposes that your experience of happiness depends not only on comparing yourself with others, but also on comparing yourself with yourself
E. An emotional experience that plays a positive and productive role in everyday life
F. Hobbes's theory claiming that we feel amused when humor makes us feel superior to other people
G. Kant's theory that states that incongruous humor brings together incompatible ideas in a surprising outcome that violates our expectations; explains why many jokes require timing
H. This theory is based on Freud's claim that humor is an outlet for anxiety caused by repressed sexual or aggressive energy
I. The main premise of the theory is that specific patterns of physiological changes are produced by emotional events
J. Theory that argues that an emotion is produced when an event or object is perceived by the thalamus, which conveys this information simultaneously to the cerebral cortex and to the skeletal and autonomic nervous system
K. Theory that holds that the mammalian brain has evolved mechanisms that counteract strong positive or negative emotions by evoking an opposite emotional response to maintain homeostasis; provides support for a "happy medium" approach
L. The theory that holds that our facial expressions affect our emotional experiences; it assumes that evolution has endowed us with facial expressions that provide different patterns of feedback of muscle tension levels to the brain
M. Stanley Schachter's theory that argues that physiological arousal and the attribution of a cause for that arousal produce the emotional experience
N. Richard Lazarus's theory that downplays the role of physiological arousal and assumes that our emotion at a given time depends on our interpretation of the situation we are in at that time

V. Thinking About Psychology: Do Lie Detectors Tell the Truth?

As mentioned at the beginning of the chapter, we infer people's emotional state from their___(113)__ behavior. However, untrained individuals tend to be very poor at detecting deceit, or___(114)__, from facial expressions. Historically, detection of lying behavior has been based on the assumption that people displayed__(115)__ physiological arousal when they lied. Modern lie-detection methods began in the late 1800s with the work of Lombroso, an Italian criminologist.

Procedures in Lie Detection: The lie detector test, or **polygraph test,** typically measures breathing patterns, heart rate, blood pressure, and___(116)__ activity (sweating). However, there are no specific patterns of physiological responses that, by themselves, indicate lying. The procedure involves asking the subject *control* and___(117)__ *questions.* The assumption is that a guilty person will show__(118)_ physiological changes in response to relevant questions, while an innocent person will show greater arousal in response to___(119)__ questions.

Issues in Lie Detection: Polygraph testing has provoked controversy due to its___(120)__. Questions about the polygraph methods include 1) individual differences in physiological___(121)__; 2) techniques to__(122)__ the polygraph; 3) the possibility that the__(123)__ will be found guilty; 4) under what circumstances and to whom should the lie detector test be administered?; 5)would alternatives such as Lykken's **Guilty Knowledge Test** be acceptable?; and 6) research findings indicating that__(124)_ rates are closer to 76 percent than 90 percent.

The "Anatomy of a Contemporary Research Study" examines research on the accuracy of lie detectors conducted by Kleinmuntz & Szucko.

Anatomy of a Contemporary Research Study: How Accurate Are Lie Detectors at Judging Guilt and Innocence? *Read the summary of the study presented on page 435-436 in your textbook and answer the following questions.*

What was the rationale for the study?

What methods did the authors use to test the hypothesis?

What was the outcome of the study and what did the authors conclude the results meant?

The _(125)____**Test** is a promising alternative to the polygraph test. The test assumes that a guilty person (who knows details of the crime), but not the innocent person, will show more physiological arousal in response to the____(126)__ words than in response to the__(127)__ words. Recent research with both college students and real criminals suggests that the test may have promise. The results indicate that the test tends to be biased toward__(128)__ results so those who are more interested in protecting the innocent would favor the test. Support for the test is, however, not universal. More research is necessary.

KEY RESEARCH FINDINGS

Provide the details of the following key research studies in psychology:

1. **Davidson (1992):** Suggested that the right cerebral hemisphere is more involved in negative emotions, while the left is more involved in positive emotions. (Page 412)
2. **Wheeler, Davidson, & Tomarken (1993):** Measured hemisphere activity while exposing subjects to positive and negative emotional stimuli. (Page 413)

3. **Fox & Davidson (1988):** Measured hemisphere activity in 10-month-olds demonstrating that the difference in processing of positive and negative emotions starts early in life. (Page 413)
4. **Lee et al. (1990):** Showed that negative emotions were more prevalent when the left hemisphere was anesthetized, and positive emotions more prevalent when the right hemisphere was anesthetized. (Page 413)
5. **Leventhal & Tomarken (1986):** Showed that damage to one hemisphere allowed the other to dominate emotional states. (Page 413)
6. **Baum, Grunberg, & Singer (1992):** Showed that emotions are based on chemistry-hormones and neurotransmitters. (Page 414)
7. **Bolm-Audorff et al. (1989):** Linked emotional responses to stressful situations to cardiovascular disease. (Page 414)
8. **Hennig, Laschefski, & Opper (1994):** Demonstrated a link between endorphin levels and feelings of euphoria. (Page 414)
9. **Goldstein (1980):** Proved that endorphins were linked to positive emotions by a double-blind test of a drug that blocks the effects of endorphins. (Page 414)
10. **Stephan, Stephan, & de Vargas (1996):** Indicated cultural differences in the expression of emotions. (Page 415)
11. **Gorelick & Ross (1987):** Study showed that people with right-hemisphere stroke spoke with an abnormal tone. (Page 415)
12. **Ross et al. (1988):** Found that injecting the right hemisphere with a barbiturate did not interfere with a person's ability to speak, but inhibited all emotion in the speech. (Page 415)
13. **Walk & Homan (1984):** Tested students' ability to discern emotions by viewing only body movements, not facial expressions or appearance. (Page 416)
14. **Sogon & Izard (1987):** Showed that females are more adept at reading emotions from body movements. (Page 416)
15. **Nowicki & Duke (1992):** Found that elementary school children who are better at decoding body movements are more popular. (Page 416)
16. **Hodgins & Zuckerman (1990):** Saw that college roommates who could read body movement rated their relationship more positive than when one or both had low ability to detect emotion. (Page 416)
17. **Hill & Stephany (1990):** Suggested that counselors who could note changes in patients' behavior through body movement were more effective. (Page 416)
18. **Goldman & Fordyce (1983):** Found a positive response with a moderate level of nonverbal interaction, as opposed to a high or low level. (Page 416)
19. **Babad, Bernieri, & Rosenthal (1989):** Studied the effect of teachers' facial expression on their students' perception of them. (Page 416)
20. **Russell & Fehr (1987):** Studied the effect of facial expressions in the context of the situation. (Page 417)
21. **Ekman, Davidson, & Friesen (1990):** Linked pleasant emotions with a natural smile. (Page 417)
22. **Hansen & Hansen (1988):** Measured ability to detect facial expressions in a crowd. (Page 417)
23. **Izard (1990):** Supported Darwin's view that facial expressions were both inborn and universal. (Page 417)
24. **Goodenough (1932):** A case study of a blind girl who exhibited appropriate facial expressions for emotions. (Page 417)
25. **Izard et al. (1980):** Studied facial expressions of young infants. (Page 417)
26. **Ganchrow, Steiner, & Daher (1983):** Showed that basic facial expressions were present in newborns. (Page 417)
27. **Balaban (1995):** Gauged the reactions of 5-month-olds to angry and happy faces. (Page 417)
28. **Ekman (1993):** Studies showed that facial expressions are universal across cultures. (Page 418)
29. **Ekman & Friesen (1971):** Studied a New Guinea tribe and their matching of descriptions of emotions to photos of Westerners displaying these emotions.(Page 418)
30. **Ekman et al. (1987):** Replicated the 1971 photo study with ten different cultural groups. (Page 418)
31. **Ekman & Heider (1988):** Found that American, Japanese, and Indonesian subjects agreed on an expression of contempt. (Page 418)
32. **Mullen et al. (1986):** Survey tried to determine if newscasters' facial expression when talking about a presidential candidate gave a more favorable impression of that candidate to viewers. (Page 418)

33. **Plutchik (1980):** Provided a model for basic emotions. (Page 418)
34. **Stone et al. (1985):** Studied the "blue monday" effect. (Page 419)
35. **Diener et al. (1993):** Studied how comparing oneself to others affects one's perception of happiness. (Page 420)
36. **Brickman, Coates, & Janoff-Bulman (1978):** Found that lottery winners had a shift in perception of happiness to a higher standard. (Page 420)
37. **Prasinos & Tittler (1981):** Found that humorous adolescents used humor to keep their distance from others. (Page 421)
38. **Mio & Graesser (1991):** Found that humor that disparages the target is perceived as funnier than that which uplifts the target. (Page 422)
39. **Wicker, Barron, & Willis (1980):** Supported the position that finds more humor when the target is one to which we can feel superior. (Page 422)
40. **Oppliger & Sherblom (1992):** Found that disparaging humor is perceived as funnier when used by someone perceived as likeable. (Page 422)
41. **Ruch, McGhee, & Hehl (1990):** Found that older and more conservative people like incongruous humor better than nonsense or disparaging humor. (Page 422)
42. **Freud (1905):** Said that humor is a cathartic release of sexual tension. (Page 422)
43. **Shurcliff (1968):** Supported the release theory of humor with a study using students and toy rats. (Page 422)
44. **Ziv (1987):** Found that students who were stimulated to laugh after taking a frustrating exam were less likely to respond aggressively than those who were not exposed to the humorous situation. (Page 422)
45. **James (1890):** Stated that emotional experience is preceded by a physiological change. (Page 423)
46. **Ekman, Levenson, & Friesen (1983):** Supported the James-Lange theory with a study that measured emotional responses of subjects while assuming facial expressions representing different emotions. (Page 423)
47. **Levenson et al. (1991):** Conducted a study that tested the ability to distinguish emotions based on constructing facial expressions associated with past emotional experiences. (Page 423-424)
48. **Cannon (1927) & Bard (1934):** Claimed that emotion is produced when the event is perceived by the thalamus. (Page 424)
49. **LeDoux, Romanski, & Xagoraris (1989):** Showed that the thalamus has a part in the process of perceiving emotion. (Page 425)
50. **Bermond et al. (1991); Chwalisz, Diener, & Gallagher (1988):** Found that persons with spinal cord injury still experience emotions, which seems to run counter to the James-Lange theory. (Page 425)
51. **Solomon (1980):** Postulated that the experience of a strong emotion produces an opposite and slightly stronger emotion to offset the initial emotion. (Page 427)
52. **Izard (1990):** Proposed that emotions were based solely on facial feedback, in contrast to the James-Lange theory of autonomic response. (Page 428)
53. **Ekman (1992):** Assumed that evolution has built patterns of sensory feedback to the brain that cause emotions. (Page 428)
54. **Adelmann & Zajonc (1989):** Measured a positive associated between facial expression and emotion. (Page 428)
55. **Buck (1980):** Found more influence of feedback from autonomic system than from facial expressions. (Page 428)
56. **McCanne & Anderson (1987):** Used biofeedback to study the facial-feedback theory. (Page 429)
57. **Schachter & Singer (1962):** Studied Schachter's two-factor theory of emotion. (Page 429)
58. **Speisman et al. (1964):** Tested the cognitive-appraisal theory of emotion. (Page 431)
59. **Kleinmuntz & Szucko (1984):** Showed that polygraph tests were not as reliable an indicator of lying as previously believed. (Page 435)
60. **Saxe, Dougherty, & Cross (1985):** Conducted a congressionally funded study that concluded that polygraphs should be used only in criminal cases. (Page 435)
61. **Bashore & Rapp (1993):** Developed a version of the Guilty Knowledge Test that measures brain-wave changes. (Page 437)
62. **Elaad (1990):** Tested the effectiveness of the Guilty Knowledge Test. (Page 437)
63. **Elaad (1994):** Found that the Guilty Knowledge Test was effective in detecting individuals with knowledge relevant to a crime. (Page 437)
64. **Bradley & Warfield (1984):** Found that the Guilty Knowledge Test might not reliably detect someone with guilty knowledge. (Page 437)

PRACTICE TEST A

1. A motivated state marked by physiological arousal, expressive behavior, and mental experience is called
   a. emotion.
   b. motivation.
   c. sensation seeking.
   d. self-actualization.

Obj.: 1 Page: 410

2. A person suffers a bullet wound to the brain and begins to respond inappropriately to threatening situations, often showing no concern for his own safety. The bullet probably damaged his
   a. amygdala.
   b. cerebellum.
   c. basal ganglia.
   d. medulla oblongata.

Obj.: 2 Page: 412

3. You return home and realize that your parents are angry at you based on the rate, pitch, and loudness of their speech--even though the words they are using are not angry words. This means that you are basing you judgment of their emotional state on
   a. prosody.
   b. kinesics.
   c. proxemics.
   d. physiognomy.

Obj.: 3 Page: 415

4. Which of the following is *not* a basic emotion as proposed by Robert Plutchik?
   a. joy
   b. anger
   c. love
   d. disgust

Obj.: 4 Page: 418

5. The emotions of elation and gladness differ along the dimension of
   a. cognitive appraisal
   b. pleasantness
   c. cognitive arousal
   d. intensity

Obj.: 5 Page: 419

6. An Olympic-class runner finds it difficult to be happy, because every time she improves her performance her standard of happiness becomes higher. This is best explained by
   a. incongruity theory.
   b. disparagement theory.
   c. adaptation-level theory.
   d. social-comparison theory.

Obj.: 6 Page: 420

7. A friend of yours amuses people by ridiculing teachers, fellow students, and public figures. The effectiveness of this kind of humor is explained best by
   a. incongruity theory.
   b. disparagement theory.
   c. adaptation-level theory.
   d. social-comparison theory.

Obj.: 7 Page: 421-422

8. A vicious dog runs after you. You run for your front door, pull it open, and escape into your home-just before the dog reaches you. You notice that you are sweating and breathing heavily and that your heart is beating rapidly. Only then do you notice that you feel terrified; this would provide circumstantial evidence for the
   a. James-Lange theory.
   b. Cannon-Bard theory.
   c. facial-feedback theory.
   d. opponent-process theory.

Obj.: 8 Page: 423

9. The assumption that an emotion is produced when an event or object is perceived by the thalamus, which conveys this information simultaneously to the cerebral cortex and the body, is called the
   a. two-factor theory.
   b. James-Lange theory.
   c. Cannon-Bard theory.
   d. opponent-process theory.

Obj.: 8 Page: 424-425

10. The relief you feel after the intense anxiety you experience during final exams is best explained by the
   a. two-factor theory.
   b. James-Lange theory.
   c. Cannon-Bard theory.
   d. opponent-process theory.

Obj.: 8 Page: 427

11. Studies supporting the facial-feedback theory of emotion have identified sensory neurons that convey information from the facial muscles to the
a. medulla oblongata.
b. corpus callosum.
c. hypothalamus.
d. motor cortex.
Obj.: 9 Page: 428-429

12. After a harrowing automobile ride to school over icy roads, you arrive physiologically aroused. You notice a fellow student and find him (her) more romantically attractive than you have in the past. The best explanation for your emotion would be provided by the
a. two-factor theory.
b. James-Lange theory.
c. Cannon-Bard theory.
d. opponent-process theory.
Obj.: 10 Page: 429-430

13. A student is turned down for a job and tells herself that "it would have meant working too many hours for too little pay," thereby making her feel relieved. Another student, turned down for the same job, tells herself that "I may never find a job," thereby making her feel depressed. The difference in the emotional responses of the two students in response to the same event is explained best by the
a. James-Lange theory.
b. Cannon-Bard theory.
c. opponent-process theory.
d. cognitive-appraisal theory.
Obj.: 10 Page: 431

14. One difficulty with the accuracy of the polygraph depends, in part, on the subject's
a. level of motivation.
b. gender.
c. age.
d. physiological reactivity.
Obj.: 11 Page: 433-437

PRACTICE TEST B

1. Both Linda and Bob receive A's on a major term paper. While Linda is happy, Bob is overjoyed. Both Ken and Carolina are rejected by someone each of them loves. While Ken is sad, Carolina is despondent. These examples demonstrate what characteristic of emotions?
a. Emotions endure over time.
b. Men and women feel different emotions.
c. Emotions vary in intensity.
d. Only internal events can elicit emotions.
Obj.: 1 Page: 410

2. As part of an ongoing research study, Debra has her blood levels of epinephrine, norepinephrine, and cholesterol tested every day. On a particular day, levels of all three of these substances are considerably elevated. Based on the findings of previous research, one could conclude that Debra
a. is experiencing positive emotions.
b. will also produce high levels of endorphins on that day.
c. has a very active parasympathetic system.
d. is feeling stressed that day.
Obj.: 2 Page: 414

3. After a threat has been met or avoided, arousal is reduced by
a. an increase in the activity of the sympathetic nervous system.
b. an increase in the activity of the parasympathetic nervous system.
c. the central nervous system.
d. the somatic nervous system.
Obj.: 2 Page: 410-414

4. During rehearsals, a talented acting coach tells her students to stop "acting like someone who is afraid." She insists that her acting students "actually be afraid." In other words, audiences will
a. attempt to decode Duchenne expressions.
b. rely more on the actors' words than on their body movements and facial expressions.
c. feel more positive emotions than negative ones.
d. be able to distinguish honest emotional expressions from insincere ones.
Obj.: 3 Page: 417

5. Which statement most accurately reflects current scientific beliefs about the universality of human facial expressions?
   a. Cross-cultural studies have shown that only love and contempt are truly universal facial expressions.
   b. While facial expressions are the same among Westerners, non-Westerners show a wider repertoire of expressions.
   c. Other than fear and surprise, no other expressions have been found to be universal.
   d. Recent findings have been too inconsistent to conclude that human facial expressions are universal.

Obj.: 3 Page: 418

6. In everyday social interactions, we prefer people who use a
   a. high level of verbal interaction.
   b. low level of verbal interaction.
   c. moderate level of verbal interaction.
   d. high level of nonverbal interaction.

Obj.: 3 Page: 415-418

7. According to Plutchik's (1980) emotion wheel, the basic emotions are fear, surprise, sadness, disgust, anger, anticipation, acceptance, and
   a. joy.
   b. despair.
   c. hostility.
   d. suspicion.

Obj.: 4 Page: 418-419

8. When Nancy is awarded a generous scholarship, she is ecstatic. When Martha is awarded the same scholarship, she is mildly pleased. Based on recent research, what else might you predict about the emotional life of these two women?
   a. Nancy is more likely to experience all the basic emotions, while Martha has a more limited repertoire.
   b. Compared to Martha, Nancy is much more likely to decode facial expressions accurately.
   c. Nancy's mood are more likely to be cyclical and predictable than are Martha's.
   d. In the face of bad news, Nancy would feel despair, while Martha is likely to be mildly unhappy.

Obj.: 5 Page: 419

9. A flood damages the town of Plutchikville. The Smith family's home is seriously damaged and many of their belongings are lost. Nonetheless, the Smiths feel happier when they recall that the Jones's home was completely destroyed. This response is in keeping with which theory?
   a. social-comparison theory
   b. fight-or-flight theory
   c. optimal-arousal theory
   d. evolutionary theory

Obj.: 6 Page: 420

10. You can make yourself happier with your own life by
    a. comparing it with the lives of those who are more fortunate.
    b. being wealthy.
    c. using humor in your everyday life.
    d. never comparing yourself with yourself.

Obj.: 7 Page: 421-422

11. Two groups of children are exposed to a very frustrating situation. Afterward, one of the groups experiences a humorous situation, while the second group does not. Later, when exposed to a second frustrating situation, the group that experienced a humorous situation is less aggressive than the other. According to release theory, this difference occurred because
    a. aggressive energy was conserved by the laughing children and will be exposed in a future, unrelated situation.
    b. those who laughed had a cathartic experience, thus releasing their aggressive energy.
    c. the basic emotions experienced by the laughing children were more diffuse than those of the other group.
    d. those who laughed felt more fortunate than those who did not laugh.

Obj.: 7 Page: 422

12. Isaac is ecstatic as he attends graduation ceremonies to receive his diploma. By the end of the ceremony, he has already begun to feel rather depressed and let down. This example is in keeping with
    a. opponent-process theory.
    b. cognitive-appraisal theory.
    c. adaptation-level theory.
    d. release theory.

Obj.: 8 Page: 427

13. Which theory supports the view that the perception of an event induces a specific pattern of physiological changes, which evokes a specific emotional experience?
    a. James-Lange theory
    b. Cannon-Bard theory
    c. facial-feedback theory
    d. opponent-process theory

Obj.: 8 Page: 423-427

14. Which theory of emotion supports the old adages that "when you smile, the world smiles with you" and "put on a happy face and you will feel happy"?
    a. two-factor theory
    b. facial-feedback theory
    c. cognitive-appraisal theory
    d. social-comparison theory

Obj.: 9 Page: 428-429

15. You are at a friend's wedding. You are dressed formally, standing in front of a number of people, and you are crying. According to Schachter's two-factor theory, your emotional experience occurs because of the outcome of two factors:
    a. psychological arousal and the attribution of a cause for that arousal
    b. physiological arousal and the misattribution of a cause for that arousal
    c. psychological arousal and the misattribution of a cause for that arousal
    d. physiological arousal and the attribution of a cause for that arousal

Obj.: 10 Page: 429-433

16. Cognitive-appraisal theory assumes that our emotion at a given time depends on our interpretation of the situation we are in at that time. In this regard, cognitive-appraisal theory is like
    a. two-factor theory.
    b. facial-feedback theory.
    c. opponent theory.
    d. no other theory.

Obj.: 10 Page: 429-433

17. How do contemporary psychologists evaluate the many theories about the nature of emotion?
    a. The cognitive theories of emotion have received the best research support.
    b. The physiological theories of emotion have proved to be the most useful.
    c. Behavioral theories such as the facial-feedback theory appear to be the strongest.
    d. While each theory explains one aspect of emotion, none can totally explain emotion.

Obj.: 10 Page: 431

18. The detectability of lying may be reduced by lowering physiological arousal. A factor that may do this is
    a. brainwashing.
    b. hypnosis.
    c. tranquilizers.
    d. stress.

Obj.: 11 Page: 433-437

19. Your friend has been accused of a crime and continually claims that she is innocent. She is given a test by the police in which she is asked questions about the victims, the site of the crime, and the commission of the crime using details that would be known only to the guilty party. The questions are asked several times, each time with different words, and your friend's physiological arousal is measured. What type of test has she been given?
    a. The Wada test
    b. The Guilty Knowledge Test
    c. Polygraph test
    d. Electroencephalograms test

Obj.: 11 Page: 433-437

20. Which item is out of place here?
    a. electrodermal activity
    b. cognitive appraisal
    c. heart rate
    d. polygraph

Obj.: 11 Page: 434

ESSAY QUESTIONS

1. Why are polygraph tests unreliable in distinguishing lying from truth telling?

Obj.: 11 Page: 435

2. You are asked to give a brief presentation to the class of the psychobiology of emotion. You have not had time to prepare adequately. You go to the classroom and are almost ready to give your presentation when your professor announces that your textbook author, Dr. Sdorow, has just arrived, unexpectedly. Since he would like to speak to

the class, your presentation will have to be postponed. Describe the various levels of emotional arousal you would experience throughout this scenario. P.S. How would you feel about him?

Obj.: 2 Page: 410-412

ANSWER RECORD FOR CHAPTER 12

Comprehensive Guided Review:

1. physiological
2. intensity
3. biopsychology
4. behavioral
5. mental
6. expression
7. sympathetic
8. norepinephrine
9. acetylcholine
10. fight-or-flight
11. less
12. more
13. adrenal
14. anxiety
15. physiological
16. limbic system
17. hypothalamus
18. amygdala
19. suppresses
20. cerebral cortex
21. subjective
22. left
23. right
24. electrical
25. anesthesia
26. lateralization
27. neurotransmitters
28. epinephrine
29. depression
30. norepinephrine
31. cholesterol
32. neurotransmitters
33. euphoria
34. descriptions
35. facial
36. wide
37. speech
38. nonverbal
39. consistent
40. Vocal
41. rejected
42. prosody
43. social
44. right
45. facial
46. dark
47. accurately
48. body movement
49. important
50. optimal
51. facial
52. pleasantness
53. social
54. females
55 males
56. sincere
57. natural
58. Darwin
59. inborn
60. basic
61. universal

Mini-review of the Biopsychology and the Expression of Emotion:

1. Q; 2. A; 3. B; 4. E; 5. J; 6. P; 7. H; 8. F; 9. I; 10. L; 11. O; 12. D; 13. N; 14. K; 15. M; 16. C; 17. G

62. Plutchik
63. opposites
64. intensity
65. elation
66. disappointment
67. immune
68. inhibiting
69. positively
70. Social-comparison
71. Adaptation-level
72. comparison
73. higher
74. happier
75. humor
76. extraverted
77. self-disclosure
78. social
79. alcohol
80. disparagement
81. incongruity
82. timing
83. Release
84. physiology
85. precede
86. James-Lange
87. physiological
88. poor
89. same
90. slow
91. thalamus
92. memories
93. same
94. Cannon-Bard
95. limbic system
96. James-Lange
97. arousal
98. brain's
99. evolved
100. opposing
101. stronger
102. moderation
103. facial-feedback
104. autonomic
105. evolution
106. several
107. attribution
108. physiological
109. determines

Anatomy of a Classic Research Study: Do Emotions Depend on the Attribution of a Cause for Our Physiological Arousal? *Read the summary of the study on pages 429-430 in the textbook and answer the questions below.*

What was the rationale for the study?

Schachter wanted to test the predictions of his two-factor theory of emotions.

What methodology did the authors use to test the hypothesis?

Three groups of college males were told they were getting an injection of a new vitamin when, in reality, they received an injection of epinephrine. The subjects then waited in a room with an accomplice who acted either happy or angry.

What was the outcome of the study and what did the authors conclude the results meant?

Informed group subjects were unaffected by the accomplice. Misinformed group subjects and uninformed group subjects experienced emotions similar to those of the accomplice.

---

110. cognitive-appraisal
111. downplays
112. experience

Mini-review of the Experience and Theories of Emotion:

1. D; 2. F; 3. M; 4. J; 5. A; 6. N; 7. G; 8. B; 9. L; 10. I; 11. K; 12. H; 13. E; 14. C

113.	expressive	116.	electrodermal	119.	control	122.	fool
114.	lying	117.	relevant	120.	imprecision	123.	innocent
115.	increased	118.	greater	121.	reactivity	124.	accuracy

Anatomy of a Contemporary Research Study: How Accurate Are Lie Detectors at Judging Guilt and Innocence? *Read the summary of the study presented on page 435-436 in your textbook and answer the following questions.*

What was the rationale for the study?
Kleinmuntz and Szucko wanted to test the accuracy of the lie detectors.

What methodology did the authors use to test the hypothesis?
Trained professional polygraphers were presented with the polygraphs of 50 thieves and innocent people.

What was the outcome and what did the authors conclude the results meant?
The results showed that the polygraphers correctly identified 76 percent of the guilty persons and 61 percent of the innocent persons. Certainly, the accuracy leaves a lot to be desired, especially the high rate of identifying innocent persons as guilty.

125.	Guilty Knowledge	126.	relevant	127.	irrelevant	128. false-negative

Practice Test A:

1. a. **Correct: Emotion is defined as a motivated state marked by physiological arousal, expressive behavior, and mental experience.**
   b. Incorrect: Motivation is the psychological process that energizes and directs our behavior.
   c. Incorrect: Sensation seeking is a type of motivation.
   d. Incorrect: Self-actualization is Maslow's need to be all you can be.

2. a. **Correct: The amygadala is a limbic system structure involved in the expression of emotional responses.**
   b. Incorrect: The cerebellum is not suggested to be involved in emotional expression.
   c. Incorrect: The basal ganglia are not suggested to be involved in emotional expression.
   d. Incorrect: The medulla oblongata has not been suggested to be involved in emotional expression.

3. a. **Correct: Prosody is defined as the changes in the vocal features of speech, and include the rate, pitch, and loudness of the speech.**
   b. Incorrect: Kinesics refers to the detection of movements.
   c. Incorrect: Prosody, not proxemics, is defined as the changes in the vocal features of speech, and include the rate, pitch, and loudness of the speech.
   d. Incorrect: Prosody, not physiognomy, is defined as the changes in the vocal features of speech, and include the rate, pitch, and loudness of the speech.

4. a. Incorrect: Joy, acceptance, fear, surprise, sadness, disgust, anger, and anticipation are Plutchik's eight primary emotions.
   b. Incorrect: Joy, acceptance, fear, surprise, sadness, disgust, anger, and anticipation are Plutchik's eight primary emotions.
   c. **Correct: Joy, acceptance, fear, surprise, sadness, disgust, anger, and anticipation are Plutchik's eight primary emotions; love is a mixed emotion.**
   d. Incorrect: Joy, acceptance, fear, surprise, sadness, disgust, anger, and anticipation are Plutchik's eight primary emotions.

5. a. Incorrect: Emotions differ on the dimensions of pleasantness-unpleasantness and intensity; elation and gladness are both pleasant emotions, thus they vary in intensity.
   b. Incorrect: Emotions differ on the dimensions of pleasantness-unpleasantness and intensity; elation and gladness are both pleasant emotions, thus they vary in intensity.
   c. Incorrect: Emotions differ on the dimensions of pleasantness-unpleasantness and intensity; elation and gladness are both pleasant emotions, thus they vary in intensity.
   d. **Correct: Emotions differ on the dimensions of pleasantness-unpleasantness and intensity; elation and gladness are both pleasant emotions, thus they vary in intensity.**

6. a. Incorrect: Incongruity theory is a theory of humor that argues that humor results when incompatible ideas come together and bring about a surprising outcome.
   b. Incorrect: Disparagement theory argues that we find things humorous when they make us feel superior to others.
   c. Correct: Adaptation-level theory argues that you compare your current circumstances with the past, and as her performance improve, her standards for happiness get higher.
   d. Incorrect: Social-comparison theory argues that happiness is the result of comparing your life circumstances with others, and deeming that yours are more favorable.

7. a. Incorrect: Incongruity theory is a theory of humor that argues that humor results when incompatible ideas come together and bring about a surprising outcome.
   b. Correct: Disparagement theory argues that we find things humorous when they make us feel superior to others.
   c. Incorrect: Adaptation-level theory argues that you compare your current circumstances with the past, and as your circumstances improve, your standards for happiness get higher.
   d. Incorrect: Social-comparison theory argues that happiness is this result of comparing your life circumstances with others and deeming that yours are more favorable.

8. **a. Correct: James-Lange theory argues that you feel an emotion because of the specific pattern of physiological arousal; you've run, you've experienced increased physiological arousal, then you are afraid.**
   b. Incorrect: Cannon-Bard theory argues that the emotion of terror comes when the thalamus perceives the event or object.
   c. Incorrect: Facial-feedback theory claims that your emotion comes from feedback about the position of the facial muscles.
   d. Incorrect: Opponent-process theory argues that strong emotions evoke an opposite emotional response to maintain homeostasis.

9. a. Incorrect: The two-factory theory of emotion argues that emotion results from the physiological arousal and the attribution of a cause for that arousal.
   b. Incorrect: James-Lange theory argues that you feel an emotion because of the specific pattern of physiological arousal; you've run, you've experienced increased physiological arousal, then you are afraid.
   c. Correct: Cannon-Bard theory argues that the emotion of terror comes when the thalamus perceives the event or object.
   d. Incorrect: Opponent-process theory argues that strong emotions evoke an opposite emotional response to maintain homeostasis.

10. a. Incorrect: The two-factor theory of emotion argues that emotion results from the physiological arousal and the attribution of a cause for that arousal.
    b. Incorrect: James-Lange theory argues that you feel an emotion because of the specific pattern of physiological arousal; you've run, you've experienced increased physiological arousal, then you are afraid.
    c. Incorrect: Cannon-Bard theory argues that the emotion of terror comes when the thalamus perceives the event or object.
    d. Correct: Opponent-process theory argues that strong emotions evoke an opposite emotional response to maintain homeostasis.

11. a. Incorrect: The support comes from studies that demonstrate that sensory neurons convey information directly to the hypothalamus, not the medulla oblongata.
    b. Incorrect: The support comes from studies that demonstrate that sensory neurons convey information directly to the hypothalamus, not the corpus callosum.
    c. Correct: The support comes from studies that demonstrate that sensory neurons convey information directly to the hypothalamus.
    d. Incorrect: The support comes from studies that demonstrate that sensory neurons convey information directly to the hypothalamus, not the motor cortex.

12. **a. Correct: The two-factor theory of emotion argues that emotion results from the physiological arousal and the attribution of a cause for that arousal; that is, you attribute your arousal to the person rather than to the drive.**
    b. Incorrect: James-Lange theory argues that you feel an emotion because of the specific pattern of physiological arousal; you've driven, you've experienced increased physiological arousal, then you are in love.
    c. Incorrect: Cannon-Bard theory argues that the emotion of terror comes when the thalamus perceives the event of object.
    d. Incorrect: Opponent-process theory argues that strong emotion evoke an opposite emotional response to maintain homeostasis.

13. a. Incorrect: James-Lange theory argues that you feel an emotion because of the specific pattern of physiological arousal; thus each individual's physiological arousal would need to be different.
 b. Incorrect: Cannon-Bard theory argues that the emotion of terror comes when the thalamus perceives the event or object.
 c. Incorrect: Opponent-process theory argues that strong emotions evoke an opposite emotional response to maintain homeostasis.
 d. Correct: Cognitive-appraisal theory argues that your interpretation of the event determines your emotion.

14. a. Incorrect: Polygraph tests measure your physiological reactions; not level of motivation.
 b. Incorrect: Polygraph tests measure your physiological reactions;there are no gender differences.
 c. Incorrect: Polygraph tests measure your physiological reactions; there are no age differences.
 d. Correct: Polygraph tests measure your physiological reactions.

Practice Test B:

1. a. Incorrect: These examples are of the differences in intensity of emotions.
 b. Incorrect: These examples are of the differences in intensity of emotions.
 c. Correct: These examples are of the differences in intensity of emotions.
 d. Incorrect: These examples are of the differences in intensity of emotions.

2. a. Incorrect: Norepinephrine, epinephrine, and cholesterol are elevated when individuals are experiencing stress.
 b. Incorrect: Norepinephrine, epinephrine, and cholesterol are elevated when individuals are experiencing stress.
 c. Incorrect: Norepinephrine, epinephrine, and cholesterol are elevated when individuals are experiencing stress.
 d. Correct: Norepinephrine, epinephrine, and cholesterol are elevated when individuals are experiencing stress.

3. a. Incorrect: This occurs in the presence of a threat and may result in the fight-or-flight response.
 b. Correct: The parasympathetic nervous system is active when the threat is removed.
 c. Incorrect: While the central nervous system may mediate and be associated with various emotional states, they are not addressed by the question.
 d. Incorrect: While the somatic nervous system may mediate and be associated with various emotional states, they are not addressed by the question.

4. a. Incorrect: A natural smile is a Duchenne smile, but there are no such things as Duchenne movements.
 b. Incorrect: Research has shown that nonverbal cues allow us to differentiate false emotions from sincere ones.
 c. Incorrect: Research has shown that nonverbal cues allow us to differentiate false emotions from sincere ones.
 d. Correct: Research has shown that nonverbal cues allow us to differentiate false emotions from sincere ones.

5. a. Incorrect: Choice d is correct; the results are too inconsistent to conclude that emotions are universal.
 b. Incorrect: Choice d is correct; the results are too inconsistent to conclude that emotions are universal.
 c. Incorrect: Choice d is correct; the results are too inconsistent to conclude that emotions are universal.
 d. Correct: This chice is correct; the results are too inconsistent to conclude that emotions are universal.

6. a. Incorrect: We tend to prefer an optimal level of nonverbal interaction in social interactions, and this optimal level appears to be a moderate level.
 b. Incorrect: We tend to prefer an optimal level of nonverbal interaction in social interactions, and this optimal level appears to be a moderate level.
 c. Correct: This appears to be the optimal level for both verbal and nonverbal interaction.
 d. Incorrect: We tend to prefer an optimal level of nonverbal interaction in social interactions, and this optimal level appears to be a moderate level.

7. **a. Correct: Joy is the eighth of Plutchik's basic emotions.**
 b. Incorrect: Joy is the eighth of Plutchik's basic emotions.
 c. Incorrect: Joy is the eighth of Plutchik's basic emotions.
 d. Incorrect: Joy is the eighth of Plutchik's basic emotions.

8. a. Incorrect: Research has shown that people who tend to experience intensely pleasant emotions also experience intensely unpleasant emotions.
 b. Incorrect: Research has shown that people who tend to experience intensely pleasant emotions also experience intensely unpleasant emotions.
 c. Incorrect: Research has shown that people who tend to experience intensely pleasant emotions also experience intensely unpleasant emotions.
 d. Correct: Research has shown that people who tend to experience intensely pleasant emotions also experience intensely unpleasant emotions.

9. **a. Correct: Social-comparison theory claims that we feel happy when we perceive our circumstances as better than those of others.**
   b. Incorrect: Fight or flight is not a theory; it refers to the response of the autonomic nervous system to threat.
   c. Incorrect: Optimal level of arousal theory is a theory of motivation, not arousal.
   d. Incorrect: Evolutionary theory argues that characteristics develop because that allows for the survival of a species.

10. a. Incorrect: Social-comparison theory claims you would be happier if you compare yourself to those less fortunate.
   b. Incorrect: Wealth does not correlate with happiness.
   c. Correct: Humor helps to make people happier.
   d. Incorrect: It is the rise in expectation for ourselves, not the act of comparison that makes us unhappy.

11. a. Incorrect: Release theory claims that laughing allowed the children to release the frustration energy that would have later produced aggression.
   b. Correct: Release theory claims that laughing allowed the children to release the frustration energy that would have later produced aggression.
   c. Incorrect: Release theory claims that laughing allowed the children to release the frustration energy that would have later produced aggression.
   d. Incorrect: Release theory claims that laughing allowed the children to release the frustration energy that would have later produced aggression.

12. **a. Correct: Opponent-process theory claims that once we feel an emotion, we will feel an opposite emotion to allow us to maintain homeostasis.**
   b. Incorrect: Cognitive-appraisal theory discusses the role of appraisal of the situation.
   c. Incorrect: Adaptation-level theory discusses our comparison of our present selves with our past selves and would not lead to that rapid a change.
   d. Incorrect: Release theory claims that an action such as laughing or crying would allow the cathartic release of energy.

13. **a. Correct: James-Lange theory argues that an event produces a specific pattern of physiological activity that evokes a specific emotion.**
   b. Incorrect: The theory states that an emotion is produced when an object or event is perceived by the thalamus, which conveys this information simultaneously to the cerebral cortex and the skeletal muscles and autonomic nervous system.
   c. Incorrect: The brain counteracts a strong positive or negative emotion by evoking an opposite emotional response.
   d. Incorrect: This is a behavioral theory of emotion.

14. a. Incorrect: Two-factor theory argues that emotions are the result of physiological arousal and the attribution of a cause to the arousal.
   b. Correct: Facial-feedback theory argues that feedback from the facial smile muscles provide different patterns of sensory feedback.
   c. Incorrect: Cognitive-appraisal theory claims that emotions come from our interpretation of the situation we are in at the time.
   d. Incorrect: Social-comparison theory claims that we experience emotions based on our comparison of our circumstances with those of others.

15. a. Incorrect: The arousal is a physiological arousal.
   b. Incorrect: We attribute, as opposed to a misattributiion, a cause.
   c. Incorrect: Neither of these choices is correct.
   d. Correct: Two-factor theory argues that emotions result from a physiological arousal and our attribution of a cause for that arousal.

16. **a. Correct: Two-factor theory also claims that emotions result from our appraisal of the situation; however, it places emphasis on physiological arousal as well.**
   b. Incorrect: Facial-feedback theory claims that emotions result from feedback from facial muscles.
   c. Incorrect: There is no opponent theory of emotions; it is known as the opponent-process theory.
   d. Incorrect: Two-factor theory also claims that emotions result from our appraisal of the situation; however, it places emphasis on physiological arousal as well.

17. a. Incorrect: The research into theories of emotions has been inconclusive, and no one theory has been able to explain them.
   b. Incorrect: The research into theories of emotions has been inconclusive, and no one theory has been able to explain them.
   c. Incorrect: The research into theories of emotions has been inconclusive, and no one theory has been able to explain them.
   d. Correct: The research into theories of emotions has been inconclusive, and no one theory has been able to explain them.

18. a. Incorrect: Brainwashing has not been examined as a factor.
   b. Incorrect: Hypnosis has not been examined as a factor.
   c. Correct: Since the polygraph test measures physiological reactivity and tranquilizers suppress reactivity, they have been shown to reduce the detectability of lying.
   d. Incorrect: Stress increases physiological reactivity and increases the likelihood of detecting lying.

19. a. Incorrect: The Wada test is used to determine lateralization of cerebral cortex function in which one hemisphere of the brain is anesthetized.
   b. Correct: The test described in the example is the Guilty Knowledge Test.
   c. Incorrect: Polygraph tests do not ask questions using details of the crime.
   d. Incorrect: The electroencephalogram is a measurement of brain-wave activity.

20. a. Incorrect: Electrodermal activity and heart rate are measured by the polygraph test, thus they are all related.
   b. Correct: Electrodermal activity and heart rate are measured by the polygraph test, thus they are all related; cognitive appraisal is not.
   c. Incorrect: Electrodermal activity and heart rate are measured by the polygraph test, thus they are all related.
   d. Incorrect: Electrodermal activity and heart rate are measured by the polygraph test, thus they are all related.

Essay Questions:

1. Polygraphs merely measure physiological reactivity. Those with low reactivity show little difference between their responses to control questions and to relevant questions. Thus, an unemotional criminal will pass the test, while a highly emotional innocent person will not. Also, reactivity can be influenced by the use of tranquilizers or the timed induction of pain (during control questions).

2. Briefly, as you enter you become more alert. Specific physiological changes occur. Also, your pupils dilate, your mouth becomes dry, goose bumps appear, and you perspire. Because the guest's presence requires that you postpone your presentation, your level of arousal subsides. Physiological changes occur.

13 Personality

LEARNING OBJECTIVES

After studying this chapter, you should be able to:

1. Define personality and explain the significance of the "Barnum Effect" in relation to personality description. (p. 442)

2. Summarize the important concepts and features of the psychoanalytic approach to personality structure and development, emphasizing the role of the various defense mechanisms. (p. 442-446)

3. Describe the important concepts and features of Alfred Adler's and Carl Jung's neo-Freudian theories of personality. (p. 447-449)

4. List and describe two psychoanalytically based personality tests, and describe the relative strengths and weaknesses of the psychoanalytic approach to personality. (p. 449-451)

5. Explain what is meant by the dispositional approach to personality and describe the important features of both Hans Eysenck's three-factor theory of personality and Gordon Allport's trait theory of personality. (p. 452-453)

6. List and describe the origins of three commonly used personality inventories, emphasizing how each of them is used today. (p. 454-456)

7. Explain the strengths and weaknesses of the dispositional approach to personality, mentioning the status of the five-factor theory. (p. 456-457)

8. Describe the main focus of behavioral approaches to personality and summarize the important features of operant conditioning and the social-cognitive theory of personality, emphasizing the concepts of reciproca determinism and self-efficacy. (p. 457-458)

9. List and describe two behaviorally oriented techniques of personality assessment, and then summarize the findings regarding the concept of locus of control. (p. 459-460)

10. Describe the main focus of the cognitive approach to personality and the important features of Kelly's personal-construct theory, emphasizing the use of the REP Test and the application of personal-construct theory in therapy. (p. 460-462)

11. Describe the main focus of the humanistic approach to personality and contrast this with the psychoanalytic and behavioral approaches. (p. 462-463)

12. Describe the important features of both Maslow's and Rogers's theories of personality, mentioning the use of the POI and Q-sort in assessing personality, and then summarize the strengths and weaknesses of the humanistic approach to personality. (p. 463-465)

13. Offer a brief overview of the history of the biopsychological approach to personality from the ancient Greeks up through the theories of William Sheldon. (p. 465-466)

14. Summarize the findings of behavioral geneticists regarding the relative influence of genetic and environmental factors. (p. 467-470)

15. Describe the controversy surrounding Walter Mischel's challenge to the traditional notion of consistency of personality. (p. 470-472)

COMPREHENSIVE GUIDED REVIEW

Your **personality** is your unique, relatively__(1)__ pattern of thinking, feeling, and behaving. To appreciate the _(2)_ of each personality, see if you recognize yourself in the following two sentences:

"You have a strong need for other people to like and admire you. You have a tendency to be critical of yourself."

Although this is admittedly an incomplete__(3)_ description, the sentences most likely are accurate. The acceptance of personality descriptions that are true of almost everyone is known as the "__(4)__ effect." This effect demonstrates that to be__(5)__, personality descriptions must distinguish one person from another. Given that you have a unique personality, how does it develop? In Chapter 1, you were introduced to the contemporary psychological __(6)__. Since then, the themes of the various perspectives have threaded their way through almost every chapter. In this chapter, the themes are called "__(7)__." Use the information to bolster your understanding of the major points of view, as well as your own.

I. The Psychoanalytic Approach:

Freud's Psychosexual Theory: Early in his career, Freud became interested in psychiatry after studying with Charcot, who demonstrated the power of__(8)__ in treating *conversion hysteria.* Freud attributed the symptoms of conversion hysteria to__(9)__ sexual conflicts, symbolized in symptoms such as deafness, blindness, or paralysis, for which there was no physical cause. Later in his career Freud expanded his theory to include inhibited __(10)__, as well as inhibited sexuality, as important determinants of personality. This led him to claim that we are __(11)__by both a life instinct, Eros, and a death instinct, Thanatos.

Levels of Consciousness: Freud divided the mind into three levels:

1) The__(12)__ *mind* is a tiny part of the mind containing continually shifting feelings, memories, and perceptions.
2) The__(13)__ *mind* is just below the conscious, containing memories that we can recall at will.
3) The__(14)__ *mind* is the bulk of the mind, containing material that we cannot recall at will.

Through__(15)__, threatening thoughts or feelings are shifted from the conscious to the unconscious. This notion led to the concept of *psychic*__(16)__, which holds that all behavior is influenced by unconscious motives. Psychic determinism is exhibited in Freudian slips.

The Structure of Personality: Freud distinguished three structures:

1) The **id,** the unconscious home of__(17)__ biological drives—primarily sex and aggression—governed by the pleasure principle and is concerned only with immediate gratification.
2) The **ego,** which is governed by the__(18)__ **principle,** which directs the expression of sex and aggression in socially acceptable ways.
3) The **superego** contains the__(19)__, which acts as our moral guide, promoting feelings of guilt for wrongdoings, and the *ego ideal,* which makes us feel good for being good.

Defense Mechanisms: The ego may resort to defense mechanisms, which distort reality, to protect itself from__(20)__ caused by id impulses, particularly those of sex and aggression. The ego may also use defense mechanisms to relieve the anxiety caused by unpleasant emotional experiences and unacceptable personal characteristics. The defense mechanisms include the following:

1) *Repression,* which is the banishment of all__(21)__ thoughts, feelings, and memories into the unconscious mind. All defense mechanisms involve repression.
2) __(22)__, which is the refusal to admit a particular aspect of personality.
3) *Regression,* which is the display of__(23)__ behaviors that have relieved anxiety in the past.
4) __(24)__, which involves providing socially acceptable reasons for our inappropriate behaviors.

5) ___(25)___, which involves reducing anxiety by reacting to emotional situations in a detached, unemotional way.
6) ___(26)___, which involves fearing the consequences of expressing our feelings toward a particular person, and expressing them toward someone less threatening.
7) ___(27)___, which is attributing our undesirable feelings to others when we cannot accept them ourselves.
8) *Reaction formation*, which involves acting in a manner___(28)___ to our true feelings.
9) ___(29)___, which is reacting to a personal deficiency by developing another talent.
10) ___(30)___, which is expressing sexual or aggressive impulses through indirect, socially acceptable outlets. Freud saw this as the most successful defense mechanism.

Psychosexual Development: Freud assumed that personality development depended on changes in the distribution of sexual energy, which he called ___(31)___, in regions of the body he called **erogenous zones.** He was concerned with the stages of___(32)___ *development.* The failure to progress smoothly through a particular stage may cause___(33)___, or the tendency to continue to engage in behaviors associated with that stage. The stages and their characteristics are as follows:

1) The first year of infancy is the **oral stage.** The important conflict is *weaning*. Inadequate weaning may produce fixation, whereas too much oral___(34)___ may lead to an oral-dependent or oral-aggressive personality.
2) At the age of 1, a child enters the **anal stage.** The important conflict is toilet training. Inadequate toilet training may lead to fixation at the anal stage. The result is either an *anal-expulsive* or ______(35)______personality.
3) Between the ages of 3 and 5, the child passes through the___(36)___ **stage,** in which pleasure is gained from the genitals. This stage involves the resolution of the **Oedipus complex,** which leads a boy to give up his desire for his mother because of___(37)___ *anxiety,* and resolution of the **Electra complex,** which leads a girl to become angry at her mother because of_____(38)_____. She then fears losing her mother's love, thus identifies with her mother, still hoping to attract her father. Freud called the process by which boys and girls adopt parental values, **identification.** Identification is what allows the child to develop a___(39)___.
4) The fifth year on to puberty is the___(40)___ **stage.** This period involves the development of social skills and friendships.
5) Finally, during adolescence, the child reaches the___(41)___ **stage.** During this stage, the child becomes sexually attracted to other people.

Freud assumed that personality was essentially fixed by the age of 5 years; thus to him the first three stages were the important determinants of personality___(42)___.

Adler's Theory of Individual Psychology: Those who made alterations in Freud's theory became known as ___(43)___. Adler was one of the most influential neo-Freudians. He deemphasized the importance of sexual motivation and the unconscious mind and developed his own theory, which he called___(44)___ psychology. Based on his own childhood experiences, Adler argued that children feel weak and dependent, and as a result they develop an _____(45)_____. This motivates them to compensate by striving for superiority.

Striving for superiority is healthiest when it leads to a concern for others, which he called_____(46)_____. This striving, however, may lead to___(47)___, as in *masculine protest.* This protest applies to both sexes, wherein individuals seek to prove themselves by ___(48)___ others. Furthermore, in the course of striving, a *style of life* based on *fictional*___(49)___ develops. He called this the "guiding self ideal." This means that we are motivated by beliefs that may not be objectively true.

Jung's Theory of Analytic Psychology: Freud's favorite disciple was Carl___(50)___. He had hoped that Jung would eventually become his successor as leader of the___(51)___ movement. However, in 1914, Jung and Freud parted ways, especially because of Jung's deemphasis of the___(52)___ motive. Jung called his version of psychoanalysis___(53)___ psychology.

Although he agreed with Freud that we each have our own unconscious mind (the___(54)___ **unconscious**), Jung claimed that people share a common unconscious mind called the ___(55)___ **unconscious:** the repository of inherited memories **(archetypes)** passed from generation to generation. Jung felt that___(56)___ influence our dreams, religious symbols, and artistic creations. He distinguished between the feminine archetype in men (__(57)__) and the masculine archetype in women (__(58)__). Jung argued that a psychologically healthy person maintains a__(59)__ between masculinity and femininity, as opposed to the extreme of a "macho" male or "prissy" female. Additionally, Jung distinguished between two personality types: the socially outgoing and environmentally attentive ___(60)___, and the socially reserved, privately directed __(61)__.

Other neo-Freudians include Karen Horney, Harry Stack Sullivan, and Erich Fromm.

Karen Horney: She was the first eminent female psychoanalyst. Horney claimed that personality develops from a child's attempt to seek security by overcoming basic__(62)__, a feeling of isolation, and helplessness. Horney disagreed with Freud's notion of____(63)____ and claimed instead that women feel envy because of men's traditionally superior rights and social status.

Harry Stack Sullivan: Placed a large emphasis on the importance of healthy__(64)__ relationships. He felt that when we reject unpleasant experiences and, as a result, fail to work at improving the inadequate social relations that caused them, we then develop__(65)__ ways of dealing with anxiety.

Erich Fromm: Based his theory on the individual's conflict between the need for__(66)__ and the anxiety that freedom brings. He presented these views in his book *Escape from Freedom*, but is most well known for his book *The Art of Loving*.

Psychoanalytic Assessment of Personality: Graphology served as a forerunner of modern psychoanalytic assessment techniques known as **projective tests.** Projective tests are based on the assumption that we will "project" our__(67)__ feelings and conflicts onto ambiguous stimuli. Examples of__(68)__ tests include the **Rorschach test** and the **Thematic Apperception Test.**

The Rorschach Test: The test consists of ten bilaterally symmetrical__(69)__. In responding to the stimuli, the person tells what he or she sees in each one and then reports the features of the inkblot that prompted the response. Scoring is relatively__(70)__, and after scoring each response, the examiner uses clinical judgment, along with an available scoring system, to write a profile of a person's motives and__(71)__. Published reviews of studies using the test reveal that it has moderately high__(72)__, making it an adequate, though not outstanding, personality test.

The Thematic Apperception Test: The__(73)__ was developed by Henry Murray and Christiana Morgan. It is comprised of cards showing people in__(74)__ situations. Responses to the following questions are scored and interpreted:

1) What is happening in the card?
2) What events led up to that situation?
3) Who are the people in the card?
4) How do they feel?
5) How does the situation turn out?

Murray and Morgan felt that the test would reveal the subjects' most important__(75)__. A recent review of the research on the TAT found that it is a moderately good predictor of__(76)__ achievement, such as career success, and has been used in psychotherapy to examine the use of defense mechanisms.

Status of the Psychoanalytic Approach: Although__(77)__ approach has been the most influential, it has received only limited support for its concepts. However, probably the greatest weakness of Freud's theory is that many of its terms refer to processes that are not__(78)__, or measurable. Nonetheless, psychoanalysis has revealed that much of our behavior is governed by irrational motives and__(79)__ forces and has contributed greatly to our understanding of personality. Additionally, it has stimulated interest in studying__(80)__ behavior and development and has demonstrated the importance of early childhood experiences.

Adler's theory has influenced cognitive and__(81)__ psychology by its emphasis on the importance of our subjective experience of reality. Current interest in Type A behavior can be traced to__(82)__ concept of a "style of life." Finally, although Jung's concept of__(83)__ has been criticized because it violates mechanisms of inheritance, his theory has received substantial research support, some of which will be discussed in Chapter 14.

Stop here and take a short study break. When you return, complete the mini-review of psychoanalytic theory provided below.

Mini-review of Psychoanalytic Theories of Personality: Match each term with its correct description.

________1. unconscious mind
________2. projection
________3. Thanatos
________4. phallic stage
________5. conversion hysteria
________6. Rorschach test
________7. collective unconscious
________8. conscience
________9. ego
________10. archetypes
________11. conscious mind
________12. reaction formation
________13. animus
________14. extravert
________15. displacement
________16. defense mechanisms
________17. personality
________18. compensation
________19. psychic determinism
________20. projective tests
________21. libido
________22. denial
________23. anal stage
________24. Oedipus complex
________25. identification
________26. Alfred Adler
________27. Eros
________28. ego ideal
________29. sublimation
________30. Harry Stack Sullivan
________31. id
________32. rationalization
________33. latency stage
________34. "Barnum effect"
________35. regression
________36. genital stage
________37. preconscious mind
________38. repression
________39. superego
________40. anima

A. Your unique, relatively consistent pattern of thinking, feeling, and behaving
B. Term for the acceptance of personality descriptions that are true of almost everyone
C. Symptoms of this include deafness, blindness, or paralysis, for which there is no physical cause
D. The tiny part of the mind containing continually shifting feelings, memories, and perceptions
E. Freud's death instinct
F. The personality structure that is the unconscious home of inborn biological drives—primarily sex and aggression—governed by the pleasure principle and concerned only with immediate gratification
G. Freud's term for the life instinct
H. The mechanism by which threatening thoughts or feelings are shifted from the conscious to the unconscious
I. The refusal to admit a particular aspect of one's personality
J. Personality structure governed by the reality principle; directs the expression of sex and aggression in socially acceptable ways
K. Is found just below the conscious, containing memories that we can recall at will
L. Mechanisms, which distort reality, used to protect the ego from anxiety caused by id impulses, particularly those of sex and aggression
M. Jung's term for the repository of inherited memories passed from generation to generation
N. This the bulk of the mind, containing material that we cannot recall at will
O. Personality structure that contains the conscience and the ego ideal
P. A socially outgoing and environmentally attentive individua
Q. Principle that holds that all behavior is influenced by unconscious motives.
R. Conflict that leads a boy to give up his desire for his mother because of castration anxiety
S. Portion of the superego that acts as our moral guide, promoting feelings of guilt for wrongdoings
T. Defense mechanism that involves providing socially acceptable reasons for our inappropriate behaviors
U. The failure to progress smoothly through a particular stage; or the tendency to continue to engage in behaviors associated with that stage
V. The important conflict during this stage is weaning
W. Portion of the superego that makes us feel good for being good
X. Mechanism that reduces anxiety by reacting to emotional situations in a detached, unemotional way
Y. Freud's favorite disciple; he deemphasized the sex motive and called his version of psychoanalysis, "analytic psychology"
Z. Involves fearing the consequences of expressing our feelings toward a particular person, and expressing them toward someone less threatening
Aa. Freud's term for changes in the distribution of sexual energy

________41. Erich Fromm
________42. introvert
________43. Karen Horney
________44. intellectualization
________45. fixation
________46. Thematic Apperception Test
________47. Electra complex
________48. Carl Jung
________49. oral stage
________50. personal unconscious

Bb. Attributing our undesirable feelings to others when we cannot accept them ourselves
Cc. The important conflict during this stage is toilet training
Dd. Involves acting in a manner opposite to our true feelings
Ee. The process by which boys and girls adopt parental values; allows the child to develop a superego
Ff. Reacting to a personal deficiency by developing another talent
Gg. Jung's term for your own unconscious mind
Hh. Expressing sexual or aggressive impulses through indirect, socially acceptable outlets. Freud saw this as the most successful defense mechanism
Ii. Jung's term for the feminine archetype in men
Jj. Freud's conflict that leads a girl to become angry at her mother because of penis envy; she then fears losing her mother's love, thus identifies with her mother, still hoping to attract her father
Kk. He was one of the most influential neo-Freudians; he deemphasized the importance of sexual motivation and the unconscious mind and developed his own theory, which he called "individual psychology"
Ll. A socially reserved, privately directed individual
Mm. In this stage, pleasure is gained from the genitals
Nn. Jung's term for a common unconscious mind that all people share
Oo. Jung's term for the masculine archetype in women
Pp. This Freudian stage involves the development of social skills and friendships
Qq. Neo-Freudian theorist who placed a large emphasis on the importance of healthy social relationships
Rr. The child reaches this Freudian stage during adolescence and becomes sexually attracted to other people
Ss. Tests based on the assumption that we will "project" our repressed feelings and conflicts onto ambiguous stimuli
Tt. She was the first eminent female psychoanalyst; claimed that personality develops from a child's attempt to seek security by overcoming basic anxiety, a feeling of isolation, and helplessness
Uu. His theory is based on the individual's conflict between the need for freedom and the anxiety that freedom brings
Vv. The test consists of ten bilaterally symmetrical inkblots
Ww. Test comprised of cards showing people in ambiguous situations
Xx. The display of immature behaviors that have relieved anxiety in the past

II. The Dispositional Approach: This approach considers the apparent stability and consistency of personality in regard to relatively enduring personal___(84)__ called *types* or *traits.*

Type Theories: Types are personality differences that are the result of an inborn___(85)__ to act in a particular fashion and are governed by a single characteristic. The most influential theory of personality types is **Eysenck's three-factor theory.** Eysenck used the techniques of____(86)____ to identify three dimensions of personality. By measuring where a person falls on these three dimensions, __(87)__ claims we can determine his or her personality type: 1) The dimension of__*(88)*__ measures stability/instability; 2) the dimension of__(89)__ measures tough mindedness/tender-mindedness; and 3) the dimension of *extraversion* measures a person's level of___(90)_/extraversion. This dimension has stimulated the most research interest. There is recent evidence that Eysenck's theory may have a__(91)__ basis. For example, studies of twins indicate that neuroticism, psychoticism, and___(92)__ all have a genetic basis.

Trait Theories: A __(93)__ is a relatively enduring, cross-situationally consistent personality characteristic that is inferred from a person's behavior. The most influencial trait theory of personality has been proposed by Gordon _(94)__. He distinguished three kinds of traits: 1) __(95)_traits are similar to personality types because they affect every aspect of a person's life; 2) __(96)_traits are the most important traits. They affect many aspects but with less pervasiveness than cardinal traits; and 3) **secondary traits** are the least important. They affect relatively__(97)__ aspects of our lives.

Dispositional Assessment of Personality: The dispositional assessment of personality relies on tests of personality __(98)__or traits. These are called **objective tests,** or__(99)_, because they present statements rather than ambiguous stimuli characteristic of projective tests. For example, the **Profile of Mood States** test is an__(100)__ test that has shown that elite athletes tend to share a personality profile.

Tests of Personality Types: The most popular objective test is the__(101)__ **Type Indicator.** It is an objective dispositional test based on__(102)__ theory. The test assesses personality__(103)__, drawing from Jung's analytical theory of personality. The test has satisfactory validity and has been used in a variety of research.

Tests of Personality Traits: The most widely used test of personality is the **Minnesota Multiphasic Personality Inventory (MMPI).** The MMPI uses an__(104)__ method to develop questions to discriminate between people who differ on the trait of interest. It was developed to diagnose psychological__(105)__ and has ten clinical scales. (*See Table 13.2 on page 455 in your textbook for a list.*) It also has four__(106)_ *scales* that test for evasiveness, defensiveness, lying to look good, and faking to look bad. Because the test was initially__(107)__ more than 50 years ago on a narrow segment of the population, it has been revised and updated as the MMPI-2.

Another popular personality assessment test is the **16 Personality Factor Questionnaire (16 PF).** Developed by Cattell, the test is used for__(108)__ personality testing rather than for diagnosing psychological disorders.

Status of the Dispositional Approach: Although successful in__(109)__ individual differences, the approach has been less successful in__(110)__ them. One of the few dispositional theories that tries to explain personality is __(111)__ three-factor theory. The existence of the three personality factors that Eysenck presents has been verified by other researchers and has received some__(112)__ support. Additionally, the introversion/extraversion dimension has received especially strong research support.

In the domain of__(113)__ theories, research on personality traits has reduced the number of basic traits from Cattell's 16 to 5. "The Big Five" include: extraversion, neuroticism,__(114)__, conscientiousness, and openness to experience. Early research has provided__(115)__ support for this "five-factor" theory. However, leading personality theorists caution that it is premature to accept it as the best approach to understanding personality.

III. The Behavioral Approach: This approach emphasizes the importance of__(116)__ and environmental factors while discounting biological factors, unconscious influences, and dispositional traits.

Operant Conditioning Theory: This theory is proposed by B. F. Skinner. Skinner is straightforward. __(117)_is merely a person's unique pattern of behavior, tied to specific situations. Accordingly, we are what we__(118)_. We tend to engage in those behaviors that have been positively or negatively__(119)__ and to avoid those that have been__(120)__ or extinguished.

Social-cognitive theory also emphasizes the role of reinforcement and__(121)__ in the development of personality but, unlike traditional behavior theory, argues that__(122)__ processes influence behavior.__(123)__'s social-cognitive theory is based on the fact that much of what we learn is derived from observing people obtaining rewards or punishments. His theory emphasizes the concept of____(124)____, which reflects his belief that neither personal dispositions nor environmental factors can by themselves explain behavior. Bandura assumes that personality__(125)__, environmental factors, and overt behavior affect one another. An important cognitive aspect in **reciprocal determinism** is___(126)__ , which is the extent to which a person believes he or she can perform behaviors necessary to bring about desired outcomes.

Self-efficacy determines our choice of activities, our__(127)__ of effort, and our persistence in the face of obstacles. But what determines whether you will have a feeling of self-efficacy in a given situation? According to Bandura there are four determinants: 1) previous__(128)__, or how well you have done in previous attempts at a given activity; 2) __(129)__experience, or how well others you know have done at a given activity; 3) ____(130)____, or the amount and type of convincing that you are given; and 4) physiological arousal.

Behavioral Assessment of Personality: There are two main approaches. One examines__(131)_ behavior, while the other examines___(132)__ that are closely connected to overt behavior.

Assessment of Overt Behavior: The methods used are as follows:

a) ____(133)____. The subject is observed in real or simulated situations, there should be more than one observer, and a main concern is reactivity. Behavioral observation is more likely to produce valid results when multiple observers are used who know the individual and observe behavior in a variety of situations.

b) ____(134)____*method.* The subject carries a portable device that beeps at random times. On hearing the beep, the subject reports his or her experiences and behaviors at that time. This method has been shown to have practical usefulness.

Cognitive-Behavioral Assessment: One example is__(135)__'s **Internal-External Locus of Control Scale.** Julian Rotter defines_____ __(136)_ _____ as the degree to which we expect that we are in control over events in our lives or that such events are controlled by factors such as fate, luck, or chance. **Locus of control** has been an extremely influential concept and has generated considerable research.

Status of the Behavioral Approach: ____(137)__'s operant conditioning theory of personality has brought attention to the roles of learning and environment but has been criticized by Eysenck for ignoring the influence of __(138)__. Additional criticisms of operant theory are that it views the individual as a___(139)__ responder to the environment and fails to consider cognitive factors. Bandura's concept of self-efficacy has been__(140)__ by research, some of which indicates that self-efficacy can be enhanced by training.

Stop here and take another well-deserved study break.
Complete the mini-review of dispositional and behavioral approaches to personality before moving on to the next section.

Mini-review of the Dispositional and Behavioral Approaches to Personality: Match each term with its correct description.

_______1. secondary traits
_______2. locus of control
_______3. Myers-Briggs Type Indicator
_______4. Eysenck
_______5. types
_______6. cardinal traits
_______7. psychoticism
_______8. Eysenck's three-factor theory
_______9. objective tests
_______10. Minnesota Multiphasic Personality Inventory (MMPI)
_______11. Social-cognitive theory
_______12. behavioral observation
_______13. experience sampling
_______14. Bandura
_______15. neuroticism
_______16. central traits
_______17. trait
_______18. Profile of Mood States
_______19. extraversion
_______20. Gordon Allport
_______21. behavioral approach
_______22. reciprocal determinism
_______23. B. F. Skinner
_______24. self-efficacy
_______25. 16 Personality Factor Questionnaire (16 PF)
_______26. Rotter's Internal-External Locus of Control Scale

A. Personality differences that are the result of an inborn predisposition to act in a particular fashion; are governed by a single characteristic
B. The most influential theory of personality types
C. He used the techniques of factor analysis to identify three dimensions of personality
D. Allport's traits that are similar to personality types because they affect every aspect of a person's life
E. Eysenck's dimension that measures stability/instability
F. The most influential trait theory of personality has been proposed by him
G. Believes that personality is merely a person's unique pattern of behavior, tied to specific situations
H. Method of personality assessment in which the subject carries a portable device that beeps at random times; on hearing the beep, the subject reports his or her experiences and behaviors at that time
I. Eysenck's dimension that measures tough-mindedness/tender-mindedness
J. Dispositional assessments of personality that present statements rather than ambiguous stimuli characteristic of projective tests.
K. The extent to which a person believes he or she can perform behaviors necessary to bring about desired outcomes
L. Eysenck's dimension that measures a person's level of introversion/extraversion
M. The most popular objective test; an objective dispositional test based on psychoanalytic theory
N. A relatively enduring, cross-situationally consistent personality characteristic that is inferred from a person's behavior
O. Allport's traits that are the most important traits; they affect many aspects but with less pervasiveness than cardinal traits
P. This approach emphasizes the importance of learning and environmental factors, while discounting biological factors, unconscious influences, and dispositional traits
Q. A cognitive-behavioral assessment tool that measures the degree to which we expect that we are in control over events in our lives or that such events are controlled by factors such as fate, luck, or chance
R. Allport's traits that are the least important; they affect relatively narrow aspects of our lives
S. Bandura's belief that neither personal dispositions nor environmental factors can by themselves explain behavior
T. Emphasizes the role of reinforcement and punishment in the development of personality but, unlike traditional behavior theory, argues that cognitive processes influence behavior
U. The degree to which we expect that we are in control over events in our lives or that such events are controlled by factors such as fate, luck, or chance
V. An objective test that has shown that elite athletes tend to share a personality profile
W. His theory is based on the fact that much of what we learn is derived from observing people obtaining rewards or punishments; emphasizes the concept of reciprocal determinism; assumes that personality traits, environmental factors, and overt behavior affect one another
X. The most widely used test of personality; uses an empirical method to develop questions to discriminate between people who differ on the trait of

interest; developed to diagnose psychological disorders

Y. Developed by Cattell, the test is used for general personality testing rather than for diagnosing psychological disorders

Z. Method of personality assessment in which the subject is observed in real or simulated situations; more likely to produce valid results when multiple observers are used who know the individual and observe behavior in a variety of situations

IV. The Cognitive Approach: This approach recognizes the influence of__(141)_ on behavior. It also pays _(142)_attention to subjective experience and__(143)_ attention to objective situations than does social-cognitive theory.

Personal-Construct Theory: This theory is the most influential cognitive theory of personality and was developed by George__(144)_. It claims that people try to make sense of the world by continually testing and revising _(145)_ about social reality. According to Kelly, each of these hypotheses is a **personal construct.** It is your characteristic pattern of__(146)___ that determines your personality. Personal constructs are___(147)_. Consequently, people are rated on categories such as *shy outgoing, safe dangerous,* or *selfish generous.*

Kelly called our ability to apply personal constructs to a given situation____(148)___, which is divided into three phases: the *circumspection-preemption-control cycle.* During the__(149)_ *phase,* we evaluate constructs. During the __(150)__ *phase,* we decide which construct is most relevant to the situation. And during the__(151)_ *phase,* we follow a course of action based on the chosen construct. This theory has been useful in researching topics such as self-esteem, ___(152)_, and mourning.

Cognitive Assessment of Personality: The most popular cognitive technique for assessment is the____ (153) ___ *Test (REP Test),* which Kelly derived from his theory. In the REP Test, the subject is presented with sets of three persons whom the subject knows and the subject must specify a way in which two of the persons are similar to each other and different from the third. The REP Test has been put to many uses and has stimulated considerable research.

Status of the Cognitive Approach: Kelly contributed a method of psychotherapy called__(154)__ therapy, which encourages clients to adopt roles that promote new, more adaptive constructs. It has been used successfully in treating people with ____(155)____ or social phobias. The cognitive approach has attracted those who believe that (156)_are more important than unconscious motives or environmental stimuli, but has been criticized by traditional behaviorists who argue that thoughts don't necessarily cause behavior.

V. The Humanistic Approach: This approach assumes that people are naturally__(157)_, quite in contrast with psychoanalytic personality theory. This approach also contrasts with the psychoanalytic and behavioral approaches by accepting conscious___(158)_ mental experience as its subject matter. Moreover, it assumes that we have__(159)__.

Self-Actualization Theory: Abraham__(160)_ presented the first humanistic theory of personality He calls the predisposition to try to reach our potential **self-actualization.** Maslow argues that__(161)_ people share personality characteristics. (Refer to Table 13.3 on page 463 in your textbook for a list of these characteristics.)

Self theory was proposed by Carl___(162)__. He claims that each of us experiences__(163)_ between the self and personal experience, which occurs as the result of the lack of **unconditional positive regard,** or complete__(164)__ during childhood. According to Rogers, psychologically healthy people have congruence between the__(165)_ *self* (Rogers's self) and the ___(166)__ *self* (the person they would like to be). The_(167)_ self-actualized a person, the __(168)_ the incongruence. Rogers claims that one way to protect the actual self is by___(169)_, in which the person notes that a task is very difficult or that factors beyond his or her control might contribute to his or her less-than-ideal behavior or performance.

Humanistic Assessment of Personality: The two main techniques of humanistic theories are the **Personal Orientation Inventory** and the **Q-sort**. The____ (170) ____ **(POI)** is used to assess the degree to which a person is self-actualized. The inventory contains items that force the person to choose between two extremes and compares the individual's responses to the characteristics of__(171)__ individuals. The__(172)__ measures the degree of congruence between a person's actual self and ideal self. In this assessment tool individuals are given a pile of cards with__(173)__ statements on them. Subjects are instructed to place the cards into various plies relating to whether the statement is most or least characteristic of their actual selves. The procedure is then repeated for the ideal self. The similarity between the two piles is compared.

Status of the Humanistic Approach: Research has produced mixed findings in regard to Maslow's concept of __(174)__. A recent view of the self put forth by Higgins (1987) considers the relationship between three selves: the *actual self*, the *ideal self*, and the__(175)__ *self*. We are motivated to reduce our personal distress by reducing the __(176)__ among these selves.

__(177)__psychology has been praised for encouraging the study of love, creativity, and other positive aspects of human experience and has contributed to the rise in interest in self-development. However, this perspective has not gone without criticism. Its critics claim that Humanism ignores both the role of the__(178)__ and the unconscious and it fails to__(179)__ define its terms. Also, some wonder whether it will produce unhappiness for those who pursue__(180)__ but do not have the essential skills or resources to achieve it. Maslow and Rogers have even been accused of unintentionally promoting__(181)__.

Mini-review of Cognitive and Humanistic Theory: Match each term with its correct description.

________1. Personal Orientation Inventory (POI)
________2. preemption phase
________3. Carl Rogers
________4. personal constructs
________5. Role Construct Repertory Test (REP Test)
________6. humanistic approach
________7. Q-sort
________8. circumspection phase
________9. self-handicapping
________10. cognitive approach
________11. unconditional positive regard
________12. personal construct theory
________13. constructive alternativism
________14. Abraham Maslow
________15. fixed-role therapy
________16. control phase
________17. the ideal self

A. This approach recognizes the influence of thoughts on behavior and pays more attention to subjective experience
B. This theory is the most influential cognitive theory of personality and was developed by George Kelly; claims that people try to make sense of the world by continually testing and revising hypotheses about social reality
C. Hypotheses about social reality that are continually tested and revised.
D. Our ability to apply personal constructs to a given situation
E. During this phase we evaluate constructs
F. The most popular cognitive technique for assessment; the subject is presented with sets of three persons whom the subject knows and the subject must specify a way in which two of the persons are similar to each other and different from the third
G. During this phase, Kelly claims that we decide which construct is most relevant to the situation
H. This approach assumes that people are naturally good; accepts conscious phenomenological mental experience as its subject matter
I. Presented the first humanistic theory of personality; argued that self-actualized people share personality characteristics
J. The person we would like to be; the "perfect" self
K. During this phase we follow a course of action based on the chosen construct
L. This is used to assess the degree to which a person is self-actualized; contains items that force the person to choose between two exteremes and compares the individual's responses to the characteristics of self-actualized individuals
M. A method of psychotherapy that encourages clients to adopt roles that promote new, more adaptive constructs
N. Proposed self theory; claims that each of us experiences incongruence between the self and personal experience
O. A way of protecting the actual self in which the person notes that a task is

very difficult or that factors beyond his or her control might contribute to less-than-ideal behavior or performance

P. Measures the degree of congruence between a person's actual self and ideal self; in this assessment tool an individual is given a pile of cards with self-destructive statements on them

Q. Rogers's term for complete acceptance

VI. The Biopsychological Approach: Biological theories of personality have been argued since ancient times. Hippocrates and Galen presented a__(182)_ view of personality when they claimed that **temperament** was reflected by the relative levels of fluids called humors. They associated__(183)_ with a cheerful, or *sanguine,* temperament; phlegm with a__(184)__, or *phlegmatic,* temperament; ____(185)____ with a depressed, or *melancholic,* temperament; and yellow bile with an__(186)__, or *choleric,* temperament. The humoral theory was joined by ___(187)___, the study of the contours of the skull, which were assumed to be associated with specific personality characteristics.__(188)___, the study of physical appearance, was also part of this early history. It assumed that ___(189)___features were associated with specific personality characteristics. Research failed to support both **phrenology** and **physiognomy,** although these views later sparked interest in the study of the biological basis of behavior, especially___(190)__.

Physique and Personality: The scientific study of this relationship began with the work of Kretschmer. But is was ___(191)__ who advanced the study of the physique-personality relationship. Sheldon's **constitutional theory** of personality centered on three types of physiques, or___(192)___, and their associated temperaments. The__(193)__ has a thin, frail body and a shy, restrained, introspective temperament called *cerebrotonia.* The ___(194)__has a muscular, strong body and a bold, assertive, energetic temperament called *somatotonia.* Finally, the__(195)__ has a soft, round body and a relaxed, sociable, easygoing temperament called *viscerotonia.*

Heredity and Personality: Even today, as a century ago, those who follow in the footsteps of__(196)__ believe that evolution has provided us with inborn behavioral tendencies that differ somewhat among us. The field that studies the relationship between heredity and behavior is known as____(197)____.

Biopsychological Assessment of Personality: How can we determine the relationship between heredity and personality? Three different methods are used to attempt to tease out the differences. These include__(198)__ studies and **twin studies.** **Adoption studies** serve to determine the relative contributions of heredity and life experiences by comparing adoptees to their__(199)__ and adoptive parents. The **Texas Adoption Study** found that children tend to resemble their__(200)__ parents more than their__(201)__ parents in personality.
Additionally, studies of__(202)__ twins reared apart provide the strongest support for the biological basis of personality. This result is shown in the "Anatomy of a Contemporary Research Study" section in the text.

Anatomy of a Contemporary Research Study: In Personality Are Identical Twins Reared Apart More Like Their Adoptive Parents or Their Biological Parents? *Read the summary of the Bouchard study on page 468-469 in your textbook and answer the following questions.*

What was the rationale for the study?

What methods did the authors use to test the hypothesis?

What was the outcome of the study and what did the author conclude the results meant?

Status of the Biopsychological Approach: Research has been unable to substantiate Sheldon's claims of a strong relationship between____(203)____ and personality, though there is a modest relationship. One of the problems was a ____(204)____one. When Sheldon conducted his research he measured both the body type and temperament of his subjects, introducing possible experimenter ____(205)____. Nonetheless, some studies have shown that mesomorphic males do tend to be more extraverted,____(206)____, and emotionally stable. Clearly, however, such findings do not indicate a ____(207)____ relationship. There are other factors. Personality differences affect diet and exercise, and these factors may cause differences in physique. Heredity also may cause differences in physique and personality.

How heritable is personality? ____(208)____ is the extent to which the variability in personality within a population is caused by heredity. Along with____(209)____ twin data, about the most that can be said is that personality is most likely determined by the combination of heredity and environment.

Mini-review on Biopsychological Theory of Personality: Match the term with its correct description.

________1. heritability
________2. endomorph
________3. behavioral genetics
________4. mesomorph
________5. Sheldon's constitutional theory
________6. humoral theory
________7. physiognomy
________8. phrenology
________9. ectomorph

A. The extent to which the variability in personality within a population is caused by heredity
B. A biological view of personality that claimed that temperament was reflected by the relative levels of fluids called humors
C. The body type that has a soft, round body and a relaxed, sociable, easygoing temperament called viscerotonia
D. The study of the contours of the skull, which were assumed to be associated with specific personality characteristics
E. The study of physical appearance; assumed that facial features were associated with specific personality characteristics
F. Personality theory centered on three types of physiques, or somatotypes, and their associated temperaments
G. Has a thin, frail body and a shy, restrained, introspective temperament called cerebrotonia
H. Has a muscular, strong body and a bold, assertive, energetic temperament called somatotonia
I. The field that studies the relationship between heredity and behavior

VII. Thinking About Psychology: Is Personality Consistent? During the past two decades, the degree of cross-situational____(210)____ in personality has been the most controversial issue in personality research.

Personality as Inconsistent: Mischel reported in 1968 that personality is much____(211)____ consistent from one situation to another than was commonly believed. He found that the____(212)____ between any two behaviors believed to represent the same underlying behavior was very low. Based on this research and a review of other research, Mischel concluded that our behavior is influenced more by the____(213)____ than by our____(214)____. (The correlation is around .30.)

This raised the question, If personality is inconsistent across situations, why do we perceive consistency in our everyday lives? There are several reasons. First, we may confuse consistency____(215)____ time with consistency ____(216)____situations. Second, we tend to avoid situations that are____(217)____ with our personalities. Third, our ____(218)____ impression of a person may make us discount later behavior that is inconsistent with that impression.

Personality as Consistent: The attacks on____(219)____ consistency have provoked responses from those who claim there is more cross-situational consistency than Mischel believes. First, individuals____(220)____ show consistency on certain traits. Second, cross-situational____(221)____ in behavior depends on whether a person is a *high self-monitor* or a *low self-monitor.* Third, many of the studies that Mischel reviewed were guaranteed to find low cross-situational consistency.

Psychologists have achieved greater success in demonstrating consistency by using____(222)____ which involves observing people's behavior across several situations. How the people____(223)____ behave, but not necessarily how they ____(224)____ behave is then determined. Using this method, the____(225)____ between traits and behaviors becomes higher (around .60). The importance of the use of behavioral aggregation is demonstrated in the study featured in the "Anatomy of a Classic Research Study" section in your textbook.

Anatomy of a Classic Research Study: Is Personality Consistent from One Situation to Another? *Read the summary of the Dudycha study on page 472 in your textbook and answer the following questions.*

What was the rationale for the study?

What methods did the authors use to test the hypothesis?

What was the outcome of the study and what did the author conclude that the results meant?

KEY RESEARCH FINDINGS

Provide the details of the following key research studies in psychology:

1. **Waldrop(1984):** Gave people personality descriptions based on astrology. (Page 442)
2. **Adler(1927):** Developed the individual psychology theory. (Page 447-448)
3. **Jung(1959/1969):** Claimed that archetypes influence our dreams, religious symbols, and artistic creations. (Page 449)
4. **Peeples(1990):** Questions the practical usefulness of graphology. (Page 450)
5. **Parker(1993):** Reviewed the Rorschach test as being an adequate but not outstanding personality test. (Page 450)
6. **Morgan & Murray (1935):** Developed the Thematic Apperception Test (TAT). (Page 450)
7. **Cramer & Blatt (1990):** Showed an association between use of defense mechanisms as revealed by TAT and a reduction in psychological symptoms. (Page 450)
8. **Potgieter & Venter (1995):** Found that students who remained in an exercise program showed less neuroticism than those who dropped out. (Page 452)
9. **Olmo & Stevens (1984):** Found more introversion in chess experts than among the general population. (Page 452)
10. **Briggs & Myers (1943):** Developed a dispositional test of personality characteristics based on Jung's analytical theory of personality. (Page 454)
11. **Smith, Munday, & Windham (1995):** Studied teaching styles based on the Myers-Briggs Type Indicator. (Page 454)
12. **Hathaway & McKinley (1943):** Developed the Minnesota Multiphasic Personality Inventory (MMPI), which measures personality traits. (Page 454)
13. **Adler (1989):** Found that the MMPI standards were too narrow to reflect society from the 1980s and beyond. (Page 455)
14. **Helmes & Reddon (1993):** Found that the new norms incorporated into the revised MMPI made for an improved test. (Page 455)
15. **Teichman & Teichman (1990):** Explained that the difficulty in overcoming depression can be linked to reciprocal determinism. (Page 458)
16. **Hillbrand & Waite (1994):** Used experience sampling to study sex offenders. (Page 459)
17. **Alliger & Williams (1993):** Used experience sampling to study clerical workers. (Page 459)
18. **Manning (1990):** Used experience sampling to study elementary school children's self-talk. (Page 459)
19. **Rotter (1966):** Developed the Internal-External Locus of Control Scale, a cognitive-behavioral assessment. (Page 459)
20. **Kelly (1963):** Developed the personal-construct theory of personality. (Page 461)
21. **Mikulincer & Peer-Goldin (1991):** Found that as students' congruence between their actual and ideal selves increased, their feelings of happiness increased. (Page 464)

22. **Bordages (1989):** Found that students who scored higher on the Personal Orientation Inventory (POI) (which measures the degree of self-actualization as described by Maslow) were more likely to perform independently on a reasoning task. (Page 464)
23. **Fogarty (1994):** Found that students who scored low on the POI at the beginning of a course found they increased in self-actualization by the end of the term. (Page 464)
24. **Hyman (1988):** Found that self-actualization in women 19-55 years old increased with age. (Page 464)
25. **Hawkins, Hawkins, & Ryan (1989):** Found that self-actualization did not increase with age in faculty members 30-68 years old. (Page 464)
26. **Andersen & Ross (1984):** Survey showed that most people would feel that others would know them best if they knew their mental experiences rather than by overt behavior. (Page 465)
27. **May (1982):** Challenged the assumption of innate human goodness. (Page 465)
28. **Kretschmer (1925):** Related the personality to physique. (Page 466)
29. **Sheldon & Stevens (1942):** Tested Sheldon's constitutional theory of personality, which divides people into somatotypes and ascribes particular temperaments to each type. (Page 466)
30. **Schonemann & Schonemann (1994):** Studied the effect of genetics on personality using identical and fraternal twin studies. (Page 467)
31. **Loehlin, Horn, & Willerman (1990):** Said that children's personalities will tend to resemble their biological parents as opposed to their adoptive parents. (Page 467)
32. **Bouchard & McGue (1990):** Found that personality is more dependent on genetics than environment, based on case studies of identical twins reared apart. (Page 468)
33. **Lester, Kaminsky, & McGovern (1993):** Found no relationship between physique and personality in day-care-age children. (Page 469)
34. **Lester & Wosnack (1990):** Found that ectomorphic infants were more emotionally responsive that infants with other physiques. (Page 470)
35. **Mischel (1968):** Theorized that personality is not necessarily consistent in all situations, and found that the correlation between any two behaviors representing the same personality trait is .30. (Page 470)
36. **Bem & Allen (1974):** Found that people who claimed a consistent personality trait were more likely to demonstrate that trait consistently. (Page 471)
37. **Herringer (1993):** Found that the correlation between personality traits and exhibition of that trait is higher when averaged across a variety of situations. (Page 472)
38. **Dudycha (1936):** Found that behavioral aggregation increased the correlation of personality traits and occurrences of that trait in general behavior. (Page 472)

PRACTICE TEST A

1. If you accepted an astrologer's description of you as "a person who is usually friendly but likes to be alone sometimes, a conscientious individual, who sometimes fails to live up to his (her) standards," you would be succumbing to the
   a. Barnum effect.
   b. "New Age" effect.
   c. pseudo-Freudian effect.
   d. intellectualization effect.

Obj.: 1 Page: 442

2. If you are giving a public speech and accidentally replace a word with a sexual word, a psychoanalytic psychologist would most likely attribute this "Freudian slip" to
   a. regression.
   b. psychic determinism.
   c. subliminal perception.
   d. reciprocal determinism.

Obj.: 2 Page: 443

3. The characters in the *Star Wars* movies may represent the concept of
   a. archetypes.
   b. somatotypes.
   c. central traits.
   d. cardinal traits.

Obj.: 3 Page: 449

4. The assumption that we will reveal our unconscious feelings when responding to ambiguous stimuli is the basis of the
   a. type test.
   b. trait test.
   c. projective test.
   d. Role Construct Repertory Test.

Obj.: 4 Page: 450

5. If you cannot predict from moment to moment whether a friend of yours will be happy or sad, he or she would most likely score high on Hans Eysenck's dimension of
   a. neuroticism.
   b. psychoticism.
   c. obsessiveness.
   d. hypochondriasis.

Obj.: 5 Page: 452

6. If your best friend had a habit of wearing a baseball cap backwards, Gordon Allport would consider this a
   a. central trait.
   b. primary trait.
   c. cardinal trait.
   d. secondary trait.

Obj.: 5 Page: 453

7. The Minnesota Multiphasic Personality Inventory (MMPI) was designed to
   a. diagnose psychological disorders.
   b. measure personality types.
   c. assist people in adjusting to changing work environments.
   d. provide an empirical measure of the unconscious.

Obj.: 6 Page: 454-455

8. Criticisms of the dispositional approach to personality have included that
   a. the approach is useful in explaining personality , but does not describe it.
   b. the approach is good for general personality testing, but not for diagnosing psychological disorders.
   c. the approach is useful in describing behavior, but does not explain it.
   d. the approach does not give operational definitions for its terms.

Obj.: 7 Page: 456-457

9. A person who typically feels happy may usually act friendly, which will, in turn, make people in his immediate environment act positively toward him. This interrelationship of the person, the person's behavior, and the person's environment is an example of Albert Bandura's concept of
   a. self-actualization.
   b. psychic determinism.
   c. reciprocal determinism.
   d. constructive alternativism.

Obj.: 8 Page: 458

10. If you assume that attending class, reading the textbook, and studying your notes will have less effect on your grades than lucky guessing and the grading biases of your professor, you would score low on what Julian Rotter calls your
   a. self-efficacy.
   b. academic flair.
   c. locus of control.
   d. learned optimism.

Obj.: 9 Page: 459-460

11. If you assume that finding out what the placement office offers, reading brochures about possible job opportunities, speaking with alumni, and assertively arranging interviews as opposed to crossing your fingers and simply hoping will increase your chances of getting the best possible job, you would score high on what Rotter calls
   a. learned helplessness.
   b. self-efficacy.
   c. locus of control.
   d. the optimism-pessimism dimension.

Obj.: 10 Page: 460-461

12. According to Carl Rogers, incongruence between the self and experience is affected by the degree of parental
   a. unconditional positive regard.
   b. self-actualization.
   c. positive reinforcement.
   d. harmony.

Obj.: 11 Page: 462-464

13. A person who always complains about minor injuries before playing basketball as an excuse for possibly playing poorly would be engaging in
   a. somatotyping.
   b. self-handicapping.
   c. reciprocal determinism.
   d. constructive alternativism.

Obj.: 12 Page: 464

14. Based on the somatotype theory of personality, tennis player Martina Navratilova, football player Jim Kelly, and basketball player Michael Jordan should share the temperament of
    a. somatotonia.
    b. musculotonia.
    c. viscerotonia.
    d. cerebrotonia.

Obj.: 13 Page: 466

15. In general the research results as to the relative influence of genetics on personality indicate that
    a. personality is inherited.
    b. personality is learned from the environment via observational learning.
    c. personality is determined both by environment and heredity.
    d. personality is learned from the environment via shaping.

Obj.: 14 Page: 470

16. Mischel (1968) found that the correlation between any two behaviors presumed to represent the same underlying personality trait rarely exceeded
    a. .10.
    b. .25.
    c. .30.
    d. .45.

Obj.: 15 Page: 471

PRACTICE TEST B

1. A "psychic reader" tells a customer, "You are likeable, and affectionate. You are sometimes shy and occasionally have trouble being assertive. You are generally honest and have an active mind." Tom accepts this as an accurate description of his personality and thus he has succumbed to the
    a. Barnum effect.
    b. Barney principle.
    c. Bandura phenomenon.
    d. Bouchard mechanism.

Obj.: 1 Page: 442

2. As she leaves the lecture hall, Nina mistakenly says to her professor, "Your lecture on Freud was really horrific . . . oops, I mean terrific." Nina's behavior is an example of
    a. the reality principle.
    b. Thanatos, or the death instinct.
    c. preconscious motivation.
    d. a Freudian slip.

Obj.: 2 Page: 443

3. Jason was a very angry and aggressive teenager. As an adult, Jason is a very successful inventor and designer of military weapons. A Freudian would call Jason's career choice an example of
    a. projection.
    b. sublimation.
    c. rationalization.
    d. regression.

Obj.: 2 Page: 446

4. Both Jane and Michelle have great business skills. Jane becomes wealthy and successful by developing and successfully marketing a new high-nicotine cigarette. Michelle becomes equally wealthy and successful by developing a solar-powered automobile. What might Alfred Adler say about these two individuals?
    a. While Jane has an inferiority complex, Michelle is clearly striving for superiority through compensation.
    b. While Jane is fixated at the oral stage, Michelle appears to have resolved her Electra complex.
    c. While Michelle is motivated by the fictional finalism "There's a sucker born every minute," Jane is not.
    d. While both are striving for superiority, Michelle is healthier because of her greater social interest.

Obj.: 3 Page: 448

5. One aspect of Jung's theory that has held up well to scientific testing is
   a. the existence of the persona and its opposite, the self.
   b. the development of the anima and animus in all human beings.
   c. the personality types: introversion and extraversion.
   d. inheritance of collective memories and archetypes.

Obj.: 4 Page: 451

6. What research finding supports Eysenck's theory?
   a. Juvenile delinquents score high in psychoticism.
   b. There are significantly more extraverts among expert chess players than in the general population.
   c. Introversion is associated with happiness.
   d. In twin studies, neuroticism and psychoticism, but not extraversion, have a genetic basis.

Obj.: 5 Page: 454-457

7. What instrument would you use if you wanted to screen applicants for positions in which people with serious psychological disorders might be dangerous, such as police officers?
   a. TAT
   b. MMPI
   c. Internal-External Locus of Control Scale
   d. Sheldon's physique profile

Obj.: 6 Page: 454

8. A researcher wants to compare the personality traits of psychology versus business majors. Most likely, she would use
   a. a projective test such as the Rorschach.
   b. behavioral observation across several situations.
   c. a personality inventory such as the Myers-Briggs.
   d. Rotter's Locus of Control Scale.

Obj.: 6 Page: 454

9. The five-factor theory of personality includes the traits of neuroticism, openness to experience, agreeableness,
   a. extraversion, and conscientiousness.
   b. self-assuredness, and timidity.
   c. seriousness, and dominance.
   d. tough-mindedness, and suspiciousness.

Obj.: 7 Page: 457

10. Rodney believes that he can succeed in college and so becomes "studious." He believes he is capable of maintaining a long-term stable marital relationship if he puts effort into it, so he attends carefully to his marriage. In at least these two areas of his life, Rodney appears to have a high level of
   a. reciprocal determinism.
   b. self-efficacy.
   c. introversion.
   d. fixation.

Obj.: 8 Page: 458

11. Those who would discount biological factors, unconscious influences, and dispositional traits would most likely favor
   a. a psychodynamic approach to personality.
   b. a behavioral approach to personality.
   c. a psychiatric approach to personality.
   d. a cognitive approach to personality.

Obj.: 8 Page: 457-458

12. A possible limitation of the method of behavioral observation is
   a. reactivity.
   b. lack of obtrusiveness.
   c. the use of a single observer.
   d. untrained observers.

Obj.: 9 Page: 459-460

13. According to George Kelly, the process by which a person applies hypotheses about social reality to a given situation is called
   a. psychic determinism.
   b. constructive alternativism.
   c. self-actualization.
   d. reality testing.

Obj.: 10 Page: 461-462

14. Woody Allen's remark, "My only regret in life is that I am not someone else" is, according to Higgins, an example of the incongruence between the
   a. actual self and the ideal self.
   b. actual self and the ought self.
   c. ought self and the ideal self.
   d. actual self and the undesired self.

Obj.: 11 Page: 465

15. David wants to be as good a nurse as he can be. He feels he is approaching this goal by mastering everything that is offered in his nursing program. He wishes to be a good father and to devote more time to his children. He strives to do this on weekends and during vacations. What might Carl Rogers say about David?
    a. David is flexible in his use of sublimation, displacement, and rationalization; thus, he is psychologically healthy.
    b. David probably has high self-esteem because he is attempting to close the gap between his actual self and ideal self.
    c. David engages in self-handicapping and is thus able to excuse his failures and protect his actual self.
    d. David is clearly detached, has need for privacy, and has democratic values; thus, he is on his way to self-actualization.

Obj.: 12 Page: 463

16. The belief that the personality is revealed by studying the features of the face is called
    a. phrenology.
    b. humoral theory.
    c. physiognomy.
    d. astrological analysis.

Obj.: 13 Page: 465-466

17. According to Sheldon, what characterizes the physiques of an endomorph?
    a. thin, frail physique
    b. muscular, strong physique
    c. soft, rounded physique
    d. soft, strong physique

Obj.: 13 Page: 465-466

18. The idea that certain physiques are associated with particular types of personalities is called
    a. phrenology.
    b. physiognomy.
    c. determinism.
    d. somatotyping.

Obj.: 14 Page: 466

19. Adoption studies have contributed to the biopsychological approach to personality
    a. by focusing on the role of the environment.
    b. with the finding that adopted infants and their biological mothers are more dissimilar in their degree of shyness than are adopted infants and their adoptive mothers.
    c. by convincingly showing that the rearing environment has a profoundly strong influence on the development of personality.
    d. by showing that, in general, the closer the genetic relationship between two persons, the more alike they will be in personality characteristics.

Obj.: 14 Page: 469-470

20. Studies using behavioral aggregation indicate that the correlation between overt behaviors and traits is approximately
    a. .05.
    b. .30.
    c. .60.
    d. .75.

Obj.: 15 Page: 472

ESSAY QUESTIONS

1 Explain the nature of the "consistency controversy" regarding personality theory. Based on your present level of knowledge, can you take a position on this debate?

Obj.: 15 Page: 470-471

2. Describe how far you have proceeded toward the goal of self-actualization. List the characteristics that apply to the current stage of your development and the next two that remain to be achieved.

Obj.: 12 Page: 463

ANSWER RECORD FOR CHAPTER 13

Comprehensive Guided Review:

1. consistent
2. uniqueness
3. personality
4. Barnum
5. useful
6. perspectives
7. approaches
8. hypnosis
9. unconscious
10. aggression
11. motivated
12. conscious
13. preconscious
14. unconscious
15. repression
16. determinism
17. inborn
18. reality
19. conscience
20. anxiety
21. threatening
22. Denial
23. immature
24. Rationalization
25. Intellectualization
26. Displacement
27. Projection
28. opposite
29. Compensation
30. Sublimation
31. libido
32. psychosexual
33. fixation
34. gratification
35. anal-retentive
36. phallic
37. castration
38. penis envy
39. superego
40. latency
41. genital
42. development
43. neo-Freudians
44. individual
45. inferiority complex
46. social interest
47. overcompensation
48. dominating
49. finalism
50. Jung
51. psychoanalytic
52. sex
53. analytic
54. personal
55. collective
56. archetypes
57. anima
58. animus
59. balance
60. extravert
61. introvert
62. anxiety
63. penis envy
64. social
65. maladaptive
66. freedom
67. repressed
68. projective
69. inkblots
70. complex
71. conflicts
72. validity
73. TAT
74. ambiguous
75. needs
76. real-life
77. Freud's
78. observable
79. unconscious
80. sexual
81. humanistic
82. Adler's
83. archetype

Mini-review of Psychoanalytic Theories of Personality:
1. N; 2. Bb; 3. E; 4. Mm; 5. C; 6. Vv; 7. Nn; 8. S; 9. J; 10. M; 11. D; 12. Dd; 13. Oo; 14. P; 15. Z; 16. L; 17. A; 18. Ff; 19. Q; 20. Ss; 21. Aa; 22. I; 23. Cc; 24. R; 25. Ee; 26. Kk; 27. G; 28. W; 29. Hh; 30. Qq; 31. F; 32. T; 33. Pp; 34. B; 35. Xx; 36. Rr; 37. K; 38. H; 39. O; 40. Ii; 41. Uu; 42. Ll; 43. Tt; 44. X; 45. U; 46. Ww; 47. Jj; 48. Y; 49. V; 50. Gg

84. characteristics
85. predisposition
86. factor analysis
87. Eysenck
88. neuroticism
89. psychoticism
90. introversion
91. biological
92. extraversion
93. trait
94. Allport
95. Cardinal
96. central
97. narrow
98. types
99. inventories
100. objective
101. Myers-Briggs
102. psychoanalytic
103. characteristics
104. empirical
105. disorders
106. validity
107. standardized
108. general
109. describing
110. Explaining
111. Eysenck's
112. cross-cultural
113. trait
114. agreeableness
115. strong
116. learning
117. Personality
118. do
119. reinforced
120. punished
121. punishment
122. cognitive
123. Bandura
124. reciprocal determinism
125. traits
126. self-efficacy
127. intensity
128. success
129. vicarious
130. verbal persuasion
131. overt
132. cognitions
133. Behavioral observation
134. Experience sampling
135. Rotter
136. locus of control
137. Skinner
138. heredity
139. passive
140. supported

Mini-review of the Dispositional and Behavioral Approaches to Personality:
1. R; 2. U; 3. M; 4. C; 5. A; 6. D; 7. I; 8. B; 9. J; 10. X; 11. T; 12. Z; 13. H; 14. W; 15. E; 16. O; 17. N; 18. V; 19. L; 20. F; 21. P; 22. S; 23. G; 24. K; 25. Y; 26. Q

141. thoughts
142. more
143. less
144. Kelly
145. hypotheses
146. personal constructs
147. bipolar
148. constructive alternativism
149. circumspection
150. preemption
151. control
152. motivation
153. Role Construct Repertory
154. fixed-role
155. social anxiety
156. thoughts
157. good
158. phenomenological
159. free will
160. Maslow
161. self-actualized
162. Rogers
163. incongruence
164. acceptance
165. actual
166. ideal
167. more
168. less
169. self-handicapping
170. Personal Orientation Inventory
171. self-actualized
172. Q-sort
173. self-destructive
174. self-actualization
175. ought
176. incongruence
177. Humanistic
178. environment
179. operationally
180. self-actualization
181. self-centeredness

Mini-review of Cognitive and Humanistic Theory:
1. L; 2. E; 3. N; 4. C; 5. F; 6. H; 7. P; 8. G; 9. O; 10. A; 11. Q; 12. B; 13. D; 14. I; 15. M; 16. K; 17. J

182. biological
183. blood
184. calm
185. black bile
186. irritable
187. phrenology
188. Physiognomy
189. facial
190. heredity
191. Sheldon
192. somatotypes
193. ectomorph
194. mesomorph
195. endomorph
196. Galton
197. behavioral genetics
198. adoption
199. biological
200. biological
201. adoptive
202. identical

Anatomy of a Contemporary Research Study: In Personality Are Identical Twins Reared Apart More Like Their Adoptive Parents or Their Biological Parents?

What was the rationale for the study?
Since 1979, Bouchard has conducted the most comprehensive study of identical twins reared apart and then reunited later in life.

What methods did the authors use to test the hypothesis?
Identical and fraternal twins reared together and identical and fraternal twins reared apart were given the multidimensional personality questionnaire and their basic personality traits were compared.

What was the outcome of the study and what did the author conclude the results meant?
The results indicated that identical twins reared together and identical twins reared apart were highly similar in intelligence. Also, identical twins reared apart were more similar than fraternal twins reared apart. Given a heritability index of .48, it appears that there is almost an even split of the role of genetics versus environment.

203. somatotype
204. methodological
205. bias
206. self-confident
207. causal
208. Heritability
209. identical

Mini-review on Biopsychological Theory of Personality:
1. A; 2. C; 3. I; 4. H; 5. F; 6. B; 7. E; 8. D; 9. G

210. consistency
211. less
212. correlation
213. situation
214. personality
215. over
216. across
217. inconsistent
218. first
219. cross-situational
220. do
221. consistency
222. behavioral aggregation
223. typically
224. always
225. correlation

Anatomy of a Classic Research Study: Is Personality Consistent from One Situation to Another?

What was the rationale for the study?
Dudycha (1936) examined personality in regard to punctuality.

What methods did the authors use to test the hypothesis?
Punctuality was assessed in six different situations on a college campus.

What was the outcome of the study and what did the author conclude the results meant?
The results seemed to indicate that the situation, not personality traits, accounted for punctuality. However, when behavioral aggregation was applied to the study, the students showed much greater cross-situational consistency in their punctuality.

Practice Test A:

1. a. **Correct: The Barnum effect refers to a passive acceptance of personality descriptions that are very vague and generalized.**
   b. Incorrect: There is no such thing as a "New Age" effect in psychology.
   c. Incorrect: There is no such thing as a pseudo-Freudian effect in psychology.
   d. Incorrect: There is no such thing as an intellectualization effect.

2. a. Incorrect: Regression is when an individual reverts back to immature behavior.
b. Correct: Psychic determinism refers to Freud's belief that all behaviors, even "accidental" statements, are the deliberate result of unconscious mechanisms.
c. Incorrect: Subliminal perception is the perception of environmental input beneath the absolute threshold.
d. Incorrect: Reciprocal determinism refers to Bandura's belief that neither personal dispositions nor environmental factors alone can explain behavior.

3. **a. Correct: Movie characters and creative actions represented various archetypes, or inherited memories that are passed down from one generation to another.**
b. Incorrect: Somatotypes are body types, not behavioral characteristics.
c. Incorrect: Central traits are traits that influence our lives but do not have a pervasive influence.
d. Incorrect: Cardinal traits are traits or characteristics that influence people's lives; an example would be altruism.

4. a. Incorrect: Type tests categorize individuals and creates a profile of the individual.
b. Incorrect: Trait tests are interested in identifying where you fit on a continuum of a specific trait.
c. Correct: Projective tests are based on the assumption that individuals will project themselves into their answers on a test.
d. Incorrect: The Role Construct Repertory test (REP test) is used by cognitive psychologists to determine how you perceive reality.

5. **a. Correct: Happiness/sadness is measured on the neuroticism scale of Eysenck's test.**
b. Incorrect: Happiness/sadness is measured on the neuroticism scale of Eysenck's test.
c. Incorrect: Happiness/sadness is measured on the neuroticism scale of Eysenck's test.
d. Incorrect: Happiness/sadness is measured on the neuroticism scale of Eysenck's test.

6 a. Incorrect: Central traits are those that have overall influence on our lives but do not have a pervasive influence.
b. Incorrect: Allport did not discuss primary traits.
c. Incorrect: Cardinal traits are similar to personality traits in that they affect every aspect of the person's life.
d. Correct: Secondary traits are characteristics that are the least important and effect a narrow portion of our lives, for example, "quirky" behaviors.

7. **a. Correct: Hathaway & McKinley created the MMPI to diagnose psychological disorders.**
b. Incorrect: should read "traits" not "types."
c. Incorrect: Hathaway & McKinley created the MMPI to diagnose psychological disorders.
d. Incorrect: Hathaway & McKinley created the MMPI to diagnose psychological disorders.

8. a. Incorrect: The theory describes, but does not explain.
b. Incorrect: The tests used by this approach are better at diagnosing than general personality measurement.
c. Correct: The theory describes but does not explain.
d. Incorrect: The theory describes but does not explain.

9. a. Incorrect: Self-actualization refers to a concept proposed by Maslow.
b. Incorrect: Psychic determinism is a Freudian concept.
c. Correct: Reciprocal determinism refers to Bandura's belief that neither personal dispositions, or environmental factors alone can explain behavior.
d. Incorrect: Constructive alternativism is a term coined by Kelly.

10. a. Incorrect: Self-efficacy refers to what Bandura claims is your belief in whether you can perform the behaviors that are necessary to accomplish a task.
b. Incorrect: Academic flair is not a term that is discussed in this unit.
c. Correct: Locus of control is Rotter's term for your belief as to whether internal or external factors control success; in this example you would be demonstrating an external locus of control.
d. Incorrect: Learned optimism is not a discussed in this chapter.

11. a. Incorrect: Learned helplessness occurs when organisms fail to respond to a situation because all of their previous attempts had not led to successful consequences.
b. Incorrect: Self-efficacy refers to what Bandura claims is your belief in whether you can perform the behaviors that are necessary to accomplish a task.
c. Correct: Locus of control is Rotter's term for your belief as to whether internal or external factors control success; in this example you would be demonstrating an internal locus of control.
d. Incorrect: This has nothing to do with the question.

12. **a. Correct: Rogers felt that incongruence was the result of the failure of the parent to provide love without any "strings", or unconditional positive regard.**
b. Incorrect: Congruence between them leads to self-actualization, not incongruence.
c. Incorrect: Rogers felt that incongruence was the result of the failure of the parent to provide love without any "strings," or unconditional positive regard.
d. Incorrect: Rogers felt that incongruence was the result of the failure of the parent to provide love without any "strings," or unconditional positive regard.

13. a. Incorrect: Somatotypes are body types, not a behavioral action.
b. Correct: Self-handicapping refers to the use of a mechanism in which the task is claimed to be harder than it is to allow for items that might contribute to less-than-ideal behavior.
c. Incorrect: Reciprocal determinism refers to Bandura's belief that neither personal dispositions nor environmental factors alone can explain behavior.
d. Incorrect: Constructive alternativism refers to our ability to apply different constructs to a given situation.

14. **a. Correct: These individuals would be considered mesomorphs by their body build, thus Sheldon would claim they would demonstrate somatotonia.**
b. Incorrect: These individuals would be considered mesomorphs by their body build, thus Sheldon would claim they would demonstrate somatotonia.
c. Incorrect: These individuals would be considered mesomorphs by their body build, thus Sheldon would claim they would demonstrate somatotonia.
d. Incorrect: These individuals would be considered mesomorphs by their body build, thus Sheldon would claim they would demonstrate somatotonia.

15. a. Incorrect: The research into the biological basis for personality has been mixed, thus researchers are concluding that personality is determined by both the environment and genetic makeup.
b. Incorrect: The research into the biological basis for personality has been mixed, thus researchers are concluding that personality is determined by both the environment and genetic makeup.
c. Correct: The research into the biological basis for personality has been mixed, thus researchers are concluding that personality is determined by both the environment and genetic makeup.
d. Incorrect: The research into the biological basis for personality has been mixed, thus researchers are concluding that personality is determined by both the environment and genetic makeup.

16. a. Incorrect: Page 470 in the textbook reports that Mischel found a correlation of .30.
b. Incorrect: Page 470 in the textbook reports that Mischel found a correlation of .30.
c. Correct: Page 470 in the textbook reports that Mischel found a correlation of .30.
d. Incorrect: Page 470 in the textbook reports that Mischel found a correlation of .30.

Practice Test B:

1. **a. Correct: The Barnum effect refers to a passive acceptance of personality descriptions that are very vague and generalized.**
b. Incorrect: There is not a psychological effect called the Barney effect.
c. Incorrect: There is not a psychological effect called the Bandura phenomenon.
d. Incorrect: There is not a psychological effect called the Bouchard mechanism.

2. a. Incorrect: The reality principle refers to the concept that the ego accepts behavior that is socially acceptable.
b. Incorrect: The death instinct results in aggressive behavior; Nina's behavior is not due to her death instinct.
c. Incorrect: The preconscious is the portion of the person that is accessible readily, but beneath conscious awareness.
d. Correct: A Freudian slip is an unintentional statement that would reveal our unconscious.

3. a. Incorrect: Projection involves the attribution of undesirable feeling to others.
b. Correct: Sublimation is the expression of a sexual or aggressive impulses through indirect, socially acceptable outlets.
c. Incorrect: Rationalization refers to providing a socially acceptable reason for an inappropriate action.
d. Incorrect: Regression is the displaying of immature behaviors.

4. a. Incorrect: Adler believed that striving for superiority is healthiest when it promotes activities that are directed towards positive social interests.
   b. Incorrect: Adler believed that striving for superiority is healthiest when it promotes activities that are directed towards positive social interests.
   c. Incorrect:Adler believed that striving for superiority is healthiest when it promotes activities that are directed towards positive social interests.
   d. Correct: Adler believed that striving for superiority is healthiest when it promotes activities that are directed towards positive social interests.

5. a. Incorrect: Jung's concept of personality types has received the most support and his concept of archetypes has received the most criticism.
   b. Incorrect: Jung's concept of personality types has received the most support and his concept of archetypes has received the most criticism.
   c. Correct: Jung's concept of personality types, introversion, and extraversion has received the most support and his concept of archetypes has received the most criticism.
   d. Incorrect: Jung's concept of personality types has received the most support and his concept of archetypes has received the most criticism.

6. **a. Correct: Research has shown that juvenile delinquents score high in psychoticism.**
   b. Incorrect: The correct term is introverts.
   c. Incorrect: The correct term is extraversion.
   d. Incorrect: Extraversion also has a genetic basis.

7. a. Incorrect: The TAT does not identify psychological disorders; it is a moderately good predictor of real-life achievement.
   b. Correct: The MMPI was specifically designed to diagnose psychological disorders.
   c. Incorrect: The Internal-External Locus of Control Scale was designed to measure the degree to which you expect that you are in control of the outcomes of your behavior.
   d. Incorrect: Sheldon's physique profile was designed to examine body type.

8. a. Incorrect: Projective tests do not measure personality traits.
   b. Incorrect: Behavioral observations do not measure traits.
   c. Correct: Personality inventories like the Myers-Briggs were specifically designed to measure personality traits.
   d. Incorrect: The Internal-External Locus of Control Scale was designed to measure your degree to which you expect that you are in control of the outcomes of your behavior.

9. **a. Correct: The last two traits of "The Big Five" are extraversion and conscientiousness.**
   b. Incorrect: This alternative is a term taken from the Cattell 16 PF Inventory and is not one of "The "Big Five."
   c. Incorrect: This alternative is a term taken from the Cattell 16 PF Inventory and is not one of "The "Big Five."
   d. Incorrect: This alternative is a term taken from the Cattell 16 PF Inventory and is not one of "The "Big Five."

10. a. Incorrect: Reciprocal determinism refers to Bandura's belief that neither inborn personal dispositions nor environmental factors alone can explain behavior.
    b. Correct: Self-efficacy is the extent to which individuals believe that they can perform behaviors necessary to achieve an outcome. This is what is being described in this question.
    c. Incorrect: Introversion is Jung's term for an individual who is shy and withdrawn.
    d. Incorrect: Fixation is a Freudian defense mechanism where an individual becomes stuck at an immature stage of development.

11. a. Incorrect: A psychodynamic theorist does not discount unconscious influences.
    b. Correct: A behavioral theorist discounts biological, unconscious, and dispositional influences.
    c. Incorrect: Psychiatrists are trained as medical doctors and therefore would not discount biological factors.
    d. Incorrect: Cognitive theorists do not deny unconscious influences.

12. **a. Correct: It occurs when subjects are aware they are being watched.**
    b. Incorrect: A limitation would be unobtrusiveness.
    c. Incorrect: More observers are more likely to produce valid findings.
    d. Incorrect: The observer should know the person(s) and conduct the observations in the situation of interest on several occasions.

13. a. Incorrect: Psychic determinism is a Freudian term for the role of the unconscious in behavior.
    b. Correct: Kelly refers to the process by which a person applies hypotheses about social reality to a given situation, constructive alternativism.
    c. Incorrect: Self-actualization is Maslow's term for an individual's full potential.
    d. Incorrect: Reality testing is not a term that was used regarding any of the theories discussed in this chapter.

14. **a. Correct: Higgins claims that this would be an example of depression resulting from an incongruence between the actual and ideal selves.**
   b. Incorrect: To Higgins, incongruence between the actual and the ought self leads to anxiety, not depression.
   c. Incorrect: Higgins does not discuss incongruence between the ideal and the ought self.
   d. Incorrect: Higgins does not discuss the "undesired self."

15. a. Incorrect: Rogers does not discuss the concepts of sublimation, displacement, or rationalization; these are Freudian defense mechanisms.
   b. Correct: Rogers claims that healthy and happy individuals have less incongruence between their actual and ideal selves.
   c. Incorrect: David would be self-handicapping if he were making excuses for possible failures by claiming his tasks were difficult.
   d. Incorrect: Rogers claims that healthy and happy individuals have less incongruence between their actual and ideal selves.

16. a. Incorrect: This is the study of contours of the skull.
   b. Incorrect: This is the claim that temperament is related to levels of body fluids called humors.
   c. Correct: Physiognomy is the study of physical appearance and the original studies dealt with the features of the face.
   d. Incorrect: Generally, astrologers would use the "Barnum effect."

17. a. Incorrect: This is an ectomorph.
   b. Incorrect: This is a mesomorph.
   c. **Correct: According to Sheldon, enodmorphs have a soft, rounded physique.**
   d. Incorrect: Soft and a strong physique are contradictions that do not characterize any one of he three types.

18. a. Incorrect: Phrenology is the study of contours of the skull.
   b. Incorrect: Physiognomy is the study of physical appearance and the original studies dealt with the features of the face.
   c. Incorrect: Determinism is the belief that there is an identifiable cause for all behavior.
   d. Correct: Somatyping is Sheldon's term for the idea that physiques are associated wi h particular types of personalities.

19. a. Incorrect: Replace "environment" with "heredity."
   b. Incorrect: Replace "dissimilar" with "similar."
   c. Incorrect: This has not been shown.
   d. Correct: When there is a closer relationship between the adoptee and his or her biological parent, this suggests a biological basis for personality. The Texas Adoption Study has shown just that.

20. a. Incorrect: Aggregate studies have suggested that the correlation between overt behaviors and traits is + .60.
   b. Incorrect: Aggregate studies have suggested that the correlation between overt behaviors and traits is + .60.
   c. **Correct: Aggregate studies have suggested that the correlation between overt behaviors and traits is + .60.**
   d. Incorrect: Aggregate studies have suggested that the correlation between overt behaviors and traits is + .60.

Essay Questions:

1. The controversy has to do with the questioning of the generally well-accepted notion that the way we are, that is, our personality, is the same across situations. Walter Mischel initiated the controversy when he pointed out the modest correlation between behaviors representing the same personality trait. In otherwords, just because a person scored high on traits such as "independent" or "honest" did not predict that the person would behave in accordance with that trait in all or even any situations. Mischel concluded that much more of our behavior is influenced by the situations we are in than by a set of traits that we carry to all situations.

2. Do you have:
   a realistic orientation?
   a self-acceptance and acceptance of others and the natural world?
   spontaneity?
   an air of detachment and need for privacy?
   a fresh rather than stereotyped appreciation of people and things?
   a tendency to have strong intimate relationships with a few special loved ones?
   democratic values and attitudes?
   no confusion of means with ends?
   a philosophical rather than a hostile sense of humor?
   a high degree of creativity?
   resistance to cultural conformity?
   transcendence of environment rather than always coping with it?

Are you:

problem-centered rather than self-centered?

autonomous and independent?

Have you had a profound mystical or spiritual experience (not necessarily religious)?

Do you identify with humankind and a strong social interest?

These are Maslow's characteristics of a self-actualized individual. You have the only correct answer about yourself.

14 Psychological Disorders

LEARNING OBJECTIVES

After studying this chapter, you should be able to:

1. Define psychopathology and describe the three traditional criteria for determining the presence of psychological disorder, indicating their weaknesses. (p. 478-480)

2. List and describe the emphases of the six major viewpoints regarding the psychological disorders. (p. 480-482)

3. Explain how the DSM-IV is used as a diagnostic tool, and briefly summarize the criticisms leveled against it. (p. 482-485)

4. List and describe the important features of four anxiety disorders and summarize how proponents of the six viewpoints account for the development of the anxiety disorders. (p. 485-490)

5. List and describe the important features of two somatoform disorders and briefly mention how proponents of the six viewpoints account for the development of somatoform disorders. (p. 490-491)

6. List and describe the important features of three dissociative disorders and briefly mention the controversy surrounding dissociative identity disorder. (p. 492-494)

7. List and describe the important features of two affective disorders, emphasizing several important points about the issue of suicide. (p. 494-497)

8. Summarize how the proponents of the six viewpoints account for the development of depression. (p. 497-501)

9. Summarize the general characteristics of all the schizophrenias and then highlight the distinctive features of four types of schizophrenia. (p. 501-503)

10. Summarize how the proponents of the six viewpoints account for the development of schizophrenia, emphasizing the findings of biopsychological researchers. (p. 503-507)

11. Define the term "personality disorder" and describe the important features of two such disorders, emphasizing what is known about antisocial personality disorder. (p. 507-509)

12. Summarize the main points in the controversy surrounding the insanity defense. (p. 509-512)

COMPREHENSIVE GUIDED REVIEW

I. The Nature of Psychological Disorders: The determination, causes, and__(1)__ of psychological disorders are the focus of the field of **psychopathology,** or the study of psychological disorders.

Criteria for Psychological Disorders: The main criteria for diagnosing a psychological disorder are **abnormality, maladaptiveness,** and **personal distress**.

Abnormality: Behavior that__(2)__ from the behavior of the "typical" person, or the__*(3)*__, is considered abnormal. A norm may be *qualitative* or *quantitative*: 1)__(4)__abnormal behavior deviates from culturally acceptable behavior; 2)__(5)__abnormal behavior deviates from the statistical average (mean). By itself, abnormality is not a sufficient condition for determining the presence of a psychological disorder. The__(6)__ in which the abnormal behavior occurs must be considered. In addition, if the criteria of ___(7)___were the sole determinant of abnormality, there is the possibility that nonconformists could be considered abnormal.

Maladaptiveness: You would have a psychological disorder if your behavior seriously disrupted your___(8)___, academic, or vocational life. As an example,___(9)___ is characterized by a fear of being in public places. This type of excessive anxiety may result in academic failure, or excessive drinking could mean the loss of one's job. But as with abnormality, ____(10)___by itself is not sufficient for determining a psychological disorder.

_____(11)____: This criterion assumes that the extent and nature of our subjective feelings of anxiety, depression, or other unpleasant emotions determine whether we have a disorder. But again, a single criterion is not always sufficient; some individuals have psychological disorders___(12)___ feeling distress.

Behavior that is maladaptive, atypical, or personally distressing might indicate a psychological___(13)___. However, there is no single point at which an individual can be declared psychologically disordered. Thus there is extensive ___(14)___ on each of the criteria, and there is a degree of___(15)___ to the identification of abnormal behavior.

Viewpoints on Psychological Disorders: Even when psychologists agree on the presence of a particular psychological disorder they may disagree on its underlying___(16)___. Currently, psychologists favor___(17)___ different viewpoints on the causes of psychological disorders.

Historically, people have tried to explain the occurrence of unusual or bizarre behavior. The Greeks attributed disorders to the actions of the___(18)___ and evil spirits. But Hippocrates argued instead that disorders had___(19)___ causes.___(20)___ was regulated by fluids he called "humors." To this day we call depressed people "melancholic," a term generated by the early notion that depression was caused by an excess of "melancholer" (black bile from the spleen) in the brain. ___(21)___ explanations remained dominant through the Middle Ages and the Renaissance. The sixteenth and seventeenth centuries saw the beginning of opposition to the supernatural view. Paracelsus attributed unusual behavior to the ___(22)___, hence the term *lunatic*. Current viewpoints, however, attribute disorders to___(23)___ causes.

The Biopsychological Viewpoint: Today, ___(24)___ researchers are interested in identifying whether psychological disorders are caused by inherited or acquired brain disorders involving imbalances in ___(25)___or damage to brain structures. What led to this current perspective? Interest in biological causes was stimulated by the discovery that *general paresis*, marked by severe mental deterioration, was caused by infection with___(26)___, and researchers in the nineteenth century found that toxic chemicals could induce psychological disorders.

The Psychoanalytic Viewpoint: Current-day psychoanalytic researchers are interested in identifying whether psychological disorders are caused by___(27)___ conflicts between inborn biological drives, particularly sex, and the norms of society that inhibit their expression. Conflicts about sex and aggression may be___(28)___ into the unconscious. ___(29)___ argued that disorders were based on unconscious unresolved conflicts, leading to feelings of___(30)___ caused by pent-up sexual or aggressive energy. We use____(31)____ to relieve this anxiety, but if they are inadequate, we may develop psychological disorders.

Both the biopsychological and the psychoanalytic viewpoint support the___(32)___ model, which assumes that abnormal behavior is symptomatic of underlying processes.

The Behavioral Viewpoint: Behavioral theorists argue that psychological disorders are caused by positive ___(33)___of inappropriate behaviors and the___(34)___ of appropriate behaviors. This perspective arose in opposition to those who looked for mental causes. Bandura stepped beyond Skinner to add that disorders may be caused by___(35)___ the behavior of others. Those who favor the behavioral viewpoint, with its emphasis on ___(36)___factors, would also more likely consider the negative effects of socioeconomic conditions on psychological well-being.

The Cognitive Viewpoint: The central assumption of this perspective was essentially stated by__(37)__ (A.D. ca. 60-120), who taught that "men are disturbed not by things, but by the views which they take of things." George Kelly argues that those who fail to maintain a fairly stable, but flexible set of____(38)____ are more likely to suffer from psychological disorders. Though most cognitivists assume that people with disorders hold irrational__(39)__, recent evidence shows that people with disorders may think even__(40)__ rationally and objectively than others about themselves and the world. People__(41)__ disorders may view the world through "rose-colored glasses."

The Humanistic Viewpoint: Humanistic theorists such as Maslow and Rogers emphasize the importance of __(42)__, or the fulfillment of one's potential. They argue that psychological disorders are the result of blocked self-actualization that results when people are discouraged from__(43)__ themselves. This __(44) *positive regard* may lead to an incongruence between one's actual self and public self and consequently to psychological disorders.

The Diathesis-Stress Viewpoint: The fact that no single viewpoint offers an adequate explanation of disorders has led to the emergence of the diathesis-stress viewpoint. This viewpoint argues that psychological disorders are caused by an individual's biological__(45)__ interacting with social__(46)__. Those with strong predispositions may succumb to __(47)__ levels of stress, and those with weak predispositions may succumb to__(48)__ levels of stress.

Classification of Psychological Disorders: Emil __(49)__ devised the first modern system of classification of psychological disorders. Today, the most widely used system of classification is the fourth edition of the *Diagnostic and Statistical Manual of Mental Disorders*, or the__(50)__.

The DSM-IV: The *Diagnostic and Statistical Manual of Mental Disorders, DSM* IV, is published by the American Psychiatric Association. It provides a means of communication among mental health practitioners, offers a __(51)__for research on the causes of disorders, and helps practitioners choose the best treatment for a particular disorder.

Unlike the DSM-I and the DSM-II versions, which endorsed a__(52)__ interpretation of disorders, this version considers the__(53)__ of biological, psychological, and social factors in diagnosing psychological disorders. DSM-IV provides__(54)__ axes for diagnosing psychological disorders:

Axis I contains sixteen major__(55)__ of psychological disorders.
Axis II contains__(56)__ disorders.
Axis III contains__(57)__ conditions that might affect a person's psychological disorder.
Axis IV contains social and environmental sources of__(58)__.
Axis V contains an estimate of a person's level of__(59)__.

Reactions to the earlier DSM-III-R provided insight into how best to develop DSM-IV. Research found that, overall, the DSM-III diagnostic categories had only modest__(60)__ (the extent to which different raters reach the same diagnosis) and__(61)__ (the extent to which a diagnosis is accurate). As a result of this and other issues, DSM-IV has a stronger research base.

Criticisms of the Diagnosis of Psychological Disorders: In spite of the widespread reliance on the DSM, some researchers continue to criticize the potential negative effects of the__(62)__ of psychological disorders and question its use. This attitude was sparked at least in part by a classic study by David Rosenhan in 1973. This research is the focus of the "Anatomy of a Classic Research Study" on page 484 in your textbook. .

Anatomy of a Classic Research Study: Can Sane People Be Recognized in a Mental Hospital? ***Read the summary of the study on page 484 in your textbook and answer the following questions.***

What was the rationale for the study?

What methods did the author use to test the hypothesis?

What results were obtained and what conclusions were drawn from them?

Mini-review of the Nature of, Viewpoints On, and Classification of Psychological Disorders:
Part I: Matching: Match each term with its correct description.

________1. Axis V
________2. personal distress
________3. *Diagnostic and Statistical Manual of Mental Disorders (DSM-IV)*
________4. Axis I
________5. psychopathology
________6. validity
________7. quantitatively abnormal behavior
________8. Axis III
________9. abnormality
_______10. Emil Kraepelin
_______11. Axis II
_______12. reliability
_______13. maladaptiveness
_______14. qualitatively abnormal behavior
_______15. Axis IV

A. The study of the determination, causes, and classification of psychological disorders
B. Critierion for behavior that examines whether a person's behavior deviates from the behavior of the "typical" person, or the norm
C. Behavior that deviates from culturally acceptable behavior.
D. The extent to which a diagnosis is accurate
E. Behavior that deviates from the statistical average (mean)
F. Criterion that determines psychological disorders by examining whether your behavior seriously disrupts your social, academic, or vocational life
G. Contains information on social and environmental sources of stress
H. Criterion assumes that the extent and nature of our subjective feelings of anxiety, depression, or other unpleasant emotions determine whether we have a disorder
I. Devised the first modern system of classification of psychological disorders
J. The most widely used system of classification of psychological disorders
K. Contains information on sixteen major categories of psychological disorders
L. The extent to which different raters reach the same diagnosis.
M. Contains information on personality disorders
N. Contains information on medical conditions that might affect a person's psychological disorder
O. Contains an estimate of a person's level of functioning

Part II: Viewpoints on Causes of Abnormal Behavior: *Provide a brief description of the major focus of each of the following viewpoints on psychological disorders.*

Viewpoint | **Claim as to cause of psychological disorders**

Biopsychological:

Psychoanalytic:

Behavioral:

Cognitive:

Humanistic:

Diathesis-Stress:

In this chapter you will read about a broad spectrum of psychological disorders. By the end of the chapter you should have a fairly solid grasp of the categories, the symptoms, and what each viewpoint has to offer. Most of you have encountered people with a disorder; this chapter should help put your interest and concern into better focus. However, it is easy to get caught in the trap of reading symptoms into your own behavior, so be cautious and intellectually objective. Many people, on occasion, experience a symptom in a mild form. If you find that you have read something that affects you or someone you know, consider discussing it with a college or university counselor.

II. Anxiety Disorders: *Anxiety* is a feeling of apprehension accompanied by increased__(63)__ nervous system activity, which produces increases in sweating, heart rate, and breathing rate. When it becomes intense, chronic, and disruptive of everyday functioning, it is a__(64)__. __(65)__ disorders include **generalized anxiety disorder, panic disorders, phobias,** and **obsessive-compulsive disorder.**

Generalized Anxiety Disorder: A person with this disorder is in a constant state of anxiety that exists __(66)__of any particular stressful situation. The anxiety is called "free floating" and has__(67)__ as its central feature. Generalized anxiety disorder is more common in__(68)__ than in__(69)__.

What accounts for the development of the disorder? __(70)__ researchers look to heredity using family and twinstudies; neurochemistry, mostly related to excess activity in__(71)__ neurons, and brain arousal using PET evidence. Psychologically,__(72)__ view it as a function of id impulses,__(73)__ theorists view it as an exaggeration of the number of threatening stimuli, and humanistic psychologists view it as a discrepancy between the__(74)__ self and the__(75)__ self.

__(76)__**Disorder:** This disorder is marked by sudden, unexpected attacks of overwhelming anxiety Panic attacks are characterized by a__(77)__ onset of overwhelming anxiety accompanied by dizziness, trembling, cold sweats, heart palpitations, shortness of breath, fears, and feelings of being detached from one's body. The attacks generally only last for a__(78)__ minutes, but are very distressing. __(79)__ theorists note that panic disorders run in families, with a __(80)__ rate among family members of about 20 percent. Based on these concordance rates, some argue that there may be a genetic __(81)__for the panic disorder, while others point to a role for the temporal lobe based on PET scans. According to cognitive theories, on the other hand, panic disorders result from faulty__(82)__ characterized by catastrophic thinking.

Phobias: A phobia is the experience of excessive, inappropriate, uncontrollable, irrational__(83)__ and is the most common form of psychological disorder. __(84)__ **phobias** are intense, irrational fears of a specific object or situation. __(85)__ **phobias** are fears of public scrutiny. **Agoraphobia** is the fear of being in __(86)__. Certain people have a biological, possibly a__(87)__ predisposition to develop phobias. Seligman argues that__(88)__ has made us biologically prepared to develop phobias of dangerous natural objects. __(89)__, however, believe that phobias are caused by anxiety displaced from a feared object or situation onto another object or situation. Hence, the true source remains__(90)__, as in the classic case of Little Hans. __(91)__theorists claim that phobias are responses to frightening situations, learned either through personal experience or through observing the behavior of others. Cognitive-behavioral explanations implicate __(92)__. They argue that phobic individuals may__(93)__ they lack the ability to cope with stressful situations.

Obsessive-Compulsive Disorder: A mild__(94)__ is a persistent, recurring thought. A__(95)__ is a repetitive action that you feel compelled to perform. People whose obsessions and compulsions interfere with their daily functioning are said to have__(96)__ disorder. Evidence from family and__(97)__ studies supports the possibility of a hereditary predisposition for this disorder. Additionally,__(98)__ scans have found that obsessive-compulsives have abnormally high activity in the frontal lobes. Psychoanalysts, on the other hand, claim that obsessive-compulsive behaviors are caused by__(99)__ at the anal stage. ____(100)____ theorists however, view these behaviors as attempts to avoid anxiety-producing situations.

III. Somatoform Disorders: Somatoform disorders are "bodylike" disorders, characterized by physical symptoms in the__(101)__ of disease or injury. The person truly believes the symptoms are__(102)__, unlike *malingering,* where the person__(103)__ symptoms to be relieved of certain responsibilities. The somatoform disorders include **hypochondriasis** and **conversion disorder**.

___(104)___**:**This is a disorder in which the person interprets the slightest physical change in his or her body as evidence of a serious illness. __(105)__ see this disorder as a defense against guilt or low self-esteem. Behavioral theorists, on the other hand, point to___(106)__, such as being lavished with attention, and ____(107)___, such as relief from work responsibilities. However,_(108)__ disagree and point to those who fear disease so much that they are overly attentive to noticing and then exaggerating bodily changes.

Conversion Disorder: An individual with a conversion disorder exhibits loss or alteration of a physical function __(109)__ any apparent physical cause. Physicians suspect the presence of this disorder when patients display *la belle indifference,* or a lack of__(110)__ about their symptoms. In searching for the cause of conversion disorders, biopsychological researchers have found a concordance rate three times higher for__(111)__ than for__(112)__ twins. While this suggests that somatoform disorders run in __(113)__, the relative impact of heredity versus life experiences is not clear. Freud, on the other hand, called such disorders *conversion hysteria,* because he felt that the disorder resulted from___(114)__ sexual impulses. However, today, to avoid the implication that it is strictly a__(115)__ disorder, it is called *conversion disorder.* Behavioral theorists assume these disorders occur because they are__(116)__ by attention or a reduction in responsibilities. __(117)__ psychologists view the disorder as a way to protect the self through self-handicapping.

IV. Dissociative Disorders: In dissociative disorders the person's__(118)__ awareness loses access to certain of his or her thoughts, feelings, and memories. The dissociative disorders include **psychogenic amnesia, psychogenic fugue,** and **dissociative identity disorders.**

___(119)____: This is characterized by the inability to recall personally significant memories, ones usually related to a traumatic event. The person usually regains the lost memories fairly__(120)__. The __(121)__perspective assumes that the defense mechanism of repression is operating in cases of psychogenic amnesia and there is some research evidence that supports this claim.

Psychogenic Fugue: This disorder is characterized by a memory loss that is characteristic of amnesia, but normally involves___(122)__ one's home and adopting a new__(123)__.

Dissociative Identity Disorder, or **Multiple Personality:** In this disorder a person has two or more distinct__(124)__ that alternate with one another. The two most famous cases of multiple personality are those of Chris Sizemore, "Eve," and Sybil Dorsett, "Sybil." Almost always there is a history of traumatic _(125)_experiences in individuals who develop a dissociative identity disorder. Some cognitive researchers believe this condition is being overdiagnosed and is simply the product of____(126)___. This claim has received some research support.

V. Mood Disorders: Individuals who are diagnosed with a__(127)__ disorder experience extreme or prolonged periods of depression or elation that are often unrelated to their everyday functioning. Classes of mood disorders include **major depression** and **bipolar disorder.**

Major Depression: Major depression is a__(128)__, intense state that causes extreme distress and disruption of everyday life for months. People with major depression may experience__(129)__, helplessness, loss of self-esteem, insomnia, loss of interest in food, chronic fatigue, poor grooming habits, withdrawal from social relations, a loss of interest in sex, difficulty in concentrating, and failing to perform up to their normal academic and vocational standards. Because of its prevalence, this disorder is considered by many to be the "common__(130)__" of psychological disorders.

Rosenthal has identified a form of__(131)__ called **seasonal affective disorder.** People with this disorder often experience extreme depression during specific__(132)__ of the year. Though typically occurring in the _(133)_, it may also occur in the summer. It has been suggested that this disorder may be caused by the inability to adjust physiologically to seasonal changes in__(134)__ levels. The most common treatment is exposure to bright__(135)__ light for a given amount of time each day.

People suffering from major depression are more susceptible to__(136)__. Baumeister believes that people commit suicide when their__(137)__ becomes so negative that it is too painful for them to bear. Suicide risk__(138)__ affected by sex, race, age, and marital status. Among the major signs are changes in__(139)__ or habits, including emotional apathy, social withdrawal, poor grooming habits, tying up loose ends in one's life, and outright threats of suicide. Shneidman suggests that since suicide__(140)__ are usually cries for help, the best way to reduce the immediate threat of an actual attempt is to provide an __(141)__response by just talking about the problem with the individual.

__(142)__**Disorder:** This disorder, formally called manic-depression, is characterized by short or long alternations of elation and major depression, typically separated by days or weeks of normal moods. The __(143)__stage is characterized by euphoria, hyperactivity, grandiose ideas, annoying and incoherent talkativeness, unrealistic optimism, and inflated self-esteem.

Causes of Mood Disorders:

The Biopsychological Viewpoint: As noted above, mood disorders have a biological basis, apparently influenced by __(144)__. At the same time, life__(145)__ also play an important role. Some studies have found support for the existence of a genetic__(146)__, while others have not. This hereditary predisposition may affect__(147)__. Major depression is related to abnormally__(148)__ levels of serotonin or norepinephrine. Mania is associated with a combination of__(149)__ levels of serotonin and__(150)__ levels of norepinephrine, as well as high levels of brain arousal. The use of PET has shown that victims of major depression tend to have relatively__(151)__ left than right hemispheric activity.

The__(152)__ Viewpoint: This viewpoint holds that the loss of a parent, or the rejection by a parent, early in childhood predisposes a person to experience depression later in life whenever he or she experiences a personal loss of some kind. There is__(153)__ research support for the position that parental loss or rejection in early childhood predisposes a person to develop depression as a response to personal loss, such as a job or lover, in later life.

The Behavioral Viewpoint: Peter Lewinsohn's__(154)__ theory assumes that depressed people lack the social skills to gain normal social reinforcement from others and, instead, provoke negative reactions from them. He points out that the depressed person is caught in a__(155)__ of reduced social reinforcement, which leads to depression, which leads to more reduced social reinforcement.

A more__(156)__ -behavioral view of depression is proposed by Martin Seligman. He originally argued that depression resulted from a *learned*__(157)__. That is, it was a condition that stemmed from experiences wherein a person had little __(158)__ over the events in his or her life. Today, however, Seligman has revised his theory and tends to explain depression in terms of the__(159)__ people make for events in their lives. Depressed people attribute negative events to three factors: a__(160)__ factor that is unlikely to change, a__(161)__ factor that affects almost all areas of one's life, and an__(162)__ factor that is characteristic of one's self rather than the environment. Cross-cultural research has provided support for Seligman's revised claims.

The Cognitive Viewpoint: Kelly's personal-__(163)__ theory has found that depressed people hold more negative constructs about themselves than do nondepressed people. But the most influential cognitive view is Beck's__(164)__ *theory.* Beck argues that depressed people exhibit a *cognitive*__(165)__: they have a negative view of themselves, their current circumstances, and their future possibilities. This triad is common to depressed psychiatric patients, but not to people with other disorders, suggesting that it is__(166)__ to depression.

Research by Lauren Alloy and colleagues has found that nondepressed individuals tend to__(167)__ the likelihood of positive events and__(168)__ the likelihood of negative ones, thus non-depressed individuals appear to have an unrealistically__(169)__ view of themselves and the world. In contrast, depressed individuals have a more accurate view of their reality, a so-called depressive__(170)__.

Susan Nolen-Hoeksema proposes yet another__(171)__ view of depression. She claims that people who constantly think about their sad state, or__(172)__, experience more severe and chronic depression than do individuals who take action to improve their lives. The "Anatomy of a Contemporary Research Study" section of the textbook focuses on a study that was designed to test the rumination theory of depression.

Anatomy of a Contemporary Research Study: Are People Who Ruminate about Their Problems More Likely to Become Depressed? *Read the summary of Nolen-Hoeksema and Morrow's study on page 500 in your textbook and answer the following questions.*

What was the authors rationale?

What methods did the author use to test the hypothesis?

What was the outcome of the study and what did the authors conclude the results meant?

A continuing problem for the ____(173)____ is the determination of whether patterns of thought are the cause, or the result, of depression. Currently, there is more evidence that depressed thinking styles accompany, or ____(174)____ the onset of depression, suggesting that they might not be the cause.

The ____(175)____ Viewpoint: Psychologists who ascribe to a humanistic viewpoint feel that depression is attributed to the frustration of self-actualization. Specifically, if the ____(176)____ self has qualities that are too distinct from those of the ____(177)____ self, the person becomes depressed.

Mini-review of Anxiety, Somatoform, Dissociative and Mood Disorders: Match the disorder with its correct description.

________1. psychogenic amnesia
________2. anxiety
________3. compulsion
________4. seasonal affective disorder
________5. simple phobia
________6. mood disorders
________7. malingering
________8. dissociative disorders
________9. anxiety disorders
________10. obsession
________11. bipolar disorder
________12. generalized anxiety disorder
________13. la belle indifference
________14. agoraphobia
________15. dissociative identity disorder
________16. hypochondriasis
________17. major depression
________18. phobia
________19. somatoform disorders
________20. panic disorder
________21. obsessive-compulsive disorder

A. This disorder is characterized by a memory loss characteristic of amnesia, but normally involves fleeing one's home and adopting a new identity
B. A form of depression in whichpeople often experience extreme depression during specific seasons of the year
C. A person invents symptoms to be relieved of certain responsibilities
D. A feeling of apprehension accompanied by increased sympathetic nervous system activity, which produces increases in sweating, heart rate, and breathing rate
E. A person with this disorder is in a constant state of anxiety that exists independent of any particular stressful situation; the anxiety is called "free floating" and has worry as its central feature
F. This disorder is marked by sudden, unexpected attacks of overwhelming anxiety; attacks are characterized by overwhelming anxiety accompanied by dizziness, trembling, cold sweats, heart palpitations, shortness of breath, fears, and feelings of being detached from one's body
G. A persistent, recurring thought
H. Fears of public scrutiny
I. The experience of excessive, inappropriate, uncontrollable, irrational fear; it is the most common form of psychological disorder
J. An intense, irrational fear of a specific object or situation
K. This disorder, formally called manic depression, is characterized by short or long alternations of elation and major depression, typically separated by days or weeks of normal moods
L. This state is characterized by euphoria, hyperactivity, grandiose ideas, annoying and incoherent talkativeness, unrealistic optimism, and inflated

________22. social phobias
________23. psychogenic fugue
________24. conversion disorders
________25. mania

self-esteem

M. This is a disorder in which a person interprets the slightest physical change in his or her body as evidence of a serious illness
N. A repetitive action that you feel compelled to perform
O. The fear of being in public
P. Disorder in which people have persistent, recurring thought and feel they must engage in a repetitive action that then interfers with their daily functioning
Q. Disorders characterized by physical symptoms in the absence of disease or injury; a person truly believes the symptoms are real
R. An individual exhibits loss or alteration of a physical function without any apparent physical cause
S. Term for a patient's apparent lack of concern about his or her symptoms
T. In these disorders a person's conscious awareness loses access to certain of his or her thoughts, feelings, and memories
U. This is characterized by the inability to recall personally significant memories, ones usually related to a traumatic event
V. A multiple personality disorder in which a person has two or more distinct personalities that alternate with one another
W. Individuals who are diagnosed with one of these disorders experience extreme or prolonged periods of depression or elation that is often unrelated to their everyday functioning
X. A prolonged, intense state that causes extreme distress and disruption of everyday life for months; people may express despondency, helplessness, loss of self-esteem, insomnia, and fail to perform up to their normal academic and vocational standards
Y. A disorder characterized by persistent anxiety that disrupts everyday life

VI. Schizophrenia: This disorder is a severe psychological disorder characterized by impaired social, ___(178)___, cognitive, and perceptual functioning. The first modern classification of schizophrenia occurred in the mid 1800s when Benedict___(179)___ used the term *demence precoce*, or premature mental deterioration, to describe the behavior of a 13-year-old boy. Kraepelin later called the disorder___(180)___. Finally, it was Eugen ___(181)___that coined the term **schizophrenia.**

Characteristics of Schizophrenia: Schizophrenia is characterized by___(182)___ disturbances. People with the disorder may display an inability to focus attention, which may account for cognitive___(183)___. They may invent words called ___(184)___, and meaningless word strings called *word salad.* Also, they often experience___(185)___, or sensory experiences in the absence of sensory stimulation. The most distinctive cognitive disturbances are *delusions,* or ___(186)___. The most common delusions are delusions of influence (*thought*___(187)___). Less common are delusions of___(188)___ in which individuals feel they are a famous or influential person. Schizophrenics typically also have inappropriate or flat emotions.

Kinds of Schizophrenia:

___(189)___schizophrenia is the category for cases that do not fall neatly into any of the following:

___(190)___ **schizophrenia** is characterized by marked personality deterioration, gibberish, outlandish dress, ritualized movement, and obscene behavior. Odd, inappropriate laughter is a hallmark.

Catatonic schizophrenia is characterized by unusual___(191)___ behavior, often alternating between *catatonic*___(192)___(frantic pacing, incoherent speech, stereotypic movement) and *catatonic*___(193)___ (may barely move, may be mute, possibly freezing in a body position, exhibiting "waxy flexibility").

___(194)___**schizophrenia** is characterized by hallucinations, delusions, suspiciousness, and argumentativeness. Because they may feel threatened by other people, people with paranoid schizophrenia may become violent.

Causes of Schizophrenia: No single viewpoint can explain all cases of schizophrenia.
The Biopsychological Viewpoint: Biopsychological theories emphasize genetic,__(195)__, and neurological causes. Schizophrenia runs in families, but to assess the relative contributions of heredity and experiences, researchers have turned to__(196)__ studies. The studies have tended to support the__(197)__ basis of schizophrenia. Biochemical research has focused on high levels of__(198)__. There are three lines of evidence to support this focus. First,__(199)__ used in treatment block dopamine receptors. Second, drugs such as amphetamines, which__(200)__ dopamine, produce schizophrenic symptoms in normal people. Third, *L-dopa,* a drug used to treat Parkinson's disease,__(201)__ dopamine levels and induces schizophrenic symptoms in people with Parkinson's. Additionally, biopsychological researchers have been struck by research findings that show that a disproportionate number of schizophrenics are born in the __(202)__ months. This led to the suggestion of a possible connection to the role of the__(203)__ virus prenatally. Various types of studies have provided indirect support for the__(204)__ basis of schizophrenia.

Another promising approach involves the study of neurological__(205)__. There are two kinds of schizophrenic syndromes. __(206)__ (active) *symptoms* and__(207)__ (passive) *symptoms* are related to a good or poor response to drug treatment, an increase or decrease in dopamine activity, and reveal no brain structure pathology; or often involve enlarged brain ventricles, respectively. __(208)__ scans show that the disorder is often associated with unusual brain activity.

The__(209)__ Viewpoint: According to this viewpoint, schizophrenics are people who have failed to overcome their dependence on their mothers and, as a result, become fixated at the oral stage. Parents who are high in __(210)__ *emotion* criticize their child, are hostile toward the child, and become emotionally overinvolved in the child's well-being. Such parents may contribute to the maintenance or relapse of__(211)__ in their child.

The Behavioral Viewpoint: This perspective assumes that schizophrenics are__(212)__ for behaving in bizarre ways.

The Cognitive Viewpoint: Proponents of this view argue that disturbances in__(213)__ and thinking are main factors. Children of parents who __(214)__ in confusing and irrational ways are predisposed to develop the irrational thought patterns of schizophrenia. And personal-construct-theory-oriented research has found that disordered__(215)__ is found in people who use either too few or too many personal-construct dimensions in perceiving social reality.

The Humanistic Viewpoint: To a humanistic psychologist, schizophrenia reflects the most extreme __(216)__between the public self and the actual self.

VII. Personality Disorders:__(217)__ of the *Diagnostic and Statistical Manual of Mental Disorders (DSM-IV)* includes the personality disorders which are longstanding, inflexible, maladaptive patterns of behavior. Individuals with a personality disorder exhibit certain personality__(218)__ to an unusual, inappropriate extreme. Table 14.4 on page 508 of your textbook summarizes the personality disorders. Currently, research into personality disorders has focused on the__(219)__ personality disorder due to its prevalence, extreme disruption, and treatment difficulties. Individuals with a borderline personality disorder tend to have inconsistent__(220)__ and are extremely unstable in their moods.

The Antisocial Personality Disorder: This disorder is characterized by maladaptive behavior beginning in __(221)__. This behavior may include lying, stealing, truancy, vandalism, fighting, drug abuse, physical cruelty, academic failure, and early sexual activity. Adults may not conform to social__(222)__. They may fail to hold a job, honor financial obligations, or to fulfill parental expectations. Normally, they are charming and can lie with a straight face, but they remain impulsive and demonstrate a remarkable lack of__(223)__. In the nineteenth century, antisocial personality disorder was referred to as "moral insanity." However throughout most of the twentieth century it has been called __(224)__ or *sociopathy.*

Causes of the Antisocial Personality Disorder: Studies have provided evidence of a__(225)__ predisposition. Heredity provides people who develop an antisocial personality an unusually low level of physiological__(226)__.

__(227)__ emphasize the influence of abusive or physically absent parents who make the child feel rejected. Because the children have no ties to their parents, they fail to develop an adequate__(228)__, including a conscience. __(229)__ believe parents reward, or fail to punish, antisocial behaviors.

Take a short study break and then complete the mini-review below.

Mini-review of Schizophrenic and Personality disorders: Match the term with its correct description.

________1. schizophrenia:
________2. word salad
________3. paranoid schizophrenia
________4. demence precoce
________5. neologisms
________6. antisocial personality disorder
________7. delusions
________8. disorganized schizophrenia
________9. Eugen Bleuler
________10. dementia praecox
________11. personality disorders
________12. undifferentiated schizophrenia
________13. thought broadcasting
________14. hallucinations
________15. catatonic schizophrenia
________16. delusions of grandeur
________17. border-line personality disorder

A. This disorder is a severe psychological disorder characterized by impaired social, emotional, cognitive, and perceptual functioning
B. Benedict Morel's term for schizophrenia and the first modern classification of schizophrenia
C. Meaningless word strings uttered by schizophrenics
D. Kraepelin's term for schizophrenia
E. The category for schizophrenic cases that do not fall neatly into any of the others
F. He coined the term *schizophrenia*
G. The invented words of schizophrenics
H. Sensory experiences in the absence of sensory stimulation
I. Subtype of schizophrenia characterized by marked personality deterioration, gibberish, outlandish dress, ritualized movement, and obscene behavior; odd, inappropriate laughter is a hallmark
J. False beliefs; the most distinctive cognitive disturbances of schizophrenics
K. Term for the most common type of delusions; delusions of influence
L. Disorders characterized by longstanding, inflexible, maladaptive patterns of behavior
M. Term for the less common type of delusions in which individuals feel they are a famous or influential person
N. Subtype of schizophrenia characterized by unusual motor behavior, often alternating between frantic pacing, incoherent speech, stereotypic movement, and behavior in which people barely move, may be mute, possibly freezing in a body position, exhibiting "waxy flexibility"
O. Subtype of schizophrenia characterized by hallucinations, delusions, suspiciousness, and argumentativeness; because they may feel threatened by other people, people with this disorder may become violent
P. This disorder is characterized by maladaptive behavior beginning in childhood; normally, people with this disorder are charming and can lie with a straight face, but they remain impulsive and demonstrate a remarkable lack of remorse
Q. Individuals tend to have inconsistent self-images and are extremely unstable in their moods

VIII. Thinking About Psychology: Should We Retain the Insanity Defense?

The Nature of the Insanity Defense: **Insanity** is a__(230)__, not a psychological or psychiatric, term attesting that the person is not responsible for his or her actions. The most widely used standard for determining insanity is that of the American__(231)__ Institute. It comprises two rules:

1) The__(232)__ *rule* says that a person was insane at the time of a crime if the person did not know what he or she did or did not know that it was wrong.
2) The __(233)__ *rule,* which presumes the reality of free will, says that a person was insane at the time of a crime if the person was not in voluntary control of his or her behavior.

Controversy Concerning the Insanity Defense:
Recent cases involving the insanity defense have provoked (234) . The cases include John Hinckley, Dan White, and Kenneth Bianchi. Were these people truly insane, or did some of them fake their symptoms?

A Proposed Alternative: The notoriety of cases such as those of John Hinkley, Dan White, and Kenneth Bianchi prompted a (235) of the insanity defense by state legislatures and professional organizations. Some states have abandoned the insanity defense entirely, while others have adopted the rule of (236) *but mentally ill.* The American Psychiatric Association, the American Psychological Association, and the American Bar Association have all taken (237) stands on the issue. The American (238) Association says that the insanity defense is a legal and moral question, not a psychiatric one. The American (239) Association has called for further research. The American (240) Association would retain the cognitive rule, but would eliminate the volitional rule. Despite the controversy, the insanity defense is rarely used and is even more rarely successful.

KEY RESEARCH FINDINGS

Provide the details of the following key research studies in psychology:

1. **Bruce, Takeuchi, & Leaf (1991):** Found that poverty is associated with a higher risk of almost all psychological disorders. (Page 481)
2. **Monroe & Simons (1991):** Found support for the diathesis-stress model by indicating that social stress interacting with physiological predisposition can cause some psychological disorders, such as major depression. (Page 482)
3. **Torgersen (1983):** Showed that the concordance rate (the likelihood that a person will develop a psychological disorder given a close relative has it) is higher for identical twins than for fraternal twins. (Page 486)
4. **Kilborn & Labbe (1990):** Studied maladaptive consequences of phobias. (Page 487)
5. **Ohman, Erixon, & Lofberg (1975):** Found that fear of inherently dangerous stimuli, such as snakes, persists longer than phobias associated with usually nonthreatening objects such as houses. (Page 488)
6. **Williams, Turner, & Peer (1985):** Indicated that a phobic person's self-efficacy is a more important factor than the person's anxiety level or perception of danger. (Page 489)
7. **Rasmussen (1993):** Provided evidence that obsessive-compulsive disorders run in families. (Page 490)
8. **Clifford, Murray, & Fulker (1984):** Study showed that almost half the variability in obsessional symptoms from one person to another were accounted for by heredity. (Page 490)
9. **Barsky et al. (1993):** Indicated that hypochondriacs presumed that being healthy meant having no medical symptoms whatsoever. (Page 491)
10. **Torgersen (1986):** Found a higher concordance rate in identical twins than for fraternal twins with somatoform disorders. (Page 491)
11. **Rothbaum & Foa (1991):** Showed that conversion disorder might be induced by severe psychological trauma, such as sexual abuse. (Page 491)
12. **Christianson & Nilsson (1984):** Indicated that psychogenic amnesia was the result of repressing unpleasant or traumatic memories. (Page 492)
13. **Spanos, Weekes, & Bertrand (1983):** Indicated that some cases of multiple personality disorder may be no more than intentional or unintentional role playing. (Page 494)
14. **American Psychiatric Association (1994):** Stated that 2-3 percent of men and 5-9 percent of women suffer from major depression. (Page 494)
15. **O'Donnell, Farmer, & Catalan (1993):** Found that the vast majority of people who commit suicide do not leave a note. (Page 495)
16. **Baumeister (1990):** Theorized that suicides are based on a self-image too negative to bear. (Page 495)
17. **Shneidman (1994):** Found that 90 percent of people who attempt suicide preceded the act by verbal or behavioral warnings. (Page 495)
18. **Daigle & Mishara (1995):** Found that counselors on suicide hotlines must tailor their responses to each individual caller. (Page 496)
19. **Lester (1993):** Found that suicide prevention centers lower the suicide rate. (Page 496)
20. **American Psychiatric Association (1994):** Found that about 1 percent of adults have bipolar disorder. (Page 497)

21. **Egeland et al. (1987):** Studied bipolar disorder in the Amish community. (Page 497)
22. **Traskman et al. (1981):** Measured serotonin (by-product) levels in the brains of persons who had attempted suicide and found that lower levels can be associated with further attempts. (Page 498)
23. **Nolen-Hoeksema, Girgus, & Seligman (1992):** Equated a pessimistic explanatory style with future episodes of depression. (Page 499)
24. **Nolen-Hoeksema & Morrow (1993):** Found that people who dwell on depression are more likely to stay depressed than those who focus on something else. (Page 500)
25. **Simons, Garfield, & Murphy (1984):** Studied the question of whether or not depression is caused by a depressed style of thinking, or if the depressed thinking is a result of depression. (Page 501)
26. **Norman & Malla (1993):** Found that while schizophrenic patients had not been exposed to unusually high levels of stress, they are more vulnerable to stressors. (Page 504)
27. **Mednick, Huttunen, & Machon (1994):** Linked higher rates of schizophrenia to prenatal influenza. (Page 505)
28. **Erlenmeyer-Kimling et al. (1994):** Failed to find a link between schizophrenia and prenatal influenza. (Page 505)
29. **Davis & Phelps (1995):** Found a higher concordance rate for schizophrenia in identical twins sharing a placenta than those who did not. (Page 505)
30. **Andreasen et al. (1995):** Found that evidence of a syndrome of negative symptoms for schizophrenia is stronger than a single syndrome of positive symptoms. (Page 506)
31. **Laing (1967):** Claimed schizophrenia is caused when a person develops a false public self to confront an intolerable situation. (Page 506)
32. **Orne, Dinges, & Orne (1984):** Described a case study of antisocial personality disorder and the insanity defense in law. (Page 511)
33. **Poulson (1990):** Showed that a guilty-but-mentally-ill verdict could reduce guilty or not guilty verdicts by two thirds. (Page 512)

PRACTICE TEST A

1. Psychopathology is the study of
   a. psychopaths.
   b. schizophrenia.
   c. psychological disorders.
   d. physiological bases of mental illness.

Obj.: 1 Page: 478

2. A student compulsively rearranges his room over and over. His psychotherapist attributes this to his desire to control an unconscious conflict over sex. The psychotherapist probably favors the
   a. cognitive viewpoint.
   b. behavioral viewpoint.
   c. humanistic viewpoint.
   d. psychoanalytic viewpoint.

Obj.: 2 Page: 480-481

3. Psychological disorders associated with maladaptive attempts to deal with anxiety, but with relatively good contact with reality, have typically been called
   a. mania.
   b. insanity.
   c. neuroses.
   d. psychoses.

Obj.: 3 Page: 482

4. While walking through a shopping center, you suddenly have an intense feeling of dread, notice your heart beating strongly, feel like you are suffocating, and find yourself running for the nearest exit. You would be exhibiting symptoms of
   a. mania.
   b. acrophobia.
   c. schizophrenia.
   d. panic disorder.

Obj.: 4 Page: 487

5. A college student faced with upcoming exams and term papers responds to his resulting feelings of anxiety by reorganizing his notes, rearranging his bookshelves, cleaning out his desk drawer, and straightening up his closet. He would be showing symptoms of
   a. claustrophobia.
   b. psychogenic fugue.
   c. disorganized schizophrenia.
   d. obsessive-compulsive disorder.

Obj.: 4 Page: 489-490

6. Just before a major singing competition, one of the singers loses his voice. A physical examination reveals no medical cause for the condition. This is most likely a case of
   a. hypochondriasis.
   b. psychogenic fugue.
   c. conversion disorder.
   d. obsessive-compulsive disorder.

Obj.: 5 Page: 491

7. A woman subjected to horrible abuse from her husband suddenly loses her memory for her self, husband, and place of employment, and begins a new life, with a new identity, in another state. This is most likely a case of
   a. hypermnesia.
   b. psychogenic fugue.
   c. psychogenic amnesia.
   d. conversion disorder.

Obj.: 6 Page: 492

8. A friend of yours suddenly changes many of his habits. He stays in bed until late afternoon, rarely leaves his room, shows little appetite for food, no longer takes daily showers, and expresses no interest in spending time with friends. This is most likely a case of
   a. agoraphobia.
   b. schizophrenia.
   c. major depression.
   d. conversion disorder.

Obj.: 7 Page: 494

9. An influential cognitive-behavioral theory of depression is based on Martin Seligman's notion of
   a. reinforcement theory.
   b. learned helplessness.
   c. the cognitive triad.
   d. incongruence between the actual and the ideal self.

Obj.: 8 Page: 499-500

10. A student returns to his dormitory room and finds his roommate immobile, staring into his closet. He maintains this pose for several hours. This is most likely a case of
    a. claustrophobia.
    b. panic disorder.
    c. somatoform disorder.
    d. catatonic schizophrenia.

Obj.: 9 Page: 503

11. Research conducted within the biopsychological framework
    a. supports the genetic basis of schizophrenia.
    b. has failed to provide any evidence of the role of heredity in schizophrenia.
    c. has shown that schizophrenia does not run in families.
    d. has failed to identify any possible biochemical or neurological causes of schizophrenia.

Obj.: 10 Page: 503

12. A young man enjoys getting into fights, has a history of stealing cars, and expresses no remorse for inflicting physical and emotional harm on others. This is most likely a case of
    a. mania.
    b. paranoid schizophrenia.
    c. multiple personality disorder.
    d. antisocial personality disorder.

Obj.: 11 Page: 507

13. Today, the insanity defense is based on
    a. a cognitive rule and a behavioral rule.
    b. a volitional rule and a behavioral rule.
    c. a cognitive rule and a volitional rule.
    d. a complex set of legal and psychological rules.

Obj.: 12 Page: 509-512

PRACTICE TEST B

1. Whatever criteria are used to evaluate the presence of psychopathology, it is important to realize that
   a. there is no sharp line distinguishing psychological health from psychological disorder.
   b. only one of the three criteria should be applied to determine psychopathology.
   c. all behavior that deviates from the norm is simple nonconformity and should be encouraged.
   d. all individuals who manifest disturbed behavior want to change that behavior.

Obj.: 1 Page: 478-80

2. What criterion for psychological disorders deals with qualitative and quantitative differences?
   a. personal distress
   b. maladaptiveness
   c. abnormality
   d. psychopathology

Obj.: 1 Page: 478

3. Some authorities believe that many persons accused of witchcraft in Salem, Massachusetts, in 1692
   a. were under the control of demonic forces.
   b. were actually suffering from psychological disorders.
   c. were sensitive to the changing high and low tides along the Atlantic seaboard.
   d. suffered from an inheritable disease.

Obj.: 1 Page: 478-479

4. Dr. Ramirez is studying how genetic factors may be involved in the occurrence of bipolar affective disorder. This approach to psychopathology is in keeping with the
   a. psychoanalytic viewpoint.
   b. diathesis-stress viewpoint.
   c. biopsychological viewpoint.
   d. cognitive viewpoint.

Obj.: 2 Page: 480

5. An electroplater who worked in an environment where he was constantly exposed to toxic chemicals began to exhibit some rather bizarre behaviors. The examining psychiatrist most likely adopted the
   a. cognitive viewpoint.
   b. diathesis-stress viewpoint.
   c. behavioral viewpoint.
   d. biopsychological viewpoint.

Obj.: 2 Page: 480-481

6. When John was asked to give a brief presentation in front of the board of directors, he felt overwhelmed by fear, panic, and anxiety, similar to what he had experienced while giving an oral class report during his sophomore year in college. The most obvious explanation for his feelings would favor the
   a. psychoanalytic viewpoint.
   b. behavioral viewpoint.
   c. humanistic viewpoint.
   d. biopsychological viewpoint.

Obj.: 2 Page: 481

7. Based on his study of eight "pseudopatients" who were admitted to mental hospitals after claiming to hear voices, Rosenhan concluded that
   a. seeing things is more diagnostic of schizophrenia than is hearing voices.
   b. most people who are in mental hospitals are not psychologically disturbed.
   c. mental patients are more interpersonally perceptive than psychologists are.
   d. psychiatric diagnoses are influenced more by preconceptions and situation than by objective symptoms.

Obj.: 3 Page: 484

8. How many axes does DSM-IV provide for diagnosing psychological disorders?
   a. three
   b. four
   c. five
   d. seven

Obj.: 3 Page: 482-483

9. An outgoing and neighborly woman suddenly begins to stay in the house. She orders her groceries by phone and has them delivered. She might be experiencing
   a. a simple phobia.
   b. agoraphobia.
   c. claustrophobia.
   d. acrophobia.

Obj.: 4 Page: 488

10. Helen and her husband have agreed they will sit down and work on their will on Saturday afternoon. That morning, Helen decides she must clean out the garage, while her husband feels the irresistible urge to begin painting the outside of their house. How would a strict behaviorist explain their compulsive activity?
   a. Each of them feels greater self-efficacy in these tasks than in completing the will.
   b. Their compulsive behavior is a symbolic "cleaning out" and "covering over" of their unconscious.
   c. Both have been frustrated in their drive to self-actualize during their lives so far.
   d. Their compulsive activity is serving to avoid the anxiety of working on the will.

Obj.: 4 Page: 490

11. Richard sees a red spot on his face and is convinced he has skin cancer. A bruise appears on his leg and he is terrified he has a blood disease. He is well known to nearly every physician in his town. Richard may be diagnosed as
   a. suffering from an obsessive-compulsive disorder.
   b. displaying a conversion disorder.
   c. having hypochondriasis.
   d. being dissociated from his normal self.

Obj.: 5 Page: 490

12. A person who interprets the slightest physical changes in his or her body as evidence of a serious illness is experiencing a disorder known as (a)
   a. hypochondriasis.
   b. conversion disorder.
   c. psychosomatic disorder.
   d. panic disorder.

Obj.: 6 Page: 491

13. Adam Jones arrives in a new city seeking work as a day laborer. About a week later, he suddenly realizes that he is Benjamin Smith and has a responsible job and a family in a far-off city. Such shifts in identity are seen in
   a. psychogenic fugue.
   b. psychogenic amnesia.
   c. dementia.
   d. disorganized schizophrenia.

Obj.: 6 Page: 492

14. Keri is headed to her room but finds that she is in the wrong residence hall. She opens her purse and finds a note signed "Vicki." The note says that Vicki was reassigned to another residence hall. Keri was upset at Vicki because Vicki didn't tell Keri that her (Keri's) room was changed. Keri is probably suffering from
   a. paranoid schizophrenia.
   b. psychogenic amnesia.
   c. a conversion disorder.
   d. multiple personality disorder.

Obj.: 6 Page: 493

15. A young man is admitted to a psychiatric emergency center after a suicide attempt. The person describes a several-year history of bouts of euphoria in which he initiates many projects and relationships, then a period of normal feelings followed by weeks of despair and despondency. The examining psychiatrist or psychologist is likely to suspect
   a. major depression.
   b. bipolar disorder.
   c. dissociative disorder.
   d. disorganized schizophrenia.

Obj.: 7 Page: 497

16. Rhonda always imagined herself proudly graduating from college and becoming a high school mathematics instructor. However, she felt she had to support her husband's military career by frequently moving from base to base. His frequent long absences left her totally responsible for their three children. Over the years, Rhonda has felt more and more depressed about her life and about herself. A humanistic psychologist would attribute Rhonda's depression to
   a. her failure to self-actualize.
   b. self-deprecating thoughts and beliefs about her life.
   c. her rigidity in depending upon rationalization and displacement.
   d. lack of reinforcement for certain behaviors.

Obj.: 8 Page: 501

17. A patient comes into the emergency room of a hospital. She complains that voices are telling her to cut herself and that her mind is racing all the time, preventing her from concentrating on anything. Her rapid-fire conversation is full of strange words. Most likely, she will be diagnosed as suffering from
    a. generalized anxiety.
    b. somatoform disorder.
    c. dissociative identity disorder.
    d. schizophrenia.

Obj.: 9 Page: 502

18. Rene is a schizophrenic. She will not speak, shows flat affect, is apathetic, and is withdrawn. Her intellectual abilities have decreased and she seems to enjoy nothing. She does not respond to drug therapy. Rene's symptoms would be described as
    a. eclectic.
    b. diffuse.
    c. negative.
    d. positive.

Obj.: 10 Page: 505-506

19. A disorder marked by impulsive, manipulative, often criminal behavior, without any feelings of guilt in the perpetrator, is called
    a. the antisocial personality disorder.
    b. psychosis.
    c. paranoid schizophrenia.
    d. the passive-aggressive personality disorder.

Obj.: 11 Page: 507

20. The association that would retain the cognitive rule, but would eliminate the volitional rule is the
    a. American Psychological Association.
    b. American Medical Association.
    c. American Psychiatric Association.
    d. American Bar Association.

Obj.: 12 Page: 512

ESSAY QUESTIONS

1. List the six major viewpoints on psychological disorders, and describe what each viewpoint claims are the causes of psychological disorders.

Obj.: 2 Page: 480

2. "People who are seriously considering suicide don't talk about it. Those who tell others they are thinking about suicide just want attention. Ignore them." Based on your present level of knowledge, how would you evaluate this bit of folk wisdom?

Obj.: 8 Page: 495

ANSWER RECORD FOR CHAPTER 14

Comprehensive Guided Review:

1. classification	13. disorder	26. syphilis	38. personal constructs	50. DSM-IV
2. deviates	14. variation	27. unconscious	39. beliefs	51. framework
3. norm	15. subjectivity	28. repressed	40. more	52. psychoanalytic
4. qualitatively	16. cause	29. Freud	41. without	53. interaction
5. quantitatively	17. six	30. anxiety	42. self-actualization	54. five
6. context	18. gods	31. defense mechanisms	43. expressing	55. categories
7. atypicality	19. natural		44. conditional	56. personality
8. social	20. Temperament	32. medical	45. predisposition	57. medical
9. agoraphobia	21. Supernatural	33. reinforcement	46. stress	58. stress
10. maladaptiveness	22. moon	34. punishment	47. low	59. functioning
11. Personal Distress	23. natural	35. observing	48. high	60. reliability
12. without	24. biopsychological	36. environmental	49. Kraepelin	61. validity
	25. neurotransmitters	37. Epictetus		62 diagnosis

Anatomy of a Classic Research Study: Can Sane People Be Recognized in a Mental Hospital?

What was the rationale for the study?
Rosenhan (1973) wondered if sane people, complaining of symptoms of schizophrenia, could gain admission to a mental hospital and, once admitted, be discovered by the professional staff.

What methods did the author use to test the hypothesis?
Rosenhan used eight "pseudopatients" who gained admission to mental hospitals by complaining of hearing imaginary voices..

What was the outcome of the study and what did the authors conclude that the results meant?
His results showed that diagnosis is influenced more by preconceptions and the context in which we find a person than by any objective characteristics of that person. Additionally, this study has been subject to criticism. Spitzer claims that Rosenhan misinterpreted the results. He claims that the admissions were justified based on the reports of the "patients," since people who report hearing voices might have schizophrenia and schizophrenics can go long periods of time without displaying obvious symptoms of the disease. Others, however, join Rosenhan in his criticism of diagnostic labels based on:

a) Critics point to the use of diagnostic labels to discredit or persecute people with unpopular ideas. These labels are, at best, inconsistent.
b) Thomas Szasz (1960) has gone so far as to call mental illness a "myth."

Mini-review of the Nature of , Viewpoints On, and Classification of Psychological Disorders:
Part I: Matching
1. O; 2. H; 3. J; 4. K; 5. A; 6. D; 7. E; 8. N; 9. B; 10. I; 11. M; 12. L; 13. F; 14. C; 15. G

Part II: Provide a brief description of the major focus of each of the following viewpoints on pscyhological disorders:

Biopsychological	*Inherited or acquired brain disorders involving imbalances in neurotransmitters or damage to brain structures*
Psychoanalytic	*Unconscious conflicts over impulses such as sex and aggression, originating in childhood*
Behavioral	*Reinforcement of inappropriate behaviors and punishment or extinction of appropriate behaviors*
Cognitive	*Irrational or maladaptive thinking about one's self, life events, and the world in general*
Humanistic	*Incongruence between one's actual self and public self as a consequence of trying to live up to the demands of others*
Diathesis-Stress	*A biological predisposition interacting with stressful life experiences*

63. sympathetic
64. disorder
65. Anxiety
66. independent
67. worry
68. women
69. men
70. Biopsychological
71. serotonin
72. psychoanalysts
73. cognitive-behavioral
74. actual
75. ought
76. Panic
77. sudden
78. few
79. Biological
80. concordance
81. predisposition
82. thinking
83. fear
84. Simple
85. Social
86. public
87. hereditary
88. evolution
89. Psychoanalysts
90. unconscious
91. Behavioral
92. self-efficacy
93. believe
94. obsession
95. compulsion
96. obsessive-compulsive
97. twin
98. PET
99. fixation
100. Behavioral
101. absence
102. real
103. invents
104. Hypochondriasis
105. Psychoanalysts
106. positive reinforcement
107. negative reinforcement
108. cognitivists
109. without
110. concern
111. identical
112. fraternal
113. families
114. repressed
115. female
116. reinforced
117. Humanistic
118. conscious
119. Psychogenic Amnesia
120. quickly
121. psychoanalytic
122. fleeing
123. identity
124. personalities
125. childhood
126 role playing
127. mood
128. prolonged
129. despondency
130. cold
131. depression
132. seasons
133. winter
134. light
135. fluorescent
136. suicide
137. self image
138. is
139. moods
140. attempts
141. empathetic
142. Bipolar

143. mania
144. heredity
145. experiences
146. predisposition
147. neurotransmitters
148. low
149. low
150. high
151. lower
152. Psychoanalytic
153. little
154. reinforcement
155. cycle
156. cognitive
157. helplessness
158. control
159. attributions
160. stable
161. global
162. internal
163. construct
164. cognitive
165. triad
166. unique
167. overestimate
168. underestimate
169. positive
170. realism
171. cognitive
172. ruminate

Anatomy of a Contemporary Research Study: Are People Who Ruminate about Their Problems More Likely to Become Depressed?.

What was the authors rationale?
Nolen-Hoeksema and Morrow were interested in whether there was a causal association between rumination and depression.

What methods did the author use to test the hypothesis?
The authors randomly assigned depressed and non-depressed subjects to spend 8 minutes either focusing attention on their current feelings (rumination condition) or descriptions of geographic locations (distraction condition).

What results were obtained and what conclusions were drawn from them?
Nolen-Hoeksema and Morrow found that the depressed subjects in the rumination condition became more depressed and the depressed subjects in the destarction condition became less depressed. Rumination did not affect the mood of the non-depressed subjects.

---

173. cognitivists
174. follow
175. Humanistic
176. actual
177. ideal

Mini-review of Anxiety, Somatoform, Dissociative and Mood Disorders:
1. U; 2. D; 3. N; 4. B; 5. J; 6. W; 7. C; 8. T; 9. Y; 10. G; 11. K; 12. E; 13. S; 14. O; 15. V; 16. M; 17. X; 18. I; 19. R; 20. F; 21. P; 22. H; 23. A; 24. Q; 25. L

178. emotional
179. Morel
180. dementia praecox
181. Bleuler
182. cognitive
183. fragmentation
184. neologisms
185. hallucinations
186. false beliefs
187. broadcasting
188. grandeur
189. Undifferentiated
190. Disorganized
191. motor
192. excitement
193. immobility
194. Paranoid
195. biochemical
196. adoption
197. genetic
198. dopamine
199. drugs
200. increase
201. elevates
202. winter
203. influenza
204. viral
205. dysfunctions
206. Positive
207. negative
208. PET
209. Psychoanalytic
210. expressed
211. schizophrenia
212. rewarded
213. attention
214. communicate
215. thinking
216. incongruence
217. Axis II
218. traits
219. borderline
220. self-images
221. childhood
222. norms
223. remorse
224. psychopathy
225. physiological
226 arousal
227 Psychoanalysts
228 superego
229 Behaviorists

Mini-review of Schizophrenic and Personality disorders:
1. A; 2. C; 3. O; 4. B; 5. G; 6. P; 7. J; 8. I; 9. F; 10. D; 11. L; 12. E; 13. K; 14. H; 15. N; 16. M; 17. O

230. legal	232. cognitive	234. controversy	236. guilty	238. Psychiatric
231. Law	233. volitional	235. reevaluation	237. different	239. Psychological
				240. Bar

Practice Test A:

1. a. Incorrect: Psychopathology is the study of all psychological disorders, not just the behavior of psychopaths.
   b. Incorrect: Psychopathology is the study of all psychological disorders, not just the behavior of schizophrenics.
   c. Correct: Psychopathology is the study of all psychological disorders.
   d. Incorrect: Psychopathologists study more than just the physiological bases of mental illness.

2. a. Incorrect: Cognitive psychologists attribute abnormal behavior to maladaptive thinking patterns, not unconscious conflicts.
   b. Incorrect: Behavioral psychologists attribute abnormal behaviors to the environment, not unconscious conflicts over sex.
   c. Incorrect: Humanistic psychologists attribute abnormal behaviors to a failure of the individual to reach their individual potential.
   d. Correct: Psychoanalytic psychologists attribute abnormal behaviors to an unconscious conflict over sex.

3. a. Incorrect: Mania is the DSM-III term for a mood disorder characterized by an extreme elevation of mood.
   b. Incorrect: Insanity is a legal term attesting that a person is not responsible for his or her actions.
   c. Correct: Neurosis is a general category no longer in use that was used for maladaptive attempts to deal with anxiety but with relatively good contact with reality.
   d. Incorrect: Psychosis is also a term that is no longer in use; it was used for severe psychological disorders associated with thought disturbances, bizarre behavior, and poor contact with reality.

4. a. Incorrect: Mania is the DSM-III term for a mood disorder characterized by an extreme elevation of mood.
   b. Incorrect: Acrophobia is an intense fear of high places.
   c. Incorrect: Schizophrenia is psychological disorder that is characterized by grossly impaired social, emotional, cognitive, and perceptual functioning.
   d. Correct: A panic disorder is characterized by the onset of sudden, unexpected attacks of overwhelming anxiety accompanied by dizziness, trembling, increased heart rate, and feelings of being suffocated.

5. a. Incorrect: Claustrophobia is an intense fear of enclosed spaces.
   b. Incorrect: A psychogenic fugue is a disorder that is characterized by memory loss the loss of one's identity, and fleeing from one's home.
   c. Incorrect: Disorganized schizophrenia is behavior marked by severe personality deterioration and extremely bizarre behavior.
   d. Correct: Obsessive-compulsive disorder is a disorder in which the person has recurrent, intrusive thoughts and recurrent urges to perform ritualistic actions.

6. a. Incorrect: Hypochondriasis is a somatoform disorder in which the person interprets the slightest physical changes as evidence of a serious illness.
   b. Incorrect: A psychogenic fugue is a disorder that is characterized by memory loss, the loss of one's identity, and fleeing from one's home.
   c. Correct: A conversion disorder is a disorder in which the person exhibits motor or sensory loss or the alteration of a physiological function without any apparent physical cause.
   d. Incorrect: Obsessive-compulsive disorder in which the person has recurrent, intrusive thoughts and recurrent urges to perform ritualistic actions.

7. a. Incorrect: Hypermnesia is not discussed in this chapter.
   b. Correct: A psychogenic fugue is a disorder that is characterized by memory loss, the loss of one's identity, and fleeing from one's home.
   c. Incorrect: Psychogenic amnesia is marked by an ability to recall personally significant memories.
   d. Incorrect: A conversion disorder is a disorder in which the person exhibits motor or sensory loss or the alteration of a physiological function without any apparent physical cause.

8. a. Incorrect: Agoraphobia is a fear of being in public.
   b. Incorrect: Schizophrenia is a psychological disorder that is characterized by grossly impaired social, emotional, cognitive, and perceptual functioning.
   c. Correct: A mood disorder marked by depression so intense and prolonged that the person may be unable to function in everyday life.
   d. Incorrect: A conversion disorder is a disorder in which the person exhibits motor or sensory loss or the alteration of a physiological function without any apparent physical cause.

9. a. Incorrect: This theory was proposed by Lewinsohn.
   b. Correct: Seligman proposed a theory of depression based on learned helplessness.
   c. Incorrect: This is a cognitive but not a cognitive-behavioral construct.
   d. Incorrect: This is the humanistic viewpoint.

10. a. Incorrect: Claustrophobia is an intense fear of enclosed spaces.
    b. Incorrect: A panic disorder is characterized by the onset of sudden, unexpected attacks of overwhelming anxiety accompanied by dizziness, trembling, increased heart rate and feeling of being suffocated.
    c. Incorrect: Somatoform disorder is characterized by physical symptoms in the absence of disease or injury.
    d. Correct: Catatonic schizophrenia is marked by an unusual motor behavior, such as bizarre actions , extreme agitation or immobile stupor.

11. **a. Correct: The research into schizophrenia has supported a possible genetic nature for the disorder through family studies, adoption studies, and twin studies.**
    b. Incorrect: The research into schizophrenia has supported a possible genetic nature for the disorder through family studies, adoption studies, and twin studies.
    c. Incorrect: The research into schizophrenia has supported a possible genetic nature for the disorder through family studies, adoption studies, and twin studies.
    d. Incorrect: The research into schizophrenia has supported a possible genetic nature for the disorder through family studies, adoption studies, and twin studies

12. a. Incorrect: Mania is the DSM-III term for a mood disorder characterized by an extreme elevation of mood.
    b. Incorrect: Paranoid schizophrenia is a subtype of schizophrenia in which the patient experiences hallucinations, delusions, suspiciousness, and argumentativeness.
    c. Incorrect: Multiple personality disorder is a disorder in which the individual has two or more distinct personalities that alternate with one another.
    d. Correct: An antisocial personality disorder is characterized by impulsive, manipulative and often criminal behavior with any feelings of guilt or remorse.

13. a. Incorrect: The cognitive rule says that a person was insane at the time of a crime if the person did not know what he or she did or that it was wrong. The volitional rule says that a person was insane at the time of a crime if the person was not in voluntary control of his or her behavior. Both of these are applied today.
    b. Incorrect: The cognitive rule says that a person was insane at the time of a crime if the person did not know what he or she did or that it was wrong. The volitional rule says that a person was insane at the time of a crime if the person was not in voluntary control of his or her behavior. Both of these are applied today.
    c. Correct: The cognitive rule says that a person was insane at the time of a crime if the person did not know what he or she did or that it was wrong. The volitional rule says that a person was insane at the time of a crime if the person was not in voluntary control of his or her behavior. Both of these are applied today.
    d. Incorrect: The cognitive rule says that a person was insane at the time of a crime if the person did not know what he or she did or that it was wrong. The volitional rule says that a person was insane at the time of a crime if the person was not in voluntary control of his or her behavior. Both of these are applied today.

Practice Test B:

1. a. **Correct: Establishing psychopathology is difficult and there are not sharp distinctions distinguishing psychological health from nonhealth.**
   b. Incorrect: All three criteria should be applied.
   c. Incorrect: Not all behavior that deviates from the norm indicates psychopathology.
   d. Incorrect: Not all individuals who exhibit abnormal behavior exhibit psychological distress.

2. a. Incorrect: This assumes that our subjective feeling of anxiety, depression, or other unpleasant emotion determines whether we have a psychological disorder.
   b. Incorrect: According to this criterion, you would have a psychological disorder if your behavior seriously interrupted your social, academic, or vocational life.
   c. **Correct: Abnormality can be qualitative, or deviate from culturally acceptable standards; or quantitative, and deviate from the statistical average.**
   d. Incorrect: This is the study of psychological disorders.

3. a. Incorrect: The behavior was attributed to this at the time, however current-day authorities suggest that their behavior may have been the result of a psychological disorder.
   b. **Correct: Although alternative a. is mentioned in the textbook, it is not an explanation offered by authorities.**
   c. Incorrect: This is not a suggested as a possible cause by psychologists.
   d. Incorrect: Authorities suggest that the behavior was the result of a psychological disorder; the cause of that disorder is not discussed.

4. a. Incorrect: Psychoanalytic psychologists attribute abnormal behaviors to an unconscious conflict over sex.
   b. Incorrect: Diathesis-stress viewpoint proposes that people may differ in their biological predisposition to determine a disorder, but that the environment must allow for the expression of the disposition.
   c. **Correct: Biopsychological theory examines the influence of genetic factors, without concern for the environment.**
   d. Incorrect: Cognitive psychologists attribute abnormal behavior to maladaptive thinking patterns, not unconscious conflicts.

5. a. Incorrect: Cognitive psychologists attribute abnormal behavior to maladaptive thinking patterns, not unconscious conflicts.
   b. Incorrect: Diathesis-stress viewpoint proposes that people may differ in their biological predisposition to determine a disorder, but that the environment must allow for the expression of the disposition.
   c. Incorrect: A behavioral viewpoint argues that the environment and the learning of maladaptive behaviors is the root cause of the abnormal behavior.
   d. Correct: Biopsychological theory examines the influence of genetic and chemical factors.

6. a. Incorrect: Psychoanalytic psychologists attribute abnormal behaviors to an unconscious conflict over sex.
   b. **Correct: A behavioral viewpoint argues that the environment and the learning of maladaptive behaviors is the root cause of the abnormal behavior, thus they would suggest that John learned the maladaptive behavior during his college period.**
   c. Incorrect: Humanistic psychologists attribute abnormal behaviors to a failure of individuals to reach their individual potential.
   d. Incorrect: Biopsychological theory examines the influence of genetic factors, without concern for the environment.

7. a. Incorrect: Rosenhan concluded that psychiatric diagnoses were influenced by preconceptions and situations more than objective symptoms.
   b. Incorrect: Rosenhan concluded that psychiatric diagnoses were influenced by preconceptions and situations more than objective symptoms.
   c. Incorrect: Rosenhan concluded that psychiatric diagnoses were influenced by preconceptions and situations more than objective symptoms.
   d. **Correct: Rosenhan concluded that psychiatric diagnoses were influenced by preconceptions and situations more than objective symptoms.**

8. a. Incorrect: The DSM-IV has five axes.
   b. Incorrect: The DSM-IV has five axes.
   c. **Correct: The DSM-IV has five axes.**
   d. Incorrect: The DSM-IV has five axes.

9. a. Incorrect: This is the fear of a specific object or situation.
   b. **Correct: Agoraphobia is the fear of being in public places.**
   c. Incorrect: This is the fear of enclosed places.
   d. Incorrect: This is the fear of high places.

10. a. Incorrect: A behavioral theorist does not discuss self-efficacy; a cognitive theorist does.
b. Incorrect: A behavioral theorist does not discuss the existence of the unconscious; a psychoanalytic theorist does.
c. Incorrect: A humanistic theorist discusses progress toward self-actualization, not a behaviorist.
d. Correct: A behaviorist would argue that the activity is negatively rewarding, by decreasing the anxiety of the will.

11. a. Incorrect: With obsessive-compulsive disorder, Richard would be engaging in recurrent, intrusive thoughts and recurrent urges to perform ritualistic actions.
b. Incorrect: If Richard had a conversion disorder his symptoms would be real physical problems without a physiological cause; this is not the case.
c. Correct: Richard is demonstrating hypochondria in that he feels that any physical problem indicates a life-threatening illness.
d. Incorrect: Richard is not dissociated from himself; he is aware of the real world.

12. **a. Correct: Hypochondriasis is a disorder in which individuals interpret even the slightest change in their physical condition as indicative of a serious illness.**
b. Incorrect: A person with this disorder exhibits loss or alteration of a physical function without any apparent physical cause.
c. Incorrect: This disorder involves the occurrence of a physical malady as a function of psychological events.
d. Incorrect: This is an anxiety disorder.

13. **a. Correct: In a psychogenic fugue disorder the person leaves their environment, experiences a memory loss the loss of their identity and establishes a new identity in an other location.**
b. Incorrect: A psychogenic amnesia is marked by an ability to recall personally significant memories however in psychogenic amnesia the individual does not leave their home and family.
c. Incorrect: In dementia the individual experiences a decline in cognitive functions.
d. Incorrect: A disorganized schizophrenic demonstrates a severe deterioration of personality and exhibits extremely bizarre behavior.

14. a. Incorrect: A paranoid schizophrenic would demonstrate hallucinations, delusions and suspiciousness, and also be argumentative.
b. Incorrect: Psychogenic amnesia is marked by an ability to recall personally significant memories; however, in psychogenic amnesia individuals do not leave their home and family.
c. Incorrect: A conversion disorder is a disorder in which the person exhibits motor or sensory loss or the alteration of a physiological function without any apparent physical cause
d. Correct: Keri/Vicki is demonstrating symptoms of a multiple personality disorder.

15. a. Incorrect: In a major depression the individual would not demonstrate the periods of euphoria.
b. Correct: In a bipolar disorder the individual's moods swing from periods of extreme euphoria to periods of extreme depression.
c. Incorrect: A dissociative disorder is characterized by thoughts, feelings, and memories that become separated from one's conscious awareness.
d. Incorrect: Disorganized schizophrenia is a disorder in which the individual has a severe personality deterioration and exhibits extremely bizarre behavior.

16. **a. Correct: Humanistic psychologists attribute depression to a failure to work toward self-actualization.**
b. Incorrect: Cognitive theorists attribute depression to self-deprecating thoughts and beliefs about one's life.
c. Incorrect: Psychoanalytic theorists would attribute depression to defense mechanisms such as rationalization and displacement.
d. Incorrect: Behavioral theories would attribute depressive behavior to the lack of reinforcements.

17. a. Incorrect: A patient with a generalized anxiety disorder would demonstrate persistent anxiety, not a conversation of strange words.
b. Incorrect: A somatoform disorder is characterized by physical symptoms in the absence of any disease.
c. Incorrect: A dissociative identity disorder is characterized by the person demonstrating two or more intact personalities.
d. Correct: Symptoms such as hearing voices, racing mind, and conversation full of strange words are indicative of a schizophrenic disorder.

18. a. Incorrect: Eclectic refers to an approach to understanding abnormal disorders that uses multiple views.
b. Incorrect: Diffuse is not a term used to refer to symptoms of schizophrenia.
c. Correct: Rene is demonstrating negative, or passive symptoms.
d. Incorrect: Positive symptoms include active symptoms such as hallucinations, delusions, thought disoders, and bizarre behavior.

19. **a. Correct: Persons demonstrating an antisocial personality disorder engage in impulsive, manipulative behavior that is often criminal and without feelings of guilt.**
   b. Incorrect: Patients who are psychotic have lost touch with reality and engage in bizarre behavior, and have severe disruptions of social relations and thought disturbances
   c. Incorrect: A paranoid schizophrenic demonstrates hallucinations, delusions, suspiciousness, and argumentativeness.
   d. Incorrect: This disorder is characterized by unassertive behavior, as in forgetting, procrastinating, being late, and being inefficient.

20. a. Incorrect: The American Psychological Association argues for more research on the effects of the insanity defense before deciding to change or eliminate it.
   b. Incorrect: The American Medical Association has not taken a position on the issue.
   c. Incorrect: The American Psychiatric Association claims the insanity defense is a legal and moral issue not a psychiatric one and that psychiatrists can testify only as to the defendant's mental status, not his or her responsibility for the crime.
   d. Correct: The American Bar Association would be the one that would eliminate the volitional rule but maintain the cognitive rule.

Essay Questions:

1.

Biopsychological	Inherited or acquired brain disorders involving imbalances in neurotransmitters or damage to brain structures
Psychoanalytic	Unconscious conflicts over impulses such as sex and aggression, originating in childhood
Behavioral	Reinforcement of inappropriate behaviors and punishment or extinction of appropriate behaviors
Cognitive	Irrational or maladaptive thinking about one's self, life events and the world in general
Humanistic	Incongruence between one's actual self and public self as a consequence of trying to live up to the demands of others
Diathesis-Stress	A biological predisposition interacting with stressful life experiences

2. According to recent research, about 90 percent of people who attempt suicide offer some verbal or behavioral warning. These warning signs include changes in moods and habits, apathy, social withdrawal, poor grooming habits, loss of interest in recreational activities, giving away cherished belongings, and tying up loose ends in their lives. Others make overt threats. When accompanied by depression, any of these signals should be taken seriously. While empathetic listening is a good immediate response, referral or accompanying the person to a suicide center is better.

15 Therapy

After studying this chapter, you should be able to:

1. Describe an important principle regarding the relationship between beliefs about the origins of psychological disturbance and the treatments to correct them. (p. 518)

2. Briefly summarize the history of treatment for psychological disorders in the West, from the early Christian era up through the eighteenth century. (p. 518-519)

3. Summarize the contributions of Philippe Pinel, Benjamin Rush, Dorothea Dix, and Clifford Beers regarding improved treatment of psychologically disturbed individuals. (p. 520)

4. Define psychotherapy, briefly describe the historical origins of psychoanalysis as well as its goals. (p. 520-521)

5. List and describe four psychoanalytic treatment techniques and summarize how psychodynamic therapy differs from classic psychoanalysis. (p. 521-522)

6. Describe the general principle underlying all behavioral therapy and then list and describe eight specific learning-theory based treatment techniques. (p. 522-527)

7. Describe the general principle underlying all cognitive therapies and describe the important features of three cognitive therapy systems. (p. 527-531)

8. Describe the general distinguishing perspective of all the humanistic therapies, and then list and describe the important characteristics of four types of humanistic therapy systems. (p. 531-534)

9. Describe the core concept of the social-relations orientation and the reasons for the development of the group approach to therapy. (p. 534)

10. List and describe the important features of seven types of group-oriented forms of therapy. (p. 535-537)

11. Describe the core assumption of family therapy and then list and describe the important features of three types of family therapy. (p. 537-538)

12. Describe the core concept underlying all biopsychological therapies and then list and describe the important features of and controversy surrounding both psychosurgery and ETC. (p. 538-541)

13. Describe the principle underlying all drug therapies and then describe the important features of four groups of medications for the treatment of psychological disorders. (p. 541-542)

14. Define deinstitutionalization and then summarize the strengths and weaknesses of this important social policy, mentioning the goals of the community mental health movement. (p. 543-544)

15. List and describe four legally established principles regarding the rights of hospitalized mental patients and therapy clients, mentioning the relevant court cases that established these principles. (p. 545-546)

16. Summarize the relevant issues in selecting a therapist. (p. 546-548)

17. Summarize the important findings evaluating the effectiveness of psychotherapy. (p. 548-552)

COMPREHENSIVE GUIDED REVIEW

I. The History of Therapy: __(1)__ Age skulls have been found with holes cut in them. Authorities believe that the act of chipping holes in the skull, or **trephining,** was done to let out__(2)__ that caused abnormal behavior. Others suggest that perhaps the holes served some unknown medical purpose. Hippocrates turned away from a __(3)__ explanation of psychological disorders. He believed that disorders were caused by imbalances in fluids he called__(4)__.

During the __(5)__era, both naturalistic treatments and supernatural treatments existed. Inhumane treatment began in the late__(6)__ Ages and continued into the Renaissance, which saw the advent of the insane__(7)__. The most humane asylum was in__(8)__. This stood in contrast to the zoolike St. Mary's, where visitors called the inmates "Tom Fools" and the asylum became known as "__(9)__."

Physician Philippe __(10)__'s **moral therapy** was uniquely kind. Benjamin__(11)__ introduced Pinel's approach in the United States. In the course of his therapy, Rush prescribed work,__(12)__, and reading in addition to physical treatments, such as whirling in special chairs. Dorothea__(13)__ shocked Congress with reports of inhumane treatment. This led to the development of __(14)__mental hospitals. Clifford__(15)__, himself an inmate, founded the mental health movement.

Today, professionals are trained in __(16)__, the verbal interaction of a professional counselor with one or more persons suffering from a psychological disorder. Most psychotherapists favor an __(17)__ orientation.

Mini-review on the History of Therapy: Match each term with its correct description.

________1. Clifford Beers	A. The Stone-Age technique in which holes were chipped in the skull, apparently to let out demons that caused abnormal behavior
________2. St. Mary's	B. He believed that disorders were caused by imbalances in fluids he called humors
________3. trephining	C. Both naturalistic treatments and supernatural treatments existed during this era
________4. Dorothea Dix	D. Inhumane treatment began late in this period and continued until the renaissance
________5. Middle Ages	E. This time period saw the advent of the insane asylum
________6. Hippocrates	F. The most humane asylum was located here
________7. Philippe Pinel	G. Asylum where visitors called the inmates "Tom Fools"; became known as "Bedlam"
________8. Christian era	H. Shocked Congress with the reports of inhumane treatment, her work led to the development of state mental hospitals
________9. Geel	I. Introduced moral therapy, in which the treatment was uniquely kind
________10. Benjamin Rush	J. Introduced the moral therapy approach in the United States; he prescribed work, travel, and reading while continuing physical treatments such as whirling in special chairs
________11. Renaissance	K. Was an inmate in a state mental hospital and wrote a book about the conditions; founded the mental health movement

II. The Psychoanalytic Orientation: Joseph__(18)__ counseled Anna O., who had symptoms of *conversion hysteria.* When she__(19)__ freely, her symptoms disappeared. She called this her "talking cure" or "__(20)__." Breuer called this process of__(21)__ release "catharsis." Freud found that childhood emotional conflicts repressed into the__(22)__ mind promoted the use of **defense mechanisms.** Helping a person gain__(23)__ into these conflicts led Freud to develop **psychoanalysis.** The goal of psychoanalysis is to make a client's __(24)__ conflicts__(25)__. In the therapy situation Freud encouraged relaxation and the reduction of inhibitions, allowing the client to speak freely. The therapist then actively__(26)__ what the client says. This is called *working through.*

Techniques in Psychoanalysis: Beginning with the main one, the techniques of psychoanalysis are:

1) The analysis of__(27)__. Here the client is urged to report any thoughts or feelings that come to mind.
2) The analysis of__(28)__. Here the psychoanalyst notes behaviors that interfere with therapeutic progress and

attempts to interpret these behaviors.

3) The analysis of__(29)__. This involves the interpretation of the __(30)__, or *manifest*, content of dreams to reveal the__(31)__, or *latent*, content -- their true meanings.
4) The analysis of____(32)__. This is the key to cure. It is the tendency of the client to act toward the therapist as he or she acts toward important people in everyday life. In__(33)__ **transference**, the client expresses feelings of approval and affection toward the therapist. In__(34)__ **transference,** the client expresses feelings of disapproval and rejection toward the therapist.

III. The Behavioral Orientation: Eysenck coined the term **behavior therapy,** an approach that favors changing maladaptive__(35)__. Behavior therapists ignore__(36)__ conflicts, emphasize the present, and assume that therapy can be accomplished in weeks. Psychoanalytic therapists, on the other hand, insisted that this approach would produce symptom__(37)__, but subsequent research has shown that is not the case.

Classical-conditioning Therapies: The goal of **classical-conditioning therapies** is the__(38)__ of the stimuli that control the maladaptive behaviors, or the promotion of more__(39)__ responses to those stimuli. The technique of **counterconditioning** replaces__(40)__ emotional responses to stimuli with__(41)__ ones. The procedure is based on the assumption that we cannot__(42)__ experience something such as anxiety and relaxation. The use of counterconditioning is demonstrated in the "Anatomy of a Classic Research Study" section.

Anatomy of a Classic Research Study: Can Phobias Be Eliminated by Counterconditioning? *Read the summary of the study by Mary Cover Jones on page 523 and answer the following questions.*

What was the authors rationale for the study?

What methods were used by the author to test the hypothesis?

What was the outcome of the study and what did the author conclude the results meant?

Systematic Desensitization: The most widely used form of__(43)__ is **systematic desensitization.** It comprises three steps. The first step involves having the client practice Jacobson's progressive__(44)__ technique. The second step is the construction of an ____(45)___. And the third step involves pairing of the scenes evoked by the hierarchy with__(46)__ relaxation. Whether caused by extinction or counterconditioning, ____(47)____ may exert its effects through the actions of__(48)__. The "Anatomy of a Contemporary Research Study" section of the textbook examines the role of endorphins in systematic desensitization.

Anatomy of a Contemporary Research Study: Do Endorphins Mediate the Effect of Systematic Desensitization on Phobias? *Read the summary of the study by Egan and colleagues on page 524-525 and answer the following questions.*

What was the rationale for the study?

What methods did the author use to test the hypothesis?

What was the outcome of the study and what did the author conclude the results meant?

The true test of systematic desensitization is the ability to face the actual source of the __(49)__. **In vivo desensitization** does this by exposing the client to__(50)__ situations listed on the hierarchy.

Aversion Therapy: The goal of aversion therapy is to make a formerly pleasurable, but maladaptive behavior __(51)__. In a sense it is the__(52)__ of systematic desensitization. In aversion therapy a stimulus that normally elicits a__(53)__ response is paired with an unpleasant stimulus. Formerly,_____(54)____ were used in the treatment of alcoholism. Today, however,__(55)__ are used. This is the better of the two treatments, a finding that supports the concept of *behavioral* __(56)__.

Operant-conditioning Therapies: Behavior modification relies on changing the behavioral contingencies of positive reinforcement and punishment and is based on the work of B. F.___(57)___. One example of an operant-conditioning technique is the use of a **token economy,** which provides tokens as __(58)__ reinforcement for desirable behaviors, such as taking showers or making beds. The tokens can be used as a form of__(59)__ to purchase desired items or privileges. The development of the____(60)___ provided a way of overcoming the problem of passivity characteristic of hospitalized patients and has been successfully applied in a variety of settings.

Although less desirable as a form of treatment,__(61)__ may be the only way to prevent maladaptive, even dangerous behavior. Once the self-injurious behavior, such as head banging, has stopped, the therapist shifts to positive__(62)__. The combination of positive reinforcement and punishment is highly effective in treating ___(63)___children.

The technique of *flooding* takes advantage of__(64)__ in the elimination of intense fears and phobias. _____(65)___ exposes the client to a situation that evokes intense anxiety. In__(66)__ flooding, the client is asked to hold the image. In _____(67)_____ flooding, the client is placed in the actual feared situation.

Social Learning Therapies: In social learning therapies the clients watch other people__(68)__ adaptive behaviors either in person or on videotape and then perform the behavior that is being modeled. Therapists may also use__(69)__ **modeling,** in which the therapist models for the client, who then attempts to perform the desired behavior. Participant modeling has been__(70)__ in helping undergraduate psychology students overcome the fear of handling rats.

Mini-review of Psychoanalytic and Behavioral Orientations: Match each term with its correct description.

_______1. aversion therapy
_______2. flooding
_______3. Joseph Breuer
_______4. social learning therapies
_______5. analysis of resistances
_______6. in vivo desensitization
_______7. behavior therapists
_______8. psychoanalysis
_______9. counterconditioning
_______10. catharsis
_______11. analysis of dreams
_______12. behavior modification
_______13. analysis of free associations
_______14. Hans Eysenck
_______15. classical-conditioning therapies
_______16. analysis of transference
_______17. systematic desensitization
_______18. token economy

A. Counseled Anna O., who had symptoms of conversion hysteria
B. This psychoanalytic technique involves the interpretation of the symbolic, content of dreams to reveal their true meanings
C. Breuer's term for the process of emotional release through talking freely
D. Therapists who ignore unconscious conflicts, emphasize the present, and assume that therapy can be accomplished in weeks
E. Freud's term for treatment aimed at helping an individual gain insight into conflicts in the unconscious mind that promoted the use of defense mechanisms
F. In this technique unpleasant emotional responses to stimuli are replaced with pleasant ones
G. In this psychoanalytic technique the client is urged to report any thoughts or feelings that come to mind
H. Therapy technique in which clients are is exposed to the actual situations listed on their anxiety hierarchy
I. Technique in which the therapist provides tokens as positive reinforcement for desirable behaviors, such as taking showers or making beds
J. In this psychoanalytic technique the psychoanalyst notes behaviors that interfere with therapeutic progress and attempts to interpret these

behaviors

K. The tendency of the client to act toward the therapist as he or she acts toward important people in everyday life; the key to cure in psychoanalysis

L. He coined the term *behavior therapy*

M. The goal of these therapies is the removal of the stimuli that control maladaptive behaviors or the promotion of more adaptive responses to those stimuli

N. This is the most widely used form of counterconditioning

O. The goal of this therapy is to make a formerly pleasurable but maladaptive behavior unpleasant; a stimulus that normally elicits a maladaptive response is paired with an unpleasant stimulus

P. Therapy that relies on changing the behavioral contingencies of positive reinforcement and punishment and is based on the work of B. F. Skinner

Q. The technique that takes advantage of extinction in the elimination of intense fears and phobias; the client is exposed to a situation that evokes intense anxiety

R. Therapies in which the clients watch other people model adaptive behaviors either in person or on videotape and then perform the behavior that is being modeled

IV. The Cognitive Orientation: The premise of the cognitive orientation is that it is not the events, but rather our __(71)__ of them, that causes maladaptive behaviors. Cognitive-behavioral therapies seek to__(72)__ the client's thinking. Aspects of ____(73)__therapy may be used in the course of treatment. A recent version of___(74)__ therapy, developed by Donald Meichenbaum, is **stress-inoculation training.** This training helps clients change their__(75)__ thinking into ____(76)__thinking and has been successful in the treatment of anxiety disorders.

Rational-Emotive Behavior Therapy: Ellis's **Rational-Emotive Therapy (R-E-T)** is based on his *A-B-C theory* of __(77)__, in which A is the activating event, B is the irrational belief, and C is an emotional consequence. Ellis points out that most of us believe that__(78)__ causes C, when, in fact,__(79)__ causes C. After identifying the client's__(80)__ beliefs, the therapist challenges the client to provide evidence supporting them. More recently Ellis had begun calling this therapeutic approach **Rational-Emotive___(81)___ Therapy,** or **R-E-B-T.**

Cognitive Therapy: Beck's cognitive therapy focuses primarily on the treatment of__(82)__, a condition he believes is caused by negative beliefs about oneself, the world, and the future. The goal of this therapy is to change such exaggerated__(83)__. Beck is__(84)__ directive than Ellis; he employs a Socratic approach.

V. The Humanistic Orientation: Unlike the psychoanalytic orientation, the **humanistic orientation** emphasizes the ____(85)__ rather than the__(86)__, and conscious experience rather than unconscious experience. Unlike the__(87)__ orientation, it stresses the importance of subjective mental experience rather than objective environmental circumstances. And unlike the cognitive orientation, it encourages the__(88)__ of emotion rather than its__(89)__. Moreover, it emphasizes the client's__(90)__ for change.

Person-Centered Therapy: Person-centered therapists help their clients by promoting___(91)_. Whereas the rational-emotive therapist is__(92)__, the person-centered therapist is__(93)__, allowing clients to find their own answers. Humanistic psychologists assume that psychological disorders arise from an__(94)__ between a person's public and private selves. The goal of **person-centered therapy** is to help individuals reduce this incongruence by expressing, and then__(95)__ their true feelings. The therapist accomplishes this through *reflection of feelings,* ___(96)__, *accurate empathy,* and *unconditional positive regard.* While *reflection of feelings* is the main technique, with the therapist serving as a therapeutic__(97)__, the most important aspect of therapy is the therapist's demonstration of *accurate empathy.* Finally, the most difficult task for person-centered therapists is the maintenance of____(98)___, or acting in a personally warm and accepting manner, regardless of how they feel about the client's actions or thoughts. The__(99)__ warmth conveyed by unconditional positive regard appears to be a key aspect of the success of the therapy.

Gestalt Therapy: __(100)__'s approach combines aspects of psychoanalysis, R-E-T, and client-centered therapy. He claimed, "The idea of Gestalt therapy is to change paper people to real people." __(101)__ people were those out of touch with their true feelings, making them live "inauthentic lives." In theory, unconscious feelings are brought forth, __(102)__changes thinking, and emotional expressiveness is increased. The two-chair exercise is one of many exercises that might be used to facilitate change. Perls has been criticized for promoting __(103)__and emotional callousness, as in his "Gestalt prayer."

Existential Therapy: Existential therapy takes a more__(104)__ approach. Existential therapies assume that emotional and behavioral problems are merely__(105)__ of an inability to come to grips with the ultimate issues of life. Yalom points to four issues that each of us must face: the inevitability of__(106)__, the responsibility for our own choices, the __(107)__ of each person from all others, and the need to find meaning in a reality that has no inherent meaning. **Logotherapy,** created by Frankl, is based on the belief that one of the most important goals is to help clients find __(108)__ in their lives. This therapeutic approach has been used to help parents deal with the __(109)__of a child.

Mini-review of Cognitive and Humanistic Therapies: Match the term with its correct description.

_______1. Beck's cognitive therapy
_______2. existential therapy
_______3. unconditional positive regard
_______4. person-centered therapy
_______5. cognitive therapy
_______6. Gestalt therapy
_______7. humanistic orientation
_______8. logotherapy
_______9. stress-inoculation training
_______10. Albert Ellis
_______11. rational-emotive behavioral therapy

A. The premise of this orientation is that it is not the events, but rather our interpretation of them that causes maladaptive behaviors; therapists seek to modify the client's interpretation of events; aspects of behavior therapy may be used in the course of treatment
B. A recent version of cognitive behavioral therapy developed by Donald Meichenbaum. Its aim is to help the client change their pessimistic thinking into optimistic thinking and has been successful in the treatment of anxiety disorders
C. In this therapy, after identifying the client's irrational beliefs, the therapist challenges the client to provide evidence supporting them
D. He proposed the *A-B-C theory* of emotion in which A is the activating event, B is the irrational belief, and C is an emotional consequence and points out that although most of us believe that A causes C, in fact B causes C
E. This approach focuses primarily on the treatment of depression, a condition he believes is caused by negative beliefs about oneself, the world, and the future; the goal of therapy is to change exaggerated beliefs; this therapy is less directive than R-E-T and employs a Socratic approach
F. This orientation emphasizes the present rather than the past, conscious experience rather than unconscious experience, and the importance of subjective mental experience rather than objective environmental circumstances; encourages the expression of emotion rather than its control and stresses the client's responsibility for change
G. This type of therapy helps clients by promoting self-acceptance; the goal is to help individuals reduce this incongruence by expressing and then accepting their true feelings
H. Acting in a personally warm and accepting manner, regardless of personal feelings about the client's actions or thoughts
I. This approach's goal is to change "paper people" to "real people"; unconscious feelings are brought forth, confrontation changes thinking, and emotional expressiveness is increased; the two-chair exercise is an exercise that might be used to facilitate change

J. This type of therapy takes a philosophical approach and assumes that emotional and behavioral problems are merely symptoms of an inability to come to grips with the ultimate issues of life

K. Created by Frankl, is based on the belief that one of the most important goals is to help clients find meaning in their lives; this therapeutic approach has been used to help parents deal with the death of a child

VI. The Social-relations Orientations: The Social-relations orientation assumes that because many psychological problems involve__(110)_ relationships, other people must be brought into the therapy process. This concept marked the beginning of__(111)___ therapy, an approach that provides a range of role models, encouragement from others with similar problems, feedback about behavior, assurance that problems are not unique, and the opportunity to try out new behaviors.

Psychoanalytic Group Therapies: Group therapies derived from psychoanalysis stress insight and emotional _(112)_. Moreno's **psychodrama** aims at achieving insight and catharsis through__(113)__ out real-life situations. One technique is *role reversal.* Berne's____(114)____ (TA) is a more recent form of therapy that centers on the thesis that we act according to one of three roles. The__(115)_, like the id in psychoanalytic theory, acts impulsively and demands immediate gratification. The __(116)__, like the superego, is authoritarian and guides moral behavior. And the adult, like the__(117)__, promotes rational and responsible behavior. Relationships with others involve transactions. __(118)_ transactions, wherein both play the same role, are normally best. __(119)_ transactions, as when one person acts as a child and the other an adult, are usually the worst. The goal of TA is to analyze transactions, or "games" that people play, that reflect our___(120)___, or pervasive themes that we follow in our social relations.

Behavioral Group Therapies: Social-skills training is a popular form of__(121)_ group therapy. Its goal is to improve social __(122)___ by improving social__(123)_. **Assertiveness training** is a form of___(124)_ training. Its goal is to help people learn to express their feelings constructively in social situations. Participants learn to distinguish among assertive behaviors,__(125)__ behaviors, and passive behaviors. The *broken-record* technique serves as a way of learning to say "no."

Humanistic Group Therapies: The humanistic group therapies encourage awareness and acceptance of__(126)_ experiences. This goal was facilitated by the development of__(127)__ groups, called *training groups,* or *T-groups.* **Encounter groups,** an offshoot of the___(128)___ *movement*, have been successful in some instances, but for the most part, studies indicate that their slight beneficial effects may be temporary and even harmful. However, the movement has led to the emergence of__(129)__ groups for drug abusers, widowed people, and others with shared problems.

Family Therapy: Family therapy brings together members of the same__(130)_. The main goals are the __(131)_ expression of feelings and the establishment of rules that family members agree to follow. One member, known as the __(132)_ patient, is assumed to bear the brunt of the family's problems. Typically, the family is brought together for ____(133)___ after that person has entered individual therapy. Minuchin developed a popular form of family therapy known as__(134)_ *family therapy.* The emphasis is on the "emotional" __(135)__ between family members. Family therapy has been shown to be effective.

VII. The Biopsychological Orientation: During the past few decades, the **biomedical orientation** has become an important approach to therapy. It is based on the assumption that psychological disorders are associated with__(136)_ dysfunctions and, consequently, will respond to treatments that alter brain activity.

Psychosurgery: Egas Moniz was impressed by a report about agitated chimps that became calmer after undergoing brain surgery separating their__(137)__ lobes from the rest of their brain. Moniz convinced neurosurgeon Almeida Lima to perform a prefrontal__(138)__ on anesthetized patients. __(139)__ was introduced in the United States by Freeman and Watts. However, they favored the technique of __(140)_ *leucotomy,* where the patient's eyesocket is anesthetized and a the frontal lobe is separated from the rest of the brain. For several reasons, the use of the once-popular technique has___(141)___ markedly. It produced unpredictable effects; had as its rival the rapidly emerging drug therapies; and was seemingly barbaric, prompting public opposition.

Electroconvulsive therapy (ECT) can be more effective than drug therapy in treating ___(142)___. It produces more rapid improvement and is the treatment of choice for depressed people in imminent danger of committing ___(143)___. The most widely accepted explanation of the mechanism of action is that ECT stimulates an increase in the level of ___(144)___ in the brain. Other studies have found that it increases the level of___(145)___ in the brain. Today, in ECT treatment muscle relaxants prevent the bodily damage caused by violent convulsions. But ECT does cause___(146)___. The ongoing debate about the desirability of ECT remains as much an ethical, emotional, and___(147)___ issue as a scientific one.

Drug Therapy: Drug therapies work by restoring___(148)___ to normal levels. Concurrent___(149)___ may be desirable, as a drug may alleviate symptoms, but it doesn't necessarily change the person's ability to adapt to everyday stressors.

Antianxiety drugs were originally called___(150)___. Today, the most widely prescribed are the benzodiazepines, such as Xanax, ___(151)___, and Valium. They work to enhance the effects of the neurotransmitter___(152)___ and may cause, as side effects, drowsiness, depression, and dependence.

Antidepressant Drugs: The early use of MAO___(153)___ has largely been replaced by the tricyclic antidepressants, such as Elavil and Tofranil. The tricyclics___(154)___ levels of serotonin and norepinephrine. Since these drugs take two to four weeks to take effect,___(155)___ patients must be closely monitored. Unfortunately, the popular new antidepressant drug ___(156)___ may, in some cases, induce suicidal behavior.

Antimania Drugs: Psychiatrists often prescribe lithium carbonate for treatment of___(157)___ disorder since it prevents extreme mood swings, but it has possible severe side effects. Patients must be monitored closely for potentially dangerous side effects such as seizures, brain damage, and irregular heartbeat.

Antipsychotic Drugs: The 1950s saw the development of ___(158)___ drugs called *phenothiazines*, such as Thorazine, for treating schizophrenia. It has been suggested that these drugs work by blocking the receptor sites for___(159)___. Long-term use of antipsychotic drugs can cause *tardive dyskinesia*, characterized by grimacing, lip smacking, and limb flailing.

Mini-review of Social-relations and Biopsychology Approaches to Therapy: Match each term with its correct description.

_______1. behavioral group therapies
_______2. antimania drugs
_______3. social-relations orientation
_______4. antianxiety drugs
_______5. family therapies
_______6. psychoanalytic group therapies
_______7. drug therapy
_______8. assertiveness training
_______9. biopsychological orientation
_______10. Berne's transactional analysis (TA)
_______11. antidepressant drugs

A. Treatment approach that is based on the assumption that psychological disorders are associated with brain dysfunctions
B. A more recent form of psychoanalytic therapy; the goal is to analyze transactions, or "games" that people play, that reflect our life scripts-pervasive themes that we follow in our social relations
C. This orientation assumes that because many psychological problems involve interpersonal relationships, other people must be brought into the therapy process; the concept marked the beginning of group therapy
D. Group therapies derived from psychoanalysis stress insight and emotional catharsis; one example is Moreno's psychodrama which aims at achieving insight and catharsis through acting out real-life situations
E. This type of group therapy encourages awareness and acceptance of emotional experiences; has been facilitated by the development of sensitivity groups, called training groups, or T-groups
F. Social-skills training is a popular form of this type of group therapy; its goal is to improve social relationships by improving social skills
G. A form of social-skills training; its goal is to help people learn to express their

_______12. humanistic group therapies
_______13. antipsychotic drugs
_______14. electroconvulsive therapy

feelings constructively in social situations; participants learn to distinguish among assertive behaviors, aggressive behaviors, and passive behaviors

H. This type of group therapy brings together members of the same family; the main goals are the constructive expression of feelings and the establishment of rules that family members agree to follow; one member, known as the identified patient, is assumed to bear the brunt of the family's problems
I. This type of therapy can be more effective than drug therapy in treating depression; it produces more rapid improvement and is the treatment of choice for depressed people in imminent danger of committing suicide; there is an ongoing debate about the desirability of this type of treatment
J. This type of therapy works by restoring neurotransmitters to normal levels
K. Originally called tranquilizers; today, the most widely prescribed are the benzodiazepines, such as Xanax, Librium, and Valium
L. They increase levels of serotonin and norepinephrine and include Prozac, Elavil, and Tofranil
M. Class of drugs that includes lithium carbonate and are used to prevent the extreme mood swings of bipolar disorder
N. Class of drugs such as Thorazine, are used for treating schizophrenia; these drugs work by blocking the receptor sites for dopamine

VIII. Community Mental Health: Since the 1950's there has been a movement toward **deinstitutionalization.** What accounts for the trend? There are four reasons: First, the introduction of__(160)__ treatments; second, mental hospitals had become __(161)__, understaffed, and crowded; third, increasing concern for the__(162)__ rights of patients; and fourth, the Community Mental Health Centers Act of 1963, advocated by President__(163)__, mandated the establishment of federally funded centers in every U.S. community. Services of the health centers include__(164)__ counseling, short-term inpatient treatment, 24-hour emergency care, consultation, and community education.

__(165)__mental health centers have three main goals. __(166)__ prevention helps by fostering social support systems and reducing stress. This might be promoted by reducing__(167)__or providing low-cost housing. Secondary prevention offers____(168)____. __(169)__ prevention helps people who have full-blown disorders to keep their conditions under control. Among the main community approaches are community residences, or____(170)____. Despite its intentions, __(171)__ has worked better in theory than in practice. One consequence is that former mental patients who lack __(172)__ support may have little choice but to live on the street. Currently, about 30 percent of the__(173)__ are former residents of mental hospitals.

IX. The Rights of the Therapy Client: People who are__(174)__ to mental hospitals lose many of their rights, including their right to vote, to marry, to divorce, and to sign contracts. In the United States, only people who are judged to be dangerous can be involuntarily committed. This law was formalized in the 1979_____ __(175)__ ____ case. Courts have also ruled that committed people have both the right to__(176)__ treatment and the right to refuse it. The 1975_____ __(177)__ _____ case ruled that patients have a right to more than custodial care.

The most significant legal decision concerning confidentiality was the__(178)__ decision, a ruling stating that a therapist who believes that a client might harm a particular person must personally warn that person. The concept of *duty to warn* has provoked concern among __(179)__ because it is difficult to predict the outcome of a threat, it may be impractical to warn potential victims, and it may keep the client from discussing his or her hostility.

X. Selecting a Therapist: At times, people may need help that requires more than just friendly__(180)__. When personal problems become unmanageable,__(181)__ help in the form of a therapist can be beneficial, or even necessary. (See Table 15.5 on page 547 in your textbook for kinds of therapists.) After finding a therapist, try to assess the therapist's credentials, reputation,_____(182)____, and interpersonal manner.

Mini-review on Community Mental Health, Rights of the Therapy Client, and Selecting a Therapist: Match each term with its correct description.

________1. secondary prevention
________2. paraprofessional
________3. *Rogers v. Commissioner of Mental Health* (1983)
________4. psychiatric nurse
________5. *Tarasoff* decision
________6. clinical psychologist
________7. primary prevention
________8. pastoral counselor
________9. deinstitutionalization
________10. psychiatric social worker
________11. Community Mental Health Centers Act of 1963
________12. counseling psychologist
________13. tertiary prevention
________14. *Addington v. Texas* (1979)
________15. *Donaldson v. O'Connor* (1975)
________16. psychiatrist

A. This act advocated by President Kennedy mandated the establishment of federally funded mental health centers in every U.S. community
B. An individual who has earned a doctoral degree in clinical psychology and has served a one-year internship
C. Level of community aid that helps by fostering social support systems and reducing stress; this goal might be promoted by reducing unemployment or providing low-cost housing
D. A registered nurse who has earned a master's degree in nursing and has specialized training in psychiatric care
E. This level of community aid involves crisis intervention
F. An individual with a high school diploma and specialized training in counseling people with specific behavioral problems
G. This level of community action helps people who have full-blown disorders to keep their conditions under control; among the main community approaches are community residences, or halfway houses
H. An individual with a master's degree in social work and training in the counseling of individuals and families
I. Court case that established that only people who are judged to be dangerous can be involuntarily committed
J. A physician who has served a three- to four-year residency in a mental hospital or psychiatric ward
K. Court's ruling that people committed have both the right to refuse treatment as well as to receive it
L. A layperson, or member of the clergy who has earned a master's degree; these individuals combine spiritual and psychological counseling in their work
M. The court case that ruled that patients have a right to more than custodial care
N. The most significant legal decision concerning confidentiality; a ruling that a therapist who believes that a client might harm a particular person must personally warn that person
O. An individual who has earned a master's or doctoral degree in counseling psychology
P. The movement toward treating people in community settings instead of mental hospitals

XI. Thinking about Psychology: Is Psychotherapy Effective?

In 1952, Eysenck reported that about 66 percent of those receiving__(183)__ improved, but he also reported that 72 percent of__(184)__ subjects who had no therapy improved! He called improvement without therapy____(185)____and concluded that psychotherapy is ineffective. However, Eysenck's__(186)__ was criticized.

Since Eysenck's original study,___(187)__ of studies have examined the effectiveness of psychotherapy. However, evaluation is difficult. The__(188)__ of what constitutes "effective" varies with each therapeutic approach. The general conclusion drawn from research since Eysenck issued his challenge is that both psychotherapy and placebo therapy are __(189)__ effective than no therapy. But more important,__(190)__ is superior to__(191)__ therapy. Up to a point, the more sessions, the more improvement. Research has shown that 75 percent of clients improved after twenty-six sessions but 50 percent improved after eight. It appears as though maximum gain occurs with relatively __(192)__therapy.

Factors in the Effectiveness of Psychotherapy: Researchers have suggested that the characteristics of the client, therapist, and nature of the therapy may be possible factors in the success of therapy.
Therapy Characteristics: The characteristics of the therapy itself have been shown to be the__(193)_ predictor of success. Most recent studies have shown that the major kinds of therapy are__(194)_ effective.
Client Characteristics: There is a_(195)_ likelihood of improvement for the educated, intelligent, and higher socioeconomic groups, as well as for those with_(196)_ severe disorders, more adequate personalities and greater motivation to change.
Therapist characteristics center on_(197)_. A major conclusion is that empathy is so important in the practice of therapy that empathetic paraprofessiionals may be as effective as _(198)_psychotherapists in treating psychological problems. Clearly, more research is necessary to determine the ideal combinations of therapy, therapist and client factors.

KEY RESEARCH FINDINGS

Provide the details of the following key research studies in psychology:

1. **Beers (1908/1970):** Described physical abuse in the Connecticut State Hospital and led to the founding of the mental health movement. (Page 520)
2. **Eysenck (1952):** Coined the term *behavior therapy* to refer to treatments that change behavior, as opposed to examining the unconscious. (Page 522)
3. **Watson & Rayner (1920):** Proposed that fear of a certain stimulus could be eliminated by introducing pleasurable stimuli--a technique called counter-conditioning. (Page 523)
4. **Jones (1924):** Used counter-conditioning to rid a 3-year-old of a rabbit phobia. (Page 523)
5. **Wolpe (1958):** Developed systematic desensitization to treat phobias. (Page 524)
6. **Egan et al. (1988):** Demonstrated that systematic desensitization may be induced by the actions of endorphins. (Page 524)
7. **Eccles, Wilde, & Marshall (1988):** Used in vivo desensitization to relieve chronic nightmares about snakes. (Page 525)
8. **Smith & Frawley (1993):** Found that 60 percent of alcoholic patients who underwent a treatment program that included aversion therapy were abstinent a year later. (Page 525)
9. **Croce (1990):** Showed that a token economy motivated mentally retarded patients to adhere to an exercise program. (Page 526)
10. **Turner et al. (1992):** Demonstrated a significant decrease in anxiety levels and heart rate in response to social phobias through the use of flooding. (Page 527)
11. **Faust, Olson, & Rodriguez (1991):** Used participant modeling to help individuals overcome fear of surgery. (Page 527)
12. **Meichenbaum (1985):** Developed stress-inoculation training. (Page 527)
13. **Salovey & Haar (1990):** Showed that more students who used stress-inoculation training were able to pass a college freshman exam. (Page 529)
14. **Ellis (1962):** Developed the first cognitive therapy, rational-emotive behavior therapy. (Page 529)
15. **Engels, Garnefski, & Diekstra (1993):** Found that R-E-B-T is more effective than placebo treatment and is as effective as other therapies. (Page 530)
16. **Gaffan, Tsaousis, & Kemp-Wheeler (1995):** Found that cognitive therapy is successful in treating depression. (Page 531)
17. **Kremer & Dietzen (1991):** Showed that accurate empathy can be learned through training. (Page 532)
18. **Hynan (1990):** Found the personal warmth of a therapist to be one of the most important factors in the patient's willingness to stay in therapy. (Page 532)
19. **Norcross, Strausser, & Faltus (1988):** Survey of 500 therapists found that personal warmth was one of the most important factors in selecting their own therapists. (Page 532)
20. **Serok & Levi (1993):** Found that prisoners that participated in a Gestalt program showed more personal responsibility than those who did not. (Page 533)
21. **Berne (1964):** Popularized transactional analysis in the book *Games People Play*. (Page 535)

22. **Minuchin (1974):** Developed structural family therapy. (Page 537)
23. **Markus, Lange, & Pettigrew (1990):** Found that people who have been in family therapy are better off than 76 percent of those who had not. (Page 538)
24. **Moniz (1937/1994):** Saw success in calming agitated patients with the surgical technique of prefrontal lobotomy. (Page 539)
25. **Cerletti & Bini (1938):** Introduced electroconvulsive therapy (ECT) as a means of calming agitated patients. (Page 540)
26. **Schwarz, Loewenstein, & Isenberg (1995):** Found that a maintenance program of ECT was effective in reducing rehospitalization of patients unresponsive to other treatments. (Page 540)
27. **Alexander (1993):** Found that patients who received Xanax showed a significantly greater reduction in panic attacks than those who got a placebo. (Page 541)
28. **Slagg et al. (1994):** Found that one third of homeless people in major cities are former residents of mental hospitals. (Page 543)
29. **Beiser et al. (1985):** Found that the availability of community mental health services helped reduce readmission of formerly hospitalized schizophrenics back into mental hospitals. (Page 544)
30. **Hermann (1990):** Discussed the case of *Rogers v. Commissioner of Mental Health,* which ruled that mental patients have the right to refuse treatment. (Page 545)
31. **Veliz & James (1987):** Found, in cases of involuntary treatment that were reviewed, the courts usually decided in favor of those prescribing the treatment. (Page 545)
32. **Eysenck (1952):** Concluded that two thirds of people undergoing psychotherapy improved, but that two thirds of patients improved by spontaneous remission. (Page 548)
33. **Bergin & Lambert (1978):** Found that rates of spontaneous remission was closer to 40 percent, rather than the 65 percent found by Eysenck. (Page 549)
34. **Smith, Glass, & Miller (1980):** Found that the typical psychotherapy client is better off than 80 percent of untreated persons. (Page 549)
35. **Luborsky et al. (1971):** Found the poorest predictor of success in therapy was the type of therapy itself. (Page 550)

PRACTICE TEST A

1. A Stone Age caveman claims he hears voices in his head, continually rants and raves, and makes bizarre movements with his hands. The tribe's medicine man treats him by using sharp rocks to cut holes in his head and release the evil spirits that are causing his behavior. This treatment is called
   a. trephining.
   b. aversion therapy.
   c. prefrontal lobotomy.
   d. transorbital leucotomy.

Obj.:1 Page: 518

2. A Stone Age technique involved using sharp stones to chip holes in the skull as a way of letting out the demons that supposedly caused abnormal behavior. The treatment is called
   a. trephining.
   b. prefrontal lobotomy.
   c. punishment therapy.
   d. the devil's demise.

Obj.: 2 Page: 518

3. Which of the following pairings is incorrect?
   a. Philippe Pinel / "moral therapy"
   b. Dorothea Dix / "mental hospitals"
   c. Benjamin Rush / "American psychiatry"
   d. Clifford Beers / "Bedlam"

Obj.: 3 Page: 519-520

4. The treatment orientation that aims at uncovering the unconscious causes of psychological disorders is called
   a. logotherapy.
   b. psychoanalysis.
   c. rational-emotive therapy.
   d. existential psychotherapy.

Obj.: 4 Page: 520

5. You dream that a person reaches down to pet a dog and the dog bites the person's hand. A psychoanalyst interprets the dream to mean that you feel unconscious guilt for treating your parents poorly after they have helped you buy a car, pay for your tuition, and take care of many of your other needs. According to a psychoanalyst, the actual dream of a dog biting a hand is its
   a. latent content.
   b. manifest content.
   c. archetypal content.
   d. preconscious content.

Obj.: 5 Page: 522

6. A therapist accompanies a client with a fear of flying on several trips to the airport. They first simply go to the terminal, eventually sit in an airplane, and finally take off on a flight. This procedure is most likely a component of
   a. psychodrama.
   b. aversion therapy.
   c. in vivo desensitization.
   d. systematic desensitization.

Obj.: 6 Page: 525

7. A person visits a therapist and complains that she is depressed because people criticize her. The therapist tries to convince her that this is caused by her unrealistic belief that she must be liked by everyone. The therapist's tactic is a component of
   a. logotherapy.
   b. moral therapy.
   c. counterconditioning.
   d. rational-emotive behavior therapy.

Obj.: 7 Page: 529-530

8. As part of a therapy session, you are asked to sit first in one chair and discuss the reasons why you wish to be married and then in another chair and discuss the reasons why you are hesitant to get married. This procedure would most likely be part of
   a. logotherapy.
   b. Gestalt therapy.
   c. counterconditioning.
   d. social-skills training.

Obj.: 8 Page: 533

9. When you attend the first session of therapy your therapist tells you that she feels that the problems you describe are the result of poor or inadequate interpersonal relationships. She does not believe that your problem can be solved with traditional client/therapist therapy and instead suggests group therapy with additional people. What type of therapeutic approach has she taken?
   a. Humanistic
   b. Gestalt
   c. Social-relations
   d. Behavioral

Obj.: 9 Page: 534

10. The founder of transactional analysis claims that we act according to one of three roles: child, parent, or adult. These elements have much in common with
   a. behavior therapy.
   b. psychodrama.
   c. psychoanalysis.
   d. cognitive therapy.

Obj.: 10 Page: 535

11. Minuchin's "structural family therapy" emphasizes
   a. the transactions between the roles of child, parent, and adult.
   b. the emotional "boundaries" between family members.
   c. assertiveness training as a way to stabilize a family.
   d. stress management.

Obj.: 11 Page: 535

12. A severely depressed person undergoes therapy and then finds that she cannot recall events that occurred during the 24 hours prior to the therapy session. She has probably undergone
   a. counterconditioning.
   b. transorbital leucotomy.
   c. in vivo desensitization.
   d. electroconvulsive therapy.

Obj.: 12 Page: 541

13. A psychiatrist prescribes a drug for a patient who claims he is Babe Ruth, hears imaginary voices cursing at him, and speaks in incoherent phrases that include words of his own invention. The drug is most likely
    a. Valium.
    b. Tofranil.
    c. Thorazine.
    d. lithium carbonate.

Obj.: 13 Page: 542

14. A community mental health center concerned with spousal abuse and child abuse institutes a stress-management program for husbands and wives. This is an example of
    a. primary prevention.
    b. tertiary prevention.
    c. secondary prevention.
    d. deinstitutionalization.

Obj.: 14 Page: 544

15. Melinda is engaging in bizarre behavior. She talks to herself, does not maintain her personal needs, cannot hold a job, and has difficulty remembering what year it is. Additionally, she has threatened to "jump off the nearest bridge." Her husband wants to admit her to a psychiatric hospital. Which of the following does Melinda not have a right to?
    a. She has the right not to be involuntary committed.
    b. She has right to treatment.
    c. She has the right to refuse treatment.
    d. She has the right to confidentiality.

Obj.: 15 Page: 545

16. Research on the effectiveness of therapy and therapist characteristics has shown that the best predictor of success in therapy was the
    a. level of empathy that the therapist demonstrates.
    b. gender of the therapist.
    c. age of the therapist.
    d. race of the therapist.

Obj.: 16 Page: 548-550

17. Spontaneous remission refers to the
    a. recovery from psychological disorders without therapy.
    b. release of sexual or aggressive drives through catharsis.
    c. elimination of phobias by maximal exposure to the feared object.
    d. voluntary return of mental patients to their hospital without asking for a formal hearing.

Obj.: 17 Page: 548

PRACTICE TEST B

1. Every therapy ever devised to treat psychological disorders
    a. has helped some problems some of the time.
    b. is based on whatever is assumed to cause the problem in the first place.
    c. has been created through trial and error and anecdotal evidence.
    d. always begins with rigorous testing in the experimental laboratory.

Obj.: 1 Page: 518

2. Hippocrates believed that psychological disorders were caused by imbalances in humors, and he would treat mania by
    a. trephining.
    b. bloodletting.
    c. exorcism.
    d. having the disordered person drink blood.

Obj.: 2 Page: 518

3. Pinel instituted a form of therapy that provided mental patients with humane treatment. The therapy was called
    a. moral therapy.
    b. deinstitutionalization.
    c. talk therapy.
    d. existential therapy.

Obj.: 3 Page: 519

4. The key to psychoanalytic cure is the analysis of
   a. dreams.
   b. free associations.
   c. resistances.
   d. transference.

Obj.: 4 Page: 520-521

5. During a therapy session, Linda reports that she dreamt she was lost in a forest and a bear told her how to get out safely. As she walked away from the bear, she could hear him laughing at her. Linda is
   a. recounting the manifest content of the dream.
   b. interpreting the sexual symbols contained in the dream.
   c. uncovering the latent content of the dream.
   d. revealing her unconscious conflicts about growing old.

Obj.: 5 Page: 522

6. Henry is severely mentally retarded. He lives in a group home where he is learning to groom and take care of himself. Behaviors such as sweeping and dusting his room or brushing his teeth are followed by plastic chips. He can use these to secure supplies and treats in a "store." Henry is involved in
   a. counterconditioning.
   b. aversion therapy.
   c. a token economy.
   d. stress-inoculation training.

Obj.: 6 Page: 526

7. Which item is out of place here?
   a. Carl Rogers
   b. REBT
   c. Albert Ellis
   d. ABC theory of emotion

Obj.: 7 Page: 529

8. Charlene has good writing skills but gets terrible grades on her papers because she procrastinates and this inevitably causes her to be penalized for handing in late papers. In the therapy hour, her therapist has Charlene create a dialogue between her "responsible self" and her "procrastinating self." Charlene moves from one seat to another to speak each of these parts of herself. This is called ____________ and is typical which therapeutic approach?
   a. in vivo desensitization; behavior therapy
   b. the two-chair exercise; Gestalt therapy
   c. stress-inoculation; cognitive therapy
   d. psychodrama; logotherapy

Obj.: 8 Page: 533

9. The form of social-skills training that teaches clients to express their feelings directly, instead of passively or aggressively, is called
   a. psychodrama.
   b. logotherapy.
   c. stress-inoculation training.
   d. assertiveness training.

Obj.: 9 Page: 535

10. Alcoholics Anonymous, Narcotics Anonymous, and rape survivor groups are examples of which type of groupwork?
    a. sensitivity training groups
    b. self-help groups
    c. transactional analysis groups
    d. encounter groups

Obj.: 10 Page: 537

11. Encounter group therapy is a form of what type of therapy?
    a. humanistic group therapy
    b. psychoanalytic therapy
    c. behavioral therapy
    d. cognitive therapy

Obj.: 11 Page: 537

12. Sal and his family are involved in a family therapy program in which their therapist encourages the family members to draw diagrams of their relationships and discuss how the relationships are maladaptive. This type of therapy is called
    a. structural family therapy.
    b. group therapy.
    c. marital therapy.
    d. thesystems approach.

Obj.: 11 Page: 537

13. How does ECT relieve major depression?
    a. It stimulates left hemisphere activity.
    b. It increases levels of serotonin and acetylcholine.
    c. Patients become less depressed to avoid ECT, which functions as a punisher.
    d. It is not known how ECT works to reduce or relieve depression.

Obj.: 12 Page: 541

14. After several serious losses and setbacks, Kim can't seem to overcome her depression. Most contemporary mental health professionals would agree that an ideal course of treatment would involve
    a. drug therapy and psychotherapy.
    b. ECT and long-term hospitalization.
    c. long-term psychoanalysis alone.
    d. hospitalization alone.

Obj.: 13 Page: 541

15. A community mental health center offers a grief and bereavement program for survivors of the Oklahoma City bombing. This is an example of
    a. primary prevention.
    b. secondary prevention.
    c. tertiary prevention.
    d. crisis prevention.

Obj.: 14 Page: 543-544

16. The need to demonstrate that a person is dangerous before that person can be committed to a mental hospital was decided in
    a. *Donaldson v. O'Connor.*
    b. *Rogers v. Commissioner of Mental Health.*
    c. *Tarasoff* decision.
    d. *Addington v. Texas.*

Obj.: 15 Page: 545

17. Under what conditions may someone be involuntarily committed to a mental hospital?
    a. if the person commits a criminal act
    b. if the person is dangerous to himself or herself, or to others
    c. if the person is behaving bizarrely and disturbing others
    d. If the person is homeless and unclean

Obj.: 15 Page: 545

18. Research has found that an important therapist characteristic for effective psychotherapy is
    a. accurate empathy.
    b. age.
    c. educational training.
    d. gender of the therapist.

Obj.: 16 Page: 546-550

19. Which of the following statements most accurately reflects the general findings of a recent large-scale study evaluating the effectiveness of psychotherapy in treating depression?
    a. Psychotherapy and drug therapy were equally effective in improving functioning in the short term.
    b. Only patients receiving drug therapy were substantially improved and remained so for an extended period.
    c. Placebo patients did as well as those receiving actual treatment of any kind.
    d. Psychoanalytic therapy was found to be the most effective treatment for depression.

Obj.:17 Page: 549

20. Research on the importance of empathy in a psychotherapeutic relationship has shown that psychotherapists may be no more effective than
    a. pastoral counselors.
    b. paraprofessionals.
    c. psychiatrists.
    d. social workers.

Obj.: 17 Page: 550-551

Essay Questions:

1. Describe briefly the psychoanalytic, behavioral, cognitive, humanistic, social-relations, and biopsychological orientations.

Obj.: 4, 6, 7, 8, 9, 12 Page: 520-541

2. Ethan has been feeling rather depressed for the past several months. He decides to seek professional help. How should he go about selecting a therapist or counselor?

Obj.: 16 Page: 546-548

ANSWER RECORD FOR CHAPTER 15

Comprehensive Guided Review:

1. Stone
2. demons
3. supernatural
4. humors
5. Christian
6. Middle
7. asylum
8. Geel
9. Bedlam
10. Pinel
11. Rush
12. travel
13. Dix
14. state
15. Beers
16. psychotherapy
17. eclectic

Mini-review of the History of Therapy:
1. K; 2. G; 3. A; 4. H; 5. D; 6. B; 7. I; 8. C; 9. F; 10. J; 11. E

18. Breuer
19. spoke
20. chimney sweeping
21. emotional
22. unconscious
23. insight
24. unconscious
25. conscious
26. interprets
27. free associations
28. resistances
29. dreams
30. symbolic
31. true
32. transference
33. positive
34. negative
35. behaviors
36. unconscious
37. substitution
38. removal
39. adaptive
40. unpleasant
41. pleasant
42. simultaneously

Anatomy of a Classic Research Study: Can Phobias Be Eliminated by Counterconditioining? *Read the summary of the study by Mary Cover Jones on page 523 and answer the following questions.*

What was the rationale for the study?
Watson had conditioned Little Albert to fear a white rat by pairing it with a loud sound. He proposed that the fear could be eliminated by pairing the rat with a pleasant stimulus.

What methods did the author use to test the hypothesis?
Mary Clover Jones set out to rid Peter, a boy with a rabbit phobia, of his fear by pairing the rabbit with candy.

What was the outcome of the study and what did the author conclude the results meant?
The process was lengthy and delicate, but it worked.

---

43. counterconditioning
44. relaxation
45. anxiety hierarchy
46. muscle
47. systematic desensitization
48. endorphins

Anatomy of a Contemporary Research Study: Do Endorphins Mediate the Effect of Systematic Desensitzation on Phobias? *Read the summary of the study by Egan and colleagues on page 524-525 and answer the following questions.*

What was the rationale for the study?
The researchers felt that the pleasurable feeling produced by endorphins might counter the anxiety produced by phobias.

What methods did the author use to test the hypothesis?
Egan et al. (1988) randomly assigned subjects with simple phobias to two groups. Prior to sessions of systematic desensitization, the experimental group received naloxone and the control group received a placebo

What was the outcome of the study and what did the author conclude the results meant?
Subjects who received the placebo experienced a significant decrease in the severity of their phobias, while the experimental group subjects did not. Because naloxone blocks the effects of endorphins, the results support the possible role of endorphins in the effects of systematic desensitization. The pleasant feelings produced by the endorphins may become conditioned to the formerly fear-inducing stimuli.

---

49. phobia
50. actual
51. unpleasant
52. opposite
53. maladaptive
54. electric shocks
55. drugs
56. preparedness
57. Skinner
58. positive
59. money
60. token economy
61. punishment
62. reinforcement
63. autistic
64. extinction
65. Flooding
66. imaginal
67. in vivo
68. model
69. participant
70. successful

Mini-review of Psychoanalytic and Behavioral Orientations:
1. O; 2. Q; 3. A; 4. R; 5. J; 6. H; 7. D; 8. E; 9. F; 10. C; 11. B; 12. P; 13. G; 14. L; 15. M; 16. K; 17. N; 18. I

71. interpretation
72. modify
73. behavior
74. cognitive-behavioral
75. pessimistic
76. optimistic
77. emotion
78. A
79. B
80. irrational
81. Behavior
82. depression
83. beliefs
84. less
85. present
86. past
87. behavioral
88. expression
89. control
90. responsibility
91. self-acceptance
92. directive
93. non-directive
94. incongruence
95. accepting
96. genuineness
97. mirror
98. unconditional positive regard
99. personal
100. Perls
101. Paper
102. confrontation
103. self-centeredness
104. philosophical
105. symptoms
106. death
107. isolation
108. meaning
109. death

Mini-review of Cognitive and Humanistic Therapies:
1. E; 2. J; 3. H; 4. G; 5. A; 6. I; 7. F; 8. K; 9. B; 10. D; 11. C

110. interpersonal
111. group
112. catharsis
113. acting
114. transactional analysis
115. child
116. parent
117. ego
118. Complementary
119. Crossed
120. life scripts
121. behavioral
122. relationships
123. skills
124. social-skills
125. aggressive
126. emotional
127. sensitivity
128. human potential
129. self-help
130. family
131. constructive
132. identified
133. family therapy
134. structural
135. boundaries
136. brain
137. frontal
138. leucotomy
139. Psychosurgery
140. transorbital
141. declined
142. depression
143. suicide
144. norepinephrine
145. endorphins
146. retrograde amnesia
147. political
148. neurotransmitters
149. psychotherapy
150. tranquilizers
151. Librium
152. GABA
153. inhibitors
154. increase
155. suicidal
156. Prozac
157. bipolar
158. antipsychotic
159. dopamine

Mini-review of Social-relations and Biopsychological Approaches to Therapy:
1. F; 2. M; 3. C; 4. K; 5. H; 6. D; 7. J; 8. G; 9. A; 10. B; 11. L; 12. E; 13. N; 14. I

160. drug
161. underfunded
162. legal
163. Kennedy
164. outpatient
165. Community
166. Primary
167. unemployment
168. crisis intervention
169. Tertiary
170. halfway houses
171. deinstitutionalization
172. family
173. homeless
174. committed
175. *Addington vs. Texas*
176. receive
177. *Donaldson v. O'Connor*
178. *Tarasoff*
179. therapists
180. advice
181. professional
182. therapeutic approach

Mini-review on Community Mental Health, Rights of the Therapy Client and Selecting a Therapist:
1. E; 2. F; 3. K; 4. D; 5. N; 6. B; 7. C; 8. L; 9. P; 10. H; 11. A; 12. O; 13. G; 14. I; 15. M; 16. J

183. psychotherapy
184. control
185. spontaneous remission
186. methodology
187. hundreds
188. definition
189. more
190. psychotherapy
191. placebo
192. brief
193. weakest
194. equally
195. greater
196. less
197. empathy
198. trained

Practice Test A:

1. a. **Correct: Trephining involved the chipping away of the skull to release demons from the head.**
   b. Incorrect: Aversion therapy is a form of behavior therapy that inhibits maladaptive behavior by pairing a stimulus that normally elicits a maladaptive response with an unpleasant stimulus.
   c. Incorrect: Prefrontal lobotomy is a surgical procedure in which portions of the frontal lobes are removed; it did not become a treatment until the twentith century.
   d. Incorrect: Transorbital leucotomy is also a surgical procedure, however it too was not developed until the twentith century.

2. a. **Correct: Trephining involved the chipping away of the skull to release demons from the head.**
   b. Incorrect: This is a relatively modern technique of surgical intervention.
   c. Incorrect: This is not mentioned in the text.
   d. Incorrect: Someone might have called it this!

3. a. Incorrect: Pinel is known for development of "moral therapy.
   b. Incorrect: Dix is know for the movement to establish state mental hospitals.
   c. Incorrect: Rush is considered the founder of American psychiatry.
   d. **Correct: Beers was a Yale university graduate who wrote the book *A Mind That Found Itself* about the treatment he received at a state mental hospital. Bedlam was a the nickname for St Mary's of Bethlehem , an insane asylum in London during the Renaissance.**

4. a. Incorrect: Logotherapy is a form of existential therapy that helps the client find meaning in life.
   b. **Correct: Psychoanalysis is the treatment orientation that aims to uncover unconscious causes of behavior.**
   c. Incorrect: Rational-emotive therapy is a form of cognitive therapy in which the client is encouraged to give up irrational beliefs.
   d. Incorrect: Existential therapy is a form of humanistic therapy that aims at helping the client overcome problems by dealing with major philosophical issues in life.

5. a. Incorrect: This is a description of the remembered part of the dream, or manifest content, not the underlying meaning.
   b. **Correct: The manifest content of the dream is the storyline that the dreamer remembers.**
   c. Incorrect: This is a description of the remembered part of the dream, or manifest content.
   d. Incorrect: This is a description of the remembered part of the dream, or manifest content.

6. a. Incorrect: Psychodrama is a form of psychoanalytic group therapy that aims at achieving insight and catharsis through acting out real-life situations.
   b. Incorrect: Aversion therapy is a form of behavior therapy that inhibits maladaptive behavior by pairing a stimulus that normally elicits a maladaptive response with an unpleasant stimulus.
   c. **Correct: In vivo desensitization is a technique that trains the client to maintain a state of relaxation in the presence of anxiety-inducing stimuli.**
   d. Incorrect: Systematic desensitization is a form of counter conditioning in which the client attempts to maintain a state of relaxation in the presence of an *imagined* anxiety-inducing stimuli.

7. a. Incorrect: Logotherapy is a form of existential therapy that helps the client find meaning in life.
   b. Incorrect: Moral therapy was Pinel's term for his humane treatment approach to therapy.
   c. Incorrect: Counter conditioning is a behavior therapy technique that applies the principles of classical conditioning to therapy.
   d. **Correct: Rational-emotive therapy is a form of cognitive therapy in which the client is encouraged to give up irrational beliefs.**

8. a. Incorrect: Logotherapy is a form of existential therapy that helps the client find meaning in life.
   b. **Correct: This procedure is known as the two-chair exercise and is used by Gestalt therapists.**
   c. Incorrect: Counter conditioning is a behavior therapy-technique that applies the principles of classical conditioning to therapy.
   d. Incorrect: Social-skills training is a form of behavioral group therapy in which the focus is to improve the client's social relationships by improving interpersonal skills.

9. a. Incorrect: The humanistic orientation generally focuses on the individual, not groups.
   b. Incorrect: The Gestalt orientation generally focuses on the individual, not groups.
   c. **Correct: The social-relations orientation assumes that psychological problems arise due to poor interpersonal relationships, and thus brings others into the therapy process.**
   d. Incorrect: The behavioral orientation generally focuses on the individual, not groups.

10. a. Incorrect: The three roles resemble, respectively, the Freudian structures of id, superego, and ego.
    b. Incorrect: The three roles resemble, respectively, the Freudian structures of id, superego, and ego.
    c. **Correct: The three roles resemble, respectively, the Freudian structures of id, superego, and ego.**
    d. Incorrect: The three roles resemble, respectively, the Freudian structures of id, superego, and ego.

11. a. Incorrect: Structural therapy stresses the emotional boundaries between family members.
    b. **Correct: Boundaries that are either too rigid or too diffuse cause or reflect problems and should be made more flexible.**
    c. Incorrect: Structural therapy stresses the emotional boundaries between family members.
    d. Incorrect: Structural therapy stresses the emotional boundaries between family members.

12. a. Incorrect: A side effect of ECT therapy is retrograde amnesia, or forgetting of events that occurred just prior to the treatment.
b. Incorrect: A side effect of ECT therapy is retrograde amnesia, or forgetting of events that occurred just prior to the treatment.
c. Incorrect: A side effect of ECT therapy is retrograde amnesia, or forgetting of events that occurred just prior to the treatment.
d. Correct: A side effect of ECT therapy is retrograde amnesia, or forgetting of events that occurred just prior to the treatment.

13. a. Incorrect: Valium is an anti anxiety drug that has a calming effect on the client.
b. Incorrect: Trofranil is an antidepressant drug that is a tricyclic antidepressant. It apparently increases the levels of serotonin and norepinephrine in the brain.
c. Correct: Thorazine is phenothiazine that is used to threat schizophrenic behavior.
d. Incorrect: Lithium carbonate is used to treat the mood swings of bi polar disorder.

14. **a. Correct: Primary prevention helps prevent psychological disorders by fostering social support systems like reducing unemployment and making low-cost housing available and providing training to help individuals deal with environmental stressors.**
b. Incorrect: Secondary prevention provides early treatment, in the form of crisis intervention, to people at immediate risk for developing a psychological disorder.
c. Incorrect: Tertiary prevention keeps people with full-blown psychological disorders from getting worse and having a relapse.
d. Incorrect: Crisis intervention is the name of the treatment used in secondary prevention.

15. **a. Correct: Since Melinda has threatened to harm herself, she can be involuntarily committed to a mental hospital.**
b. Incorrect: Melinda does have the right to treatment.
c. Incorrect: Melinda does have the right to refuse treatment.
d. Incorrect: Melinda does have the right to confidentiality.

16. **a. Correct: The degree of empathy you feel with a therapist is a good predictor of therapy effectiveness.**
b. Incorrect: There does not appear to be a predictable relationship between the therapist's gender, age, or race and effectiveness of therapy.
c. Incorrect: There does not appear to be a predictable relationship between the therapist's gender, age, or race and effectiveness of therapy.
d. Incorrect: There does not appear to be a predictable relationship between the therapist's gender, age, or race and effectiveness of therapy.

17. **a. Correct: Spontaneous remission is Eysenck's term for apparent recovery from psychological disorders without treatment.**
b. Incorrect: Spontaneous remission is Eysenck's term for apparent recovery from psychological disorders without treatment.
c. Incorrect: Spontaneous remission is Eysenck's term for apparent recovery from psychological disorders without treatment.
d. Incorrect: Spontaneous remission is Eysenck's term for apparent recovery from psychological disorders without treatment.

Practice test B:

1. a. Incorrect: Not all forms of therapy practiced have been successful.
b. Correct: All therapeutic approaches are based on assumptions as to the cause of the problem.
c. Incorrect: Therapeutic approaches have developed through systematic research.
d. Incorrect: Research into therapy is not done in a lab.

2. a. Incorrect: Hippocrates believed mania was the result of too much blood; trephining involved the chipping away of the skull to release demons from the head.
b. Correct: Bloodletting was used to decrease the level of blood; which Hippocrates believed to be the cause of mania.
c. Incorrect: Exorcism was used to scare the devil away; Hippocrates believed in a natural, not supernatural cause of abnormal behaviors.
d. Incorrect: Hippocrates believed that mania was the result of too much blood, not too little.

3. **a. Correct: Pinel called his therapy "moral therapy" due to its premise that humane treatment would promote mental well-being.**
b. Incorrect: Pinel was not involved in the deinstitutionalization movement.
c. Incorrect: Pinel used "talk therapy," but he called the therapeutic approach "moral therapy."
d. Incorrect: Existential therapy was not developed until the late nineteenth century.

4. a. Incorrect: While all of these alternatives play a significant role in psychoanalytic therapy, transference (positive or negative) is the key.
   b. Incorrect: While all of these alternatives play a significant role in psychoanalytic therapy, transference (positive or negative) is the key.
   c. Incorrect: While all of these alternatives play a significant role in psychoanalytic therapy, transference (positive or negative) is the key.
   d. Correct: While all of these alternatives play a significant role in psychoanalytic therapy, transference (positive or negative) is the key.

5. **a. Correct: The manifest content of the dream is the storyline that the dreamer remembers.**
   b. Incorrect: This is a description of the remembered part of the dream, or manifest content, not the sexual symbolism.
   c. Incorrect: This is a description of the remembered part of the dream, or manifest content, not the underlying meaning.
   d. Incorrect: This is a description of the remembered part of the dream, or manifest content, not unconscious symbolic content.

6. a. Incorrect: The use of chips as rewards for desired behavior is the use of a token economy.
   b. Incorrect: The use of chips as rewards for desired behavior is the use of a token economy.
   c. Correct: The use of chips as rewards for desired behavior is the use of a token economy.
   d. Incorrect: The use of chips as rewards for desired behavior is the use of a token economy.

7. **a. Correct: Carl Rogers is a humanistic theorist and is not involved in any of the other theories.**
   b. Incorrect: REBT and the ABC theory of emotion are both proposed by Albert Ellis.
   c. Incorrect: REBT and the ABC theory of emotion are both proposed by Albert Ellis.
   d. Incorrect: REBT and the ABC theory of emotion are both proposed by Albert Ellis.

8. a. Incorrect: In vivo desensitization is a technique that trains the client to maintain a state of relaxation in the presence of anxiety-inducing stimuli.
   b. Correct: This procedure is known as the two-chair exercise and is used by Gestalt therapists.
   c. Incorrect: Stress-inoculation therapy is a type of cognitive therapy that helps clients change their pessimistic thinking into more positive thinking.
   d. Incorrect: Psychodrama is a form of psychoanalytic group therapy that aimed at achieving insight and catharsis through acting out real-life situations and logotherapy is a form of existential therapy that helps the client find meaning in life.

9. a. Incorrect: Psychodrama is a form of psychoanalytic group therapy aimed at achieving insight and catharsis through acting out real-life situations.
   b. Incorrect: Logotherapy is a form of existential therapy that helps the client find meaning in life.
   c. Incorrect: Stress-inoculation therapy is a form of cognitive therapy that helps clients change their pessimistic thinking to more positive thinking.
   d. Correct: Assertiveness training involves training clients to express their feelings more directly.

10. a. Incorrect: AA, NA, and rape survivor groups are examples of self-help groups, not sensitivity-training groups.
    b. Correct: AA, NA, and rape survivor groups are examples of self-help groups.
    c. Incorrect: AA, NA, and rape survivor groups are examples of self-help groups, not transactional analysis groups.
    d. Incorrect: AA, NA, and rape survivor groups are examples of self-help groups, not encounter groups.

11. **a. Correct: Encounter groups are a form of sensitivity-training groups that are an offshoot of the human potential movement, a humanistic type of therapy.**
    b. Incorrect:Encounter groups are a form of sensitivity-training groups that are an offshoot of the human potential movement, a humanistic type of therapy.
    c. Incorrect:Encounter groups are a form of sensitivity-training groups that are an offshoot of the human potential movement, a humanistic type of therapy.
    d. Incorrect:Encounter groups are a form of sensitivity-training groups that are an offshoot of the human potential movement, a humanistic type of therapy.

12. a. Incorrect: Structural family therapy involves the identification of boundaries between family members.
    b. Incorrect: Group therapy involves therapy with others, not specifically family members.
    c. Incorrect: Marital therapy involves the attempt to improve the relationship between a couple, not a family.
    d. Correct: The systems approach involves the family members drawing diagrams of their relationships and discussing how the relationships are maladaptive.

13. a. Incorrect: The research into the cause of the effects of ECT has been inconclusive; increases in norepinephrine and endorphins, among others, have been suggested.
    b. Incorrect: The research into the cause of the effects of ECT has been inconclusive; increases in norepinephrine and endorphins, among others, have been suggested.
    c. Incorrect: The research into the cause of the effects of ECT has been inconclusive; increases in norepinephrine and endorphins, among others, have been suggested.
    d. Correct: The research into the cause of the effects of ECT has been inconclusive; increases in norepinephrine and endorphins, among others, have been suggested.

14. **a. Correct: Research suggests that the best treatment for major depression is a combination of drug therapy and psychotherapy.**
    b. Incorrect: Research suggests that the best treatment for major depression is a combination of drug therapy and psychotherapy.
    c. Incorrect: Research suggests that the best treatment for major depression is a combination of drug therapy and psychotherapy.
    d. Incorrect: Research suggests that the best treatment for major depression is a combination of drug therapy and psychotherapy.

15. a. Incorrect: Primary prevention helps prevent psychological disorders by fostering social support systems like reducing unemployment and making low-cost housing available and providing training to help individuals deal with environmental stressors.
    b. Correct: Secondary prevention provides early treatment, in the form of crisis intervention, to people at immediate risk for developing a psychological disorder, as in the example in this question.
    c. Incorrect: Tertiary prevention keeps people with full-blown psychological disorders from getting worse and having a relapse.
    d. Incorrect: Crisis prevention is not the term that is used; crisis intervention is the correct term.

16. a. Incorrect: This was a decision dealing with the right to have treatment.
    b. Incorrect: This was a decision dealing with the right to refuse treatment.
    c. Incorrect: This was a decision concerning confidentiality.
    d. Correct: *Addington v Texas* is the court case that established the need to demonstrate that a person is dangerous before that person can be committed to a mental hospital.

17. a. Incorrect: Criminal activity is not grounds for admission to a mental hospital.
    b. Correct: For involuntary commitment to a mental institution it must demonstrated that the person is potentially harmful to self or others.
    c. Incorrect: Bizarre behavior is not ground for admission to a mental hospital.
    d. Incorrect: Homelessness and uncleanseliness are not grounds for commitment.

18. **a. Correct: Empathy may, in many cases, be the key to success in therapy. Indeed, even empathetic professors may be as effective in helping others as professional psychotherapists.**
    b. Incorrect: Empathy may, in many cases, be the key to success in therapy. Indeed, even empathetic professors may be as effective in helping others as professional psychotherapists.
    c. Incorrect: Empathy may, in many cases, be the key to success in therapy. Indeed, even empathetic professors may be as effective in helping others as professional psychotherapists.
    d. Incorrect: Empathy may, in many cases, be the key to success in therapy. Indeed, even empathetic professors may be as effective in helping others as professional psychotherapists.

19. **a. Correct: Psychotherapy and drug therapy have been shown to be equally effective in improving functioning in the short run.**
    b. Incorrect: Psychotherapy and drug therapy have been shown to be equally effective in improving functioning in the short run.
    c. Incorrect: Psychotherapy and drug therapy have been shown to be equally effective in improving functioning in the short run.
    d. Incorrect: Psychotherapy and drug therapy have been shown to be equally effective in improving functioning in the short run.

20. a. Incorrect: Empathy may, in many cases, be the key to success in therapy. Indeed, even empathetic professors may be as effective in helping others as professional psychotherapists.
    b. Correct: Empathy may, in many cases, be the key to success in therapy. Indeed, even empathetic professors may be as effective in helping others as professional psychotherapists.
    c. Incorrect: Empathy may, in many cases, be the key to success in therapy. Indeed, even empathetic professors may be as effective in helping others as professional psychotherapists.
    d. Incorrect: Empathy may, in many cases, be the key to success in therapy. Indeed, even empathetic professors may be as effective in helping others as professional psychotherapists.

Essay Questions:

1. Briefly, the psychoanalytic orientation emphasizes the importance of the analysis of free association, dreams, resistances, and transference so that the client may gain insight into unconscious conflicts and experience catharsis. The behavioral orientation emphasizes the importance of learning and environment, employing the models of classical conditioning, operant conditioning, and observational learning. The cognitive orientation assumes that thoughts, rather than events themselves, cause psychological disorders. The humanistic orientation emphasizes the importance of being aware of one's emotions and feeling free to express them. The social-relations orientation assumes that people cannot be treated as isolated individuals. The biopsychological orientation uses medical procedures to treat psychological disorders.

2. Because most therapists have an eclectic orientation, the therapist's personal qualities are more important than the particular type of therapy he or she practices. For a college student, the college counseling center, a trusted and knowledgeable professor, or a relative, could recommend a therapist. Other sources include community mental health centers and state psychological associations; a pastor or other clergy member can also be of help. Once Ethan meets the therapist, he should attend to the therapist's credentials, reputation, and interpersonal manner. It is preferable that the therapist be licensed. Ethan should also attend to his own feelings of comfort and confidence in the therapist. Because most therapists have an eclectic orientation, the therapist's personal qualities are more important than the particular type of therapy he or she practices.

16 Psychology and Health

After studying this chapter, you should be able to:

1. Describe how the major causes of illness and death have changed since the beginning of the twentieth century. (p. 558)

2. Describe the domain of health psychology and the significance of the biopsychosocial model. (p. 558)

3. Define stress and then give examples of the three major categories of stress. (p. 558-561)

4. Distinguish between the stress that arises from life changes versus that from everyday hassles, mentioning the concept of posttraumatic stress disorder. (p. 561-564)

5. Describe the important features of the general adaptation syndrome, and explain how it is related to susceptibility to noninfectious diseases. (p. 565-566)

6. Explain the relationship between stress and infectious diseases and then explain how studies in psychoneuroimmunology add to our knowledge about that relationship. (p. 566-569)

7. Explain the relationship between stress and cancer. (p. 569)

8. List and describe six factors that moderate our reactions to stress. (p. 570-574)

9. List and describe five approaches to coping with stress. (p. 574-575)

10. List and describe the impact of four health-impairing habits, emphasizing how tobacco use may be both prevented and treated, and how behavior-modification techniques are useful in changing high-fat dietary habits. (p. 575-582)

11. Summarize the results regarding the efforts of health psychologists to encourage individuals to seek appropriate medical treatment, reduce patient distress, and increase patient adherence to medical regimens. (p. 582-586)

12. Summarize the strengths and weaknesses of research on the Type A personality. (p. 586-589)

COMPREHENSIVE GUIDED REVIEW:

Health psychology is the field that studies the role of__(1)__ factors in the promotion of health and the prevention of illness. Health psychologists favor a__(2)__ model, which emphasizes the interaction of biological, psychological, and social factors, quite in contrast to the__(3)__ model, which neglects the psychological and social factors.

I. Stress and Illness: What is stress? According to Selye, **stress** is the__(4)__ response of the body to physical and psychological demands, known as **stressors.** Stress acts as a__(5)__ to make us adjust our behavior to meet changing demands. Stress can even be__(6)__, as when using this *Course Success Guide* and doing well, or __(7)__, as in not having any systematic approach to study and doing poorly. Seyle called unpleasant stress, "__(8)__," and pleasant stress, "__(9)__."

Types of Stress: There are three general categories of psychological stressors:

1) __(10)__, which occurs when you are blocked from attaining a goal. The intensity of **frustration** varies from minor frustration, such as having to wait in line, to major frustration, such as losing one's job or flunking out of school.

2) ___(11)__, which occurs when you must face demands that tax your abilities to meet them.
3)___(12)___, which occurs when you are torn between two or more courses of action. Kurt__(13)_ identified three kinds of conflicts: **approach-approach,** which occurs when you are torn between two__(14)_ courses of action; **avoidance-avoidance,** when you are forced to choose between two___(15)__ courses of action; and **approach-avoidance,** which occurs when you are__(16)__ drawn to and repelled by the same goal.

Types of Stressors: Frustration, pressure, and **conflict** are often the results of life events. These include both __(17)_ life changes and everyday__(18)__. Interest in the relationship between life changes and illness began when Holmes and Rahe developed the_____(19)____ *Rating Scale*. From their research, a list of forty-three kinds of____(20)_____ was generated. (See Table 16.1 on page 563 in your textbook for the items and their ratings.) From the list, you can find your *life change score,* or the sum of the scores for your life changes that occurred in a given period of time. Research has indicated that there is a___(21)__ between the amount of life change and illness; but remember, the positive correlation that exists between your life change score and illness indicates only that there might be a____(22)_ between life events and illness.

In developing the Social Readjustment Rating scale, Holmes and Rahe assumed that any degree of life change, whether positive or negative would induce__(23)__. However, subsequent research has shown that it is the__(24)__ of the events that induces stress, not just the change. Traumatic__(25)__ events are often associated with **posttraumatic stress disorder,** associated with chronic overarousal and an increased risk of physical illness.

Although major life changes are important stressors, the__(26)__ of everyday life were also identified by Lazarus as stress-inducing events. Research has shown that the more daily hassles, the more___(27)___. Thus, it has been suggested that major life changes may promote illness indirectly by__(28)__ everyday hassles. Most research makes it difficult to determine whether hassles are merely__(29)__ with, or whether they actually promote, illness. This is because, at this time,__(30)__ **prospective** studies have been conducted. __(31)__ studies investigate whether one's current level of hassles is predictive of future health. The prospective studies that have been done indicate that__(32)__ experiences are associated with depression and poor health, but only when there is also a lack of__(33)__ circumstances, or *uplifts,* that may buffer the negative effects.

The Biopsychology of Stress: Whatever the causes of stress, it is marked by physiological__(34)__ Selye identified three stages that organisms go through in reacting to__(35)__. Collectively, he called these stages the **general adaptation syndrome.** During the first stage, or the___(36)____ stage, the body prepares to cope with the stressor by increasing the level of activity in the sympathetic nervous system and adrenal glands. This is known as the__(37)__ response. During the second phase, or the **stage of resistance,** the body becomes more__(38)__ to continued exposure to the stressor. During the final phase, or the stage of__(39)__, resistance to disease collapses and, in extreme cases, death may follow.

Stress and Noninfectious Diseases: While the__(40)__ response is a helpful evolutionary trait in response to periodic stressors, such as an occasional attack by wild animals; in the twentieth century, when stress is usually more__(41)__, its repeated activation can take its toll on the human body, possibly causing or aggravating infectious or noninfectious diseases. Stress-related__(42)__ diseases include asthma, headache, diabetes, gastric ulcers, rheumatoid arthritis, ulcerative colitis, and essential hypertension. These diseases are *psychosomatic illnesses* and are based on the assumption that they are caused, or worsened, by__(43)__ factors.

In the domain of noninfectious diseases and stress, most attention has been given to the role of stress and____(44)___ disease, which is caused by **atherosclerosis** and, in turn, is promoted by__(45)__ deposits in the coronary arteries. __(46)__has been linked to cholesterol levels, as well other factors in heart disease, such as elevated heart rates and blood pressure.

Stress and Infectious Diseases: The realization that stress can impair the__(47)__ system led to the emergence of **psychoneuroimmunology,** the interdisciplinary field that studies the relationship between psychological factors and

__(48)__. This field recognizes that stress effects the immune system through mediation of the brain and __(49)__ system. The most fully understood immune mechanism is the one in which the __(50)__ secretes a hormone that stimulates the pituitary gland to secrete *ACTH*, which then stimulates the adrenal cortex to secrete *corticosteroids*. The hypothalamus also increases activity in the __(51)__ nervous system, which stimulates the adrenal medulla to secrete the hormones epinephrine and norepinephrine. (Remember that although corticosteroids, epinephrine, and norepinephrine make us more resistant to stressors, they also impair our immune systems!) The white blood cells, called __(52)__, which attack invading bacteria, and __(53)__, which attack viruses, cancer cells, and foreign tissues, are chiefly responsible for the immunological response to infections.

The relationship between stress and the immune system is of special importance to victims of acquired immune deficiency syndrome (__(54)__), who suffer stress not only from the disease but also from social reactions to it. This may further impair the immune system. Research has shown that the immune response may be enhanced or suppressed by __(55)__ conditioning. A study by Robert Ader demonstrated conditioned suppression of the immune system and is the focus of the "Anatomy of a Contemporary Research Study" section on page 568 in your textbook.

Anatomy of a Contemporary Research Study: Can the Immune Response Be Altered by Classical Conditioning? *Read the summary of Ader's study presented on page 568 in your textbook and answer the following questions.*

What was the rationale for the study?

What methods did the author use to test that hypothesis?

What was the outcome of the study and what did the authors conclude the results meant?

Stress and Cancer: In the second century, the Greek physician __(56)__ noted that depressed women were more likely to get cancer than happy women. Contemporary research has suggested that stress does not __(57)__ cancer, but rather it affects the ability of the immune system to destroy cancerous cells. Although the evidence is not clear, if we can assume that emotions can influence the __(58)__ of cancer, what mechanism might account for this phenomenon? Currently, scientists suggest that when the body is under pressure, there is a __(59)__ in the activity of natural killer cells. This appears to be due to a decrease in __(60)__. However, remember the research indicates that stress can *impair* the immune system's ability to __(61)__ cancer cells, but does *not* suggest that stress __(62)__ normal cells to become cancerous.

Mini-review of Stress and Illness: Match each term with its correct definition.

_______1. distress
_______2. frustration
_______3. general adaptation syndrome
_______4. T-lymphocytes
_______5. health psychology
_______6. approach-approach
_______7. biopsychosocial
_______8. stress
_______9. approach-avoidance
_______10. prospective studies
_______11. posttraumatic stress disorder

A. The field that studies the role of psychological factors in the promotion of health and the prevention of illness
B. Selye's term for unpleasant stress
C. A theoretical model that emphasizes the interaction of biological, psychological, and social factors
D. The type of stress of psychological stressors that occurs when you must face demands that tax your abilities to meet them
E. A theoretical model that neglects psychological and social factors
F. The physiological response of the body to physical and psychological demands.
G. Selye's term for pleasant stress
H. Type of conflict that occurs when you are forced to choose between two unpleasant courses of action
I. Blood cells that attack viruses, cancer cells, and foreign tissues and are chiefly responsible for the immunological response to infections
J. The type of stress of psychological stressors that occurs when you are blocked

________12. medical model
________13. psychoneuroimmunology
________14. alarm reaction stage
________15. eustress
________16. B-lymphocytes
________17. pressure
________18. *Social Readjustment Rating Scale*
________19. conflict
________20. stage of resistance
________21. avoidance-avoidance
________22. stage of exhaustion
________23. psychosomatic illnesses

from attaining a goal

K. Type of conflict that occurs when you are torn between two desirable courses of action
L. The second stage of the body's reaction to stress; the body becomes more resistant to continued exposure to the stressor
M. Type of conflict that occurs when you are simultaneously drawn to and repelled by the same goal
N. Identifies an individual's life change score, or the sum of the scores for that individual's life changes that occurred in a given period of time
O. Psychological illness characterized by chronic overarousal and an increased risk of physical illness that follows the occurrence of a traumatic negative event
P. Selye's term for the three stages that organisms go through in reacting to stressors
Q. The first stage of the body's reaction to stress. The body prepares to cope with the stressor by increasing the level of activity in the sympathetic nervous system and adrenal glands
R. The type of stress that occurs when you are torn between two or more courses of action
S. Research that investigates whether one's current level of hassles is predictive of future health
T. The final phase of the body's reaction to stress; stage in which resistance to disease collapses and, in extreme cases, death may follow
U. Diseases that are believed to be caused or worsened by emotional factors.
V. White blood cells that attack invading bacteria
W. The interdisciplinary field that studies the relationship between psychological factors and illness

II. Factors That Moderate the Stress Response: ____(63)____noted 2, 000 years ago that it was more important to know what sort of person had a disease than what the disease was. What accounts for____(64)____ in response to stress? There are a variety of factors, including **physiological reactivity, cognitive appraisal, explanatory style, feeling of control, psychological hardiness,** and **social support.**

Physiological reactivity refers to the extent a person displays____(65)____ in heart rate, blood pressure, stress hormone secretion, and other physiological factors in response to stressors. Individual differences in____(66)____ can be attributed to the sex of the subject, degree of physical fitness, or the use of stimulant drugs.

Cognitive appraisal refers to the fact that two people may respond to the same stressor differently based on how they ____(67)____ the stressor. In *primary appraisal*, you judge whether the situation is____(68)____. In____(69)____ appraisal, you estimate whether you have the ability to cope with the stressor. Research has shown that lower reactivity is linked to higher____(70)____, an idea from Chapter 13 that is similar to secondary appraisal.

Another difference in people in their reaction to stress is their____(71)____. The____(72)____ explanatory style, as discussed in chapter 14, where subjects attribute unpleasant events to stable, global, and internal characteristics of themselves, is characteristic of most depressed people. Research has also shown that a **feeling of**____(73)____ is one of the most important factors mediating the relationship between stress and illness. The poorer recuperative powers of some patients are associated with their feelings of____(74)____, the acquired feeling that one has little control over events in one's life. The ultimate response to lack of control is ____(75)____. This is a state of mental, emotional, and physical exhaustion caused by subjection to chronic____(76)____ stressors.

Psychological hardiness refers to a set of____(77)____ characteristics that represent a measure of the degree of responsiveness to stressors. Hardy people face stressors with a sense of____(78)____, challenge, and control, especially in terms of how these elements affect health habits. Finally, people with good____(79)____ are less likely to suffer illness. **Social support** may be____(80)____, in the form of money or practical help, or____(81)____, in the form of advice or encouragement. There is evidence that social support____(82)____ the immune response, thus promoting health.

III. Coping with Stress: Since stress is unavoidable, and sometimes harmful,__(83)__ with stress is an important part of everyday life. Strategies for coping with stress vary. One approach identifies__(84)__, *emotion-oriented,* or *avoidance-oriented* coping behaviors. Stress __(85)__ training is a formal method of coping with stress, and stress-__(86)__ training is the most common form. Two additional ways of coping with stress are the use of__(87)__ exercise and relaxation training.

The effects of__(88)__ on stress management was shown in a longitudinal study of students. It is suggested that exercise has a direct effect on stress reduction by reducing__(89)__, and an indirect effect by increasing one's sense of __(90)__ over stressors. There is also evidence that exercise enhances the__(91)__ system.

Because stress is associated with__(92)__, **relaxation techniques** have proved effective in coping with stress by reducing physiological or psychological arousal. Techniques include hypnosis; __(93)__; biofeedback; slow, rhythmic breathing; progressive relaxation, and restricted environmental stimulation, or REST. The most basic technique is __(94)__, which involves the successive tensing and relaxation of the major muscle groups. It reduces activity in the__(95)__ nervous system, as well as the muscles, which can relieve anxiety. Progressive relaxation may also enhance the immunological response.

Mini-review of Factors that Moderate Stress and Coping with Stress: Match each term with its correct description.

_______ 1. pessimistic explanatory style
_______ 2. physiological reactivity
_______ 3. learned helplessness
_______ 4. secondary appraisal
_______ 5. psychological hardiness
_______ 6. cognitive appraisal
_______ 7. social support
_______ 8. explanatory style
_______ 9. burnout
_______10. relaxation training
_______11. primary appraisal
_______12. stress-management training
_______13. progressive relaxation

A. The extent a person displays increases in heart rate, blood pressure, stress hormone secretion, and other physiological factors in response to stressors
B. Refers to the subjective interpretation of the severity of a stressor
C. Subjects attribute unpleasant events to stable, global, and internal characteristics of themselves; is characteristic of most depressed people
D. The stage of cognitive appraisal in which you judge whether the situation is stressful
E. Refers to a set of personality characteristics that represent a measure of the degree of responsiveness to stressors
F. The stage of cognitive appraisal in which you estimate whether you have the ability to cope with the stressor
G. Class of stress-coping techniques that have proved effective by reducing physiological or psychological arousal; includes hypnosis; meditation; biofeedback; slow, rhythmic breathing; progressive relaxation; and restricted environmental stimulation, or REST
H. The tendency to explain things either optimistically or pessimistically
I. A factor that moderates stress; it may be tangible, in the form of money or practical help, or intangible, in the form of advice or encouragement
J. The acquired feeling that one has little control over events in one's life
K. This is a state of mental, emotional, and physical exhaustion caused by subjection to chronic uncontrollable stressors and is the ultimate response to lack of control
L. A formal method of coping with stress
M. Technique that involves the successive tensing and relaxation of the major muscle groups; it reduces activity in the sympathetic nervous system as well as the muscles, which can relieve anxiety

IV. Health-Impairing Habits: Habits as varied as smoking, overeating, avoiding exercise, and failing to wear seat belts sharply__(96)__ the chances of illness, injury, or death. Yet a majority of people still engage in these habits because they don't believe that they are__(97)__ to the risks. A most important factor that determines whether people are motivated to engage in health-promoting behavior is__(98)__, or people's belief in their ability to do the task at hand. Research has shown that people high in self-efficacy believe that their behaviors will be__(99)__, and are more likely to downplay the barriers and engage in the behaviors. Those low in self-efficacy are more likely to engage in health-impairing habits, including unsafe sex practices, lack of__(100)__, smoking, and poor nutrition.

Unsafe Sexual Practices: Many health psychologists have turned their attention to unsafe behaviors related to the spread of__(101)__, which is caused by human immunodeficiency virus (HIV). Today, no group is safe from it, irrespective of age, gender, race, or_____(102)___. AIDS is spread by blood or__(103)_. Since it may take up to 10 _(104)__to develop AIDS after being infected, people can infect others without realizing that they have the disease themselves. Therefore,__(105) techniques are crucial. Workshops and prevention education have been increasingly successful.

Exercise: People who exercise regularly are healthier and live__(106)__ than those who do not. Exercise accomplishes this, in part, by boosting the__(107)__ system. The consequences of lack of exercise are numerous; among them, people are more likely to suffer from infectious disease, obesity, and__(108)__ disease. A concern is to get people involved in programs of regular exercise and then get them to__(109)__ to the program. Programs that are aimed at getting people to adhere to exercise programs do help more people to stay with an exercise regime after a lapse.

Smoking: Despite the preponderance of information that smoking is__(110)__ and hazardous to health, millions of people continue (or start) to smoke tobacco. Clearly,__(111)__ is addictive. Smoking causes__(112)__ and contributes to stroke, cancer, emphysema, and heart disease. Although many smokers say they smoke to relieve anxiety or be more alert, continuing to smoke is also way of avoiding the unpleasant symptoms of__(113)__. Worldwide smoking may be reduced by programs aimed at __(114)__, and those to help people stop smoking. *Prevention programs* __(115)__ people, especially children, about the ill effects of smoking, and also encourage them to resist peer pressure and advertisements.

Quitting smoking is difficult. One study showed that only__(116)__ percent succeeded over the course of two years. __(117)__techniques include the use of *nicotine gum* and, more recently, the *nicotine patch*. These techniques will not help smokers overcome their__(118)__. Their chances of overcoming it will be increased by a feeling of__(119)__ and the presence of social support. For those who are motivated, the technique of___(120)___ is useful. Another technique is rapid smoking as a form of__(121)_therapy. Another approach to smoking cessation is **self-management programs,** which use___(122)___ to promote smoking cessation. Still another way is to train physicians how to help their patients stop.

Nutrition: Health psychologists are particularly concerned with the relationship between__(123)__ and health. They are especially concerned about the risk factor of__(124)__ diets in cardiovascular disease. __(125)__is also a topic of concern to psychologists, since it is a health risk for both men and women. Clearly, there is a great deal of__(126)__ among cultures in terms of how people perceive the ideal body type.

A common approach to weight__(127)__ and weight loss is dieting. For the most part, however, dieting by itself is __(128)__and unhealthy. Obese people may resort to medical treatments. Diet pills, however, eventually lose their effectiveness and can cause insomnia, high blood pressure, and symptoms of__(129)__ schizophrenia. Surgery is another approach. Morbid obesity is best treated by __(130)_means. Formal approaches to weight loss include __(131)__therapy in conjunction with aerobic exercise and self-monitoring with guidance. The need for__(132)__ cannot be overemphasized.

V. Reactions to Illness: Everybody, including those who lead a__(133)__ lifestyle, will occasionally become ill. The importance of seeking appropriate medical help has encouraged some psychologists to study factors that__(134)__ people to seek treatment. An important factor is___(135)___. One's__(136)__ style (optimistic versus pessimistic) may affect the decision to seek treatment, as well as how the symptoms are interpreted.

If a condition is chronic, or requires surgery, it may induce ___(137)__in the patient. One important factor in coping with distress is__(138)__. Among the most effective means of preparing patients for stressful medical procedures is for __(139)__medical practitioners to inform them of the procedures they will undergo, telling them how to cope with the sensations they will experience, and by __(140)__. Distress may also be__(141)__ by knowing about the successful surgery of a hospital roommate.

Recovery from illness or surgery may include adherence to a medical regimen, such as __(142)__ drugs, a restricted diet, or an exercise program. Patients are less likely to adhere to regimens prescribed by physicians they__(143)__.

Physicians who are emotionally__(144)__ and expressive are more likely to achieve patient compliance. Some patients may abandon a regimen prematurely because they no longer experience the symptoms. This can have serious effects. Lastly,__(145)__ reinforcement may be helpful.

Mini-review of Health-impairing Habits and Reactions to Illness:

1. Describe the four most important health impairing habits in today's society.

2. What are the most important factor in determining whether a person will be motivated to engage in a health-promoting habit?

VI. Thinking About Psychology: Does Type A Behavior Promote Coronary Heart Disease?

A person exhibiting____(146)____ behavior can be characterized by impatience, rapid speech, becoming easily angered, and being highly competitive and driven to do more and more in less time. By contrast, ____(147)____behavior is characterized by patience, an even temper, and a willingness to do a limited number of things in a reasonable amount of time. The Type A person might also show____(148)____, chronic activation, and multiphasic activity. Research has shown that the overall pattern of Type A behavior is__(149)__ to coronary heart disease but is related to a specific component of behavior, known as **cynical hostility.** This is characterized by outbursts of anger, rudeness, and an __(150)__ manner. People who display ____(151)____are more physiologically reactive.

Anatomy of a Classic Research Study: Is There a Relationship Between Behavior and Heart Disease? *Read the summary of Friedman and Rosenman's study presented on page 586 in your textbook and answer the following questions.*

What was the rationale for the study?

What methods did the author use to test that hypothesis?

What was the outcome of the study and what did the authors conclude the results meant?

In 1975, Friedman, Rosenman, and colleagues reported the results of a__(152)__ study that began in 1960 and lasted 9 years with the same results: Those men classified as Type__(153)__ were more than twice as likely to have developed coronary heart disease than those classified as Type__(154)__. More recently, however, the role of Type A behavior in ____(155)____has been brought into question by a follow-up study of the subjects in Friedman et al.'s 1975 study. This most recent result found no__(156)__ between overall Type A behavior and coronary heart disease. They did, however, also suggest that____(157)____ was most related to the disease.

Whether it is cynical hostility or Type A behavior in general, how does Type A behavior promote coronary heart disease? One explanation is that there is a significant increase in the production of stress__(158)__. Second, Type A people have a tendency to__(159)__ the symptoms of illness. There is also evidence that Type A behavior runs in families and that it may be related to__(160)__ practices, where children are given no standards except "Do better." Research has shown that there are__(161)__ differences, with Type A behavior being more common in men.

Since there is a possible link between health problems and Type A behavior, programs to change that behavior have been developed. _____(162)____ programs to help university teachers (they are particularly prone to Type A behavior) have been shown to be successful!

KEY RESEARCH FINDINGS

1. **Selye (1980):** Noted that stress can be good (eustress) or bad (distress). (Page 558)
2. **Baumeister & Steinhilber (1984):** Archival study found that NBA teams were more likely to lose deciding championship games when they were thehome team. (Page 559)
3. **Schlenker et al. (1995):** Found no difference in home-team results in championship games. (Page 560)
4. **Lewin (1935):** Defined three types of conflict (approach-approach, approach-avoidance, and avoidance-avoidance). (Page 560)
5. **Holmes & Rahe (1967):** Developed the Social Readjustment Rating Scale to describe the relationship between life changes and illness. (Page 561)
6. **Stone et al. (1992):** Showed that students who had more life changes were more susceptible to developing colds when exposed to a rhino virus than those who had fewer changes. (Page 562)
7. **Norris & Uhl (1993):** Found that the daily hassles due to the aftereffects of a hurricane were more stressful than the storm itself. (Page 563)
8. **Siegel & Brown (1988):** Found that illness in adolescent girls increased with negative circumstances, but only when there was also a lack of positive circumstances (uplifts). (Page 564)
9. **Snyder, Roghmann, & Sigal (1993):** Found that university students who had experienced more positive stress had a higher immune response when exposed to an antigen. (Page 564)
10. **Selye (1936):** Conducted rat study that led to the concept of the general adaptation syndrome. (Page 565)
11. **Schleifer et al. (1983):** Showed impaired immune system functioning in men whose wives had died of breast cancer. (Page 566)
12. **Kiecolt-Glaser & Glaser (1995):** Described the physiological mechanisms of the effects of stress on the immune system. (Page 566)
13. **Stone et al. (1987):** Showed daily changes in immune response of dental students due to positive and negative stress. (Page 567)
14. **Cohen (1982):** Demonstrated that the immune response in rats could be classically conditioned. (Page 568)
15. **Shaffer et al. (1987):** Conducted longitudinal study that linked lack of emotional expressiveness with cancer. (Page 569)
16. **Hiramoto et al. (1987):** Classically conditioned rats' immune response. (Page 569)
17. **Dandoy & Goldstein (1990):** Replicated a study by Lazarus et al., showing how students using cognitive appraisal developed less physiological arousal to a stressful film. (Page 571)
18. **Peterson, Seligman, & Vaillant (1988):** Conducted retrospective study that showed that graduates who used a pessimistic explanatory style became less healthy later in life. (Page 571)
19. **Kobasa, Maddi, & Kahn (1982):** Found a set of personality characteristics called psychological hardiness in a 5-year study of business executives. (Page 572)
20. **Jemmott & Magloire (1988):** Found higher levels of immunoglobulin in students who reported more-adequate social support. (Page 574)
21. **Brown & Siegel (1988):** Found that adolescents under a high level of stress who exercised regularly had a significantly lower level of illness that those who did not exercise. (Page 574)
22. **Kiecolt-Glaser et al. (1986):** Found a decrease of natural killer cells in students who did not practice a relaxation program. (Page 575)
23. **Belisle, Roskies, & Levesque (1987):** Found that those who participated in a program to motivate adherence to an exercise program were more likely to continue their exercise programs. (Page 578)
24. **Hennrikus, Jeffery, & Lando (1995):** Found that only 16 percent of smokers who wanted to quit were able to do so. (Page 579)
25. **Fiore et al. (1994):** Found that 22 percent of smokers trying to do so abstained for 6 months by using a nicotine patch, and that the nicotine patch was more effective than a placebo patch. (Page 580)
26. **Stapleton et al. (1995):** Found that a nicotine patch was twice as effective as a placebo. (Page 580)
27. **Wadden, Foster, & Letizia (1994):** Found that rapid weight loss does not guarantee long-term weight loss. (Page 582)
28. **Lin & Peterson (1990):** Found that students with a pessimistic explanatory style were less likely to seek medical attention. (Page 583)

29. **Cameron, Leventhal, & Leventhal (1995):** Found that older adults, when faced with ambiguous medical symptoms, were less likely to seek medical attention if they had a stressful life event in the preceding three weeks. (Page 583)
30. **Redd et al. (1987):** Found that children undergoing chemotherapy reported less anxiety and nausea if they played video games during treatment. (Page 584)
31. **Putnam et al. (1994):** Showed that patients who made oral and written commitments to adhere to a medical regimen were more likely to do so than those who did not make such commitments. (Page 585)
32. **Friedman & Rosenman (1959):** Identified a set of personality characteristics called Type A behavior, and linked this behavior to heart disease. (Page 586)
33. **Rosenman et al. (1975):** Reported on the Western Collaborative Group Study, which concluded that men with Type A behavior were twice as likely to develop coronary heart disease than those with Type B. (Page 587)
34. **Ragland & Brand (1988):** This 22-year follow-up on the Western Collaborative Group Study showed no relationship between Type A behavior and coronary heart disease mortality. (Page 588)
35. **Williams et al. (1982):** Found that Type A students displayed a significantly higher level of adrenal stress hormones while performing a stressful task. (Page 588)
36. **Thurman (1985):** Found that behavior modification and assertiveness training changed Type A behavior in college teachers. (Page 589)

PRACTICE TEST A

1. In the early 1900s the leading causes of death were
   a. heart disease, alcohol abuse, and obesity.
   b. influenza, alcohol abuse, and tuberculosis.
   c. influenza, pneumonia, and tuberculosis.
   d. obesity, pneumonia, and tuberculosis.

Obj.: 1 Page: 558

2. The field that studies the role of psychological factors in the promotion of health and the prevention of illness is called
   a. immunopsychology.
   b. health psychology.
   c. psychomicrobiology.
   d. environmental psychology.

Obj.: 2 Page: 558

3. An example of what Hans Selye called "eustress" would be
   a. vacationing in Hawaii.
   b. experiencing insomnia.
   c. taking a series of final exams.
   d. having a flat tire on a desolate road.

Obj.: 3 Page: 559

4. A major fire wipes out your entire community. Months later, residents of the community suffer higher rates of generalized anxiety disorder, sleep disturbances, and physical illnesses. This would be an example of
   a. burnout.
   b. Type A behavior.
   c. learned helplessness.
   d. posttraumatic stress disorder.

Obj.: 4 Page: 562

5. A student develops true migraine headaches when under the stress of studying for exams or writing term papers. This is most likely an example of
   a. malingering.
   b. hypochondriasis.
   c. conversion hysteria.
   d. psychosomatic illness.

Obj.: 5 Page: 565

6. The field that studies the relationship between psychological factors and physical illness is called
   a. biofeedback.
   b. biopsychology.
   c. psychophysiology.
   d. psychoneuroimmunology.

Obj.: 6 Page: 566

7. Psychological factors such as stress have been linked to cancer. Recent research suggest that this is because
   a. stress leads the hypothalamus to secrete a hormone that stimulates the pituitary to release ACTH, leading to abnormal cell growth.
   b. stress leads the hypothalamus to secrete a hormone that stimulates the sympathetic nervous system to release epinephrine and norepinephrine, leading to abnormal cell growth.
   c. stress leads the hypothalamus to secrete a hormone that stimulates the adrenal medulla to release B-lymphocytes and T-lymphocytes, leading to abnormal cell growth.
   d. stress impairs the immune system's ability to destroy cancer cells.

Obj.: 7 Page: 569

8. A student who believes that exam grades depend on lucky guessing, biased grading, and student cheating instead of attending class, reading assignments, and studying hard would most likely be exhibiting
   a. Type A behavior.
   b. learned helplessness.
   c. psychological hardiness.
   d. posttraumatic stress disorder.

Obj.: 8 Page: 572

9. A professor feels in complete control of her courses, challenged by the need to prepare lively lectures, and committed to the teaching profession. She would most likely be high in
   a. burnout.
   b. Type A behavior.
   c. psychological hardiness.
   d. physiological reactivity.

Obj.: 8 Page: 572

10. The three formal methods of coping with stress are
   a. relaxation, exercise, and stress management.
   b. exercise, relaxation, and drug therapy.
   c. relaxation, stress management, and drug therapy.
   d. relaxation, social support, and stress management.

Obj.: 9 Page: 574-575

11. A person tests positive for the AIDS virus. He most likely
   a. kissed someone with AIDS.
   b. ate food prepared by a cook with AIDS.
   c. used a toilet after a person with AIDS.
   d. used a hypodermic needle after a person with AIDS.

Obj.: 10 Page: 576

12. Aerobic exercise promotes weight loss by
   a. causing the lateral hypothalamus to atrophy.
   b. increasing the level of insulin in the blood.
   c. reducing the number of fat cells in the body.
   d. elevating the basal metabolic rate for hours afterward.

Obj.:10 Page: 581

13. What technique has been effective in reducing the distress of surgery patients?
   a. biofeedback
   b. stress-inoculation training
   c. standard hospital instructions
   d. providing no information about the impending surgery

Obj.: 11 Page: 527-529

14. A student takes a course overload, volunteers to be on several committees, writes checks while speaking on the telephone, and becomes upset when forced to wait in line at the bank. She is exhibiting
   a. burnout.
   b. Type A behavior.
   c. learned helplessness.
   d. psychological hardiness.

Obj.:12 Page 586-587

PRACTICE TEST B

1. How have the causes of illness and death changed for members of our society during the twentieth century?
   a. More people now die of infectious diseases such as HIV.
   b. More young people now die because of drunk driving and drug use.
   c. More people now die of lifestyle-related illnesses rather than infectious diseases.
   d. More people now die because of environmental toxins and pollution effects.

Obj.: 1 Page: 558

2. Jenny is exploring potential career avenues within psychology. She tells you that she is interested in the role of psychological factors in the promotion and prevention of illness, specifically the relationship between stress and illness. Which of the following types of psychology should she most likely pursue?
   a. stress psychology
   b. biopsychosocial psychology
   c. psychiatry
   d. health psychology

Obj.: 2 Page: 558

3. The biopsychosocial model of health and illness is the currently favored alternative to the more traditional
   a. biomedical model.
   b. psychophysiological model.
   c. psychosomatic model.
   d. biopsychological model.

Obj.: 2 Page: 558

4. Isaac really dislikes attending college, but the low-level jobs available as an alternative are equally unappealing. His solution is to tell his parents he is going to classes, but he spends his time and allowance drinking beer and playing video games. Such behavior has been found to be associated with
   a. approach-avoidance conflicts.
   b. learned helplessness.
   c. avoidance-avoidance conflicts.
   d. general adaptation syndrome.

Obj.: 3 Page: 560

5. When you must fulfill responsibilities that tax your abilities you will experience
   a. frustration.
   b. pressure.
   c. conflict.
   d. confusion.

Obj.: 3 Page: 559

6. A *causal relationship* between life changes and illness was demonstrated in a study in which
   a. all subjects were exposed to a cold virus, but only the high life-change subjects developed colds.
   b. a relationship was found between life changes and illnesses among a group of elderly people.
   c. medical patients indicated the type of life changes they had experienced in the previous 12 months.
   d. subjects were asked to assign a numerical value to particular life changes.

Obj.: 4 Page: 562

7. According to the *Social Readjustment Rating Scale,* the life event that requires the most adjustment is (are)
   a. a change in the health of a family member.
   b. the death of a spouse.
   c. a divorce.
   d. sex difficulties.

Obj.: 4 Page: 563

8. Which item is out of place here?
   a. pressure
   b. resistance
   c. exhaustion
   d. general adaptation syndrome

Obj.: 5 Page: 565

9. You have been looking forward to your vacation to the mountains since the beginning of the term. For two weeks prior to leaving you "burned the candle at both ends," going to class, taking final exams, working long hours, and socializing with friends when you could. Your vacation finally arrives, and you spend it in bed with the flu. What sage of Selye's general adaptation syndrome are you experiencing?
   a. exhaustion
   b. resistance
   c. alarm
   d. illness

Obj.: 5 Page: 565

10. The interdisciplinary field that studies the relationship between psychological factors and physical illness is called
    a. psychophysiology.
    b. biopsychology.
    c. psychoneuroimmunology.
    d. physiological psychology.

Obj.: 6 Page: 566

11. According to recent research, how does the suppression of emotion come to be associated with the risk for cancer?
    a. Corticosteroids stimulate the growth of abnormal cells in other parts of the body.
    b. Stress and emotional inhibition result in the rejection of the body's own cells.
    c. Elevated levels of ACTH and cyclophosphamide stimulate abnormal cell reproduction.
    d. Emotional suppression is associated with immunosuppression, thus increasing risk of cancer.

Obj.: 7 Page: 569

12. Many students report that they feel less stressed about a difficult examination if they have more choices about which questions to answer. Having more options may increase their
    a. feeling of social support.
    b. sense of control.
    c. psychological hardiness.
    d. alarm reaction.

Obj.: 8 Page: 571

13. The so-called "good patient" in the hospital, who adopts a passive, compliant role will have poorer recuperative power and a feeling of
    a. psychological hardiness.
    b. being in control of one's life.
    c. learned helplessness.
    d. anger.

Obj.: 9 Page: 571

14. Sally has a strong sense of commitment to her job, she views the stresses and roadblocks that face her as challenges and opportunities for personal growth. Additionally, she believes that she has the personal resources and strength to overcome any obstacles. Suzanne Kobasa would say that Sally would score high in
    a. social support.
    b. psychological hardiness.
    c. explanatory style.
    d. physiological reactivity.

Obj.: 9 Page: 572

15. A major way to prevent the spread of HIV is by
    a. engaging in safer sex practices.
    b. avoiding contact with hemophiliacs and homosexuals.
    c. refusing to donate or receive blood transfusions.
    d. preventing infected individuals from working or studying.

Obj.: 10 Page: 576

16. Rose has been a heavy smoker for several years. She enters a smoking cessation program. What two psychological factors are associated with the likelihood of her success?
    a. high self-control and a pessimistic explanatory style
    b. low sensation-seeking and psychological hardiness
    c. adequate social support and high self-efficacy
    d. low reactivity and an internal locus of control

Obj.: 10 Page: 580

17. Greater ability to cope with surgery or other painful procedures has been found to be related to
    a. a more pessimistic explanatory style.
    b. higher degrees of self-efficacy.
    c. greater physiological reactivity.
    d. cardiovascular fitness.

Obj.: 11 Page: 584

18. A study of children undergoing chemotherapy for cancer (Redd et al., 1987) found that those who played video games during their chemotherapy
    a. reported less anxiety and nausea.
    b. reported more anxiety but less nausea.
    c. reported less anxiety but more nausea.
    d. reported more anxiety and nausea.

Obj.: 11 Page: 585

19. A problem with attempting to change the behavior of Type A individuals is that
   a. most are not troubled by their behavior and our society rewards it.
   b. there are few reliable techniques for modifying self-destructive behaviors.
   c. other behaviors place people at greater risk for coronary heart disease.
   d. some aspects of Type A behavior are actually health-enhancing.

Obj.: 12 Page: 589

20. You are driving along a two-lane country road at a speed consistent with the traffic ahead of you. When you look in your rear-view mirror, you see a vehicle close behind you veering from right to left, clearly driven by an impatient driver. The driver speeds by you in a no-passing zone. Upon reaching the next turn you see the vehicle overturned and burning. Tragically, the driver was killed. Evidence showed that the person had plenty of time to reach his or her goal and that taking such a chance was unnecessary. This situation can be explained by knowing that the driver was
   a. a Type A personality.
   b. a Type B personality.
   c. Personality type plays no role in driving behavior
   d. obsessive-compulsive.

Obj.: 12 Page: 588

ESSAY QUESTIONS

1. When it comes to the psychology of health and illness, "It is more important to know what kind of person has a disease than it is to know what kind of disease a person has." Do you agree or disagree with this statement? Support your response with scientific evidence.

Obj.: 8 Page: 570-573

2. Define Type A behavior and discuss its effects. Be sure to explain how it develops , and whether it can be modified?

Obj.: 12 Page: 586-589

ANSWER RECORD FOR CHAPTER 16

Comprehensive Guided Review

1. psychological	12. Conflict	22. relationship	33. positive	44. coronary heart
2. biopsychosocial	13. Lewin	23. stress	34. arousal	45. cholesterol
3. medical	14. desirable	24. nature	35. stressors	46. Stress
4. physiological	15. unpleasant	25. negative	36. alarm reaction	47. immune
5. motivator	16. simultaneously	26. hassles	37. fight-or-flight	48. illness
6. pleasurable	17. major	27. health problems	38. resistant	49. endocrine
7. unpleasurable	18. hassles	28. increased	39. exhaustion	50. hypothalamus
8. distress	19. Social Readjustment	29. correlated	40. fight-or-flight	51. sympathetic
9. eustress	20. life changes	30. few	41. constant	52. B-lymphocytes
10. Frustration	21. correlation	31. Prospective	42. noninfectious	53. T- lymphocytes
11. Pressure		32. negative	43. emotional	54. AIDS
				55. classical

Anatomy of a Contemporary Research Study: Can the Immune Response Be Altered by Classical Conditioning?

What was the rationale of the study?

Ader was interested in whether a chemical could be used as the basis for classically conditioning the immune response.

What methods did the author use to test the hypothesis?

Ader and Cohen used cyclophosphamide, a drug that suppresses the immune response, and paired it with flavored water in a classical conditioning procedure with mice.

What was the outcome of the study and what did the authors conclude the results meant?
The mice developed an aversion to the sweet-tasting water and when later forced to drink it, several mice developed a serious illness and died. Ader and Cohen attributed this to a conditioned suppression of the mice's immune response.

---

56. Galen 57. cause 58. progress 59. reduction 60. interferon 61. destroy 62. causes

Mini-review of Stress and Illness:
1. B; 2. J; 3. P; 4. I; 5. A; 6. K; 7. C; 8. F; 9. M; 10. S; 11. O; 12. E; 13. W; 14. Q; 15. G; 16. V; 17. D; 18. N; 19. R; 20. L; 21. H; 22. T; 23. U

63. Hippocrates
64. individual differences
65. increases
66. physiological reactivity
67. interpret
68. stressful
69. secondary
70. self-efficacy
71. explanatory style
72. pessimistic
73. control
74. learned helplessness
75. burnout
76. uncontrollable
77. personality
78. commitment
79. social support
80. tangible
81. intangible
82. boosts
83. coping
84. task-oriented
85. management
86. inoculation
87. aerobic
88. exercise
89. physiological reactivity
90. control
91. immune
92. arousal
93. meditation
94. progressive relaxation
95. sympathetic

Mini-review of Factors That Moderate Stress and Coping with Stress:
1. C; 2. A; 3. J; 4. F; 5. E; 6. B; 7. I; 8. H; 9. K; 10. G; 11. D; 12. L; 13. M

96. increase
97. susceptible
98. self-efficacy
99. effective
100. exercise
101. AIDS
102. sexual preference
103. semen
104. years
105. prevention
106. longer
107. immune
108. cardiovascular
109. adhere
110. addictive
111. nicotine
112. fatigue
113. withdrawal
114. prevention
115. educate
116. 16
117. Nicotine-replacement
118. addiction
119. self-efficacy
120. nicotine fading
121. aversion
122. behavior modification
123. diet
124. high-fat
125. Obesity
126. variability
127. control
128. ineffective
129. paranoid
130. surgical
131. behavior
132. social support
133. healthy
134. motivate
135. social support
136. explanatory
137. distress
138. self-efficacy
139. empathetic
140. modeling
141. reduced
142. prescription
143. dislike
144. warm
145. positive

Mini-review of Health-impairing Habits and Reactions to Illness:
1. Unsafe sex, lack of exercise, smoking and poor nutrition.

2. Self-efficacy. Research has shown that people high in self-efficacy believe that their behaviors will be effective, and are more likely to downplay the barriers and engage in the behaviors. Those low in self-efficacy are more likely to engage in health-impairing habits, including unsafe sex practices, lack of exercise, smoking, and poor nutrition.

146. Type A 147. Type B 148. time urgency 149. unrelated 150. uncooperative 151. cynical hostility

---

Anatomy of a Classic Research Study: Is There a Relationship Between Behavior and Heart Disease?

What was the rationale for the study?
Friedman had noticed that the majority of his heart disease patients tended to show particular personality characteristics that he called type A. He and Rosenman wanted to determine if lifestyle and personality characterisitcs were associated with greater risk of heart disease.

What methods did the author use to test the hypothesis?
Friedman and Rosenman (1959) asked managers and supervisors to identify colleagues who fit the description of Type A and Type B behavior patterns.

What was the outcome of the study and what did the author conclude the results meant?
They found that Type A's had significantly higher levels of blood cholesterol, smoked much more, and had a higher incidence of coronary heart disease in their parents. Clearly, a person's behavior pattern contributes to one's health and life expectancy.

---

152. longitudinal
153. A
154. B
155. heart disease
156. relationship
157. cynical hostility
158. hormones
159. ignore
160. child-rearing
161. gender
162. Cognitive behavior modification

Practice Test A:

1. a. Incorrect: Obesity, heart disease, and drug abuse are leading causes of death in today's society.
   b. Incorrect: Alcohol abuse was not a leading cause of death in the early 1900s.
   c. Correct: In the early 1900s flu, pneumonia, and TB were the leading causes of death.
   d. Incorrect: Obesity was not a leading cause of death in the early 1900s.

2. a. Incorrect: Immunopsychology is not an area of study; psychoneuroimmunology examines the relationship between psychological factors and illness.
   b. Correct: Health psychology is concerned with the role of psychological factors in health and the prevention of illness.
   c. Incorrect: Psychomicrobiology is not an area discussed; psychoneuroimmunology examines the relationship between psychological factors and illness.
   d. Incorrect: Environmental psychology concerns itself with the use of psychological principles to improve the physical environment.

3. **a. Correct: Eustress is Selye's term for positive stress; a vacation in Hawaii would be a good example of "positive stress."**
   b. Incorrect: Eustress is Selye's term for positive stress; insomnia is not an example of "positive stress."
   c. Incorrect: Eustress is Selye's term for positive stress; final exams would not be considered an example of "positive stress."
   d. Incorrect: Eustress is Selye's term for positive stress; having a flat tire is not an example of "positive stress."

4. a. Incorrect: Generalized anxiety, sleep disorders, and physical illnesses after a traumatic event are symptomatic of posttraumatic stress disorder.
   b. Incorrect: Generalized anxiety, sleep disorders, and physical illnesses after a traumatic event are symptomatic of posttraumatic stress disorder.
   c. Incorrect: Generalized anxiety, sleep disorders, and physical illnesses after a traumatic event are symptomatic of posttraumatic stress disorder.
   d. Correct: Generalized anxiety, sleep disorders, and physical illnesses after a traumatic event are symptomatic of posttraumatic stress disorder.

5. a. Incorrect: Malingering occurs when an individual continues to demonstrate symptoms after treatment.
   b. Incorrect: Hypochondriasis occurs when individuals consistently feel that every pain they experience is indicative of a serious illness.
   c. Incorrect: Conversion disorders occur when individuals experience a physical symptom without any physical cause.
   d. Correct: A psychosomatic illness is an illness brought on by psychological stresses.

6. a. Incorrect: Biofeedback is a method in which patients monitor their own physiological arousal and attempts to control them.
   b. Incorrect: Biopsychology is a field of psychology that examines the biological basis of behavior.
   c. Incorrect: Psychophysiology is not an area of study.
   d. Correct: Psychoneuroimmunology is the field of study that examines the relationship between psychological factors and illness

7. a. Incorrect: Research has shown that stress impairs the ability of the immune system to destroy cancer cells; it does not lead to the growth of abnormal cells.
   b. Incorrect: Research has shown that stress impairs the ability of the immune system to destroy cancer cells; it does not lead to the growth of abnormal cells.
   c. Incorrect: Research has shown that stress impairs the ability of the immune system to destroy cancer cells; it does not lead to the growth of abnormal cells.
   d. Correct: Research has shown that stress impairs the ability of the immune system to destroy cancer cells; it does not lead to the growth of abnormal cells.

8. a. Incorrect: Type A behavior is behavior that is characterized by impatience, an uneven temper, and a highly competitive nature.
   b. Correct: Learned helplessness occurs when individuals feel that they have no control over their life.
   c. Incorrect: Psychological hardiness refers to the individual's resistance to stressors; people with high psychological hardiness have feelings of commitment, challenge, and control.
   d. Incorrect: Individuals who demonstrate posttraumatic stress disorders show symptoms of generalized anxiety disorders, sleep disorders, and physical illnesses after a traumatic event.

9. a. Incorrect: Burnout occurs when individuals experience a sense of a loss of control over their environment; this professor is demonstrating complete control.
   b. Incorrect: Type A behavior is behavior that is characterized by impatience, an uneven temper, and a highly competitive nature.
   c. Correct: Psychological hardiness refers to the individual's resistance to stressors; people with high psychological hardiness have feelings of commitment, challenge, and control.
   d. Incorrect: Physiological reactivity refers to the physical responsiveness of an individual; this individual would not show high levels of physical reactiveness.

10. **a. Correct: Relaxation, exercise, and stress-management techniques are examples of formal methods for coping with stress.**
   b. Incorrect: Drug therapy is not a method of coping with stress.
   c. Incorrect: Drug therapy is not a method of coping with stress.
   d. Incorrect: Social support is a factor that moderates the stress response, but is not a formal technique for coping with stress.

11. a. Incorrect: You cannot contract AIDS by kissing.
   b. Incorrect: You cannot contract AIDS by eating food prepared by someone with AIDS.
   c. Incorrect: You cannot contract AIDS by using the toilet after someone with AIDS.
   d. Correct: You can contact AIDS by sharing body fluids with and individual with the HIV virus, as you would in sharing a hypodermic needle.

12. a. Incorrect: Aerobic exercise does not promote the lateral hypothalamus (a brain structure) to shrink.
   b. Incorrect: Aerobic exercise does not promote the increase of insulin.
   c. Incorrect: Aerobic exercise does not promote the decrease of fat cells.
   d. Correct: Aerobic exercise elevates the basal metabolic rate of the individual for hours after the exercise.

13. a. Incorrect: Biofeedback has been used to reduce stress, not relieve patient distress.
   b. Correct: Stress-inoculation techniques help relieve patients' distress and help relieve patient pain after surgery.
   c. Incorrect: The more self-efficacy patients have, the better their recovery, thus standard hospital instructions are generally insufficient.
   d. Incorrect: More information given rather than less is best to improve recovery.

14. a. Incorrect: Burnout occurs when individuals experience a sense of a loss of control over their environment; this student is demonstrating complete control.
   b. Correct: The behavior described in this question is typical of a Type A personality.
   c. Incorrect: Learned helplessness occurs when individuals feel that they have no control over their life.
   d. Incorrect: Psychological hardiness refers to the individual's resistance to stressors, people with high psychological hardiness have feelings of commitment, challenge and control.

Practice Test B:

1. a. Incorrect: In the 1900s people also died of infectious diseases such as influenza and pneumonia.
   b. Incorrect: Drunk driving and drug use kill young and old.
   c. Correct: Deaths as the result of lifestyle-related illnesses have increased.
   d. Incorrect: Environmental toxins and pollution effects have increased, yet not many deaths are directly related to these phenomena.

2. a. Incorrect: Stress psychology is not an identified career field in psychology.
   b. Incorrect: Biopsychosocial is a model of thinking in psychology that emphasizes the interaction of biological, psychological, and social factors.
   c. Incorrect: Psychiatry is a specialization in the medical field.
   d. Correct: Health psychology is field that studies the role of psychological factors in the promotion of health and the prevention of illness.

3. a. **Correct: This model emphasizes biological factors and neglects psychological and social ones.**
b. Incorrect: Psychophysiological is not a formal name given to a model in psychology.
c. Incorrect: Psychosomatic is not a name given to a model in psychology.
d. Incorrect: Biopsychological is not a name given to a model in psychology.

4. a. Incorrect: Isaac is experiencing a conflict between two equally unattractive things; this is an avoidance-avoidance conflict.
b. Incorrect: Learned helplessness results when individuals feel they have no control over their life.
c. **Correct: Isaac is experiencing a conflict between two equally unattractive things; this is an avoidance-avoidance conflict.**
d. Incorrect: The general adaptation syndrome is Selye's term for the stages that an organism goes through when faced with a stressor.

5. a. Incorrect: Frustration results when you are blocked from achieving a goal.
b. **Correct: Pressure results when you must fulfill responsibilities that tax your abilities.**
c. Incorrect: Conflict results when an individual is torn between two or more potential courses of action.
d. Incorrect: Confusion occurs when an individual is unable to understand a situation.

6. a. **Correct: The causal relationship was indicated in this prospective experimental study that manipulated level of stress; all of the other studies were correlational.**
b. Incorrect: The causal relationship was indicated in this prospective experimental study that manipulated level of stress; all of the other studies were correlational.
c. Incorrect: The causal relationship was indicated in this prospective experimental study that manipulated level of stress; all of the other studies were correlational.
d. Incorrect: The causal relationship was indicated in this prospective experimental study that manipulated level of stress; all of the other studies were correlational.

7. a. Incorrect: With a score of 100, the death of a spouse requires the most adjustment according to the Social Readjustment Scale.
b. **Correct: With a score of 100, the death of a spouse requires the most adjustment according to the Social readjustment scale.**
c. Incorrect: With a score of 100, the death of a spouse requires the most adjustment according to the Social Readjustment Scale.
d. Incorrect: With a score of 100, the death of a spouse requires the most adjustment according to the Social Readjustment Scale.

8. a. **Correct: Pressure is not a stage in the general adaptation syndrome; resistance and exhaustion are.**
b. Incorrect: Pressure is not a stage in the general adaptation syndrome; resistance and exhaustion are.
c. Incorrect: Pressure is not a stage in the general adaptation syndrome; resistance and exhaustion are.
d. Incorrect: Pressure is not a stage in the general adaptation syndrome; resistance and exhaustion are.

9. a. **Correct: Selye claims that if you succumb to an illness you have entered the stage of exhaustion in the general adaptation syndrome.**
b. Incorrect: Selye claims that if you succumb to an illness you have entered the stage of exhaustion in the general adaptation syndrome.
c. Incorrect: Selye claims that if you succumb to an illness you have entered the stage of exhaustion in the general adaptation syndrome.
d. Incorrect: Selye claims that if you succumb to an illness you have entered the stage of exhaustion in the general adaptation syndrome.

10. a. Incorrect: Psychoneuroimmunology is the field of study that examines the relationship between psychological factors and physical illness.
b. Incorrect: Psychoneuroimmunology is the field of study that examines the relationship between psychological factors and physical illness.
c. **Correct: Psychoneuroimmunology is the field of study that examines the relationship between psychological factors and physical illness.**
d. Incorrect: Psychoneuroimmunology is the field of study that examines the relationship between psychological factors and physical illness.

11. a. Incorrect: Corticosteroids do not stimulate growth of abnormal cells; they decrease the immune system response.
b. Incorrect: Stress does not lead to rejection of body tissue.
c. Incorrect: Increased levels of ACTH do not stimulate the production of abnormal cells, they suppresses the immune system response.
d. **Correct: Emotional suppression does suppress the immune system, thus preventing the body from fighting the disease effectively.**

12. a. Incorrect: Increased choices increase perceived sense of control over a situation, and a high sense of control is a factor that moderates the effects of stress.
  b. Correct: Increased choices increase perceived sense of control over a situation, and a high sense of control is a factor that moderates the effects of stress.
  c. Incorrect: Increased choices increase perceived sense of control over a situation, and a high sense of control is a factor that moderates the effects of stress.
  d. Incorrect: Increased choices increase perceived sense of control over a situation, and a high sense of control is a factor that moderates the effects of stress.

13. a. Incorrect: This is a personality characteristic marked by feelings of commitment, challenge, and control, which promote resistance to stress.
  b. Incorrect: This is normally not the case with a passive, compliant person.
  c. Correct: This is a feeling of futility caused by the belief that one has little or no control over events in one's life, which may make one stop trying and develop feelings of depression.
  d. Incorrect: This may be the case, although the anger would not necessarily be overtly expressed. Certainly this does not serve as a viable alternative in this question.

14. a. Incorrect: Social support refers to the availability of support from other people.
  b. Correct: Psychological hardiness refers to the personality characteristic that is marked by feelings of commitment, challenge, and control and promotes resistance to stress, all characteristic of Sally.
  c. Incorrect: Explanatory style refers to the tendency to explain results either optimistically or pessimistically.
  d. Incorrect: Physiological reactivity refers to the physiological responsiveness of the individual.

15. **a. Correct: Safe sex practices are the most effective way to reduce the spread of AIDS.**
  b. Incorrect: Safe sex practices are the most effective way to reduce the spread of AIDS.
  c. Incorrect: Safe sex practices are the most effective way to reduce the spread of AIDS.
  d. Incorrect: Safe sex practices are the most effective way to reduce the spread of AIDS.

16. a. Incorrect: Those smokers who are the most successful in quitting have a good social support system and believe in their abilities to control their behavior, that is, they have high self-efficacy.
  b. Incorrect: Those smokers who are the most successful in quitting have a good social support system and believe in their abilities to control their behavior, that is, they have high self-efficacy.
  c. Correct: Those smokers who are the most successful in quitting have a good social support system and believe in their abilities to control their behavior, that is, they have high self-efficacy.
  d. Incorrect: Those smokers who are the most successful in quitting have a good social support system and believe in their abilities to control their behavior, that is, they have high self-efficacy.

17. a. Incorrect: Pessimistic explanatory style would make the person less able to deal with stress.
  b. Correct: People with higher degrees of self-efficacy are better able to cope with painful procedures.
  c. Incorrect: Physiological reactivity refers to the physiological responsiveness of the individual; those high in this would be more reactive to stress.
  d. Incorrect: Cardiovascular fitness, although linked to healthy lifestyle, does not affect ability to cope with surgery.

18. **a. Correct: The children who played the video games reported less nausea and anxiety.**
  b. Incorrect: The children who played the video games reported less nausea and anxiety.
  c. Incorrect: The children who played the video games reported less nausea and anxiety.
  d. Incorrect: The children who played the video games reported less nausea and anxiety.

19. **a. Correct: It is true that most Type A persons do not find anything wrong with their behavior and it is rewarded by society.**
  b. Incorrect: It is true that most Type A persons do not find anything wrong with their behavior and it is rewarded by society.
  c. Incorrect: It is true that most Type A persons do not find anything wrong with their behavior and it is rewarded by society.
  d. Incorrect: It is true that most Type A persons do not find anything wrong with their behavior and it is rewarded by society.

20. **a. Correct: Type A driving has been shown to be related to traffic accidents and fatalities. You can't change a Type A while driving, but you can certainly drive defensively. And, just because you might be a Type A doesn't mean that you are an irresponsible driver.**
  b. Incorrect: Type B personalities tend to be calm, patient, and even-tempered and would tend not to engage in the type of behavior described.
  c. Incorrect: Personality type has been shown to be related to driving behavior.
  d. Incorrect: Obsessive-compulsive individuals repeatedly engage in behaviors and do not tend to be impulsive.

Essay Questions:

1. Researchers in health psychology have shown that no matter what the illness or dysfunction, there are six factors that will determine our response to that problem and the treatment for it. These are:
   a) physiological reactivity
   b) cognitive appraisal
   c) explanatory style
   d) feeling of control
   e) psychological hardiness
   f) social support

2. Type A behavior is a syndrome that is marked by impatience, hostility and extreme competitiveness and it promotes coronary heart disease via stress hormones. Type A people tend to ignore symptoms of illness, but may be more stress-resistant than others. The syndrome tends to run in families, originates in child-rearing practices, and is more common in men. Programs that try to alter Type A behavior focus on impatience, hostility, and competitiveness. One program was successful with college teachers who received cognitive behavior modification and assertiveness training.

17 Social Behavior

LEARNING OBJECTIVES

After studying this chapter, you will be able to:

1. Describe the domain of social psychology, and explain what is meant by social cognition. (p. 594)

2. Distinguish between dispositional and situational attributions and summarize the important features of two theories about when each type of attribution is made. (p. 594-596)

3. List and explain three biases that enter into the attribution process, and mention a flaw in our usual process of person perception. (p. 596-597)

4. List and describe five factors that influence the process of person perception. (p. 597-599)

5. List and describe five factors that influence our attraction or liking for another person. (p. 600-602)

6. Distinguish between the important features of two theories of romantic love, briefly summarizing any research that supports them. (p. 602-604)

7. Summarize the scientific evidence in support of the three factors that promote romantic love. (p.604)

8. Define attitude, explain the three components of an attitude, and summarize the important features of three theories that attempt to explain how attitudes are formed. (p. 604-606)

9. Describe the elaboration likelihood model and how the qualities of the source, message and audience influence the persuasion process. (p. 606-608)

10. Describe how two theories attempt to explain the relationship between behavior and attitudes. (p. 608-610)

11. Distinguish between prejudice and discrimination and summarize the factors that have been found to promote and reduce prejudice. (p. 610-612)

12. Define group and then describe three factors that influence the process of group decision making. (p. 612-615)

13. Explain the resolution of the controversy that surrounded the concept of social facilitation, and then explain the concept of social loafing. (p. 615-616)

14. Describe three types of social influence and explain the significance of the obedience research. (p. 616-622)

15. Distinguish between prosocial and altruistic behavior and explain the bystander intervention model. (p. 622-626)

16. Define aggression and describe several theories that attempt to account for aggressive behavior, emphasizing the strengths and weaknesses of each theoretical approach. (p. 627-628)

17. Summarize the findings regarding the relationship between television and aggression, pornography and sexual violence, and the nature of group violence. (p. 628-632)

COMPREHENSIVE GUIDED REVIEW

Social psychology is the field of psychology that studies behavior in its___(1)__ context; that is, how people affect one another's thoughts, feelings, and behaviors.

I. Social Cognition: The study of social___(2)__ is concerned with how we perceive, interpret, and predict social behavior.

Causal Attribution: According to Heider, when we engage in social___(3)__ we determine the extent to which a person's behavior is caused by the person or by the person's circumstance. When you decide that a person is primarily responsible for his or her own behavior, you are making a___(4)__ *attribution.* When you decide that a person's circumstances are primarily responsible for his or her behavior, you are making a___(5)__ *attribution.*

The 1970s were considered the decade of__(6)__ psychology since so much research was done on causal attribution. The most influential theorist in the study of attributions was Harold___(7)__. Kelley identified factors that determine when we make___(8)__. Kelley found that causal attributions depend on

1) *consistency,* or the extent to which a person behaves in the___(9)__ way in a given situation on different occasions;
2) ___(10)__, or the extent to which a person behaves in the same way across different situations; and
3) ___(11)__, or the extent to which, in a given situation, other people perform the same behavior as the person being observed.

Bernard__(12)__ found that estimating the relative impact of dispositional and situational factors could not by itself account for causal attribution, Thus, Weiner developed his own theory in which he attempted to explain successes and failures. Weiner identified three dimensions that govern social___(13)__:

1) __(14)__*dimension.* This is similar to Kelley's distinction between dispositional and situational attribution;
2) ___(15)__*dimension.* This refers to the degree to which we attribute behaviors to a factor that is stable or unstable; and
3) ___(16)__*dimension.* This indicates the extent to which we attribute behaviors to a factor that is controllable or uncontrollable.

Since human beings are not always rational and objective, social psychologists have observed that__(17)__ are often expressed in causal attributions. A____ ___(18)___ ____ is a bias in which the tendency is to attribute other people's behavior to dispositional factors. The **actor-observer bias** is the tendency for observers to make___(19)___ attributions for the behavior of others but___(20)___ attributions for their own behavior. Finally, the **self-serving bias** is the tendency to make dispositional attributions for our own___(21)__ behaviors and situational attributions for our own ___(22)__ behaviors. It is suggested that the use of these biases is what helps individuals maintain a positive____(23)__.

Person Perception: In addition to making attributions, we also make__(24)__ about other people. Any deliberate attempt to control the impressions that others formabout us is called_____ _(25)____. A common technique in **impression management** is the use of_____(26)___, or letting others know that we are performing under the handicap.

In making judgments about others we use social ____(27)__. A **social schema** comprises the presumed ___(28)__of a role, event, person, or group. Since we use schemas to___(29)__ and predict the behavior of others, they bring order to an otherwise chaotic social world. Upon the occasion of first meeting someone we do not know, we have little information other than the person's sex, age, and physical appearance. This information might then activate a particular social__(30)__, which, in turn, will create a first impression. Thus, first impressions serve as a social schema to __(31)__ our predictions of that person's behavior. If, however, we are given additional information, such as this person is "warm and friendly" as opposed to "cold and aloof," we will assimilate that information into our schema.

A___(32)__ is a social schema that incorporates characteristics, which may be both positive and negative, that supposedly belong to virtually all members of a group. In part, **stereotypes** are based on our tendency to view members of our own group (___(33)__) as more variable than members of another group (___(34)__). Stereotypes are used to make predictions about the behavior of group members, and our stereotypic expectations may induce a______(35)_____. The **self-fulfilling prophecy** is one of the most important effects of _______(36)_______. It is the tendency for one person's___(37)__ to make a second person behave in accordance with them. In a classic study, Rosenthal & Jacobson (1968) investigated the effects of teachers' expectations of students labeled "late bloomers" and demonstrated that teachers' expectations were based on their first impressions and led them to treat students differently.

II. Interpersonal Attraction:

Liking: In addition to causal attribution, social psychologists also study the development of interpersonal __(38)__, or why we like certain people and not others. Five factors have been identified that determine who you like:

1) ___(39)__. The closer people live to one another, the more likely they are to become friends.
2) ___(40)__. The more we interact with particular people, the more we tend to like them. This mere exposure effect holds only when the people do not behave in negative ways.
3) ___(41)____. We tend to like physically attractive people more than physically unattractive people. This effect has been shown to have strong cross-cultural consistency. Physical attractiveness has been shown to be an important factor in dating relationships. Physical attractiveness is also relative to that of other persons who might be present, and although we may prefer more attractive people, thy might reject us. Thus, social sorting leads us to have friends who are similar in attractiveness to us.
4) ___(42)___. Although we do tend to develop relationships with people who are similar to us in physical attractiveness, it has also been shown that we are also attracted to people with attitudes similar to ours. However, research has shown that we are likely to associate with people who hold similar attitudes merely by default, because we are repulsed by those who have dissimilar ones.
5) ___(43)___. To find out whether we share similar attitudes, interests, and activities, we must engage in self-disclosure, in which we reveal our beliefs, feelings, and experiences. Timing is important. If people disclose highly personal information too early, we may become uneasy and less attracted to them.

Romantic Love: The concept of love has "fuzzy boundaries," thus making it difficult to___(44)__, especially in an operational manner. That is, we know love when we see it but cannot define it by a single set of features without finding that there are exceptions.

Hatfield & Berscheid make a distinction between___(45)__ love and____(46)__ love. **Passionate love** is commonly known as sexual love. It involves intense emotional arousal, including sexual feelings. **Companionate love** involves feelings of__(47)__ and commitment to the relationship. __(48)__ research has been conducted on passionate love than compassionate love. According to Berscheid & Hatfield,__(49)__ love depends on three factors:

1) The culture must promote passionate love.
2) The person must experience a state of intense emotional arousal.
3) The emotional arousal must be associated with a romantic partner.

This theory incorporates aspects of Schachter's ___(50)__ theory of emotion. You will experience a particular emotion when you perceive that you are ___(51)__aroused and__(52)__ that arousal to an emotionally relevant aspect of the situation in which you find yourself.

Another prominent theory of love has been proposed by Robert___(53)__. The **triangular theory of love** argues that the experience of love depends on the__(54)__ of three components: __(55)__, which encompasses the drives that lead to romance, physical attraction, and sexual relations; __(56)__, which encompasses the feelings of closeness, bondedness, and connectedness; and decision/commitment, which refers to the__(57)__, in the short term, that the individual loves the other person, and___(58)__ to maintain that love in the long term. According to Sternberg, the __(59)__ of love depends on the individual strengths of the three components and the __(60)__of love depends on the strengths of the components relative to one another. __(61)__ is strong passion with little intimacy and weak decision/commitment, while___(62)__ love is strong passion and great intimacy and weak decision/commitment.

In addition to attempting to define romantic love, social psychologists have been concerned with the question "What are the factors that promote romantic love?" A number of factors have been identified that promote romantic love. One is __(63)__. We tend to date and marry people who are similar in age, race, religion, ethnic background, and educational level. Additionally, a sense of__(64)__, sensation-seeking levels, self-disclosure levels, and equity, or the belief that each partner is contributing equally to the relationship are important factors.

Mini-review of Social Cognition and Interpersonal Attraction: Match each term with its correct description.

________1. social psychology
________2. consistency
________3. situational
________4. actor-observer bias
________5. social cognition
________6. internal-external dimension
________7. distinctiveness
________8. self-handicapping
________9. social attribution
________10. stable-unstable dimension
________11. dispositional
________12. social schemas
________13. fundamental attribution error
________14. consensus
________15. self-serving bias
________16. impression management
________17. physical attractiveness
________18. controllable-uncontrollable dimension
________19. decision/ commitment
________20. person perception
________21. passionate love
________22. self-fulfilling prophecy
________23. interpersonal attraction
________24. companionate love
________25. infatuation
________26. proximity
________27. familiarity
________28. intimacy
________29. passion
________30. triangular theory of love
________31. similarity
________32. romantic love

A. The field of psychology that studies behavior in its interpersonal context; that is, how people affect one another's thoughts, feelings, and behaviors
B. How we perceive, interpret, and predict social behavior
C. We determine the extent to which a person's behavior is caused by the person or by the person's circumstance
D. Attribution in which you decide that a person is primarily responsible for his or her own behavior
E. Weiner's dimension of social attribution that refers to the degree to which we attribute behaviors to a factor that is stable or unstable
F. Attribution in which you decide that a person's circumstances are primarily responsible for his or her behavior
G. The factor in interpersonal attraction that states that we must share similar attitudes, interests, and activities; we must reveal our beliefs, feelings, and experiences
H. The tendency for observers to make dispositional attributions for the behavior of others but situational attributions for their own behavior
I. Kelley's factor that claims that we make attributions based on the extent to which a person behaves in the same way across different situations
J. The process of making judgments about other people
K. A common technique in impression management; letting others know that we are performing under a handicap
L. The tendency to make dispositional attributions for our own positive behaviors and situational attributions for our own negative behaviors
M. Weiner's dimension of social attribution similar to Kelley's distinction between dispositional and situational attribution
N. Refers to the decision, in the short term, that the individual loves the other person, and commitment to maintain that love in the long term
O. A bias in which the tendency is to attribute other people's behavior to dispositional factors
P. Encompasses the feelings of closeness, bondedness, and connectedness
Q. A deliberate attempt to control the impressions that others form of us
R. Used in making judgments about others, it comprises the presumed characteristics of a role, event, person, or group; used to interpret and predict the behavior of others, they bring order to an otherwise chaotic social world
S. A social schema that incorporates characteristics, which may be both positive and negative, that supposedly belong to virtually all members of a group
T. Why we like certain people and not others
U. The tendency for one person's expectations to make a second person behave in accordance with them
V. Commonly known as sexual love, involves intense emotional arousal, including sexual feelings
W. The factor in interpersonal attraction that states that the closer people live to one another, the more likely they are to become friends
X. According to this theory the experience of love depends on the interaction of three components, intensity of love depends on the individual strengths of three components, and the kind of love depends on the strengths of the components relative to one another
Y. Kelley's factor that claims that we make attributions based on the extent to which, in a given situation, other people perform the same behavior as the person being observed
Z. Weiner's dimension of social attribution that indicates the extent to which we attribute behaviors to a factor that is controllable or uncontrollable
Aa. A concept that has "fuzzy boundaries," thus making it difficult to define, especially in an operational manner; that is, we know it when we see it but cannot define it by a single set

________33. stereotype

of features without finding that there are exceptions

Bb. Involves feelings of affection and commitment to the relationship

Cc. The factor in interpersonal attraction that states that we tend to like physically attractive people more than physically unattractive people

Dd. Encompasses the drives that lead to romance, physical attraction, and sexual relations

Ee. The factor in interpersonal attraction that states that the more we interact with particular people, the more we tend to like them; this mere exposure effect holds only when the people do not behave in negative ways

Ff. According to Sternberg this is strong passion with little intimacy and weak decision/commitment

Gg. Kelley's attribution factor that claims that we make attributions based on the extent to which a person behaves in the same way in a given situation on different occasions

III. Attitudes: ___(65)___are evaluations of ideas, events, objects, or people. They have three components: an emotional component, a cognitive component, and a behavioral component.

The Formation of Attitudes: Attitudes are learned through___(66)__ *conditioning, operant conditioning,* or, according to *social learning theory,* through___(67)__ others.

The Art of Persuasion:___(68)__ is the intentional attempt to influence the attitudes of other people. According to the elaboration likelihood theory of Petty & Cacioppo (1981), persuasive messages take either a ___(69)__route or a ___(70)__ route. A message that takes a central route relies on clear,___(71)__ arguments, whereas a message that takes a peripheral route relies on factors such as the source or the___(72)__ context. The more___(73)__we think about an argument the more lasting any attitude change that occurs will be. The central and peripheral routes are related to three main factors in persuasion; the *source*, the *message*, and the *audience*.

1) **The Source:** This is a___(74)__ factor. The greater the credibility of the source, the greater the ___(75)___of the message. Two important factors that determine the___(76)__ of the source are the expertise and trustworthiness of the source. An additional factor is attractiveness. Sources that are *attractive* are also more appealing.
2) **The Message:** Presenting only arguments that support your position is not always desirable or effective. If the listener already___(77)__ your position, or has no counterarguments handy, arguments favoring your position alone will be more effective. But if the listener___(78)__ your position, arguments that acknowledge both sides of the issue will be more persuasive.___(79)__ arguments are superior in persuasive appeals, in part because they enhance the credibility of the source and decrease counterarguing by the listener.
3) **The Audience:** People of relatively high intelligence are more likely to be influenced by messages supported by rational argument—the___(80)__ *route*—while people of relatively low intelligence are more likely to be influenced by messages supported by factors other than rational arguments—the ___(81)__*route*. Also, when a message has high___(82)__ to an audience, the central route will be more effective; otherwise the peripheral route will be more effective.

Attitudes and Behavior: Until the 1960s psychologists believed the commonsense idea that you could accurately predict an individual's behaviors from his or her___(83)__ or vice versa. However, the relationship between behavior and attitudes is not that simple.

Influence of Attitudes on Behavior: Attitudes that are strongly held or are personally important are better ___(84)__ of behaviors. Attitude-behavior consistency is also affected by the___(85)__ of the attitude and the behavior; your attitudes and behaviors are more consistent with one another when they are at similar levels of specificity.

Influence of Behavior on Attitudes: Leon___(86)__ and his colleagues were intrigued by a sect whose members believed that they would be saved by aliens prior to a worldwide flood predicted to occur on a specific date. When the prophesied event did not occur, surprisingly the members did not lose their faith; they simply changed their belief to justify their actions. To explain this phenomenon, Festinger developed the ____(87)___theory. **Cognitive dissonance** is an unpleasant state of___(88)__ associated with high physiological arousal, which is caused by the realization that one has cognitions that are___(89)__ with each other. Festinger felt that we are motivated to___(90)__ the unpleasant state by making our cognitions consistent. Additionally, the more___(91)__ we feel for the inconsistencies between our cognitions, the stronger the feelings of cognitive dissonance, and the more motivated we will be to change them.

The **cognitive dissonance theory** has been challenged by other theories. Bem's___(92)__ theory states that attitude change is not motivated by our need to reduce cognitive dissonance. Instead, we___(93)__ our attitudes from our behavior in the same way that we infer other people's attitudes from their behaviors. While cognitive dissonance theory appears to be better at explaining the effect of behavior on ____(94)___attitudes, self-perception theory appears to be better at explaining the effect of behavior on___(95)__ attitudes.

Social Prejudice: ___(96)__ is a positive or negative attitude toward a person based on his or her membership in a particular group. The behavioral component of prejudice is___(97)___, which involves treating people differently, whether positively or negatively, based on their group membership.

What factors account for the origin and maintenance of prejudice? Clearly,___(98)__ plays an important role. Adorno et al. (1950) discovered what they called the *authoritarian personality*. These individuals tend to be obedient toward their superiors and domineering toward subordinates (____(99)___), prejudiced in favor of their own groups and against other groups (____(100)___), and unwilling to accept their own faults but willing to place them on members of other groups (___(101)__). Remember that ___(102)___is one of the most important factors in social attraction and prejudiced people perceive stereotyped groups as having attitudes that are different from those of their own groups. In fact, when there is little or no pressure to discriminate, race or ethnicity is____(103)____ important than attitude similarity in determining discrimination.

Social psychologists have also been interested in finding ways to____(104)__ prejudice and have attempted to identify factors that reduce prejudice. According to Gordon ____(105)___, prejudice can be reduced by increasing social contact between members of different social groups. However, research has shown that social contact alone is not enough. For contact to reduce prejudice, the contact must be between group members of equal____(106)___; otherwise, prejudice may actually increase. Promoting intergroup___(107)___ is another way to reduce prejudice.

IV. Group Dynamics: According to social psychologists a____(108)___ is a collection of two or more persons who interact and have mutual influence. Social psychologists who study groups are interested in group___(109)___ making, group effects on performance, and social influence.

Group Decision Making: Decisions are not simply the outcome of____(110)___ discussion but of other factors as well. There are three: *group polarization, minority influence,* and *groupthink.*

Group polarization is the tendency for group decisions to be more____(111)___ decisions than would be made by the individual members. The tendency for groups to make decisions that were ____(112)___than the group became known as the *risky shift*. It was originally thought that____(113)___ behavior was always riskier than____(114)___ behavior; however, more recent research has shown that groups tend to make decisions in either a risky or a____(115)___ direction, rather than only in a risky direction. Thus the term *group*____(116)___ is used. What accounts for group polarization? It probably is best explained by two theories:

1) *Persuasive argumentation theory.* This theory assumes that group members who initially hold a____(117)___ position about an issue will move toward the more____(118)___ arguments, which will move the group toward risky or cautious decisions;
2) *Social-comparison theory* states that group members want to be viewed as socially____(119)___, perhaps by agreeing with the norm favored by group members. As a consequence, when a group member determines the position that a group seems to favor, that member will adopt a slightly more extreme position in that direction.

Minority influence refers to the influence of the____(120)___ in group decisions. In general, the majority determines the outcome of a group's decision. However, under certain circumstances minorities may influence group decisions. Principles of influence by a minority in group decisions include:

1) presentation of ____(121)___, rather than emotional, reasons for the position; taking the central rather than the peripheral, route of persuasion;
2) appear absolutely____(122)__ in the position;
3) be____(123)__ in the position over time;
4) try to bring at least one other person over to the minority side; and
5) patience.

Groupthink is a decision-making process in small, cohesive groups that places____(124)__ ahead of critical thinking and aims at a premature consensus. Groupthink is promoted by several factors: 1) a____(125)__ leader; 2) feelings of invulnerability by the group; 3) discrediting contrary evidence; 4)fear of criticism for disagreeing; 5) the desire to maintain group____(126)__; 6) isolation from outside influences; and 7) disparaging outsiders as incompetent.

The concept of____(127)__ has received support from experimental studies on group decision making. The research has shown that groups with more____(128)__ leaders consider fewer alternatives and that in groups with high cohesiveness and other conditions of groupthink, groupthink is actually promoted. However, groupthink does not occur in all cases and it does not always lead to____(129)__ outcomes. Thus, more research needs to be conducted to determine the robustness of the phenomenon and the factors that promote it.

Group Effects on Performance: One of the first topics to be studied by social psychologists was the influence of groups on the____(130)__ of their members. Social psychologists have been particularly interested in the effects of *social facilitation* and *social loafing*.

Social facilitation is the ____(131)__in performance caused by the presence of other people. However, there are data to show the opposite effect: This process is called *social*____(132)__. Both social facilitation and inhibition may be best explained by Zajonc's____(133)__ *theory*. According to Zajonc, the presence of others increases the____(134)__ arousal, which energizes the performer's most likely responses to the task. Thus, for those who are good at a task, what they do best will cause them to perform____(135)__. However, for those who are not good at a task, what they do best will cause them to perform____(136)__. Our drive level may increase in the presence of others because of *evaluation* ____(137)__. This means that arousal increases because of concern with having one's performance evaluated.

Social____(138)__ is concerned with the effect of others on individual performance; however, psychologists are also concerned with the effect that working in a group has on the common goal. In the 1880s, Ringelmann observed that as the number of men in a rope-pull____(139)__, individual effort____(140)__. This is known as the *Ringelmann effect.* Today, as applied to groups, this effect is known as **social loafing.** According to the concept of *diffusion of responsibility,* ______(141)______occurs when group members feel anonymous and believe that their individual performances are dispensable. One way to reduce social loafing is to convince group members that they will be held____(142)__ and that their individual efforts will be evaluated.

Social Influence: When we work in groups, social influences such as subtle prodding and direct demands influence our behavior. Social psychologists have studied the effects of____(143)____ such as conformity, compliance, and obedience on behavior.

Conformity, as demonstrated in the classic experiments by Solomon Asch, describes the phenomenon in which people behave in accordance with group____(144)___ with little or no ____(145)__ pressure to do so. Their main reason for conforming was their need for social____(146)__—they feared social rejection.

Compliance involves agreeing to a request that is backed by little or no threat of____(147)__. Two techniques of compliance are the *foot-in-the-door technique* and the *door-in-the-face technique*. The ____(148)__techniques refers to the fact that a person who complies with a small request is more likely to comply with a larger request. The effectiveness of the foot-in-the-door technique is explained by____(149)__ theory, which assumes that we infer our personal characteristics from observing our own behaviors. If you give a little, you are a giver. The ___(150)___ technique refers to the fact that individuals are more apt to respond to a smaller request after refusing a larger one. That is, ____(151)____ is fostered by presenting a smaller request after a larger request has been denied. This technique depends on social____(152)____ that require concessions offered by one negotiating party to be met by concessions from the other party. However, the____(153)____ technique is more effective overall than the door-in-the-face technique.

Obedience involves following orders given by an____(154)____. The surprising extent to which people will obey orders to harm others was demonstrated in a classic study by Stanley____(155)____. This study is the focus of the "Anatomy of a Classic Research Study" section on page 620 in your textbook.

Anatomy of a Classic Research Study: Would You Harm Someone Just Because an Authority Figure Ordered You To? *(Read the summary of Milgram's study presented on page 622 in your textbook and answer the following questions.)*

What was the rationale for the study?

What methods did the author use to test the hypothesis?

What was the outcome of the study and what did the author conclude the results meant?

Mini-review of Attitudes and Group Behavior: Match each term with its correct description.

_______1. central
_______2. social inhibition.
_______3. attitudes
_______4. door-in-the-face technique
_______5. cognitive dissonance
_______6. discrimination
_______7. persuasive-argumentation theory
_______8. compliance
_______9. group
_______10. persuasion
_______11. groupthink
_______12. authoritarian personality
_______13. foot-in-the-door technique
_______14. diffusion of responsibility
_______15. obedience
_______16. group polarization
_______17. peripheral
_______18. social-comparison theory
_______19. cognitive dissonance theory
_______20. elaboration likelihood theory
_______21. prejudice
_______22. conformity

A. Evaluations of ideas, events, objects, or people
B. Theory that argues that persuasive messages take either a central route or a peripheral route
C. The intentional attempt to influence the attitudes of other people
D. A message that takes this route relies on clear, explicit arguments
E. Term for actions that include subtle prodding and direct demands and influence our behavior
F. A message that takes this route relies on factors such as the source or the situational context
G. An unpleasant state of tension associated with high physiological arousal that is caused by the realization that one has cognitions that are inconsistent with each other
H. A positive or negative attitude toward a person based on his or her membership in a particular group
I. Festinger developed this theory that argues that we are motivated to reduce the unpleasant state by making our cognitions consistent
J. Theory that states that attitude change is not motivated by the inference of our attitudes from our behavior
K. This is the behavioral component of prejudice, it which involves treating people differently, whether positively or negatively, based on their group membership
L. These individuals tend to be obedient toward their superiors and domineering toward subordinates, prejudiced in favor of their own groups and against other groups, and unwilling to accept their own faults but willing to place them on members of other groups
M. A collection of two or more persons who interact and have mutual influence
N. The tendency for groups to make decisions that are riskier than the decisions made by individuals who compose the group
O. This theory assumes that group members who initially hold a moderate position about an issue will move toward the more persuasive arguments, which will move the group toward risky or cautious decisions
P. This theory states that group members want to be viewed as socially desirable, perhaps by agreeing with the norm favored by group members
Q. Term that refers to the influence of the minority in group decisions

________23. Bem's self-perception theory	R. A decision-making process in small, cohesive groups that places unanimity ahead of critical thinking and aims at a premature consensus
________24. social influence	S. Term for the improvement in performance caused by the presence of other people
________25. social loafing	T. According to this theory the presence of others increases the physiological arousal, which energizes the performer's most likely responses to the task
________26. evaluation apprehension	U. Term for an increase in arousal because of concern with having one's performance evaluated
________27. Zajonc's drive theory	V. The decline in performance caused by the presence of other people
________28. social facilitation	W. Term for the *Ringelmann effect;* as the number of men in an event increases, individual effort decreases
________29. minority influence	X. According to this concept, social loafing occurs when group members feel anonymous and believe that their individual performances are dispensable
________30. risky shift	Y. The tendency for group decisions to be more extreme decisions than would be made by the individual members
	Z. Term for behaving in accordance with group expectations with little or no overt pressure to do so; the main reason for the behavior is the need for social approval
	Aa. This involves agreeing to a request that is backed by little or no threat of punishment
	Bb. A technique of compliance in which a person who complies with a small request is more likely to comply with a larger request
	Cc. A technique in which individuals are more apt to respond to a smaller request after refusing a larger one
	Dd. This involves following orders given by an authority

V. Prosocial Behavior: The heroic act of James Patridge detailed on page 622 in the textbook is both an example of ____(156)__ behavior (the helping of others in need) and altruism.

Altruism: Helping others without the expectation of reward is defined as___(157)___. Social psychologists have focused on the role of *empathy* in altruism, where___(158)__ is defined as the ability to feel the emotions that someone else feels. Some researchers have found that prosocial behavior associated with feelings of empathy are truly altruistic, while prosocial behavior associated with feelings of___(159)__ is not. Research studies on the role of empathy in prosocial behavior have provided contradictory findings. One study that showed that subjects' willingness to help was related more to their___(160)__ score than their empathy score and provided scientific support for Robert Cialdini's *negative state relief theory* of prosocial behavior. However, another study found that the rate of helping among high-empathy subjects was no lower when they anticipated mood enhancement than when they did not and that high-empathy subjects were more likely to help than low-empathy subjects, supporting the___(161)__ hypothesis. Thus, it is still unclear whether prosocial behavior is motivated by more than empathy for others.

Bystander Intervention:_____(162)_____is the act of helping someone who is in immediate need of help, as in the classic case of Kitty Genovese. Social psychologists Darley & Latané set out to determine what factors affect the ___(163)___ of bystanders to intervene in emergencies. They identified a series of five steps. The intervention process could continue or stop at any one.

1) ____(164)__*the Victim.*
2) *Interpreting the Situation as an*__(165)__.
3) *Taking*__(166)__ *Responsibility.* A major finding was that as the number of bystanders increases, the likelihood of a bystander intervening decreases. This is true only in situations involving strangers. The relationship noted in the major finding is known as diffusion of responsibility.
4) *Deciding on a Course of Action.* The decision to intervene depends on whether the bystander feels ___(167)___ to meet the demands of the situation.
5) *Taking Action.* The decision to take action is influenced by the degree of____(168)___that the situation presents, and the degree to which the victim appears to be responsible for his or her predicament also influences bystander intervention.

VI. Aggression: In addition to examining prosocial behavior, social psychologists have studied___(169)__ behavior. The most extreme form of antisocial behavior is__(170)__, or verbal or physical behavior aimed at causing harm to another person.

Theories of Aggression: Psychologist have identified three classes of theories on aggression. One views aggression as a product of___(171)__; a second views aggression as the product of____(172)__; and the third views it as the product of the interaction of the two.

Aggression as the Product of Physiology: The earliest theories on aggression viewed it as___(173)_, or an inborn tendency, unaffected by learning, to engage in a relatively complex behavior. Freud concluded that aggression is caused by an instinct he called____(174)__. *Thanatos* causes a buildup of aggressive energy, which must be__(175)__ periodically through a process called *catharsis.* Lorenz's more recent instinct theory states that both humans and animals have__(176)__ an instinct for aggression as a means of promoting their survival. Research has __(177)__to support the belief, shared by Freud and Lorenz, that aggression can be reduced through catharsis. In fact, people who engage in aggression usually become___(178)__ likely to engage in it.

Although few psychologists accept instinct theory, many do believe that aggression has a___(179)__ basis. Such is the case with the relatively new field of *sociobiology.* Studies of__(180)__ have supported the hereditary nature of aggression. Additionally, the physiological basis of aggression has been linked to brain structures (the___(181)__ system) and testosterone.

Aggression as a Product of Experience: Psychologists who look to life experiences concluded that aggression is caused by__(182)__. This became known as the *frustration-aggression hypothesis.* It argues that we experience frustration when we are blocked from reaching a goal and thus become aggressive. The___(183)__ hypothesis, though widely known, appears inadequate because experiences other than frustration can cause aggression, and frustration does not always lead to aggression. This led to the___(184)__*frustration-aggression hypothesis,* proposed by Berkowitz. This revision states that frustration directly provokes___(185)_, which, in turn, will provoke aggression when stimuli that are associated with aggression are present.

Social learning theory argues that we learn by___(186)__ the behavior of others. This stands today as the most widely researched and accepted theory of aggression.

Television and Aggression: Research conducted over the past 20 years has seen a yet-unresolved controversy about the effects of televised violence on real life. A recent meta-analysis found that there is a significant ___(187)___ correlation between television violence and aggressive behavior. Another study suggest that the relationship between television violence and aggression is ___(188)__, suggesting that more exposure to violence leads to increased aggression *and* that more aggressive people choose to watch more violent television. And yet, still another possibility exists: that ___(189)__influences both television watching and aggression.

Group Violence: Psychologists are also interested in why normally peaceful individuals become___(190)__ in groups. One suggestion is that when we are in groups, we become less___(191)__ of ourselves and less concerned about being socially___(192)__. Festinger called this process___(193)___, wherein our behavior may no longer be governed by our social values. This is especially true when the group is large, when the group members feel___(194)__, and when the group members are emotionally aroused.

Take one of your study breaks. When you return, be sure to complete the mini-review before you go on to the "Thinking of Psychology" section.

Mini-review on prosocial behavior and aggression: Match each term with its correct description.

________1. altruism	A. Helping others without the expectation of reward
________2. frustration-aggression hypothesis	B. The ability to feel the emotions that someone else feels
________3. social learning theory	C. The act of helping someone who is in immediate need of help
________4. prosocial behavior	D. Behavior that helps others in need
________5. aggression	E. States that frustration directly provokes anger, which, in turn, will provoke aggression when stimuli that are associated with aggression are present
________6. negative relief theory	F. Verbal or physical behavior aimed at causing harm to another person
________7. frustration	G. The theory that states that we engage in prosocial behavior to relieve our own state of emotional distress at another's plight
________8. Thanatos	H. An inborn tendency, unaffected by learning, to engage in relatively complex behavior
________9. catharsis	I. Freud's term for the aggression instinct
________10. sociobiology	J. Festinger's term for the process in which we become less aware of ourselves and less concerned about being socially evaluated when we are in a group
________11. deindividuation	K. Field of study that believes aggression has a hereditary basis
________12. instinct	L. The emotional state induced when one is blocked from a goal
________13. empathy	M. It argues that we experience frustration when we are blocked from reaching a goal
________14. revised frustration-aggression hypothesis	N. The emotional release of repressed energy
________15. bystander intervention	O. Argues that we learn by observing the behavior of others

VII. Thinking about Psychology: Does Pornography Cause Aggression Against Women?

One in eight American women is raped during her lifetime, and "date rape" appears to be on the increase. Among the possible and potentially causal or correlated factors that researchers have studied and continue to study is___(195)___, or sexually explicit material intended to incite sexual arousal.

Government Reports on Pornography and Aggression: The 1970 President's Commission on Obscenity and Pornography concluded that men exposed to pornography are___(196)___ likely to commit sexual aggression. However, the 1985 Attorney General's Commission on Pornography, written by Attorney General Edwin Meese and published in 1986, concluded that exposure to either violent or nonviolent pornography may___(197)___ aggression against women. The report was criticized for assuming a___(198)___link. Another report of the Surgeon General's Workshop on Pornography and Public Health, written by Surgeon General C. Everett Koop and relying on the testimony from___(199)___ in the field concluded that pornography might have some adverse effects. Specifically, the effects reported were on children and___(200)___ who participate in the production of pornography. It did not, however, conclude that nonviolent pornography definitely___(201)___ aggression against women.

Empirical Research on Pornography and Aggression: A study by Donnerstein & Berkowitz indicated that portrayals of violent sexual attacks may condition people, especially males, to associate sex and aggression. This is the focus of the "Anatomy of a Contemporary Research Study" section in your textbook.

Anatomy of a Contemporary Research Study: Do Pornographic Films Promote Aggression Against Women?
Read the summary of Donnerstein and Berkowitz's study presented on page 631 in your textbook and answer the following questions.

What was the rationale for the study?

What methods did the author use to test the hypothesis?

What was the outcome of the study and what did the author conclude the results meant?

____

There is little evidence that ___(202)___ pornography causes sexual aggression against women. There is stronger evidence that___(203)___ pornography may cause aggression against women. The issue remains not only a scientific one but a moral, social, and___(204)___ dilemma as well.

KEY RESEARCH FINDINGS

Provide the details of the following key research studies in psychology:

1. **Triplett (1898):** Found that boys competing against other boys performed faster than if competing against time. (Page 594)
2. **Heider (1944):** Defined causal attribution as either dispositional or situational. (Page 594)
3. **Zucker & Weiner (1993):** Found that political liberals tended to make situational attributions, while conservatives make dispositional. (Page 594)
4. **Kelley (1973):** Found that causal attribution depends on consistency, distinctiveness, and consensus. (Page 595)
5. **Forsyth, Pope, & McMillan (1985):** Found that students who were manipulated into cheating on a test made situational attributions, and those who did not cheat made dispositional. (Page 595)
6. **Schuster, Forsterling, & Weiner (1989):** Identified three dimensions of attribution: internal-external, stable-unstable, and controllable-uncontrollable. (Page 596)
7. **Schoeneman & Rubanowitz (1985):** Survey showed that people attribute their own problems to situational factors, and rate other people's as dispositional. (Page 596)
8. **Kelley (1950):** Demonstrated that first impressions could be influenced by a prior description. (Page 599)
9. **Rosenthal & Jacobson (1968):** Showed that a "self-fulfilling prophecy" could be created in a classroom experiment. (Page 599)
10. **Mita, Dermer, & Knight (1977):** Tested the "mere exposure effect," and found that people preferred familiar images. (Page 601)
11. **Cunningham et al. (1995):** Found high correlation in ratings of attractiveness across cultural and racial lines. (Page 601)
12. **Dutton & Aron (1974):** Found a link between physiological arousal and sexual or romantic arousal. (Page 603)
13. **Insko (1965):** Found that attitudes could be operantly conditioned. (Page 605)
14. **Hovland, Lumsdaine, & Sheffield (1949):** Found that prior beliefs influenced the outcome of persuasion attempts. (Page 607)
15. **Zuwerink & Devine (1996):** Found that the more important a message was personally, the more successful were rational arguments in persuasion. (Page 607)
16. **LaPiere (1934):** Found that attitudes about Chinese people were not necessarily exhibited in behavior toward them. (Page 608)
17. **Festinger & Carlsmith (1959):** First experimental study of cognitive dissonance found that the subjects' attitude about a task did not match the prediction based on reward. (Page 609)
18. **Leonard (1970):** Reported the results of an experiment by a third-grade teacher (Elliott) on prejudice based on eye color. (Page 610)
19. **Wood et al. (1994):** Meta-analysis of research studies showed that a minority can influence a group when the minority maintains a consistent position. (Page 614)
20. **Janis (1983):** Coined the term *groupthink* to describe a premature consensus brought about by group polarization due to isolation, feeling of invulnerability, discrediting of contrary evidence, fear of criticism for disagreeing, and desire to maintain harmony. (Page 614)
21. **Bond & Titus (1983):** Found that performing tasks in front of others improves performance when the task is simple or well learned and inhibits performance with a complex or poorly rehearsed task. (Page 615)

22. **Kravitz & Martin (1986):** Described the "Ringlemann Effect," a study of social loafing that found people sharing a task performed at a lower level than if doing it alone. (Page 616)
23. **Asch (1955):** Found that choices that a subject made would often conform to ones made by the experimenter's confederates, even if the choice was incorrect. (Page 617)
24. **Freedman & Fraser (1966):** Found that people who agreed to a small request were more likely to agree to a larger request later. (Page 618)
25. **Cialdini et al. (1975):** Found that people who refused to do a large task were more likely to do a smaller task later. (Page 619)
26. **Milgram (1963):** Found that subjects told to administer incrementally larger shocks to a confederate would continue to do so, to an apparently dangerous level, when absolved of responsibility by the experimenter. (Page 620)
27. **Cialdini et al. (1987):** Found that people given the opportunity to help someone did so more from a desire to avoid negative moods rather than empathy. (Page 623)
28. **Darley &Latané (1968):** Showed that as the number of bystanders increases, the likelihood that anyone will help in an emergency deceases. (Page 624)
29. **Bandura, Ross, & Ross (1963):** Found that children who saw adults punching an inflatable doll were more likely to punch the doll themselves. (Page 628)
30. **Liebert & Baron (1972):** Found that children who watched a violent television show were more aggressive than ones who watched a nonviolent track-and-field event. (Page 628)
31. **Donnerstein & Berkowitz (1981):** Concluded that men who had been angered by female confederates and then watched a film in which a woman was enjoying being raped behaved most aggressively toward the women in a later task. (Page 631)

PRACTICE TEST A

1. Your friend Tony expresses interest in studying the behavior of people within its interpersonal context. He has heard that this is a field of psychology and comes to you for advice as to what type of psychology he should pursue. Which field would you tell him to examine?
   a. sports psychology.
   b. social psychology.
   c. aggression psychology.
   d. interpersonal psychology.

Obj.: 1 Page: 594

2. If you decide that a fellow student has performed well on an exam because she is intelligent and conscientious, you have made a
   a. free will attribution.
   b. situational attribution.
   c. deterministic attribution.
   d. dispositional attribution.

Obj.: 2 Page: 594-595

3. If you tend to blame other students' academic failures on their own lack of intelligence or effort, while blaming your own failures on unfair exams and biased grading, you would be committing the
   a. self-serving bias.
   b. actor-observer bias.
   c. fundamental attribution error.
   d. self-fulfilling prophecy effect.

Obj.: 3 Page: 596

4. A basketball coach believes that one player is better than another player--even though they are equal in ability. The coach proceeds to treat the players differently, and the first player ends up playing better than the second player. This is an example of
   a. social loafing.
   b. deindividuation.
   c. self-serving bias.
   d. self-fulfilling prophecy.

Obj.: 4 Page: 599

5. What social attraction factor is the "mere exposure effect" most closely associated with called?
   a. proximity
   b. similarity
   c. familiarity
   d. liking

Obj.: 5 Page: 600

6. According to the Hatfield-Berscheid theory of love, love characterized by feelings of affection and commitment to the relationship is called
   a. passionate love.
   b. "spring fever."
   c. companionate love.
   d. romantic love.

Obj.: 6 Page: 602

7. A survey found that when males and females were asked to rate the factors that would make someone attractive as a romantic partner, the most important was
   a. intelligence.
   b. a sense of humor.
   c. integrity.
   d. adventurism.

Obj.: 7 Page: 604

8. What theory states that attitude change is motivated by the desire to relieve the unpleasant state of tension caused when one holds cognitions that are inconsistent with each other?
   a. social facilitation
   b. self-perception
   c. attribution
   d. cognitive dissonance

Obj.: 8 Page: 608

9. A presidential candidate accuses his opponent of being ungodly, anti-American, and hedonistic. In regard to the theory of Richard Petty and John Cacioppo (1981), this persuasive message takes the
   a. direct route.
   b. central route.
   c. indirect route.
   d. peripheral route.

Obj.: 9 Page: 606

10. A person believes that he is not prejudiced, but finds himself laughing at racist and ethnic jokes. This contradiction between his attitudes and his behavior makes him feel anxious, a feeling best explained by
   a. self-perception theory.
   b. social facilitation theory.
   c. cognitive dissonance theory.
   d. impression management theory.

Obj.: 10 Page: 608

11. Which of the following is *not* a method of reducing prejudice?
   a. the use of the jigsaw method
   b. increasing cognitive dissonance in prejudiced individuals
   c. increasing social contact between members of equal status
   d. promoting intergroup cooperation

Obj.: 11 Page: 611

12. The individual members of the academic affairs committee of a college would like to make minor revisions in the college's curriculum. Yet, after discussing the topic for several meetings, arguing every side of the issue, and working independent of any powerful administrator, they produce a radical revision that changes every aspect of the old curriculum. This would most likely be an example of
   a. groupthink.
   b. group polarization.
   c. social facilitation.
   d. self-fulfilling prophecy.

Obj.: 12 Page: 613

13. A basketball player is a notoriously poor "practice player," but performs well during actual games. This would most likely be attributable to
   a. social loafing.
   b. social facilitation.
   c. cognitive dissonance.
   d. self-fulfilling prophecy.

Obj.: 13 Page: 615

14. A decrease in the individual effort exerted by group members when working together on a task is called
   a. social loafing.
   b. deindividuation.
   c. group polarization.
   d. social facilitation.

Obj.: 13 Page: 616

15. Behaving in accordance with group expectations with little or no overt pressure to do so is called
   a. obedience.
   b. compliance.
   c. conformity.
   d. groupthink.

Obj. 14 Page: 618

16. According to research by John Darley and Bibb Latané, a person who collapsed on the street would be most likely to be helped if
   a. there are many witnesses to the event.
   b. there is a single witness to the event.
   c. witnesses are strangers rather than acquaintances.
   d. witnesses assumed that the person was drunk, rather than a diabetic suffering from insulin shock.

Obj.: 15 Page: 624

17. Pornography involves
   a. any material involving nudity.
   b. only material depicting sexual intercourse.
   c. only material depicting abnormal sexual behavior.
   d. sexually explicit material intended to incite sexual arousal.

Obj.:17 Page: 630

PRACTICE TEST B

1. Which of the following pairing is correct?
   a. Health psychology: the study of the development of illness.
   b. Environmental psychology: the study of the influence of the environment on the person.
   c. Social psychology: the study of behavior in its interpersonal context.
   d. Cognitive psychology: the study of the biological basis of thinking.

Obj. 1 Page: 594

2. If you determine that your professor included rather difficult questions on this exam because she enjoys watching students struggle and fail their courses, you are
   a. attributing her behavior to situational factors.
   b. making a dispositional attribution.
   c. engaging in social loafing.
   d. anticipating negative state relief.

Obj.: 2 Page: 594

3. Suppose you submit a term paper late. According to Weiner, your excuse would be more effective if you attribute your behavior to a family emergency than if you attribute it to difficulty in budgeting your time. Why? A family emergency comprises
   a. external, stable, controllable factors.
   b. internal, unstable, uncontrollable factors.
   c. external, unstable, uncontrollable factors.
   d. internal, stable, controllable factors.

Obj.: 3 Page: 596

4. Jeff has the tendency to always make dispositional attributions for his success and situational attributions for his failures. Social psychologists would call this a
   a. self-fulfilling prophecy.
   b. actor-observer bias.
   c. fundamental attribution error.
   d. self-serving bias.

Obj.: 3 Page: 596-597

5. When Nina asks Charles out to lunch, he accepts. When they are at the restaurant, he carefully asks, "Nina, is this a date, or just lunch?" In social psychological terms, he is asking
   a. whether he needs to engage in impression management.
   b. whether his attribution should be dispositional or situational.
   c. which schema to apply to this event.
   d. if he has committed the fundamental attribution error.

Obj.: 4 Page: 598

6. A relatively unknown person is running for mayor of your town. Her campaign manager blankets the city with numerous television, radio, and newspaper ads. This campaign manager is attempting to increase liking for the candidate
   a. by implying great similarity between the candidate and the voters.
   b. by appealing to bias against out-groups.
   c. through the mere exposure effect.
   d. through increased proximity.

Obj.: 5 Page: 600

7. Which item is out of place here?
   a. intimacy
   b. commitment
   c. triangular theory
   d. two-factor theory

Obj.: 6 Page: 603

8. A computer dating study conducted at the University of Minnesota (Walser et al., 1966) revealed that the most important factor in initial social attraction was
   a. similarity.
   b. proximity.
   c. familiarity.
   d. physical attractiveness.

Obj.: 7 Page 601

9. Advertisements for a new passenger van always associate a smiling, happy, and attractive family with this van. This advertiser is attempting to have the audience form a positive attitude toward the van through
   a. operant conditioning.
   b. classical conditioning.
   c. impression management.
   d. social facilitation.

Obj.: 8 Page: 605

10. Several people are trying to persuade Jan to purchase a particular car. Which of the following individuals is likely to be the most persuasive and why?
    a. Aunt Mary, who has owned several of these cars, because she is credible and trustworthy.
    b. Jack Smith, who sells these cars, because he is attractive and has expertise.
    c. Anne Jones, who is a recent buyer, because she is familiar and similar to Jan.
    d. John Johnson, who wrote the advertising material for this car, because he has expertise and intelligence.

Obj.: 9 Page: 606

11. George knows that drinking and driving is very dangerous. Yet he drives away from the party while intoxicated. He tells himself that it is okay to do this because he has only a short distance to drive. What would Leon Festinger say about George's behavior?
    a. He is trying to reduce his negative state.
    b. He is attempting to reduce his cognitive dissonance.
    c. He is taking the peripheral route.
    d. He is applying the actor-observer bias.

Obj.: 10 Page: 609

12. If Professor Smith has a negative attitude toward JoAnn because JoAnn is female, then Professor Smith
    a. has an acceptable personal dislike.
    b. is prejudiced.
    c. is applying the self-serving bias.
    d. is experiencing dissonance.

Obj.: 11 Page: 610

13. You are a member of a collection of six persons. You interact and have mutual influence on one another. Your collection is called a____________ by social psychologists.
    a. couple
    b. cohort
    c. clan
    d. group

Obj.: 12 Page: 612

14. The causes of the 1986 explosion of the space shuttle *Challenger* has been attributed to the group process called
    a. groupthink.
    b. group polarization.
    c. self-fulfilling prophecy.
    d. self-serving bias.

Obj.: 12 Page: 612

15. Social loafing is more likely to occur when the
    a. group leader is directive, and the members are cohesive and dedicated to maintaining harmony.
    b. task is unfamiliar and the members are concerned about impression management.
    c. group members feel anonymous and the outcome responsibility is diffused among members.
    d. number of people in the group exceeds ten.

Obj.: 13 Page: 616

16. Your teenage daughter tells you that she just has to have a specific type of jeans or her friends will not be her friends anymore. When you ask her if her friends have told her this she says that no, she just knows that it is true. Your daughter's behavior illustrates the psychological concept of
   a. obedience.
   b. compliance.
   c. social loafing.
   d. conformity.

Obj.: 14 Page: 616

17. A telemarketer calls you at home and asks you to donate $100 to send four underprivileged children to a day camp. When you say no the telemarketer then asks for a $10 dollar donation that would send one child to a basketball game. If you agree to the $10 dollar donation the telemarketer has successfully used which technique of inducing compliance?
   a. the foot-in-the-door technique
   b. the door-in-the-face technique
   c. the face-in-the-door technique
   d. the foot-in-the-face technique

Obj. :14 Page: 618

18. You observe a man and a woman arguing on the corner of a busy intersection. Which of the following factors have been shown to influence whether or not you are likely to offer assistance?
   a. the number of other people in the general area
   b. whether or not you felt the confrontation was an emergency
   c. your assessment of your ability to successfully offer help
   d. all of the above

Obj.: 15 Page: 625

19. Pertaining to the cause of aggression, revised social learning theory states that
   a. frustration does not directly provoke aggression.
   b. aggression always provokes anger.
   c. frustration always leads to aggression.
   d. aggression is caused by frustration.

Obj.: 16 Page: 627

20. According to social psychological research, does exposure to television violence increase aggressive behavior among children?
   a. Yes, it has been clearly shown that watching television violence causes increased aggressive behavior among children.
   b. No, it is clear that parental and peer behaviors have much more influence on aggression levels than does televised violence.
   c. Only children who are already aggressive select to watch violent television shows.
   d. Psychological research findings and the opinions of psychologists are divided about this complex issue.

Obj.: 17 Page: 628-629

ESSAY QUESTIONS

1. An ancient Greek philosopher said that for success in life, a good face is more powerful than any letter of introduction. Do you agree? Support your position with social-psychological evidence.

Obj.: 5 Page: 601-602

2. Discuss the research you believe would be most helpful in understanding the nature of the Los Angeles riots.

Obj. 12, 13, 14 Page: 625, 632, 642

ANSWER RECORD FOR CHAPTER 17

Comprehensive Guided Review:

1. interpersonal
2. cognition
3. attribution
4. dispositional
5. situational
6. social
7. Kelley
8. attributions
9. same
10. distinctiveness
11. consensus
12. Weiner
13. attribution
14. Internal-external
15. stable-unstable
16. controllable-uncontrollable
17. biases
18. fundamental attribution error
19. dispositional
20. situational
21. positive
22. negative
23. self-image
24. judgments
25. impression management
26. self-handicapping
27. schemas
28. characteristics
29. interpret
30. schema
31. guide
32. stereotype
33. in-group
34. out-group
35. self-fulfilling prophecy
36. first impressions
37. expectations
38. attraction
39. Proximity
40. Familiarity
41. Physical Attractiveness
42. Similarity
43. Self-disclosure
44. define
45. passionate
46. companionate
47. affection
48. More
49. passionate
50. two-factor
51. physiologically
52. attribute
53. Sternberg
54. interaction
55. passion
56. intimacy
57. decision
58. commitment
59. intensity
60. kind
61. Infatuation
62. romantic
63. similarity
64. humor

Mini-review of Social Cognition and Interpersonal Attraction:

1. A; 2. Gg; 3. F; 4. H; 5 . B; 6. M; 7. I; 8. K; 9. C; 10. E; 11. D; 12. R; 13. O; 14. Y; 15. L; 16. Q; 17. Cc; 18. Z; 19. N; 20. J; 21. V; 22. U; 23. T; 24. Bb; 25. Ff; 26. W; 27. Ee; 28. P; 29. Dd; 30. X; 31. G; 32. Aa; 33. S

65. Attitudes
66. classical
67. observing
68. Persuasion
69. central
70. peripheral
71. explicit
72. situational
73. elaborately
74. peripheral
75. persuasiveness
76. credibility
77. favors
78. opposes
79. Two-sided
80. central
81. peripheral
82. relevance
83. attitudes
84. predictors
85. specificity
86. Festinger
87. cognitive dissonance
88. tension
89. inconsistent
90. reduce
91. responsible
92. self-perception
93. infer
94. well-defined
95. poorly defined
96. Prejudice
97. discrimination
98. learning
99. authoritarianism
100. ethnocentrism
101. projection
102. similarity
103. less
104. reduce
105. Allport
106. status
107. cooperation
108. group
109. decision
110. rational
111. extreme
112. riskier
113. group
114. individual
115. cautious
116. polarization
117. moderate
118. persuasive
119. desirable
120. minority
121. rational
122. confident
123. consistent
124. unanimity
125. charismatic
126. harmony
127. groupthink
128. directive
129. negative
130. performance
131. improvement
132. inhibition
133. drive
134. physiological
135. better
136. worse
137. apprehension
138. facilitation
139. increased
140. decreased
141. social loafing
142. accountable
143. social influences
144. norms
145. overt
146. approval
147. punishment
148. foot-in-the-door
149. self-perception
150. door-in-the-face
151. compliance
152. norms
153. foot-in-the-door
154. authority
155. Milgram

Anatomy of a Classic Research Study: Would You Harm Someone Just Because an Authority Figure Ordered You To?
Read the summary of Milgram's study presented on page 620 in your textbook and answer the following questions.

What was the rationale for the study?
Milgram (1963) researched the issue of whether people who obey orders to hurt innocent people are unusually cruel, or whether most humans are susceptible to obeying such orders. Surveys of psychiatrists and Yale students had predicted that less than 2 percent of the subjects would reach the maximum (faked) shock level.

What methods did the author use to test the hypothesis?
Milgram used adult men who had responded to an advertisement. Each participant was introduced to another man (a confederate) who was also to participate in the study. The true subject was always assigned the role of teacher. The subject was then instructed to administer progressively higher amounts of shock to the learner whenever the learner made an error. The confederate responded to higher levels of shock with cries of pain. If the subject expressed discomfort, the experimenter would say: "You have no other choice, you must go on."

What was the outcome of the study and what did the author conclude the results meant?
To Milgram's surprise, two thirds of the subjects reached the maximum level of shock, and none stopped before reaching 300 volts. The results of this most famous and controversial study, showing that the average citizen is capable of extreme obedience, remain disturbing and highly criticized. The study has been successfully replicated.
Baumrind has been the most outspoken critic, claiming that Milgram's use of deception increased distrust of psychological researchers and that his subjects' self-esteem was damaged by the realization that they might harm an innocent person simply because an authority figure told them to do so.

Mini-review of Attitudes and Group Behavior:
1. D; 2. V; 3. A; 4. Bb; 5. G; 6. K; 7. O; 8. Aa; 9. M; 10. C; 11. R; 12. L; 13. Cc; 14. X; 15. Dd; 16. Y; 17. F; 18. P; 19. I; 20. B; 21. H; 22. Z; 23. J; 24. E; 25. W; 26. U; 27. T; 28. S; 29. Q; 30. N

156. prosocial
157. altruism
158. empathy
159. distress
160. sadness
161. empathy-altruism
162. Bystander intervention
163. willingness
164. Noticing
165. Emergency
166. Personal
167. competent
168. danger
169. antisocial
170. aggression
171. physiology
172. experience
173. instinctive
174. Thanatos
175. released
176. evolved
177. failed
178. more
179. hereditary
180. twins
181. limbic
182. frustration
183. frustration-aggression
184. revised
185. anger
186. observing
187. positive
188. bidirectional
189. heredity
190. violent
191. aware
192. evaluated
193. deindividuation
194. anonymous

Mini-review of Prosocial Behavior and Aggression:
1. A; 2. M; 3. O; 4. D; 5. F; 6. G; 7. L; 8. I; 9. N; 10. K; 11. J; 12. H; 13. B; 14. E; 15. C

195. pornography
196. not more
197. cause
198. casual
199. researchers
200. adolescents
201. causes

Anatomy of a Contemporary Research Study: Do Pornographic Films Promote Sexual Aggression? *Read the summary of Donnerstein & Berkowitz's study presented on page 631 in your textbook and answer the following questions.*

What was the rationale for the study?
The authors wanted to examine several factors related to violence against women induced by erotic films. In this study they examined whether the film was violent and whether the victim seemed to enjoy being raped.

What methods did the author use to test the hypothesis?
Male undergraduate students were assigned to one of four film conditions: a talk-show interview, a young couple making love, a woman enjoying being raped by two men, and a woman suffering during a rape by two men. Additionally half the men in each group had been insulted and angered by women prior to observing the film. The men were then given the opportunity to retaliate against the women by giving them electric shocks when women made mistakes on a memory task.

What was the outcome of the study and what did the author conclude the results meant?
This study by Donnerstein & Berkowitz (1981) showed that men who had seen a neutral or nonviolent erotic film displayed relatively little aggression. Both angered and nonangered men who had seen a rape film in which the woman enjoyed it displayed higher levels of aggression. And, of the men who had seen a rape film during which the woman suffered, those who had been angered behaved more aggressively than those who had not.

---

202. nonviolent
203. violent
204. political

Practice Test A:

1. a. Incorrect: Sport psychology is the field of psychology associated with the application of psychological principles to help amateur and professional athletes to improve their performance.
   b. Correct: Social psychology is the field of psychology that examines the behavior of individuals within the context of their interpersonal environment.
   c. Incorrect: Social psychologists are interested in aggression, but it is not a separate field of psychology.
   d. Incorrect: Social psychologists are interested in interpersonal behaviors, but it is not a separate field of psychology.

2. a. Incorrect: This is not a defined type of causal attribution.
   b. Incorrect: Situational attribution is based on circumstances.
   c. Incorrect: Deterministic attribution is not a defined type of causal attribution.
   d. Correct: This type of attribution is based on personal qualities.

3. a. Incorrect: This refers to attributing one's own positive behavior as dispositional and negative behaviors as situational.
   b. Correct: This bias results when one attributes others' behavior to dispositional causes and your own to situational.
   c. Incorrect: This refers only to the tendency to attribute others' behavior as dispositional.
   d. Incorrect: This is not a type of causal attribution error.

4. a. Incorrect: Social loafing is a group dynamics phenomenon where individuals do not exhibit peak performance because of anonymity of effort.
   b. Incorrect: Deindividuation is becoming less aware of self and less concerned about societal evaluation.
   c. Incorrect: This is a type of attribution error that believes that positive personal traits are dispositional, and negative behaviors are situational.
   d. Correct: This effect is produced when one person's expectations influences another's behavior to meet those expectations.

5. a. Incorrect: Proximity refers to how physically near people live, work, or attend school with each other as a factor in developing relationships.
   b. Incorrect: This factor is based on liking people who are similar in physical attractiveness, have similar attitudes, and enjoy the same activities.
   c. Correct: Familiarity means that the more we are exposed to and interact with particular people, the more we will like them.
   d. Incorrect: This is not a social attraction factor, but a result of such factors.

6. a. Incorrect: This is characterized by intense emotional arousal, including sexual feelings.
   b. Incorrect: This is not mentioned in the text.
   c. Correct: This type of love may start out as passionate and develop over time.
   d. Incorrect: This is not a concept employed in this theory.

7. a. Incorrect: For this study, intelligence was not mentioned as an outcome.
   b. Correct: For this study (Buss, 1988), this was the only outcome mentioned.
   c. Incorrect: For this study, integrity was not mentioned as an outcome.
   d. Incorrect: For this study, adventurism was not mentioned as an outcome.

8. a. Incorrect: This refers to an improvement in individual performance due to the presence of other people.
   b. Incorrect: This theory suggest that we use behavior as a way of making inferences about attitudes-our own as well as others'.
   c. Incorrect: Attribution is an attempt to define the cause of behavior.
   d. Correct: Cognitive dissonance occurs when one's beliefs do not match reality, behavior, or other beliefs.

9. a. Incorrect: This theory does not mention such a route.
   b. Incorrect: The central route is one in which arguments are clear, logical, and easily supported.
   c. Incorrect: This theory does not mention such a route.
   d. Correct: The peripheral route focuses on the source of the message or the situational context.

10. a. Incorrect: This theory infers attitudes from behavior.
   b. Incorrect: This refers to an improvement in individual performance due to the presence of other people.
   c. Correct: Cognitive dissonance occurs when one's beliefs do not match reality, behavior, or other beliefs.
   d. Incorrect: Impression management is not discussed in the text.

11. a. Incorrect: This is not mentioned anywhere in the text.
   b. Correct: Increasing dissonance would not reduce prejudice.
   c. Incorrect: A study showed reduction of prejudice using this technique.
   d. Incorrect: A study showed showed reduction of prejudice using this technique.

12. a. Incorrect: A form of group polarization, groupthink places unanimity ahead of critical thinking and aims at premature consensus.
  b. **Correct: Characterized by the tendency to make more extreme decisions than the members would individually.**
  c. Incorrect: This refers to an improvement in individual performance due to the presence of other people.
  d. Incorrect: This effect is produced when one person's expectations influence another's behavior to meet those expectations.

13. a. Incorrect: Social loafing is a group dynamics phenomenon where individuals do not exhibit peak performance because of anonymity of effort.
  b. **Correct: This refers to an improvement in individual performance due to the presence of other people.**
  c. Incorrect: Characterized by the tendency to make more extreme decisions than the members would individually.
  d. Incorrect: This effect is produced when one person's expectations influence another's behavior to meet those expectations.

14. a. **Correct: Social loafing is a group dynamics phenomenon where individuals do not exhibit peak performance because of anonymity of effort.**
  b. Incorrect: Deindividuation is becoming less aware of self and less concerned about societal evaluation.
  c. Incorrect: Characterized by the tendency to make more extreme decisions than the members would individually.
  d. Incorrect: This refers to an improvement in individual performance due to the presence of other people.

15. a. Incorrect: Obedience is following orders given by an authority.
  b. **Correct: This is going along with the group with little or no threat of punishment.**
  c. Incorrect: Conformity means behaving in accordance with real or imagined group pressure.
  d. Incorrect: A form of group polarization, groupthink places unanimity ahead of critical thinking and aims at premature consensus.

16. a. Incorrect: The more bystanders there are, the less the likelihood that anyone will help (if they are strangers).
  b. **Correct: A lone bystander is more likely to help in some way.**
  c. Incorrect: If bystanders are friends or relatives, the probability of help goes up as the number of bystanders goes up.
  d. Incorrect: If bystanders did not attribute the situation to an emergency, they were less likely to help.

17. a. Incorrect: Sexual arousal may be stimulated by material depicting certain types of clothing, e.g., leather.
  b. Incorrect: Sexual arousal may be stimulated by material depicting acts other than intercourse.
  c. Incorrect: Sexual arousal may be stimulated by material depicting normal or abnormal sexual encounters.
  d. **Correct: Pornography is any material intended to incite sexual arousal.**

Practice Test B:

1. a. Incorrect: Health psychology is the field of psychology that applies principles to the prevention and treatment of illness
  b. Incorrect: Environmental psychology is the field of psychology that applies psychological principles to help improve the physical environment.
  c. **Correct: Social psychology is the field that studies behavior in its interpersonal context.**
  d. Incorrect: Cognitive psychology is the field that studies how the mind organizes perceptions, processes information, and interprets information.

2. a. Incorrect: Situational factors are factors that attribute behavior to the circumstances, not to the personality of the individual.
  b. **Correct: Dispositional attributions attribute the behavior of the individual to the personality of the person.**
  c. Incorrect: Social loafing refers to a decrease in the individual effort exerted by group members when working together on a task.
  d. Incorrect: Negative state relief refers to a theory of prosocial behavior that argues that we engage in the behavior to relieve our own state of emotional distress at another's plight.

3. a. Incorrect: Family emergencies are considered external, unstable, and uncontrollable factors.
   b. Incorrect: Family emergencies are considered external, unstable, and uncontrollable factors.
   c. **Correct: Family emergencies are considered external, unstable, and uncontrollable factors.**
   d. Incorrect: The excuse of having difficulty budgeting your time would be an internal, stable, and controllable factor.

4. a. Incorrect: The tendency to always make dispositional attributions for your own successes and situational attributions for your own failures is called a self-serving bias by social psychologists.
   b. Incorrect: The tendency to always make dispositional attributions for your own successes and situational attributions for your own failures is called a self-serving bias by social psychologists.
   c. Incorrect: The tendency to always make dispositional attributions for your own successes and situational attributions for your own failures is called a self-serving bias by social psychologists.
   d. **Correct: The tendency to always make dispositional attributions for your own successes and situational attributions for your own failures is called a self-serving bias by social psychologists.**

5. a. Incorrect: A self-fulfilling prophecy is the tendency for one person's expectation to influence another person to behave in a particular way. This is not what Charles is doing.
   b. Incorrect: Charles is not concerned with whether he should attribute behavior to personality or circumstances.
   c. **Correct: Charles is trying to determine which cognitive structure he should apply to the event of the lunch date.**
   d. Incorrect: A fundamental attribution error is a bias to attribute other people's behavior to dispositional factors. Charles is not attributing Nina's behavior to anything.

6. a. Incorrect: By just presenting the candidate the campaign manager is attempting to increase liking by having the public be familiar with the candidate, or the use of the mere exposure effect.
   b. Incorrect: By just presenting the candidate the campaign manager is attempting to increase liking by having the public be familiar with the candidate, or the use of the mere exposure effect.
   c. **Correct: By just presenting the candidate the campaign manager is attempting to increase liking by having the public be familiar with the candidate, or the use of the mere exposure effect.**
   d. Incorrect: By just presenting the candidate the campaign manager is attempting to increase liking by having the public be familiar with the candidate, or the use of the mere exposure effect.

7. a. Incorrect: Sternberg's triangular theory of love discusses both intimacy and commitment; the two-factor theory does not.
   b. Incorrect: Sternberg's triangular theory of love discusses both intimacy and commitment; the two-factor theory does not.
   c. Incorrect: Sternberg's triangular theory of love discusses both intimacy and commitment; the two-factor theory does not.
   d. **Correct: Sternberg's triangular theory of love discusses both intimacy and commitment; the two-factor theory does not.**

8. a. Incorrect: This early study on dating examined the importance of physical attractiveness in dating relationships.
   b. Incorrect: This early study on dating examined the importance of physical attractiveness in dating relationships.
   c. Incorrect: This early study on dating examined the importance of physical attractiveness in dating relationships.
   d. **Correct: This early study on dating examined the importance of physical attractiveness in dating relationships.**

9. a. Incorrect: If the advertisers were using operant conditioning they would be rewarding the public for buying or using the van.
   b. **Correct: The advertisers were attempting to develop the association of "happiness" with their particular car; this is an example of classical conditioning.**
   c. Incorrect: Impression mamagement is the process by which we deliberately attempt to control the impression that individuals form of us, but it is not a specific technique.
   d. Incorrect: Social facilitation refers to the improvement of a person's task performance when in the presence of another individual.

10. **a. Correct: The credibility and trustworthiness of the source are two important factors in persuasion.**
   b. Incorrect: Jack, although attractive and credible, is however not trustworthy and thus would be less persuasive.
   c. Incorrect: Familiarity and similarity are not factors that influence persuasion.
   d. Incorrect: Expertise is not enough without trustworthiness and thus his credibility is not high.

11. a. Incorrect: Festinger proposed the theory of cognitive dissonance to explain why people justify the occurrence of behavior that differs from their beliefs. Thus he would explain this behavior in terms of cognitive dissonance.
   b. Correct: Festinger proposed the theory of cognitive dissonance to explain why people justify the occurrence of behavior that differs from their beliefs. Thus he would explain this behavior in terms of cognitive dissonance.
   c. Incorrect: Festinger proposed the theory of cognitive dissonance to explain why people justify the occurrence of behavior that differs from their beliefs. Thus he would explain this behavior in terms of cognitive dissonance.
   d. Incorrect: Festinger proposed the theory of cognitive dissonance to explain why people justify the occurrence of behavior that differs from their beliefs. Thus he would explain this behavior in terms of cognitive dissonance.

12. a. Incorrect: A negative attitude toward an individual based on membership in a particular group is a prejudice.
   b. Correct: A negative attitude toward an individual based on membership in a particular group is a prejudice.
   c. Incorrect: A negative attitude toward an individual based on membership in a particular group is a prejudice.
   d. Incorrect: A negative attitude toward an individual based on membership in a particular group is a prejudice.

13. a. Incorrect: This is not the correct choice because a couple consists of only two people.
   b. Incorrect: A cohort is a group of people of the same age. You are not told the age of the individuals in this question.
   c. Incorrect: *Clan* is not a term used by social psychologists.
   d. Correct : A group is defined as a collection of two or more individuals who interact and influence each another.

14. **a. Correct: The explosion has been linked to groupthink, or the tendency of small, cohesive groups to place unanimity ahead of critical thinking in making decisions. The group that made the decision ignored information in an attempt to please the public and Congress.**
   b. Incorrect: Group polarization refers to the tendency for groups to make more extreme decisions than individual members would otherwise make.
   c. Incorrect: A self-fulfilling prophecy is the tendency for one person's expectation to influence another person to behave in a particular way. This is not what happened.
   d. Incorrect: The tendency to always make dispositional attributions for your own successes and situational attributions for your own failures is called a self-serving bias by social psychologists, this is not what happened.

15. a. Incorrect: Social loafing occurs more often if the group members feel that they are anonymous and the outcome responsibility is diffused.
   b. Incorrect: Social loafing occurs more often if the group members feel that they are anonymous and the outcome responsibility is diffused.
   c. Correct: Social loafing occurs more often if the group members feel that they are anonymous and the outcome responsibility is diffused.
   d. Incorrect: Social loafing occurs more often if the group members feel that they are anonymous and the outcome responsibility is diffused.

16. a. Incorrect: Your daughter is following orders of an authority; she is behaving in accordance with implied group expectations, which is conformity.
   b. Incorrect: Your daughter is not behaving in accordance with a request; she is behaving in accordance with implied group expectations, which is conformity.
   c. Incorrect: Your daughter is not demonstrating a decrease in individual effort because she is a member of a group; she is behaving in accordance with implied group expectations, which is conformity.
   d. Correct: Your daughter is behaving in accordance with implied group expectations; this is conformity.

17. a. Incorrect: The foot-in-the-door technique involves the increased likelihood of compliance with a request by first getting someone to comply with a smaller request. The telemarketer asked for a large request first, then countered with a smaller.
   b. Correct: The door-in-the-face technique involves increasing the likelihood of compliance by first asking for a large request that the individual will reject and following it up with a smaller one.
   c. Incorrect: This is not a term for a technique identified by psychologists.
   d. Incorrect: This is not a term for a technique identified by psychologists.

18. a. Incorrect: The number of people, whether you feel the situation is an emergency, and your assessment of your ability to help are all factors that determine whether a bystander is likely to offer aid.
   b. Incorrect: The number of people, whether you feel the situation is an emergency, and your assessment of your ability to help are all factors that determine whether a bystander is likely to offer aid.
   c. Incorrect: The number of people, whether you feel the situation is an emergency, and your assessment of your ability to help are all factors that determine whether a bystander is likely to offer aid.
   d. Correct: The number of people, whether you feel the situation is an emergency, and your assessment of your ability to help are all factors that determine whether a bystander is likely to offer aid.

19. a. **Correct: The key word is "revised." Otherwise, c. would be the correct choice. The revised frustration-aggression theory argues that frustration leads to anger, which leads to aggression.**
b. Incorrect: The key word is "revised." Otherwise, c. would be the correct choice. The revised frustration-aggression theory argues that frustration leads to anger, which leads to aggression.
c. Incorrect: The key word is "revised." Otherwise, this. would be the correct choice. The revised frustration-aggression theory argues that frustration leads to anger, which leads to aggression.
d. Incorrect: The key word is "revised." Otherwise, c. would be the correct choice. The revised frustration-aggression theory argues that frustration leads to anger, which leads to aggression.

20. a. Incorrect: The research on this complex issue has been inconclusive and psychologists are still divided.
b. Incorrect: The research on this complex issue has been inconclusive and psychologists are still divided.
c. Incorrect: The research on this complex issue has been inconclusive and psychologists are still divided.
d. Correct: The research on this complex issue has been inconclusive and psychologists are still divided.

Essay Questions:

1. For positions of agreement:
   a) Infants as young as four months prefer attractive faces.
   b) Physically attractive people are perceived as more intelligent.
   c) Physically attractive people are perceived as more socially competent.
   d) Physically attractive people are more likely to be hired for jobs than less attractive people with equivalent qualifications.
   e) Physically attractive defendants are less likely to be convicted of crimes, and if convicted, they get less punishment.
   f) Mothers play more with their attractive infants.

2. Members involved in the riots might be behaving in accordance with group norms when there is little or no overt pressure to do so; that is, they are influenced by conformity, or they may be behaving in accordance with a direct request that is backed by little or no threat of punishment; that is, their behavior is the result of compliance. Finally, they may be influenced by obedience, and be behaving in accordance with orders given by an authority.